*A Jewish
Woman of
Distinction*

T0366808

ChaeRan Y. Freeze
A Jewish Woman of Distinction: The Life and Diaries of Zinaida Poliakova

Chava Turniansky
Glikl: Memoirs 1691–1719

Dan Rabinowitz
The Lost Library: The Legacy of Vilna's Strashun Library in the Aftermath of the Holocaust

Jehuda Reinharz and Yaacov Shavit
The Road to September 1939: Polish Jews, Zionists, and the Yishuv on the Eve of World War II

Adi Gordon
Toward Nationalism's End: An Intellectual Biography of Hans Kohn

Noam Zadoff
Gershom Scholem: From Berlin to Jerusalem and Back

*Monika Schwarz-Friesel and Jehuda Reinharz
Inside the Antisemitic Mind: The Language of Jew-Hatred in Contemporary Germany

Elana Shapira
Style and Seduction: Jewish Patrons, Architecture, and Design in Fin de Siècle Vienna

ChaeRan Y. Freeze, Sylvia Fuks Fried, and Eugene R. Sheppard, editors
The Individual in History: Essays in Honor of Jehuda Reinharz

Immanuel Etkes
Rabbi Shneur Zalman of Liady: The Origins of Chabad Hasidism

*A Sarnat Library Book

HBI SERIES ON JEWISH WOMEN

Sylvia Barack Fishman, General Editor
Lisa Fishbayn Joffe, Associate Editor

The HBI Series on Jewish Women, created by the Hadassah-Brandeis Institute, publishes a wide range of books by and about Jewish women in diverse contexts and time periods. Of interest to scholars and the educated public, the HBI Series on Jewish Women fills major gaps in Jewish Studies and in Women and Gender Studies as well as their intersection.

The HBI Series on Jewish Women is supported by a generous gift from Dr. Laura S. Schor.

For the complete list of books that are available in this series, please see www.brandeis.edu/hbi

CHAERAN Y. FREEZE
Translated by Gregory Freeze

A Jewish Woman of Distinction

◆ ◆ ◆ ◆ ◆ ◆

THE LIFE & DIARIES OF

Zinaida Poliakova

Brandeis University Press ◆ *Waltham, Massachusetts*

Brandeis University Press
http://www.brandeis.edu/library/bup.html
© 2019 Brandeis University
All rights reserved
Manufactured in the United States of America
Designed by Eric M. Brooks
Typeset in Whitman by Passumpsic Publishing

For permission to reproduce any of the material in
this book, contact Permissions, Brandeis University Press,
415 South Street, Waltham MA 02453, or visit
http://www.brandeis.edu/library/bup.html

Library of Congress Cataloging-in-Publication Data
available upon request
Cloth ISBN: 978-1-68458-002-6
Paperback ISBN: 978-1-68458-001-9
Ebook ISBN: 978-1-68458-003-3

5 4 3 2 1

Dedicated to

Rabbi Ben Zion Gold, *z"l*, Merav Gold, and

Hannah Gold; Samuel and Shirley Goldin, *z"l*,

beloved friends who took me under their wings

and

in honor of Valya Shapiro, a diarist and

world traveler, a woman of distinction in

her own right

CONTENTS

The discovery of a Jewish woman's diaries in Russia is exceedingly unusual—
not to mention the fact that they span nearly three-quarters of a century and
several countries. Zinaida Lazarevna Poliakova (1863–1952), who hailed from
one of the wealthiest Jewish banking families in the Russian Empire but lived
in France and England after her marriage in 1891, would have been bemused
to learn that her diaries found their way back to her beloved Russia in the post-
Soviet era. The diaries first went to the actress Vera Poliakoff (the granddaughter of Zinaida's cousin Lazar Iakovlevich), then to the Russian-born electronics
engineer Alexander Poliakoff, and last to Sir Martyn Poliakoff, a distinguished
British chemist. He then donated them to the Manuscript Division of the Russian State Library in Moscow, where they are now preserved. Parts of the diaries were published in 1995 along with the memoirs of Alexander Poliakoff.[1]

Zinaida Poliakova was twelve years old when she began writing her diaries
"for nothing to do" at the family dacha in Sokol'niki (just outside of Moscow).
Childish boredom gradually gave way to a serious resolve to record the details
of her life "so that I will enjoy reading it in a few years." As she matured, Zinaida poured her emotions and impressions into her diaries,[2] which became a
space where she could express her rage, hurt, scorn, or amusement without
fear of reprisals. On some days (especially when she lived in France), she simply scribbled trivial notes about the weather or her bad headaches. After all,
Zinaida wrote the diaries for herself, never imagining that an audience outside
her immediate family or friends might read them.

Her ten surviving diaries represent a treasure trove for historians and are
unique in several respects. First, although Jewish women wrote diaries in Imperial Russia, few have survived the ravages of war, migrations, or purges by
heirs or zealous cleaners who did not understand the value of the notebooks.
In fact, the only other known diaries of a Jewish woman from this period (although others certainly survived in private archives or family documents) are
those of the writer Rashel Mironovna Khin (1861–1928), who described her
social, intellectual, and cultural life in Moscow from 1891 to 1917.[3] She converted to Christianity to escape an unhappy marriage and married a fellow

convert, Osip Goldovsky, a Moscow lawyer. Like Zinaida, she was immersed in Russian culture but socialized more with the leading intellectual and literary figures of her day rather than with aristocrats and bureaucrats.

Second, the remarkable time span of Zinaida's diaries affords a rare glimpse into the entire trajectory of one woman's life. She wrote her first entry on 13 August 1875 as a young girl and her final entry sometime in late 1949, when she was eighty-six years old.[4] She lived through the period when aristocratic society in Moscow was at its apogee, under the general-governorship of Prince Vladimir Dolgorukov; experienced the fall of the tsarist regime and the arrest of her family members by the Bolshevik regime (albeit from afar in Paris); survived both catastrophic world wars and the loss of her closest relatives and friends during the Holocaust; and managed to live through the difficult post-war years with the help of her husband's relatives in England. It is possible to trace how her aristocratic upbringing influenced her life from childhood to old age, as well as the impact of life-changing events like the Holocaust on her attitudes toward religion and family.

Third, the diaries reveal how Jews were integrated into Russian high society in prerevolutionary Russian capitals without submitting to pressures to convert. Zinaida and her family lived according to both Jewish and Russian calendars; they were as intimately familiar with Russian Orthodox holidays and name days as they were with Jewish time. The Poliakovs, who welcomed wealthy Jews (like the Gintsburgs and Brodskiis) and poor aspiring artists and musicians into their home, felt just as comfortable hosting Russian bureaucrats, military figures, and aristocrats. Their deep engagement with the vibrant world of music, art, and theater placed the Poliakovs at the heart of imperial culture. The diaries provide a window into the elite female world of sociability and the decline of female participation in business from one generation to the next. Whereas her grandmother and mother actively engaged in trade, commerce, and banking, Zinaida took no interest in such matters, which the family left solely to her brothers. The inability to handle her own finances had dire consequences after World War II, when she lived beyond her means and forced her daughter—who took over her debts—to declare bankruptcy. Zinaida's daily records also show how Jewish women navigated issues of kashrut, religious observance, and modesty (in dress) to participate in Russian social life.

Significantly, other family records complement and elucidate Zinaida's diaries. Most important are the lengthy diaries of Zinaida's uncle, Iakov Solomonovich Poliakov, preserved in the Central Archives for the History of the Jewish People in Jerusalem. Valuable supplements are also to be gleaned from Alexander Poliakoff's *The Silver Samovar: Reminiscences of the Russian Revolu-*

tion,[5] Russian archival materials, and Russian and Western newspapers that help fill in the years of silence.

This volume is divided into two parts. The first part places Zinaida's diaries in the context of the rise of the Poliakov family from its obscure roots in Dubrovno in the Pale of Settlement to immense wealth and high status in Moscow until a global economic crisis overtook Russia at the turn of the twentieth century. It follows Zinaida's life after she emigrated to France, where she created her own brilliant salon in French-Jewish high society but suffered from unrequited love in a difficult marriage to Reuben Gubbay, the grandson of Sir Alfred Sassoon. The couple had one daughter, Annette (on whom Zinaida doted), who became a popular socialite in Paris during the interwar years. A wartime diary and her final postwar diary help us understand how Zinaida and Annette survived World War II (they were even exchanged for a German prisoner in England) and lived out the final years of their lives, traumatized by their losses during the war and financial need.

The second part of the book consists of translations of the first four diaries that Zinaida wrote while she lived in Russia. These contain the most coherent narratives, with a continuity of people and historical context. They portray the integration of the Poliakovs into the world of the Russian aristocracy through philanthropy, politics, social interactions, and culture. Zinaida's post-Russian diaries (for the periods 1894–98, 1901–2, 1902–4, 1904–11, 1944, and 1945– 49), by contrast, are more fragmented and less attentive to the broader context. She wrote the four pre–World War II diaries mainly during her summer holidays, when she had more time, and some entries read like brief travel or weather logs. The wartime diary is remarkable—especially since it was written in 1944, a year before the end of conflict—and the final diary represents Zinaida's attempts to make sense of her losses during the war. However, the post-Russia diaries are elliptical and laconic, replete with allusions to obscure things and people. It is impossible to fill in the blanks completely, but important details in the diaries, contextualized by supplementary sources, will be incorporated in the first part of the book.

Myths and legends about the Poliakovs—the Rothschilds of Moscow— abound in Jewish memory and literature. As Sholem Aleichem once wrote, "Why, just look at the Poliakovs in Moscow. . . . Even in ordinary times, it's not hard to crave an easy ruble, and who can resist becoming a Poliakov quicker than it takes to say one's bedtime prayers?"[6] Even Leo Tolstoy included a portrait of Zinaida's uncle Samuil in his novel *Anna Karenina*—the protagonist who perished by throwing herself in front of a train (the symbol of the Poliakovs). In his eulogy for Zinaida's father, Rabbi Iakov Maze of Moscow proclaimed that the name Poliakov "has become a legend for all Jews of the Pale of Settlement and when blessing their children before a wedding, our hapless brothers pray, 'May God make you like Poliakov.'"[7] Zinaida's diaries are invaluable precisely because they reveal the mundane, everyday life experiences behind the legendary family through a sharp female lens (often judgmental and rarely nostalgic), scrutinizing her parents and society in the context of late Imperial Russia.

◆ ◆ ◆ ◆ ◆ ◆ ◆

NOTES

1. Zinaida Poliakova and Alexander Poliakoff, *Sem'ia Poliakovykh*, ed. Larisa Nikolaevna Vasil'evna (Moscow: Atlantida, 1995).

2. The book will refer to some people by their first names because there are too many individuals with the same surname.

3. Rashel Mironovna Khin's thirty-two diaries are located in Rossiiskii gosudarstvennyi arkhiv literatury i iskusstva, fond 128, opis' 1, dela, list 32. For a sample from these diaries, see R. M. Khin-Gol'dovskaia, "Iz dnevnikov 1913–1917," edited and compiled by E. B. Korkina and A. I. Dobkin, *Minuvshee: Istoricheskii al'manakh* 21 (1997): 521–96.

4. Zinaida did not include dates in her final diary, but there were clues about the year from her writing. Near the end of the final diary, Zinaida mentioned that she was turning eighty-seven in a few months, so she must have written it at the end of 1949.

5. Alexander Poliakoff with Deborah Sacks, *The Silver Samovar: Reminiscences of the Russian Revolution* (Moscow: Atlantida Press), 1996.

6. Sholem Aleichem, *Tevye the Dairyman and the Railroad Stories*, trans. Hillel Halkin (New York: Schocken, 1987), 185.

7. Iakov Maze, *Pamiati L. S. Poliakova* (Moscow: Tipografii M. O. Attai i Ko; 1914), 9–10.

ACKNOWLEDGMENTS

The process of writing this book was like putting together a complex jigsaw puzzle: at first, it was unknown how many siblings Zinaida Poliakova had (let alone their full names). However, it eventually proved possible to identify most of the myriad personalities who appear in her diaries. Critical help came from Professor Martyn Poliakoff, who identified the location of the diaries in Moscow and provided a copy of his father's memoirs. To my astonishment, I learned that Martyn had spent some time in Ethiopia (my childhood home), where he filmed videos for his award-winning YouTube series, *The Periodic Table of Videos*. The project was surely fated to be. Martyn put me in touch with his cousin Elisabeth (Betka) Bérard, who was researching the history of her mother, Mouma Vitalevna Laporte (née Poliakoff). We corresponded regularly, piecing together the family history like detectives, and she made every discovery feel like finding a precious gem. I also thank other distant relatives for their stories and photographs, including Diana von Sachsen, a relative of Alma Reiss (the wife of Daniil Poliakoff); Alain Guggenheim, who is related to the Raffalovich family; and Pierre-Daniel Beguin, whose godmother was a close friend of Clare (Visha) Poliakoff.

I am truly grateful to Ol'ga Sobolevskaia, whose work alerted me to the diaries of Iakov Poliakov; Veniamin Lukin at the Central Archives for the History of the Jewish People in Jerusalem, who gave me permission to copy the documents; and Dafna Dolinko for photographing the diaries. Shaul Stampfer, a steadfast friend and colleague, helped me make all these connections and supported me in more ways than it is possible to express. Elisheva Ansbacher, an attorney who represented the great-niece of Xenia (Khaia) Levy-Poliakoff in the Holocaust Victims Assets Litigation, provided important information about Xenia's death in Auschwitz. My dear friend Leonid Vaintraub of Moscow transcribed some of the diaries, which was an enormous help.

This book was made possible by the generous support of the former Brandeis Genesis Institute for Russian Jewry and the support of the Genesis Philanthropy Group, which enabled the translation of the diaries by Gregory Freeze. Gregory's research was supported by Grant N 15-18-00119 from the Russian

Science Foundation. He is enormously grateful for their belief in the vision for this book and related projects. The Hadassah-Brandeis Institute was very supportive. I especially thank Lisa Fishbayn Joffe for the special book cupcakes. We are also grateful to the Tauber Institute for the Study of European Jewry and especially to its executive director, Sylvia Fuks Fried, for her involvement at every stage of this book and her immense editorial wisdom. We also thank Jeanne Ferris for her heroic and meticulous work on this text, with countless names spelled in multiple ways, and Ann Brash for keeping us on track. I am especially grateful for the kindness and support of my friends and colleagues Eugene Sheppard, Jonathan Decter, Ilana Szobel, Laura Jockusch, Bernadette Brooten, Alice Nakhimovsky, Marion Kaplan, and Lois Dubin, who provided encouragement and feedback along the way. This book is also a reminder of a memorable friendship with Rena Olshansky, who supported my work and always wrote to me, "In Celebration!"

To our family: thank you, Sebastian, for your beautiful gift of cello music that uplifted our spirits and our little bear, Natalia, for bringing sunshine into our lives with your beautiful singing and dedicated craft of thrift shopping! We also thank our parents Min Chul and Suk Za Yoo; Jun, Zooyeon, and baby Yeonjun; and, of course, Katie, Christopher, and Ruth. This book is dedicated to six remarkable people whom I was privileged to meet in my life. Samuel and Shirley Goldin provided a second home for me in Binghamton, where I held my first job. Their home-cooked meals, tales of prewar Nesvizh, and immense kindness will be remembered with fondness and appreciation. I will always be grateful to Rabbi Ben Zion Gold (z"l) who gave of his precious time to read Yiddish with me. When we were translating Ita Kalish's *A rebishe heym in amolikn Polyn* together, I looked forward to those moments when he spontaneously broke into a *niggun* from his childhood. His daughters Hannah and Merav are very dear to me. I especially thank Merav for her kindness to me whenever I visited and for her steadfast friendship and support. I hope that their father's memory will shine brightly through this very small gesture. This book also honors the generosity of Valya Shapiro, whose genuine interest in my work and encouragement helped me see the end of the tunnel. Like Zinaida Poliakova, she will always be a "woman of distinction" in my mind.

Zinaida Poliakova's Life & Times

◆ ◆ ◆ ◆ ◆ ◆

AN INTRODUCTION

"What are you writing, Marya?" Nikolai asked. Countess
Marya blushed. She was afraid that what she was writing would
not be understood or approved by her husband. She had wanted to
conceal what she was writing from him, but at the same time was
glad he had surprised her at it and that she would now have to tell
him. "A diary, Nicolas," she replied, handing him a blue exercise
book filled with her firm bold writing. "A diary?" Nikolai repeated
with a shade of irony, and he took up the book. It was in French.

—LEO TOLSTOY, *War and Peace*

. . . .

"Why, just look at the Poliakovs in Moscow. . . . [W]ho can resist
becoming a Poliakov quicker than it takes to say one's bedtime prayers?"

SHOLEM ALEICHEM, *Tevye the Dairyman and the Railroad Stories*

. . . .

N 1895, ZINAIDA POLIAKOVA marked the beginning of the new year by
starting a new diary in Milan, Italy, where she was vacationing with her
husband Reuben ("Ruby") Gubbay. Born on 27 January 1863 (Old Style),[1]
Zinaida was the eldest daughter of Lazar Solomonovich Poliakov (1843–
1914), one of three brothers who dominated Russian big business and
finance, with banking houses in Moscow and St. Petersburg, and who built
almost a quarter of the railroad lines in Imperial Russia. Known as the Russian
Rothschild, Lazar Poliakov was among the few Jews who attained the coveted
status of hereditary nobility, earned mainly through his family's philanthropy
—especially contributions to Russian hospitals, schools, and prominent charities. Zinaida's husband hailed from a very different, though no less illustrious, family: he was the grandson of a British entrepreneur, Sir Albert Abdullah
David Sassoon (1818–96),[2] and grew up in Bombay, India, where his father
worked for Messrs. David Sassoon and Co. and as controller of currency in the
Indian Civil Service.[3] The Sassoons established an empire in Asia through the

opium trade and other enterprises and became known as the Rothschilds of the East.[4] According to a popular aphorism, "silver and gold, silks, gums and spices, opium and cotton, wool and wheat—whatever moves over sea or land feels the hand or bears the mark of Sassoon and Company."[5] Superficially, it was a perfect match: Zinaida was descended from a "Russian Rothschild" and Reuben from a "Rothschild" of the East.

As Zinaida's diary entry that day revealed, their marriage was anything but ideal. Her sullen husband watched Zinaida's bustling preparations for the upcoming Russian New Year with unconcealed displeasure. And that was but the calm before the storm. "It goes without saying that we are not celebrating the Russian New Year," Zinaida wrote, "but Ruby did not even wish me a [happy new year] and raged the whole time. Only now will he permit me to drink champagne after dinner in honor of Berta Grigor'ieva Abramovich.[6] He calls me a Jew, not a Russian; generally speaking, he wanted to turn today into the most dismal day so that I would forget about the New Year. Now he has gone to his room to pray."[7] The next day, when the couple went out in their carriage, "Ruby wished me three times, 'May God kill you! [in English].'" Still furious about the spoiled holiday, Zinaida fumed: "Yesterday, he suggested that I drink champagne after dinner—but if in his opinion, I should not drink in celebration of the Russian New Year, and there was no champagne—then why? He is not right in the head. . . . Scoundrel [in English], as the English would say."[8] The intimacy that she so desired was conspicuously absent in their marriage. The casus belli of their immediate conflict was not the champagne but Reuben's rejection of his wife's Russian elite culture that her family had so painstakingly cultivated. As her diaries reveal, the aristocratic lifestyle that Zinaida had internalized during her youth shaped the tastes and habits of her life abroad as an émigrée in France, even during her difficult years in Paris in World War II. This elite habitus—her dispositions, aesthetic sensibilities, habits, and social practices—became central to her identity even as her privileged life in Russia receded into the past and much of the family wealth disappeared (figure 1).[9]

Zinaida's ten extant diaries, spanning more than three-quarters of a century (1875 to circa 1952), offer rich insight into the inner world of the Russian Jewish elites from a female perspective. Her first four diaries (1875 to 1887), which are translated in part 2 of this volume, describe her privileged childhood and young adulthood in Moscow—a period of economic prosperity and political security for her family under a protective governor-general of Moscow, Prince Vladimir Andreevich Dolgorukov (1810–91). The diary provided a space where Zinaida could record daily events and reflect on them; it was her refuge from the glitter of the ballrooms and her bustling, and often conflicted, household.

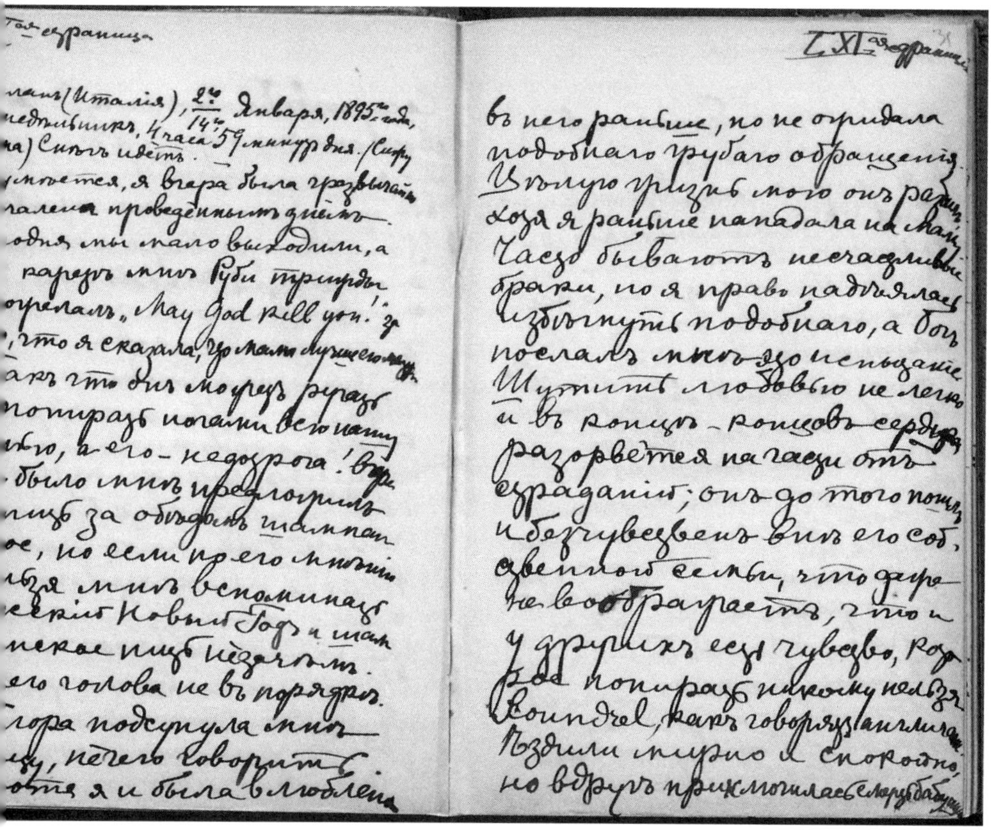

FIGURE 1

Diary entry of Zinaida Poliakova (2 January [Old Style]/14 January [New Style], 1895).
"Nauchno-issledovatel'skii otdel rukopisei Rossiiskoi gosudarstvennoi biblioteki,"
f. 743, op. 138, d. 1, ll. 30 ob–31.

Although the word "diary" implies privacy and secrecy, keeping one's diary under lock and key was not always the practice in Russian high society. In fact, Zinaida realized that her mother, who routinely opened her letters, had access to the diaries.[10] She took pleasure in sharing the diary with relatives and friends, asking them to read entries aloud or soliciting their opinions about her writing. Thus her diary became what might be termed "a literary form of sociability."[11] It provided a venue through which a woman could express certain emotions and desires[12]—an important facet of Russian diary writing—to her family without openly transgressing the social conventions and scripts of her class and gender. Indeed, Zinaida may have written certain entries, such as those about her longings for greater autonomy or her choice of groom, with her parents as her audience. Like letter writing (in which writers develop and express their subjectivity[13]), the very act of committing daily experiences to paper served both to construct and reinforce Zinaida's sense of her elite self. Drawing on literary models like Leo Tolstoy's *War and Peace* (the author's wife gave Zinaida a copy), Zinaida could write herself into narratives of Russian aristocratic ballrooms. Silence too was important: Zinaida deliberately excluded herself from stories of Jewish suffering during the pogroms of 1881, which she almost totally ignored.[14]

Read in the context of other sources (documents of family members,[15] newspapers, and various archival sources), Zinaida's diaries shed light on the complex and conflicted process of acculturation. They show how the Poliakovs became Russian aristocrats, first de facto and then de jure, as chronicled in Zinaida's diaries. Historians have long contrasted the bourgeoisies of Moscow and St. Petersburg, including people in the banking sector. Whereas the Petersburg financial elites were closely connected with the state, the Moscow banks belonged to industrialists and focused on "the region's industrial development."[16] Lazar Poliakov breaks that simplistic dichotomy. In contrast to other Moscow bankers, he had a banking and entrepreneurial empire that more closely resembled those of the Petersburg financial world—not only because his networks were more global, but also because of his close ties to the Ministry of Finance and the State Bank.[17] This intimate nexus with the state facilitated the Poliakov integration into aristocratic society. Ties to high-ranking officials and influential publishers, along with generous philanthropy, brought the Poliakovs into the world of aristocrats and royals and ever further from the community of merchants and industrialists of Moscow. The Poliakovs collaborated with other Jewish banks in Russia (especially where there were family connections through marriage), but lucrative profits and political connections took precedence over ethnic solidarity at times—a behavior that provoked criticism from some Jewish coreligionists.

Zinaida's diaries provide a fascinating narrative about a Jewish family that lived in central Moscow and forged intimate relationships with the Russian cultural, bureaucratic, and aristocratic elites. The "political economy of intimacies" in which the Poliakovs participated involved a complex calculus of capital, aristocratic sociability, and imperial philanthropy.[18] In recent years, critical studies have challenged the traditional approach to modernity that demarcates the intimate from "the state and the market," presupposing that it "belongs to the local level and private sphere."[19] Rather, as Ann Laura Stoler writes, "To study the intimate is not to turn away from structures of dominance, but to relocate their conditions of possibility and relations and forces of production."[20] Criticial to personalizing this political intimacy were the Polia-kov women, who were active as hosts of their aristocratic salon and munificent patrons of the arts. They invited both distinguished and obscure artists and musicians to their home for private performances before influential guests. In this respect, the Poliakovs did have some equivalents in Moscow (notably, the Tret'iakovs and Riabushinskiis), but in sheer scale and diversity they were out-standing—especially with respect to music. The Poliakovs aspired to create a new imperial elite culture: that culture was *rossiiskii*, not ethnic *russkii*,[21]—one that was inclusive and accommodating of their Jewishness. Through this new culture, they longed for an affective merger with Russia, not simply acquiring legal privileges due to wealth.

Yet the Poliakovs' acculturation and integration into Russian society had limits and boundaries. Alexander II's policy of selective integration of "use-ful" Jews meant freedom from onerous residency laws and the acquisition of new privileges, while aristocratic sociability opened doors for the Poliakovs to enter high society. Yet the nature of the confessional empire precluded conju-gal or familial intimacies: imperial Russian law prohibited Jews from marrying Christians without converting. For their part, the Poliakovs had no desire to cross these strict confessional lines even as they forged intimate friendships. Instead they affirmed their Jewishness through endogamous marriages, active engagement in the Jewish community, and devoted (but selective) observance of Judaism. This strategy enabled the family to construct the dual habitus that characterized the Poliakovs' bicultural Russian-Jewish identity and lifestyle. Zinaida's aristocratic habitus, constructed in the summer dachas and ball-rooms of Moscow, continued to inform her sense of distinction in France, even as her family's prosperity and prestige faded. Antisemitism in the bureaucracy and conservative Russian newspapers (owned by close friends of the Polia-kovs) also served as a constant reminder that they were not fully accepted. The Poliakovs were not immune from the expulsion of Jews from Moscow in 1891: two relatives without proper resident permits were forced to return to the Pale of Settlement. Neither were they spared attacks in the press for their alleged economic power, as we shall see below.

Zinaida's dairies, fascinating in their own right, provide rich insights into this world of Jewish elites and their intimate ties to Russian officialdom. How, even during the age of rampant antisemitism (not only popular but official), did the Poliakovs succeed? And how did they not just survive but flourish, becoming fabulously rich, influential, beloved by some Russian bureaucrats,[22] and even ennobled? And they did so as Jews: they neither converted nor inter-married, even insisting on the observance of Jewish rites, building synagogues, and supporting Jewish causes. In the final analysis, what counted was imperial *rossiiskii*, especially for a family so heavily engaged in supporting the secular elite culture. But intimacy was not simple, even within the family. As Zinaida's dairies show, tensions were indeed pervasive over where those boundaries ought to be drawn. This was especially true in the case of the changing gender roles in the sphere of business and family. The explosive conflict between Zinaida and Reuben, representing the two "Rothschild" branches, symbolize tensions within the Poliakov family itself as it sought to nurture conflicting intimacies with the family, Judaism, and Russian state and society.

• • • • • • •

From the Pale of Settlement to the Capitals

The Poliakov family originated in Poland, but in 1793 the patriarch, Lazar Samuilovich Poliakov (1748–1833), and his family moved to the small town of Dubrovno in Mogilev province. According to Iakov Poliakov, his grandfather was "considered a wealthy individual who had a store with expensive goods" that catered to wealthy landowners.[23] Following the patriarch's death, his son Solomon (Shlomo) (1812–97) opened a broadcloth shop with two older brothers,[24] and after they liquidated the business, he ran a small store with his wife, Zlata (née Rabinovich, 1812–51), who came from Minsk.[25] Hard times, however, impelled Solomon to journey to Moscow "in search of fortune" in 1842.[26] Although Jewish merchants could not reside there,[27] in 1826 the governor-general of Moscow permitted Jews from Shklov and Orsha (a town close to Dubrovna) to stay temporarily at the Glebov compound[28] in Zariad'e—a downtown commercial hub of Moscow. The compound's owner stipulated in his will that all revenues from the property be used for philanthropic purposes.[29] From the authorities' perspective, the compound not only generated funds for charity but also facilitated surveillance of the Jews. Regulations were strict and differentiated: merchants of the first and second guilds could stay for two months, but those of the third guild were limited to one month. Moreover, Jews could only purchase (not sell) goods and could do so only at this inn and one other designated building.[30] Iakov described his father's first trip to Moscow as the first step toward acculturation: "At this time, Jews still wore special clothing, and I remember what preparations were made for father's impending trip to Moscow, how they made for father clothing like that worn by the Russians—boots (Jews wore *bashmaki* [ankle boots]), a *furazhka* or peaked cap (Jews wore special *shliapy* [hats] and *shapki* [caps]."[31] In 1846 the police tightened the clothing regulations: "Jews arriving in Moscow must not appear in public places and on the streets in inadmissible clothing."[32] The attempt to blend into the Russian milieu was telling. It marked the first step toward the lifestyle of the next generation, whose members would don smart imported attire, such as the latest Charles Frederick Worth dresses from Paris.

In Solomon's absence, Zlata, like other Jewish female merchants of her generation, single-handedly ran the family's small retail store in Dubrovna. She later moved to Orsha to sell the merchandise—tailored to the "tastes and demands of her clients"—that her husband sent from Moscow.[33] Zlata gave her sons a traditional Jewish education but also arranged for them to have a tutor for Russian and arithmetic "at a time [the mid-1840s] when there was nothing special apart from the *hadarim* (elementary Jewish schools) and *melamdim* (Jewish teachers)."[34] Her initiative was extraordinary because most Jews were wary of secular education during the Nikolaevan era of "compulsory enlightenment," but it enabled her sons later to work for Russian bureaucrats newly appointed in the provinces.[35]

With respect to marriage, Zlata observed traditional norms—early and arranged marital unions with families that boasted *yikhus* (lineage) and learning.[36] "In the winter of 1849," wrote Iakov, "when I was fifteen and a half, mother married me off to the maiden Khasia Mera, the daughter of Moisei Nokhimovich Berlin from the town of Rudni," whom Iakov described as a scholar who "devoted himself exclusively to study and did not engage in other work."[37] The bride's grandfather, who "enjoyed special respect and honor among the Jews and local residents," engaged in the trade of grains and small goods, but "this did not prevent him from being a scholar in the Jewish sense of the word."[38] For her son Samuil, Zlata chose Avdot'ia Epshtein, whose father bequeathed a large house to the family upon his death. The youngest son, Lazar (Zinaida's father), was only eight years old when his mother suddenly died of pneumonia in 1851 (a tragedy that Iakov blamed on Dr. Mezer, who continued playing cards when Zlata's tearful sons ran to his house pleading for help). When Lazar came of age, his family betrothed him to the daughter of a certain Shakhno of Chausy in Mogilev province. The girl—whom none of the Poliakovs had actually seen—was reputed to be a "phenomenon—beautiful, intelligent, educated, and so forth."[39] To their dismay, within a few months the prospective bride suddenly died—a tragedy that the brothers concealed from Lazar, merely informing him that they had annulled the match because certain unspecific conditions had not been met. According to Iakov, his father quickly found another bride, who was to become Zinaida's mother: "After this, being present in Moscow, father betrothed Lazar to Rozaliia, the daughter of P[avel] Vydrin. Vydrin was also in Moscow; both fathers probably met by chance and matched one's son to the other's daughter."[40] Despite the absence of the customary care that his mother had put into matchmaking, Iakov praised the result, especially the bride's business acumen: "The Vydrins ran an iron goods business in Mogilev. The bride Rozaliia managed a store and was considered knowledgeable in her business."[41] Rozaliia remained active in the family's finances after her marriage, to Iakov's chagrin—especially when she refused to back risky loans to rescue his failing banks or chided him about previous loans that he had not repaid.

Like other first-generation Jewish entrepreneurs such as the Gintsburgs,[42] the Poliakov brothers initially worked for Jewish tax farmers[43] and later became tax farmers in their own right.[44] They took advantage of opportunities created by a Russian state that was eager to consolidate its power in the western provinces. As Iakov observed, the Polish uprising of 1863 was a disaster for Poles, who had previously dominated the local administration. They were replaced by a "new class of [Russian] state excise officials" whom Iakov held in high regard as "young people, almost all with higher education with the best views and inclinations, honest without a doubt."[45] By cultivating intimate ties with enlightened Russian bureaucrats (first in the provinces and then in the capitals), the Poliakov brothers made themselves indispensable by intertwining their finances with those of officials at the highest levels of government.

Their fortunes rose exponentially when Ivan M. Tolstoi (1806–67), the minister of posts and telegraphs, hired Samuil to manage a vodka distillery on his estate and several postal stations in Riazan. Samuil in turn subcontracted the business to his brother Lazar, and the Tolstoi patronage opened the door to other lucrative state contracts (for example, to supply the army during the Russo-Turkish War of 1877–78) and to the new business of private railway construction. As a result, in the 1860s and 1870s Samuil became the "founder, concessionaire, and owner" of several private railroad lines, including the Kozlov-Voronezh-Rostov-na-Donu, Kursk-Khar'kov-Azov, Tsarskoe Selo, Orenburg, Fastov, and other lines.[46] Although most railway companies remained private until the 1890s, the state guaranteed and regulated them. One major commission for the Poliakovs was the Bender-Galats railway line for the military, which cost an estimated 5,550,000 silver rubles.[47] Iakov, who oversaw its construction in 1878, proudly described how he met Tsarevich Alexander (the future Alexander III) during the train's maiden voyage from Galats to Bender: "The heir shook my hand . . . and thanked me very courteously for the successful trip, [and] asked about the health of my brother [Samuil, who was ill]. I presented him with the album [of the Bender-Galats railroad]. He remembered that I had also presented him with an album in Cherkassy. He

FIGURE 2

Samuil Solomonovich Poliakov (uncle of Zinaida Poliakova).

Zinaida Poliakova and Alexander Poliakoff, *Sem'ia Poliakovykh*, ed. Larisa Nikolaevna Vasil'evna (Moscow: Atlantida, 1995).

began to examine the album at great length and asked for explanations and clarifications. This continued for more than half an hour and then he again shook my hand."[48] As recognition for the speed with which he constructed the Russian railroads, Samuil received a medal at the Paris World Exhibition in 1878 (figures 2 and 3).

FIGURE 3
Samuil Poliakov and his son Daniil (Daniel) Poliakov.
Poliakova and Poliakoff, *Sem'ia Poliakovykh*.

However, not everyone was impressed with the pace of construction. Critics complained that Samuil, the "Railway King,"[49] enriched himself by inflating costs, engaged in influence peddling (allocating railway shares to state ministers), and used shoddy construction materials. "Not for any amount of money will I go into business with Poliakov," declared a rival railroad contractor, Fedor Chizhov, who refused to "soil" his name by having any contracts with Poliakov.[50] Accusations of "substandard railway construction" proliferated after the notorious Borki train accident in 1888, when the imperial family was on board but miraculously escaped unharmed. Despite evidence that excessive speed was the real cause, many placed the blame on the railway builders—the Poliakovs.[51] Iakov recorded the disaster in his diary:

> One can say that 1888 is deemed the most unfortunate year, which reached its acme in the catastrophe of 17 October on the Kursk-Khar'kov railroad with the tsar's train. In a flash, twenty years of work was lost, and what labor it was. The Poliakov name was vilified in all the newspapers (with few exceptions they rushed off to write) . . . but as God is my witness, only a zealous bureaucrat, without paying any attention, put together the schedules, and others with the same amount of attention, wanted—no matter what, seeking to get medals and awards—to meet that insane schedule. No one had the courage to speak up. And such a train, and such a schedule should never have existed, still less carry the emperor with the tsarist family. But thank God they were saved by a miracle, and not by the precautions of those whose duty it was to protect, warn, and foresee.[52]

This incident only reinforced the emperor's disdain for Jews. According to Sergei Witte, Alexander III viewed railway lines run by Jewish companies as abominable and called Ivan Blokh's Southwest Railway an example of a "Yid's railroad (*zhidovskaia doroga*)."[53] The link between the railroad and Jews, indeed, also found its way into both Russian and Jewish literature.[54]

Samuil Poliakov was spared the humiliation of Borki: he had died of a sudden heart attack six months earlier on the way to the funeral of his close friend and in-law, Abram (Anton) Varshavskii (Warshawsky) (1821–88).[55] Malicious rumors blamed Varshavskii's suicide on the refusal of his son Leon (Samuil's son-in-law) "to provide money to pay a bill of exchange that had come due."[56] Although silent about Varshavskii's suicide, Iakov noted that his death "had a staggering impact on [my] brother who loved him from his soul." The loss was all the more painful for Samuil, whose twenty-five-year-old daughter Roza (married to Leon Varshavskii [Warshawsky]) had died a few years earlier, leaving behind her newborn son Ignatii (Ignace)[57] and daughter Marie

(Maroussia)[58] — an event that Zinaida describes in her diaries. At the time of his death, Samuil's net worth was 31,425,546 rubles, including a mansion on the English Quay assessed at 532,050 rubles. After taxes, however, the amount distributed to his heirs — mainly his immediate family and two brothers — was 16,360,200 rubles.[59]

Samuil's funeral procession was described by his neighbor Ivan Alekseevich Shestakov (1820–88), the minister of the navy: "I was only able to witness such a mass of people as at the Poliakov's send-off. The entire space from my house, up to my window, through the Senate Square was densely packed with people."[60] The Hebrew press captured the extravagance of the event — from the "expensive, metal coffin adorned with palm branches" and covered with a "black cloth lined with a silver border" to the "magnificent carriage" pulled by three pairs of horses.[61] In attendance were state dignitaries,[62] leaders of the St. Petersburg Jewish community (such as Baron Horace Gintsburg), representatives from the railroad companies and banks, and students and teachers from educational institutions that Samuil had helped establish. Jewish communities such as Kovno, Dinaburg, Grodno, and Vil'na that had benefited from his generosity also sent emissaries. Laudatory obituaries emphasized Samuil's contributions to Russian society (for example, he helped create Russia's first railroad school in the town of Elets[63]) and stifled criticism that the "Railway King" was more interested in hobnobbing with Russian elites than with his own people.

Among Samuil's harshest critics was Genrikh Sliozberg. An influential lawyer and public figure in St. Petersburg, Sliozberg castigated Poliakov for his aloofness from the Jewish community, drawing a sharp contrast between the railway magnate and Horace Gintsburg — a model of communal leadership in Sliozberg's view: "He [Samuil] avoided relations with St. Petersburg Jewry [and] stood like a private mansion apart from them; but then he gave a cordial reception to all high officials, princes, counts, seeking his favor in their material interests. . . . His business influence brought no benefits for Jews; this did more to irritate him than to make him better disposed toward them. His participation in Jewish institutions was almost imperceptible, but he was glad to participate in imperial institutions of general utility."[64] Sliozberg was especially critical of Samuil's donations to create student dormitories in memory of Alexander II at the St. Petersburg University at a time "when they did not accept Jews at all."[65] Sliozberg acknowledged Samuil's participation in the creation of an organization in 1880 that evolved into the Society of Artisanal and Agricultural Labor among Jews in Russia,[66] which aimed to make Jews productive through crafts and agriculture. But the real force behind the initiative, claimed Sliozberg, was not Poliakov (who received some credit for the

FIGURE 4

Iakov Solomonovich Poliakov (uncle of Zinaida Poliakova).
https://blog.nli.org.il/en/the_brothers_polyakov/, Yakov Polyakov, The Abraham Schwadron
Portrait Collection at the NLI. Segula, *The Jewish History Magazine*, Issue 97, June 2018.
National Library of Israel.

project) but a professor of medicine named Nikolai Ignat'evich Bakst (1842–1904).[67] While Sliozberg's hostility may have been personal (stemming from a cold reception by a Poliakov), it reflected the broader sentiment that Jews should not donate large sums to their oppressors. That view would also plague Zinaida's father, Lazar, because of his connections to antisemitic publishers and politicians. Even in the West, the *Jewish Messenger* emphasized Samuil's contribution of more than two million rubles to Russian institutions (schools, "hospitals, churches, and asylums of every kind"), before adding that "his co-religionists have not been neglected."[68]

Iakov mourned the death of "a dear brother to whom we owed everything from beginning to end."[69] It was at Samuil's initiative that, in 1865, Iakov had first moved to Voronezh to help him manage Count Tolstoi's liquor and textile factories[70]—a decision that Rebbe [Menachem] Mendel of Lubavitch (whom Iakov sought out for advice) allegedly assured him he would not regret.[71] Just as he felt settled with his family in Voronezh, having purchased a grand two-story house and developed ties to local administrators, in 1868 Iakov had to move to Taganrog at Samuil's request to work on the Kursk-Khar'kov-Azov railway line, while Lazar relocated to Khar'kov.[72] In Taganrog, Iakov registered as a first-guild merchant, and in 1871 he earned the Order of St. Stanislav of the Third Degree that conferred the status of hereditary honorary citizen.[73] With his new capital and prestige, Iakov purchased the Novomar'inskoe estate in Taganrog,[74] opened his first banking house,[75] and oversaw various ventures—such as a newly founded Azov shipping company, a coal mine on his estate in Krasnopol' (using engineers trained abroad at his expense),[76] and other businesses in Persia undertaken jointly with Lazar.

The two older Poliakov brothers accumulated enormous wealth, but Zinaida's father, Lazar, surpassed both of them. His assets included a bank (which owned securities valued at forty million rubles in the late 1890s) and the majority of shares "in joint-stock companies and banks controlled by the Moscow financier himself."[77] Like his brothers, Lazar began his career in Orsha as a petty merchant, but he soon became involved in Samuil's enterprises, including the profitable management of postal stations in Riazan in the 1860s.[78] According to Iakov, Lazar suffered from poor health during these early years: on one trip Iakov found his brother sick, looking "thin, withered, pale." The doctors diagnosed Lazar with tuberculosis and advised him to take the koumiss cure. Iakov took him to Count Tolstoi's dacha and, on the advice of acquaintances, purchased a mare and engaged a Tatar woman to brew high-quality koumiss. After two months of treatment, Lazar "went home absolutely healthy."[79] As the diaries of Iakov and Zinaida show, Lazar was later repeatedly forced to have prolonged bed rest and extensive treatment. In 1863, during this Riazan phase, Zinaida was born—Lazar and Rozaliia's first child, named after her grandmother (Zinaida is the Russian equivalent of the Yiddish Zlata). Five years later the family moved to Khar'kov so that Lazar could oversee construction of the Kursk-Khar'kov-Azov railroad line.

Taking advantage of his opportunities, Lazar worked diligently to acquire wealth and status. He registered as a first-guild merchant's brother in Taganrog (based on Iakov's capital) and in 1870 independently attained the status of hereditary honorary citizen (together with the Order of St. Stanislaw, third degree) for his role in the construction of the Kursk-Khar'kov-Azov railway line.[80] He raised his status in the society of Riazan by contributing to various charities and became an honorary member of the Riazan Provincial Guardianship of Children's Shelters. With his newfound status and wealth, Lazar was ready to move upward—to Moscow, the old capital and heart of the Russian empire.

The Dolgorukov Era

In 1870, seven-year-old Zinaida and her family arrived in a Moscow with golden cupolas, white stone cathedrals, and colorful streets that presented "a bizarre mix" of East and West.[81] Although Peter the Great had relocated the capital to St. Petersburg in 1713, Moscow represented what was truly Russian, with little of the Western veneer of St. Petersburg. "Every Russian looking at Moscow feels her to be a mother; every foreigner who *sees* her, even if ignorant of her significance as the mother city, must feel her feminine character and Napoleon felt it," wrote Tolstoy in *War and Peace*—a novel that influenced Zinaida's sense of belonging to Moscow.[82]

Even before the 1870s, Moscow was being transformed from a "big village" into a modern metropolis based on railroads, commerce, and industry. Indeed, Moscow increasingly came to resemble "a big construction site," with new buildings packed vertically into the old blocks of the medieval city.[83] New structures—railroad terminals, multistory rental houses, public buildings, and offices—rose up between the Muscovite facades, giving an ambience of jumbled modernity.[84] The wealth of the center quickly gave way to the poverty of the periphery, where shantytowns of impoverished workers sprawled for miles. Drawn by the economic opportunities of the city, migrant workers lived if not in barracks, then in one-story wooden houses, without running water or sewer systems.[85]

Jews had begun to settle in Moscow in the late 1850s, when the state gave people in "useful categories" (initially retired soldiers, first-guild merchants, skilled artisans, and university students and later pharmacists, dentists, paramedics, and midwives) the right to reside outside the Pale of Settlement.[86] By 1871 Moscow—which long resisted the presence of Jews—had 5,319 registered Jews, and that number would triple over the next decade.[87] The heart of Jewish Moscow was Zariad'e, the downtown district (and site of the Glebov compound), but after 1856 Jewish residents were no longer restricted to this area. As the writer Ivan Belousov recalled, the Zariad'e of his childhood resembled an exotic bazaar of some remote Jewish shtetl in the Pale of Settlement: "Along the lanes were small Jewish meat and sausage stores and bakeries, in which they baked an enormous quantity of *matzah*—dry flat bread from unleavened dough—for Jewish Passover. The Zariad'e bakers baked *matzah* not only for the local population but for sale in other cities."[88] Artisans and retired soldiers also lived there, renting modest premises from wealthy owners. In the long summer months, cobblers and furriers worked at their trades on the long access balconies that the apartments shared and that led to the sole entrance to the building. Belousov recalled the illegal residents who also found their way into the neighborhood: "Many fortune tellers took shelter in the dark, dirty cellars of the Zariad'e houses; a few of them were renowned in all of Moscow, and wealthy female merchants from the Moscow environs came to them to have their fortunes told. These 'famous' fortune tellers occupied decently furnished apartments and practiced their trade openly, thanks to bribes to the police who should have expelled them according to the law."[89] The wealthy predictably left Zariad'e: for example, the Vysotskii (Wissotzky) tea merchants took up residence on the picturesque Miasnitskaia Street (one of the first to have gas lighting installed in the 1870s).

Zinaida's father, Lazar, moved his growing family into a house on the fashionable Tverskoi Boulevard—popular among the nobility—that Samuil had purchased from a merchant and later put in Lazar's name.[90] The house witnessed many magnificent events, like the winter ball of 1857–58, which has been described by Count Dmitrii Nikiforov (who later lost his bid to Lazar, the Poliakov's rival group, to establish the Moscow Land Bank), and it was where a prominent military commander, Nikolai Obolenskii, met his future wife.[91] Zinaida grew up on Tverskoi Boulevard with her nine younger siblings: Khaia (Ksenia or Xenia), Mikhail (Misha or Michel), Aaron (Ronia), Il'ia (Il'iusha or Elie), Raisa (Raechka, Raia, or Rachel), Isaak (Satia), Iakov (Iasha or Jacques), Aleksandr (Sasha), and Beniamin (Baby or Benjamin). The second oldest child, Avgust (Azi or August), had died suddenly from illness on the eve of the High Holidays in 1872, when the family was vacationing in Geneva, Switzerland. Zinaida's Uncle Iakov remembered Lazar's and Rozaliia's "misfortune, losing their oldest, most beloved son."[92] Perhaps growing up in a household full of children—her siblings and Vydrin relatives on her mother's side[93]— helped console Zinaida, who was nine at the time of her brother's death and rarely wrote about the loss. She did insert a poem about him in her diary and described his gravestone in 1902, when she visited the Jewish cemetery in Geneva to pay her respects at the boy's grave and saw how his memorial had been restored at the order of her brother Mikhail.[94]

• • • • • • •

The Poliakov Financial Empire

When twelve-year-old Zinaida began her diary in 1875, she took little interest in the banking revolution that her father had initiated in the financial world. It was during her adolescence that Lazar lay the foundations for the family's

FIGURE 5

Lazar Solomonovich Poliakov (father of Zinaida Poliakova).

Poliakova and Poliakoff, *Sem'ia Poliakovykh*.

wealth and privilege. Two years after attaining the status of a Moscow first-guild merchant in 1871, Lazar established the L. S. Poliakov Banking House, which was to serve as the hub for his empire of joint-stock and commercial banks, railroad and insurance companies, and other enterprises in Russia and abroad.

Private banking houses emerged after the Crimean War and an international financial crisis compelled the government to close its state banks and launch far-reaching monetary and credit reforms. One of the earliest Jewish financial institutions to appear was the I. E. Gintsburg Banking House in St. Petersburg, founded by Evzel' Gintsburg in 1859 (with an international branch in Paris).[95] That was the model for Lazar's own banking house and fueled his lifelong aspiration to become a baron just like Gintsburg.[96] Until the 1890s, private banking houses were virtually unregulated, enjoying a special status that exempted them from the obligations to incorporate, file a governing charter (*ustav*), and issue public financial statements about their activities and account balances.[97] Free from state regulation, the banks played a critical role in providing affordable private and commercial loans at a time when credit was expensive and scarce.[98] At the time Lazar's bank began operations, the credit market was still a weak sector, but it was beginning to develop.[99] Bills of exchange (*vekseli*), which had functioned as the primary instrument of credit transactions among merchants, became accessible in 1852 as private loan documents to almost all social groups (with the exception of the clergy, noncommissioned officers, and women). Although the easing of restrictions aimed to "liberalize Russian private credit," deregulation actually made "credit even more dependent on personal connections" and difficult to obtain.[100] Traditionally, large-scale foreign loans were only accessible through court bankers in St. Petersburg like the Stieglitz family (Jewish converts to Lutheranism) with ties to international banks. However, rates on short-term loans were exorbitant because of the frequent bankruptcies of Russian merchants.[101] After the middle of the nineteenth century, the new State Bank (established in 1860) and private banking houses increasingly displaced the court bankers, offering better terms and gradually developing a more reliable system of credit and deposits.[102]

The Poliakov Banking House more closely resembled the financial institutions in St. Petersburg than did the Moscow banks that were founded at the same time but known as the "old ones."[103] Influenced by ideas of the economic historian Ivan K. Babst (1823–81), the Moscow banks catered almost exclusively to the established industries in Moscow, shunning speculation on the stock market and risky new ventures.[104] The Moscow banks filled their boards with industrialists, not professional bankers.[105] In the words of Vladimir Riabushinskii, an Old Believer financier from an established mercantile family, "The native Moscow banks were very specific and differed significantly from St. Petersburg ones: their major goal was solidity. . . . Moscow traditions implied the rejection of the speculative establishment of new enterprises, in which Petersburg banks were so active. The risk of such a policy was excessively close dependence of the bank's destiny on that of the establishments patronized by it. Moscow was afraid of this."[106] Old Believers—archconservative religious dissenters who broke with the Russian Orthodox Church in the mid-seventeenth century over liturgical and ritual reform—were strongly attracted to the Moscow model of banking, which dovetailed with their ideals of self-discipline, strict business ethics, disdain of usury, and commitment to supporting the enterprises of coreligionists. As one historian has observed, bankers like the Riabushinskiis sought to harness the power of capitalism to "a system of communal credit" that could serve to "ensure their community's survival in a hostile environment."[107] The founders of these "old banks" exhibited an intense animus toward Jewish competitors like the Poliakovs and accused them of unscrupulous business practices. When the Riabushinskiis opened a branch office in St. Petersburg, they warned their employees about the dangers of the capital city, where "exchange orgies and unprincipled brokers, mainly of Jewish origin, . . . were masters of the game."[108] Reinforced by the traditional animosity of Old Believers toward the state and tsar,[109] resentment of the Poliakovs may have also had to do with their close connections to government officials, whom they openly courted to win special concessions.

The nobleman Dmitri Nikiforov (1833–1907), who was not an Old Believer, echoed Riabushinskii's accusation of Jewish influence when he wrote about his failed attempt, with four other partners, to create the Moscow Land Bank. Despite assurances of a positive outcome from state officials, Nikiforov learned that a rival group had submitted an identical proposal to the Ministry of Finance, and that the group had invited two of his partners to join them. Petr G. Vol'kov, one of those invited, warned Nikiforov to abandon the project and "not to struggle against such forces as Prince [Vladimir] Cherkasskii[110] and the railroad man [Lazar] Poliakov," the leaders of the rival group with twenty investors.[111] When Nikiforov complained to the minister of finance, the latter suggested that the two groups unite and split the stocks among themselves rather than sell shares to the public as they had planned. According to Nikiforov, disagreements over the value of land in Riazan and intimidation by Cherkasskii pressured one investor in his group named Konoplin to cede his stock to Lazar, "who immediately doubled his quantity of shares." Then another investor declined to buy all his allotted shares, and these had to be divided among the other investors. In the end, claimed Nikiforov, "the entire business was controlled by Cherkasskii jointly with Poliakov, and there was nothing left for us to do but sell our shares because we did not have any influence on the course of business"—and in fact his partners sold most of their shares.

Lazar's connections to high officials were indeed central to his success in building his banking network. As a result that empire came to include the Orlov Bank (1870), the Riazan Commercial Bank (1871; later renamed the Moscow International Commercial Bank), the Moscow Land Bank (1872), the Iaroslavl'-Kostroma Land Bank (1873), the Petersburg-Moscow Bank (1884), and the Southern Russian Industrial Bank (1897). To manage this financial empire, Lazar placed his sons Mikhail, Isaak, and Aleksandr strategically on the administrative boards. Although his wife Rozaliia played a central role in his banks as a major stockholder, none of their daughters had a place at the business table. Now armed with easy access to capital, Lazar could control transactions among his various enterprises[112] and arrange things for his personal benefit. For instance, he allowed the Moscow Lumber Company (which he founded) to acquire estates with mortgages from his Moscow Land Bank, thereby receiving "hundreds of thousands [of rubles] in the form of additional mortgage loans."[113] Lazar also speculated on mortgage bonds on the stock exchange and made unheard-of profits. Although such transactions were risky, domestic mortgage banks like Poliakov's played a valuable role in Russia's economic development by promoting the creation of a land market, private peasant farms, and urban construction.[114] At the beginning of the twentieth century, the Moscow Land Bank had 10.5 million rubles in fixed capital and 6.6 million rubles in reserve—a formidable sum, which prompted the board, on the occasion of the bank's fortieth anniversary, to praise Lazar for "raising [the bank] to its highest acme in Russia."[115]

While Lazar's success owed much to favorable market conditions (until the recession of the late 1890s), contemporaries were more disposed to link his good fortune to his intimate friendship with Prince Dolgorukov. And the ties were very public. Prince B. A. Shchetinin, for example, called Poliakov an "indispensable guest" at Dolgorukov's famed lavish balls "with [their] sea of champagne, the tried and true Riabov orchestra,[116] and magnificent live flowers from Nice."[117] It was at these balls that mothers of the *haut monde* presented their daughters for their first dances. These sumptuous affairs required capital, and "malicious tongues" gossiped that Poliakov had opened an account for Dolgorukov "in his Land Bank for any sum" (which Shchetinin found entirely credible): "That the Prince was in need of money—of this there can be no doubt, because he had transferred his entire fortune (which was invested in substantial real estate) to his son-in-law, General-Adjutant N. V. Voeikov, who only paid him the annual stipulated sum." That income was hardly sufficient, claimed Shchetinin: "The Prince loved to live in grand style, and to exercise charity with a generous hand. He was not shy about donating tens and hundreds of rubles from his own means for the benefit of needy students, poor artists, and various almshouses, shelters, etc." Given this state of affairs, he argued, Dolgorukov's "friendly disposition to the Jewish millionaire could surely inspire a certain suspicion, all the more so because year after year, the latter was showered with every honor and mark of distinction."[118] Shchetinin relished repeating an anecdote about Lazar after he received the title of state councilor:[119] when one of his clerks greeted him, "Hello, Lazar Solomonovich," the new state councilor allegedly retorted: "I am no longer Lazar Solomonovich to you—but Your Excellency!" Thanks to Lazar's ties to Dolgorukov, claimed Shchetinin, "the Jews of Moscow could feel the firm ground beneath their feet, because in case of need, they could always turn to their influential patron, requesting him for protection or patronage."[120] He claimed that almost any Jew could obtain a residence permit if he or she registered in the service of a first-guild merchant: "As a result, some bizarre things happened: one fine day it turned out that the same Poliakov had 34 cooks in his service!"[121] Perhaps this was an exaggeration, but Lazar did manage to obtain residency rights for his stepmother's two nieces (who took care of their blind aunt until their expulsion from Moscow in 1891) and a family cook (whose son was in the choir at Lazar's synagogue).

Jewish contemporaries offered their own versions about the intimate friendship between Poliakov and the "boss of Moscow" (*khoziain Moskva*). Roza Vinaver, the daughter of a wealthy merchant in Moscow and wife of Maksim Vinaver (a Jewish lawyer and liberal Kadet deputy in the first State Duma), recalled her first thoughts when she heard about the assassination of Alexander II: "I was nine years old but I already understood that something extremely terrible had happened which could have an impact on all our lives. However, while the governor-general Prince Dolgorukii [sic] remained at his post, it could be possible to live peacefully under his protection. The fact that Dolgorukii [sic] was friends with the Jewish banker, Lazar Poliakov, had an especially soothing effect on my childish imagination. We children were convinced that no one could touch us as long as Dolgorukii [sic] went to the Poliakovs for dinner."[122]

Zinaida's diaries offer abundant evidence of the two men's intimacy. On 2 August 1884, for instance, she recounted how her father accompanied Prince Dolgorukov to the railway station: "Papa was given the prince's portrait with the inscription 'it is a matter of railway cars,' i.e., it is a question of in whose

FIGURE 6

Rozaliia Pavlovna Poliakova, née Vydrina (mother of Zinaida Poliakova).

Poliakova and Poliakoff, *Sem'ia Poliakovykh*.

car he will travel in—that of Fon Derviz or ours. In the end he traveled as usual in a Fon Derviz car, and thinking Papa will be offended by this, made his apologies and invited Papa to lunch." Zinaida's references to balls at Dolgorukov's echo Shchetinin's stories, as do similar descriptions in other Jewish memoirs. According to one relative, Zinaida's mother opened the winter ball for Dolgorukov, who was grateful for "Lazar helping the governor-general's adjutant with his debts."[123] Sliozberg claimed that Russian women in high society strongly disliked Rozaliia because of the special attention that she received from the prince: "Rumor had it that at one ball at the palace of Governor-General Prince Dologorukov, he and Madame Poliakova led the polonaise as the first couple."[124]

Sliozberg observed that until the creation of the State Noble Land Bank in 1885, Poliakov's Moscow Land Bank was a key source of credit for noble landowners in the central provinces and had a virtual monopoly over these services. "Poliakov had many friends but no lack of enemies," Sliozberg concluded.[125] "The bank was all the more important because there was not a noble landowner who had not mortgaged his estate or in some measure become dependent on the bank." To secure mortgages, the nobility ingratiated itself with Lazar, and the latter "made himself available to them." In contrast to his brother Samuil, writes Sliozberg, Lazar "considered it his duty to do a service for everyone possible and was in the position to do so." Lazar's generosity notwithstanding, the fact that a Jewish banker held the debts of Russian noble landowners and industrialists contributed to the "antisemitic atmosphere of the time, creating pent-up hostility against the 'Jew Poliakov'," and animosity that extended from Poliakov to Jews in general.[126]

The image of a Jewish banker holding reception hours for debt-ridden Russian nobles elicited an unflattering portrayal in Tolstoy's *Anna Karenina* (1877). Anna's brother Stepan Oblonsky, who finds that "his affairs were in very bad way," asks his brother-in-law, Aleksey Karenin, to put in a good word with Pomorsky to appoint him secretary of the Committee of the Amalgamated Agency of the Southern Railroad and Banking.[127] Karenin responds, "But I imagine it's more in Bolgarinov's hands." The sound of that name suddenly sullies the image of "new, genuine, and honest public body" that Oblonsky has just described in glowing terms to Karenin, when he recalls his unpleasant meeting with the Jewish financier that morning:

Whether he was uncomfortable that he, a descendant of Rurik, Prince Oblonsky, had been kept waiting two hours to see a Jew, or that for the first time in his life he was not following the example of his ancestors in serving the government, but was turning off into a new career, anyway he was very uncomfortable. During the two hours in Bolgarinov's waiting room, Stepan Arkadevich, stepping jauntily about the room, pulling his whiskers, entering into conversation with the other petitioners, attempting to invent a pun he would repeat afterwards—how he was *jewing* his cud at the Jews'—tried very hard to hide from others and even from himself the feeling he was experiencing.[128]

To add insult to injury, when Oblonsky finally was admitted for his appointment, Bolgarinov "with exaggerated politeness and unmistakable triumph at his humiliation" refuses to grant his request for the position.[129] Tolstoy may have modeled Bolgarinov after one of the Poliakov brothers (most likely Samuil, given the characterization) and evidently took pleasure in using a Jewish character to punish Oblonsky—the privileged profligate who cares so little about his family. Oblonsky, who humiliated his wife Dolly (with an affair that opens the novel), is thoroughly humiliated by a Jew who (he believes) is below his station yet holds the fate of his career in his hands. The irony of the inverted power relations between a blue-blooded Russian ("a descendant of Rurik") and the Jew who now presides over granting positions makes Oblonsky's mortification all the more conspicuous and painful.

Zinaida, an avid reader of Tolstoy, must have read this blockbuster novel but does not refer to it in her diaries. Rather, she cites *War and Peace*—a novel that celebrated the cultural practices of the nobility that her family so diligently emulated. Although her family did not become hereditary nobles until 1897 and remained in the modest rank of a first-guild merchant, the Poliakovs hobnobbed mainly with Russian aristocrats, not merchants.

✦ ✦ ✦ ✦ ✦ ✦ ✦

Emulating Russian Aristocrats

The Poliakovs, who were neither native Muscovites nor hereditary aristocrats, raised their children to be members of the cultured Russian elite. That Russianness, ironically, required mastery of foreign languages, and Zinaida's mother therefore engaged foreign tutors and governesses to teach her children multiple languages—English, German, and especially French, an indispensable marker of gentility for Russian nobles.[130] Nevertheless, Russian was the family's everyday language and served to demonstrate their national belonging. Even at the acme of Francomania in the late eighteenth century, but especially after the Napoleonic Wars, Russian nobles came to emphasize Russian as their native tongue.[131] Zinaida's mother tongue was indubitably Russian: her English, French, and German were fluent but flawed (with misspellings and lapses in grammar and syntax), but her Russian was impeccable, rich in diction, permeated with references to belles lettres (especially the work of Tolstoy), and given to invoking popular proverbs. She was well aware of her limited command of foreign languages. On 13 March 1885, for example, the twenty-two-year-old Zinaida did not mince words about her English nanny: "All the children have forgotten how to speak English; Russian now reigns in our household." Her diaries show that she regularly read conservative Russian publications,[132] with a particular eye for news about her father and their friends. Significantly, Zinaida used her Russian-language skills to judge the intelligence of Jewish acquaintances, as shown in this diary entry from 30 January 1886: "Every day we have guests: G[rigorii] Rozenberg and wife, and L[azar] Izr[ailevich] Brodskii[133] with his male cousin. The latter is not attractive: he wrote yesterday in my album, and I found him more stupid than I previously thought. First, although he is Russian, he does not know how to speak Russian. Second, despite the fact that he has a law degree, he cannot answer the simple questions posed in my booklet. I invite all young people to write in it."

After Zinaida emigrated to France in 1891, Russian proved to be her intimate companion, a portable sanctuary that provided a way to decode and describe her experiences. Deeply offended by Reuben's coldness after the New Year's fight, Zinaida wrote: "You can't take love lightly, and in the end, the heart breaks into pieces from suffering (*stradanie*). . . . These regrettable circumstances agitated his weak nerves and gall, and again I must endure his verbal abuse." Her use of *stradanie* was revealing: the word signifies "effort and painful labor" and also implies "passion" (*strast'*), an "elevated moral value" rooted in Russian spirituality.[134]

Russianness also expressed itself as an intimate, organic bond to the land. During a visit to her father's estate of Tsurikovo in Smolensk province in 1881 (the year of violent pogroms in Ukraine), Zinaida was in raptures over the idyllic beauty of the Russian countryside: "Just now I passed out sweets to peasant women and children. I very much liked the view today: the manor house built on an elevation, with the balcony opening for a view of the mountains that are dotted with peasant houses on the slope (villages that belong to the estate). To the right of our house is an old path leading to the church, and a hill is to the left" (30 July 1881). Chancing upon a picturesque place, a family friend "insisted on naming [it] after me ('Zinino')" in her honor—much to her pleasure. Her mother, Rozaliia, extended the joy of communing with Russian nature to her side of the family, the Vydrins, who spent their summers at Tsurikovo, away

FIGURE 7

Entrance to a Poliakov dacha in Russia.

Courtesy of Pierre-Daniel Beguin, who received it from Claire [Visha] de Poliakoff,
wife of Aleksandr Poliakov [de Poliakoff]).

from the heat of the Moscow summers.[135] The family eventually acquired six
other estates in four different provinces: Novo-Pavlovsk and Goguansk (Orel'
province), Zumruk and Koz'e (Tauride province), Kavkazskoe (Chernomorsk
province), and Serebriansk (Khar'kov province). It was at once a show of prosperity and of connection with the land.

The Poliakovs purchased a summer dacha closer to home—in the popular
pastoral nook of Sokol'niki, on the outskirts of Moscow. By the last third of
the nineteenth century, the dacha had become an indispensable part of the
privileged lifestyle, evolving from a modest vacation cottage to a full-fledged
summer house. Urban elites found respite from their daily lives and an escape
from the "heat, dirt, and diseases of the city in the summer."[136] In 1886 Anton
Chekhov admonished a friend for failing to observe this summer ritual: "You
should be ashamed of staying in stuffy Moscow. . . . Living in town in summer
is worse than pederasty and viler than bestiality."[137] To the dacha the Poliakov
family also fled, spending their leisure time in warm-weather sociable activi-

ties: gathering nuts, playing games like croquet, taking strolls in nature, and horseback riding (Zinaida's brother Il'ia became an equestrian as an adult in France).[138] Free from studies and social obligations, Zinaida wrote at length about visits to neighbors (such as the merchant-banking family of Artem Liamin) with children her age. The city was close enough that she could take day trips to Moscow, including one on 17 July 1881 to see Alexander III and the imperial family: "I was at the royal audience in the Kremlin palace and saw the Sovereign, his wife, the heir, and [his brother] Georgii. They very cordially bowed, but the heir and his brother Georgii Aleksandrovich were looking upward. Then we drove to Tverskoi Boulevard to our house and at 5 pm returned to Sokol'niki." It was inconvenient, however, to attend synagogue services in the city, so the family built a private synagogue at their dacha.

Although Zinaida spent her early childhood in Riazan and Khar'kov before coming to Moscow in 1870,[139] she regarded the capital as her real home. In a diary entry of 25 September 1887, she invoked Tolstoyan language about the maternal character of Moscow: "For the first time [my brother] Il'ia and I went out in the carriage for a half hour and breathed the fresh, but not clean air of our dear capital, mother Moscow." Even after Zinaida moved abroad, she continued to identify with events in Russia: On 13 July 1906, for example, she wrote: "A revolution is taking place now at home (*u nas*)," and only as an afterthought did she refer to the infamous Dreyfus case that earlier preoccupied France.[140] Zinaida's patriotism was evident during World War II, when she found herself under German occupation. "The courageous Russians are fighting like lions," she wrote on 8 April 1944. As the tide of war turned, she wrote proudly on 11 June 1944: "My motherland (*rodina*)—Russia—is now fighting magnificently." Despite her fear of communists, Zinaida praised the victory of the Red Army in her final diary (in an undated entry probably written in 1950): "The bravery of the Russian soldiers is indisputable, and it is therefore possible that the U.S.S.R. will conquer the whole world."[141] There was some irony that this statement came from the daughter of Moscow's famed capitalist.

Zinaida's upbringing, which fostered love of tsar and country, included none of the business skills so typical of previous generations of women in her family. That, however, reflected a general pattern: the engagement of Russian merchant women in business declined significantly in the late imperial period, reflecting the onset of new "bourgeois family" norms and the rise of organized business with male predominance.[142] It was all quite different from the time of Zinaida's grandmother, Zlata, who had single-handedly run the family's retail store in Dubrovna and later in Orsha. Zinaida's own mother, Rozaliia, had likewise managed a store in Mogilev before her marriage to Lazar. Even after the marriage, she insisted on being directly involved in the family's financial enterprises and held her own stocks in Lazar's banks. For example, out of the 2,000 shares (worth 1,000 rubles each) of their lumber company, 500 shares belonged to Rozaliia.[143] Iakov complained bitterly that Rozaliia kept a tight hand on the purse strings when his banks began to fail at the turn of the century. When Iakov met the couple at the Moscow railway station in May 1900, "Rozaliia Pavlovna complained about Lazar Solomonovich for his many squandered deals."[144] Knowing full well that Iakov was in no position to repay any loans, she strongly opposed her husband's decision to grant his brother's desperate pleas for a bill of exchange.[145] When she proved right about the ill-advised loan and Lazar found himself in financial difficulty, Rozaliia never missed an opportunity to remind Iakov that he had helped to drive Lazar to the verge of bankruptcy.[146] She was deeply involved in the family's lumber, rubber, and stationery factories. Rozaliia was not unusual: Jewish female entrepreneurs were a numerically significant group until the late nineteenth century. In 1879, for example, Jewish women made up 3.9 percent of the proprietors of industrial enterprises, predominantly in the Pale of Settlement. Some, like Sof'ia Brodskaia, even owned their own factories: in her tobacco factory in Voronezh, Brodskaia employed "twenty workers and produced goods up to the value of 20,000 rubles." As Galina Ulianova has shown, Jewish women engaged in various enterprises, from the production of lard candles and matches to that of porcelain.[147] In contrast to the West, Russian women—of any ethnicity or religion—"enjoyed the same property right as men." They could "sell their own property without the consent of [their] husbands, acquire new and separate property, transfer assets, enter contracts, and receive inheritances."[148] Yet alongside these broad rights in property laws were strict patriarchal family laws that "imposed severe restictions on women's autonomy," creating "one of the most intriguing paradoxes in Russian history," in the words of Adele Lindenmeyr.[149]

Zinaida was deliberately cut from a very different cloth than her mother: Rozaliia raised her daughter to be a cultured lady of leisure and consumption, not a merchant and entrepreneur like herself. In contrast to their brothers who sat on the boards of the Poliakov banks, Zinaida and her sisters played no role in the family business. Rather, it was important that the Poliakov daughters be aristocrats—that Zinaida perform this new elite identity. To this end, her mother organized an elite home education that rivaled that of other aristocratic daughters. As the diaries show, Zinaida and her siblings took music lessons with the talented violinist and concertmaster of the Bolshoi Theater orchestra, Vasilii Vasil'evich Bezekirskii (1835–1919), and extraordinary pia-

FIGURE 8
Raia Lazarevna
Poliakova (sister of
Zinaida Poliakova).
Poliakova and Poliakoff,
Sem'ia Poliakovykh.

nists like Emiliia Isaakovna Ogus-Shaikevich (b. 1872) and Max Erdmansder-fer [Erdmansdörfer] (1848–1905). The girls studied Latin and Greek with the author of the widely used grammar books on these ancient languages, Emi-lii Viacheslavovich Chernyi, and the coauthor of a Russian-Latin dictionary, Iurii Khodobai. The children's education also included history, mathematics, penmanship, and several languages (including Russian, English, French, and German, as noted above). Zinaida also studied Hebrew and Yiddish, allowing her to read *maskilic* literature and write letters to her grandparents. In addition to their formal lessons, the children socialized in the evenings with renowned professors such as Avgust Iul'evich Davydov, a mathematics professor from Moscow University (who was also the brother of the illustrious cellist and head of the St. Petersburg Conservatory, Karl Iul'evich Davydov).

Being aristocrats also entailed ostentatious indulgence, not for its own sake, but as a public display of creditworthiness. The family lived in a magnificent house on the prestigious Tverskoi Boulevard in Moscow and later on the fash-ionable Avenue du Bois de Boulogne in Paris. They became regulars at the most prized—and pricey—spas and hotels in Europe.[150] On 21 September 1880, the *Ischler Cur-Liste* reported that the family of Lazar Solomonovich Poliakov and servants had arrived at their hotel in Ischler.[151] The *Wiener Salonblatt* listed Lazar, his wife, Zinaida, and son as guests at Franzensbad, and later the *Prager Abendblatt* announced that the family was taking the cure at Marienbad.[152] At Baden-Baden, the Poliakovs received the Jewish historian Heinrich Graetz in 1883, a meeting that was duly reported in the press. The society pages also reported the aristocratic company with whom the Poliakovs were traveling, a valuable enhancement to their prestige. For instance, the *Deutsches Volksblatt* announced on 2 January 1885 that "Lazar Poliakov and family, who came from Paris, traveled with Princess Marie Dolgurukoff and Princess Sophie Scherba-toff, who came from Italy. The Russians are staying at the Hotel Imperial."[153] Identified as distinguished "Russians" (with no allusion to their Jewishness), the Poliakovs had publicly established themselves as part of the aristocratic elite. Ironically, socializing with Russian nobles did nothing to advance the task of Jewish matchmaking—a primary purpose of the trips to spas. Indeed, when Zinaida finally met her prospective groom, he may have been more in-terested in her family's ostentatious spending than in her.

What Zinaida lacked in business acumen, she made up in high culture. Her parents' patronage of leading artists, musicians, and theater performers, who often frequented their house, created a milieu that instilled in her a lifelong dedication to the arts. Music was in the very air she breathed. As one English governess observed in 1879, members of the Russian nobility attended con-certs and operas religiously, a model that the Poliakovs enthusiastically em-ulated. Zinaida's diary is as much a cultural chronicle as a personal journal. On 15 January 1886, she raved about Anton Rubinstein,[154] whose concerts she faithfully attended: "Yesterday we went to a concert of Anton Rubinstein. This pianist-giant distinguished himself in performing nine sonatas of L[ud-wig] Beethoven, and of these I very much liked the *Appasionata*. Why is there no one like him up to now? Not one of the young pianists gives great hopes for such a brilliant talent in our nineteenth century. Perhaps the lone excep-tion is D. Albert Elzhen,[155] who has strongly distinguished himself." And on 5 February 1886, she commented: "I did not write in this book yesterday be-cause I went to the Rubinstein concert in the evening. The enchanting sounds of his powerful genius were resounding somewhere far away. And when he played, I thought that this was not his fingers striking the keys, but that he had wings, fluttering in the air." Rubinstein wanted the state to endow musi-cians with "the civic status of musician" and envisioned a "free artist," an estate that would consist of "Russian music teachers, Russian orchestral musicians, and Russian singers of both sexes who will work the way a person works for whom his art is a livelihood, the key to special respect, a means of achieving fame, and a way of surrendering himself completely to his divine calling."[156] Privately, the Poliakovs afforded this privilege to musicians through generous financial support and patronage. In the long winter months, the Poliakov home regularly hosted *soirées musicales* where accomplished musicians gave private concerts.[157] "Yesterday evening there was a performance at our house by Al'fred Gr[ü]nfeld and his brother, along with the small female pianist E[i]bensh[ütz] [Ilona Eibenschütz]; she was accompanied by her brother, a conductor," wrote Zinaida on 18 December 1883. She observed that a large number of guests attended the performance and that only on a Friday night (Sabbath!) did the brothers play for the family alone. These musical gatherings provided a venue for Zinaida and her sisters to perform as well and inspired Zinaida to become a better musician. On 14 January 1886 she wrote: "It seems that I have a new desire to play piano with Emiliia Isaakovna [Ogus-Shaikevich]. Until now I have played only once in public and by myself, but now I especially want to distinguish myself with art." As intimidating as it was to perform before such illustrious musicians, their presence also encouraged Zinaida to practice more and to appreciate the arts.

Like any good aristocratic family, the Poliakovs had season tickets to the ballet and opera.[158] The opera was an opportunity to socialize with elites but also a venue to experience national belonging, especially when attending quintessential Russian operas like Mikhail Glinka's *A Life for the Tsar* (1836), as Zinaida and her family did in 1887. On 9 February 1887 Zinaida wrote that she was elated because the prima donna Aleksandra Panaeva-Kartseva (1853–1942), "who will debut in the role of Antonina," had sent them tickets for the performance. The singer and her husband had been guests at the Poliakovs' home in St. Petersburg a few days earlier when Zinaida noted she was expecting them on 5 February for dinner. And on 22 February she was in raptures over the soprano's beauty: "Yesterday evening [Panaeva-]Kartseva was at the concert; she could not have been more beautiful in a red velvet dress with a train." Another memorable concert was a performance of Valentina Serova's first opera *Uriel Acosta*, which premiered at the Bolshoi Theater in 1885. It inspired a diary entry on 22 April 1885: "[My sister] Raechka went with us last week to the opera. They performed Serov's *Uriel Acosta*. The wife of a well-known composer staged this opera, and it was a great success." Curiously, Zinaida assumed that Serova's famous husband, Alexander Serov, was the composer and that the wife had merely staged, not written the opera—an adaptation of Karl Gutzow's German play.[159] In fact, Serova—a convert from Judaism—had written the last act of her late husband's opera *The Power of the Fiend* before composing her own haunting opera about the excommunication of a Jewish skeptic (sometimes seen as the precursor to Baruch Spinoza) in Amsterdam seeking reconciliation with the community but without the shackles of rabbinic authority. The protagonist, humiliated by a public lashing and abuse from the Sephardi congregation, committed suicide. Herbert Lindenberger once described the opera as a productive site to observe "the interactions between the aesthetic order and the social order."[160] Operas like Serova's articulated the painful and incongruous position of the Jewish convert, trapped between two worlds in this "space for cloak-and-dagger manifestations of the forbidden."[161] Perhaps less enamored of a performance that did not feature her favorite prima donna, Zinaida had little to say about the content of the opera, even about the presence of Jewish figures on stage.

Famous opera singers were not the only recipients of Poliakov generosity: impoverished, unknown musicians like Berta Abramovich—a talented vocalist who was a lifelong friend of Zinaida—also earned the family's support. Born in 1872 in Vil'na, Abramovich's lyrical voice quickly became legendary. According to the Hebrew press, even when the three-year-old Abramovich was staying at a dacha on the outskirts of Vil'na, a large crowd gathered outside to hear her sing. At the age of ten, Abramovich was accepted to the music school of Zeev Eban, who could not have been more proud of his prize student: "I am confident that in one musical soirée I will be recompensed seven-fold with pleasure for all the effort I put into her education during the course of time."[162] So impressed were the famous Polish opera singer Prakseda Marcelina Kochanska (known by her stage name of Marcella Sembrich)[163] and her husband, Wilhelm Stengel, when they passed through Vil'na that they advised Abramovich's parents to have her learn music theory so that she could attend the conservatory by age sixteen. The Hebrew press reported that when Abramovich arrived in Moscow in 1888, the renowned cellist and rector of the St. Petersburg Conservatory, Karl Davydov (1838–89)—a Riga-born Jewish convert whom Peter Tchaikovsky described as the "tsar of violoncellists"[164]—agreed to give her an audition. After the audition, he immediately wrote to the opera singer Princess Elizaveta Lavrovskaia (known by her married name of Tsetelev) to help arrange Abramovich's acceptance at the conservatory. Davydov reportedly increased the number of Jewish students at the conservatory during his directorship, despite state pressure to restrict admissions to those with "exceptional musical abilities."[165] Matriculation at the conservatory, however, was challenging: paying expensive tuition fees and obtaining permission to reside in Moscow seemed impossible. To the rescue came that Poliakov confidant, Prince

Dolgorukov, who resolved the red tape while the Poliakovs assumed responsibility for Abramovich's tuition and financial needs. In addition to paying the 300 rubles for tuition, the Poliakovs "did not withhold anything that her eyes desired."[166] Their reward was the lyrical beauty of a voice that enriched their salon and a deep friendship that sustained Zinaida during her troubled marriage with Reuben. By supporting musicians like Abramovich at the Moscow conservatory, the Poliakovs ensured that imperial music now included Jews —who would have otherwise languished in the provinces.

Cultivating and demonstrating aesthetic sensibility thus entailed substantial contributions to the fine arts.[167] The Poliakovs' fame traveled far, earning coverage even in the *Jewish Advocate* in America: "Thanks to her [Rozaliia's] generosity as well as that of her husband, Moscow was endowed with museums and art treasures."[168] Rozaliia and Lazar were early supporters of the Museum of Fine Arts in Moscow (now the Pushkin State Museum of Fine Arts) as an imperial institution for the general public and the advancement of art education. Its founder, Ivan Tsvetaev, a professor at Moscow University, sought to raise funds by naming exhibition halls in honor of donors. In contrast to some Moscow merchants who did not participate either because of niggardliness or cultural conservatism, Lazar promptly agreed to support the venture. Over time the relationship between Lazar and Tsvetaev developed from a business to a personal one, as reflected in their correspondence with its exchanges of family news—births, illnesses, and deaths. Lazar generously put his public support behind Tsvetaev's project:

> Owing to Your Excellency's letter of 28 May, I have the honor to report that, sympathizing with the useful goal for the building of the Museum of Fine Arts (in honor of Emperor Alexander III) at the Moscow Imperial University, I expressed my wish to donate a sum of 22,944 rubles for the building of exhibit hall No. 12 of Greek relief sculptures from the 5th and 6th centuries BC. I sent a deposit of ten thousand rubles to the treasurer of the committee, I. Iu. Shul'ts, in accordance with our agreement. The receipt is attached. I will send the balance of 12,944 rubles as needed.[169]

That contribution led to Lazar's name being inscribed on the wall of the Greek exhibition hall. Rozaliia made her own contributions of cultural artifacts, including two amphoras and bronze vessels from Greek antiquity. Apparently, such pieces had been found near the town of Kerch and in various places on the coast of the Black Sea.[170] The Greek hall also boasted a nearly complete cast of the Ionic frieze from the Temple of Apollo Epicurus at Bassae.[171] The ties between the Poliakovs and Tsvetaevs continued into the next generation:

in a letter of 1927 the famous poet Marina Tsvetaeva asked her friend to find out "without fail the surname and, if possible, the address of the Poliakova who is married to the Frenchman and resides, if I am not mistaken, on Boulogne (perhaps on Champs Elysees?—in any case, not on Vilette!)."[172] Tsvetaeva was not wrong: Zinaida, now known as Gubbay, her married surname, lived on Avenue du Bois de Boulogne.

The Poliakovs also funded the Jewish sculptor Mark Antokol'skii (1840–1902), a frequent guest in their home and prominent figure in Zinaida's diaries. Antokol'skii was an artist of some renown: he received the *Medaille d'honneur* and *Legion d'honneur* at the Paris World Exhibition in 1878, the same year that Samuil Poliakov received a medal for his speedy railroad construction. On 3 September 1884, Zinaida—an admirer of the imperial family—expressed a desire to impress Antokol'skii with her sculpture of Alexander II:

> I also made my first attempt at sculpting (a bas-relief of the late emperor) —which people say was not so bad. . . . I shall try to justify Mr. Antokol'skii's opinion that I have a talent for making models. Tomorrow I shall begin working on a small head if I do not go into the city with Papa. . . . They say that Luiza [Louise Gintsburg]'s fiancé [Joseph Sassoon] is neither nice nor handsome. Those are the words of the sculptor Antokol'skii and, consequently, someone well versed in physiognomy.

The artist had already made several busts and one statue of Samuil's family members.[173] Not to be outdone, Zinaida's uncle Iakov commissioned Antokol'skii to make two bronze busts, not of his family members but rather of Nicholas II and the empress, for 10,000 rubles—ironically, the very same tsar who repeatedly rejected Iakov's petition for the status of hereditary noble specifically because he was Jewish.[174] By employing a Jewish artist to create sculptures not only of the royal family but also of themselves, the Poliakovs succeeded in expanding the ethno-religious boundaries of imperial Russian art that now included Jewish subjects. In his article "Twenty-Five Years of Our Art," the art critic Vladimir Stasov declared that while Antokol'skii created many impressive sculptures, his full-body statue of Samuil Poliakov "stood above the rest," adding this explanation: "This statue is a real living person. In its life-like naturalism, simplicity, the astonishing reality of the body and dress, this statue has no parallel in all of European sculpture."[175] The Poliakovs could have asked for no better proof of their contribution to the creation of an imperial Russian art that even transcended national boundaries.

The Poliakovs also became enamored of the Russian artist, Konstantin E. Makovskii (1839–1915), who painted their portraits in 1882 and 1883 (now in the State Historical Museum). This was before Makovskii won the gold medal at the 1889 World's Fair in Paris for three paintings: "The Death of Ivan the Terrible," "The Judgment of Paris," and "Demon and Tamara." He also painted the portraits of several Poliakov acquaintances, including Zinaida's favorite prima donna of opera, Panaeva-Kartseva (1889).

When not attending a performance or entertaining artists, Zinaida sought leisure time between routine social calls, outings, soirées, and dances. However, for women in the privileged class, leisure time did not mean that they had freedom of choice but that they could do "what was permitted" within the constraints of propriety and respectability.[176] One acceptable practice was diary writing, and for women of privileged status the act of recording their daily experiences had become a sign of elite status by the early eighteenth century.[177] For many women, the diary was a form of sociability that allowed them to express their emotions and desires. But diaries could speak to broader issues, and Zinaida was perfectly aware that the diaries of some women went beyond their personal experiences. In April 1885 she asked her sister Raisa to search through the conservative newspaper *Grazhdanin* (which routinely published diaries and memoirs) for Ol'ga Novikova's diaries.[178] A prominent journalist and frequent guest at Poliakov social gatherings, Novikova once cited Prime Minister William Gladstone to reassure Zinaida that there would be no war between Britain and Russia over the tensions in Afghanistan.[179]

Reading novels, another preoccupation of aristocratic women, provided an important means of self-cultivation and self-criticism, and to this task Zinaida applied herself diligently. She even tried to calculate how many chapters constituted a legitimate amount of reading and considered whether to abide by her "one-chapter-a-day rule" or to stay up reading in bed. Finding time to read was difficult in the bustling Poliakov household, however, and Zinaida sometimes bemoaned the long intervals between readings. On 2 February 1886, after a long week of visitors, she wrote: "We are finally free of tiresome guests, who did send us a bouquet today as a reward. . . . I can now read L[eo] Tolstoy's novel, *War and Peace* with a clear conscience. I have an original edition with the French phrases. I intend to acquire all his works." Writing about Tolstoy's novel gave Zinaida an opportunity to ponder the meaning of personal ordeals, above all her increasingly acrimonious conflicts with her mother. At times Zinaida referred to books as her "true friends" and showed a fondness not only for Tolstoy but also for Alexandre Dumas.[180] Books provided a refuge from hostile female alliances in her household. When her sister Khaia and Lidiia Stepanovna Zotova, a family companion, grew very close during her parents' absence, Zinaida fled to her books, noting on 4 May 1887: "I positively do not come out of my monastic cell. I have now taken up reading and want to finish Dickens's *David Copperfield*, which I began shortly after arriving from abroad." Zinaida evidently never indulged in "bad reading"—the forbidden political novels or scandalous literature that induced some noble girls to join the revolutionary movement. Time for reading, however, was limited. Zinaida's social responsibilities meant endless streams of guests (many of whom were actually calling because of business matters) and making dutiful calls on multitudinous friends and acquaintances. Zinaida took her duties seriously. For instance, on 20 July 1886, she found herself tasked with the responsibility of entertaining a very important guest:

> Yesterday we were very much animated because of dinner—eleven people came. Moreover, the chief of police [Aleksandr A. Kozlov] dined along with [Gennadii V.] Grudev—the youngest person of the ancient capital. Also present were the Podgoretskiis, the engineer [Andrei Nikolaevich] Gorchakov, P. Naumenko, Kondrat'ev, Semen S., Sof'ia Ivanovna Slezkina and her sister, and [Dr.] Iu[lii] Gol'denbakh. And that was all our guests. I will say one thing: I was very flattered by the fact that it fell to my lot to entertain A[leksander] Kozlov, and they say that I performed the role well. Because Mama was busy with Grudev, I had to hold a conversation with my neighbor so that he not become bored.

Since her mother was busy attending to the ninety-year-old honorary justice of the peace Grudev (1796–1895), Zinaida drew on her conversation skills to entertain the chief of police of Moscow, an important figure who had power over residency permits in Moscow.[181] Sometimes she resented the fact that the burden of entertaining fell completely on her shoulders. On 17 January 1887 she criticized her sister Khaia for failing to do her part: "Yesterday I had to entertain all the guests because Khaia refused to come to dinner (claiming a headache). I was nevertheless dissatisfied with her rude behavior toward the honored guests who were here at our house." But on 17 February 1887 Zinaida breathed a sigh of relief for a break in all the socializing: "I can finally take a rest from the seasonal chores, the entertaining, and the balls!"

Zinaida was particularly fond of private balls, which allowed her to demonstrate her dancing skills and indulge in society gossip, an important performance of aristocratic intimacy. Some male acquaintances were fair game for gossip, and on 25 January 1886 she wrote: "Edmond Rudnitskii danced the first quadrille with me again at the Spiridinovs. Mashen'ka Perevozchikova finds him similar to a pig, because he says 'gm...'—like that very animal." The best part of the ball was to show off the latest fashions from Paris and flaunt her family's wealth. On 1 March 1886, she expressed her delight at an invitation that had just arrived:

> We have an invitation for Tuesday evening. It reads as follows: "Count and Countess Brevern de Lagarde [de Lagardi] most humbly ask that you come on Tuesday evening, 8 March, at 9 p.m." I think that after the music part there will be dancing—despite the Lenten fast. Therefore one should be dressed décolleté. But I am happy to say that it does not have to be a tulle dress. I simply do not have such, but there is a blue silk dress, very beautiful, from the famous [Charles Frederick] Worth. Of course I shall use this occasion to wear the dress.

This is the same Countess Brevern de Lagarde whose hat Zinaida subjected to savage irony in her diary on 23 April 1886: "Countess Brevern de Lagarde . . . arrived to show us her new hat (which had been brought from Paris by M[aria] I[vanovna] Fon Derviz). It is really very beautiful—a gray hat from tulle, which suits her about as much as a saddle does a cow. But it is a splendid saddle."

The fact that Zinaida successfully performed her elite Russian identity was evident in a visit to the Trinity-Sergius Monastery[182] with Semen Sergeevich Podgoretskii and his family in the summer of 1884. "As a historical site, the Lavra [monastery] deserves attention, and also because of the incalculable riches in its sacristy," she wrote on 7 August. Her group was told, however, that they must wait to see the sacristy until vespers were over. The visitors threatened to complain to the metropolitan and pretended to be from the imperial court, and "open sesame!"—the party promptly gained access. Zinaida showed a particular interest in sacred art with connections to her beloved monarchy: "After viewing the sacristy (where I especially liked the portraits of Alexander I, Alexander II, and Nicholas I that had been given to the metropolitan), there was the icon of the Mother of God [made] from rose coral with precious stones donated by the late empress on the first confession of M[aria] A[leksandrova]. There was an unusually natural depiction of Christ's head on one stone, and also an agate bearing a natural portrayal of a praying monk at the feet of the cross of crucifixion."

As the eldest daughter of an aristocratic family Zinaida had to navigate tangled relationships that included family companions, governesses, and domestic servants. These "family dramas" figure significantly in her diaries. The elite patriarchal family structure offered little autonomy, but Zinaida had some authority—in the hiring and firing of her servants. On 14 January 1886, for example, she was trying to decide whether to dismiss her servant Katia, "who has become so spoiled that it did not occur her to tidy up in advance, and she will be away tomorrow." Her decision to discharge Katia was made easier when the family companion, Lidiia Stepanovna, whom Zinaida thoroughly detested, suggested that the woman stay: "I absolutely do not want to humiliate myself —despite the fact that, after she has spent six years with me, it will be difficult to adjust to someone else." Zinaida was determined to "show my will."

Unquestionably, however, Zinaida's most difficult relationship was with her strong-willed mother. The daughter did not mince words, writing on 19 April 1884: "I do not always get along with Mama, and we do have little in common." But the norms of patriarchal family order demanded submission and obedience from an unmarried daughter, even one of legal age. Zinaida's main strategy to avoid conflict was to withdraw and, as she put it on 13 March 1885, "do everything possible to avoid being constrained in my actions." Zinaida's key tactic was to claim poor health as the pretext for refusing to participate in some unwanted social occasion. On 15 January 1886, for instance, the twenty-three-year-old informed her mother that she must decline an invitation to attend the symphony because "I do not wish to make my cold still worse"; it was, in fact, the third Saturday in a row that she had invoked this excuse. Although generally dutiful, Zinaida sometimes exploded in rage. One such outburst led to a violent confrontation: the casus belli this time was the interception of her personal mail. After returning from St. Petersburg, Zinaida realized that some letters were missing. She recorded what happened on 12 March 1885: "It turned out that Mama not only has been opening my letters but has not even been giving them to me. I said that was swinish, and she hit me with blows to the head. I don't care in the least about all this, but yesterday she came into my room twice and left notes: 'I don't give a damn about you, Zina.' They were dated 11 March 1885. I tore them up and threw them into the wastepaper can."

Conflict with her mother was exacerbated by sibling rivalry with her sister Khaia, whom Zinaida regarded as her mother's favorite. Bickering with Khaia was a common refrain in her diaries, but one incident was particularly bitter. In May 1886 the family decided to go to their dacha in Sokol'niki "in accordance with the Muscovite custom," as Zinaida put it on 2 May. This time Zinaida decided to stay home, citing a headache as the pretext. In reality, she simply could not bear the idea of spending time in the company of her mother and sister, and this time the issue was a hat: "But as they were leaving, I noticed Khaia wearing a hat similar to the one that I had bought for myself. The affair with this hat began already in Paris. I was the first to claim the hat, but Khaia wanted to buy it. And when I proposed to them (i.e., Mama and Khaia) to transfer my right, Papa gave me his word that he would not buy Khaia exactly the same hat. Despite this, Mama deliberately—to do something unpleasant to me—bought it for her." Zinaida could barely hide her feelings of self-pity following the hat incident: "To live means to fight. And so long as struggle is possible and I am alive, then I shall not bow down to higher injustice. My mother does not want to know me, and in fact I cannot be her scapegoat. Her love for Khaia means nothing to me; so be it. But only do not pity me, for otherwise I will completely wither and fade away." Zinaida's conviction that her mother favored Khaia resurfaced decades later when she learned that her sister was one of the executors of her mother's will, along with Isaak—Zinaida's least favorite brother.[183] Perhaps seeking to offset her mother's affronts, Zinaida idealized her father as a protector and true companion, although in reality, as she admitted, he remained a warm but inaccessible figure. He spent much of his time in St. Petersburg, where they owned a second home. The annual sum that she and Reuben received from her father until his financial collapse was not only a financial necessity but also a sign of his solicitous care for which she yearned.

◆ ◆ ◆ ◆ ◆ ◆ ◆

Being Jewish

The Poliakovs' immersion in Russian culture inevitably challenged their Judaism, but the family refused to convert to Christianity. They had been closely associated with Habad Hasidim before they moved to Moscow. Before leaving for the Russian interior, Iakov had asked the Lubavitch rebbe for a blessing, and in 1898, he wrote: "I received the Lubavitch rabbi Schneerson (the grandson of the great rabbi of Lubavitch, this young rabbi was an acquaintance of my father), and what his grandfather said to me and his blessing came to pass as did what he said about my deceased brother Samuil."[184] Despite their religious devotion, the quotidian difficulties of observance had commenced the moment the Poliakovs left the Pale. Iakov recounted how, in the early years, when the brothers traveled to remote areas to supervise railroad construction, they often found themselves without a minyan for prayers. That proved especially stressful in 1871, when a trip to open the Voronezh-Rostov railroad line overlapped with his mother's yahrzeit (anniversary of a death):

> Lazar and I were in despair at the time of the journey with the commission. During the trip there was the anniversary of our mother's death, and on that day we were deprived of the possibility of holding prayers. Until then we had never failed to pray on this day for the peace of our mother's soul. But thanks to the energy of Fainberg, who was the contractor at the time for the Voronezh railway, we were taken to a postal station with fewer than

ten Jews. So we and the commission arrived at a stone station to spend the night. All the members of the commission sat down to play cards, but we went to the home of some Jewish clerk whom Fainberg had hired and prayed in the evening. The following morning, while the members of the commission were tired, we managed to pray and were perfectly happy that this time we succeeded in not missing our annual moral-religious duty.[185]

The resourcefulness of people like Fainberg ensured that even in remote parts of Russia, Jews could gather a minyan for a mother's yahrzeit.

Complying with kashrut (Jewish dietary laws) was another serious challenge. Iakov recalled that one of his earliest jobs—working for a Jewish tax farmer, Levin Zalmanson—required him to live in a peasant house in a Smolensk village, "far from the Jewish population." He could eat meat only once a week (presumably when he went home to his family for the Sabbath) and was content to subsist on "milk and kvass" the rest of the week, so long as he could regularly earn twelve rubles to take home.[186] Even after a decade in Moscow, Zinaida's mother insisted on strict observance of kashrut. According to a synagogue chorister whose mother worked as the family housekeeper, Rozaliia "entertained a great deal, and had two kosher kitchens, one 'fleishik' [meat] and one 'milchik' [dairy]."[187] While the imperious Rozaliia prevailed (and inspired endless grumbling from Zinaida about tasteless food), the dietary rules ignited war at the family dacha in 1887, when Lazar lay gravely ill and his frightened children feared for his life. One son (Mikhail) made bold to ask the family's Russian doctor if "Papa can eat meat fried in [pork] lard," and Zinaida took the liberty to opine that this unkosher concoction would hasten her father's recovery. Rozaliia exploded, and Zinaida wrote on 3 September: "This made [Mama] so furious that she brazenly even went in to Papa and began to curse us every possible way, so that Papa asked her to leave his room in order to avoid any further problems that might occur. But she is still revolving, as the astronomer Galileo put it"—to which Zinaida added her unkosher metaphor: "like meat patties in lard!" The firestorm inspired a furious tirade from Zinaida: "I am totally convinced that Mama's fanaticism will enter into the history of Yid-ism [zhidovstvo]." The enraged Zinaida used two choice epithets from the antisemitic lexicon—fanatizm and zhidovstvo. The conflict escalated when her mother even refused to serve her ailing husband food that the doctor had prescribed and that did not violate kashrut, and Zinaida wrote the following day: "Yesterday we had a pure 'Sodom and Gomorrah' because of Mama's impossible and quite fanatical, stubborn tendency to deny Papa nutritious and easily digestible food contrary to the Law of Moses. For her, that is more important than the question of love for one's neighbor and anonymous benevolence (charity that does not trumpet oneself). It is said that fanaticism is stupidity. Indeed, I agree totally, all the more because it makes people stupid. If one calculates the number [of] Jewish fanatics, it is easy to compile a percentage for the level of intellectual development." The battle over kashrut only added to the ongoing, even increasing, tension between an observant mother and a daughter who cared more about taste and nutrition. Kashrut, however, remained engrained in Zinaida's life: on 22 March 1907, her uncle Iakov, who had breakfasted at her home in Paris, observed that her holiday kitchen was "set up according to all the [halakhic] regulations" for Passover.[188]

Although Rozaliia set rigid boundaries around Jewish holidays, she was more accommodating on Sabbath observance and even permitted socializing on Saturdays (though limited to their home on Friday nights). It would have been difficult to do otherwise: Saturday was prime time in Russia for balls, soirées, parties, theater performances, and other forms of aristocratic sociability. For Zinaida, however, even this compromise did not go far enough. For example, on 1 March 1884 she made this plaintive entry: "Tomorrow is the [anniversary of Alexander III's] accession to the throne[189] and therefore a celebratory performance is on our subscription tickets. But alas!—it is Friday, so we cannot go." As a member of a family determined to demonstrate loyalty to the Russian autocracy (despite its antisemitic policies), Zinaida found it painful to forgo so important a public event. At some point even Rozaliia became so acculturated that she abandoned the *sheitel* (wig), which was no longer fashionable among Jewish women in Moscow.

No compromises were to be tolerated, however, with respect to religious rituals of death and mourning. The Poliakovs were no strangers to tragedy: the brothers lost their mother early in life and observed her yahrzeit dutifully, no matter what. Each brother lost at least one child[190] and grandchildren,[191] and each death earned a detailed description from Iakov, the family chronicler. Indeed, Iakov experienced two such tragedies. Because his wife Khasia could not nurse their first son (born in 1850), the infant was sent to a wet nurse from a poor family, but he fell ill and died.[192] And just when Iakov and his second wife's family began to enjoy their newfound prosperity in Taganrog, tragedy struck again. Their eight-year-old daughter, who delighted her parents with her fluency in German, French, and Russian and an uncanny ability to sing and dance, came down with a fever that the doctor ignored and died suddenly. Amaliia, who could "not live a minute" without the little girl, "went out of her mind for a long time."[193]

The death of Zinaida's grandfather in 1897 showed the family's unbending determination to observe traditional rites no matter what—in spite of the challenges of travel and pressing business, even at a time when Iakov's banks were teetering on the brink of bankruptcy. Iakov received a telegram from his nephew Mikhail on a Saturday morning that Solomon was dangerously ill. Although Mikhail was clearly trying to prepare him for the inevitable, Iakov willfully chose not to believe the worst. Only when he met his son-in-law Leon did he learn that his father had already passed away. The next day Iakov and his sons and son-in-law went to the mikvah (ritual bath) and traveled to Moscow to make arrangements for the funeral. Zinaida received news about the "sudden death of our poor grandfather Solomon Lazarevich Poliakov" in Paris, where her father was staying at the time.[194] The burial had to be held on Sunday—which Iakov declared that he was "in no condition to describe." Instead of sitting shiva (week-long mourning period) at his brother's house in Moscow, where Solomon had resided, Iakov sent his oldest son ahead to St. Petersburg to prepare his house for mourning. Traveling after *mincha* prayers on the postal train, Iakov arrived in St. Petersburg at 9:00 a.m. and rushed to morning services. Having just received the status of hereditary noble from the emperor, Iakov faced a difficult decision on New Year's Day: "On account of the mourning—shiva—I do not go anywhere and do not receive anyone; although the spiritual rabbi took the sin upon himself and advised me to go, by all means, to the palace for the imperial reception, I nonetheless decided not to go."[195] Even the temptation to meet the imperial family (with the dispensation of his rabbi) could not entice Iakov to ignore the duty to mourn his beloved father.[196]

Religiosity meant not only observance of family rituals, but also *tsedekah* (charity) to the Jewish community. The liberal Austrian weekly *Die Neuzeit* pointed out that the Poliakov family remained devoted to Judaism despite their immense wealth and credited the women as the wellspring of the family's generosity: "Inspired by their wonderful, religious wives, they [the Poliakov brothers] seek through their prominence and visibility, to advance culture among the Russian Jews and to support Hebrew literature."[197] Most notable was Rozaliia's charitable work to aid the poor in the Old Yishuv in Palestine. In 1897 *Hamelits* reported that Rozaliia had "sent a considerable sum to money" to Rabbi Yehoshua Yehudah Leib Diskin of Brisk (1818–98) in Jerusalem to organize a beggars' feast "in honor of her gentle daughter Zlata's [Zinaida's] birthday."[198] Rabbi Diskin, who had moved from Brest-Litovsk to Palestine in 1877, established an orphanage with capital from the dowry of his second wife, Sonia (Sarah, the Brisker *rebbitsen*), a woman renowned for her sharp mind and tongue.[199] The public hall for the beggars' feast was filled with more than three hundred indigent residents of Jerusalem, who "praised the virtuous woman, her husband, and the entire family of the honored girl."[200] "Year after year," Rozaliia sent a telegram to "our rabbi of Jerusalem" (R. Shmuel Salant, chief rabbi of the Ashkenazi community),[201] directing the administrators of the General Soup Kitchen in Jerusalem to feed 250 indigent Jews at her expense on the 22 and 23 of Tammuz—her birthday and the yahrzeit of her mother.[202] According to Yitshak Shiryon [Zalkind] (1871–1941), a relative of R. Moshe Wittenberg (a Hasidic banker who also gave generously to the Diskin orphanage), the soup kitchen opened its doors to the needy from any community and provided a hot meal for a *grush* [penny].[203] Wittenberg, who bought and sold Russian government securities on the Russian stock exchange, was probably acquainted with the Poliakovs (who also shared ties with Habad rabbis from the Vitebsk region, such as R. Yosef Yitzhak Shneerson) and solicited their support for his charities. Not only did Rozaliia teach her children about charity by example, but she also reminded them of their responsibilities when they visited various Jewish communities. When Zinaida was vacationing in Rome, for instance, she visited a synagogue, which she found "horribly dirty because everyone spits on the floor." Yet she set out to "give francs to the poor" because "Mother entrusted me to give [money] to the poor here."[204]

Rozaliia and Lazar donated greater sums of money to build a hospital in Tiberius, probably in memory of their son Aaron (Ronia), who became ill in Eygpt and died in France (as discussed below).[205] The Hebrew press reported some initial conflicts about the hospital's medical staffing,[206] and funding remained a perennial problem despite the Poliakovs' generosity. According to the Society for the Settlement of Jewish Toilers on the Land, many poor Jews living in Tiberius had no trade or occupation, and tropical diseases were a significant threat to the Jewish residents. The Poliakovs had pledged 2,000 francs per year for the hospital, but the director complained that the funds were insufficient: the fifteen staff members (including the doctors) alone required 6,000 francs (400 per person). Thus, the hospital needed 4,000 francs in addition to the Poliakov contribution.[207]

The Poliakovs received numerous requests not only from the Old Yishuv but also from their hometown in the Pale. They willingly obliged. For instance, when impoverished *tallis* (prayer shawl) weavers in Lazar's hometown of Dubrovno asked for assistance, he helped create the Joint-Stock Society of Dneprovsk Manufacturing (in collaboration with the Jewish Colonization Association). Dubrovno had been the center of tallis weaving since the eighteenth century, but the weavers found themselves at the mercy of merchants who marketed their fine goods throughout Russia, Western Europe, and even America. The growing competition from factories forced talented weavers—

who had numbered some 660 in 1847—to leave their homes in search of work. The Hebrew press praised Lazar for providing work for the weavers (many of who came "streaming in every day to ask for work") and noted that this labor helped them sustain their faith.[208] The training and temporary work actually commenced in 1889, and the institution opened officially in 1901. Rabbi Yosef Yitzhak Schneerson was involved in a large weaving factory that employed Jewish workers and closed on the Sabbath and other Jewish holidays.[209]

The Poliakovs were especially active in the Jewish religious institutions of Moscow. The institutions addressed an important need: Alexander II's policy of "select emancipation" made no provision for religious servitors such as rabbis, cantors, and ritual slaughterers. In 1857 the office of the Grand Kremlin Palace reported that Nosel' Naifel'd, a rank-and-file member of the Veteran Fire Brigade who had joined the army in 1840, requested permission to serve as a rabbi for Jewish soldiers in Moscow. Having "neither a permanent rabbi nor another guardian" to perform the rites of their faith, he argued, the soldiers needed someone to conduct services, circumcise infants, and perform marriage and burial ceremonies. The state approved his request.[210] By the 1860s the community had obtained permission to invite the distinguished R. Chaim Berlin (1832–1912), the son of R. Naftali Zvi Yehudah Berlin of Volozhin, to serve as the spiritual rabbi of Moscow.

When the Poliakovs arrived in Moscow, the religious community had just begun to build its basic institutions. According to the historian and demographer Samuil Vermel' (1860–1935), the vast differences among Jews (who came from diverse social strata, geographic regions, and subcultures) generated considerable antagonism and resentment. Retired Nikolaevan soldiers, who considered themselves the true veteran residents of the city, looked warily at newcomers (mainly merchants and artisans) from Shklov, Berdichev, and other small towns in the Pale of Settlement. In the veterans' view, the new arrivals had not earned the right of residency through blood and service. The new arrivals, "being more educated in all respects, wealthier, and engaged [in business]," regarded the veterans as intellectually and culturally inferior. But the migrants themselves were diverse. Those from the Baltic province of Courland, with cultivated European manners and mastery of German, looked with condescension on the rest, while those with a traditional Jewish education dismissed the "Germans" as ignoramuses.[211] To unite these disparate populations required an exceptional rabbinic leader, and such was Rabbi Zelig (Shlomo Zalkind) Minor (1826–1900).[212] After being invited by Moscow's Jewish community to serve as the state rabbi in that city, in 1854 Minor left his position as the rabbi of Minsk (where he was one of the first to deliver sermons in Russian). When the cornerstone of the new synagogue on Solianka Street[213] was laid on 8 March 1870, Minor expressed his deep faith that Alexander II would realize the promise of Jewish emancipation:

> By the will of God and our august Monarch, we embark on laying the foundation of God's house—a house of prayers, a house of tears, a house of joy. But where? In the heart of Russia! At last, the barriers have fallen, separating us, the children of Israel, from our native land, the heart of Russia, and henceforth by the compassion of the Monarch, we raise up our modest but warm prayers here, without terror, without fear, openly and festively. . . . And how can we not rejoice at this event, when we are convinced that the strength, fortitude, glory, and grandeur of our beloved homeland depends fully on the present and future prosperity of our people?[214]

Refusing to function as the mere registrar of metrical books (the usual role of state rabbis), Minor built a vibrant religious community that could interact openly with general Russian society. According to Leo Tolstoy's wife Sof'ia, Minor became a familiar presence in their home after the writer "all of a sudden took into his head to learn Hebrew. He wanted to read the Bible and Gospels in Hebrew." Minor's son Lazar recollected arguments between his father and the famous writer "about one or another understanding of a Jewish text." One conversation remained indelibly etched in Minor's memory: "For about a half hour, we worked as teacher and student. . . . Once, we came to his understanding of the world of love. He said, 'There is not a word about it in the Bible.' I pointed him to the third line of Psalm 89 which I translated as 'the world exists with love.' He was very surprised by such an understanding of this well-known passage."[215] It was precisely this kind of rapprochement that Minor sought as he built the foundational institutions to strengthen Jewish religious observance and communal solidarity.

Minor found willing partners in the Poliakovs, who made increasing contributions to support the community. In 1878, for instance, Rozaliia contributed 250 rubles to the Moscow Jewish School for Poor and Orphaned Children, a generous donation second only to the 800 rubles donated by Mina Abramovna Malkiel'.[216] According to Vermel', this "Talmud Torah for both sexes," which opened in October 1872, was one of the few institutions to combine traditional Jewish education with Russian-language instruction, in addition to practical training in a trade.[217] In 1884–85 the Poliakovs contributed 3,000 rubles (equal to the donation of the Malkiel's) to the Aleksandrov artisan school and shelter, established in 1880 in honor of Alexander II's twenty-five-year reign.[218] This school prepared poor children for "work in a mechanized factory or for independent labor as a master mechanic," while teaching them the fundamentals of Judaism, Hebrew, Jewish history, and the Bible.[219] In 1882 Rozaliia raised funds for meals and medicine for poor Jews in hospitals or their own homes; the food was to be prepared at an inexpensive Jewish cafeteria on Old Square.[220] In 1886, to ensure that Jewish women had a proper place to immerse themselves, the Poliakovs (along with several other prominent Jews) laid the foundation for Mikvah Mayim.[221] As the financial records of the mikvah reveal, the religious community provided the basic necessities for observance of the ritual—scissors for clipping nails, candles, firewood, kerosene, lamps, mops, rugs, and a watchman to stand guard outside. Women either used the mikvah for free or paid a minimum fee according to their ability (15, 30, or 50 kopecks, or a ruble). It is unclear from Zinaida's diaries whether Rozaliia personally observed the laws of *niddah* as strictly as she maintained kashrut. However, the family's role in the building of the communal mikvah reflected their commitment to "all the institutions needed to observe the laws of the Jewish faith" in Moscow.[222]

Perhaps the most significant event for the Poliakovs was the opening of a private synagogue in 1886,[223] for which Lazar had obtained permission in 1883. In his petition of 6 May 1883 to the Building Department of the Moscow Provincial Board, Lazar explained:

> Wishing to move the existing Jewish prayer house from my private building on Tverskoi Boulevard to my other residence on Bronnaia Street no. 5 (Arbat district, 2nd section) and proposing to convert this building for such purposes, [and] presenting with this [petition] the plans of the locale and detailed designs for the reconstruction of the aforesaid building, I have the honor to ask humbly to grant me permission for this construction. In addition, I have the honor to add that for his part, the Moscow chief of police sent me permission to construct a prayer house in the above building. For this purpose, I am soliciting a permit from the Chancellery of the Chief of Police.[224]

The couple hired the prominent Russian architect Dmitrii N. Chichagov (1835–94), best known for his modern, nationalistic, and eccentric designs. Not everyone in the family approved the choice, however. According to Zinaida's diary entry for 27 February 1886, her brother "Il'iusha [Il'ia] expresses sharp criticism of the architectural shortcomings of the new house of worship and is even excessive in his abuse of its builder, Chichagov." She also observed that "the latter is really not qualified to design a Jewish synagogue: he himself is [Russian] Orthodox and has hardly seen such buildings." In her view, only a

FIGURE 9
The private Poliakov synagogue on Bronnaia Street.
"Sinagoga na bolshoi Bronnoi," accessed 7 May 2019, http://www.bronnaya.ru/.

Jewish architect could understand the proper aesthetics required for a Jewish house of worship. However, *Hamelits* praised the grandeur of the "Temple of the Lord of Hosts" that Lazar Poliakov built in the Tverskoi neighborhood, the heart of aristocratic Moscow: "I went to pray there, and what a very marvelous thing it was to view this building from within and without." The writer described the tall, quadrangular edifice as "pleasing to the eye" and noted the ornate *luhot habrit* (tablets of the covenant) engraved with the Ten Commandments in gilded Hebrew letters that stood above the arched entrance.[225] The grand, conspicuous synagogue in the heart of the Moscow urban landscape proclaimed that Judaism was as much a part of the imperial fabric as Russian Orthodoxy.

Equally attentive to the aesthetics of sacred music at the synagogue, the Poliakovs hired Nahum Maten'ko, and his magnificent baritone voice even attracted Christians to the Friday evening services.[226] Born into a Hasidic family in Kalarash (in Kherson province), Maten'ko "awed worshippers with the sweetness of his voice and warmth of his singing."[227] When he was ten years old, his musical talents came to the attention of Nissl Belzer (Nissan Spivak, 1824–1906), who was renowned for his choral arrangements and compositions.[228] Maten'ko moved with Belzer to Kishinev and later to Berdichev, where the chorister made a name for himself. Boris Thomashevsky, who also sang in

Belzer's choir in Berdichev (and later became a star on the Yiddish stage), remembered Maten'ko as a striking figure: "He had a rare bass-baritone voice. He was a very handsome man, and he donned a top hat and the most modern clothing. His long hair, artistic brow, and graceful deportment elicited great respect for him. Looking at Nahum, one might assume that he was an artist of the imperial opera rather than a chorister in Reb Nissi [Nissl] Belzer's choir."[229]

Following his marriage, Maten'ko moved to Odessa at the invitation of Jacob Bachman (1846–1905) to serve as the second cantor of the Great Choral Synagogue. With a touch of hyperbole, Thomashevsky claimed that "the millionaire Poliakov from Moscow heard Nahum praying at the Odessa shul [and] was so impressed by his singing and personality that he built a synagogue in his courtyard and installed Nahum as cantor. He gave him a lifelong contract."[230] Lazar most likely sought out Maten'ko in Moscow—where, according to one account, the cantor had moved to attend the Moscow Imperial Conservatory. The talented singer allegedly made many enemies at the conservatory and found his career path blocked, so the invitation to serve as the cantor of the new Poliakov synagogue (with a salary of 1,800 rubles a year, plus 4,000 rubles to assemble and direct a choir) must have proved irresistible.[231] At the choir rehearsal on 26 February 1886, before the opening of the synagogue, Zinaida observed that Maten'ko resembled a Russian Orthodox "priest in his broad black cassock." She complained about the new boys' choir, especially one "boy with a very strong soprano [voice]." Disappointed, Zinaida observed the following day that "no foreigners are at the opening of the synagogue," but she consoled herself with the thought that "the authorities will be invited at some other time on an appropriate occasion." The dedication of the synagogue needed to be "simple and modest, as is required." On 1 March Zinaida could not help but write proudly that "the opening of the synagogue had a remarkable impact," especially when her two grandfathers (Solomon Poliakov and Pavel Vydrin), her father, her brother Mikhail (dressed in his school uniform with a sword!), Rabbi Minor, and the family's trusted financial officer Efim Epstein carried the Torah.

However, the Poliakovs were not content to build a private synagogue without ensuring that the community had a proper place to worship. Whereas construction of a private synagogue was relatively easy, the battle to obtain permission for the new Choral Synagogue on Spasoglinishchevskii Lane was fierce. In 1879 members of the Moscow Jewish religious community filed paperwork arguing that their current synagogue on Solianka Street had become overcrowded and was unable to accommodate worshippers, especially during holidays. Citing a state law permitting one synagogue per eighty Jewish households (the basis on which the St. Petersburg community had built its choral synagogue a decade earlier), Rabbi Minor and the synagogue board requested permission for the community to acquire land for the new building.[232] Notwithstanding Prince Dolgorukov's staunch support, authorities in St. Petersburg denied the petition on the ground that "at the present time they are considering the basis for the organization of the Jewish religious community outside the Pale of Settlement," and hence the question of purchasing land was "completely untimely."[233] Seven years later, buoyed with confidence in Dolgorukov's patronage, in 1886 Lazar Poliakov purchased two adjoining buildings and their plots of land for 80,000 silver rubles, and then he donated the properties to the community. This time the Moscow provincial board approved construction.

With the permit (signed personally by Dolgorukov) in hand, the Jewish community hired the architect Semen Eibushits (1851–98) to construct a magnificent choral synagogue based on a Greek architectural style. The towering edifice immediately provoked complaints from the Russian Orthodox community.[234] In a letter to the chief procurator of the Holy Synod, Konstantin Pobedonostsev, a Moscow resident named A. Shishkov lodged this complaint: "The main thing that strikes Muscovites in this case, irrespective of the fact that the synagogue is situated in such a central place in the city, is that the erected building resembles an extremely beautiful Russian Orthodox church with columns and cupolas, crowned with a special symbol in the shape of two intersecting triangles in lieu of a cross." Shishkov urged Jewish leaders to eliminate the cupola and change the exterior facade so that it would not resemble a Christian church. To his surprise, he received an invitation from Dologorukov, who "accepted me cordially" and expressed his wish that the matter would end "without noise." After that meeting, Shishkov sent a warning to Pobedenostsev: "He [Dolgorukov] strongly protects Poliakov and [the synagogue warden] Shneider,[235] and his pride is wounded."[236] After traveling to Moscow to view the building, Pobedonostsev filed a formal complaint with the deputy minister of internal affairs, stating that the image of the facade sent by Dologorukov was inaccurate because it did not reveal the entire exterior, especially the portico supported by columns.[237] The chief procurator's crusade to protect the honor of Russian Orthodoxy soon bore fruit.

In the summer of 1891, following Dolgorukov's dismissal and the expulsion of some 20,000 Jews from Moscow, the chief of police, Aleksandr Vlasovskii (1842–99), ordered that the cupola be removed—the first in a series of administrative actions against the synagogue.[238] Vermel' recalled how "the cupola was torn down to the accompaniment of clamorous and bellowing hurrahs and replaced by an ugly patch that disfigured the entire appearance of the building."[239] According to an anonymous memoir in Rabbi Minor's archive, Lazar and his family were in Paris at this time, and the synagogue did not have sufficient funds to pay the rent on its old premises. Shneider and the building committee decided to terminate the land lease and informed the chief of police that "we have temporarily started to pray in the side room of the new building." Vlasovskii "did not say anything definitive against this."[240] However, when a doctor attempted to hold his wedding at the synagogue in June 1892, the police expelled all the guests and locked the building. Vlasovskii informed Rabbi Minor that because "so few Jews remained after the expulsion," there was no longer any need for a synagogue on Spasoglinishchevskii Lane. In his view, the "existence of a Jewish synagogue in Moscow, the first capital of the Russian empire and Russian Orthodoxy, is indecent (neprilichno)." He gave the rabbi until 1 January 1893 to either turn the synagogue into a "philanthropic institution" or sell the property. The memoirist bemoaned the fact that "Poliakov was not in Moscow" at the time because, "as a very prudent individual, he would have understood at once that there was nothing to be done; of necessity, one needed to comply and accept the proposal." Instead, based on the "strength of the law, especially in the interior of Russia," Rabbi Minor decided to petition the emperor with an appeal based on the freedom of religion in Russia—a document that only Shneider agreed to cosign.[241] The response was swift and decisive: Minor was dismissed as state rabbi and permanently expelled from Moscow to the Pale of Settlement, while Shneider received a lesser punishment—exile from the city and Moscow province for two years. To prevent a sale, the community transformed the synagogue into an orphanage and canteen for poor Jews. It was only after the decree on religious liberty was issued on 17 April 1905 that the community received permission to reopen the synagogue—which it did on 1 June 1906.[242] "The Jews of Moscow received His Imperial Majesty's permission to open the synagogue," wrote Zinaida in Paris on 28 June 1905. "It is only a pity that now there are disorders by the revolutionaries."[243]

Rabbi Iakov Maze (1859–1924), who replaced Minor as the state rabbi of Moscow,[244] recalled the opening of the synagogue with great emotion. During the nearly two decades when the synagogue could not function as a house of worship, Lazar had comforted the new rabbi: "This too will pass" (in Hebrew, Gam zeh yaavor).[245] The two had become especially close during the years of hardship over the synagogue. After Maze's election 1893, Lazar had invited him to his private synagogue on Hanukkah, when a "crowd of men and women gathered" to listen to a three-hour sermon by the new rabbi. Vermel' recalled:

"This was an event that raised the spirits of the demoralized community, which responded as if to say: 'Never mind, we'll get by.'"[246] As they approached the entrance of the newly opened synagogue, Maze handed Lazar—the head of the Jewish community—the keys, which bore this inscription: "I opened the doors of the House of the Lord and repaired them" (2 Chronicles 29:3). When the Temple was destroyed for the first time, Maze explained, the priests threw their keys to the heavens saying, "Master [of the Universe], since we did not merit being faithful guardians of these keys, we return them to you" (Babylonian Talmud Taanit 29a).[247] He turned to Lazar and reminded him, "When it was necessary to close our synagogue and give over its keys, your hands reached out and accepted the keys." To this Lazar replied, with tears in his eyes, "The hand of God also accepted our keys, and it is now giving them back to us," and he wept bitterly as he entered the sacred space.[248] In his eulogy for Lazar in 1914, Maze cited an "obscure text"[249] with this description of the deceased: "Here I entered the city of Rome and saw children studying, [the ritual of] the morning bathers, and evening, morning, and afternoon prayers, and I asked who established these? An old man responded to me, 'one man was among us and when he died, we cried [in the words of the Prophet Jeremiah 6:25]: Mourn, as for an only child; wail bitterly.'" Like the traveler who entered the city of Rome, Maze remembered that when he arrived in Moscow—another imperial capital—he "saw schools for Jewish children, Talmud Torahs, and an artisan school . . . all the institutions which are necessary for the observance of the Jewish faith." When he asked, "Who built all these institutions in the heart of Russia?," they cited Exodus 18:4: "and the other was named Eliezer" —Lazar Solomonovich Poliakov.[250] All this does much to correct the contemporary view that the Poliakovs were "less Jewish" than the Gintsburgs (a view propagated by Sliozberg and others). In fact, the Poliakovs played a central role in establishing, financing, and promoting Jewish religious institutions in Moscow and making them visible as part of the imperial landscape. That is why Lazar was elected the first head of the community's Financial Board when it was founded in 1893 by Maze.[251]

Although professing and observing Judaism, the Poliakovs did adopt some Russian Orthodox customs, chiefly so that their children could participate in cultural practices that would make them feel Russian. For example, they designated one child to serve as the godparent (*krestnyi*) for each newborn infant—a kind of secular variant of Orthodoxy. At age thirteen Zinaida proudly wrote: "Yet another brother was born on 13 December but they have not named him yet: it appears that they will call him Genrikh. Ronia and I will be his godparents. Ronia is terribly pleased that he will be the godfather of our brother."[252] Mindful of her duties to another godchild, a cousin on her mother's side, she wrote on 21 March 1884: "Aleksandr Vydrin, my godson, should be celebrating his birthday any day now." The family also celebrated saints' name days with friends, as reflected in Zinaida's diary entry for 3 February 1887: "At last, I managed to go with Papa to an exhibition of Aivazovskii's paintings on Vasil'evskii Island [in St. Petersburg]. There was a total of twenty-two paintings. I did not particularly like any of them, but the best, in my opinion, is 'The Surf at Gurzov Cliff,' a small but precise painting. In addition, we went to Mme. Messarosh, and it turned out that today is her name day. In honor of this solemn day we had chocolate at their house, but quite inadvertently." One of Zinaida's favorite holidays was Russian New Year, with its *elka* (Christmas tree), festive parties, and exchange of gifts. She wrote fondly of one such event on 4 January 1887, when she was fourteen: "In recent days we were at the Malkiels for the holiday tree; it was very cheerful there, and the children received gifts. Khaia received a glass box for small items; Misha—an architectural construction; Ronia—little fish, small boats, and tiny ducks with magnets; Il'iusha —a horse with hussar astride, which is wound up by a key (which they lost, promised to send tomorrow, but forgot to do)." Such practices, associated not only with New Year's but also with Christmas, prompted the Jewish poet and composer Eliakum Zunzer to complain about the so-called Jewish aristocrats: "Like apes, they imitate the manners and customs of Christians; thus, as Christians, they would have a Christmas tree in their homes."[253] Zunzer would not have been surprised to learn that the Poliakovs also participated in the holiday of *maslenitsa* (Shrovetide, popularly known as *bliny* or crepe week), when Christians consumed dairy products before the fast of Lent. On 15 February 1887 Zinaida attributed the latter to Judaism: "Great Lent begins tomorrow, so we shall say goodbye to Shrovetide! That is not bad, since it is unhealthy to eat a lot of hotcakes, and I think that Moses established the fast so that people not gorge themselves excessively on tasty foods. And he was right. But what was good and appropriate for our predecessors is not good for us, and therefore I do not observe [these rules]." This hybridity—the secular observance of Russian Orthodox holidays and selective observance of Judaism—differed significantly from Reuben Gubbay's upbringing in the Baghdadi Jewish community in India. In her final postwar diary, Zinaida wrote: "Ruby was very religious and fastidiously observed all of our holidays and fasts."[254] One can imagine the tensions when Zinaida celebrated the birthday of Annette, their only daughter, on 23 December 1904 with a small Christmas tree.

The selective association with Russian Orthodoxy, however, did not extend to marriage: the Poliakovs married off their children to members of the Jewish elite in the Russian Empire and Western Europe. Samuil's children boasted the most illustrious marriages. In 1880, his oldest daughter, Zinaida Samuilovna, married Baron James de Hirsch (1843–96). The *American Hebrew* noted that their fathers "chiefly made their money out of railroads, and both are conspicuous by their philanthropy in behalf of their Jewish coreligionists." [255]Samuil's third daughter, Rachel, married the lawyer Georges Elie St. Paul, the son of a wealthy banker and a distinguished member of the Jewish community in Paris.[256] His second daughter, Roza (Rosille), found a partner closer to home —Leon Varshavskii [Warshawsky], the son of a St. Petersburg banker and close family friend, Abram Varshavskii [Warshawsky]. The marriage of the latter's daughters (Marie and Louise) into elite French families (the Kanns and Cahen d'Anvers) would help connect the Poliakovs to an important social circle, as will be seen below. Zinaida mentions Samuil's children in her diaries but writes mainly about their latest news, rarely about personal interactions with them (except for Daniil, who was close to her family because of business ties). Relations between Samuil's and Iakov's children were not even cordial. When Lazar and Liza (Iakov's children from his first marriage) were eighteen and fourteen, respectively, their Uncle Samuil had invited them to live with his family in St. Petersburg. Lazar needed to prepare for his exams to matriculate in the Railways, Road, and Communications Institute, and Liza was to develop a closer relationship with Samuil's daughter Zinaida, who was around the same age. Iakov, who had misgivings about sending his children away in the first place, explained with regret that they quarreled and "their relationship is bad up to the present time."[257]

Zinaida enjoyed more intimate relationships with Iakov's children, who married into prominent families in the Russian Empire but spent more time in France, especially at the family villas in Nice and Biarritz.[258] Iakov's older children Lazar (1851–1927) and Elizabeth (Liza or Elena, 1855–1937) married two Raffalovich siblings from Odessa: Anna (Annette) Leonino (the widow of Edward E. B. Leonino)[259] and Lev (Louis) Raffalovich. Iakov was elated when Elizabeth and Lev announced their engagement. In 1873 he wrote a glowing report about his future son-in-law, describing him as "an educated and cultivated young man [who] speaks *all* the European languages." Yet he expressed some misgiving: "However, all that glitters is not gold"—a sadly accurate prophecy of Lev's financial future. Still, the Poliakovs were susceptible to dazzling first appearances. "At this time, all the Raffaloviches made the best impression on us," Iakov reported. "[They have] an enormous, European office; everyone lives like royals." He noted that Abraham Raffalovich's three sons had built "*for themselves* and [their] *children* an enormous house for 200,000–300,000 rubles" and had received the status of honorary citizens long before other Jews.[260] Unfortunately, Lev's father quarreled with his brothers and went his separate way, forcing Lev to beg Iakov for financial assistance in 1875. In despair, Iakov wrote: "I received a letter from him [Lev] that if I do not allow him to take the 100,000 rubles belonging to Liza (it is deposited in the bank for five years, and it is not possible to withdraw it without my permission), then he would not be able to endure his father's disgrace and shoot himself."[261] The couple decided to move abroad while the family put Lev's father's affairs in order.[262]

Iakov found a more successful son-in-law in Iosef Landau, son of the wealthy Warsaw banker Wilhelm Landau (1833–99).[263] Impressed with the young man, whom he met in Marienbad, Iakov urged his wife to bring their daughter Isabella (Bella) to Vienna and then travel together to an exhibition in Brussels, for the purpose of making the prospective couple acquainted: "I introduced [Iosef] to my wife and Bella; my wife knew who he was but Bella did not. She only asked the following day who he was and what [was his] nationality, not presuming that he was a Jew. He made a good impression, as did she on him and his parents."[264] Zinaida gave an unsparing impression of the new couple on 16 August 1881: "Mrs. Mozer told me that Bella's fiancé is not bad looking, but very overweight; I replied that the fiancée is not skinny ('birds of a feather flock together')." Isabella and Iosef married in Taganrog on 17 January 1882 and had a very close relationship, according to all accounts.[265] Seven years later, Iakov celebrated the wedding of his youngest daughter, Anna (Niuta), to Grigorii (George) Rubinshtein, a member of a reputable banking family in Khar'kov (although he belonged to the less successful branch).[266] Iakov's diaries constantly bemoaned the financial failures of Grigorii's side of the family:

He had in his blood the deficiency of one part of the Rubinshtein family, for whom "money is nothing"—in spite of the fact that they themselves never amassed any money and so have none. But that's all the same to them. He should buy, order, do something as he sees fit, but then how it is to be paid for—about that they don't give a thought. And in spite of the fact that he extracted 25,000 rubles from the modest means of Niuta, and the house itself has been double mortgaged, he still needs 10,000 rubles (so he says, but I do not believe him) to finish the house, or otherwise it has to be mortgaged as unfinished. So Niuta spoke to me before her departure about selling part of her stock and transferring 10,000 rubles. Thus the visit of the children is one part satisfying, nine parts dissatisfying.[267]

But the real black sheep in Iakov's family was his son Boris, who converted to Christianity to marry a Russian Orthodox divorcée called "P." There were hints that Iakov was anxious about his two unmarried sons, for example in this telegram of 31 August 1898: "Telegram from Avdot'ia [Samuil's wife] that Kotia [Daniil Poliakov] is marrying Alma Reiss from Czernowitz, Galicia. Thank God, thank God. May God help us so that [my sons] Boria [Boris] and Samuil will also marry Jewish women."[268] When Iakov got wind of alarming rumors (including an anonymous letter sent to his wife about Boris),[269] he inserted a clause in his will disinheriting Boris if he did not marry a Jewish woman —but this was to no avail. He learned about his son's secret marriage during a conversation with an "*orel*" (derogatory Hebrew for an "uncircumcised one") in Taganrog:

> The *orel* asked me if it was true that Boria [Boris] had married. I replied that if this happens, he is not my son. He crossed himself and said, thank God that you look on it in that way. Stepanov was breakfasting, and related how Kovalev had told him based on Foti's words that his daughter has already married Boria. . . . Stepanov told me that the former teacher Somov said that in Kiev they told an anecdote about me (a good anecdote)—that God came to me in a dream and said, "don't grieve, you have three sons but I had only one, and that one was baptized."[270]

Iakov and his wife disowned their "wayward" son and, in response to pleas of their children to reconcile with Boris, they always responded with a resounding "*nikogda, nikogda*" (never, never).[271] Although at home in Russian society, the Poliakovs drew a red line at conversion. It bears noting that the state generally disapproved of conversions, especially from the mid-nineteenth century on, because it created problems of governance and prosecution for apostasy in cases of reconversion. Recognizing the realities of a multiconfessional empire and affirming the priority of *raison d'état*, the state simply preferred that all people retain their confessional status.[272] In his despair over Boris and fears of a similar scenario occurring with his youngest son, Iakov proposed that his granddaughter Alice[273] marry his son Samuil. However, his daughter Bella rejected the idea, saying that she did "not want to give her daughter [in marriage] to a family in eternal mourning [because it disowned Boris]."[274] When she finally got married, Alice invited Boris, his Russian wife, and their son to her wedding, which must have upset her father, Iakov, immensely.[275] Zinaida often corresponded with her cousin Boris because "I take an interest in his fate." She expressed sympathy for Boris's wife and son, who "must suffer from his uncertain position in society and in his family because the majority do not acknowledge him now as a result of this unfortunate marriage."[276]

In contrast to their cousins, Lazar's children married relatively late in life.

Russian by culture and aristocratic by class, the family expected the children to marry Jewish spouses within their social circles, but that greatly limited their choices. As Zinaida approached her early twenties, the gaiety of the Russian balls and parties began to fade and she developed a sense of futility: there were simply no eligible Jewish partners at these grand affairs. To broaden their choices, the family sought marriage partners at the spas—Jewish hives of matchmaking. However, Zinaida complained on 13 October 1886 that European Jews "are very stand-offish, especially toward us Russian Jews, who regard themselves as not the least better or worse than they (the "cibilized"[277] ones, as Mme. Malkiel' says). She always tries to use pompous, stilted words. But it is excusable for her not to know how to speak Russian." The prejudice against Russian Jews could be overcome by titles like baron—as in the case of the Gintsburgs, whose children married Rothschilds, Sassoons, and Warburgs. But the Poliakovs never attained the coveted status of titled aristocracy and could only resort to using "de Poliakoff" as their surname in Europe, thereby staking a claim to aristocratic status if not a title. Fluent in French and English, the Poliakov daughters met eligible bachelors at spas and resorts, ever hoping to find a good match. On 23 December 1885, Zinaida cautiously described meeting Reuben Gubbay but did not even mention his name, referring only to his family: "We spent five months abroad. So I was two and a half months with Mama in Paris after the treatment in Franzensbad and in Nachhut (in the Swiss mountains)[278] and made a pleasant new acquaintance. I initially did not like the Gabbe [Gubbay] family, but later became close to them." She pondered long hours about Gubbay's opinion of her because, as she noted on 6 November 1886, "he is very cool toward everyone, with the exception of I[da] A. Rubinshtein." Concerns about Gubbay's financial position, however, put a damper on her hopes as of 24 November 1886: "Gabbe [Gubbay] is a very nice, handsome young man, in my opinion. One regret: he is without means. He is very strongly praised by his relatives and by those who know him."

A long-awaited letter from Gubbay's sister Flora[279] encouraged Zinaida to discuss matters of the heart with her aunt on 13 February 1887: "Masha is sitting here and in a very humorous vein has begun to ponder my love life. First she began to analyze Robin Gabbe [Reuben Gubbay] and then even tried to convince me that it will come to pass." Zinaida resented her grandfather's attempts to arrange her marriage through a former teacher at the State Rabbinical School in Vil'na, so that "even the lowliest teacher [melamed] at the Glebov compound has access [here]." She complained bitterly on 18 May 1887, "But I have great antipathy toward this, since—under no circumstances—do I believe in happiness that has been prearranged, calculated, and decided in advance."[280] To express her desires, she worked up the courage to consult her father on 18 August, but Lazar preferred a groom of greater financial substance:

> Today I talked about Gabbe [Gubbay] with Papa, who finds that Jacques Rozenberg is better. To be sure, the former is much more attractive, but the latter is much wealthier and better-looking (if one ignores the attractiveness of the personality). So when Uncle Samuil comes here shortly, we will find out what Robin Gabbe [Reuben Gubbay] intends to do and whether, after the wedding of his uncle (a Sassoon), he is really going to China, to which he "is drawn by some unknown power." I think he will go, since he has no work or business here in Europe, and he is just twiddling his thumbs.

After much debate about the advisability of the match (the groom was after all a Sassoon on his mother's side, despite his lack of means), Zinaida and Reuben finally became engaged on 11 July 1891. Zinaida's existing diaries do not include any entries about the engagement or wedding, but her Uncle Iakov recorded these important family events: "Zina, the daughter of Lazar Solomonovich, and Gubbay from Paris were engaged. Thank God. It's time."[281] *Le Figaro* published the formal announcement on 25 July 1891: "Mr. Reuben Gubbay, son of Mr. and Madame Gubbay, was engaged with Mademoiselle Zenaide de Poliakoff, daughter of the Russian banker. The fiancé is the grandson of Sir Albert Sassoon. His sister is married to the director of the Messageries Fluviales de Cochinchine [The River Shipping Company of Cochinchina], Mr. Jules Rueff."[282] News of the engagement traveled quickly to friends and family in India. As the *Times of India* reported: "By a telegram from Paris, dated yesterday, we learn that Mr. Reuben Gubbay, son of Mr. A. M. Gubbay of Messrs. E. D. Sassoon and Co., has been betrothed to the daughter of Baron [sic] Poliakoff, a very rich Russian banker of Moscow."[283] The Parisian edition of the *New York Herald* also announced that the grandson of Sir Albert Sasson was betrothed to "the daughter of the great Russian banker."[284] When the couple finally wed on 10 September 1891, Iakov remarked, "Thank God for brother and for his domestic peace, which is now established. Yes, it's about time and very much about time. It appears that she's already twenty-eight years old."[285]

Zinaida's sisters married even later, but all within the Jewish fold. Khaia (Xenia) married the engineer Georges Levi (who did eventually earn the title of baron) of Venice[286] when she was thirty-one.[287] The groom was a relative of Zinaida's close friend Madame Enrichetta Levi, whom she had met during her travels in Italy. In 1895, Zinaida wrote in her diary: "I have one friend here [in Florence], Madame Adolfo Scander Levi to whom we dropped by for a visit today, but did not find her home and only left a box of confectionery with her daughter Nina which we bought for her in Milan."[288] The Levis, a prominent aristocratic Florentine family, were affectionate to the Gubbays, sending toys for their daughter Annette and inviting them to vacation, where they played tennis together.[289] Zinaida envied her sister's warm marriage, though the couple lived in a small house (by her standards) in Florence. "Khaia's husband, Georges Levi, was a very handsome Italian and exquisite gentleman in general," she recalled in her final diary.[290] Zinaida's youngest sister, Raisa, finally decided to marry Adolphe de Hirsch of Munich, a nephew of their close friend Jacques Rozenberg, when she was thirty-three.[291] She had had several suitors, including her brother-in-law Marco Levi, "who serves in the regiment." Although her father found him "almost suitable," Raisa did not want to marry a military man.[292] "Better to have business with one's compatriot," wrote Zinaida, approving her sister's choice. "The young man, Adolphe von Hirsch Gereuth, is from the family of Baron Hirsch, but only a 'von' [not a baron] and his mother was Mlle. Rozenberg."[293] The official engagement took place in Marienbad in September 1903. Zinaida remembered fondly, "Skinny Raia married a fat Bavarian and was, nonetheless, very happy with him always."[294]

Zinaida's brother Jacques, a famous doctor in Biarritz, was twenty-five in 1901 when he wed Claire (Clairette) Brodskaia,[295] daughter of Leon Brodskii of Kiev, with whom he had three daughters. In Zinaida's view, her other brothers seemed too preoccupied with business to consider matrimony: "Isaak is serious and works a lot at the banks and does not intend to marry for now."[296] She added later, "Il'iusha [Il'ia] works in Moscow,"[297] but in her mind, he was the eternal family playboy who "wastes everything on women and horses of course!"[298] Zinaida observed wryly: "Shcherbatov's daughter, they say, has become a very beautiful young woman; how would Il'ia not have fallen in love with her?"[299] He maintained a long-term relationship with Countess de Buffon, with whom Zinaida kept in touch during World War II. Zinaida was also not optimistic about her other brothers, because they were wedded to the family banks and businesses: "Isaak and Misha also [work] at the banks and office. It goes without saying that Sasha also intends to find himself a suitable friend for life [sarcastic tone]."[300] She thought he should get married "now rather than later because he can get accustomed to married life" and the "discipline of a woman." Zinaida added that "Mama provided the example, and now the husbands are chafing under this control, of course, because everyone loves complete freedom."[301] Aleksandr (who joined the Kadet Party during the 1905 revolution)[302] eventually married Klara Solomonovich Khishin (better known as Visha), a divorcée of whom Rozaliia strongly disapproved—so much so that she cut him out of her will.[303] Mikhail eventually married Vera Nikolaevna

FIGURE 10

Zinaida Lazarevna Poliakova on her wedding day.

Poliakova and Poliakoff, *Sem'ia Poliakovykh*.

Boitchevsky, about whom Zinaida worried during World War II.[304] In any case, when Zinaida traveled back to Moscow for family events and visits, she must have recalled the bittersweet memories of her own wedding that took place in one of the blackest years of Moscow Jewry.

. . . .

After Dolgorukov: Decline and Crisis, 1891–1914

The year 1891 proved to be most inauspicious for a Jewish wedding in Russia. As the Poliakovs prepared to lead their eldest daughter under the huppah, they were still reeling from the shock of Prince Dologorukov's dismissal as governor-general of Moscow and the appointment of Grand Duke Sergei Aleksandrovich as his successor. As long as Dolgorukov stood at the helm, the Jews of Moscow were safe from the antisemitism that engulfed the empire in the 1880s—including pogroms, the May Laws, and discriminatory university quotas. Vermel' claimed that "the concord between the police on the one hand, and the artisan board on the other, established a more or less tolerable *alliance*; the police and artisan board, on which the fate of the Jews depended after all, maintained the principle of *un accord tacite*—and both sides were satisfied." The tolerance was not free: bribes for residence rights lined the pockets of police, some of whom received a "regular salary from the Jews (a thousand rubles or more a month)."[305] Contemporaries noted that the campaign against Dolgorukov assumed antisemitic hues. According to Sliozberg, "the highest authorities accused him [Dolgorukov] of being indulgent, filling Moscow with Jews."[306] Rumors spread that Alexander III even asked Dolgorukov, "Tell me, who is governor-general in Moscow—you or Poliakov?"[307]

The conservative Russian press played on the antisemitic fervor, increasing the visibility and vulnerability of the Jews. In 1889 E. L'vov wrote in *Novoe vremia* that he would "stake his life" on the proposition that Moscow would "soon turn into Vil'na" because it was so overrun by Jews:

> If some curious tourist turned to me—a Moscow lawyer—with the question, could I visually persuade him in just twenty-four hours that contemporary Moscow is overpopulated with Jews, instead of an answer, I would take this gentleman to the best Moscow avenue—Tverskoi Boulevard—and some of the other busiest trading streets of the first capital. I would point out to him to the vast proportion of the finest, colossal houses belonging to the Jews; the mass of Jewish banks, shops, offices, loan offices; the Jewish house of worship on Solianka Street; the sumptuous synagogue on Bron-

naia Street next to *Poliakov's* house (and on his land); twenty-one Jewish prayer houses spread throughout the town; the eateries of the *zhidy* [yids] and meat shops; the immense percentage of *zhidy*—their sharp, unusual eyes on the Kremlin and [downtown] Kitaigorod. . . . One part [of high society and the middle classes] puts the blame on the person who, at the time, played a prominent role in the administration, but now after [his] resignation,[308] all that blame is placed on the person who is openly the head of the financial management—Poliakov.[309]

In his next installment L'vov accused two unnamed Russian newspapers[310] of being overrun by Jews (in terms of their "advertisements and Jewish sympathy")—one was even "sold off to the local Jewish king"—the "genius of Jewish *shakhermakherstva* [a Russified Yiddish word for shady dealings], . . . His Highness Rebbe Poliakov with his millions, banks, houses, railroads."[311]

Despite (or perhaps because of) such attacks, Lazar Poliakov made lavish financial contributions to the editors of archconservative antisemitic newspapers, including Vladimir P. Meshcherskii of *Grazhdanin.* In the 1880s Meshcherskii published a series of articles in *Grazhdanin* that blamed all of Russia's economic woes on a "Prussian-Jewish plutocracy." He pressed for reform "to centralize the credit system in a state bank" so that the "mass of the people's capital . . . would not go into the bottomless pockets of the zhidy, plutocrats, and other swindlers."[312] Meshcherskii, of course, had no qualms about taking rubles from those very "bottomless pockets" that he denounced. In fact, he judged the "Jewish question" to be the greatest social problem facing Russia: "Everything is hidden in it, its satanic goals; with its genuinely satanic attributes, it flies under a false flag to conceal its main intention—which is, sooner or later, to destroy the Orthodox Church, the autocracy, and the integrity of the people (*narod*)—in a word, Russia."[313] Meshcherskii warned against the complete "Judaization" of Russia:

> Take the past half-century. How many measures were devised against the Jews, starting with the Pale of Settlement and ending with quotas on Jews in educational institutions! . . . Meanwhile . . . both capitals became big Berdichevs; in Moscow a vast majority of merchants and trading firms became Jewish; in St. Petersburg, entire markets became exclusively Jewish; all the banks (except one) became Jewish; tens of thousands of Jews penetrated into all the small cracks of life of the capital; they knew ways to evade the law unbeknownst to anyone. All the educational institutions accepted Jews with the help of the most extensive evasion of the quotas. . . . Who was it that did all these things for the Jews? It was we ourselves.[314]

At the same time, Meshcherskii continued to court the Poliakovs for their financial support. After the brothers attained their status of hereditary nobility, Iakov boasted, "Prince Meshcherskii displayed his friendship to me. He wrote a remarkable article about our nobility. The article made a great impression on everyone."[315] Outraged by the unholy alliance of Poliakov and Meshcherskii, the Jewish press was fit to be tied. In its coverage of the fiftieth anniversary of *Grazhdanin*, the Yiddish daily *Der fraynd* alluded to Meshcherskii's rumored homosexual philandering in a lead article titled "The Great Love." It questioned how Poliakov could congratulate the "antisemitic publicist" and hope that the newspaper "would flourish for many years for the good of society." Asking "Is Poliakov a Jew?," the article concluded: "He's more a financial magnate than a Jew."[316] Lazar even made headlines in New York: "Poliakov sends a blessing to Prince Meshcherskii." *Der morgen zhurnal* reported that Poliakov wished the "famous Judeophobe (*yidn freser*)" a long life so that "he can continue his 'useful work'—that is, besmirch[ing] Jews."[317]

The antisemitic campaign in the press, royal court, and higher administration generated foreboding among the Jews of Moscow in 1891. After the appointment of Vlasovskii as chief of police (a man Vermel' described as "coarse and cruel"), the local police began to "cleanse" Moscow of Jews residing illegally in the city.[318] According to Vermel', most vulnerable were those whose right of residency was conditional on employment in a trade as craftsmen and their apprentices, midwives, feldshers, chemists, and pharmacists. Clerks and agents of first-guild merchants, whose residency depended on special permission from the administration, also found themselves prime targets.[319] Amid all the expulsions, the decree of 29 March 1891 ("On the prohibition of Jewish artisans, distillers, brewers and, in general, craftsmen and artisans to settle in Moscow and Moscow province") nevertheless came as a shock. The end to selective integration seemed complete in October 1892 when descendants of Nikolaevan soldiers—the oldest, most established residents of the city—received expulsion notices. "People who had lived in Moscow for twenty, thirty, forty years," wrote the jurist Onisim Gol'dovskii (1865–1922), "had to sell off their belongings in a short period and leave."[320] Roza Vinaver observed that Moscow never witnessed direct violence against the Jews, but the expulsions were a kind of "bloodless pogrom."[321] Vermel' recalled that the winters of 1891 and 1892 in Moscow were especially harsh, with the "thermometer showing 31 degrees below freezing in January." The chaos at the train station where the "crowds of expelled [Jews]—women, children, elderly, the infirmed, crippled, the manifestly impoverished, and more or less affluent people" waited for their trains was horrific.[322] As the *New York Times* reported, the material possessions accompanying their owners "spoke eloquently of a people torn up by the roots,"with "carpets, picture frames, candlesticks, big leather-bound books, even bird cages, all made into as portable parcels as possible." Then there were the faces of the refugees: the parting of "two young sisters who clung, sobbing to each other through the window till the train moved;" the one left behind in Moscow "fainting as the train left the station."[323] The Poliakovs also came to the train station in the summer of 1891 to bid farewell to the sister and two nieces of Lazar's blind stepmother, Breine—relatives "who had never left her side." Lazar's father, Solomon, was so upset by the expulsions that his face broke out with "eczema," and "he almost did not leave [the house]." There must have been family discussions about intervening on behalf of Breine's relatives, but Iakov admitted, "It was awkward for Lazar Solomonovich to intercede for them."[324] Lazar's influence had vanished with Prince Dolgorukov's departure and left him cautious and reluctant to ask for any favors.

The Poliakovs' fall from favor was evident in the fate of their private synagogue on Bronnaia Street, which had served as a place to worship for the city's mercantile, cultural, and intellectual elites. According to the records of the Financial Board, in 1896 the authorities denied Lazar's petition to hold public Rosh Hashanah and Yom Kippur services in his prayer house.[325] That same year the director of a Moscow bank also received this brusque note from the Moscow chief of police: "I am informing the honorary citizen Sh., regarding his request for permission to hold his daughter's wedding ceremony at the Poliakov synagogue, that I have rejected the petition because the Poliakov prayer house is permitted exclusively for members of his family."[326] The Poliakovs nonetheless remained loyal to the emperor and attached to the Russian people, even while decrying the discrimination against Jews. Iakov expressed these sentiments in a diary entry during the fateful year of 1891:

> The Jews in Paris have celebrated the centenary of their equal rights, but the unfortunate Jews of Russia . . . are equal only in the performance of all obligations. They are killed and wounded in wars like all the other subjects. Each year they are taken as soldiers to man the troops, and we need say nothing about their monetary obligations. At the same time, they are being driven out of here, and there is no end to the legal restrictions on them. And what is more worthy of amazement, the tsar is honest and just; the Russian people are incomparable, good, welcoming, receptive, and tolerant. All the misfortunes of the Jews [lie with the] administration (which is generally ready to accommodate them). . . . The only hope is for God alone [to] soften the heart of the administration and mitigate the fate of the unfortunate Jews in Russia.[327]

Despite their strong allegiance to the tsar and people, the Poliakovs must have been shocked in 1899 when the state ruled that Jews could not constitute more than a third of the first-guild merchants in Moscow.[328]

In the face of increasing antisemitism, Zinaida's parents and relatives not only continued to associate with infamous conservatives but also maintained intimate friendships with them. That included luminaries close to the throne, such as Konstantin P. Pobedonostsev (chief procurator of the Holy Synod) and publishers like Meshcherskii and Mikhail N. Katkov. So intimate was their friendship with the Katkovs that the latter even inquired if they could attend synagogue with the Poliakovs, who were happy to send them tickets for Friday night services on 24 March 1887. The prominence of such connections is particularly striking in the diary of Iakov Poliakov. On 17 January 1893, for example, he boasted: "Yesterday I was at the Minister of Transportation [Apollon K.] Krivoshein, who promised to speak to several senators about our ennoblement. He already knew that Prince Meshcherskii dined with us and told me that Pobedonostsev had said many good things about me."[329] One incentive for fostering intimacy with conservative Russian bureaucrats was an interest in imperial philanthropy, which reflected a genuine charitable instinct but also provided an opportunity to hobnob with Russian elites. As in France, the economic capital of the banking elites like the Poliakovs allowed them to engage in philanthropic activities that emulated aristocratic practices, facilitating their inclusion in high society.[330] The charitable activities included the construction of hospitals (desperately needed in an undermedicalized country with high rates of infant and child mortality) and donations to high-quality educational facilities (such as the Katkov Lycée, where Lazar's sons gained admission).[331] The Poliakovs gave generously to charities important to the royal family, such as the Imperial Russian Music Society[332] and the Imperial Philanthropic Society.[333] Iakov proudly recorded that he "received several heartfelt letters" after a 500-ruble donation to a Meshcherskii philanthropy.[334] His donations to the charities of Pobedonostsev's wife made him welcome in their home—or at least he so believed, with this frequent refrain in his diary: "I was at Madame and Monsieur Pobedonostsev's. As always, they were infinitely courteous."[335] The Poliakovs and Pobedonostevs even socialized together abroad. For instance, in 1897, Iakov wrote a series of entries about their friendship during their sojourn at the spas of Carlsbad and Marienbad:

> 21 July 1897 [Carlsbad]: Madame Pobedonostsev herself came up to my wife to become acquainted with her; it went well.
>
> 24 July 1897: I went on a stroll and had coffee with the Pobedonostsevs.

26 July 1897: I was at the theater with the Pobedonostsevs.

29 July 1897 [Marienbad]: The Pobedenostsevs were at my place and then we were at the theater.

30 July 1897: I accompanied the Pobedenostsevs to the train station; the farewell was heartfelt. They both asked me to send regards to my wife.[336]

Such intimate ties reflected not only philanthropic interests but also political views—especially an aversion to the revolutionary movement, with its terrorism and socialism.[337] As early as 1879, in response to Fyodor Dostoevesky, who had claimed that the Jews had thoroughly Judaized Germany, infusing it with "the spirit of speculative realism,"[338] Pobedonostsev wrote echoing his words:

What you write about the Yids is absolutely fair. They take over everything, they undermine everything, but behind them is the spirit of the age. They are at the root of the revolutionary-social movement and regicide. They control the periodical press, the financial markets are in their hands, the common masses fall into financial slavery to them, they guide the foundations of contemporary science, striving to place it outside of Christianity. And besides all this, a question barely arises about them when a chorus of voices arises for the Jews allegedly in the name of civilization or toleration—indifferent to faith. In Romania and Serbia as well as with us, no one dares to say a word that the Jews are taking over everything. Our press is already becoming Jewish. *Russkaia Pravda, Moskva, Golos*, if you please, are all Jewish organs; yes, they have even begun special journals: *Evrei* and *Vestnik [russkikh] evreev* and *Evreiskaia biblioteka*.[339]

The increasing number of Jews in the revolutionary movement only reinforced Pobedonostsev's belief that the Jews planned to take over Russia. His categorical rejection of political reform found reflection in his harsh words: "I see a lot of people of various ranks and titles [here in St. Petersburg]. All the local official and learned people have made me sick to my stomach—as if I were in the company of half-crazed people or perverted apes. Everywhere I hear the same trite, false, and accursed word: constitution."[340] Although the Poliakovs must have been aware of Pobedonostev's antisemitic views, as mutual defenders of autocracy, the public order, and philanthropic work, they made common cause in a complex "political economy of intimacies."

Paradoxically, it was during an age of rising antisemitism that the Poliakov brothers acquired the status of hereditary nobility—to be sure, after several years of tireless campaigning. They originally submitted petitions to the Senate in 1890, and six years later Iakov recounted all the highly placed people whom they had mobilized on their behalf: "Everyone is making efforts on [our] behalf about the nobility through Golitsyn, Kutuzov, Sipiagin, Pobedonostsev, Delianov, Durnovo, Taneev." For years, their efforts went for naught. Iakov finally appealed to Andrei N. Markovich (1830–1907), a ranking member of the Senate and an active participant in imperial charities, and it was Markovich who persuaded the emperor to grant the Poliakov brothers hereditary nobility. On 20 May 1897 Iakov wrote triumphantly: "I received congratulations from [my children] Lazar, Boris, Samuil, and Annette that the sovereign has approved Markovich's report and granted me and [my brother] Lazar the right and privilege of the rank of active privy state counselor and, through the Order of Anna Stanislav of the first degree, hereditary nobility. Thank God, finally!" The next day, a bit more soberly, he bemoaned the exorbitant cost: "But a lot of expenditures—all preliminary and unsuccessful. I promised Markovich to contribute 25,000 rubles to the [Imperial] Philanthropic Society. Nevertheless, I least of all expected to receive [the status of nobility] through him, so I made persistent efforts through so many highly placed people but did not succeed; no matter whom I asked, no matter who acted on my behalf, no matter what means were employed, it was all in vain. God helped and Markovich did it, thank God."[341]

Lazar and Iakov received official confirmation of their new status on 27 May 1897. Zinaida, who was already married to a British subject and had surrendered her Russian citizenship, was ineligible to share in the family's newfound noble status. When her cousins Isabella and Elizabeth formally acquired the status of hereditary nobility, Zinadia wrote: "Of course, they were registered to the nobility through Uncle [Iakov], as Russian citizens, and Raia was registered before her wedding. Thus Khaia and I are excluded as a result of losing Russian citizenship. But the misfortune is not great."[342] In any case, the family's surname abroad, de Poliakoff, now matched their legal status at home, as did their coat of arms—a shield decorated with golden lions holding silver arrows and scarlet winged wheels, a golden crown decorated with ostrich feathers, and a star of David. The motto "God is my help," in gold Hebrew letters, graced with a blue ribbon.[343]

Navigating the conservative bureaucracy proved easier than turning a profit in volatile world markets. Eager to expand into the international market, in the 1890s Lazar embarked on several risky ventures in Persia and Central Asia, but this all led to huge losses when the global boom turned into a global bust at the turn of the century.[344] The three Poliakov brothers had first become engaged in

Persian business two decades earlier: in 1871 they became "consuls of Persia" and acted as representatives for Persian trade negotiations with Russia. Iakov remarked that this status lent him prestige not only in Russia but also abroad, for he could bypass customs control altogether by flashing his "consulate calling card."[345] The brothers also hoped to gain the title of baron in Persia, but to no avail: the Russian state did not recognize the title if granted by a country that did not possess traditional barional titles of its own.[346]

Lazar, who served on the executive board of a Belgian company, La Société Anonyme des Chemins de Fer et Tramways en Perse (founded in 1887 in Brussels), quickly learned about the challenges of operating in a country like Persia, with its poor transportation infrastructure. The Belgian company, which had a concession to build a railway line from Qazvin to Qom (via Tehran), had to transport all its equipment "by sea from Antwerp to Batumi on the Black Sea, then by land through the Transcaucasian Railway to Baku, then by sea again to Anzali on the Caspian, and from there once more by land and on the backs of animals through difficult terrain."[347] In 1890 Lazar received a concession from Naser el-Din Shah to establish the Companie d'Assurance et de Transport en Perse, a Persian insurance and transportation company with an initial capital of two million francs (170,000 rubles) in stocks.[348] The concession, which was valid for seventy-five years, stipulated: "No one [else] shall have the right within the borders of our Lands to interfere in affairs which concern insurance. And likewise no one [else] shall have the right under any pretext whatsoever under any title or form to found a transportation company."[349] There were early signs of trouble. According to Iakov, "Lazar Solomonovich left Moscow. He had sharp words with the minister of finance about the Persian roads."[350] Unwilling to run the company on his own, Lazar partnered with the Ministry of Finance, which took out a loan from the State Bank in 1901 to establish a company called Nadezhda to share the concession while holding three-quarters of the board votes. In 1902, almost a decade after Witte became minister of finance, he attempted to buy out Lazar's shares and gain complete control of the company. When the parties failed to reach an agreement, Witte sold the state's shares to the Discount Loan Bank.[351]

Lazar's company first sought to address the problem of transportation in "a country without roads."[352] Initially, the Russian government was reluctant to provide the requested funding, and Lazar's representative in Tehran, Captain Anatolii Bostelman, offered two explanations to the British chargé d'affaires: "He [Poliakov] has till now been hindered by the Russian Government from carrying out the work, partly on account of his being of Jewish extraction, and partly in consequence of the opposition of the Caucasus and Mercury Steam

Navigation Company, which owns practically the whole of the steamships ply-
ing the mail and passengers on the Caspian Sea and has up till lately enjoyed
a large subvention from the Imperial government."[353] Despite his Jewish ethnicity and the stiff competition from an established firm, Lazar succeeded in
securing the "exclusive right to build the carriage road from Qazvin to the Bay
of Anzali."[354] Although the expense and time to construct the road exceeded
the original budget, Lazar recouped some of the costs from the high tolls after
the road opened in January 1889. According to one report, the Rasht-Tehran
road alone yielded £270 to £300 daily—tolls that Russia's rival, Britain, paid to
transport its goods by land from the Caspian coast to the Persian interior. Abraham Jackson traveled on the 250-mile road in 1903 and described it as "the
best I had seen in Persia, because [it was] built and managed by Russians."[355]
The Russian state was less sanguine about the investment. The Russian chargé
d'affaires in Tehran conceded that his government "never expected any road of
theirs to pay, but that they kept up their roads at a loss in order to maintain the
necessary communications and in hope of thereby benefitting the country."[356]
In 1897 Lazar's company also received "a concession to build quays, piers, and
hotels at Anzali," but by then it was perilously overextended.[357]

Lazar's financial empire, despite his furtive attempts to conceal business
losses, steadily disintegrated. Lazar had known failure earlier: his gold mining venture in Nechersk (1878–79) had been an unmitigated disaster. But the
failures began to snowball in the 1890s. A perfect example of bad business
judgment was his match factory in Tehran, which he built for 400,000 rubles in 1889 through a newly organized Persian and Central Asian Industrial
and Commercial Society. It was a failure from the outset. Critics observed that
the ill-advised location of the factory (far from cheap supplies of wood), inferior quality of the matches, and high production costs meant that the Poliakov matches could not possibly "compete with the Austrian import."[358] Rather
than cut his losses, Lazar chose to expand: in 1893 he used funds from his Moscow International Bank to enter the Persian cotton market. His losses steadily
mounted. To mask all the red ink and losses, Lazar resorted to bookkeeping
tricks: he acquired a textile mill in Pärnu (which was neither incorporated
nor even fully built), had it purchase three of his unprofitable Persian cotton factories, and thereby reduced the book debt of his Persian and Central
Asian Society.[359] Lazar was not through. He also speculated on American cotton, planning to buy cheap and sell dear in New York, Liverpool, and Alexan-
dria (which explains why Aaron was in Egypt in 1894, where he contracted
tuberculosis). As long as the global markets were on an upswing, Lazar's risky
enterprises managed to stay afloat. As one historian observes, Lazar plunged

ever deeper into speculative ventures: he "mortgaged shares of his own companies at a preferential rate in his own banks, and immediately invested the bank loans he received into new stock-exchange transactions."[360] But Lazar's fraudulent operations to mask his losses caught up with him in 1899, when European markets slid into a deep recession. That misery was compounded by bad timing: the Moscow State Bank's bonds came due in 1900 and 1901. The catastrophic losses caused the bank stockholders—three-quarters of whom were small investors—to demand that the state hold Poliakov accountable.[361]

The complaints led to an audit of the Poliakov Banking House in 1901, conducted by the State Bank and the Special Chancellery of the Credit Division. The audit found that Lazar had inflated the book value of his securities and stocks, and that in fact there was a discrepancy of 15,798,000 rubles between the declared book value of his assets (53,513,000 rubles) and their real market value (37,715,000). That liability, moreover, far exceeded his personal assets: Lazar had "squandered all the founding capital" (5 million rubles) and therefore was short 10.8 million rubles to pay off creditors.[362] In a memorandum to Nicholas II in October 1901, Witte warned that the heavy losses sustained by just three of the Poliakov banks (the Moscow International, Southern Russian, and Orlov Banks) could "lead Poliakov to bankruptcy."[363] But the banks were not only too big to fail but also too intimately connected to fail, for Poliakov had cleverly nurtured financial ties to influential patrons and investors. In self-defense, Poliakov's supporters elevated the discourse from personal to state interest. Witte, for example, warned that failing to assist the Poliakov banks could lead to catastrophic consequences: "The situation is different with regard to private banks—the solvency of which is of interest not only to stock-holders but also depositors. . . . A cessation of payments by these banks, which have existed about thirty years, would ruin not only a multitude of depositors all across Russia, but would deal a heavy blow to private credit, undermining confidence in private banks that has already been shaken."[364] In short, argued Witte, Poliakov's problems were threatening to create a general economic crisis.[365]

Lazar's commercial banks had already come under investigation by the Commission on the Question of Registration of Russian Promissory Notes for speculating on credit granted by foreign banks in the 1890s. The findings revealed that cheap foreign credit and high interest rates in Russia had given the banks a windfall while providing little benefit to local merchants.[366] The commission denounced several commercial banks (such as the Volga-Kama, St. Petersburg International, and Warsaw Banks) but singled out the Poliakov banking group, claiming that it supported Jewish smuggling in the Pale of Settlement by providing a banking structure and credit for these illicit activities:

Meanwhile, the Jewish trade of the western provinces is the main distributor of Jewish contraband imports. Before the settling of the Jewish population (which in the past decade has reached the capitals themselves), western contraband was limited to the known area. With the spread of the Jewish population and of Jewish trade to central Russia, contraband warehouses have sprung up in the most distant centers, and thereby the volume of smuggling that paralyzes our [trade] balance must have increased. The network of local departments with which the Jewish banks have recently shrouded European Russia so zealously is one of the powerful means of encouraging contraband trade.[367]

All this was grist for antisemitic discourse. Criticism of Jewish economic activities pervaded debates in the Committee of Finances, which sought to sort out the crisis of the Poliakov Banking House. Some state officials opposed state intervention to bail out the Poliakovs, insisting that Lazar had acted "exclusively with profit as the end" and had created a "powerful center and bulwark of Jewry" in Moscow.[368] Other officials, however, argued that the Jewish ownership of a banking firm "cannot serve as an obstacle to lending him [Poliakov] support" and pointed to more urgent geopolitical concerns of maintaining the highways in Persia that could "pass into the hands of foreign capitalists."[369] Nicholas II weighed in, expressing his desire to remove the Poliakov Banking House and Poliakov himself "once and for all" from the picture and liberate "Moscow from the Jewish den."[370] In the end, the committee decided to place the Poliakov Banking House under the State Bank, authorize it to service his debts, and thus provide a lifeline to keep his enterprises afloat. According to one calculation, Poliakov received up to 22.5 million rubles in credits and loans to avoid bankruptcy, but this assistance came at a heavy cost: as collateral, the bank seized not only all of Lazar's unencumbered assets (securities and bills of exchange) but also those of his wife Rozaliia (who promptly filed a lawsuit). Notably, Zinaida noted that her Uncle Genrikh Vydrin had advised her mother to leave Russia "to preserve her capital" in 1902. She reasoned that her mother "must therefore have opened a checking account at the branch of the Credit Lyonnais."[371] Alexander Poliakoff also recalled his father-in-law Gerald Montagu's story of "Lazar's wife, unaccompanied by Lazar, descending on London with a retinue complete with a chef." As Montagu recounted: "At the bank, an office had to be left empty for her to undress partially and take out all the bonds which she had been concealing on her body."[372] These stories would account for the suspicions of the State Bank that the Poliakovs had hidden their assets abroad when it sought to recover payments for its loans.[373]

Lazar's financial troubles were compounded by Iakov's pleas to rescue his failing Bank Azov. Iakov had already approached the state, but to no avail. After a tense meeting with Witte, on 30 April 1899, Iakov wrote that the minister of finance refused to help because "everyone reproaches him that the Poliakov brothers are seizing all of Russia with their expansion of their banks."[374] Witte was especially sensitive to accusations that he favored Jews because of his marriage to a Jewish convert. "When I married a divorced woman, my wife was not accepted into court for more than ten years, and I considered this completely natural and correct," Witte rationalized, "because at the time the court in general did not permit the presentation of divorced wives."[375] The issue was not her divorced status but her Jewish origins, according to state officials like State Controller Tertii I. Filippov. Public loathing intensified, claimed Filippov, when Witte "transferred her sisters' husbands—the engineer Bykhovets and the doctor Levi, who were living in Novgorod—to new positions with enormous salaries and travelling expenses, much to the amazement of all Novgorod."[376] Witte was already detested by noble landowners for his merciless industrialization, which, in their view, came at the expense of the agricultural sector. Disheartened by Witte's attempt to dissociate himself from Jewish bankers, Iakov inserted his favorite line in the diary: "In general, he [Witte] was coldly courteous as usual."[377] Despite his own liabilities, Lazar could not refuse his older brother's request for a bill of exchange. The main obstacle was Rozaliia, who fought to prevent adding to her husband's debt. Her opposition proved fully justified: amid the financial crisis that beset the country, Iakov's banks collapsed. In her 1901 diary, Zinaida described a visit from her cousin Samuil (Iakov's youngest son) who described his family's latest financial calamity: "It seems that [business at] Uncle's bank is going poorly. Rubinshtein[378] gave up all his possessions to help . . . but they appear to be on the brink of bankruptcy. This is difficult especially for my uncle and aunt, who are used to living in luxury and being well cared for; and if they have to deny themselves everything in their old age, it will be difficult for them, poor things, of course."[379] In the summer of 1902, she noted that her Uncle Iakov no longer had business in St. Petersburg (though this was not the case, as is evident from his diaries) after the liquidation of his bank: "He suffered very much in this collapse and now simply lives peacefully at [his daughter] Bella's in Nice."[380]

In contrast to Iakov's Bank Azov, Lazar's banks managed to avoid liquidation, but they remained under strict state control. Vladimir N. Kokovtsov, appointed minister of finance in 1904, urged the Committee of Finances to proceed "gradually and cautiously" with the Poliakov banks because of the "extreme circumstances precipitated by the events in the Far East" and hence the need to stabilize the markets.[381] However, Lazar's financial difficulties made it difficult to fulfill family obligations, such as the regular allowance he gave Zinaida and Reuben in Paris. As early as March 1898, Zinaida wrote that her father "suffers because of the expenses." She acknowledged the need to reduce expenditures but admitted that "it is not easy when you see a certain way of life and want to enter society."[382] In 1901, Zinaida became anxious when her father failed to send the promised funds, which she needed for daily expenses such as the dresses for which she had been measured:[383] "I did not sleep all night because I was very agitated about Ruby's nasty disposition, screaming all day. The funds are to blame!"[384] The situation had not improved by 1905, when Zinaida complained, "I am very dissatisfied with the letter from Misha to Ruby saying that Papa cannot provide us with the annual allowance, as earlier."[385] Her youthful animosity toward her mother reappeared as well: "Mama, of course, is satisfied that now they will give [us] less support as a result of the bad business affairs at the present time."[386] Her brother Il'ia explained to Reuben that "everything is going badly in Moscow" and that Isaak was now managing the family finances. "Everyone is angry that we waste [money]," wrote a very distraught Zinaida in the summer of 1905. "It seems that we cannot reduce our expenses unless we move. It is better to live modestly in Paris than in Moscow. Mama very much wants to move here herself, and therefore is jealous that we are well established. Our apartment is not large but quite good, and the location is the very best in all of Paris, although it now lacks a room for Annette's governess."[387] Zinaida's grasp of her family's desperate financial straits was limited, perhaps due to the lack of news (of which she often complained). Whenever possible, she noted her father's visits to Witte or Kokovstov on bank business or resignations from their banking house.[388] Her father was the only one who sent any real details about his banking affairs, while her brothers wrote more generally about the financial crisis in Russia.

The revolution of 1905 greatly complicated things: "They themselves do not know what will happen in Russia now!" That sober judgment was followed by a cheerful report on Zinaida's daily regimen: "Yesterday, we traveled to Paris in the automobile and had breakfast there."[389] But Zinaida was deeply concerned about her family's safety, as news hit closer to home. She began to hear about "shrapnel, bombs, and gun shots everywhere" and worried about "the welfare of [my] brothers who are now in Moscow on account of the necessity of their work at the banks."[390] On 18 June 1905, several guests (including a Brodskii) told her about a "revolutionary demonstration on Tverskoi Boulevard in the evening."[391] Her alarm increased when she received news from her mother that she "was afraid that there was sure to be a pogrom in Moscow because the newspapers spread these rumors."[392] A few months earlier, Zinaida had reassured herself that a close family friend, Nikolai Shcherbatov, had "organized protection of the Russian people against the revolutionaries. This is an anti-liberal party and it supports autocratic power."[393] She preferred his conservative monarchism to the revolutionaries, whom she despised. On 25 July 1906, Zinaida wrote with satisfaction: "Shcherbatov's monarchist party has triumphed so far and the Sovereign has dispersed the State Duma!"[394]

Despite the chaos of 1905–6, the Russian economy soon recovered and began another period of rapid growth. Even the *Economist*, which had been critical of Witte and Kokovstov's policies, was forced to admit:

> The present situation in Russia is one of hopeful suspense. Just now there is a lull in the revolutionary activity, and the country is quiet. The Duma, it seems, has really come to stay, and though its discussions are still of the academic order rather than practical, it is beginning to make its influence felt on the administration. Internal conditions in the country are almost entirely dependent on the state of the harvest, and this year the yield is exceeding all records. . . . Russia, in spite of the grossest mismanagement has, so far, always succeeded in weathering the worst financial storms.[395]

It was a powerful recovery, with a strong surge in the stock market, an enormous increase in industrial production, bountiful harvests and substantial grain exports, and an increase in foreign direct investment.[396]

As Lazar's securities began to recover, his goal was to regain control over his banks and properties, and he undertook some reorganization (including the merger of his ailing banks into a single Union Bank, with sixty-eight regional branches, in May 1908). Now, however, he had to contend with foreign investors, "who were quick to smell opportunity amidst the financial ruins."[397] Western financiers like Théophile Lombard (senior manager of the Banque du Nord, a Russian and French joint venture), sought to expand operations in Russia and proposed "a merger with two of the three 'zombie' banks of Poliakov's erstwhile empire."[398] The London and Midland Bank of Great Britain also sought to take over Poliakov's ailing banks, "presumably at a distressed price."[399] These overtures met with opposition from the head of the Union Bank, Vladimir S. Tatishchev, and the de facto head of the Credit Chancellery, Leonid F. Davydov, who claimed that the bank was "now adequately capitalized."[400] Seeking new markets and partnerships, Lazar proposed to attract Japanese capital by opening branches of the United Bank at "various points in Japan." He convinced the minister of foreign affairs, Aleksandr P. Izvol'skii, that such operations would provide an "enormous service" for the empire by developing economic relations between Russia and Japan. A skeptical Kokovtsov, however, warned Izvol'skii (who had deigned to call Poliakov a "well-known financial figure") in 1908: "I consider it my duty to convey that Poliakov's position is not only beyond hope, but his liabilities in terms of his debt to the State Bank are considerably greater than his assets." The minister of finance was incredulous that Lazar would even propose such "fantastical plans."[401]

In the eyes of his critics, Poliakov had evaded any responsibility let alone punishment for the financial crisis.[402] On 29 November 1912, Lazar succeeded in reacquiring some of his real estate (four houses in Moscow and five estates) for an "insignificant sum." However, his bid to regain control of the banks failed when the state reminded him of his outstanding debt to the State Bank (a tidy sum of 1,416,691.48 rubles in principal and 8,243,803.08 rubles in interest).[403] Before he could deal with these debts, Lazar died suddenly in January 1914 in Paris. The state had kept Lazar's bankruptcy a secret and withheld information about his finances from the public, but a year after Lazar's death, the State Bank filed a suit against the Poliakov Banking House for the sum of 9,660,494.55 rubles and tacked on provisions to seize some of his real estate as well as securities and cash from various institutions. Lazar's son Mikhail attempted to resolve the claims (to no avail) but declined to help the State Bank identify his father's assets in Russia and abroad. Mikhail could only propose to repay a million rubles: 100,000 immediately and the rest in installments over the next ten years—offering the Poliakov Banking House's troubled Persian stocks as security for prompt payments (which the State Bank rejected as unreliable).[404] In the end, the State Bank never recouped its loans to the Poliakovs. The October Revolution of 1917 eliminated the bank officials' authority, putting an end to the battle between the Russian and Poliakov empires. Both collapsed in the fires of the Bolshevik Revolution.

◆　◆　◆　◆　◆　◆　◆

Life in Paris

The failure of the Poliakov banks and attendant loss of income and prestige was a devastating blow to Zinaida, whose identity had rested on family wealth and cultural patronage. However, her diaries suggest that until World War II, Zinaida continued to live fairly comfortably at 34 (and later 40) Avenue du Bois de Boulogne in the sixteenth arrondissement, which she described as the "best location in Paris."[405] The Bois de Boulogne, with its botanical gardens, lake, zoo, and restaurants, was the ideal site for long promenades and family outings.[406] Now, as Madame Zineide Gubbay (née de Poliakoff)[407]—or Zina to her friends—she began another chapter of her life in Paris, cultivating new ties in high society, especially through her and Reuben's involvement in the Alliance Israélite Universelle, where he was elected to the board and she served on women's charity committees and initiated the creation of an organization to assist Russian-Jewish war victims.[408] When Alfred Lévy succeeded Zadok Kahn as chief rabbi of Paris, Zinaida wrote with pride: "We are going today for the installation ceremony of the chief rabbi at the Grand Synagogue on Rue de la Victoire. This will be a very festive event, and based on the special invitation from the Consistory, both of us will have the most honored positions."[409] The intimacy that Zinaida enjoyed in her religious community and tight-knit salon society proved to be elusive in her marriage, in part due to the significant cultural divide between the couple. The English she used to converse daily with Reuben did not come as naturally to her as her native Russian (which no doubt led to some misunderstandings), and consuming French food and English tea was less satisfying than indulging in her beloved Russian shchi (cabbage soup) and kvass. For that reason, Zinaida continued to write her diaries in Russian to express her emotions, desires, and experiences in the language and cultural idiom in which she felt most at home. Above all, intimacy meant togetherness for Zinaida—living, traveling, eating, and breathing together even if it was suffocating at times (as in her own family: "Mama was never apart from Papa")[410] —something she felt was missing in Reuben's upbringing and family.

In the first years of their marriage, Zinaida traveled to England to reacquaint herself with Reuben's large extended family, which she discovered was very different from her own. They had traveled to England in 1886 so that her family could determine the desirability of the match with Reuben and meet his extended Sassoon family. Brighton—once described by Henry Labouchère as a "seacoast town, three miles long and three yards broad, with a Sassoon at each end and one in the middle"—was the home of Reuben's family.[411] Zinaida recalled fondly in her final diary: "Ruby understood that there was no comparison between life in England and France, and, as a result, we moved there [Paris]. Before this, we went to stay with his grandfather Sir Albert Sassoon in Brighton, and he accepted me very graciously."[412] This "white-haired, white-whiskered gentleman, with a kindly manner and pleasant voice, speaking English with a slight foreign accent," was the head of the Sassoon family.[413] Having succeeded his father as head of David Sassoon & Co. in Bombay, Sir Albert Sassoon was knighted and made a member of Order of the Star of India in 1872, in part for "his heroic entertainment of a difficult guest: the Shah of Persia."[414] In 1890, the queen "was [also] pleased to confer the dignity of a Baronetcy of the United Kingdom" on him for his commercial and philanthropic achievements.[415] Zinaida did not have the pleasure of meeting Reuben's grand-mother, Hannah Meyer Sassoon, who resided in Bombay because "she was unable to stand the severity of the European winters"[416] and "the different style of living." [417]As a result, "she was reluctantly compelled to abandon her intention of permanently joining her husband."[418] During their vacation in Milan in 1895, Reuben learned of his grandmother's unexpected death. "Ruby left," wrote Zinaida. "He is very saddened by the news of the death of Lady Sassoon in Bombay. Apparently she was sick with a fever and bronchitis and died suddenly because two days ago I received a letter from her. She was seventy years old, of course, but nonetheless she seemed to be younger than her age, judging from her latest portrait that she sent to us with her signature and invitation to visit [their mansion] Sans Souci in Bombay."[419] Sans Souci was renowned for its grand parties, especially the brilliant ball given by Sir Albert and Lady Sassoon in November 1872 for the Earl of Northbrook (the viceroy of India) and the governor of Bombay: "The mansion and its fine garden were illuminated on a scale hitherto unknown, the illuminated foundation being a special feature of the beautiful scene. The 1,400 guests included nearly all the native Princes and Rajahs of India then in Bombay, and one and all expressed themselves enchanted with the glimpse of fairyland which their hosts had given them." In addition, the Sassoons had a country house in Poona and another residence in Mahabashwar, and "all three were kept up for Lady Sassoon's use when her husband had taken up his abode in England."[420] When Hannah Sassoon died, the editor of the newspaper *Israel Dharmadeep* described her as "one of the most large-hearted and influential Jewesses of western India."[421] Although she admired Sir Albert Sassoon, Zinaida was critical of his relationship with his wife. After an acrimonious quarrel with Reuben, she wrote: "As regards to the Sassoons, it is still worse. Sir Albert does not pretend to be saddened by the death of his wife. In general, the Sassoons look upon the wife as a completely inanimate object"—an observation that she obviously applied to herself.[422] In general, Zinaida claimed that she could not understand what she disparagingly called an "eastern nature."[423]

Zinaida also expressed her surprise that Reuben's brother David Gubbay still lived in Bombay in 1906, especially since his wife Hannah (née Ezra, his first cousin from Calcutta) lived in England. "But now all the Indian relatives of Ruby have already gotten out of there to Europe where they seem to like it better!" she explained.[424] It seemed inconceivable to Zinaida, who had never traveled outside of Europe, that David chose to live in India, where he had been born and where he headed the family firm David Sassoon & Co. until his death in 1928. Meanwhile, Hannah Gubbay seemed to live in another world

—helping her cousin Philip Sassoon host a lavish salon at his Trent Park mansion; entertaining British royalty like the Prince of Wales and Queen Mary; and collecting magnificent eighteenth-century English furniture, fine porcelain, textiles, and other decorative arts.[425] Whatever criticisms she had of the Sassoons, connections to such illustrious relatives got Zinaida an invitation to the royal palace. "By command of the Queen, a Drawing Room was held yesterday afternoon at Buckingham Palace by Her Royal Majesty, the Princess of Wales," announced the *Morning Post* in 1897. In attendance was "Mrs. Reuben Gubbay, [presented] by Mrs. Panmure Gordon."[426]

Reuben's parents, Rachel (née Sassoon) and Aaron Moses Gubbay, also lived on two different continents. Born in Bombay, Aaron had traveled to China at the age of fifteen to work for the firm Messrs. Sassoon, which was almost like a rite of passage. According to the *Times of India*: "It is almost an article of faith in a family knit together in the closest bonds that every male member must pass a certain time in China towards the eastern extremity of the vast network of banking and mercantile correspondence, the centre of which is Bombay."[427] Upon his return to Bombay, Aaron married Sir Albert Sassoon's eldest daughter, and after another stint in China he returned to the center during "troublous days of the share mania until he was relieved by S[assoon] D[avid] Sassoon."[428] Instead of living in India, Rachel and the children moved to Paris, where they bought a home on the Boulevard Malesherbes. In 1885, "after a happy spell of rest with his family in Paris," Aaron returned to India "and succeeded Jacob Sassoon as the head of the other major family firm—Messrs. E[lias] D[avid] Sassoon & Co.—on the latter's departure to England."[429] When Reuben claimed that "there was never any unpleasantries between [my] mother and father" during one of his quarrels with Zinaida, she retorted sardonically: "At such a far distance, it is possible to live peaceably with one another."[430] Shortly after his return to Europe (a few months after Reuben and Zinaida's wedding), Aaron passed away on 29 August 1894.[431] Zinaida had barely had a chance to know him, but she enjoyed warm relations with her mother-in-law, who appears as "Ruby's mother" or "mamasha" in her diaries. Rachel Gubbay died in 1913, leaving 100,000 francs to each of her six children and 10,000 to each grandchild.[432] In attendance at her funeral were the "ministers of Chile and Serbia, Barons and Baronesses James and Robert de Rothschild," Pierre de Gunzburg, Jules Ephrussi, the Weisweillers (including their nephews Edmond and Gustave), Halphens, Singers, Foulds, and many other prominent members of the close-knit Parisian Jewish elite.[433]

Like any family, Reuben's had a few skeletons in the closet, and Zinaida learned that her Uncle Iakov was not the only one with a black sheep in the family: "[Rachel] Sassoon married Jacques [Ricardo] Marrot and is expecting a new addition to the family. Because her husband is Catholic, her father, Reuben, does not recognize her marriage and does not want to know her anymore ever since her wedding."[434] Other relatives also intermarried. For example, Reuben's glamorous relative Sybil Sassoon (daughter of Edward Sassoon and Aline Rothschild) married George Cholmondeley, the Earl of Rocksavage and heir to the Marquess of Cholmondeley, in 1913. Although Sybil did not convert to Anglicanism for the wedding (but did so after World War II),[435] the historian Cecil Roth mused: "On the day of the wedding, scientific observers might have discerned slight seismological disturbances in different parts of the earth's surfaces, for the pious founders of both families had turned in their graves."[436] The Cholmondeleys claimed few Jewish friends, but they were close to Reuben's sister-in-law, Hannah Gubbay, and Zinaida mentioned Sybil in familiar and somewhat envious terms.

Reuben also visited Russia—the first time for his wedding in 1891, the infamous year of the brutal expulsion of the Jews from Moscow. His experiences in Russia soured further during a vacation in May 1893, which Iakov Poliakov reported in his diary: "[I'm] in Moscow and it turns out that L[azar] S[olomonovich]'s son-in-law is ill." It did not help that Lazar had just "had a misunderstanding with Professor Zakhar'in," the family doctor.[437] Nonetheless, Reuben agreed to his wife's plan to take a long trip through Russia in 1895 with stops in "Feodosia, Yalta, Sevastopol and other cities in the Crimea" as well as "Evpatoriia and Odessa on the sea and then to Vienna on the Orient Express."[438] Zinaida was disenchanted with Yalta, where "there are many hotels and a big restaurant, [and] halls but very little that is pleasant because there are many malnourished infants and their emaciated and painful appearance makes an onerous impression." When Zinaida was eight years old, her uncle Iakov had rented two dachas in Yalta—one for his family and another for Lazar's—where they had spent their summer holidays, but it seemed like a different place to her now.[439] The couple also traveled to Voronezh, where the Poliakovs had lived while they were building the Kozlov-Voronezh-Rostov-na-Donu railway line. "We were very surprised by the decent appearance of the local rabbi [Rabbi Chaim Geselevich Feigin, 1852–95]," remarked Zinaida. "He is better than our Moscow [rabbi]! He has served as the state rabbi here for many years and remembers how Papa drank koumiss in Voronezh thirty years ago. They say he was very sick then. And now the old man [rabbi] is 80–90 years old. Mama would like him. He brought us a book for the donation; he received 100 rubles from us for different charitable organizations." She wrote with pride, "In a quarter century, European civilization will probably enlighten [the people] here in the middle of nowhere [and] we began this by laying the foundations—the railroads."[440]

After their daughter, Annette, was born the following year, the Gubbays traveled less frequently to Russia, fearful of the cold winters and political instability. In 1901, for example, Zinaida's brother Mikhail explicitly warned them "not to come to Moscow."[441] However, the entire family returned to Moscow in 1912 to celebrate Rozaliia and Lazar's golden wedding anniversary with the Jewish community. On this occasion, all the major Jewish institutions paid tribute to the couple for their generous social and philanthropic activities. Annette "charmed the audience by reading a poem by a Miss Myrtil from Paris, dedicated to Mr. de Poliakoff," and the three grandchildren (Annette, Elizabeth, and Olga)[442] presented their grandparents with a manuscript decorated with the Poliakov seal to commemorate their wedding on 6 March 1862.[443] Zinaida returned for her father's funeral in 1914 but did not stay long in Russia—unlike her sister Khaia, who witnessed the horrors of World War I there.

Zinaida's post-Russia diaries focused primarily on her travels in Europe and ostentatious consumption, reinforcing the creditworthy face of the family and her sense of distinction. Holidays often provided the rare moments when she found time to write in her diary. During a vacation in Italy in 1894, Zinaida waxed ecstatic about the art on sale: "They are selling Andrea del Sarto's painting of the 'Madonna with Child' for 4,000 francs and also Tiziano [Vecelli's] 'Deposition from the Cross' for 90,000 francs at the Manni Art Gallery. . . . Of course, yesterday we purchased samples of Venetian glass in Mignano. The year that Uncle Samuil was here in Venice, he probably also bought a lot of goods. *I want to purchase a great deal.*"[444] On another occasion, she wrote about a new purchase in Bordeaux that reflected her fine taste compared to that of her sister-in-law: "Today I bought a doll because we have a collection of national dolls. We already have quite a few of them, and Ruby acquired a display case for them. [His sister] Flora, of course, laughs at us. Although she only owns rather strange things, her husband [Jules Rueff] does nothing to improve her taste."[445]

Weddings provided the perfect occasion to flaunt prestige and wealth, especially when the society pages covered the event. Zinaida must have been pleased to read in *Le Gaulois* on 23 June 1896 that Mrs. Gubbay "in a gray satin dress, pearls, [and] a white tulle hat with feathers" attended the wedding of her sister Khaia (Xenia) and Georges Levy in Moscow.[446] In 1895, she grudgingly bought a gift in Paris for Mathilde Weisweiller (even though "she did not give me a present at my wedding") on the occasion of her nuptials to Henry James de Rothschild, "who is a very young person and fell in love with her apparently at his sister Mademoiselle Jeanne's."[447] With more affection, Zinaida selected a beautiful ruby and diamond watch for her niece Alice Landau (her cousin Bella's daughter), who married Osmond d'Avigdor-Goldsmid of England, a gift listed alongside "Lady and Lord Rothschild's three silver dessert plates" in *Le Figaro's* high-society pages in 1907.[448] Weddings expanded Zinaida's social circles to include the Jewish elites in England and America with whom her father worked in the Jewish Colonization Association. For instance, when her uncle Genrikh Vydrin wed Roza Vilenkin (whose brother was married to Irma Seligman), Zinaida met the American banking families of the Seligmans and Schiffs.[449] She mingled with the "large and fashionable crowd" that attended the wedding of Gladys Goldsmid and Lewis Samuel Montegu at the New West End Synagogue in London and was "regaled with white Palestine wine from Rishon le Zion."[450]

Aristocratic Parisians socialized and displayed the latest fashions at the horse races and equestrian shows, where Zinaida watched her brother Il'ia perform. "Today everyone went to the horse races at the Longchamp [Race Course]," she wrote in 1903. "[Daniel dit] Constant Dreyfus was there.[451] There are mostly high society people there, and they show off their new spring dresses and hats. Of course, they are always the first to wear them because it does not cost them much."[452] Zinaida in her "tailor-made dress altered to fit together with the frock coat and black straw hat enhanced with egret plumes" caught the attention of *Le Figaro* in the spring of 1909.[453] It was on these occasions that she could also show off her jewelry, like the beautiful anniversary bracelet with pearls and small rubies that Ruby had bought for her from the House of Boucheron. Meanwhile, *L'Intransigeant* drew attention to Annette ("Mademoiselle Reuben Gubbay"), who was dressed "in grand blue with a blue straw hat" at the horse races at the Grand Palais in 1913.[454]

Following her move to Paris, Zinaida formed intimate friendships with members of French high society at the salon of Julie Kann née Koenigswater (1845–1917)—the second wife of the banker Isaac Eduard (Sacki) Kann (1830–87), who had been an influential leader of the Alliance Israélite Universelle.[455] Zinaida had first become acquainted with the Kanns during a family vacation to Paris in 1886. In 1892, *Le Sport* reported on a "lovely ball at Madame Sacki Kann's," which was "led by the daughter of the house in a charming white taffeta dress with thin pink stripes."[456] In attendance with Zinaida were "Baron S. de Ginzburg, Jules Koenigswater, Dollfus, Baron de Précourt, the Count of Andigné, Count Ducos," and others." Zinaida's elegance, noble manners, and refinement, which she had cultivated to perfection in Russia, allowed her to blend seamlessly in with the distinguished company. She soon took the initiative to branch out on her own, hosting members of the aristocracy like Baroness Jeanne Leonino Rothschild, who "finally accepted our invitation!"[457] In 1902, *Le Figaro* had only the highest praise for Zinaida: "A very lovely dinner at Madame Reuben Gubbay's whose guests included Madames Sulzbach and Vanderheym, the Morpurgos, Ullmans, Rosenheims, Martignans, Rueffs, Count de Tinseau, the Marquis de Torre Alfina, Mr. Masse, and Mr. de Poliakoff [most likely Il'ia]."[458] Jeanne Edwards (née Charcot), the sister of the famous Antarctic explorer Jean-Baptiste Charcot (1867–1936), was a familiar figure at Zinaida's salon. When the Grand Duke Konstantin summoned her father — Jean-Martin Charcot, a famous neurologist — to Moscow in 1891, one of his private patients was Lazar Poliakov. Zinaida's father hosted the French family in the old Russian capital with such "warmth and sumptuous splendor" that Jeanne wrote, "Papa has such a happy look." The Poliakovs invited them to return to Paris in their luxurious private rail car and covered Jeanne in "a bouquet of flowers composed of the French colors."[459]

As she had done in Moscow, Zinaida held regular reception hours[460] at her private domicile — one of the many Jewish salons on the fashionable Avenue du Bois de Boulogne. The French aristocratic salons not only persisted after 1789 but also served to make high society "more distinctive and attractive as a cultural model" at a time when the power of the aristocracy was in a precipitous decline.[461] The persistence of the salon represented an active strategy of resistance and adaptation, not a merely an act of survival.[462] As in earlier times, the salon was a powerful institution that helped "link private interests to political power and public influence."[463] Charles Ephrussi, who collected netsuke "at the height of the Parisian rage for all things Japanese," found that each "formidable salon" was a "minefield of fiercely contested geographies of political, artistic, religious, and aristocratic taste."[464] In the drawing rooms of these Parisian salons, guests — "poets, playwrights, painters, 'clubmen,' *mondains*" — met at the set reception hours under the "patronage of a hostess to engage in conversation around issues of note, or purposeful gossip, or to listen to music, or see a new society portrait unveiled."[465]

The intimacy of salon culture helped women cultivate genuine friendships, which sustained Zinaida through her homesickness for her family and difficult marital moments. Touched that "Madame S[acki] Kann purposefully dropped by to congratulate me on Raia's engagement," Zinaida wrote with genuine appreciation: "She is such an attentive lady, really! No one else did this. This is praiseworthy!"[466] They often attended cultural events together, like a performance of Paul Hervieu's play *L'Enigme*, which first opened at the Comèdie Française on November 1901. "The theater was full because this was only the third performance," observed Zinaida. "Madame Kann was so kind to invite us to her box together with her two sons Reginald and Antony [sic]."[467] Through the Kanns, Zinaida befriended the Reinarch brothers—members of the French-Jewish intelligentsia who became deeply involved in the Dreyfus affair.[468] In turn, Zinaida provided solace for the women whom she received at her salon. In 1901, she described a visit by "Mademoiselle Walter Behrens,"[469] who brought her friend Sonia Montefiore (née Antokol'skaia). The latter related that her "unfortunate husband" was at the mental hospital in Suresnes because he "wanted to strangle her in a fit of fury." The wife lamented the fact that they were forced to "lock him up in an insane asylum, albeit a private one." Expressing the proper empathy for her troubles, Zinaida remarked, "She is very unhappy, of course."[470] All these diary entries on sociability reveal how faithfully Zinaida maintained this institution of aristocratic civility, which represented a form of security and continuity even as her family's banks teetered on the brink of bankruptcy.

Zinaida also hosted politicians, bankers, and the industrial *haute bourgeoisie* in her salon, cementing alliances for both the Poliakovs and her husband as he embarked on new entrepreneurial enterprises. She played a critical role in personalizing the political intimacy as she had done in Russia. On 17 March 1904, *Le Figaro* reported, "On Monday, Madame Reuben Gubbay gave a brilliant dinner party with twenty-four place settings in honor of His Excellency, Monsieur Kartsov, the very distinguished Consul General of Russia in Paris, who learned the day before about the exploits of his son at Port Arthur."[471] Political news about Russia from their guests and Zinaida's family in Moscow spurred Reuben to write a letter to the *Jewish Chronicle* in 1905 to protest the unfair expulsion of a Jewish soldier named Schwartz, who had received four St. George Crosses. According to the *New York Times*, "one of them, the gold cross for bravery in Manchuria, was questioned by Mme Ol'ga Novikoff [Novikov]," a close friend of the Poliakovs. Nonetheless, Reuben insisted that not only had the authorities unjustly given Schwartz twenty-four hours to leave Moscow but also had expelled all wounded Jewish soldiers who had been sent to Moscow hospitals for recovery. The newspaper cited Mr. Gubbay, who claimed that a "dying Jewish soldier was unable to see his wife, though charitable ladies subscribed her railway fare, because the woman being a Jewess, could not obtain the official permission to visit her expiring husband."[472] Clearly, there was a dispute about the facts between Reuben and a close confidant of the Poliakov family, leaving one to wonder how Zinadia's family perceived the letter—given their precarious financial and political position under Nicholas II. Not only did the Gubbays host foreign dignitaries from Russia, but they were also invited to events like a concert organized by the newspaper *Le Figaro* in April 1907 during the visit of Prince Fushimi Hiroyashi of Japan (1875–1946) to Paris. The prince expressed great satisfaction with this "very intimate Parisian visit" to the editor of the newspaper, Gaston Calmette (1858–1914), who would be assassinated seven years later in a sensational murder case.[473]

Business associates of the family such as the Proppers, a prestigious banking family originally from Prague,[474] Henri and Philippe Brüll,[475] and the English stockbroker Alex Waley and his wife, Marguerite, were also familiar figures at the Gubbays' home. Marguerite (who went by Margot) was Zinaida's close friend and the granddaughter of Léopold Louis-Dreyfus, who had established a lucrative trading house in Basle in 1851 that moved its operations to France and expanded its networks to Eastern Europe and Russia.[476] Iakov Poliakov's diaries are filled with entries about seeing various branches of the Dreyfus family at the Gubbays' home.[477] Iakov's business connections with Ruben Dreyfus in Russia acquainted Zinaida with the latter's wife, Minette, and her brothers Joseph, Nathan, and Daniel dit Constant—half-siblings of Léopold Louis-Dreyfus. In October 1897, Iakov recounted an unpleasant conversation between Leopold Dreyfus and Ruben Dreyfus in Paris over the latter's "deposit of 40,000 francs" in the Bank Azov; Léopold clearly understood that Iakov's bank was a sinking ship and disapproved strongly of the imprudent investment.[478] The marriage of Reuben Gubbay's sister Louise to Antoine (Tony) Dreyfus (grandson of Isaac dit Adolphe Dreyfus) solidified their family ties to another branch of the family. The Gubbays attended balls with the Dreyfuses (along with the Levis, whom Zinaida had befriended in Italy, and the Knoffs) at Marthe Emden's on the Rue de Pantheon.[479] In the summer of 1906, Zinaida looked forward to traveling with the Dreyfuses to Saint-Germain-en-Laye, where the Waleys also planned to visit.[480] Family and business did not always mix well, however, as will be seen below.

Like the French aristocracy that "deployed social and symbolic forms of capital," through their patronage of the performing arts, Zinaida cultivated her ties to Parisian artists, musicians, and theater celebrities to cement her place in cultured society.[481] She often invited artists to perform at her salon to promote their plays. For instance, on 13 March 1903, *Gil Blas* announced "a soirée de comédie at Madame Reuben Gubbay's salon on Avenue du Bois de Boulogne."[482] On 14 March 1903, *La Presse* promised that the guests of "this charming hostess" would be treated to "a performance of a small scene about the *montmartrois* [the inhabitants of Montmartre]."[483] A few days earlier, she took her daughter, Annette, to two of the most fashionable musical salons in Paris: "Today we were at the children's matinee at Madame Maurice Sulzbach's."[484]

This was the same Madame Sulzbach whom Marcel Proust mentioned in a letter to a friend in 1895. Regarding Madame Sulzbach's eternal devotion to Gabriel Fauré, who dedicated several pieces to her, Proust observed: "I chatted at length last night with Fauré who is indeed very nice. Madame Sulzbach didn't manage to spoil it for me by saying that she would trade all of Beethoven for just one of Fauré."[485] Following the matinee at the Sulzbachs, Zinaida went to the salon of Angelika Koenigswarter, who had organized a musical evening for the performance of compositions by her son-in-law, Fernand Halphen (1872–1917). The latter was a student of Fauré's before he matriculated at the Paris Conservatory to study with Ernest Guirand (who had also taught Claude Debussy). Zinaida took great pride in socializing with the Koenigswaters, whom she described as "one of the large Jewish [banking] houses here after the family of Baron Rothschild of course."[486] She also accepted invitations from Princess Maria Della Rocca (1836–1908)[487] to musical matinees, including a performance by the English singer Madame Florence Meredith.[488] After Zinaida attended "a very good matinee at the publisher's [of] Le Figaro," where the Spanish violist Pablo de Sarasate (1844–1908) performed along with many other artists, she admitted cynically: "It goes without saying that the main attraction of this [event] is that they will publish the names of the invited [guests] the next day."[489] As a Russian, Zinaida also took great interest in the émigré artists like Leopold Sinaeff-Bernstein and was friendly with art collectors like Nikolai Ivanovich Shchukin (1851–1910), but it is unknown if she collected art like her parents.[490]

As a member of the Society of the Friends of the Louvre,[491] Zinaida's curiosity was piqued by the scandal of the Tiara Saitapharnes, which involved her close family friend Theodore Reinach (1860–1928). "They say that Theodore Reinach lent the Louvre 50,000 francs to buy a tiara, which is now deemed to be a fake," she wrote in 1903. Zinaida was incredulous that Reinach wrote a letter in Le Figaro stubbornly maintaining "that it is an antique!"[492] In June, Zinaida expressed her relief that "Theodore Reinach acknowledged his own mistake. And today there was an official announcement that the tiara was made by Rouchomovsky [a Jewish goldsmith from Odessa]. It was embarrassing for the Louvre Museum and French archaeology to admit its lack of authenticity." In general, she concluded: "Antiques and ancient objects are a mystery. It is said that there now exist factories everywhere for fake rarities."[493] She preferred to avoid the folly of dealing in counterfeits and instead attend the lectures of Theodore's brother Salomon Reinarch, a renowned archeologist, which she intended to do "punctually."[494]

To her dismay, Zinaida's husband shared neither her cultural values nor desire for intimacy. Having waited almost a decade to marry Reuben, Zinaida was shocked at his crude and barbaric treatment. After their fight over champagne on New Year's, he vehemently exclaimed, "May God kill you!"—not once but thrice.[495] After a lovely time at the theater, where they saw *La fille de Madame Angot*, a comedic opera in three acts by Charles Lecocq, Zinaida's evening was ruined when "Ruby declared to me that I am repulsive to him."[496] This was not the first time that he had denigrated her in this manner. Three years earlier, she had described a similar episode in which "Ruby directly declared to me that I am repulsive to him, and no matter where he sees me, it's unbearable." She could not conceal her feelings: "Of course, this is very painful to hear."[497] She blamed their quarrels in part on Reuben's violent temper, which caused her many sleepless nights. "[The Moscow art collector] Nikolai Ivanovich Shchukin married his cousin late, but then again, they say that they have peace in their home, but we have Sodom and Gomorrah," she admitted. "Ruby is constantly agitated about one thing or another, and everything falls on me to bear. . . . I did not sleep all night because I was very upset by the bad mood of Ruby, who yelled all day." In this case, she blamed his anger squarely on her family's failure to send them money.[498] On another occasion, she imagined that had Dr. Charcot been alive, he would "have recognized Ruby as not legally responsible [for his actions]; yesterday he went into a rage and began to curse. The fact of the matter is that he is sick of being with me and he wants to change his way of life. As a result of this, he began to swear and wished me everything good [sarcastic]. I did not close my eyes all night and today am completely ill, so that I do not know how I will be in any condition to get up."[499]

After endless conflicts about everything—from trivial matters like a change in the brand of sugar for their tea to more serious issues like the family budget—Zinaida confessed that Reuben fell radically short of her expectations: "I always dreamed of finding myself a companion but I erred in my judgment. The point is that for complete mutual harmony, above all, one needs to have, at the very least, an equivalent education. But that, he absolutely did not have because, when he was sixteen, they sent him to get rich in Hong Kong, where he spent the best time of his life, sitting at the table smoking and selling opium."[500] Behind the not-so-veiled reference to the Sassoons' lucrative opium trade[501] was a sharp critique of Reuben's shortcomings when it came to his responsibilities. Zinaida was disappointed by Reuben's tendency to ignore and even disparage social obligations—so unlike her father, who enjoyed a widespread reputation for his promptness and cordiality: "Ruby had a letter from Libanskov from Nice, which was very courteous, asking to inform him about his health. It goes without saying that he has not yet fulfilled this because Ruby

FIGURE 11

Zinaida Lazarevna Poliakova and Reuben Gubbay.

Poliakova and Poliakoff, *Sem'ia Poliakovykh*.

has a lot of business: praying, smoking, and playing patience [a card game] —on the whole, [he has] an Eastern nature, completely different from the European way and much of it is incomprehensible to me."[502] Zinaida, the ever-gracious hostess who went to great lengths to accommodate the needs of her family and friends, was devastated when Reuben demanded that she cancel a visit from his brother Maurice (which she had spent much time organizing) so that his mother could come instead. Unable to hold back her tears, she broke down: "I simply cannot endure his screaming. . . . It goes without saying that . . . [his] swearing is even worse. Today, I did not say anything in response to him, but I don't know how he can take the liberty because, in reality, he owes me everything and treats me worse than a slave."[503] If Zinaida had expected "polite, civilized attention to the ladies" as an expression of aristocratic civility, she did not find it in Reuben.[504]

Zinaida valued the intimacy of togetherness, and she was distressed by Reuben's constant threats to leave her whenever they quarreled. "He has ruined my whole life," she wrote wearily in 1895. "He has nothing better with which to frighten me other than [threats that] he will run off to some distant region like India, China, Australia, or even further."[505] She admitted to being terribly unhappy because Reuben refused to reciprocate her love: "Life is sown with quarrels and no one envies such unpleasantness. So, if you have a misanthropic character like Ruby and the presence of the wife is a burden, then you should live alone and not have anything to do with a being who can feel and love!"[506] A few years later, she still found herself dealing with his "constant threats . . . to leave me and to ask for a divorce."[507] Observing his niece's marriage during their first visit to Moscow in 1892, Iakov Poliakov wrote, "It is impossible to say that Zina and her husband Gabe [Gubbay] were very happy."[508]

At the root of their problems was Zinaida's suspicion that Reuben had married her only for money, not for love. Her father had not been enthusiastic about the match because, as she wrote on 15/27 September 1886, he feared that Reuben's "pockets are empty" and "he has neither shelter nor a fortune." Reuben's own family had chosen not him but his younger brother David to head their firm David Sassoon & Co. Reuben first worked as an administrator for the Society of Commerce and Industry in Paris—a position that clearly did not pay enough to support his and Zinaida's lifestyle. The couple relied heavily on the regular stipend from the Poliakovs—which led to severe marital conflicts during the Russian financial crisis, as described above. Their finances became more complicated after Reuben opened his own office in connection with a company that he ran with Messieurs d'Abnour, Trousselle, and Philippe Brülle—the Nickel of New Caledonia, a mining and metallurgical company created in 1907 that sought to exploit the region's rich deposits of nickel, cobalt, copper, and other metals. Its goal was to acquire rights to the mines; purchase foundries in which to smelt, refine, and process the precious metals and ores; and engage in the commercial, banking, transportation, and other operations related to the business. Headquartered at 4 Boulevard Malesherbes in Paris, the company had a share capital of 7,000,000 francs, divided into 70,000 shares of 100 francs each.[509] Despite the promise of success given the region's rich resources, the business did not thrive. The first hints of problems appeared in Zinaida's diaries in the summer of 1910: "I am yearning for when Ruby will be free. Worries about his offices pursue him everywhere."[510] On 22 June 1910, Zinaida complained bitterly about her brother-in-law, who had been drawn unwillingly into the company's financial crisis: "Nasty Tony [Dreyfus] wanted Ruby to close his office last year and, because he did not do so, he grumbles that in order to get out of financial difficulties, he and Ruby's two sisters had to provide surety for 600,000 francs, and now they torment us at every step as though we are under their guardianship."[511] She was furious that "Shylock (Tony Dreyfus) wrote me a impudent letter before our departure" and complained that "vile Tony follows us as though he were our guardian."[512] Although her husband had put his family in an untenable position by having them back his enormous loan, Zinaida resented them for what she perceived as meddling. Whereas her mother, a merchant and major stockholder, understood the operations of the Poliakov banks, Zinaida did not claim to have any knowledge of finances, which would have devastating consequences after World War II when she and Annette fell deeply into debt yet expected to live in the manner to which they were accustomed.

Despite their heated arguments, the Gubbays enjoyed a few moments of harmony. Zinaida was delighted to receive a bracelet made of pearls and rubies from Boucheron's for their tenth anniversary, which they picked out together (but "unfortunately it did not have the date of our wedding").[513] In 1906, she wrote: "I was made extremely happy on the morning of July 22 to receive a ring from Ruby [for] . . . our engagement [anniversary]. This gave me great pleasure because it [the custom of gift giving on this occasion] has been out of fashion lately."[514] But diary entries about happiness or love were quite exceptional. Although Zinaida may have written only in moments of despair, the entries suggest that there were deep-rooted problems, not just momentary outbursts or quarrels. Yet the couple never became a statistic in the "divorce epidemic" that Zinaida observed had infected her circle of friends.[515]

Reuben and Zinaida did share one powerful bond—their daughter, Annette, born on 23 December 1896. Zinaida had neglected to keep a diary for over two years, but she found a moment during a vacation in St. Germain to record her daughter's birth date and complain that "Annette will soon be eight months old but only has two teeth."[516] Iakov Poliakov, who faithfully recorded family events, exclaimed: "Zina Gabbe [Gubbay] gave birth to a daughter. Nobody expected this."[517] He had imagined that the couple could never have been intimate given their hostile relationship! *Le Figaro* had published a formal announcement: "Madame Reuben Gubbay has given birth to her first child, a girl, who is doing well, as is her lovely mother."[518] During Annette's early childhood, Zinaida was preoccupied with securing the best nannies and tutors to prepare her for high society. In 1897, she hired Marie Foin, a young peasant girl from the village of Lingoult (Yonne), who served as a *nourrice sur lieu* and traveled with the family on their vacations to the Poliakoff mansion in Biarritz, a seaside city where the family had financed the building of the synagogue. Annette kept in touch with Foin throughout her life, offering financial assistance when her childhood caretaker fell ill.[519] Zinaida had also hired an Italian nanny, Henriette Pignatelli di Cerchiare ("from one of the first Neapolitan families"), who came highly recommended by an old Russian friend, N. B. Spiridonov.[520] However, Reuben did not like her and forced Zinaida to let her go, even though his wife clearly appreciated the woman's assistance with their young daughter. Unfortunately, Zinaida's new domestic servant Louisa raised some unpleasant dilemmas. Their family friend Theodore Klein warned that she was "too young, and Mama was frankly fearful that some kind of romance would take place in our house." Zinaida herself felt uncomfortable "seeing Louisa turn red, as often happens among *fräuleins* [sic]."[521] Given her painfully difficult relationship with Reuben, it is not surprising that both friends and family members advised Zinaida against keeping the young woman as a nanny.

Like her mother, Zinaida took great care to organize Annette's religious and cultural education. Relying on her friendship with Rabbi Zadoc Kahn (the chief rabbi of France since 1890) and his wife, Ernestine, Zinaida hired their son-in-law Julien Weill (who was married to Hélène Kann) to teach her daughter Hebrew and the fundamentals of Judaism (what she called *Zakon Bozhii*—a Russian term used to describe religious education). "He is a very nice charming gentleman and extremely decorous," wrote Zinaida in 1906, very pleased with her choice.[522] Weill (1873–1950) would be the chief rabbi of Paris when the Germans invaded the city during World War II.[523] Annette studied French dictation and reading with Mademoiselle Gerfaut and English with Miss Springley but did not take Russian-language lessons, judging from Zinaida's secret longing ("if only Annette could speak Russian").[524] As the champagne incident suggests, Ruby would have disapproved of teaching Annette the Russian language, which he clearly saw as irrelevant to their lives. Then there was her daughter's cultural education, which consumed Zinaida's energies. She was eager to purchase a piano that she had seen on display at the Exposition de l'Enfance at the Petit Palais on the Champ Elysees in 1901, which cost 400 francs.[525] Zinaida proudly noted that Annette "very much loves to listen to music" and "is partial to [Sigismond] Thalberg" (1812–71)—the virtuoso pianist and composer. Re-creating her own childhood, Zinaida hosted extravagant costume balls for her daughter, which captured the attention of the fashion magazine *Les Modes* in 1903: "A lovely morning costume ball at Madame Reuben Gubbay (née de Poliakoff) who gathered the little friends of her charming daughter, age six. The *cotillion*, which was full of charming surprises, was led by Mademoiselle Annette Gubbay, a ballerina, and Monseiur Roger Seligman, a drum major."[526] In 1909 the magazine also highlighted the "lovely holiday party for children and youth on the occasion of Christmas and the New Year hosted by Madame Marcelin Singer, Madame Reuben Gubbay, and Madame Paul Moeller."[527] On 28 December 1904, *Gil Blas* described "Madame Reuben Gubbay's children's matinee dance" as "brilliant." The dance was "led by Monseiur Jean de Morpurgo and Mademoiselle [Annette] Gubbay."[528] As the names indicate, Zinaida had her daughter socialize with children of the most elite families: the Morpurgos, for instance, were a prestigious Sephardic banking family from Trieste. Like her mother, Annette learned how to be the perfect hostess. In 1905, *Le Figaro-Modes* praised Annette, who was "just eight years old," for playing her role "as an ambassador well versed in the matter of receiving [guests]" and grouping her little friends so that they could enjoy the party as much as possible.[529]

The Gubbays took Annette to the most fashionable spas and hotels in Europe from an early age. "Today, I write from Bourboule where we are taking the cure with the waters," wrote Zinaida on 28 July 1902. "Baby [Annette] has already taken eight or nine baths today, and the doctor said that eight to ten baths altogether would be sufficient for her."[530] While they were in Bourboule, they took a day trip to Mont-Dore, best known for its thermal spas, where they saw Beatrice Ephrussi de Rothschild (1864–1934), who was married to Maurice Ephrussi (1849–1916), and Baronness Lambert. Zinaida noted that the former refused to take the cure in Bourboule because "they did not give her a *cabine de luxe* like she wanted."[531] Sometimes Zinaida left her daughter at home—for example, when they took an excusion to Rochers-de-Naye in the Swiss Alps for fear that the "excessive height (2,045 meters) would affect her [Annette]."[532] Zinaida was also a very protective mother who tried to avoid places with outbreaks of infectious diseases. "Flora and Mozelle Sassoon and the children are in Cabourg," she explained in the summer of 1903. "Although this is not far

FIGURE 12

Annette Gubbay (daughter of Zinaida Poliakova Gubbay, *front center*) at a
children's costume ball at the family home on Avenue du Bois de Boulogne.
"A Travers le monde," *Les Modes: Revue mensuelle illustrée des arts décoratifs
appliqués à la femme*, February 1903, 19.

from Trouville, all the same, we were not at their home, being afraid of the
whooping cough."[533] Zinaida also took Annette to Fontainebleau, where they
stayed at the Hôtel de France et d'Angleterre with Zinaida's brother Aleksandr
and Dr. Jacques (Iakov) Bandaline. "Fontainebleau is a very quiet place and
the forest is delightful. Although I do not like too quiet a life, I am completely
taking advantage of it after the noise and din of the capital," she wrote.[534] Other
favorite vacation sites for the Gubbays included the spas of Ischel, Interlaken,
Franzensbad, and Marienbad, as well as Dieppe (a fishing town on the Normandy coast) and Puyz, which she described as the "former summer residence
of Lord Slossberg and the French writer Alexandre Dumas."[535] But life was not
only about holidays for Zinaida's only daughter.

When Annette turned seventeen, her grandfather Lazar wanted to arrange
her marriage. At the time, however, Zinaida lamented the fact that "there
were no suitable Jews" and "we did not expect her [to marry] a Christian." Her
friend "Madame [Hélène] Allatini [née Kann][536] proposed a match with Nini

[Nissim] de Camondo" (1892–1917)—one that pleased Annette immensely.[537] The prospective groom hailed from an illustrious Sephardi banking family from Istanbul that had moved to Paris in 1869. In 1911, Nissim's father, Moïse Camondo (1860–1935), bought a property on the Rue de Manceau, which he renovated as an "artistic family residence."[538] This neighborhood in Paris had become home to a "burgeoning financial and commercial elite" from Russia and the Levant—"a virtual colony, a complex of intermarriage, obligation, and religious sympathy."[539] Camondo intended the house, with its lavish furnishings and decorative arts (judiciously selected on the advice of the curators of the Musée de Louvre and Musée de Arts Décoratifs), to serve as "the setting for his own family history."[540]

The Poliakovs and Camondos had become well acquainted with each other long before Madame Allatini suggested the match. Nissim's grandmother, Louise Cahan d'Anvers, was a relative of the Poliakovs by marriage: she was the daughter of Abram Varshavskii [Warshawsky] and sister of Leon Varshavskii [Warshawsky], the husband of Zinaida's cousin Roza, who died soon after childbirth. Roza's father, Samuil, had served as one of the founding members of the Société des Études Juives, together with Baron de Rothschild, David Gintsburg, and Nissim Camondo (Moïse's father) in 1880.[541] The French society pages often cited the Sassoons, Gubbays, Poliakovs, and Camondos as being at the same weddings and funerals.[542] For instance, at the signing of the marriage contract between Zinaida's sister-in-law Mozelle Gubbay and Meyer Sassoon on Boulevard Malesherbes in 1892, "Count and Countess de Camondo" presented the couple with "two carafes of crystal and vermeil."[543] Reuben had also served on the board of the Paris Israelite Consistoral Association with Nissim's father. In 1911, the board voted to replace the outgoing members "M[onsieur] Gubbay and M[onseiur] M[oïse] Camondo with [M]onseiur Achille Bloch."[544]

Zinaida was also privy (as was much of the public, admittedly) to the scandalous divorce of Nissim's father from Irène Cahen d'Anvers ("Little Irène" in Renoir's portrait),[545] who had a tumultuous affair with Count Charles Sampieri in 1902 and later became his wife. "Isaac Camondo has a 'collage' [of women]," Zinaida wrote in her diary, "but his cousin Moïse got divorced. How strange to see his former wife with the second husband. It is better, of course, to suffer as much as possible than to tear the first ties [of marriage], although this is not easy."[546] Irène's mother Louise also had a lover—none other than Charles Ephrussi (described in *The Hare with the Amber Eyes*), who had advised Moïse on his early art purchases.[547] Nissim's sister, Beatrice, eventually married (and divorced) Leon Reinach, the son of Theodore Reinach—a close family friend of the Gubbays.

Nissim was discharged from military service in 1913 and had just commenced his training as a securities banker when World War I broke out. His father had hoped that the son would take over the family business, but Nissim rejoined the military and asked for a transfer to the air force from the trenches. Obtaining his pilot's license in 1916, he was promoted to the rank of lieutenant. According to Zinaida, everything "seemed to go well" for Annette and Nissim until "he courageously was killed in his airplane during the time of war."[548] His plane was shot down near Embermenil on 5 September 1917.[549] "Therefore, everything collapsed, unfortunately," wrote Zinada, as she looked back on Annette's life during World War I with deep grief.[550] The year that Nissim's plane went down, Marcel Proust sent a moving condolence letter to the bereaved father: "Monsieur, I learn with profound sadness that you are tormented about the fate of your son. I do not know if my name means anything to you, but I used to dine with you at Madame Cahan's, and more recently (although it is still long ago) you once took me to dine with dear Charles Ephrussi, whom I loved deeply. These memories are very old. They were enough, however, for my heart to be crushed with anguish when learning that you were without news about your son."[551]

Devastated by the death of his only son, Moïse bequeathed the house to the state at the time of his death, "wishing to perpetuate the memory of my father Count Nissim de Camondo and that of my unfortunate son, Lieutenant Pilot Nissim de Camondo, killed in aerial combat on 5 September 1917. . . . My house is to be given the name of Nissim de Camondo, the name of my son for whom this house and its collections were intended."[552] According to his final wish, the exquisite Musée Nissim de Camondo remains a memorial to his son's memory in Paris today. Strangely, neither Annette Gubbay nor her parents were listed among the prominent members of the aristocracy and banking families (many of whose names appear in Zinaida's diaries) who attended Nissim's funeral, as described in *Le Figaro* or *Le Gaulois*. They were relegated to the "etc." at the end of the list of prominent figures such as the prince of Monaco and Quinones de Léon (the "minister of Spain"), the titled aristocracy, the industrial haute bourgeoisie, and military officials.[553]

Zinaida, who had grown up in a large, close-knit family, was disappointed that Annette never married and took after her father when it came to family intimacy: "Ruby did not value closeness; his family was always apart." Here, again, she recalled Reuben's grandparents and parents who lived separately in Bombay, London, and Paris. Waxing nostalgic about her own parents, she wrote, "Mama was never apart from father," and Zinaida claimed that she "never left Ruby's side." However, "Annette—is absolutely the opposite."[554]

After she left Russia, Zinaida kept in touch with all of her siblings and her parents regularly through letters and telegrams, visiting them on her many travels around Europe. In fact, one of the most common complaints in her Parisian diaries is about the absence of news from home, especially during the crisis years in Russia. Jealous that her mother wrote to her sister-in-law Claire "but did not even answer me," Zinaida ruminated bitterly: "In our family, it's for certain that they look after the daughter-in-law more than the daughter."[555] Yet she could hardly contain her excitement when her family decided to visit her in Paris. "Mama and Papa, Raia and her fiancé, Sasha and Baby [Benjamin] are in Marienbad," she wrote in 1903, "but in a few days they will probably already be in Paris again, where I wait for them with great impatience."[556]

Holidays at the Poliakoff (the name they went by in France) mansion—the Villa Oceana—in Biarritz provided the perfect place for reunions of the family, now living in Russia, France, Italy, England, and Belgium. Zinaida's brother Jacques (Iakov) and his wife, Claire, lived year-round in Biarritz, where the former founded a hospital that became a surgical center for military casualties during World War I. Biarritz was very "popular with Russians," and "the fall season was known as *la saison russe*."[557] Following the Russian crowd, Zinaida arrived in Biarritz for the entire month of September 1902 to "recover there with my parents" after a busy summer of traveling.[558] The Poliakoff parties for the members of high society, hosted by Jacques and Claire, were so brilliant that even in August 1939, *Le Petit Journal Parti Social Français* recalled the "unforgettable receptions" at the "Villa Poliakoff" in prewar Biarritz.[559] In 1904, the Poliakoff family celebrated the opening of the Biarritz synagogue on 3 Rue Pellot, which had been financed primarily by Lazar—who initially pledged 5,000 francs as early as 1895.[560] Unfortunately, neither Lazar nor Rozaliia was able to attend the consecration of the building, but they were represented by their "honorable family members." According to *L'Univers Israélite*, the synagogue, which was "located in the most beautiful areas of the city," was both Romanesque and Oriental in style. On the facade of the synagogue were Tablets of the Law "and the beautiful words from the Pentateuch, 'You shall love your neighbor as yourself.'"[561] Iakov described the event on 25 August 1904: "The opening of the synagogue. I am glad that it was my initiative and my first donations in francs. Lazar Solomonovich followed [my example] and [donated] a lot [of money]. A modest, small, and very nice synagogue, close to us." The Consistory of Bayonne was present along with the Grand Rabbi, Emile Lévy. They presented Iakov with "a key to open the *aron kodesh* [holy ark] where they placed the Holy Torah" for the first time.[562] The Gubbays were not present for this event but spent many High Holidays in Biarritz in the interwar period.

It was easier to meet Zinaida's immediate family in Biarritz than in other spa towns because of Lazar and Rozaliia's habit of making last-minute plans due to their complicated financial affairs and family events in Russia. Zinaida, who liked to arrange her vacations in advance, was often frustrated by what she viewed as indecisiveness and poor planning: "Mama and Papa will take the cure in Marienbad, but in my opinion, it is already too late, and the [spa] season there is over. They put everything off from day to day and finally left for Marienbad after Genrikh [Vydrin]'s wedding. Perhaps they will not make it to Biarritz before Yom Kippur. Raia, of course, is also with them and surely Khaia and George too because they stayed in Sokol'niki all this time with them."[563] As she surmised, Raisa wrote that when they arrived in Marienbad, "no one was there already except for the permanent residents of Marienbad."[564]After several telegrams passed back and forth about their plans, Zinaida wrote in frustration: "It seems that the day of our wedding [anniversary] is on Rosh Hashanah. It would be better if our family did not spend the holidays in Biarritz. . . . Mama always makes it appear like she is going to remain in Paris when we go there; however, now she is making haste to go to Biarritz. It is a pity that they always manage to leave so late from home to go abroad. Of course, it is always difficult for Papa to manage to leave, but in general, they somehow drag it out and indecisively prepare for their annual trip abroad, but why?"[565] Although Zinaida never mentioned it directly, her diary entries showed that her sister Khaia seemed to coordinate her vacations more successfully with her mother and managed to be at the same spas and resort towns.

Zinaida made a conscious effort to take Annette to visit relatives like her cousin Isabella, who had a lovely home in Nice. "It is a nice, large villa," she observed, but she expressed her astonishment that "it still appears not to be furnished at all." Always the charming *salonnière*, Zinaida remarked, "I am surprised at their inattentiveness to the needs of the guests who come here exclusively for the sun."[566] When the Gubbays visited Khaia and her husband, Georges Levi, in Rome, Zinaida's sense of distinction led her to observe that they owned a "beautiful house, but in eighteenth-century style." She could not restrain her judgment that "everything is somewhat old (the furniture)" and "they both have little taste."[567] To make matters worse, Zinaida was mortified by her sister's lack of style: "Yesterday evening, we went to the opera, where they put on *La Bohème* with a new Italian tenor Alexandre Bonei. Khaia was in an old-fashioned dress, but I wore a [Jeanne] Paquin dress from Paris and found that it was not worthwhile at all because in Rome, everyone dresses poorly."[568] Paris had only made Zinaida more fashion conscious, while Khaia apparently had settled into a modest Italian way of life (at least in her older sister's eyes).

When the Gubbays were not traveling, their house in Paris was always bustling with Russian relatives and friends, acquainting Annette with members of her mother's old social circles. "Today we had a visit from the Vilenkins. Now we are busy preparing for our dinner party for twenty," Zinaida wrote in 1903.[569] That same day, she had missed an important communication about a visit from their St. Petersburg relatives: "Leon Abramovich Varshavskii [Warshawsky] and his oldest brother came by yesterday. To our regret, we were not home and thus we did not see Mark who, it appears, was essentially alone; Leon had already left. [My cousin] Zina [de Hirsch] said that she put him [Mark] on the train, and this was supposedly five days before I received their visiting cards! How strange this is!"[570] Zinaida was very fond of the Brodskiis, who became related to her through her brother Jacques's marriage to Claire Brodskaia: "We spent the whole day here today with Sasha, [Dr. Jacques] Bandalin, L[eon] I[sraelovich] Brodskii and Masha Brodskaia."[571] On another occasion, touched by the Brodskiis' sending her a beautiful basket of flowers, she wrote: "Because they had dinner at our home, they probably repaid us with this kindness!"[572] Her connection to the Brodskiis, however, led to some unpleasant exchanges with guests like the sculptor Leopold Sinaeff-Bernstein (1867–1944),[573] who dropped by before dinner to lodge a complaint: "He was very displeased with Brodskii who promised to come to the studio with his wife but did not fulfill his promise. He is very angry with him about this of course and wants to sue him."[574] She had no complaints about the Shcherbatovs (who organized the conservative Party of Law and Order in Russia), whom she mentioned frequently in her diaries as though they were family members: "The Shcherbatovs are always very good to our family, although he serves at the Moscow Land Bank. They are very attached to our house and it turns out that in 'difficult moments,' render great service to Papa. We were very glad to receive them at our home in Paris."[575]

News from her mother's side of the family seemed incredibly sad even as there were moments to celebrate (like her Uncle Genrikh's wedding). On 10 February 1903, the family received word from Raisa that their stepgrandmother Rozaliia Vydrin (who had the same name as Zinaida's mother) had died in Berlin. She had been ill with cancer at a clinic there. "One often hears now about this dreadful disease," wrote Zinaida. "Here, we have a lot of acquaintances who are sick from it. They say that the Princess of Wagram [Bertha Clara née Rothschild, 1862–1903] is dying of it unfortunately."[576] Zinaida learned from Liza Vydrin (who was studying at a polytechnical institute in Zurich) that her aunts (close friends from childhood as seen in her diaries) were suffering from serious conditions. Mariia (Masha) was ill, and "it turned out that Fania was in Vienna at Madame Smolensk; she took her from the hospital so that it would be more pleasant for her. They say that sometimes she becomes very agitated and screams and so on! I do not know, of course, if this is right. Although she is nervous, there is no need to keep her locked up. She has been imprisoned for an entire *fifteen years*."[577] Yet there was nothing she could do to help. Interestingly, she did not mention all the Vydrins (like her uncle Isaak Il'ich Vydrin) who became revolutionaries.[578] Fears that her cousin Liza had become a revolutionary in Zurich as well vanished after spending time with her. "She is extremely mature and has come to look like the rest of the students," observed Zinaida with a newfound respect. They traveled together from Ischl to Vienna, where they met up with Liza's mother, Sonia, and Zinaida's sister Raisa.

Zinaida increasingly spent more time with Ruby's family, especially his mother and siblings. She spent evenings at the Gubbays' home on the grand Boulevard Malesherbes near Parc Manceau, where the Camondos also resided: "We had dinner at my mother-in-law's where the whole family and Dreyfuses were there for some reason."[579] Zinaida was very solicitous toward her mother-in-law, who included her family members at social gatherings: "We are going for breakfast at Ruby's mother's. She invited us with Raia, [Khaia] and Georges, the young Montegues, and maybe Madame Sacki Kann." Of course, Zinaida always reciprocated. An evening at her home included her "mother-in-law, Il'ia, sisters-in-law Flora and Louisa Dreyfus, and Mr. Waley and his wife [Marguerite]."[580] Her family schedule on 19 October 1903 reflected their tight-knit family relations: "We have dinner at Louisa Dreyfus' on Monday. Flora Rueff returns to Paris on [October] 28 and Mozelle with her husband [Meyer Sassoon] should return on the 27th. . . . Yesterday we had breakfast with Frederick and Jenny Sassoon. . . . It is very convenient now because no one has begun to receive [guests], of course! We left cards at Madames Valbreque and Sassoon."[581] Perhaps Zinaida found that Reuben treated her better in front of his relatives than when they were alone.

To please Reuben's family, however, Zinaida had to overcome some cultural differences, especially in the sphere of gastronomical tastes and ideas about child care. She worried about what to prepare for her sister-in-law Flora and Jules Rueff because "no one likes Russian cuisine, and I do not know what the [menu] should be."[582] While Zinaida constantly longed for shchi, kvass, black bread, bliny, and kasha, her English relatives did not share her tastes.[583] The problem, she diagnosed, was that "our cook makes an excellent shchi and kasha, but French cuisine, not so well."[584] Although "there are only a few people coming," Zinaida still fretted, "it is all the same, a luncheon."[585] In another entry she wrote, "Flora and her husband are coming next Friday evening (after dinner); we will have 24 people for dinner this time. I do not know how we got so many guests; it was completely unexpected! All families with daughters."[586] Accustomed to her close, even suffocating, relationships with her Russian family, she was highly critical of Flora who "is always intoxicated by the presence of the Rothschilds in Chantilly and thinks that she has also become a member of this rich and proud family, but we are nothing, although [to be sure] we aren't millionaires!"[587] Zinaida, whose family had always traveled together on vacation, could not understand "why Flora so religiously travels every year to spend a month with Mozelle [in London] and abandons her children." When Flora's husband also left for London "to have dinner with Lord-maire [the Lord Mayor of London]," she thought that "it would be better if Flora did not travel there and leave the children alone."[588] Perhaps she felt excluded from the Sassoons' social events in England, especially when she received a letter from Flora saying that "all of our family members were at the horse races." Mozelle Sassoon, who was a frequent guest at Philip Sassoon's glamorous parties at Trent Park for English royalty, politicians, artists, and literary figures, was a "great London hostess herself."[589] Zinaida conceded, "Although I do not regret that we will not go there, [I realize that] we have not been there for a long time. It has been a whole year already since we traveled there for the coronation of the English king [Edward VII]."[590] In general, Zinaida was extremely sensitive to any kind of family snub, even the most minor one. For instance, she complained one summer: "Today, I had a visit from Louisa, Ruby's sister. She invited us to dinner on Monday because [Yvonne Sophie] Emden and her groom and Madame Vanderheym are coming for dinner. They refused to come to dinner recently when we had the Brodskiis and Count and Countess Verney della Valetta."[591] However, judging from her diaries, it appears that Louisa often visited her home, and this was an exceptional case. In any case, Zinaida began to adapt to the lifestyle of the Gubbays and pick up nuances of the English language and mannerisms: when her sister Raisa got engaged, she wrote in English: "It's high time for N!"[592]

Attentive to family and society in her diary, Zinaida rarely engaged in discussions about politics except to mention a few key events such as the 1905 revolution in Russia (discussed above) and the peace agreement following the Russo-Japanese War: "We were very glad about the conclusion of Witte's peace with Japan in Portsmouth on 29 August.[593] . . . Fedor [Theodore] Roosevelt, the president of the United States, successfully arranged the peace. However, Japan is apparently dissatisfied with the terms because Russia will not pay a kopeck of compensation understandably; but this is not at all what Jefferson

Levy wrote in the American newspaper, the *New York Herald.*[594] Her interest in the Dreyfus affair came naturally through her circle of friends like the Reinarch brothers and Rabbi Zadoc Kahn, who were working for the exoneration of Captain Alfred Dreyfus:

> Only France could change its own verdict! It is true that Captain Dreyfus' supporters moved heaven and earth for this. All of the prominent people worked for this to show the world the mistake of the court about this officer. His wife worked without fail until she secured such a desirable [outcome]. A similar mistake occurred it appears in Voltaire's time when he publicly declared that the court appeared to be wrong. At home [Russia], there is a revolution now, but in France they are changing the approved verdict of Captain Dreyfus and proclaiming him innocent to register him in the army again and award him the Legion of Honor.[595]

Forever enamored of the Romanov dynasty, Zinaida devoted many more pages of her diary to the visit of Nicholas II to Paris in 1901: "Paris is apparently preparing for arrival of the Sovereign and Her Highness. They will probably be here on Friday, [September] 20th, for a few hours in Paris [to] see the Alexander III Bridge and then go directly to the Russian consulate where there will be a reception it seems, judging from the information in the newspapers [*Le*] *Figaro* and [*Le*] *Gaulois*." She carefully followed the news of the imperial visit to Compiègne with the French president and chose to have breakfast at the Restaurant Paillard in the Champs Elysées, where she met her brother-in-law Tony Dreyfus (who was married to Reuben's sister Louise).[596] Together they "set up chairs on the Champs Elysées to see the Sovereign," but they were disappointed not to see him.[597]

There was a long silence between 1910 and 1944, when Zinaida either stopped writing her diaries or lost them, but some details of her life appeared in newspapers and journals. During World War I, she assumed an important leadership role in the Alliance Israélite Universelle (AIU), for which she had served as a patroness for lotteries and fund-raisers.[598] At the end of 1915, the AIU announced that "Mme Reuben Gubbay, née de Poliakoff, initiated the creation of the Society to Aid Jewish Victims of the War" and had become its president.[599] Moved by horrifying accounts from her sister Khaia (Xenia, as she was known in Italy), "who witnessed the forced evacuations personally," Zinada resolved to act quickly.[600] In an appeal for funds, the new society described the horrors of the war: "The German invasion drove out an immense multitude of Jewish families from Poland. Some are still wandering in neighboring areas, where they are dying of hunger; others, evacuated to the interior [of Russia] or even in Siberia, are waiting for help, which is slow in coming." The society called on Jews of the world to "relieve the distress of their brethren."[601] Zinaida used her English family connections to appeal to Lord Swaythling (Louis Montagu), who was the treasurer of the newly formed Jewish Committee for the Relief of War Victims in Russia (whose board included the Rothschilds, Sassoons, Israel Zangwill, Moses Gaster, and Lucien Wolf) for assistance.[602] In a letter to Zinaida, Lord Swaythling assured her that the organization was collecting donations for their unfortunate Russian coreligionists. Notably, the English appeal letter described a Pale of Settlement "ravaged with a completeness unparalleled in other vast battlefields of the war" but failed to mention "pogroms, hostage taking, the summary execution of 'spies,' and deportations" —the brutal targeting of Jews that had propelled Zinaida to act urgently in the first place.[603]

Having shown little interest in the fate of her coreligionists during the pogroms of the 1880s, Zinaida increasingly felt responsible for their welfare, especially following the Kishinev pogroms in 1903. She expressed surprise that her mother had written nothing to her about the tragedy while the newspapers were "filled with different narratives about the furious mobs raging in Kishinev." In her view, if measures had been taken to "calm the agitation" from the beginning, "the Kishinev pogroms would not have occurred."[604] Zinaida had been attentive to the fund-raising efforts of Rabbi Zadoc Kahn for the Alliance Israélite Universelle (the Paris-based international Jewish organization) to support widows and orphans. As the conditions of Jewish refugees from Poland grew desperate during World War I, Zinaida used her family connections with the imperial government and fluency in the Russian language to assume a leadership role in organizing the relief effort. The war took a heavy toll on Zinaida, who was devastated by the traumatic experiences of her coreligionists in Russia and Poland. She was also shattered by the death of Nissim de Camondo, which was a significant loss for Annette and for his family: because he was their only son, "with his death, the family became extinct."[605] There were also some moments of pride: her brother Dr. Jacques de Poliakoff received the insignia of Commander of the Legion of Honor along with his colleague Dr. Bandaline for their innovative surgical treatment of soldiers.[606] She must also have been proud of her niece Marie Varshskaia (Warshawsky), who courageously worked as a Red Cross nurse treating soldiers in Russia before she emigrated to France in 1922.[607]

During the interwar years, Zinaida's daughter, Annette, stole the limelight as a popular socialite in Paris. Her glamorous photograph graced the pages of the *Sketch*, a London newspaper, where she was featured with other members

FIGURE 13

"Popular in Parisian
Society, Annette
Gubbay" (*top right*).

"London, Paris, and
New York: A Page of
Society Élégantes," *Sketch*,
6 April 1927, 23.

of the high society of London, Paris, and New York, including Mrs. Reginald Vanderbilt, "one of America's leading hostesses"; the Grand Duchess Boris of Russia (née Rachevsky); Miss Peggy Flake, "one of the leading hostesses of the American colony in Paris"; and Madame de Munoz, "the daughter-in-law of the Spanish Ambassador in Rome," among others. "Popular in Parisian Society, Annette Gubbay," the paper announced, was the "cousin of Sir Philip Sassoon."[608] It was not lost on her that she was connected to the "best known and most glamorous figures in Britain in the first forty years of the twentieth century" and the youngest member of Parliament, elected in 1912.[609] Sporting short bobbed hair, Annette was a portrait of the ideal new woman of the 1920s —a "young, sexy, independent 'garçonne' or 'femme moderne.'"

A radical departure from the ideal "voluptuous curvaceous woman" of the past, the "sinuous, smooth, 'modernist' woman" preferred the minimalist style pioneered in the *haute couture* world by Paul Poiret.[610] Although some historians have dismissed postwar fashion as "mere consumerist frivolity" or the objectification of women as sex objects, Mary Louise Roberts argues that women who donned "scandalously abbreviated dresses and short hair" helped create a new "political imaginary" in which dress became the political language for challenging gender norms—"a visual analogue of female liberation" that emerged at the end of World War I.[611] She observes that the blurring of gender differences exacerbated social anxieties that emerged at the fin de siècle—especially among natalists and Catholics, who feared that women "were becoming like men and rejecting their traditional domestic role."[612] Short stories like Pierre Drieu la Rochelle's "Le pique-nique" (1924) equated the modern woman with the loss of innocence, pleasure, and maternal warmth. In the story, a disaffected war veteran named Liessies describes his girlfriend, Gwen, as "extremely thin, mere skin and bones. . . . Women are cutting their hair as a sign of sterility. . . . She walks with empty hands; she wears no jewelry; she is completely uncovered." Roberts observes that the critique was as much a commentary on the "spiritual impotence and malaise felt by the veteran Liessies" (and the author) as it was of the new woman.[613]

Despite the vitriol in conservative society, Annette enthusiastically embraced the new aesthetic, especially the *style sportive* created by the designer Coco Chanel, which further simplified Poiret's style. This "sporty, casual style" was popular in the sea resorts La Baule-Escoublac in southern Brittany, Évian-les-Bains, and of course Biarritz—where the Gubbays vacationed every year.[614] The artistic director of the house of Doeuillut described his rationale for shifting from the elaborate tradition of haute couture with its beading, appliqué, and other decorative elements: "The big principle . . . is simplicity. Gone are the decorations of the past, 'rich decorations.' We make a dress in three seams. All of the refinement is placed on that which, before, held the least important: the form and the fabric. . . . None of the luxury is lost."[615] Traveling to Biarritz gave Annette the perfect occasion to wear the latest styles and throw lovely parties with her parents for their "charming friends" at the Hotel Lefèvre. Among their guests were some familiar figures like Baron and Baroness Gunzburg [Gintsburg], but there were also others whose names were not in Zinaida's pre–World War I diaries, like "Madame Siviecinska, Madame d'Hosville, Mrs. Godfray, Madame Pastor, Pedro de Candamo," and many others.[616]

In 1926, Annette had an opportunity to wear her sporty riding outfit at the "first meet for stag hunting [which] was held at Arbonne last Friday at Château de Pony [Biarritz], the country residence of Madame Borotra and children." The entire village had come to observe the "magnificent spectacle," including the sleek scarlet coats—which were "a splash of color against the gre[e]n backgrounds of the lawns." Reginald Wright, an Englishman who acted as "Master of the Biarritz hunt," and Senator Paul Lederlin added a new feature to entertain the young people: "They brought a red deer from England to be carted and hunted in the manner employed by several famous hunters in that country." Then the party "enjoyed another excellent sport, running after a fox across the valleys covered with golden oak leaves and gorgeous autumn gorse and heather." At the end of the day, "the brush was presented to Mlle. Borotra and the mash to Mlle. Gubbay." The "gay hunting people were soon gathered around the luncheon table at the château."[617] The local gazette also reported on a "pajama contest"—one of the lively parties for members of high society in Biarritz. The guests included Mademoiselle Annette Gubbay, Baron Henri de Rothschild, and many counts and countesses.[618] Annette continued to participate in high-society events like charitable fund-raisers in Paris in the 1930s. *Le Figaro*, for instance, reported on a successful benefit organized by Madame André Schwov d'Héricourt in December 1932, at which Annette was present —along with Madame Allatini (who had tried to arrange her marriage with Nissim Camondo) and many elite figures.[619]

During the interwar years, the family frequently traveled abroad to visit relatives in Brighton, Rome, Brussels (where Mikhail worked as a banker),[620] and Zurich (where Raisa lived with her husband).[621] Zinaida especially loved Monte Carlo and Nice because of her fondness for gambling at the casinos, which she dreamed about in the last years of her life.[622] But the optimism of the postwar years was tempered by the loss of Zinaida's closest family members. When her father, Lazar, died of a heart attack in 1914, Zinaida traveled to Moscow for his funeral.[623] Rabbi Maze, who delivered a long eulogy, remarked, "This name has become a legend in the mouths of all Jews in the Pale of Settlement, and when blessing their children before a wedding, our unfortunate brothers pray, '*Yesimcha Elohim kePoliakov*' [May God make you like Poliakov]."[624] He praised Lazar for being "an exceptional spouse, [an] affectionate, loving father, who was able to have pure, friendly relations with his children, spreading his love to all his relatives."[625] As her diaries reveal, Zinaida felt the closest to her father, who sent her regular telegrams with the latest news even when he was terribly preoccupied with the failure of his banks or in poor health. Lazar passed away before the Russian Revolution of 1917, which proved to be both a blessing in disguise and a disaster for her family. On the one hand, the Bolsheviks did not force the Poliakovs to repay the millions of rubles in loans to the State Bank. On the other hand, as the most visible capitalists in Russia, the Poliakovs represented the greatest enemies of the working class. Zinaida's brother Aleksandr, who had been elected to the Duma as a Social Democrat, received a death sentence by the new Bolshevik state; however, he was lucky enough to escape to France.

Rozaliia had apparently remained in Moscow during the revolution and had tried join her sons in Kiev "but was unfortunately recognized by the Bolsheviks who arrested her in Mogilev." She fell severely ill on her return trip to Moscow and never recovered. She died in 1919 at the age of seventy-seven.[626]

L'Univers Israélite, which announced the death of this "elite woman, founder of many charities, hospitals, asylums, etc.," praised her as a "fervent admirer of France and faithful friend of Biarritz where she came for forty years with her many family members."[627] The newspapers announced the settlement of Rozaliia's estate, instructing anyone with any claim against her estate to send a detailed letter to her solicitor, Frederick Arnold Biddle. His firm, Biddle, Thorne, Welsford, and Galt, was located in London. Notably, Rozaliia had named Khaia (Xenia) and Isaak as her executors instead of her oldest children, Zinaida and Mikhail.[628] It is unclear what happened to Rozaliia's estate, but Zinaida mentioned in passing in her final diary that she wished Annette would not travel alone to Italy, so that the family assets would not "disappear like Mama's money."[629]

Over a decade after her mother's death, Zinaida unexpectedly lost her husband. *Le Figaro* announced the death of Reuben Gubbay on 3 February 1931 and informed the public that, according to the wishes of the deceased, the funeral would be private.[630] In her final diary, Zinaida explained that her husband died from "an unforeseen accident" during a procedure performed by a professor named Abram. "Nothing could have predicted this," she explained, "because he felt well" with the exception of problems with his prostate.[631] The AIU described Reuben as a man "dedicated to tradition and philanthropy" who had served on the board of the Israelite Central Consistory of France for several years. At the end of February 1931, Zinaida donated 5,000 francs "in memory of her husband" to the AIU, to which he had been very devoted.[632] The day after Yom Kippur in some year around 1948, Zinaida sat in a hotel in London, reflecting on the fact that neither she nor Annette had fasted. She recalled that "Ruby was very religious and fastidiously observed all our holidays and fasts. Poor [Ruby]. He is buried in Paris in our family vault in the Montparnasse Cemetery."[633] Looking back at the decade before she got married in Moscow, Zinaida wrote nostalgically, "I fell in love with Ruby from afar." Despite their stormy marriage, she stayed with him for forty years and remembered him with bittersweet fondness. After Reuben's death, a man named Gedalia "very much desired to marry me but I did not like him; none of my suitors were attractive to me. I only liked Ruby and Baron Armin von Propper . . . and afterwards George Jeidels." In retrospect, she declared, "I really liked George Jeidels." But she chose not to remarry and "now I remain completely alone . . . unfortunately."[634] In 1937, a few years after Ruby's death, Zinaida's brother Isaak, president of the Persian Railway and Tramway Company, passed away.[635] This was only a few years before the greatest tragedy befell Zinaida's large and close-knit family.

World War II and the Postwar Years

The outbreak of World War II found Zinaida in Paris. Her diary picked up again on 25 February 1944: "Today I have begun to write a new journal and hope that it will be a good hour."[636] The past few years had been a nightmare for her family and community. When the French government declared defeat on 11 June 1941, the Jewish leaders of the Israelite Central Consistory and some 100,000 Jews fled Paris for the south of France. "Visha [Clara Solomonovich] and [my brother] Sasha left [for Nice] at the time of the occupation. Almost everyone fled from Paris then," Zinaida recalled of those early days. "It was simply horrid to be left alone at the Place des États Unis."[637] Annette's former Hebrew teacher, Julien Weill, now the chief rabbi of Paris, returned to the capital in August 1940 to provide support and guidance to his community. The signs of Nazi occupation were now visible everywhere: a café on Rue de Châteaudun was one of the first to put up a placard with the foreboding words "Israelites forbidden on these premises."[638] In September 1940, the German military administration issued an ordinance that defined a Jew "as a person belonging to the Jewish religion or having more than two Jewish grandparents."[639] The newspapers announced that Jews must report to various police stations in Paris to submit to a Jewish census in October 1940. Zinaida and her daughter, Annette, must have complied since they suffered from the anti-Jewish legislation that followed; besides, it was apparently rare for Jews to evade the order.[640] However, they would be treated as British citizens throughout the war based on the passports that they had obtained through Reuben. Zinaida had planned to travel to Switzerland to live out the war with her sister Raisa, but "Annette did not want to abandon the house," which turned out to be a disastrous decision.[641]

In 1941, the Nazis arrested Annette and sent her to the internment camp in Vittel, where she joined other British prisoners of war, whom the Nazis hoped to exchange for German officers captured by the Allies. When Annette first arrived in Vittel, a resort town in the Vosges Mountains with thermal baths, the camp included three hotels (the Grand Hotel, the Vittel Palace, and the Continental) as well as pavilions, theaters, churches, and other buildings—all of which were surrounded by a double fence of barbed wire so that the prisoners could not escape.[642] From its beginnings as a single-sex internment camp for British citizens and then a site that included older men from the camp in Saint-Denis who were reunited with their wives, Vittel expanded to accommodate new prisoners, including Americans in October 1942. Although they cheered the American internees as they arrived, the British prisoners were none too happy to share rooms with these new inmates while the authorities renovated the Hôtel Central to accommodate the influx of newcomers. According to the Swiss consul, "Additional beds were placed in these rooms so that altogether four persons were accommodated." Nonetheless, he claimed that "each of these rooms had a private toilet and bath. . . . Everywhere the conditions of sanitation and ventilation were perfect."[643]

Indeed, the Red Cross claimed that Frontstalag (prisoner-of-war camp) 194 in Vittel was one of the best internment camps in Europe: the prisoners lived in luxurious hotel rooms with running water (hot and cold) and received proper rations of bread, potatoes, and soup as well as mail and packages of food from the Red Cross and family members.[644] "Poor Annette," wrote Zinaida in 1944, "she was so happy to speak with me." Her daughter was able make phone calls, send telegrams, and receive visitors like her mother.[645] She was also able to obtain packages from the outside. "A true friend, Count Guiche sends Annette books," wrote Zinaida. "It is important to know when I will pay back my debt to him."[646] As Annette discovered after she injured her foot, prisoners had access to proper medical services either at the camp or at a hospital in Nancy. The doctors at the camp were prisoners of war themselves, while most of the other medical personnel, like the nurses, were nuns. For entertainment, the camp allowed the prisoners to organize theatrical performances and musical concerts and engage in sports like tennis and volleyball. But what set Vittel apart from the other camps was the absence of terror by the Schutzstaffel (ss). In fact, some even described Otto Landhauser, the German officer in charge of the camp, as incredibly humane. This was perhaps not surprising, because the Nazis wanted to showcase Vittel with its exemplary living conditions and treatment of prisoners to the world.[647]

Eighty-one years old in 1944, Zinaida found it difficult to live from day to day without her daughter: "I am complaining about the fact that they took away Annette; here it is already three years. It is impossible to imagine how difficult it is for me without her—[it is] as though [I am] completely without hands."[648] Hopeful that the Nazi authorities would approve her daughter's request for their repatriation to England, Zinaida focused on surviving from day to day. Her quality of life deteriorated when the Nazis began to implement their program of expropriation. In the spring of 1941, new measures blocked access to Jewish bank accounts so that it became impossible to withdraw funds and cash.[649] For the first time in her life, Zinaida felt the physical deprivations of war and financial need, although she clearly had some access to money: "I grew up in luxury and now find myself in reduced circumstances."[650] On 10 April 1944, Zinaida was worried: "I have little money and food costs a lot. It is a minimum of 100 francs for breakfast. Yesterday I ate at a modest Jewish restaurant. I absolutely do not know how I will manage."[651]

At the beginning of the war, Zinaida retained ownership of her apartment. However, a new decree of 22 June 1941 established that Jewish properties could be confiscated and sold, including valuable articles of furniture.[652] It is not clear when she lost her apartment, but Zinaida recalled that fateful day: "The Nazis came to me a few times. On our Paris home, there was a sign '*Reguisizionesh* [*sic*; requisitioned].'[653] We did not live long in it; Annette—all of one year only. After the requisitioning [of the apartment], I moved to the Pension de Family."[654] She was horrified to think about the fate of their beloved possessions that Annette had refused to part with and to flee to Switzerland: "They have probably taken away all the furniture. This is a second debacle [written in English] for us!"[655] Having selected each piece of furniture and material object to furnish their beautiful apartment, the violent confiscation of her personal belongings was a terrible blow. Nonetheless, she admired her own resilience: "I spent the past winter in Paris courageously. It goes without saying that I was without heat at the pension."[656]

To survive, Zinaida put her language skills to work. "I worked at the time of the occupation at the Red Cross," she admitted, "and translated documents for the Nazis."[657] Yet it was a very lonely existence because "no one wanted to have relations with the English during the period of the German occupation."[658] Zinaida was quite offended when her sister-in-law "Clara (Visha) Solomonovna asked me not to write. She has broken off relations with all members of Sasha's family."[659] Later, she acknowledged that Clara's reluctance to be associated with her was because "no one wants to be compromised. And as a relative she could be."[660] At least in Paris, friends nonetheless came to visit her occasionally, like Armand and Suzanne Kohn, Marcel Goldshmidt, Madame Weiller (who was later sent to Poland), Sonia Melmeister, and Madame von Wiezel.[661]

Armand Kohn (a nephew of Philippe de Rothschild) and his wife, Suzanne, who corresponded faithfully with Zinaida when she moved to Vittel and Nancy to await repatriation to England, appear frequently in her diary. Kohn was a banker until the war, and when the Second Statute on the Jews excluded him from his profession in 1941, he became the director of the Rothschild Hospital in Paris. Like some other members of the old French Jewish elite, Kohn had refused to flee France with his family when the war broke out and became a member of the Union Général des Israélites de France (UGIF), a compulsory representative body that was charged with managing all Jewish social and charitable organizations. In contrast to others who rejected the UGIF as a "treacherous Nazi-created organ of collaboration," Kohn believed that strict obedience to the law was the way for Jews to survive. Although he secured exemptions for his hospital personnel from internment and deportation, the great lengths to which Kohn went "to comply with discriminatory and cruel directives" shocked the staff at the hospital. For instance, he maintained a list of the exact ages of the infants so that they would return to Drancy Transit Camp with their mothers when they turned six months old.[662] He enacted "prison-like regulations and punishments" to prevent patients escaping from the hospital and even requested that barbed wire be placed around the pavilions.[663] Kohn's dedication to Zinaida's welfare until his deportation from France was remarkable, given the gravity of his work at the hospital. He may have been the one who helped organize her translation job with the Nazis, given his polititcal connections.[664] Perhaps an old family connection was responsible for this bond: in 1886, Kohn's mother was acquainted with the Poliakovs because her father, George Daniel von Weisweiller, visited them in Moscow (as noted in Zinaida's diary on 12 February 1886). Despite the occasional visits from friends like the Kohns, Zinaida's deep loneliness was obvious. "It is an extreme pity that I am doomed to solitude," she wrote on the eve of her trip to Vittel. "It would be desirable to have one of my relatives [with me]."[665]

In addition to her unbearable solitude, Zinaida was extremely anxious about her health, which had deteriorated during the war. "I have struggled with my chronic bronchitis for three years already," she explained. "I will seriously carry out the doctor's orders. I have severely neglected my illness. The critical issue of tuberculosis. Tomorrow Madame Sassoon will come. I think she will bring me something to eat. As soon as the weather improves, I will get better. It is impossible to get treatment."[666] A week later, she reported some hopeful news: "I have very inflamed lungs at their base. It does not matter if I receive treatment or not because it is chronic. . . . Armand Kohn recommended to me a radiologist, Dr. Lifschits. Maybe as a result of the treatment, I will still get better."[667] But her illness continued to linger and perhaps even got worse. On 9 June 1944, she complained: "I am very tired from coughing. I am alone all day in a room in this small hotel. I cough all night and often wake up. I need to think of something for this. How soon will it be possible to treat this? It is difficult to think of something."[668]

Problems with her health and finances were compounded by Zinaida's anxiety about the fate of her family and friends. As the status of the Jews in France deteriorated, Zinaida kept a diary to make sense of the chaos swirling around her, keeping track of the location and welfare of each individual. The massive roundup of Jews in Paris began following the Soviet Union's entrance into the war, which spelled catastrophe for Zinaida's family. In 1943, "Baby [Benjamin] disappeared without a trace after his arrest and transport to Nancy and then to an unknown place in Germany."[669] On 8 April 1944, Zinaida received news from her sister Khaia and Georges in Florence and was hopeful that they would be safe. "The rest of the members of our family are now scattered," she wrote. "As soon as the war ends, we will lower the count. Probably only three sisters and two brothers will remain."[670] A month later, she was alarmed because "I have not received any news about Khaia for a long time already here." She tried to reassure herself: "It is good that she and Georges remained in Italy. What they live on now, I do not know because they do not have revenues."[671]

Zinada was grieved when two of her brothers died during the war in France: Aleksandr, who had fled to the south, passed away in Nice in 1942, and Il'ia died in a freak accident and was buried in Neuilly-sur-Seine. "Poor Il'iusha perished as a victim of his own carelessness," she wrote. He had recommended that Zinaida switch to gas appliances in her house, and "other people around me also recommended that I do this. He [Il'iusha] fell asleep and left a saucepan on the stove and it overflowed." The water put out the flame, and her brother died from the toxic fumes of the gas. While she mourned his death, Zinaida could not help but resent the fact that her brother did not leave part of his estate to Annette (who, as we shall see below, needed the resources after the war) but rather opted to leave everything to his other nieces Olga and Elizabeth (Jacques's daughters).[672] She hoped that Il'ia's partner, Countess de Buffon, would support them after the war.[673] Zinaida's brother Mikhail had died in Brussels, but she kept in touch with his widow, Vera Nikolaevna, as often as she could[674] and wrote: "Poor Misha, in Brussels in a temporary grave. Maybe after the war I will be able to move him."[675] Ensuring that each brother had a proper gravestone became her main preoccupation after the war.

As she contemplated the welfare of her family, Zinaida regretted not moving to Switzerland to be with her youngest sister. "Poor Raia is completely alone in Geneva," she wrote on 22 May 1944. "I will be glad to see her again." She suddenly remembered that she had forgotten to send birthday wishes to Raia, "who is very sick."[676] Zinaida also fretted about the fate of her brother Jacques's family, with whom she had lost touch for a long time: "It is unknown where Keta [Claire] and Lili [Elizabeth] are now."[677] Unbeknown to her, they had already been deported to the Auschwitz-Birkenau camp in the fall of 1942.[678] Zinaida found out on 5 June 1944 that "Elizabeth and her mother have been deported somewhere."[679] Fortunately, Claire's daughter Olga Lindenbaum had moved safely to America after her marriage to Leo Lindenbaum, while the youngest daughter, Marie Hélène, had died in 1940 at the age of twenty-eight.[680] Zinaida received more bad news about her relatives on 13 May 1944:

"Liulia Varshavskaia [Alice Warshawsky] was interned near Bourdeau." "Lazar [Iakovlevich]'s son Mitia [Dmitrii] and his wife have been deported."[681] Two of her cousins died in Biarritz, which had recently undergone heavy bombing. On 8 April 1944 she reported: "Biarritz suffered very heavily as a result of the bombing. . . . Officially, 113 were killed and many injured. I am very sad about our dear Biarritz."[682] One year before this disaster, Samuil Iakovlevich Poliakov had died at this favorite sea resort.[683] "Niuta [Anna] is buried with her husband [Grigorii Rubinshtein] in Biarritz," Zinaida explained. "She built a burial vault beforehand for both of them. Grieved by the death of her husband [in 1929], she led a secluded life."[684] Her cousin Daniil [Kotia] Poliakoff's wife Alma had taken her own life in 1940.[685] As her losses mounted, Zinaida mourned her beloved family: "My brothers, unfortunately, are almost no more. We were eight people, but now, maybe only two remain. What a misfortune that they have all disappeared! Now only Khaia, Raia, and me alone are left."[686]

The noose tightening around the Jews caused Zinaida great consternation, especially since she had evaded the deportations: "The Jews are all hiding now. They will probably arrest them. . . . They are catching Jews (like rats) on the streets."[687] She observed that the "Jewish question is becoming more and more acute,"[688] and soon "the Christians will be left without the Semites."[689] For instance, in Vittel, she noticed that "here, Jews are absolutely not visible, and I have not seen a single [yellow] star."[690] She bemoaned how "the Jews suffer from expropriations. Hardly any of them will return home."[691] Zinaida castigated people who collaborated with the Nazis, like "Madam Wolf who probably handed over Zoberheim." Describing the latter as a member of a "fifth column," she convinced herself that "time will reveal everything that she did during the war. Previously, she did favors, but all this was only a deception."[692] She also had harsh words for Jews like Marthe Emden (1862–1945),[693] who "lives alone and has three servants" but refused to help her: "For some reason, Emden does not want to know me. It is simply inconceivable what a boor she is. She needs to suffer and no one must acknowledge her. Strangers are far more courteous than family."[694]

The absence of her Parisian friends (many of whom were related to her distantly by marriage) left a gaping hole in Zinaida's life, which had revolved around the intimacy of friendships and salon culture. Perhaps recording the most recent news about her social circle helped Zinaida to keep track of the scattered remnants:

25 February 1944: "They deported Philippe Halphen to Silesia.[695] . . . Almost all the Rothschilds left for America at the beginning of the

war. They will probably remain there until the end of the military hostilities. Oppenheim and Propper are in Cannes at their estates. Irene [Monferrato] bought a dacha there as well and lives with her mother and husband. Katherine Raffalovich [née Lightner] left for the United States after the death of Koli [Nicholas Raffalovich]."[696]

9 April 1944: "Fabienne de Villain and her husband are spending Passover in Monte Carlo. It must be very pleasant there now. . . . Dreyfus and his mother are in Monte Carlo now. . . . T. Blumenthal is in the free zone with the family. The Brodskiis were deported for labor. . . . Nobel and Gintsburg were in Nice. Ida Helbronner and her brother are in the free zone."[697]

14 April 1944: "Dreyfus of Basel [Switerland] is taking in the entire family of Gintsburgs."[698]

2 May 1944: "Alexandra Raffalovich does not send news about herself. The barons Levi[699] all reassembled in the United States. Suffice it to say, [George] Landau probably preserves their interests. [Reuben] Gubbay laughed at him but he forged a good partnership, despite his idiotism."[700]

18 May 1844: "Leo Lindenbaum [husband of her niece Olga Poliakoff] is in the United States. They deported Lorsch and Hochstadter a long time ago."[701]

28 May 1944: "Esther [Bensliman] Oulman is in Lisbon with her son and relatives.[702] Her one son died when he was a young man. . . . Gaston Rueff is in Indochina (with his new wife)."[703]

Reminiscing about old elite Russian families like the Brodkiis and Gintsburgs brought Zinaida both pleasure and sadness as she sat alone waiting for news:

Bibka [Anna] Prevot is married a second time to a surgeon [Robert Merle d'Aubigné].[704] Before, she was married to her father's friend [Vladimir Gintsburg]. The rest of her brothers and sisters are also settled. The only Jew is her brother-in-law Valabrègue, a relative of Dreyfus. Volodia [Vladimir] Gintsburg had three daughters and one son. [Jules] Dreyfus in Basel is married to the sister [Marie] of the deceased Clara Gintsburg. He is probably doing a lot for their family now. The rest—each for himself, of course. Keta [Claire Poliakoff] very much praised her deceased cousin Clara. Getia alone is confined with her husband in Brussels.[705] The Gintsburgs are all scattered.[706]

Zinaida finally received a telegram from her daughter in Vittel that they would be repatriated to England, and she prepared hastily to leave the war behind her. She described this episode of her life in her diary but also in an essay titled "My Journey to England during War-Time," which she wrote in English after the war in the hope of getting it published: "On the 18th of April 1944, I received a telegram from my daughter from the internees' camp in Vittel that we were [to be] exchanged. Thereupon I immediately telephoned my doctor asking his advice whether I could undertake this tiring journey. I received a favorable answer and engaged my old Italian cook [Serafina] to accompany me to Vittel."[707] The prisoner exchange process entailed a meeting with Nazi authorities and the journey to Vittel, which proved to be quite an ordeal:

> Receiving a telephonic [sic] call from the Gestapo in Paris to call upon them as soon as possible, I went to 74 Avenue Foch and was received by a German officer who announced to me that my daughter was [to be] exchanged, whereupon I asked him whether I was authorized to [go to] her in Vittel in order to accompany her. According to this, he told me that I could do so. Therefore I decided to leave Paris for Nancy the day after and left by the Gare de Lyon. I did the journey very well, although during the night there was the bombardment of the Chaumont and they stopped our train and put out all the lights. During the 24 hours I spent in Nancy, they told me that the next train for Vittel would leave the day after. Taking a room at the Hotel d'Angleterre, I started the next morning for Vittel. Arriving there a few hours later, I settled down at the Hotel des Tilleuls. I met my daughter in the afternoon. Nobody had the permission to see their [sic] relatives more than once a week. Having announced myself to the Gestapo, I was told that my daughter would meet me there in the afternoon.[708]

As soon as Zinaida arrived in Vittel, she was arrested for attempting to communicate with Annette from across the street. The sentry informed her that it was forbidden to talk to the internees. She was released an hour later but was terribly annoyed. When she finally reunited with her only daughter, Annette broke the bad news to her mother: "Since then I heard that the repatriation would not take place at the present time as England had to close her frontiers. Till a new order would issue [sic], one had to wait [in] Vittel." Regretting her decision to bring her cook with her, Zinaida wrote in her diary: "Tomorrow, Serafina will return to Paris. There was no need for this expenditure on her. There is nothing to do here: this is a big prison."[709] As a farewell gift, Zinaida gave Serafina her fur coat, only to realize later that she would not have a winter coat if their repatriation were delayed. "I have no one who can help me now," she wrote in resignation.[710]

Taking stock of her surroundings, Zinaida found the contradictions of the internment camp disconcerting: "There are a great number of children here: in general, all nationalities and ages. The greenery is fresh; Germans are on every corner; Italians. The lovely lilacs are blooming, and our hotel is under lime trees."[711] The radio kept warning people to stay away from the railway stations, which were targets for Allied bombing, but life had a strange semblance of normalcy: "Yesterday I went to eat ice cream. The circus is in Vittel. I do not know who goes there."[712] Nonetheless Zinaida was shocked to see barbed wire and prison bars in a place that she had always associated with spa culture: "This place should be very lively during the hydropathic season. Few people of modest means could receive treatment here because of the high prices. As a result even now the hotels are expensive. . . . It is hard to imagine what Vittel is. Sirens are not heard here, but there is a mass of soldiers. Marvelous greenery and amazing air. . . . Pale prisoners behind iron bars."[713] Even prisoners (mainly American and Latin American citizens) who arrived from the Warsaw ghetto in 1943 found the barbed wires very jarring. The writer Itzhak Katzenelson explained in his *Vittel Diary*: "I looked out of the window and saw a barbed-wire all along the length of the opposite pavement. . . . Although I have come from Warsaw, this fence creates a painful impression."[714] Zinaida imagined that "Ruby would have been upset to see Annette among the prisoners. . . . Other camps are still much worse, and it is impossible to complain too much. It would be better to say that I am very upset about this."[715] She longed to see one of their acquaintances among the Polish Jewish internees but saw only desperate prisoners: "Poor things, many of them have tried to take their own lives. There, a doctor's wife tried to throw herself out the window—an isolated case that is very sad."[716]

Their circumstances became further complicated when Annette dislocated her foot during an excursion with the other internees, leading to her transfer to a hospital in Nancy.[717] Zinaida accompanied her daughter to Nancy and stayed in a hotel during her two-month recovery. Nancy was under heavy bombardment when the Gubbays arrived at the train station. "It is difficult to imagine the catastrophe of the bombing of the station," Zinada wrote on 12 May 1944.[718] "The powerful bombs destroy everything around." She faced the impossible task of finding a hotel that was located farther from the train station—a tall order, since the Nazis had requisitioned almost all the hotels. She blamed "the crude Americans" who do not discriminate "and "throw bombs wherever they fall."[719] In contrast, she praised the Soviet Red Army, which she predicted would come out on top at the end: "The Russians carry on like lions."[720]

In her haste to be reunited with her daughter, Zinaida had neither made proper financial arrangements for the trip nor packed her luggage properly. She had not anticipated being delayed for two months in Nancy and feared running out of money even while she was in Vittel: "I am extremely anxious about my financial position. I paid Weisel for her bag that she sold to me. I, of course, did not surmise that I would be left without a penny. It's an extreme pity that Annette has upset me. I am waiting with impatience for the arrival of the funds from the bank."[721] Dealing with her finances from afar was far more challenging than she had imagined. On 8 June 1944, she wrote in Nancy: "Armand Kohn sent me a telegram yesterday about the money. It is extremely disagreeable that a change of address slowed down the sending [of the money]. Nothing was foreseen, and I am without a penny this month."[722] A week later, Zinaida was satisfied that "Armand Kohn—is the only one who helps me. . . . Armand fulfilled all of my instructions thoroughly. His musical daughter Rose-Marie asked for cigarettes."[723] To obtain some funds, Zinaida asked Countess de Buffon (her brother Il'ia's partner) to sell her ermine blanket. "They will sell all my other possessions," she concluded.[724] She looked to Reuben's sisters for assistance, reassuring herself: "I think that Flora will send me money for expenses. As soon as the circumstances improve, all will be well."[725] After much anxiety, the monetary assistance finally arrived, and Zinaida decided, "I must purchase rubber stockings for myself without fail when I change the money that I received from [my sister-in-law] Flora."[726] She also anticipated funds from Adolphe Oppenheim's son-in-law, Marcel Goldshmidt, who had established an account for her, but he had not been in touch.[727] She needed her pension to pay for her hotel bills and food.

Zinaida felt even more isolated in Nancy, where she hardly knew anyone: "Life moves slowly. In Nancy, there are no acquaintances. Silence in the room, and I am in solitude the entire day." She had a few visitors, like Madame Fru-hingolz or Regina Clurrson—who sent her groceries[728]—but she could not engage in her former leisure activities. "My vision is severely weakening," she admitted. "It is a torment to read; it is better not to pay attention to this. I do not like to read foreign books; i.e., I read slowly. I completed the novel, *Argyle*, which is very interesting. I have not read Russian books in a long time. I don't read anything except for French books now."[729] She must have also missed doing her crossword puzzles: in 1902, she had been so proud when "today I read my name among those who received an honorable mention for solving a puzzle. Out of 4500! 300 people received [the mention]. . . ." The winner, "it goes without saying," was a French novelist.[730] Having been surrounded by friends and family, she complained: "A quiet life is too monotonous for me." She corresponded with friends like Suzanne and Armand Kohn, but soon even the letters from Paris ceased to arrive, which Zinaida attributed to the bombings.

Finally, Annette's foot healed sufficiently to warrant their return to Vittel, and their repatriation to England began just hours after their motorcar arrived at the camp. Annette was to be exchanged for a General von Armhem [Arnim], "a prisoner at Trent Park, which belonged to Mrs. David Gubbay, Annette's aunt Hannalia [Hannah Gubbay]."[731] Hannah had inherited the mansion at Trent Park from her relative Philip Sassoon in 1939, only to have it requisitioned during the war "as a residence for airmen (because of the airfield nearby) both British and foreign."[732] She may have played a role in the exchange of her niece because she was so well connected to members of the British government.

According to Zinaida, trains in Vittel were rare in those days, so they had to take a motorbus for the first part of their trip, which was "most disagreeable." Among the travelers on the train on the next leg of their journey was a Swiss delegate "who was appointed to conduct the English internees to the frontier." On their first day, the heavy rain brought down some big trees, and the party had to stop to clear them to continue their journey. But this was the least of their problems: "Till we crossed the Rhone, we were not at all certain of our safety. What happened at Saiacaise [sic] is this: American bombers came to bombard a German train with petroleum, which was stopping next to ours. Hearing the alert, we all came out of the train and laid [sic] down in the fields. Till the bombardment stopped, we remained lying down there and noticed that all the new-mown [sic] hay was on fire, and our cars also."[733] The authorities informed the travelers that the luggage train had burned and had damaged one of the cars next to Zinaida's. She observed that many of the passengers suffered nervous attacks. Now the frightened party traveled only by night and stopped in the fields during the day. When they reached Station Marguerity in the south of France, they had to transfer to motorcars because the railroad was destroyed. In Madrid, Spain, the English ambassador welcomed the repatriated British citizens and presented them with twenty cigarettes each. From there, Zinaida traveled in a sleeping car for the aged and infirm to Portugal, where a Red Cross representative met them. "On our arrival in Lisbon, the British colony [there] greeted us and offered us a magnificent lunch" and presented them with useful toiletries. Zinaida called a friend (probably Esther Oulman, who lived in Lisbon), who came "almost at once" to the station and "offered us hospitality during the ten days" until the next transport took them to Liverpool. In the meantime, Zinaida and Annette sent a telegram to relatives to send money but received it only when they disembarked in England.

During their first three days in England, they stayed at the Adelphi Hotel and then moved to the country estate in Popes Manor (Bracknell) of Zinaida's sister-in-law Mozelle Sassoon. Zinaida's first diary entry in England, dated 16 August 1944, relived the terrifying bombing that they had experienced on the trip from France. "Not surprisingly, . . . after this, we need rest," she wrote. "Only I prefer to be at home. The furious bombadiers are always flying above us."[734] Although the Gubbays had escaped the nightmare in France and landed safely with their relatives, the war was not over.

After the initial adjustment, Zinaida's most pressing problem was to find a place to live, and she first relied on the generous hospitality of family members. In Liverpool, she visited a Poliakov relative—her Uncle Iakov's great-granddaughter Vera Poliakoff (1911–92), a Shakespearean actress who went by the stage name Vera Lindsay.[735] Her father, Vladimir (Volodia) Poliakoff, Zinaida noted proudly, "is Lazar [Iakovlevich]'s son in England; he was a reporter for the *Times* but now writes for provincial newspapers."[736] Known by his pseudonym "Auger," Vladimir was a respected diplomatic correspondent until he became the "center of public controversy in 1937 when he sold the German émigré newspaper *Pariser Tagenblatt* of which he was [the publisher]," prompting the editor Georg Bernard to accuse him of selling out to Nazi interests. Vladimir not only vehemently denied the accusations but also pursued libel suits against any paper that dared to publish Bernard's allegations.[737] According to *Life* magazine in 1938, he was an austere man: "He neither smokes nor drinks, gets up at 5:30, goes to bed at midnight, and has insomnia. He has two Afghan hounds called Rib (for the German Foreign Minister, Ribbentrop) and Rab (for Rabinovich for fun)." The article added that Vladimir admired "power politics, Mussolini, big doings, tough talk, and Britain's imperial mission."[738] Mireille, the wife of Vladimir's grandson Richard Burton, described him as "a terrifying figure."[739] Vladimir's daughter Vera was first married to Major Percy Basil Harmsworth Burton and then to Sir Gerald Barry, the editor of the *News Chronicle* and director general of the Festival of Britain.

Apart from visits to Vera Poliakoff, the Gubbays spent most of their time at Mozelle Sassoon's estate in Popes Manor, which suited neither Zinaida nor Annette as they did not like living in the countryside. "We will probably move from here [Popes Manor] to Forkey," explained Zinaida. "Madame Burton will remain in Liverpool. . . . Lady Burton is a very sweet woman: a lot of assets but no cash in hand."[740] On 21 September 1944, they relocated to Brighton, where they stayed for about two months. "No one stays here long," observed Zinaida. "The winter season in Brighton seems extremely harsh. The sea wind is extremely unpleasant but healthy—i.e., drives away microbes." But Zinaida's health deteriorated in the windy climate. "I am coughing severely still, un-

FIGURE 14
Zinaida Lazarevna
Poliakova-Gubbay.
Poliakova and Poliakoff,
Sem'ia Poliakovykh.

fortunately," she lamented. As lovely as it was to live by the seaside, she was dissatisfied with their living conditions and worried about how the sea air affected Annette's nephritis (an inflammation of the kidneys). "The garden here is small, and the rooms [in the hotel] are disgusting," grumbled Zinaida. "It will be impossible to remain in them during the winter, in my opinion. . . . We have made a mess of things here, not having good accommodations in the hotel. The place is pretty but the food is bad. The sun shines sometimes, and it is fortunately still not very cold as it tends to be on the seashore. And after the doodlebugs [Vergeltungswaffen bombs],[741] we want to move to London. It is impossible to find anything now; yesterday we asked an agent, but it was all useless, of course."[742] Annette wanted to move to London where opportunities and friends beckoned. "We must move from this hotel to another," Zinaida reasoned, "because they do not want to support us anymore."[743] It was unclear who was reluctant to help pay the hotel bills in Brighton, but Zinaida felt that it was time to move. "It is hard to live without means," she concluded sadly.[744] "No news from Paris; almost all my things remain there, and I do not know if they will be returned."[745]

Their trip to London to explore new prospects proved to be both fruitful and painful because of the constant reminders of the war. Zinaida had lunch with Mozelle's daughter, Violet FitzGerald (née Sassoon),[746] at the Hotel Ritz and learned that her son "Desmond FitzGerald has been lightly wounded in the knee and Jack d'Avigdor Goldsmid in the head; Alice d'Avigdor Goldsmid is in Leicester where [her son] is in the hospital."[747] Zinaida was very fond of her cousin Isabella's daughter Alice Goldsmid, "who is very friendly to me."[748] She also had breakfast with her old friends Mozelle Hayeem (1855–1952), who was "completely deaf" as she was almost ninety years old, and Louise Boyle, describing to them her and Annette's journey to England. "I want to publish it in some newspaper," wrote Zinaida. "It's not likely they will remunerate me [for the article]."[749] After meeting with the manager of the Hotel Rembrandt, who agreed to give them "a suite of rooms for an extended time," the Gubbays decided to move right away to London: "Our second apartment will be in Hotel Rembrandt on Brompton Road, not far from Hyde Park Hotel. We were there not long ago and found a suite of rooms, consisting of two rooms, another room, bathrooms and a salon. It is a little expensive for us. But Annette arranged with Mozelle to supplement our rent. One does not hear sirens here."[750] Although Zinaida complained that it was not "comfortable to live in a hotel," she expressed some optimisim that "perhaps we will finally be settled somewhere in England."[751] As she walked down the streets, she observed happily that Paris had migrated with her to London. "It is impossible to turn around and not hear the French language now," she exclaimed. Zinaida even found an excellent hairdresser—Antoine from Paris—who was in great demand.

Unfortunately, the doodlebugs that the Gubbays had desired to escape in Brighton followed them to London. On 19 October 1944, Zinaida reported that the Germans had bombed the city at night. "Annette excitedly explained when I woke up: she heard the explosions of the bombs. Previously, they had not flown up to London.[752] The rest of the 'doodlebugs' perished at sea. The others, no. 3 and 4, it appears are prepared to attack England. And the entire night, they sounded the alarm with sirens." The bombing hit too close to home for Ziniada, who learned that the destruction directly affected her family: "The city was destroyed in different quarters. Entire streets with houses have been destroyed: everyone suffered a lot. The houses of Mozelle [Hayeem], Violet [FitzGerald] and Hannah [Gubbay] were all destroyed. They had proposed that we move to the Service Flats on Hertford Street across the street from Hannah. All the houses there were destroyed, [and] it will be unpleasant to live there now."[753] Zinaida's friends, who had recommended this prestigious neighborhood, clearly did not realize how limited her resources were since Nazis had confiscated her assets in Paris. Finding a residence that she could afford and, more importantly, where Annette would agree to live, proved to be challenging.

Although she was preoccupied with housing, Zinaida was even more weighed down by fears about the fate of her family members. "I know nothing about Khaia," she wrote anxiously. "She was in Florence. When she left from there is unknown. Visha must be somewhere in the south probably."[754] She was alarmed when the post office returned her letter to Khaia in October 1944. During the Jewish holidays, thoughts about her family tormented her: "It is terrible to think about where our family members are. It is simply incomprehensible that there is not any news about them. No one knows where they are sending the deportees. But, of course, it is probably not very good."[755] Due to the chaos of her trip to England, "I forgot to inform Khaia about our safe arrival here. Will she surmise this or not?"[756] She also remembered, "Baby [Benjamin] spent the last Yom Kippur in Paris with me before they arrested and deported him. Now, God knows, is he alive or not?" The fate of her youngest sister in Switzerland also worried her: "I am waiting hungrily to receive news from Raia. Her life in Geneva is extremely difficult."[757] A few days later, she became increasingly worried about her sister's welfare: "I am very worried about poor Raia. Her address there has remained the same. I wrote to Mimi Halphen to inqure about her at her maid Marta's, who took good care of her."[758]

By the time Zinaida wrote her final diary in 1948, she had discovered the fate of her family through extensive inquiries to the Red Cross and other organizations. "Baby [Benjamin] disappeared after his arrest and [was] transported to Nancy and then to Germany, somewhere unknown," she reported. The records reveal that Benjamin de Poliakoff "had been deported from Drancy Transit Camp to Auschwitz on Convey 46 on 9 February 1943"—a fact she learned closer to 1950.[759] Coming to terms with the cold reality of her sister's fate, Zinaida wrote: "It is an empty hope to see Khaia and Georges again; they both perished in Auschwitz. They arrested them in Florence."[760] According to the records of Yad Vashem and the Claims Resolution Tribunal, Khaia and her husband, Georges, were first detained in the Fossoli Concentration Camp in early April 1944 and then deported to Auschwitz, where they were both killed on 10 April 1944.[761] This is why Zinaida had not received any news from them. "Khaia's friends in Italy did not help her hide from their [the Nazis'] mad savagery," she wrote angrily.[762] What she demanded to learn from the Red Cross was "did they suffer or not?"[763] Zinaida discovered that her cousin Isabella's son George and his wife, Lina Landau (née Levi), who had hid at their rural estate near Florence, had been more fortunate and somehow evaded the deportations. Among all of Zinaida's siblings, only her sister Raisa had survived the war, but before Zinaida could visit her, "poor Raia died suddenly from a heart attack last Monday on 26 April [1948]." Fears of traveling alone and her inability to obtain Swiss francs prevented Zinaida from attending Raisa's funeral. "I no longer have anyone left in my family now, unfortunately. Yesterday, they buried her in Geneva for sure," mourned Zinaida.[764] She grieved over the unknown graves of seven relatives who were deported to Auschwitz.[765]

During the war—but especially after her harrowing journey to England—Zinaida paid closer attention to religious holidays and rituals, which brought her comfort and organized her chaotic sense of time: "The memory of my deceased parents will be [observed] on the great fast of Yom Kippur. Before then, I will go by the synagogue and give the names of everyone. The day of the great fast will be Wednesday. I must go to pray."[766] As the last remaining member of her immediate family, Zinaida felt a tremendous sense of responsibility to honor their memories: "Unfortunately, I did not fast yesterday on Yom Kippur. I heard nothing at the time of the prayers for the deceased at the synagogue. But, of course, they pronounced the names of my family. Apart from me, no one prays for them now."[767] She even wrote about God in a personal way, which she had not done in her Paris diaries: "I believe in God's mercy, that he will yet give me life."[768] At the same time, Zinaida still chafed against the strict laws that governed the Jewish holidays, as she had done as a young woman in Russia: "For sure, I go to synagogue. In truth, I do not observe the holidays at the present time. It's nonsense—the prohibition to travel and write on the days of our holidays and on the Sabbath."[769] In fact, she confessed to violating a Jewish holiday for her personal care needs: "Simhas Torah is today, and I regret that I accepted a rendezvous with the hairdresser Antoine. It is difficult to get him and thus I did not want to put it off. The Jewish holidays end today until Hanukkah, only in December, on the eve of Papa and Baby's birthdays. Purim is in March and after that the month of our Passover."[770] Zinaida regretted the loss of her old Jewish calendar, which had included all the important dates of family life events.

During this difficult adjustment to her new life, Zinaida's relationship with her daughter became severely strained. In part, she blamed Annette's problems on the trauma that she had experienced in the Vittel during the war: "Annette cannot forget her internment. The strong nervous shock has made her very irritable. No one can contradict her about anything now. But, of course, Mozelle can argue with her."[771] Zinaida recalled that recently films had been shown "depicting the arrival of a steamer with immigrants from the camps." Annette "sat for a long time in the cinema" but did not see her fellow inmates from Vittel on the screen.[772] Still, Zinaida could not help but comment, "The ideal daughter—is not Annette, of course. Other children take care of their elderly parents. Yes, of course, the internment has made her still more embittered. It is an extreme pity that she did not get married when there was time."[773]

Annette's "failure" to get married was deeply disappointing to Zinaida, who desired to see her daughter settled and financially secure. When the proposed match with Nissim Camondo vanished with his death in World War I, there were very few potential grooms in their small, elite social circle. She recalled that their friend Dr. Bandaline "made efforts to find grooms for [my brother] Jacques's daughters and only Olga got settled extremely well. It is good that she married Leo Lindenbaum from Vienna and now resides in New York."[774] Like her cousins Hélène and Lily, Annette could not find a suitable partner. Naturally, Zinaida could not help but envy family members who had married well and even had grandchildren: "Edward Sassoon's daughter, Sybil [Cholmondeley] has already become a grandmother through her oldest son [George] Hugh. Gray [haired], she is a little older than Annette but well settled; now everyone is getting married."[775] She marveled at Francine Halphen (sister of Philippe and Fabienne Halphen, mentioned above) who had married below her station: "Francine is well settled in England. Her courage allowed her to get married. There is a difference between high and low society. She grew up among Rothschilds and married a self-made man [Charles Clore]. Only one thing remains—it is not known where [her brother] Philippe is." It bears noting that Francine's marriage did not last long, partly because she was homesick for France, according to her daughter.[776] Although Annette attemped do meaningful social work after the war, her mother saw it as only a distraction from the serious task of finding a spouse. "Annette will probably return here from Paris to finish her business with the lawyers. But now she is traveling to the hospital to inspect the children for the government. Only all of this is not her business," Zinaida complained.[777] "It is important to prolong my existence! Annette remained an old maid and dreams about the past. The shallowness of her life! She is already fifty-two years old now, and there is little chance that she will get married. Living life is not like crossing a field [life is not easy] as the Russian saying goes."[778] As she got closer to her eighty-seventh birthday, Zinaida was critical of Annette for not trying hard enough: "The shallowness of Annette's life taught her to think only of external beauty; all the rest interests her but little. Her life flowed by without any serious acts and, unfortunately, she did not marry. If she would still meet someone suitable, I would be very happy to know that she is settled."[779] Like a good meddling mother, Zinaida had some prospects in mind: "Baron de Worms [sic] will have breakfast with Annette in London. He takes great care of her. He must be hopeful of persuading her to marry him." Clearly, Annette resented her mother's constant interference in her love life, prompting Zinaida to protest: "I courageously endure Annette's disgusting treatment of me. She curses and fights. Why—this is incomprehensible to me. I did everything for her to get married and she reproaches me about this."[780]

Zinaida's expectation that Annette would move to Paris to take care of her proved to be another thorny issue of contention. They lived in England in the period 1944–48 in various locations. A diary entry in early 1948 mentioned that "this is our second year in London, and instead of an improvement, there is nothing unfortunately for now." For Zinaida, the grass seemed much greener on the Parisian side: "Absolutely no one remains alive from our former friends and acquaintances. However, the French climate and way of life in Paris is more pleasant for me all the same, of course. It is an extreme pity that Annette insists on settling in England for social work. It would be desirable for her to change her mind and rent a small apartment in Paris for us both. She does not like Brighton and the London climate is harmful for me, and I was sick all the time with bronchitis."[781] Zinaida longed for the prewar years, holding onto every connection to the past: "Not long ago [in 1947], Henri Rothschild died near Lausanne. I sent [his daughter] Nadine Thierry a telegram of condolence. It is a major loss for her; now, the only one who remains of the old [generation] is Edouard [Alphonse James de Rothschild, 1868–1949]. True, the young are not interested like all new generations; it is difficult to reconcile with this."[782] Annette, like many survivors of the internment camp, had little time to pine for the past as she struggled to survive in the new postwar world.

Eventually, Zinaida moved back to Paris on her own just before Passover in 1948, hoping that Annette would follow. Instead, her daughter "rented an apartment for herself in the detached house of Dulcie Sassoon [in London]."[783] Dulcie was the daughter-in-law of Zinaida's old friend Louise Gintzburg (whose marriage to Joseph Sassoon was mentioned in her Moscow diaries). Zinaida was convinced that Annette was working hand in glove with Mozelle Sassoon to force her back to London and lamented: "I live alone, without servants, and my daughter does not acknowledge me." She was resentful of Annette for uprooting her from the life that she was accustomed to living: "Ruby and I lived here for forty years. Annette takes into her head to move to London—what for?"[784] Zinada was glad at least to have her brother Aleksandr's widow Clara in France (although she lived in Versailles at the time) as well as some old friends: "Apart from Clara Solomonovich [Visha], I have no other family members here. Annette will not return from London. Of course, this worries me. . . . Edouard Helbronner's widow [Cècile Paule Marthe] came by to see me, but I was not home and then her sister Denise [Marie-Louise] Goldschmidt came by."[785] Zinaida's loneliness was compounded by her inability "to read because my eyes are very weak, and thus I am very bored sitting alone all day in my room. I sleep badly at night and am forced to wake up every two hours unfortunately." She used to love reading French novels with Reuben, like *Le supplice d'un père* (1895) by Louis Letang—the author of *Les deux frères*, which some suggested may have inspired the tactics employed in the Dreyfus trial.[786] But she had been especially fond of novels by female authors like *Ève victorieuse* (1900) by Pierre de Coulevain (the pen name for Jeanne-Philomène Laperche)[787] and *L'amour est mon péché* (1899) by Hermine Lecomte du Nouy, which she described as a "wonderful book of masterful talent and a deep knowledge of the soul of women!"[788] Considering her dire circumstances, Zinaida concluded that "all of this would not be important if there were money."[789]

Money—or more precisely, the lack thereof—was an endless point of contention between Zinaida and Annette. At some point, Zinaida had given Annette power of attorney over their finances, which she immediately regretted because Annette put everything in her own name.[790] Having lost their apartment, furniture, and assets during the war, they sought to claim the belongings of their deceased relatives. Although Annette had assumed her debts, Zinaida became increasingly suspicious that her daughter intended to steal her money and squander it: "She [Annette] is about to go to Italy [to claim Khaia's estate] but I don't want her to travel there alone without me so that Khaia's ring does not disappear like Mama's money."[791] They traveled to Italy together but could not agree on anything. For instance, Zinaida complained that Annette "sold Khaia's estate—a diamond ring—for 5,000,000 francs when it cost then up to 10,000,000 francs. I will never get the slightest amount of the inheritance because Annette always puts everything away."[792] In another entry, she was convinced that her daughter took her money frivolously: "It is true that Annette is very carefree and puts me in a difficult position in relation to money. Just when I have a little bit of cash, she comes and takes it away."[793] However, it was clear from Zinaida's own grievances that Annette was desperate to pay off their debts. "Simon sold Annette's sealskin coat for 75,000 francs," wrote Zinaida, "which is very low in my opinion." Zinaida even admitted that creditors were hounding Annette to collect their debts: "The conspiracy against Annette in London continues; she must go there to settle her affairs."[794]

Zinaida had hoped that her sister Raisa had left some assets, but she was sorely disappointed when she arrived in Geneva in the summer of 1948. "Judging from everything, nothing will be left to anyone from Raia's inheritance because there are a lot of debts," she wrote. A visit to "Raia's empty apartment" confirmed her fears: "Apart from books and photographs, there is nothing in it, unfortunately. In addition, a mass of accumulated dust is everywhere. I was there once, and today I went to the cemetery with Marta [Raisa's maid]. Baron [de] Hirsch of Basel must come to inspect the books."[795] Raisa was supposed to be buried next to her husband, Adolphe, but Zinaida explained that it was "dangerous to move [her] there now." Instead, she decided it was better "to establish a suitable grave for her in the Cemetery Verrier." Having spent a month in Geneva to sort out Raisa's estate, Zinaida began to run out of money: "I need to rely on God's mercy because I only have forty francs left in my pocket from the money [given to me] by the notary. Not long ago, Annette telephoned me that she would send the entire check [of 100,000 francs], but I have received not one centime, and she wanted to send the rent. . . . Apart from the notary, no one wants to care about my hopeless situation! A few days remain until my trip from Lausanne to Paris, but I have not paid anything to the hotel."[796]

This would not be the last time that Zinaida had to negotiate her hotel bill, much to her great humiliation. "My funds are slow to arrive," she wrote, very agitated. "I am very worried about today's meeting with the director [manager] of the hotel. Its results will be extremely important to me. I hope for a successful outcome." She was upset that no one offered to help her, especially her old friend Armand Kohn: "Armand Kohn and his new wife [Margrethe, née Pederson] are on vacation. Yes, he did nothing to help me during the time of the occupation," she wrote, conveniently forgetting how she had praised him for being the only person to provide her with assistance.[797] At least this time, Zinaida seemed to have managed to work out a plan with the hotel manager, because she was already planning to fix her teeth when she arrived in Paris in September. She also wanted to spend Rosh Hashanah in Biarritz as was the family custom, but she wrote, "Of course, Annette will not agree to accompany me; she lives like a free young woman."[798]

However, it was clear that Annette could no longer fend off their creditors, let alone send money to her mother for her expenses (such as a month's worth of hotel fees and living expenses). On 13 August 1948, the *London Gazette* announced her bankruptcy hearing: "Gubbay, Annette (Spinster), 3 Holland Park, London w 11 of independent means. Court—HIGH COURT OF JUSTICE.

No. of Matter—195 of 1948. Date of First meeting—August 25, 1948, 12 noon. Place—Bankruptcy Buildings, Carey Street, London w c 2. Date of Public Examination—October 21, 1948, 11 a.m. Place—Bankruptcy Building, Carey Street. London w c 2."[799]

Annette's address indicates that she lived in a fashionable neighborhood where several Sassoon relatives resided—including the writer Siegfried Sassoon, at 23 Camden Hill Square (in Holland Park), and Sybil Cholmondeley, who acquired 12 Kensington Palace Gardens in the "millionaires' row."[800] On 19 October 1948, the court appointed a trustee, Torquil Macleod, and a certified accountant, John Murdoch of 4 Bucklebury, London, to settle Annette's affairs.[801] It is unclear how she resolved her debts, but it is evident from Zinaida's diary (in an entry dated around the last few months of 1949) that Annette was still struggling with their finances because she was "summoned back often to London regarding her [financial] affairs."[802] Although Reuben's wealthy family clearly helped them with rent and other expenses, they did not intervene to save the Gubbays from bankruptcy. Zinaida clearly felt that they could have done more: "No one helps us, unfortunately; everyone only thinks about oneself."[803]

Zinaida did not live long enough to obtain restitution for the Nazis' confiscation of their apartment and other assets. Having lived in Paris most of her adult life, Zinaida was determined to spend her last years in her beloved city full of memories: "I am going to settle again in Paris if God still gives me life for some time. I have but few means, and I am only able to take a room with a living room and bathroom in a small hotel. I do not intend to kill myself, so I want to get a decent place so that I can receive friends. . . . In a few months I will be eighty-seven years old."[804] Zinaida remained disappointed with her daughter as the the last two pages of her final diary reveal: "The repulsive attitude of Annette to the memory of my family disgusts me, although she acquired a lot from them. . . . Between Annette and myself there is not the slightest intimacy, unfortunately; I feel very bad now."[805] After she visited the lonely grave of Raisa—the last of her siblings to pass away—Zinaida became suddenly aware that "I remain one of the last of our family."[806] Living with Annette in France (who must have been persuaded to return sometime around 1950–52), Zinaida received the final insult, which she recorded in the last few lines of her diary: "Not long ago, I received from the director [manager] of this hotel a bill of 300,000 francs for the second half of our stay. I am falling over from exhaustion."[807]

Zinaida, who had lived a life of distinction among the most elite Jewish families in Europe, found herself completely in debt. However, she had one

FIGURE 15
Family vault of Reuben, Zinaida, and Annette Gubbay,
Montparnasse Cemetery, Paris.
Courtesy of Elizabeth Bérard.

remaining comfort: when her husband died in 1931, she had purchased a family vault in Montparnasse Cemetery—the final resting place of artists, intel-
lectuals, and wealthy elites—where she was buried in style after her death on
28 April 1952 in Grosbois.

Her life had been like the meteor that she had witnessed in Vevey, Switzerland, on 3 August 1924. As she reported to the Astronomy Society of France,
the meteor that fell from the heavens created a "whirlwind of water that

seemed to be 300 to 400 meters high."[808] Similarly, she confessed during the war: "I grew up in luxury and now find myself reduced in circumstances."[809] The devastating whirlwind had deprived her of almost everything—including her family and friends—and strained her relationship with her only daughter. Zinaida probably never imagined that she would go from being the daughter of Russia's wealthiest banker to a mere guest who owed a tremendous debt to a hotel. "It is sad to think that after my death none of my loved ones will mourn me," she wrote near the end of her final diary. Yet Zinaida left her diaries for posterity, which ended up with her relative Alexander Poliakoff, who described them as a "rare document of the social history of wealthy Russian Jews."[810] Ten diaries—in various shapes and sizes and with different locks—had survived two world wars, traveled to several countries (including Russia, France, Italy, Switzerland, and England), and eventually ended up back in Russia—donated by Alexander Poliakoff's son Sir Martyn Poliakoff to the Russian State Library in Moscow.

* * * * * * *

NOTES

Leo Tolstoy, *War and Peace*, trans. Louise and Aylmer Maude (Oxford: Oxford University Press, 2010), 1261.

1. Until 1 February 1918, Russia used the Julian (Old Style) calendar, which lagged behind that of the Gregorian calendar used in the West by twelve days in the nineteenth century and thirteen days in the twentieth. Strangely, Zinaida's grave in Paris has her birth date as 27 January 1865.

2. Reuben Gubbay (6 September 1860–1 February 1931), born in Shanghai, was the grandson of Sir Albert Abdullah David Sassoon (first Baronet of Kensington Gore). Sir Albert was the oldest son of David Sassoon (1792–1864), who served as the principal finance minister and banker to the governor of Baghdad until he fell out of political favor during the rule of the Mameluke governor Daud Pasha. The family escaped to India and established a successful economic empire in Asia in 1833. Albert Sassoon took over his father's firm and played a key role in the development of the textile industry in Bombay. He was "knighted as a member of the Star of India in 1972" for his philanthropic work in Bombay (Peter Stansky, *Sassoon: The Worlds of Philip and Sybil* [New Haven, CT: Yale University Press, 2003], 6). He and his brothers moved to England in the second half of the nineteenth century and became "central figures in the the the social life of the times . . . specifically, they joined other rich Jews such as the Rothchilds" (ibid., 12). See also Joan G. Roland, *Jews in British India: Identity in a Colonial Era* (Hanover, NH: University Press of New England, 1989), 15.

3. Aaron Moses Gubbay (Reuben's father), born in Baghdad in 1832, married Rachel Sassoon (daughter of Albert Sassoon), with whom he had six children. He was engaged in commercial enterprises as well as the family's charitable organizations. See below in the text for more details. See also "The E. D. Sassoon Benevolent Institution," *Times of India*, 11 March 1891.

According to Joan Roland, Gubbay was one of only two Baghdadis accepted into the Indian Civil Service. He retired in 1895 and died a year later in Paris (*Jews in British India*, 304 n. 88).

4. In *Vanity Fair*'s famous caricature of Sir Albert Sassoon, he received the designation "the Indian Rothschild" (*Vanity Fair*, 16 August 1879). However, Cecil Roth disagrees with the appellation, asserting that the Sassoons were "nothing of the kind" (*The Sassoon Dynasty* [London: Robert Hale, 1941], 11). In contrast to the Rothschilds, who were "essentially financiers with subsidiary interests," he argues that the Sassoons were mainly merchants. The Rothschilds were "neatly distributed among five centers" in Europe, while the Sassoons were "untidily scattered about the Levant" and "had never strayed from Asia . . . until they were brought to England in the nineteenth century." Roth also contends that the Rothschilds were "of undistinguished origins" and emerged from ordinary money changers, whereas the "progenitor of the Sassoons was a Prince in Captivity" whose descendants were "able to take their rank in Society and at Court as in the manner born. . . . [T]hey were re-entering as it were into their birthright." This narrative of the Sassoons as having descended from royalty or noble blood is reminiscent of Jewish preoccupations with royal genealogy in the Islamic Near East in the medieval period. See also Arnold E. Franklin, *This Noble House: Jewish Descendants of King David in the Medieval Islamic East* (Philadelphia: University of Pennsylvania Press, 2012).

5. Quoted in Stansky, *Sassoon*, 6.

6. Berta Abramovich, born in 1872 in Vil'na, was a talented and famous singer who received support from Zinaida's family when she began her musical career at the Moscow conservatory. Zinaida and Abramovich remained close friends throughout their lives ("Halel lezimrah," *Hatsefirah*, 22 February 1893).

7. "Nauchno-issledovatel'skii otdel rukopisei Rossiiskoi gosudarstvennoi biblioteki" (hereafter NIOR RGB), fond 743, opis' 138, delo 1, list 29 ob. The standard Russian archival notation will be used hereafter: f. (fond), op. (opis'), k. (karton), d. or dd. (delo or dela), l. or ll. (list or listy), ob. (oborot), and g. (god).

8. Ibid., ll. 30 ob.–31 (2 January 1895). Ruby later claimed that he had intended to leave her on New Year's, and Zinaida responded that she wished his desires would be fulfilled, "that I would free him and others from my useless existence on this earth" (ibid., l. 36 ob. [22 January 1895]).

9. Pierre Bourdieu's concept of habitus links practices to positions, which seems applicable to Zinaida's life (*The Logic of Practice* [Stanford, CA: Stanford University Press, 1990], 53–56).

10. "Lock and key" did exist, but only nominally. In 2016 staff members of the Manuscript Division of the Russian State Library (now custodian of the diaries) could not find the key to one diary (so that it could be opened and read), but one member was able to unlock the diary using a high-tech solution—a paper clip!

11. Irina Paperno, "What Can Be Done with Diaries?" *Russian Review* 63, no. 4 (October 2004): 561.

12. On the "emotional work" of diaries, see Martha Tomhave Baluveit, "The Work of the Heart: Emotion in the 1805–35 Diary of Sarah Connell Ayer," *Journal of Social History* 35, no. 3 (2002): 577–92.

13. Jürgen Habermas, *The Structural Transformation of the Public Sphere: An Inquiry into a Category of Bourgeois Society*, trans. Thomas Burger with the assistance of Frederick Lawrence (Cambridge, MA: MIT Press, 1989), 48. See also Dena Goodman, "Letter Writing and the Emergence of Gendered Subjectivity in Eighteenth-Century France," *Journal of Women's History* 17, no. 2 (2005): 9–37.

14. Zinaida paid little attention to her coreligionists in the Pale of Settlement. The pogroms had little bearing on her personal life, so she does not discuss them. Her one comment was short and matter-of-fact: "There was recently a pogrom in Nizhnii Novgorod, where Beselmann perished. He was beaten to death" (6 July 1884). Her uncle Iakov also ignored the pogroms in his memoir and diaries—among the most important but neglected sources—that were intended to trace the family history starting in the mid-eighteenth century. He boasted about his election as deputy from the city of Taganrog and his being designated to take bread and salt to Alexander III and attend his coronation on 27 May 1883. Iakov's wife, Amaliia, was afraid to let him go because of rumors that bombs would be thrown at the new tsar, like those that killed his father, Alexander II. See Iakov Poliakov, "Istoriia semeinye nachinaia [s]1748 goda" (hereafter "Istoriia"), Central Archives for the History of the Jewish People, l. 94.

15. These include Iakov Poliakov, "Istoriia"; Alexander Poliakoff with Deborah Sacks, *The Silver Samovar: Reminiscences of the Russian Revolution* (Moscow: Atlantida, 1996); and Marie Warshawsky's unpublished and untitled memoir at the United States Holocaust Memorial Museum, Accession Number 2010.405. For a transcription of Iakov's diaries, see "Poliakov, Iakov Solomonovich, 1832-1909," *Prozhito*, accessed 29 July 2018, http://prozhito.org/person/953.

16. Yuri [Iurii] A. Petrov, "The Banking Network of Moscow at the Turn of the Twentieth Century," in *Commerce in Russian Urban Culture, 1861–1914*, ed. William Craft Brumfield, Boris V. Anan'ich, and Yuri A. Petrov (Washington: Woodrow Wilson Center, 2001), 50.

17. Boris V. Anan'ich and Sergei G. Beliaev, "St. Petersburg: Banking Center of the Russian Empire," in *Commerce in Russian Urban Culture*, 14–18.

18. I borrow the concept of a "political economy of intimacies" from Lisa Lowe's *The Intimacies of Four Continents* (Durham, NC: Duke University Press, 2015), 18.

19. Ara Wilson, "Infrastructure of Intimacy," *Signs* 41, no. 2 (January 2016): 250. For examples of critical gender studies that engage the intersection of intimacy and broader structures of power, see Nayan Shah, *Stranger Intimacy: Contesting Race, Sexuality, and the Law in the North American West* (Berkeley: University of California Press, 2011); Eileen Boris and Rhacel Salazar Parreñas, eds., *Intimate Labors: Cultures, Technologies, and the Politics of Care* (Stanford, CA: Stanford University Press, 2010); Elizabeth Povinelli, *The Empire of Love: Toward a Theory of Intimacy, Genealogy, and Criminality* (Durham, NC: Duke University Press, 2007).

20. Quoted in Wilson, "Intrastructure of Intimacy," 250.

21. The terminology defies easy translation but is of great importance. Whereas *russkii* means specifically "ethnic Russian," *rossiiskii* refers to the supra-ethnic state and all that is within its territory. The latter is used today to distinguish *Rossliane* (citizens of the Russian Federation regardless of ethnicity) from *russkie* (ethnic Russians).

22. For the most intimate relationship, see Iakov Poliakov's diary entries about his friendship with Prince Nikolai Ivanovich Sviatopolsk-Mirskii (1833–98), a cavalry general and politician. The prince was the ataman of the Don Cossack Voisko. Since Iakov could not attend the prince's funeral, he sent a wreath for his coffin ("Istoriia," l. 272 [16 July 1898]).

23. Ibid., l. 1. The patriarch Lazar was married twice and had four children from the first marriage and five from the second. See the family tree in the appendix. According to Iakov, Lazar's sons were all very pious—especially the oldest, Samuil, who lived in Shklov. He was best known for his interest-free loan society for the poor, known as the *gemilat hesed*. He also had a business that traded iron goods, which his wife probably ran because "from morning to night he engaged inclusively in the interest-free society for the poor—the *gemilat [hesed]*" (ibid.).

24. Solomon opened the store with Veniamin, a son from Lazar's first marriage, and Aron, who was an official representative of the Jewish community in Dubrovno (ibid., l. 2).

25. The couple had a daughter, who died after her caretaker fell with her on ice during a fair in Besenkevich. See ibid.

26. Ibid.

27. Despite restrictions, Jewish merchants evidently made their way to Moscow in the late eighteenth century. According to a petition to the mayor of Moscow on behalf of Moscow merchants on 13 February 1790, Jews in Moscow were routinely selling foreign goods at lower prices. The petition triggered a decision by Catherine II to ban Jewish residence in the capital: "We find that the Jews do not have any right to register in the merchant estate in the towns and ports of the Russian interior, and only by Our ukase are they permitted to have the rights of citizenship and petty townspeople status in Belorussia" (*Polnoe sobranie zakonov Rossiiskoi Imperii*, 1-e sobranie [Moscow, 1830], 23: no. 17,006 [23 December 1791]).

28. The Glebov compound, the sole inn open to Jews, became the center of a district that grew into a Jewish "ghetto."

29. Margarita Lobovskaia, "Putevotidel' po evreiskoi Moskve," in *Moskva evreiskaia*, ed. K. Burmistrov (Moscow: Dom evreiskoi knigi, 2003), 12–13.

30. Efim Naumovich Ulitskii, *Istoriia Moskovskoi evreiskoi obshchiny: dokumenty i materialy* (Moscow: KRPA OLIMP, 2006), 30.

31. Iakov Poliakov, "Istoriia," l. 2.

32. Quoted in Lobovskaia, "Putevoditel' po evreiskoi Moskve," 15.

33. Iakov Poliakov, "Istoriia," l. 3.

34. Ibid. l. 4. So that her sons would not be bored, Zlata arranged for them to take lessons with the sons of David Dynin, whose mother, Esther, had run the postal station in Orsha alone after her husband's death. According to town lore, Esther, renowned for her beauty and skills, enjoyed the title *pochterin* (postmistress) and even hosted Alexander I, who presented her with a valuable ring.

35. Michael Stanislawski, *Tsar Nicholas I and the Jews: The Transformation of Jewish Society in Russia, 1825–1855* (Philadelphia: Jewish Publication Society of America, 1983).

36. See ChaeRan Y. Freeze, *Jewish Marriage and Divorce in Imperial Russia* (Waltham, MA: Brandeis University Press, 2002), 11–74.

37. To fend off criticism about the early marriage, Iakov Poliakov offered this explanation: "I was identical in height and build as when [I was] 20–25 years old, and up until my wedding, in the midst of studying, I was already occupied with my parents' business, traveled to Mogilev and to the fair in Lubavitch to sell goods that father sent directly from Moscow" ("Istoriia," l. 5).

38. Ibid.

39. Pavel Vydrin became a first-guild merchant in Moscow and tried to expand his business by hiring assistants to do business for him in the province of Orel'. After a complaint was brought against Vydrin, the Senate deliberated in 1885 and 1886 on whether assistants of Jewish first-guild merchants who did not hold the same rank had the right to conduct business for their employers outside the Pale of Settlement. See "Hahlatat hasenat," *Hamelits*, 4 March 1898.

40. Iakov Poliakov, "Istoriia," l. 5.

41. Ibid., l. 16.

42. See Ilya Vovshin, "Mishpahat Gintsburg veyetsirat haplutokratiya hayehudit ba'imperi-yah harusit," PhD diss., Haifa University, 2015.

43. A tax farmer (*otkupshchik*) was a person who received a contract to collect taxes for the state in return for having the right to gain commercial profit from monopolies such as the alcohol trade.

44. Iakov Poliakov worked for his wife's uncle, Moisei Niselson, and his partner, Levin (Levi) Zalmanson (the son-in-law of Rabbi Menachem Mendel Shneerson of Lubavitch). Iakov made his early breakthrough when he became the managing tax farmer of Orsha and Babinovich. In January 1855 he wrote, "At [age] nineteen, I became a very important person in my own town where yesterday I had been but a young boy" ("Istoriia," l. 9). It bears noting that non-Jewish entrepreneurial elites in Moscow also accumulated their initial capital as tax farmers. See Alfred Rieber, *Merchants and Entrepreneurs in Imperial Russia* (Chapel Hill: University of North Carolina Press, 1982), 153.

45. Iakov Poliakov, "Istoriia," l. 17.

46. Boris V. Anan'ich, *Bankirskie doma v Rossii, 1860–1914 gg.* (Moscow: ROSSPEN, 2006), 101. Iakov Poliakov often complained in his memoirs that Samuil enthusiastically accepted the contracts but left all the real work to his brothers. Iakov also stressed his role in cultivat-ing relations with local elites (which made the negotiations possible), as in the case of the Voronezh zemstvo (local self-government): "Thanks only to my acquaintance with each of them, as described above, this business succeeded with the zemstvo" ("Istoriia," l. 29). Iakov evidently resented the fact that his brother received all the credit while his contribution and sacrifices (such as living separately from his family in remote regions of Russia) did not garner the same recognition. For example, after the Kozlov-Voronezh-Rostov-na-Donu railroad had been completed, the local zemstvo awarded Samuil the status of commercial councilor and the Order of St. Stanislav (second degree) but merely bestowed on Iakov a silver medal. The Hebrew press likewise emphasized Samuil's successes, for example, reporting his donation of 30,000 rubles for a railway school in the town of Elets ("Maasei Poliakov," *Hakarmel*, 4 March 1869).

47. Anan'ich, *Bankirskie doma v Rossii*, 101.

48. Iakov Poliakov, "Istoriia," l. 82.

49. Sergei Iu. Witte referred to Samuil Poliakov as a "Railway King" in his memoirs (*Vospom-inaniia* [Moscow: Izadatel'stvo sotsial'no ekonomicheskoi literatury, 1960], 1:116). See also "Foreign Gleanings," *Jewish Messenger*, 19 February 1886. Samuil Poliakov not only controlled almost a quarter of Russia's railroads but also represented Russia as the "bridge and railroad engineer and member of the international jury" at the Paris World Exhibition in 1878. See Comité Central des Congrès et Conférences, *Congrès international des architectes* (Paris: Im-primerie Nationale, 1878). 37.

50. Quoted in Thomas C. Owen, *Dilemmas of Russian Capitalism: Fedor Chizkov and Corpo-rate Enterprise in the Railroad Age* (Cambridge, MA: Harvard University Press, 2005), 172.

51. Ibid., 173.

52. Iakov Poliakov, "Istoriia," ll. 102–3. Although no criminal charges were filed, rumors circulated that "greedy Jewish railway magnates were responsible for the accident" (Vladimir Meshcherskii, *Moi vospominaniia* [St. Petersburg: Tipografiia V. P. Meshcherskogo, 1897–1912], 3:302). See also Frithjof B. Schenk, *Russlands Fahrt in die Moderne: Mobilität und sozialer Raum in Eisenbahnzeitalter* (Stuttgart: Franz Steiner Verlag, 2014).

53. Witte, *Vospominaniia* 1:129.

54. Leo Tolstoy's novella *The Kreutzer Sonata* (1889), published a year after the Borki accident, described a third-class railroad compartment (frequented by Jews) as a "dirty, smoky, third-class car, littered with shells of sunflower seeds" (trans. Michael R. Katz [New Haven, CT: Yale University Press, 2014], 60). It was seen as symbolizing the dissoluteness of Jews, whom the main character Vasilii Pozdnyshev equated with women. "It's like the Jews," pontificates Pozdnyshev (who later kills his wife for taking a lover), "just as they pay us back for their oppression of them by their financial power, so it is with women" (ibid., 20). Sholem Aleichem also used third class as a Jewish space. If one could not "get rich quick" building a railroad ("who can resist becoming a Poliakov quicker than it takes to say one's bedtime prayers?"), one could always travel in "a car full of Jews." In this Jewish space, "everyone knows who you are, where you're bound for and what you do, and you know the same about everyone" (*Tevye the Dairyman and the Railroad Stories*, trans. Hillel Halkin [New York: Schocken Books, 1987], 283). For more on the railway car as Jewish space in Yiddish literature, see Leah Garrett, "Trains and Train Travel in Modern Yiddish Literature," *Jewish Social Studies* 7, no. 2 (2001): 67–88.

55. For the Hebrew obituary, see "Hadashot beyisrael," *Hatsefirah*, 25 April 1888.

56. Quoted in Anan'ich, *Bankirskie doma v Rossii*, 72.

57. According to the memoirs of one of Ignatii Varshavskii's [Warshawsky's] classmates at the Tsarskoe Selo Nikolaevskii Gymnasium, A. Otsupa, "There was a kind of puffed and stuffed Varshavskii [Warshawsky]. So round and draped in a castor-cloth coat and trousers was he that everyone wanted to touch him [to see if he were real]" ("Varshavskii, Ignatii Leonovich, 1883–1916," Sotsial'naia set' goroda Pushkin," accessed 31 March 2019, https:// tsarselo.ru/yenciklopedija-carskogo-sela/istorija-carskogo-sela-v-licah/varshavskii-ignatii -leonovich.html#.VYMdyqZigyE.

58. Roza's oldest daughter, Marie (Maroussia) Varshavskaia [Warshawsky], was born in 1881 in Paris. According to her unpublished memoirs, she lived in St. Petersburg on 4 English Quay (presumably at her Poliakov grandparents' home) and later in Tsarskoe Selo. Like other educated women of her generation, she developed a strong social conscience, influenced by Russian writers such as Leo Tolstoy, Nikolai Chernyshevsky, and Dmitrii Pisarev. Varshavskaia [Warshawsky] studied to be a nurse and worked in an orphanage in St. Petersburg, where she created a sewing atelier. Every year, she brought back new dress patterns from Paris for the girls to use. From 1914 to 1922, she ran a military hospital in Tsarskoe Selo. She lost her brother, Ignatii, during the war. She left Russia with her father in 1922 and lived in Paris at 111 Quai d'Orsay. She adored her father (who never remarried) and took care of him until his death. In Paris, she graduated from the École des Surintendantes d'Usines et de Services Sociaux (school for superintendents of factories and social services) and then worked for the fashion designer Jean Patou. She insisted on maintaining an in-store training atelier and providing minimum wages and vacations for the workers. In 1928, she joined the Ministry of Labor as an inspector of conditions for workers. Following her father's death, she bought an apartment on the Avenue de Saxe in Paris, where she lived until 1964 (presumably she paid for it from the large bequest that she received from Samuil Poliakov's daughter, her aunt Zinaida de Hirsch). Interestingly, Zinaida Lazarevna Poliakova does not mention Maroussia very often in her diaries. See "Marie Warshawsky manuscript," accession number 2010.405, United States Holocaust Memorial Museum. For Zinaida Hirsch's property and will, see Monika Klepp, "Zenaide von

Hirsch auf Gereuth und die Schule im Schloss Bergheim," *Jahrbuch des Oberösterreichischen Musealvereines, Gessellschaft für Landeskunde* 158 (2013): 279–96.

59. Rossiisskii Gosudarstvennyi Istoricheskii Arkhiv (hereafter RGIA), f. 626, op. 1, d. 1073, ll. 217–24. For details about his estate, see Anan'ich, *Bankierskie doma v Rossii*, 109.

60. Quoted in Anan'ich, *Bankierskie doma v Rossii*, 109.

61. "Halvayat hamet," *Hamelits*, 25 April 1888.

62. These included Minister of War Petr Vannovskii and Minister of Public Education Count Ivan Delianov.

63. The Hebrew press reported that Samuil had donated 30,000 rubles for the railway school in Elets ("Ma'asei Poliakov," *Hakarmel*, 4 March 1869). According to Anan'ich, Samuil was very late in fulfilling his other promises to the zemstvo to build a classical gymnasium and a road between El'tsa and Orla, and the frustrated residents of the town published a complaint about him in the satirical magazine *Iskra* on 13 December 1870 (*Bankirskie doma v Rossii*, 103).

64. Genrikh Sliozberg, *Dela minuvshikh dnei: zapiski russkago evreia* (Paris: Izdanie komiteta po chestvovaniiu 70-ti letniago iubeleiia G. B. Sliozberga, 1933), 1:142.

65. Ibid. In November 1882 students demonstrated against the Poliakov dormitories after fellow students were expelled for protesting the closing of Kazan University. According to the *Grazer Volksblatt*, 250 students were involved ("Russland," *Grazer Volksblatt*, 30 November 1882). The *Morgen-Post* reported that 277 students were detained, of whom 172 were released ("Bezüglich der studenten-Krawelle," 28 November 1882).

66. Obschestvo remeslennogo i zemledelcheskogo truda sredi evreev v Rossii, known by its abbreviation ORT.

67. ORT, founded with support from Samuil Poliakov, Horace Gintsburg, Abram Varshavskii, Abram Zak, and other members of the St. Petersburg Jewish elite, finally received legal recognition of its charter in 1906, after long delays by the state. Sliozberg argues that Samuil Poliakov "paid little attention to Jewish affairs" and that he was influenced heavily by the ideas of Nikolai Bakst (to whom the author gives credit for the ideas of ORT). See Sliozberg, *Dela minuvshikh dnei*, 1: 267.

68. "Samuil Poliakov," *Jewish Messenger*, 11 May 1888.

69. Iakov Poliakov, "Istoriia," l. 101.

70. Iakov observed that this was the first time he found himself in a "new region in a genuinely Russian environment" (ibid., l. 21).

71. Ibid., l. 19.

72. Ibid., ll. 30–32.

73. The status of honorary citizen (*pochetnyi grazhdanin*), established in 1832 by Nicholas I, created a social estate midway between the nobility and the merchant guilds: it conferred many of the privileges of the nobility (such as exemption from the poll tax, military conscription, and corporal punishment) without the honor of nobility. The status could either be personal or hereditary (applying to offspring as well); it was the latter that was conferred on Iakov in 1871.

74. For details about Iakov Poliakov's estate, see I[akov]. S[olomonovich] Poliakov, *Statisticheskiie svedeniia za 20 let, ot 1874 po 1894, po imeniiu 'Novomar'inskoe'. Taganrogskogo okruga, oblasti voiska Donskogo (byvsh. Taganrogskogo gradonachal'stva) na beregakh Azoskogo moria i reki Miusa* (St. Petersburg: Tipografiia i litografiia Berman, 1897). The main challenge was finding an efficient and honest manager to run the estate (Iakov Poliakov, "Istoriia," l. 69).

75. Iakov Poliakov, "Istoriia," ll. 49–51. The bank had a portfolio of eight million rubles and

gave out big dividends in the first two years, but a series of bad investments led to the loss of credibility in the bank. The losses were especially great in 1878–79.

76. Iakov attributed the problem of supplying the Azov railroad to the high price and poor quality of coal (ibid., ll. 53–55). According to a document outlining his twenty-five years of activities in Taganrog and Prizaovskii District, he outlined his contributions to the coal mining industry by developing a sophisticated coal mine. See RGIA, f. 720, op. 1, d. 1209, ll. 2–3 ob. See also Anan'ich, *Bankirskie doma v Rossii*, 111–12.

77. Petrov, "The Banking Network of Moscow," 55.

78. Iakov Poliakov, "Istoriia," ll. 16 and 32.

79. Ibid., l. 22.

80. Anan'ich, *Bankirskie doma v Rossii*, 86. See also RGIA, f. 40, op. 1, d. 26; f. 20, op. 2, d. 1209, l. 2.

81. Konstantin Nikolaevich Batiushkov, *Sochineniia* (Moscow: Gosudarstvennoe izdatel'stvo khudozhestvennoi literatury, 1955), 308–9.

82. Tolstoy, *War and Peace*, 935.

83. Natalia Datieva, "The Architecture of Moscow Banks in the Late Nineteenth and Early Twentieth Centuries," in *Commerce in Russian Urban Culture*, 139.

84. Ibid.

85. Petrov, "The Banking Network of Moscow," 48.

86. The State Council, which reviewed all acts before the emperor signed them into law, confirmed on 16 March 1859 that first-guild merchants who had maintained their status for at least ten years, their families, and a limited number of their clerks and servants could settle permanently in the interior provinces of Russia. The State Council had agreed to the inclusion of first-guild merchants partly because the minister of internal affairs (Sergei S. Lanskoi) and the minister of finance (Aleksandr M. Kniazhevich) assured them that only 108 Jews were eligible. Students who received a "learned degree—doctor, magister, or candidate" were granted residency rights and the right to enter civil service on 27 November 1861. And on 19 January 1879 all students with higher education regardless of degree, such as pharmacists, dentists, paramedics, and midwives, could reside in the interior. On 28 June 1865 the government extended residency rights to Jewish artisans, mechanics, distillers, and apprentices, but the law included many restrictions whereby they could be returned to the Pale of Settlement (that is, for selling anything but their own handmade goods). See Simon Dubnow, *History of the Jews in Russia and Poland* (Philadelphia: Jewish Publication Society of America, 1918), 2:162–67; Ulitskii, *Istoriia Moskovskoi evreiskoi obshchiny*, 33–34; Anan'ich, *Bankirskie doma v Rossii*, 54.

87. Samuil Vermel', "Evrei v Moskve," in *Moskva evreiskaia*, 155.

88. Ivan Belousov, "Zariad'e (iz knigi 'Ushedshaia Moskva')," in *Moskva evreiskaia*, 474.

89. Ibid., 475.

90. Lobovskaia, "Putivoditel' po evreiskoi Moskve," 29. Lazar Poliakov's name was listed in Moscow address books, such as the 1896 edition of *Vsia Moskva: Adres-spravochnik g. Moskvy XXVI-i god* (Moscow: Gorodskoe izdanie Adres-kalendaria g. Moskvy, 1896), where it appeared on page 247.

91. Dmitrii Nikiforov, *Vospminaniia D. Nikiforova: Moskva v tsarstvovanie Imperatora Aleksandra II* (Moscow: Universitetskaia tipografiia, 1904), 44.

92. Iakov Poliakov, "Istoriia," l. 57.

93. According to the Vydrin family, Rozaliia provided for the education and upbringing of her father's children as well as her own. Her father, Pavel, remarried and had children who were the same age as Zinaida and her siblings, including Genrikh, Roman, and Masha. Many of the Vydrins, despite their capitalist kin, became involved in the revolutionary movement as Bolsheviks, Mensheviks, and Socialist Revolutionaries. See Evgeniia Iaroslavskaia-Markon, "Klianus' otomstit' slovom i krov'iu," *Zvezda* 2 (2008): 127–59. In 1903, Zinaida received word from her aunt Sofiia Vydrin that her youngest daughter, Liza, had traveled to Switzerland to study. Zinaida wrote, "She was always such a reticent and quiet girl, and now she is falling to God knows what kind of company" (NIOR RGB, f. 743, k. 138, d. 3, ll. 40–40 ob). Zinaida worried, of course, about the radical revolutionary circles that Liza might join. See also "Rafael Vydrin, der arbeter tuer, geshtorbn," *Undzer ekspres*, 26 December 1928, about the death of Rafael Vydrin (son of Il'ia and Sofiia Vydrin), Rozaliia's nephew. The article states that he was a cousin of Rozaliia Poliakova.

94. NIOR RGB, f. 743, k. 138, d. 3, l. 12 ob. (20 September 1902).

95. Vovshin, "Mishpahat Gintsburg veyetsirat haplutokratiya hayehudit ba'imperiyah harusit," 111–38.

96. On 19 March 1875 Alexander II allowed Evzel' Gintsburg to accept the title of baron bestowed by the Grand Duke of Hesse. Anan'ich, *Bankirskie doma v Rossii*, 55.

97. Boris V. Anan'ich, "Russian Private Banking Houses, 1870–1914," *Journal of Economic History* 48, no. 2 (1988): 401.

98. Ibid., 403.

99. Anan'ich and Beliaev, "St. Petersburg," 12.

100. Sergei Antonov, *Bankrupts and Usurers of Imperial Russia* (Cambridge, MA: Harvard University Press, 2016), 27.

101. Sergei K. Lebedev, "European Business Culture and St. Petersburg Banks," in *Commerce in Russian Urban Culture*, 23. The interest sometimes devoured profits and left merchant-debtors in dire financial straits.

102. Anan'ich and Beliaev, "St. Petersburg," 11–13.

103. The old Moscow banks included such institutions as the Merchant's Bank (founded in 1866), the Discount Bank (1870), and the Trade Bank (1871). See Petrov, "The Banking Network of Moscow," 50.

104. On Babst's economic nationalism, see Owen, *Dilemmas of Russian Capitalism*.

105. Yuri Petrov, "'Moscow City': Financial Citadel of Merchant Moscow," in *Merchant Moscow: Images of a Vanished Moscow Bourgeoisie*, ed. James L. West and Yuri Petrov (Princeton, NJ: Princeton University Press, 1998), 46.

106. Quoted in ibid., 47.

107. Aleksandr V. Pyzhikov, *Grani russkogo raskola: Zametki o nashe istorii ot XVII veka do 1917* (Moscow: Drevlekhranilishche, 2013), 84. See also Alfred Rieber, *Merchants and Entrepreneurs in Imperial Russia* (Chapel Hill: University of North Carolina Press, 1982).

108. Anan'ich and Beliaev, "St. Petersburg," 19.

109. On the Old Believers' hostility toward the state and tsar, see Roy Robson, *Old Believers in Modern Russia* (DeKalb: Northern Illinois Press, 1995).

110. Cherkasskii (1824–78) was an influential figure in Moscow and served as the city's mayor in 1869–71.

111. Dmitrii Nikiforov, *Moskva v tsarstvovanie imperatora Aleksandr II*, 144–47. Lazar re-

mained the head of the Moscow Land Bank's board until his death in 1914, at which point his son Isaak took over his position.

112. In addition to a lumber enterprise, Lazar invested in a Riazan factory for agricultural machinery, a stationery factory and a rubber factory in Moscow, and several industries in Persia and other countries.

113. Anan'ich, *Bankirskie doma v Rossii*, 122–23.

114. Natalia Proskuriakova, *Ipoteka v Rossisskoi imperii* (Moscow: Izd. Dom vysshei shkoly ekonomiki, 2014).

115. Quoted in Boris V. Anan'ich, *Chastnoe predprinimatel'stvo v dorevoliutsionnoi Rossiii* (Moscow: ROSSPEN, 2010), 413.

116. Stepan Riabov (1831–1919) was the conductor of the Malyi Theater in Moscow (1873–75) and then the conductor for ballet performances at the Bolshoi Theater (1875–1900). In addition, he created his own Riabov orchestra, which performed at social functions such as the Dolgorukov balls.

117. B. A. Shchetinin, "Khoziain Moskvy," *Istoricheskii vestnik* 148 (1917): 458.

118. Ibid., 459.

119. Lazar reached the rank of privy councilor, like his brother Samuil.

120. Shchetinin, "Khoziain Moskvy," 459.

121. Ibid., 459–60.

122. Roza G. Vinaver, "Vospominaniia" (unpublished memoir, 1944, folder 3, box 15, Collection V. Maklakov, Hoover Institute Archives, Stanford, California), 9. See also ChaeRan Y. Freeze, "The Evolution of Roza Georgievna Vinaver: The Making of a Jewish Liberal Politician's Wife in Imperial Russia," in *The Individual in History*, ed. ChaeRan Y. Freeze, Sylvia Fuks Fried, and Eugene Sheppard (Waltham, MA: Brandeis University Press, 2015), 317–34.

123. Alexander Poliakoff, *The Silver Samovar*, 23.

124. Sliozberg, *Dela minuvshikh dnei*, 2:45.

125. Ibid.

126. Ibid., 2:44–45.

127. Leo Tolstoy, *Anna Karenina*, trans. Constance Garrett, revised by Leonard J. Kent and Nina Berberova (New York: Modern Library, 2000), 813.

128. Ibid., 817.

129. Ibid.

130. Michelle L. Marrese, "'The Poetry of Everyday Behavior Revisited: Lotman, Gender, and the Evolution of Russian Noble Identity," *Kritika* 11, no. 4 (2010): 729.

131. See, for example, the importance of Russian for the Decembrists, in Hans Lemberg, *Die nationale Gedankenwelt der Dekabristen* (Cologne: Böhlau, 1963).

132. For example, the newspaper *Moskovskie vedomosti* and the journal *Russkii vestnik*, both published by Mikhail Katkov, a close family friend.

133. Lazar Izrailevich Brodskii (1848–1904), a prominent entrepreuneur in the family's sugar businesss in Kiev who created one of the largest wheat mills in Kiev. See the memoirs of Alexandra Fanny Brodsky, *Smoke Signals: From Eminence to Exile* (London: I. B. Tauris, 1997); Natan Meir, *Kiev, Jewish Metropolis: A History, 1889–1914* (Bloomington: Indiana University Press, 2010), 30–38.

134. Zulfia Karimova and Andriy Vaslychenko, "Stradanie," in *Dictionary of Untranslatables:*

A *Philosophical Lexicon*, ed. Barbara Cassin (Princeton, NJ: Princeton University Press, 2014), 1064.

135. Ol'ga Vydrin, a relative of Rozaliia, met her husband (a second cousin), Bentsian I. Sheftel', at Tsurikovo. See "Sheftel', Bentsian Il'ich (1886–1968), Semeinye istorii, accessed 9 August 2017, http://www.famhist.ru/famhist/sheftel/00054d9e.htm. For a photograph of the Vydrin family at the estate, see "Foto sem'iakh Vydrinykh," Semeinye istorii, accessed 1 April 2019, http://www.famhist.ru/famhist/sheftel/001947f4.htm.

136. Stephen Lovell, *Summerfolk: A History of the Dacha: 1710–2000* (Ithaca, NY: Cornell University Press, 2003), 60.

137. Quoted in Caroline Brooke, *Moscow: A Cultural History* (Oxford: Oxford University Press, 2006), xviii. Several years later, Chekhov wrote a novella titled *Three Years*, which featured a country dacha at Sokol'niki (to which the Laptevs moved in May because Yulia was expecting a baby). See Anton Chekhov, *The Complete Short Novels*, trans. Larissa Volonkhovsky and Richard Pevear (New York: Everyman's Library, 2004).

138. In April 1901, Il'ia, who had run a brilliant race with his horse, Nikita Judeei, was injured when the horse kicked him on his right temple. He was transported to the medical station and survived the accident. See "Concours Hippique," *Le Radical*, 1 April 1901.

139. Iakov Poliakov, "Istoriia," l. 44.

140. NIOR RGB, f. 743, k. 139, d. 1, l. 72 (13 July 1906).

141. Zinaida Poliakova and Alexander Poliakoff, *Sem'ia Poliakovykh*, 255 and 272–73; NIOR RGB, f. 343, k. 138, d. 7, l. 44.

142. Muriel Joffe and Adele Lindenmeyr, "Daughters, Wives, and Partners: Women of the Moscow Merchant Elite," in *Merchant Moscow*, 104.

143. Anan'ich, *Bankirskie doma v Rossii*, 123.

144. Iakov Poliakov, "Istoriia," l. 304.

145. Ibid., l. 322.

146. Ibid., l. 344.

147. Galina Ulianova, *Female Entrepreneurs in Nineteenth-Century Russia* (2009; repr., London: Routlege, 2016), 122.

148. Ibid., 2. See also the meticulous research by Michelle Marrese, *A Woman's Kingdom: Noblewomen and the Control of Property in Russia, 1700–1861* (Ithaca, NY: Cornell University Press, 2002).

149. Quoted in Ulianova, *Female Entrepreneurs in Nineteenth-Century Russia*, 3. William Wagner argues that "such proprietary power could provide wives with a counterweight to their complete personal subordination to their husbands" (*Marriage, Property, and Law in Late Imperial Russia*, 2nd ed. [Oxford: Clarendon Press of Oxford University Press, 2001], 66).

150. On Jewish spa culture, see Mirjam Zadoff, *Next Year in Marienbad: The Lost Worlds of Jewish Spa Culture* (Philadelphia: University of Pennsylvania Press, 2012).

151. *Ischler Cur-Liste*, no. 32 (21 September 1880).

152. "Präsenzliste von Franzensbad," *Wiener Salonblatt*, 19 August 1888; *Prager Abendblatt*, 27 July 1894.

153. *Deutsches Volksblatt*, 2 January 1895.

154. On Anton Rubinstein, who was baptized in Berdichev as an infant, and his musical career, see James Loeffler, *The Most Musical Nation: Jews and Culture in the Late Russian Empire*

(New Haven, CT: Yale University Press, 2010), 15–55. Rubinstein was the court pianist for Elena Pavlovna and later founded the St. Petersburg Conservatory.

155. Probably Eugene d'Albert, a Scottish-born composer and pianist.

156. Quoted in Loeffler, *The Most Musical Nation*, 29.

157. For a description of the *soirées musicales*, see Amy Coles and Vera Urusov, *Letters of Life in an Aristocratic Russian Household before and after the Revolution*, ed. Nicholas Tyrras (New York: Edwin Mellen Press, 2000), 159 and 165.

158. Julie A. Buckler, *The Literary Lorgnette: Attending Opera in Imperial Russia* (Stanford, CA: Stanford University Press, 2000), 8.

159. The Yiddish theater first performed the play, based on Yehuda Yosef Lerner's translation (which relied heavily on the Russian text), at the Mariinskii Theater in Odessa in 1885.

160. Quoted in Buckler, *The Literary Lorgnette*, 8.

161. Ibid. For the difficulties of transitioning between worlds for family ties, see ChaeRan Y. Freeze, "When Chava Left Home: Gender, Conversion, and the Jewish Family in Tsarist Russia," *Polin: Jewish Women in Eastern Europe* 18 (2005): 153–88.

162. Quoted in "Halel lezimrah," *Hatsefirah*, 22 February 1893.

163. Ibid. *Hatsefirah* used the name Sembrich-Kochanska (1858–1935).

164. Quoted in Dimitry Markevitch, *Cello Story*, trans. Florence W. Seder (Los Angeles: Summy-Birtchard Inc, 1984), 94. The Davydov Stradivarius, presented to Davydov by his patron, Matvei Weilhorski, came into the possession of the famous cellist Jacqueline du Pré, whose godmother, Ismena Holland, purchased it for $90,000. In 1988, the Vuitton Foundation bought the instrument and loaned it to Yo-Yo Ma, who still plays it as one of his two cellos.

165. Loeffler, *The Most Musical Nation*, 43.

166. "Halel lezimrah."

167. John E. Bowlt, "The Moscow Art Market," in *Between Tsar and People: Educated Society and the Quest for Public Identity in Lat Imperial Russia*, ed. Edith Clowes, Samuel Kassow, and James West (Princeton, NJ: Princeton University Press, 1991), 108.

168. "Foreign News," *Advocate: America's Jewish Journal* 58 (22 November 1919): 379–80.

169. Quoted in R. Lobovskaia, "Poliakovskii zal v Musee iziashchnykh iskusstv v Moskve," *Vestnik evreiskogo universiteta v Moskve*, no. 3 (1993): 135.

170. N. Shcherbakov, "K voprosy ob odinakovykh risunkakh na drevne-grecheskikh raspisannykh sosudakh," in *Sbornik v chest' Matveia Kuzmicha Liubavskogo* (Petrograd: Tip. B. D. Brukera, 1917), 120.

171. Lobovskaia, "Poliakovskii zal v Musee iziashchnykh iskusstv v Moskve," 135. The Poliakovs also gave a considerable sum to the Rumiantsev Museum, a collection that became the basis for the manuscript division of the Russian State Library (formerly the Lenin Library) in Moscow.

172. "Tvetaeva, M. I., to Andronikovoi-Gal'pern, S. N.," 25 February 1927, Marina Ivanovna Tsvetaeva, accessed 1 April 2019, http://tsvetaeva.lit-into.ru/tsvetaeva/pisma/letter-566.htm.

173. In 1937, an engineering institution in charge of the canal system was directed to melt down the ten bronze busts and statue, but they were rescued and placed in the Russian State Museum. See Musya Glants, *Where Is My Home? The Art and Life of the Russian-Jewish Sculptor Mark Antokolsky, 1843–1902* (Lanham, MD: Lexington Books, 2010).

174. Iakov Poliakov, "Istoriia," l. 199.

175. Vladimir V. Stasov, "Dvatsat' piat' let nashego iskusstva," in *Izbrannye sochineniia v trekh tomakh. Zhivopis'. Skul'ptura. Muzyka* (Moscow: Gosudarstvennoe izdatel'stvo "Iskusstvo," 1952), 498. See also Glants, *Where Is My Home?*

176. Ruth Robbins, "A Woman's Work Is Never Done? Women and Leisure in the Nineteenth Century and Beyond," Routledge History of Feminism, 3 August 2016, https://www .routledgehistoricalresources.com/feminism/essays/a-womans-work-is-never-done-women -and-leisure-in-the-nineteenth-century-and-beyond.

177. See David Ransel, *A Russian Merchant's Tale: The Life and Adventures of Ivan Alekseevich Tolchenov* (Bloomington: Indiana University Press, 2009).

178. As the editor of the newspaper in 1873, Fyodor Dostoevsky had launched a monthly column devoted to the "diaries of a writer," which he transformed into a literary genre with his own "Writer's Diaries." See Gary Saul Morson, *Boundaries of Genre: Dostoevsky's 'Diary of a Writer' and the Tradition of Literary Utopia* (Austin: University of Texas Press, 1981).

179. See Zinaida's diary entry of 8 April 1885. The reference was probably to the Panjdeh incident in 1885, when Russia conquered a border fort in Afghanistan, which the British interpreted as a threat to their colony of India. The incident almost caused a war, but the two sides resolved the conflict through negotiations and diplomacy.

180. See Zinaida's diary entry of 3 June 1886.

181. Aleksandr Kozlov's term ended in 1887, before the infamous expulsion of Jews from Moscow in 1891.

182. The Trinity-Sergius Monastery, founded in 1377, has long been a premier institution of Russian monasticism—rich in spiritual leaders as in worldly possessions. For its development in prerevolutionary Russia, see Scott M. Kenworthy, *The Heart of Russia: Trinity-Sergius, Monasticism, and Society after 1825* (New York: Oxford University Press, 2010).

183. "Succession Mme V[eu]ve Rosalie Pavlovna Poliakoff," *Le Temps*, 28 July 1923; "Succession Mme Veuve: Rosalie Pavlovna Poliakoff," *Journal officiel de la République française. Lois et décrets*, 2 August 1923.

184. Iakov Poliakov, "Istoriia," l. 286 (17 February 1899).

185. Ibid., l. 52 (3 September 1871).

186. Ibid., l. 8 (1851).

187. Geoffrey L. Shisler, "The Choral School of Moscow in Pre-Revolutionary Days," March 1972, http://geoffreyshisler.com/the-cantors-review/choral-shul-of-moscow.

188. Iakov Poliakov, "Istoriia," l. 455 (22 March 1907).

189. The editor of the published diary questions Zinaida's reference, given that the coronation of Alexander III was in May 1883. However, Zinaida was referring to 1 March 1881 (when Alexander II was assassinated and his son Alexander ascended the throne).

190. Lazar and Rozaliia lost their first son, Avgust (Azi), who died in Geneva in 1872, and Aaron (Ronia) who died of pulmonary tuberculosis at 9:30 p.m. on 5 May 1895 in Beaulieu-sur-Mer in the French Riviera. He was buried in Moscow in the Dorogomilovskoe Jewish Cemetery on 15 May 1895. See Irina Ryklis and Andrei Shumkov, "Poliakovy: Nekotorye voprosy genealogii roda i soslovnogo statusa," *Trudy po evreiskoi istorii i kul'tury: Materialy XIX mezhdunarodnoi ezhegodnoi konferentsii po iudaika* (Moscow: Tsentr Sefer, 2012): 3:212.

191. Lazar Iakovlevich Poliakov and his wife, Annette, lost their daughter Ol'ga and son Victor at an early age—both unexpectedly. Zinaida, who sent the announcement of Victor's death to *Le Figaro*, described her cousin Lazar's grief: "Lazar is very saddened by the death of his son

Victor who did not complain of anything; upon returning home, he lay in bed and died in the night" (NIOR RGB, f. 743, k. 139, d. 1, l. 53 [1 April 1906]).

192. Iakov Poliakov, "Istoriia," l. 8.

193. Ibid., l. 39. When the other children developed symptoms of scrofula, Amaliia insisted that they travel to Khar'kov and receive first-class medical care.

194. NIOR RGB, f. 743, op. 138, d. 1, l. 153 ob.

195. Iakov Poliakov, "Istoriia," l. 255.

196. For Solomon's memorial service, the reading of psalms in his honor, and praise for his contributions to the establishment of the Talmud Torah for the poor in Orsha and other charitable acts, see "R. Shlomo bar Eliezer Poliakov, z"l," *Hamelits*, 18 January 1898.

197. *Die Neuzeit*, 5 August 1881. It added that "as is often the case among wealthy Jews, they are not alienated from Jewish life."

198. "Yerushalayim," *Hamelits*, 29 January 1897.

199. On Sarah Diskin's resentment of the prayer "who has not made me a woman," see Joseph Tabory, "The Benedictions of Self-Identity and the Changing Status of Women and Orthodoxy," in *Kenishta: Studies on the Synagogue*, ed. Joseph Tabory (Ramat-Gan, Israel: Bar-Ilan University Press, 2001), 1:130–31.

200. "Yerushalayim," *Hamelits*, 29 January 1897.

201. Rozaliia probably made a connection with R. Salant through R. Chaim Berlin, the spiritual rabbi of Moscow, who corresponded with R. Salant regularly. When R. Berlin emigrated to Palestine in 1906, his friend R. Salant helped him get elected to the rabbinate of the Ashkenazi community in Jerusalem.

202. H. Rivlin, "Mikhtavei sofrenu," *Hatsefirah*, 18 August 1898. Rozaliia also sent an emissary on her behalf to visit cities in Galilee, the settlements, Jerusalem, and the charitable houses. See "Naveh yafah," *Hatsefirah*, 20 March 1898.

203. Yitzhak Shiryon, "Zikhronot Yitzhak Shiryon," accessed 5 April 2019, https://benyehuda.org/shiryon/.

204. NIOR RGB, f. 743, op. 138, d. 1, l. 68 (13 February 1895).

205. "A sheyne matoneh," *Der teglikher herald*, 2 March 1896; "Jerusalem," *Die Neuzeit*, 20 March 1896. Iakov first learned that Ronia had contracted tuberculosis on 4 August 1894. He later wrote that Mikhail had taken Aaron (Ronia) to Cairo on 27 August 1874. On 30 April 1895, Lazar, Rozaliia, and Khaia went abroad to see Ronia, who was apparently gravely ill.

206. "Mikhtavei sofrenu," *Hatsefirah*, 17 November 1896.

207. "Totzaot mehaprotokolim shel yeshivot havaad lehevrat temikhah beovdei adamah," *Hatsefirah*, 4 October 1889. Since the hospital also treated farmers and poor craftsmen, the director wanted the same salary as the person holding the same position in Jaffe. The society decided to give the hospital 400 francs.

208. "Me'arei hamedinah," *Hatsefirah*, 19 November 1899; Yehuda Slutsky and Shmuel Spector, "Dubrovno," in *Encyclopedia Judaica*, 2nd ed., ed. Fred Skolnik (Detroit, MI: Macmillan Reference USA, 2006), 6:39. See also YIVO Institute for Jewish Research, RG 236, folder 26, for reports of the manufacturing company for 1902–3.

209. Slutsky and Spector, "Dubrovno," 6:39. During World War I, some thirty thousand prayer shawls accumulated in Dubrovno that could not be shipped because of the violence; they were sent to Berlin after the war. The Bolsheviks closed the factory in the 1920s.

210. Ulitskii, *Istoriia Moskovskoi evreiskoi obshchiny*, 35.

211. Vermel', "Evrei v Moskve," 145–46.

212. Born in 1826, Minor received a traditional education and attended the Vil'na rabbinical school, where he later taught Talmud. With the support of *maskilim* like Lev Levanda, he was elected the state rabbi of Minsk.

213. According to archival sources, Aron Efremov Shneider, Mordukh Izrailovich Ioffe, and other merchants had petitioned to build this synagogue, which was financed primarily by Samuil Poliakov. There were complaints from the Russian Orthodox community that the synagogue bordered the house of a priest serving at the Chapel of St. Boris and Gleb. See Tsentral'nyi gosudarstvennyi arkhiv goroda Moskvy (hereafter TsGAM), f. 16, op. 25, d. 111, ll. 13, 88, and 89.

214. Quoted in Vermel', "Evrei v Moskve," 149.

215. Quoted in Vladimir Porudominskii, ". . . ravenstvo vsekh liudei—aksioma," *Zhurnal'nyi zal*, 9 October 2001, http://magazines.russ.ru/october/2001/9/porud.html.

216. Ulitskii, *Istoriia Moskovskoi evreiskoi obshchiny*, 42.

217. Samuil Vermel', "Iz nedavnego proshlogo," in *Moskva evreiskaia*, 263. See also Ulitskii, *Istoriia Moskovskoi evreiskoi obshchiny*, 40–41.

218. Ulitskii, *Istoriia Moskovskoi evreiskoi obshchiny*, 41–42 and 43.

219. Ibid., 42. The chief of police, Aleksandr A. Vlasovskii, closed the school in 1895.

220. Ibid., 47.

221. "Be'aretsenu," *Hamelits*, 16 August 1886. For the budget of the mikvah in 1910, see TsGAM, f. 1457, op. 1, d. 128, ll. 1–9.

222. Iakov Maze, *Pamiati L. S. Poliakova* (Moscow: Tipografii M. O. Attai i Ko., 1914), 9–10.

223. Secondary sources date the official opening to 1888, but Zinaida's diary entries and reports in the Hebrew press give the date as 1886.

224. A photograph of this archival document can be found in Vilen Stolovitskii and Leonid Gomberg, *Sinagoga na Bol'shoi Bronnoi: do i posle sta dvadtsati* (Moscow: Agudas Khasidei Khabad, 2015), accessed 31 March 2019, http://jewish.kiev.ua/files/Books/Book_sinagoga_na _bolshoj_bronnoj.pdf.

225. "Leyisharim naveh tehilah," *Hamelits*, 23 August 1886.

226. The Russian newspaper *Novosti* announced that "lovers of music and hymns" could hear Cantor Maten'ko every Friday night at the Poliakov synagogue ("Bearatsenu," *Hamelits*, 25 April 1887).

227. Moshe Bick, "Nahum Matenko, z"l," in *Dubosari: Sefer zikaron*, ed. Iosif Rubin (Tel Aviv: Irgun yotse Dubosari beamerikah), 321.

228. "Di tragedye fun dem vunderbarn khazn Nohum Matenko," *Der Yiddisher bihne*, 1 December 1909.

229. Quoted in Bick, "Nahum Matenko," 321.

230. Ibid., 322.

231. "Maasim bchol yom," *Hamelits*, 25 August 1886.

232. RGIA, f. 821, op. 8, d. 69, ll. 33–36 and 31–32 ob.; Ulitskii, *Istoriia Moskovskoi evreiskoi obshchiny*, 110–15.

233. RGIA, f. 821, op. 8, d, 68, l. 39–39 ob. See also Ulitskii, *Istoriia Moskovskoi evreiskoi obshchiny*, 116–17.

234. Lobovskaia, "Putevoditel' po evreiskoi Moskve," 38.

235. Aron E. Shneider, a first-guild merchant.

236. Quoted in Ulitskii, *Istoriia Moskovskoi evreiskoi obshchiny*, 122–23.

237. Quoted in ibid., 124.

238. Vermel' contended that the cupola in question was "the most common kind that one could see on many buildings," but Pobedenostsev's intervention led to its destruction ("Evrei v Moskve," 181). In his account, the pharmacist and public activist Aleksandr Katsenel'son (d. 1930) pointed out that "the enormous cupola with the star of David," which had been included in the approved architectural plan, took several days to tear down. See Samuil Vermel', "Iz martirologa Moskovskoi obshchiny (Moskovskaia sinagoga v 1891–1906 gg.)," in *Moskva evreiskaia*, 411). This article was first published in *Evreiskaia starina* 2 (1909): 175–88.

239. Vermel', "Evrei v Moskve," 181.

240. Quoted in Ulitskii, *Istoriia Moskovskoi evreiskoi obshchiny*, 128.

241. Quoted in ibid. According to Vermel', the exact text of the petition is not extant, but Minor apparently cited a law providing that "the freedom of religion is not only asserted by Christians of the foreign faiths but also by Jews, Muslim, and heathens" ("Evrei v Moskve," 182–83).

242. Ulitskii, *Istoriia Moskovskoi evreiskoi obshchiny*, 147–53.

243. NIOR RGB, f. 743, k. 139, d. 1, l. 67 ob.

244. On Iakov Maze's [Jacob Mase] appointment as state rabbi, including his interview with Aleksander Bulygin, governor of Moscow (1893–1902), see Maze's memoirs (*Zikhronot* [Tel Aviv: Yalkut, 1936], 2:5–56). A university-educated jurist, Maze was about thirty years old at the time of his election and was already well known for his oratorical skills. He was elected unanimously but had to deal with some criticism by M. N. Levin, who would have preferred a state rabbi who was "a more modest, humble, and submissive person" (Vermel', "Evrei v Moskve," 187).

245. Iakov Maze, *Pamiati L. S. Poliakova* (Moscow: Tipografii M. O. Attai i Ko., 1914), 9.

246. Vermel', "Evrei v Moskve," 187.

247. Maze paraphrased the text, which read: "When the Temple was destroyed for the first time, many groups of young priests gathered together with the Temple keys in their hands. And they ascended to the roof of the Sanctuary and said before God: 'Master of the Universe, since we did not merit to be faithful treasurers, let the keys be handed back to you.' And they threw them upward, and a palm of a hand emerged and received [the keys] from them" (Maze, *Pamiati L. S. Poliakova*, 9–10).

248. Ibid.

249. According to Sid Leiman, this quote is probably not from a classical Jewish text but may be a late Hebrew translation of an original Aramaic aggadic passage or a fictional passage created for a textbook or reader for children in simplified, rabbinic Hebrew. I thank Sid Leiman and Yehuda Mirsky for their assistance in identifying this quote.

250. Maze, *Pamiati L. S. Poliakova*, 3–4.

251. Vermel', "Evrei v Moskve," 188. Other members included Lazar's son, Mikhail; E. Ia. Rubinshtein; O. G. Khishin; Vladimir O Garkavi; and S. I. Cheplivetskii.

252. December 1876.

253. Eliakum Zunzer, *A Jewish Bard* (New York: Zunzer Jubilee Committee, 1905), 28–29.

254. NIOR RGB, f. 343, k. 138, d. 7, l. 5 ob.

255. The wedding announcement in the *American Hebrew* read in part: "On the 29th of April, a marriage was solemnized at Planegg near Munich between Baron de Hirsch, son of the

great financier and a daughter of M. Poliakoff, the equally great railroad contractor" ("Foreign News," *American Hebrew*, 28 May 1880). James de Hirsch was the adopted son of Maurice de Hirsch. Baroness Zinaida de Hirsch was involved in promoting the Jewish colonization scheme of Baron de Hirsch to resettle Russian Jews to other countries such as Argentina ("Baron de Hirsch's Emigration Scheme," *American Israelite*, 28 July 1892).

256. In the obituary of Victor Aron St. Paul (a retired Jewish banker), it mentions that his surviving son Georges St. Paul was married to a "a daughter of M. Poliakoff, the famous Russian railway king" ("Foreign News," *American Hebrew*, 9 March 1888). For the marriage contract between Rachel Poliakoff and Georges St. Paul, see Cyril Grange, *Une élite parisienne: Les familles de la grande bourgeoisie juive, 1870–1939* (Paris: CNRS Éditions, 2016), 186.

257. Iakov Poliakov, "Istoriia," l. 40.

258. Iakov purchased a villa in Biarritz for 130,000 francs in 1896 as a present for his wife. He renamed it the Villa Poliakoff Amalie (ibid., l. 236). Lazar and Rozaliia, whose son Jacques was a famous doctor in Biarritz, donated generously to the building of the synagogue there.

259. Lazar met Anna (Annette) Anisimovna Leonino when he was visiting his sister Elizabeth (Liza), in Odessa, and they were married on 11 January 1880.

260. Iakov Poliakov, "Istoriia," l. 65. For more on the Raffalovich family, especially on the pioneering educator Elena Raffalovich in Italy, see Asher Salah, "From Odessa to Florence: Elena Comparetti Raffalovich: A Jewish Russian Woman in Nineteenth-Century Italy," *Quest* 8 (November 2015), http://www.quest-cdecjournal.it/focus.php?id=365.

261. Iakov Poliakov, "Istoriia," l. 70.

262. After his father (the Odessa banker Anisim Raffalovich) died, Lev (Louis) worked for the Abramov firm and lost 75,000 of the 100,000 rubles of Liza's money that Iakov had deposited for her. Samuil Solomonovich helped him get appointed as a board member of the Moscow–St. Petersburg Bank with a salary of 8000 rubles a year. See ibid., l. 88.

263. Wilhelm Landau created a major commercial bank in Warsaw. His gravesite is graced by a famous modern sculpture: "The mantle-draped sarcophagus of the banker Wilhelm Landau . . . follows the pattern of Amschel Mayer von Rothschild's in Frankfurt" (Frederic Bedoire, *The Jewish Contribution to Modern Architecture, 1830–1930* [Jersey City, NJ: KTAV Publishing House, 2004], 404–5).

264. Iakov Poliakov, "Istoriia," l. 90.

265. Iosef had many health problems (including a heart attack and edema of the leg), and he grew very ill in 1900. Iakov recalled that he did not want to say farewell to the family in Paris on 23 October. Apparently he "cried all day." Iosef died on 24 November, leaving his wife, Isabella, and two children: Alice (Liulia) and George (Georzhik). They held the funeral in Warsaw (ibid., l. 314).

266. Rubinshtein attended funerals for various family members, including Leon Rubinshtein (the father of the ballerina Ida Rubinstein [ibid., l. 155]) and Adolf Romanovich Rubinshtein (the brother of Leon Romanovich Rubinshtein [ibid., ll. 183–84]).

267. Ibid., l. 160.

268. Ibid., l. 276. In 1889, Iakov had heard rumors about Daniil's affair with a certain Kozlova and confronted him about his intention to marry a Russian, which his nephew denied. Iakov remarked that his brother Samuil would have died had he still been alive to hear this news (ibid., l. 108 [10 August 1889]).

269. Ibid., l. 292 (25 January 1898).

270. Ibid., l. 271. He asked his children, who claimed they did not know anything about the conversion and marriage, but it is evident from other entries that they knew about their brother's decision. On Iakov's refusal to reconcile with his son at Daniil Poliakov's request, see ibid., l. 292. Isabella also refused to seek treatment for her mental illness unless her parents reconciled with her brother (see ibid., l. 355).

271. Ibid., l. 293.

272. See Gregory Freeze, "Religioznaia politika Rossiiskoi imperii v Pribaltike," *Vestnik S. Peterburgskogo Universiteta*, Seriia 2: Istoriia, no. 4 (2017): 777–806.

273. Alice (Liulia) Landau (1883–1968) was the daughter of Isabella and Iosef Landau. She eventually married Osmond d'Avigdor Goldsmid.

274. Iakov Poliakov, "Istoriia," l. 311.

275. *Le Figaro*, 25 October 1907.

276. NIOR RGB, f. 343, k. 138, d. 2, 12 ob. However, Zinaida apparently misunderstood why the family had disowned him and thought that the issue was the wife's divorced status: "His wife was married earlier to an officer in Taganrog and was divorced from him; this is why everyone is opposed to this marriage" (ibid.).

277. Malkiel evidently mispronounced "civilized," and Zinaida sardonically reproduced her mistake.

278. On the spas, see Zadoff, *Next Year in Marianbad*.

279. Flora Gubbay married Jules Reuff, a French businessman who—according to some accounts—founded the Messageries Fluviales de Cochinchine (River Shipping Company of Cochinchina) in 1881. See J. Ka., "Rueff, Jules," in *The Jewish Encyclopedia: A Descriptive Record of the History, Religion, Literature, and Customs of the Jewish People from the Earliest Times*, ed. Isidore Singer, (New York: Funk and Wagnalls Company, 1964), 10:509.

280. Poliakova and Poliakoff, *Sem'ia Poliakovykh*, 231 (19 May 1887).

281. Iakov Poliakov, "Istoriia," l. 139.

282. "Carnet de mariage," *Le Figaro*, 25 July 1891.

283. *Times of India*, 25 July 1891.

284. "Echos Mondains," *New York Herald, Paris*, 25 July 1891.

285. Iakov Poliakov, "Istoriia," l. 140.

286. "Mariages," *Le Figaro*, 5 July 1896. The witnesses were Jacques Caponi and Marc Levi for the groom and Reuben Gubbay and Michel de Poliakoff for the bride.

287. *Le Gaulois* announced the celebration of the wedding that took place on 4 June 1896 in Moscow at the private Poliakov synagogue, with Rabbi Maze officiating.

288. NIOR RBG, f. 743, op. 138, d. 1, l. 32 (16 January 1895). Zinaida also became acquainted with Madame Levi's brother-in-law, Sir Georgio Enrico Levi, whose daughter Lina married Isabella Landau's son, George Landau. Zinaida observed that their friend Rosenau's daughter, Nina Levi, went out a lot and suspected that she had fallen in love with a Christian "because she herself says that religion does not play any role, only the Italian nationality" (NIOR RGB, f. 743, k. 139, d. l., l. 2 [2 January 1904]).

289. For example, see NIOR RGB, f. 743, k. 138, d. 3, ll. 50, 61 ob.–62.

290. NIOR RGB, f. 343, k. 138, d. 7, l. 48 ob.

291. *Le Figaro* reported the wedding, which took place on 31 January 1904 in Moscow. It noted that delays in the Russian post due to censorship led to problems with the invitations

and announcements ("Mariages," 1 February 1904). On 24 August 1903, Iakov Poliakov had written in his diary about Raia's engagement: "Thank God, it's already time. She's thirty-two years old" ("Istoriia," l. 365).

292. NIOR RGB, f. 743, k. 138, d. 3, l. 73 (12 September 1903).

293. Ibid., l. 68.

294. NIOR RGB, f. 343, k. 138, d. 7, l. 48 ob.

295. "Mariages," *Le Matin*, 23 January 1901.

296. NIOR RGB, f. 743, k. 138, d, 3, l. 64.

297. Il'ia was also an avid equestrian whose feats were publicized in the French papers. See "Concours Hippique," *Le Radical*, 1 April 1901; NIOR RGB, f. 343, k. 138, d. 2, l. 47 ob.

298. NIOR RGB, f. 343, k. 138, d, 2, l. 47 ob. (n.d., 1901).

299. NIOR RGB, f. 743, k. 139, d. 1, l. 13 ob. (26 August 1904).

300. Ibid., l. 71.

301. NIOR RGB, f. 743, k. 138, d. 3, l. 72–72 ob. (12 September 1903).

302. NIOR RGB, f. 743, k. 139, d. 1, l. 60 (1 May 1905).

303. Grange, *Une élite Parisienne*.

304. The marriage was registered in England in 1908 at St. George's Hanover Square Church, in London. See "All Marriage and Divorce Results for Michel Poliakoff," Ancestry, accessed 1 April 2019, https://www.ancestry.co.uk/search/categories/bmd_marriage/?name=michel_Poliakoff&location=3257.3250&name_x=_1&priority=united-kingdom.

305. Vermel', *Evrei v Moskve*, 158.

306. Sliozberg, *Delo minuvshikh dnei*, 2:43.

307. Quoted in ibid., 2:162.

308. The reference is to the head of police, E. O. Iankovskii, who was called "the whip of Jewry" (E. L'vov, "Evrei v Moskve," in *Evrei v Moskve: Sbornik materialov*, ed. Iu. Snopov and A. Klempert [Moscow: Mosty kul'tury, 2003], 274).

309. Ibid., 272 and 274.

310. Some claim that one newspaper that L'vov was referring to here was Abram Ia. Lipskerov's *Novosti dnia*, although it did not have a Jewish character. See ibid., 279.

311. Ibid., 278–79.

312. Quoted in Ivan E. Dronov, "Rasrabotka konservativnoi kontseptsii razvitiia Rossii v tvorchestve V. P. Meshcherskogo," Kand. diss., Moscow State Humanitarian University, 2002, 208.

313. Quoted in John Klier, *Imperial Russia's Jewish Question, 1855–1881* (Cambridge: Cambridge University Press, 1995), 448. Iakov Poliakov also claimed to be very close to Meshcherskii. For instance, he wrote in his diary on 14 January 1897: "Meshcherskii gave a dinner to all those who congratulated him on his twenty–fifth jubilee. He treated me most graciously" ("Istoriia," l. 239).

314. Quoted in Dronov, "Rasrabotka konservativnoi kontseptsii razvitiia Rossii v tvorchestve V. P. Meshcherskogo," 269.

315. Iakov Poliakov, "Istoriia," l. 239 (10 July 1897).

316. T. D. G., "Di groyse libe," *Der fraynd*, 2 February 1910.

317. "Poliakov shikt a broche tsu kniaz Meshcherski," *Der morgen zhurnal*, 15 February 1910.

318. Vermel', "Evrei v Moskve," 174. Vlasovskii was the chief of police in Moscow from 1891 to 1896.

319. Ibid., 167–68.

320. Onisim Gol'dovskii, "Evrei v Moskve: stranitsa iz istorii sovremennoi Rossii," in *Evrei v Moskve*, 284. Gol'dovskii's memoirs were originally published anonymously in Berlin in 1904 and in the journal *Byloe* in 1907.

321. Vinaver, "Vospominaniia," 9.

322. Vermel', "Evrei v Moskve,"190.

323. Harold Frederic, "An Indictment of Russia: Trying to Tear an Entire People up by the Roots," *New York Times*, 7 December 1891.

324. Iakov Poliakov, "Istoriia," l. 133.

325. Vermel', "Evrei v Moskve," 190.

326. Quoted in Katsnel'son, "Iz martirologa Moskovsoi obshchiny," 417.

327. Iakov Poliakov, "Istoriia," l. 140 (15 September 1891).

328. Gol'dovskii, "Evrei v Moskve," 394–410. See also Lev Aizenberg, "Veliki Kniaz' Sergei Aleksandrovich, Vitte, i evrei—Moskovskie kuptsy (iz istorii izgnaniia evreev iz Moskvu)," in *Evrei v Moskve*, 302.

329. Iakov Poliakov, "Istoriia," l. 161.

330. For a comparative view, see Elizabeth C. MacKnight, "Faiths, Fortunes, and Feminine Duty: Charity in Parisian High Society, 1880–1914," *Journal of Ecclesiastical* History 58, no. 3 (2007): 482–506.

331. Konstantin Petrovich Pobedenostsev wrote to Alexander III that Katkov had made efforts to secure subsidies for his school from P. M. Leont'ev and "mainly S[amuel] S[olomonovich] Poliakov" (*Pis'ma k Aleksandru III* [Moscow: Izdatel'stvo "Direkt-Media," 2014], 1:401). Sergei Witte also wrote: "In general, Katkov had nothing against the Jews and not only had nothing against [them], but even had good relations with the Jews. So, for example, the Katkov Lycée in Moscow (the so-called Lycée of the Tsarevich Nicholas) was founded on considerable assistance from Poliakov and Jewish money in general" (*Iz arkhiva S. Iu. Vitte: Vospominaniia*, ed. Boris V. Anan'ich and Rafail Sholomovich Ganelin [St. Petersburg: Sankt-Peterburskii institut istorii RAN, 2003], 1:283).

332. *Otchet Moskovskago otdeleniia imperatorskogo russkogo muzykal'nogo obshchestva, 1904–1905* (Moscow: Tovarishchestvo "Pechatnia S. P. Iakovleva," 1906), 25.

333. *Vsepodanneishii otchet soveta Imperatorskogo chelovekoliubivogo obshchestva za 1904 god* (St. Petersburg, 1904), 109.

334. Iakov Poliakov, "Istoriia," l. 165.

335. Ibid., ll. 140–41.

336. Iakov Poliakov, "Istoriia semeinye nachiniaia [s] 1748, ll. 335–36. The ties between the Poliakovs and Pobedonostsev went back to the 1870s, when Samuil Solomonovich Poliakov submitted his first petition to donate a two-story building and funds to establish a school of the Russian Voluntary Fleet. Pobedonotsev brought the petition to the attention of Alexander III. See Konstantin Petrovich Pobedonostsev, *Konstantin Petrovich Pobedonostsev i ego korrespondenty* [Minsk: Kharvest, 2003), 1:18–19; Pobedonostsev, *Pis'ma k Aleksandru III*, 1:180 and 252–53. Pobedonostsev also supported Samuil Poliakov's proposal to build railroads in Turkey, Bulgaria, and Persia to counter the British (who were being supported by the Austrians). See Pobedonostsev, *Pis'ma k Aleksandru III*, 1:122–25.

337. Iakov Poliakov, who had been elected a deputy of Taganrog, planned to take bread and

salt to greet Alexander III for the coronation, but his wife Amaliia "cried, afraid to let me go because there were rumors that ill-intended plotters were going to throw explosive bombs" ("Istoriia," l. 94 [8 May 1883]).

338. Quoted in L. Grossman, "Dostoevskii i pravitel'stvennye krugi," *Literaturnoe nasledstvo* 15 (1934): 142.

339. Quoted in ibid.

340. Pobedonostsev, *Pis'ma k Aleksandru III*, 1:247.

341. Iakov Poliakov, "Istoriia, l. 232.

342. NIOR RGB, f. 743, k. 139, d.1, l. 24 (17 December 1904).

343. A. N. Khmelevskii, "Gerb Lazaria Poliakova," Obshchii grebovnik, dvorianskikh rodov vserossiiskiia imperii, accessed 31 March 2019, https://gerbovnik.ru/arms/2919.

344. When Iakov Poliakov informed his brother that his son Boris and son-in-law Lev (Louis) Raffalovich had just been to Persia to establish a railroad company in 1889, he observed, "He [Lazar] apparently did not expect this but did not say anything, so there was [a] pause" ("Istoriia," l. 113). According to John Galbraith, Lev Raffalovich and Boris Poliakov "appeared in Tehran under the auspices of Dolgoruki [*sic*] to seek a railroad concession" (John S. Galbraith, "British Policy on Railways in Persia, 1870–1900," *Middle Eastern Studies* 25, no. 4 [October 1989]: 498). However, Iakov did not state that his son and son-in-law went to Persia for the Russian state. Rather, they went on Iakov's initiative, which clearly surprised or displeased Lazar.

345. Iakov Poliakov, "Istoriia," l. 48. Iakov (as consul in Taganrog) credited himself for helping Samuil become the Persian consul in St. Petersburg and Lazar in Moscow.

346. Ibid., l. 104. Iakov learned that he had received the title of baron for himself and his two sons-in-law Iosef Landau and Grigorii (George) Rubinshtein, on 25 February 1890 and for his son Lazar Iakovlevich on 2 March 1890. When Iakov asked his brother Lazar if he also wanted the title, the latter responded that he already had the title but "it does not impart any significance" (ibid., l. 118 [15 March 1890]).

347. Soli Shahvar, "Railroads i. The First Railroad Build and Operated in Persia," *Encyclopaedia Iranica*, 7 April 2008, http://www.iranicaonline.org/articles/railroads-i.

348. Anan'ich, *Bankirskie doma v Rossii*.

349. Quoted in Firuz Kazemzadeh, *Russia and Britain in Persia, 1864–1914* (New Haven, CT: Yale University Press, 1968), 275.

350. Iakov Poliakov, "Istoriia," l. 239 (29 March 1897).

351. Anan'ich, *Bankirskie doma v Rossi*, 119.

352. Kazemzadeh, *Russia and Britain*, 276.

353. Quoted in ibid., 277.

354. Ibid.

355. Quoted in ibid., 76.

356. Quoted in ibid., 279.

357. Guive Mirfendereski, *A Diplomatic History of the Caspian Sea: Treaties, Diaries, and Other Stories* (New York: Palgrave, 2001), 79.

358. Anan'ich, *Bankirskie doma v Rossii*, 200.

359. Ibid.

360. Petrov, "The Banking Network of Moscow," 56.

361. Anan'ich, *Bankirskie doma v Rossii*, 122.

362. Ibid., 127.

363. Quoted in ibid., 125.

364. Quoted in ibid.

365. Hassan Malik, *Bankers and Bolsheviks: International Finance and the Bolshevik Revolution* (Princeton, NJ: Princeton University Press, 2018), 179.

366. Lebedev, "European Business Culture and St. Petersburg Banks," 30–31.

367. Quoted in ibid., 32. The two records of the commission's meetings on 27 May and 12 June 1893 can be found in RGIA, f. 588, op. 3, d. 10.

368. Lebedev, "European Business Culture and St. Petersburg Banks," 129. Poliakov's detractors included the state controller, Pavel L. Lobko; the minister of the interior, Dmitrii S. Sipiagin; and the minister of justice, Nikolai V. Murav'ev.

369. Ibid., 130. Those who supported giving Poliakov state assistance included Dmitrii M. Sol'skii, Fyodor G. Terner, Anatoli P. Ivashchenkov, and Petr A. Saburov.

370. Quoted in ibid.

371. NIOR RGB, f. 743, k. 138, d. 3, l. 3 (30 July 1902).

372. Alexander Poliakoff, *The Silver Samovar*, 23.

373. NIOR RGB, f. 743, k. 138, d. 3, l. 3 (30 July 1902).

374. Iakov Poliakov, "Istoriia," l. 288.

375. Witte, *Vospominaniia*, 1:422–23. See also Freeze, "When Chava Left Home," 176–77.

376. Quoted in Witte, *Vospominaniia*, 536, n. 63.

377. Iakov Poliakov, "Istoriia," l. 288 (30 April 1899).

378. This is a reference to Iakov's son-in-law Gregorii (George) Rubinshtein, who was married to his daughter Anna (Niuta).

379. NIOR RGB, f. 343, k. 138, d. 2, l. 56 ob.

380. Ibid., l. 11. This was not quite accurate. Iakov wrote constantly about his business affairs in his diaries until his death. His son Samuil seems to have been in charge of the family business.

381. Quoted in Anan'ich, *Bankirskie doma*, 132.

382. NIOR RGB, f. 743, op. 138, d, 1., l. 151 ob.

383. NIOR RGB, f. 343, k. 138, d. 2, l. 47–47 ob.

384. Ibid., l. 50.

385. NIOR RGB, f. 743, k. 139, d. 1, l. 62 (26 February 1905). Zinaida's allowance may have already been reduced, because when she received a letter thanking her for her donation from a philanthropic organization, she wrote: "I often have to give to various philanthropic bazaars and lotteries and now we need to decrease [these donations] a bit" (ibid., 19 February 1905).

386. Ibid., l. 69 (4 July 1905).

387. Ibid., l. 69 ob. (6 July 1905).

388. NIOR RGB, f. 743, k. 138, d. 3, l. 14 ob. (8 February 1903). Zinaida noted that her mother always went with her father to St. Petersburg for business meetings.

389. NIOR RGB, f. 743, k. 139, d. 1, l. 71 ob. (11 July 1905).

390. Ibid., l. 28 ob. (28 December 1904).

391. Ibid., l. 66 (18 June 1905).

392. Ibid., l. 70 ob. (8 July 1905).

393. Ibid., l. 29 (1 January 1906). Shcherbatov's Party of Law and Order was positioned

somewhere between the moderate Union of 17 October Party (which supported a constitutional monarchy) and the right-wing Black Hundreds.

394. NIOR RGB, f. 743, k. 139, d. 1, l. 76 (25 July 1906).

395. Quoted in Malik, *Bankers and Bolsheviks*, 93.

396. Ibid., 93–94.

397. Ibid., 106.

398. Ibid., 102.

399. Ibid., 103.

400. Ibid., 105.

401. Quoted in Anan'ich, *Bankirskie doma*, 135.

402. Malik, *Bankers and Bolsheviks*, 103.

403. Ibid., 136.

404. Ibid., 137.

405. NIOR RGB, f. 743, k. 139, d. 1, l. 69 ob. (6 July 1905). For her address, see *Tout-Paris: Annuaire de la société parisienne: Noms & addresses, classés par noms, par professions, et par rues . . . suivis d'un dictionnaire des pseudonymes* (Paris, 1905), 263. See also Patrice de Moncan, *Les jardins du baron Haussmann* (Paris: Les Éditions du Mécène 1992), 24–32.

406. Grange, *Une élite parisienne*. Zinaida's home was also steps away from her parents' apartment on 50 Rue de Bois de Boulogne, where Lazar and Rozaliia were registered in the *Livre d'or des salons* in 1899—although they primarily resided in Russia (*Livre d'or des salons: Addresses à Paris et dans les châteaux* (Paris: E. Bender, 1899).

407. In France, the "de Poliakoffs" went by their French names.

408. For example, Reuben Gubbay was elected as a new member of the central committee of the Alliance Israélite Universelle in 1902. See "Election des membres du Comité central de l'Alliance," *L'Univers Israélite*, no. 41 (27 June 1902): 465.

409. NIOR RGB, f. 743, k. 139, d. 1, l. 107 ob. (6 April 1907).

410. Poliakova and Poliakoff, *Sem'ia Polikovykh*, 267 (21 May 1944).

411. Quoted in Gerry Black, *Lender to the Lords, Giver to the Poor* (Chicago: Vallentine Mitchell, 1992), 128.

412. NIOR RGB, f. 343, k. 138, d. 2, l. 47 ob. She also visited Lady Leontine and Sir Edward Elias Sassoon in 1898.

413. "Sir Albert Sassoon at Home," *Times of India*, 22 January 1885.

414. Stansky, *Sassoon*, 6. After the shah arrived in Brighton and was received by the mayor, he "at once drove off to the residence of Sir Albert Sassoon at the Eastern Terrace, Marine Parade. . . . Sir Albert's house was in a perfect blaze of light. In addition to the large assemblage of persons on the streests, the windows and tops of the houses in the vicinity were crowded with persons anxious to get a a view of His Majesty, and coloured lights burned in profusion" ("The Shah's Tour," *Times of India*, 20 August 1889). Incidentally, the Poliakovs also had dealings with this shah as they expanded their business into his realm.

415. "Sir Albert Sassoon, Bart, C.S. I.," *American Hebrew*, 24 January 1890.

416. Ibid.

417. "Sir Albert Sassoon," *American Israelite*, 19 November 1896.

418. Ibid.

419. NIOR RGB, f. 743, op. 138, d. 1, l. 29.

420. "Sir Albert Sassoon [obituary]," *American Israelite*, 12 November 1896.

421. Quoted in Roland, *Jews in British India*, 70.

422. NIOR RGB, f. 743, op. 138, d. 1, l. 35 ob. Zinaida also found it cruel that when Solomon Sassoon died a year earlier in Bombay, her sister-in-law "Flora was angry at her father for weeping" over the death of his half-brother.

423. Ibid., l. 27 ob.

424. NIOR RGB, f. 743, k. 139, d. 1, l. 64 ob. (9 June 1906).

425. Stansky, *Sassoon*, 19 and 21. Hannah Gubbay was close to English royalty, especially the Prince of Wales (who called her frequently to share gossip and confidences) and Queen Mary.

426. "The Queen's Drawing Room," *Morning Post*, 19 May 1897.

427. "Sir Albert Sassoon at Home."

428. "Death of Mr. A. M. Gubbay," *Times of India*, 29 August 1894.

429. Ibid.

430. NIOR RGB, f. 743, op. 138, d. 1, l. 35 (22 January 1895).

431. "Nécrologie," *Le Gaulois*, 24 August 1894.

432. "Wills and Bequests," *Illustrated London News*, 7 March 1914.

433. "Nécrologie," *Le Gaulois*, 31 December 1913.

434. NIOR RGB, f. 743, op. 138, d. 1, l. 170. Zinaida wrote this entry in London.

435. In an interview for a film, Sybil reflected on her conversion: "I changed because I thought that—I had children, and I thought it was better for them to belong to the religion of the country. . . . I don't think that [my family] thought very much of my [oath of conversion]. First of all a great many of them were not there any more, either had died or were far away. . . . My family were not at all what they call orthodox. But we went naturally to services but we never kept very much to the religious things (quoted in Stansky, *Sassoon*, 34–35). See also Roth, *The Sassoon Dynasty*, 231.

436. Quoted in Stansky, *Sassoon*, 34.

437. Iakov Poliakov, "Istoriia," l. 165 (14 May 1893).

438. NIOR RGB, f. 743, op. 138, d. 1, l. 120 ob (1 August 1895).

439. Iakov Poliakov, "Istoriia," l. 51 (13 August 1871).

440. NIOR RGB, f. 743, op. 138, d.1, ll. 120 ob. (1 August 1895).

441. NIOR RGB, f. 343, k. 138, d. 2, l. 32 (1901).

442. Elizabeth (Lily) and Olga were Iakov (Jacques) and Claire de Poliakoff's daughters. The couple had another daughter, Hélène, later.

443. "Distinctions," *L'Univers Israélite*, no. 39 (12 June 1912), 30.

444. NIOR RGB, f. 743, op. 138, d. 1, ll. 1–2 ob. (27 December 1894) (my emphasis).

445. Ibid, l. 140 ob. (2 November 1895). See also "Au jour le jour: Le mariage Rothschild," *Le Figaro*, 23 May 1895.

446. "Mariages," *Le Gaulois*, 23 June 1896.

447. NIOR RGB, f. 743, op. 138, d. 1, 1. 119 (17 April 1895).

448. "Mariages," *Le Figaro*, 25 October 1907. Alice Landau and her brother, George, had visited Zinaida in Paris for meals with the family. For example, Iakov Poliakov mentioned on 30 October 1903 that "my wife with Alice and George were at Zina Gabbe's [Gubbay's]" ("Istoriia," l. 367).

449. NIOR RGB, f. 743, k. 138, d. 3, l. 5 (8 September 1902), and l. 7 (9 September 1902).

450. "The Montagu-Goldsmid Wedding: Description of the Ceremony, Guests, Dress, and Presents," *Jewish World*, 11 February 1898.

451. "Dit" in French refers to an alias. In this case, Daniel went by Constant Dreyfus in France rather than by his Hebrew name.

452. NIOR RGB, f. 743, k. 138, d. 3, l. 22 (March 1903).

453. "Le Concours Hippique," *Le Figaro*, 9 April 1909.

454. "Le Concours Hippique: La mode au Grand–Palais," *L'Intransigeant*, 24 March 1913.

455. Grange, *Une élite parisienne*, 83.

456. "La vie à Paris," *Le Sport*, 2 January 1892.

457. NIOR RGB, f. 743, k. 138, d. 3, l. 24 ob. (6 May 1903).

458. "Le monde et la ville," *Le Figaro*, 16 March 1902. Zinaida also published her reception hours, which were 5:00–7:00 p.m. on Sundays in 1906 ("Le monde et la ville," *Le Figaro*, 2 December 1906). On 15 May 1909, she announced in *Le Figaro* that she would not be receiving guests at her salon on Monday night "because it was a sad anniversary" ("Le monde et la ville: Salons," *Le Figaro*, 15 May 1909).

459. Quoted in Christopher G. Goetz, Michel Bonduelle, and Tony Gelfand, *Charcot: Constructing Neurology* (New York: Oxford University Press), 299.

460. Interestingly, the language she used—"*moi priyemnyi den*"—was the same term for the reception hours held by a Russian bureaucrat.

461. Steven D. Kale, "Women, the Public Sphere, and the Persistence of the Salon," *French Historical Studies* 25, no. 1 (2011): 142.

462. Ibid., 142.

463. Ibid., 146.

464. Quoted in Edmund de Waal, *The Hare with the Amber Eyes: A Family's Century of Art and Loss* (New York: Farrar, Straus and Giroux, 2010), 39.

465. Ibid., 40.

466. NIOR RGB, f. 743, k. 139, d. 1, l. 7 ob. (9 September 1904).

467. Ibid., l. 44–44 ob. Antony was not one of Julie's sons (who were Arthur Emile Kann [1874–1943], Reginald Salomon Kann [1876–1925], and Andre Maximillian Kann [1884–1910]) or stepsons. Perhaps Antony was a nickname.

468. Zinaida and Ruby were especially close to Theodore Reinach, who was married to a stepdaughter of Madame Sacki Kann.

469. The daughter of Walter Behrens.

470. NIOR RGB, f. 343, k. 138, d. 2, l. 40 (1901).

471. "Salons," *Le Figaro*, 17 March 1904. Viktor Kartsov was the commander of the torpedo boat *Vlastnyi* at Port Arthur.

472. "Treatment of Jewish Hero: Winner of Four George's Crosses Ordered out of Moscow," *New York Times*, 18 November 1905.

473. "Le 5'o'clock du 'Figaro,'" *Le Figaro*, 4 April 1907. Calmette was assassinated by Madame Henriette Caillaux, whose husband Joseph Caillaux—"leader of the Radical party and nemesis of nationalists"—had been a target of *Le Figaro*'s "campaign of libel and character assassination that was dirty even by the decidedly lax standards of the Third Republic" (Edward Berenson, "The Politics of Divorce in France in the Belle Epoque: The Case of Joseph and Henrietta Caillaux," *American Historical Review* 93, no. 1 [1988]: 32). Henriette, his second wife, was afraid that the newspaper would publish her love letters, written to Joseph while he was still married to his first wife, Bertha Gueydan. Her fears were well-founded because a few months earlier it had published a facsimile of a love letter that he had written to his first wife.

Henriette was acquitted by a jury for shooting Calmette, which she claimed happened during a momentary derangement.

474. Iakov Poliakov also mentions the Proppers. For instance, he wrote on 11 April 1903: "I met with Propper in Vienna; he passionately praised Samuil [Iakov's youngest son]" ("Istoriia," l. 360).

475. In 1906, Zinaida wrote that Philipp Brüll was at their home for business negotiations with her father to combine his three banks into one commercial company (NIOR RBG, f. 743, k. 139, d. 1, l. 88 ob.).

476. Grange, *Une élite parisienne*, 91.

477. On Iakov Poliakov's difficult Azov-Don Bank affairs with Ruben and Constant Dreyfus, see Iakov Poliakov, "Istoriia," ll. 156, 157, and 171 (3 and 11 October and 16 November 1892 and 23 September 1893). On social events, see ibid. (24 February 1894). "In general, the Dreyfuses have cost me a lot in both money and health, and there is no accounting," Iakov wrote on 19 July 1895 (ibid., l. 208).

478. Ibid., l. 240 (6–7 October 1897).

479. NIOR RGB, f. 743, k. 138, d. 3, l. 15. These were the Levis from Florence, who were related to Zinaida's brother-in-law Georges Levi. She had become very close to Madame Enrichetta Levi during her travels to Italy, as noted above. Through her ties to Madame Levi, she became acquainted with Levi's brother-in-law Sir Georgio Enrico Levi (whose daughter Lina married Isabella Landau's son George). Zinaida observed that Nina Levi went out a lot and suspected that she had fallen in love with a Christian "because she herself says that religion does not play any role, only the Italian nationality" (NIOR RGB, f. 743, op. 139, d. l., l. 2 [2 January 1904]).

480. NIOR RGB, f. 743, k. 139, d. 1, l. 76 (25 July 1906).

481. MacKnight, "Faith, Fortunes, and Feminine Duty," 486.

482. "Réceptions mondains," *Gil Blas*, 13 March 1903.

483. "Nos Echos," *La Presse*, 14 March 1903.

484. NIOR RGB, f. 743, k. 138, d. 3, l. 16 ob. (8 March 1903).

485. Quoted in Michel Duchesneau, "The Triumph of Genre: Fauré's Chamber Music through the Looking Glass of Music Criticism," in *Regarding Fauré*, ed. and trans. Tom Gordon (Amsterdam: Gordon and Breach Publishers, 1999), 69.

486. NIOR RGB, f. 743, k. 138, d. 3, l. 18 (8 March 1903).

487. Maria Emden Heine, niece of the German-Jewish writer Heinrich Heine.

488. NIOR RGB, f. 743, k. 138, d. 3, l. 26 ob. (9 May 1903).

489. NIOR RGB, f. 743, k. 138, d. 3, l. 24 ob. (6 May 1903). She also hosted a dinner party at which Madame Roth "sang some songs of Schumann and Schubert after dinner" ("Le monde, salons," *Gil Blas*, 12 January 1905).

490. NIOR RGB, f. 343, k. 138, d. 2, l. 50 ob. (1901). Zinaida also mentioned that Shchukin had informed her mother that her relative, Vera Livshits, had married a Christian (ibid., k. 139, d, 1, l. 121 ob. [7 July 1909]).

491. *Annuaire de la Société des amis du Louvre* (Paris: Imprimerie Générale lahure, 1903), 21.

492. NIOR RGB, f. 743, k. 138, d. 3, l. 28 (9 May 1903).

493. Ibid., l. 30 (6 June 1903).

494. Ibid. For a lawsuit filed by Reuben Gubbay, Serge Zarine (the Russian consul in Paris), Viscount Rene Vigier, and an antique dealer named Lejeune against Victor Menage for objects

and art that they placed with a M. Wollmann, an antique dealer at 64 Rue du Faubourg Saint-Honoré, see "Un référe," *Le Matin*, 4 August 1915.

495. NIOR RGB, f. 743, op. 138, d. 1, l. 30 ob. (24 January 1895).

496. NIOR RGB, f. 743, k. 139, d. 1., l. 16 ob. (4 September 1904).

497. NIOR RGB, f. 343, k. 138, d. 2, l. 110 ob. (1901).

498. Ibid., l. 50 (1901).

499. Ibid., l. 63, ob. (1902).

500. NIOR RGB, f. 743, op. 139, d. 1, ll. 27–27 ob. (11 January 1895).

501. Stansky observes that in the nineteenth century, "opium accounted for one-seventh of British income in India—and the Sassoons eventually controlled 70 percent of the trade" (*Sassoon*, 6).

502. NIOR RGB, f. 743, op. 138, d. 1, l. 27 ob.

503. Ibid., l. 150 (8 August 1897).

504. Steven D. Kale, "Women, the Public Sphere, and the Persistence of the Salon," *French Historical Studies* 25, no. 1 (2002): 147. Kale argues that "pleasing women" became an "ethical cornerstone" of aristocratic society, which saw women's "ability to civilize as not merely a feminine attribute but a social and potlical responsibility."

505. NIOR RGB, f. 743, op. 138, d. 1, l. 53 ob. (31 January 1895).

506. NIOR RGB, f. 743, k. 138, d. 2, l. 64 (1901).

507. NIOR RGB, f. 743, op. 139, d. 1, l. 8 (15 May 1904).

508. Iakov Poliakov, "Istoriia," l. 158 (7 December 1892).

509. "Le Nickel de la Nouvelle-Calédonie," *Annuaire Desfossés: Valeurs cotées en banque à la Bourse de Paris* (Paris: E. Desfossés & Fabre Fréres, 1910), 538–39.

510. NIOR RGB, f. 743, op. 139, d. 1, l. 115 (20 June 1910).

511. Ibid., l. 127, ob. (22 June 1910).

512. Ibid., l. 129 (13 July 1910).

513. NIOR RGB, f. 343, k. 138, d. 2 (1901).

514. NIOR RGB, f. 743, k. 139, d. 1, l. 77 ob. (1 August 1906).

515. NIOR RGB, f. 743, k. 1, 139, d. 1, l. 38 ob. (8 February 1906). Zinaida expressed surprise at every announcement of a divorce among their friends: "In general there is now an epidemic of divorces: Constance [Dreyfus], [Anna Gould and Boni de] Castellane, Jourdanne, Shteilin, and many others with whom we are not acquainted" (ibid.).

516. Ibid., l. 145.

517. Iakov Poliakov, "Istoriia," l. 238 (11 December 1896). The birthday is noted as 11 December 1896 according to the Old Style calendar in Iakov's diary.

518. "Renseignements mondains," *Le Figaro*, 24 December 1896.

519. "Semur-en-Auxois: La nourrice morvandelle qui a côtoyé un conseiller du tsar," 15 May 2017, http://www.bienpublic.com/edition-haute-cote-d-or/2017/05/15/la-nourrice-morvandelle-qui-a-cotoye-un-conseiller-du-tsar.

520. NIOR RGB, f. 743, k. 138, d. 3, l. 37 (22 June 1903).

521. Ibid.

522. NIOR RGB, f. 743, k. 139, d. 1, l. 74 (18 July 1906).

523. Renée Poznanski, *Jews in France During World War II* (Hanover, NH: University Press of New England, 2001), 25.

524. NIOR RGB, f. 743, k. 138, d. 3, l. 83 (19 October 1904).

525. NIOR RGB, f. 343, k. 138, d. 2, l. 54 ob. (1901).

526. "A Travers le monde," *Les Modes: Revue mensuelle illustrée des arts décoratifs appliqués à la femme*, February 1903, 17.

527. "A Travers le monde," *Les Modes: Revue mensuelle illustrée des arts décoratifs appliqués à la femme*, February 1909, 2.

528. "Le Monde," *Gil Blas*, 28 December 1904.

529. "Causerie Mondaine," *Le Figaro-Modes a la ville, au theater, arts décoratifs*, 15 January 1905.

530. NIOR RGB, f. 743, k. 138, d. 3, l. 2-2 ob. (28–30 July 1902).

531. Ibid.

532. Ibid., l. 6 (9 September 1902). While they were in Switzerland, Zinaida visited the grave of her brother Avgust, as noted above.

533. Ibid., l. 67 ob. (24 August 1903). She was not always successful, because Annette caught scarlet fever.

534. Ibid., ll. 27–32.

535. NIOR RGB, f. 743, k. 139, d. 1, l. 14 ob. (28 August 1904).

536. Hélène Kann Allatini (1887–1943) was the daughter of Zinaida's close friend Julie Sacki Kann. She was married to Moïse Allatini (1809–82) and was the sister-in-law of Marie Kann Varshavskia [Warshawsky], the sister of Louise Cahen d'Anvers. In other words, she was a relative of Nissim Camondo, who knew about the family connection between Annette's family and the Camondos through the Varshavskiis [Warshawskys].

537. Poliakova and Poliakoff, *Sem'ia Poliakovykh*, 2.

538. Elizabeth Rodini, "Preserving and Perpetuating Memory at Musée Nissim de Camondo," *Museum History Journal* 7, no. 15 (2014): 36. See also Pierre Assouline, *Le dernier des Camondo* (Paris: Gallimard, 1997).

539. De Waal, *The Hare with Amber Eyes*, 27.

540. Ibid., 40.

541. *Annuaire de la Societé des etudes juives* (Paris: Librairie A. Durlacher, 1883), 2:207. For more on the Camondo family, see Assouline, *Le dernier des Camondo*; Aron Rodrigue, "Abraham de Camondo of Istanbul: the Transformation of Jewish Philanthropy," in *Profiles in Diversity: Jews in a Changing Europe, 1750–1870*, ed. Francis Malino and David Sorkin (1991; repr., Detroit, MI: Wayne State Unversity Press, 1998), 46–56.

542. For instance, see "Le Suicide de M. de Gunzburg," *Le XIXe siècle* (20 September 1905); "Nécrologie," *Le journal* (19 September 1905).

543. "Mondanités," *Le Gaulois*, 5 June 1892. See also "Le vie mondaine," *Le Matin*, 6 June 1892; *Revue Mondaine Illustrée*, 6 June 1892.

544. "Nouvelles Diverses," *L'Univers Israélite* 67, no. 8 (3 November 1911): 245.

545. For the marriage of Moïse de Camondo and Irène Cahen d'Anvers, which was celebrated with the greatest pomp and circumstance at the synagogue on Rue de la Victoire, see Grange, *Une élite parisienne*, 151–52.

546. NIOR RGB, f. 743, k. 138, d. 3, l. 66 ob. (24 August 1904).

547. De Waal, *The Hare with the Amber Eyes*, 83. See also Rodini, "Preserving and Perpetuating Memory at Musée Nissim de Camondo," 39.

548. Poliakova and Poliakoff, *Sem'ia Poliakovykh*, 76–77 (23 June 1944).

549. "Nissim de Camondo (1892–1917)," Musée Nissim de Camondo, accessed 3 April

2017, https://madparis.fr/en/museums/musee-nissim-de-camondo/the-camondo-family-1599/genealogy/nissim-de-camondo-1892-1917.

550. Poliakova and Poliakoff, *Sem'ia Poliakovykh*, 277 (23 June 1944).

551. Quoted in Assouline, *Le dernier des Camondo*, 232–33.

552. Quoted in Rodini, "Preserving and Perpetuating Memory at Musée Nissim de Camondo," 38.

553. "Deuil," *Le Figaro*, 13 October 1917. See also Assouline, *Le dernier des Camondo*, 234–36.

554. Poliakova and Poliakoff, *Sem'ia Poliakovykh*, 267 (21 May 1944).

555. NIOR RGB, f. 743, k. 139, d. 1, l. 71 (9 July 1906).

556. NIOR RGB, f. 743, k. 138, d. 3, l. 69 (9 September 1903).

557. John Richardson, *A Life of Picasso: The Triumphant Years, 1917–1932* (New York: Alfred A. Knopf, 2010), 92.

558. NIOR RGB, f. 743, k. 138, d. 3, l. 9–9 ob. (17 September 1902).

559. *Le Petit Journal Parti Social Français*, 15 August 1939.

560. "Un temple Israélite a Biarritz," in *Archives Israélite*, ed. Isidore Cahen and H. Prague (Paris: Bureau des Archives Israélite, 1895): 331–32.

561. "Inauguration de la Synagogue de Biarritz," *L'Univers Israélite* 59, no. 52 (16 September 1904): 818–19.

562. Iakov Poliakov, "Istoriia," ll. 389–90. Iakov died in Biarretz in 1909. See "Poliakov geshtorben," *Di varhayt*, 30 November 1909; "Iakov Poliakov geshtorben," *Yidishes tagesblat*, 30 November 1909.

563. NIOR RGB, f. 743, k. 138, d. 3, l. 8 ob. (17 September 1902).

564. Ibid., l. 13 ob. (29 September 1902).

565. Ibid., ll. 51–51 ob. (24 July 1903).

566. NIOR RGB, f. 743, op. 139, d. 1, l. 2 (1 January 1904). On one occasion, Isabella came to Paris but without informing Zinaida, who discovered her whereabouts by reading the *New York Herald*, which announced that she was staying "at the Hotel Meurice, registered as Josephine Landau from Basel." The pseudonym (easily decipherable because of the feminized name of her husband) suggests that perhaps Isabella—who suffered from depression—wanted some privacy, away from her large, extended family (NIOR RGB, f. 743, k. 1, d. 138, l. 18 ob. [1901]).

567. Ibid., f. 343, op. 138, d. 2, l. 75 (1901).

568. Ibid., l. 78 (1901).

569. NIOR RGB, f. 743, d. 3, l. 7-7 ob. (9 September 1902). Zinaida was referring to Gregorii Vilenkin and his wife, Irma Seligman, who were scheduled to travel from England to Dieppe (in northern France) and then to stay with Irma's mother in the countryside before coming to Paris.

570. NIOR RGB, f. 743, op. 138, d. 3, l. 18 (8 March 1903).

571. Ibid., l. 35 (21 June 1903). Leon's niece Marie Lazarevich née Brodskii (who was married to Jules Dreyfus) also came to visit the Gubbays (ibid., d. 2, l. 26 ob. [summer 1901]).

572. Ibid., l. 78 ob. (8 October 1903).

573. Ibid., l. 37 ob. Leopold Sinaeff-Bernstein (1867–1944) began his art education in Vil'na. He moved to Paris when he was fourteen and studied sculpture with Aimé-Jules Delou.

574. NIOR RGB, f. 743, k. 138, d. 2, l. 37 (1901).

575. NIOR RGB, f. 743, k. 138, d. 3, l. 35.

576. Ibid., l. 16 (10 February 1903).

577. Ibid., ll. 59 ob.–60 (28 June 1903).

578. See Veronica O. Shapovalov, *Remembering the Darkness: Women in Soviet Prisons* (Lanham, MD: Rowman and Littlefield, 2001), 23–70. According to Shapovalov, the uncles and aunts of Evgeniia Iaroslavskaia Markon (1901–31)—on the side of her mother, Roza Vydrin —took an active role in the political movements in Russia as Bolsheviks, Social Democrats, Octoberists, and Kadets. Markon's uncle Isaak Il'ich Vydrin went into exile together with Iakov Mikhailovich Sverdlov (a prominent Bolshevik leader).

579. NIOR RGB, f. 343, op. 138, d. 2, l. 62 ob. (1901).

580. Ibid., ll. 51 and 54. The newspapers also reported brilliant dinners at Zinaida's home that included relatives and friends: "A very nice dinner at the home of Madame Reuben Gubbay whose guests were Mmes. Sulzbach and Vanderheym, M. and Mme. Morpurgo, M. and Mme. Ullmann, M. and Mme. Rueff, comte de Tinseau, M. Masse, marquis de Torre Alfina, M. de Poliakoff" ("Le monde et la ville," *Le Figaro*, 16 March 1902).

581. NIOR RGB f. 743, k. 138, d. 3, l. 81 ob.

582. NIOR RGB, f. 743, k. 139, d. 1, l. 59 (26 April 1906).

583. For example, "I am searching for kasha and black bread," she wrote in 1906 during a vacation in Nice. "Maybe they will have it at the Restaurant du Casino Municipal" (Ibid., d. 1, l. 46 [26 February 1906]). Apparently, she had greater luck finding foods like her favorite shchi and kasha in Nice than in Paris.

584. Ibid., l. 76 ob.

585. Ibid., l. 59.

586. NIOR RGB, f. 743, k. 138, d. 3, l. 16 ob. (8 March 1903).

587. Ibid., l. 11 ob. (17 September 1902). Of course, Zinaida was just as enamored of the Rothschilds. During the family's treatment in La Bourboule in 1902, she took a day trip to Mont-Dore and reported that "we saw Béatrice Ephrussi [née Rothschild, 1864–1934] and Baronness Lambert from the window" of the hotel (ibid., l. 2 [28 July 1902]). Their relative Edward Sassoon and his wife, Aline Rothschild (daughter of Baron Gustave de Rothschild), also spent time with their children (Philip and Sybil) at the Château Laversine, which was near Chantilly. See Stansky, *Sassoon*, 15.

588. Ibid., ll. 34 ob. and 39 (18 and 25 June 1903).

589. Stansky, *Sassoon*, 170.

590. NIOR RGB, f. 743, k. 138, d. 3, l. 33 ob. (14 July 1903).

591. Ibid., l. 84 ob.

592. Ibid., l. 7 (9 September 1902).

593. The peace treaty, which was negotiated in August, was finally signed on 5 September 1905.

594. NIOR RGB, f. 743, k. 139, d. 1, l. 13 ob. (3 September 1905).

595. Ibid., l. 72 ob. (13 July 1906). Dreyfus was officially exonerated on 12 July 1906.

596. Antoine "Tony" Dreyfus (b. 1867).

597. NIOR RGB, f. 343, k. 138, d. 2, ll. 17 ob.–20 ob. (circa 18–20 September 1901).

598. For instance, see NIOR RGB, f. 743, k. 139, d. 3, l. 24 (6 May 1905).

599. "Au secours!," *L'Univers Israélite* 71, no. 22, (4 February 1916): 561.

600. "Pour les juifs russes, victimes de la guerre," *L'Univers Israélite* 72, no. 35 (25 March 1917): 224.

601. "Appel de la sociéte de secours aux Juifs victimes de la guerre en Russie," *L'Univers Israélite* 71, no. 23 (11 February 1916): 571–72.

602. For more on the organization, see Sam Johnson, "Breaking or Making the Silence: British Jews and East European Jewish Relief, 1914–1917," *Modern Judaism* 30, no. 1 (2010): 95–119.

603. Ibid., 108. For more on these brutal measures taken by the Russian military against the Jews, see Eric Lohr, "The Russian Army and the Jews: Mass Deportation, Hostages, and Violence During World War I," *Russian Review* 60, no. 3 (2001): 404–19.

604. NIOR RGB, f. 743, k. 138, d. 3, l. 57 (27 July 1903).

605. "Nissim de Camondo (1892–1917)."

606. "Legion d'honneur," *L'homme libre*, 20 July 1919. For a sample of Jacques de Poliakoff's medical articles, see "Quelques modifications à la technique de localisation des corps étrangers à l'aide du compas de hirtz," *Archives d'électricité médicale* 402 (1 April 1916): 7–109; Jacques Bandaline and Jacques Poliakoff, "Douches d'air chaud contre les brûlures par l'ypérite," *Recueil de médecine vétérinaire*, 15 March 1919, 160.

607. According to Zinaida, Marie (Maroussia) Varshavskaia [Warshawsky] was supposed to marry Robert Cahen [d'Anvers, possibly] in Paris when she was sixteen, but she never married. It appears that Marie's cousin Sonia Alice [Liulia] Varshavskaia [Warshawsky] ended up marrying Robert Cahen d'Anvers (grandparents of the writer Christian de Mombrison). Marie is buried in one plot with Olga Raffalovich, with whom she lived in Paris (NIOR RGB, f. 743, op. 138, d. 1, l. 159 [Cannes, 28 March 1898]).

608. "London, Paris, and New York: A Page of Society Élégantes," *Sketch*, 6 April 1927, 23.

609. Stansky, *Sassoon*, 1.

610. Mary Louise Roberts, "Samson and Delilah Revisited: The Politics of Women's Fashion in 1920s France," *American Historical Review* 98, no. 3 (1993): 658. See also Madeline Ginsburg, *Paris Fashions: The Art Deco Style of the 1920s* (London: Bracken Books, 1989), 12.

611. Roberts, "Samson and Delilah Revisited," 665.

612. Ibid., 660.

613. Quoted in ibid., 672.

614. Jaclyn Pyper, "*Style Sportive*: Fashion, Sport and Modernity in France, 1923–1930," *Apparence(s)* 7 (2017), https://journals.openedition.org/apparences/1361.

615. Quoted in ibid.

616. "Receptions," *Gazette de Bayonne, de Biarritz et du Pays Basque*, 18 October 1930.

617. "English and American News: Biarritz Notes," *Gazette de Bayonne, de Biarritz et du Pays basque*, 1 December 1926.

618. "Concours de Pyjamas," *Gazette de Bayonne, de Biarritz et du Pays Basque*, 6 September 1930.

619. "Bienfaisance," *Le Figaro*, 5 December 1932.

620. During the interwar years, Mikhail (known as Michael in the English-language press) was the head of the General Mortgage Bank, created by Keren Hayesod, for projects in Palestine. The *Jewish Advocate* reported: "The [General] Mortagage Bank is now in operation under the management of Mr. Michael Poliakoff, who is a recognized authority in banking matters and belongs to a family with wide banking experience and reputation" ("Houses for Palestine," *Jewish Advocate*, 24 August 1922). The headquarters of the bank was in Tel Aviv.

621. For a few examples, see "Déplacement et villégiatures," *Le Figaro*, 23 July 1914, 10 July 1918, 3 August 1920, 3 September 1924, 5 July 1930, and 27 August 1931; "Déplacement et villégiatures," *Le Gaulois*, 14 September 1917, 19 August 1919, 22 September 1921, 19 July 1923, and 29 July 1928.

622. In her final diary, Zinaida wrote, "I love to play in the casino and hope to do so in Nice" (NIOR RGB, f. 343, k. 138, d. 7, l. 39).

623. "A L'etranger," *Le Figaro*, 3 February 1914.

624. Maze, *Pamiati L. S. Poliakova*, 6.

625. Ibid., 13.

626. "Foreign News," *Advocate*, 22 November 1919; "Echos et Nouvelles," *L'Univers Israélite* 75, no. 4 (17 October 1919): 81.

627. "Echos et Nouvelles," *L'Univers Israélite* 75, no. 4 (17 October 1919): 81–82. For the commemoration of Rozaliia's yahrzeit at the Temple Israelite on Rue de la Victoire, at which Zinaida, Iakov (Jacques), and Aleksandr (Sasha) were present, see "Nécrologie," *Le Temps*, 18 March 1920.

628. "Succession Mme. Vve. Rosalie Pavlovna Poliakoff," *Le Temps*, 28 July 1923; "Succession Mme Veuve: Rosalie Pavlovna Poliakoff," *Journal official de la Republique français. Lois et décrets*, 2 August 1923.

629. NIOR RGB, f. 343, k. 138, d. 7, l. 17 (circa 1948).

630. "Deuils," *Le Figaro*, 3 February 1931.

631. NIOR RGB, f. 343, k. 138, d. 7, l. 68.

632. "Dons et offrandes," *L'Univers Israélite*, 27 February 1931.

633. NIOR RGB, f. 343, k. 138, d. 7, l. 5-5 ob. Zinaida traveled to Venice six months after Reuben's death, as noted in *Le Figaro*, 27 August 1931.

634. NIOR RGB, f. 343, k. 138, d. 7, l. 48 ob. (circa 1948).

635. "Deuils," *Gazette de Bayonne, de Biarritz et du Pays Basque*, 2 April 1937.

636. Poliakova and Poliakoff, *Sem'ia Poliakovykh*, 243 (25 February 1944). It is possible that she had kept a diary during the entire war period, since the diary picks up as though there had not been a long break between entries.

637. Ibid., 254 (25 February 1944).

638. Poznanski, *Jews in France During World War II*, 25.

639. Quoted in ibid., 31.

640. Ibid., 32.

641. Poliakova and Poliakoff, *Sem'ia Poliakovykh*, 260 (4 May 1944).

642. Claire Soussen, "Le Camp de Vittel, 1941–1944," *Le Monde Juif* 51, no. 153 (1995): 106–7.

643. Quoted in Charles Glass, *Americans in Paris: Life and Death under Nazi Occupation* (New York: Penguin Press, 2010), 253–54.

644. Soussen, "Le Camp de Vittel," 110–13.

645. Poliakova and Poliakoff, *Sem'ia Poliakovykh*, 254 (30 March 1944).

646. Ibid., 263 (10 May 1944).

647. Soussen, "Le Camp de Vittel," 110–13.

648. Poliakova and Poliakoff, *Sem'ia Poliakovykh*, 254 (24 February 1944).

649. Jacques Adler, *The Jews of Paris and the Final Solution* (New York: Oxford University Press, 1987), 22.

650. Poliakova and Poliakoff, *Sem'ia Poliakovykh*, 276 (21 June 1944).

651. Ibid., 255.

652. Adler, *The Jews of Paris*, 23.

653. Perhaps she meant "*requisitionné*."

654. Poliakova and Poliakoff, *Sem'ia Poliakovykh*, 280 (16 August 1944).

655. Ibid., 260 (4 May 1944). The first debacle must have been Annette's arrest and incarceration in the Vittel internment camp.

656. Ibid., 276 (20 June 1944).

657. NIOR RGB, f. 343, k. 138, d. 7, l. 38 (1948–49).

658. Ibid., l. 8 (circa 1948).

659. Poliakova and Poliakoff, Sem'ia Poliakovykh, 272 (10 June 1944).

660. Ibid., 274 (17 June 1944). She also explained that "Visha asked me not to write her anymore because she was in danger of trouble from the Nazis" (ibid., 289 [15 October 1944]).

661. NIOR RGB, f. 343, k. 138, d. 7, l. 8.

662. Anne Landau, "Rothschild: The Rothschild Hospital," Pipcus, accessed 1 May 2018, http://picpus.mmlc.northwestern.edu/mbin/WebObjects/Picpus.woa/wa/essayPageFor AtomID?id=52493.

663. Ibid.

664. Poliakova and Poliakoff, Sem'ia Poliakovykh, 272 (10 June 1944). Zinaida was also indebted to Fabienne de Vilain for all the efforts she made on Zinaida's behalf. During her sojourn in Nancy, she asked Fabienne "to send me two Jewish calendars. Before the [Jewish] holidays, I must order a new calendar" (ibid.).

665. Ibid., 257.

666. Ibid., 254 (30 March 1944).

667. Ibid., 254 (8 April 1944).

668. Ibid., 272 (9 June 1944).

669. NIOR RGB, f. 343, k. 138, d. 7, l. 6.

670. Poliakova and Poliakoff, Sem'ia Poliakovykh, 255 (8 April 1844). She must have been thinking of Khaia, Raisa, and herself as the three sisters and Benjamin and Il'ia (Elie) as the two brothers.

671. Ibid., 262 (9 May 1944).

672. Ibid., 77 (25 June 1944).

673. Ibid.

674. Ibid., 266 (19 May 1944).

675. Ibid., 268 (22 May 1944).

676. Ibid.

677. Ibid., 263 (12 May 1944).

678. Claire de Poliakoff was deported with Transport 45, Train DA 901-38, from Drancy Transit Camp to Auschwitz-Birkenau Extermination Camp on 11 November 1942. Elizabeth was deported with Transport 7, DA Train 901-2, from Drancy Transit Camp to Auschwitz-Birkenau Extermination Camp on July 19, 1942. See the information about Claire de Poliakoff and Elizabeth de Poliakoff in "Central Database of Shoah Victims' Names," Yad Vashem, accessed 1 April 2019, https://yvng.yadvashem.org/index.html?language=en&s_lastName=poliakoff&s_firstName=&s_place=&s_dateOfBirth=&s_inTransport=.

679. Poliakova and Poliakoff, Sem'ia Poliakovykh, 271 (5 June 1944).

680. Zinaida wrote, "Leo Lindenbaum and his family are in the United States" (ibid., 265 [18 May 1944]). Olga Lindenbaum later sent her "a package of provisions from the U.S." (NIOR RGB, f. 343, k. 138, d. 7, l. 12). On Hélène's death, see "Avis de décès," Gazette de Bayonne, de Biarritz et du pays Basque, 4 November 1940.

681. Poliakova and Poliakoff, Sem'ia Poliakovykh, 254 (13 May 1944). In his memoirs, Alex-

ander Poliakoff described Dmitrii as "Lazar's playboy son" who bought clothing designs from Mouma (*The Silver Samovar*, 25).

682. Poliakova and Poliakoff, *Sem'ia Poliakovykh*, 254 (8 April 1944).

683. "Décès," *Gazette de Bayonne de Biarritz et du pays Basque*, 4 May 1943. His address was listed as 18 Rue Alcide Augey.

684. Poliakova and Poliakoff, *Sem'ia Poliakovykh*, 259 (3 May 1944). Anna (Niuta) died on 22 May 1942.

685. I thank Diana Sachsen, a relative of Alma Reiss, for this information.

686. Poliakova and Poliakoff, *Sem'ia Poliakovykh*, 280 (9 July 1944).

687. Ibid., 255 and 256 (10 April 1944).

688. Ibid., 250.

689. Ibid., 257.

690. Ibid., 262 (10 May 1944).

691. Ibid., 257 (30 April 1944).

692. Ibid., 272 (10 June 1944).

693. Marthe Emden was the mother of Tony Emden and Yvonne Sophie Marie Oppenheim and the grandmother of Denise Marie-Louise Goldshmidt, whose husband, Marcel Goldshmidt, helped Ziniada during the war.

694. Poliakova and Poliakoff, *Sem'ia Poliakovykh*, 265 (16 May 1944).

695. Zinaida wrote on 5 June 1944 that Fabienne sent her brother, Philippe Halphen, provisions (ibid., 271). Fabienne, Philippe, and Francine Halphen (mentioned later in the postwar diaries) were the grandchildren of Zinaida's sister-in-law Louise Dreyfus (née Gubbay).

696. Ibid., 253 (25 February 1944). Nikolai (Nicholas) was the son of Louis and Liza Raffalovich (Iakov Poliakov's daughter). He was first married to his cousin Maria (Marie) Raffalovich (daughter of Arthur Raffalovich), who died in 1918. See "Deuil," *Le Figaro*, 2 September 1918.

697. Poliakova and Poliakoff, *Sem'ia Poliakovykh*, 255 (9 April 1944). The Helbronners were related by marriage to the St. Pauls—the family of Zinaida's cousin Rachel. For instance, Rachel's sister-in-law Hermace Rebecca St. Paul was married to Horace Oscar Louis Helbronner.

698. Ibid., 256 (14 April 1944). Zinaida mentions again how the wealthy Dreyfus family took in the Gintsburgs (ibid., 271 [8 June 1944]).

699. Zinaida is referring to Georgio Enrico Abrams Levi; his wife, Nina Leia; and their children, Anthony, Emma (who married Louis Dreyfus), Angelo Adolphe, and Giacomo Levi. Their daughter Lina, who married George Landau (Iakov Poliakov's grandson), remained in Italy during the war. See ibid., 259 (2 May 1944).

700. Ibid., 259 (2 May 1944).

701. Ibid., 265 (18 May 1944). She may be referring to the family of Elise Lorsch and Henri Höchstadter, who were married in 1900.

702. Ibid., 268 (28 May 1944). Zinaida was probably referring to Esther Bensliman Oulman—née Bensaude, the wife of Camile Alphonse Oulman (1863–1965)—and her son Albert Emile Oulman. Her son Jose Paul Oulman died in 1914. In 1901, Zinaida described a visit from the Oulmans, who stayed until 7:30 p.m. and talked about nothing in particular: "As a result, it was evident that they want to marry their brother to Raia or some other young woman with money, as she herself put it!" (NIOR RGB, f. 343, k. 138, d. 2, ll. 42, 60 ob. [1901]). Zinaida also attended a performance of the opera *Faust* with Camile Oulman and Madame Regeure and sat in the loge with them.

703. Poliakova and Poliakoff, *Sem'ia Poliakovykh*, 258 (28 May 1944).

704. Robert Merle d'Aubigné (1900–89) was best known as a pioneer of orthopedic surgery. He became the chair of orthopedic surgery at the Hôpital Cochin (in Paris) in 1948. See "Merle d'Aubigné, Aime Robert (1900–1989)," *Royal College of Surgeons: Plarr's Lives of Fellows*, accessed 1 May 2018, https://livesonline.rcseng.ac.uk/biogs/E007501b.htm.

705. This is a reference to Margarita [Getia] Brodskaia, who was married first to Dmitrii Gintsburg and then to Alfred Goldschmidt. For the controversy over the marriage to Gintsburg, see Geraldine Gudefin, "The Civil and Religious Worlds of Marriage and Divorce: Russian Jewish Immigrants in France and the United States, 1881–1939," PhD diss., Brandeis University, 2018, 49–59.

706. Poliakova and Poliakoff, *Sem'ia Poliakovykh*, 273 (15 June 1944). For more on this family, which originated with the Brodskiis of Kiev, see Brodsky, *Smoke Signals*.

707. NIOR RGB, f. 343, k. 138, d. 8, l. 1.

708. Ibid.

709. Poliakova and Poliakoff, *Sem'ia Poliakovykh*, 247.

710. Ibid., 260 (6 May 1944).

711. Ibid., 258 (31 April 1944).

712. Ibid., 261 (7 May 1994).

713. Ibid., 258 (1 May 1944).

714. Itzhak Katzenelson, *Vittel Diary* (Tel Aviv: Ghetto Fighters' House, 1962), 43–44.

715. Poliakova and Poliakoff, *Sem'ia Poliakovykh*, 258 (31 April 1944).

716. Ibid., 258 (1 May 1944).

717. Ibid., 259 (2 May 1944).

718. Ibid., 265 (12 May 1944).

719. Ibid., 266 (19 May 1944).

720. Ibid., 268 (25 May 1944).

721. Ibid., 260–61 (6 May 1944).

722. Ibid., 271 (8 June 1944).

723. Ibid., 273 (15 and 16 June 1944). Two months later, on 17 August 1944, the Kohn family was included among the fifty-one Jews deported on the last transport from the Drancy Transit Camp. During the journey, eighteen-year-old Rose-Marie and her twenty-one-year-old brother, Philippe, jumped from the train to their safety in defiance of their father, who feared reprisals to the other prisoners. Their little brother, twelve-year-old Georges André, wanted to join them but his father prevented him from doing so. His wife, Suzanne, and daughter Antoinette died in Bergen-Belsen. Georges André was one of the children sent to Neuengamme to be subjected to cruel medical experiments, injected with pathogens that caused diseases like tuberculosis. He was hanged with the other children on 12 April 1945 in the cellar of the Bullenhauser Damm School. See Susan Zuccotti, *The Holocaust, the French and the Jews* (Lincoln: University of Nebraska Press, 1993), 202–3; "The 20 Children," Children of Bullenhuser Damm Association, accessed 3 April 2019, http://www.kinder-vom-bullenhuser-damm.de/_english/georges -andre_kohn.php.

724. Poliakova and Poliakoff, *Sem'ia Poliakovykh*, 271 (8 June 1944).

725. Ibid., 263 (10 May 1944).

726. Ibid., 276 (21 June 1944).

727. Ibid., 259.

728. Ibid., 265 (16 May 1944) and 266 (19 and 20 May 1944).

729. Ibid., 270 (1 June 1944).

730. NIOR RGB, f. 743, k. 138, d. 3, l. 12 ob. (20 September 1902).

731. NIOR RGB, f. 343, k. 138, d. 8, l. 2. This note was added to the text by someone other than Zinaida.

732. Stansky, *Sassoon*, 162. Hannah Gubbay, née Ezra, was married to David Gubbay.

733. NIOR RGB, f. 743, k. 138, d. 8, l. 2.

734. Poliakova and Poliakoff, *Sem'ia Poliakovykh*, 260 (16 August 1944).

735. Vera Lindsay was the granddaughter of Lazar Iakovlevich Poliakov (not Zinaida's father) and the daughter of Vladimir (Volodia) Poliakov. Vladimir Poliakov worked for the *Times* in England and had purchased a grand house in Queens Gate Gardens, Kensington.

736. NIOR RBG, f. 343, k. 138, d. 7, l. 77 (circa 1950).

737. "Vladimir Poliakoff, Publisher, Dead in France at 74," *Jewish Telegraphic Agency*, 24 May 1939.

738. "Europe's Four Best Reporters Interpret the Continent's Bluff and Guff," *Life*, 15 August 1938, 26–27.

739. Quoted in Alexander Poliakoff, *The Silver Samovar*, 25. Vera's son Richard Burton was an acclaimed architect and a pioneer in designing for energy conservation. See Elain Harwood, "Richard Burton Obituary," *Guardian*, 16 February 2017, https://www.theguardian.com/artanddesign/2017/feb/16/richard-burton-obituary.

740. Poliakova and Poliakoff, *Sem'ia Poliakovykh*, 281 (17 August 1944).

741. From 13 June 1944 to 29 March 1945, Hitler launched a new assault on London, employing the new V-1 flying bombs, which the Londoners called doodlebugs.

742. Poliakova and Poliakoff, *Sem'ia Poliakovykh*, 283 (29 September 1944).

743. Ibid., 286 (7 October 1944).

744. Ibid., 282 (26 September 1944).

745. Ibid., 290 (18 October 1944).

746. Violet FitzGerald was married to Derek FitzGerald, a clerk to an exchange broker.

747. Poliakova and Poliakoff, *Sem'ia Poliakovykh*, 287 (9–10 October 1944).

748. NIOR RGB, f. 343, k. 138, d. 7, l. 34.

749. Poliakova and Poliakoff, *Sem'ia Polikovykh*, 288 (12 October 1944).

750. Ibid.

751. Ibid., 289 (15 October 1944).

752. The first German air offensives against London began in September 1940, but the first V-1 bombs launched against London fell on 13 June 1944.

753. Poliakova and Poliakoff, *Sem'ia Poliakovykh*, 290 (19 October 1944).

754. Ibid., 281 (17 October 1944).

755. Ibid., 281 (24 September 1944).

756. Ibid., 282 (25 September 1944).

757. Ibid.

758. Ibid., 287 (9 October 1944).

759. "Benjamin Poliakoff," Holocaust Survivors and Victims Database, United States Holocaust Museum, accessed 5 January 2018, https://www.ushmm.org/online/hsv/person_view.php?PersonId=5357830.

760. NIOR RGB, f. 343, k. 138, d. 7, l. 6.

761. I thank Elisheva Ansbacher, a lawyer in Jerusalem, who had filed a claim on behalf of Georges Levi's great-niece, Mirella (Mira) Goss (Gus) Vivante, for this information. Zinaida also discovered this tragic fact after the war. See the information about Xenia Levi Delle Trezz in "Central Database of Shoah Victims' Names," Yad Vashem, accessed 1 April 2019, https://yvng .yadvashem.org/index.html?language=en&s_lastName=poliakoff&s_firstName=&s_place= &s_dateOfBirth=&s_inTransport=.

762. NIOR RGB, f. 343, k. 138, d. 7, l. 42 ob.

763. Ibid., l. 64.

764. Ibid., l. 20–20 ob.

765. These were her brother Benjamin; sister Khaia and her husband, Georges Levi; sister-in-law Claire and her daughter Elizabeth (Lily); Alice Warshawsky; and Dmitrii Poliakov.

766. Poliakova and Poliakoff, *Sem'ia Poliakovykh*, 281 (24 September 1944).

767. Ibid., 283 (28 September 1944).

768. Ibid.

769. Ibid., 385 (3 October 1944).

770. Ibid., 287 (9 October 1944).

771. Ibid., 281 (2 September 1944).

772. Ibid., 284 (1 October 1944). Zinaida confessed that she preferred to "sit on the seashore and tan in the sun."

773. Ibid., 282 (26 September 1944).

774. NIOR RGB, f. 343, k. 138, d. 7, l. 45 ob. See also "Mariages," *Ambassades et consulats: Revue de la diplomatie international*, April 1929, 459.

775. The granddaughter, born 20 March 1948, was named Rose Aline Cholmondeley (NIOR RGB, f. 343, k. 138, d. 7, l. 13).

776. Poliakova and Poliakoff, *Sem'ia Poliakovykh*, 284 (29 September 1944). Francine's aunt Noémie Claire Alice was married to Maurice Edmond de Rothschild. There were other marriages between the Halphens and Rothschilds, such as that of Edouard de Rothschild and Germain Halphen. Francine's daughter Dame Vivien Duffield recalled that her father, Charles Clore, was the son of immigrants from Riga. He was a "self-made man, establishing his name and wealth through an array of retail ventures, notably the department store Selfridges and the ubiquitous high street store brands of the British Shoe Corporation." She remembered that her parents' marriage did not last long: "She [Francine] missed France and returned there. She was much more cultured, from a wealthy Parisian family." Her uncle Philippe Halphen "survived Auschwitz and testified at the Nurenberg Trials" (quoted in David Russell, "The Benefactors: An Occasional Series," *Jewish Renaissance* [October 2013]: 7–8, https://www.jewishrenaissance .org.uk/october-2013). As noted above, Francine was the granddaughter of Louise Dreyfus, Zinaida's sister-in-law.

777. NIOR RGB, f. 343, k. 138, d. 7, l. 8.

778. Ibid., l. 29 ob.

779. Ibid., l. 45 ob.

780. Ibid., l. 30. ob.

781. Ibid., l. 2 ob.

782. Ibid., l. 8.

783. Ibid., l. 12.

784. Ibid., l. 13–13 ob.

785. Ibid., l. 22–22 ob. These sisters were the daughters of Adolphe Félix and Yvonne Sophie Marie Oppenheim.

786. NIOR RGB, f. 343, k. 138, d. 2, l. 63 ob. (1901). See also Christopher E. Forth, *The Dreyfus Affair and the Crisis of French Manhood* (Baltimore, MD: Johns Hopkins University Press, 2004), 125.

787. Laperche's first novel, written under the pen name Hélène Favre de Coulevain and titled *Noblesse américaine* (1898) won the Montyon Prize in 1899, and her second novel, *Ève victorieuse* (1900), won the Montyon Prize in 1902 (NIOR RGB, f. 343, k. 138, d. 2, l. 15 [1901]).

788. NIOR RGB, f. 743, k. 138, d. 3, l. 38 (26 June 1903).

789. NIOR RGB, f. 343, k. 138, d. 7, l. 18 ob.

790. Ibid., l. 37.

791. Ibid., l. 17.

792. Ibid., l. 35.

793. Ibid., l. 24 ob.

794. Ibid., l. 40.

795. Ibid., ll. 23 ob. and 26 ob.

796. Ibid., l. 27 ob.

797. Ibid., l. 27 ob.

798. Ibid., l. 26.

799. "First Meetings and Public Examination," *London Gazette*, 13 August 1948.

800. For more on the Cholmondeleys at Kensington Palace Gardens, see Stansky, *Sassoon*, 179.

801. "Appointments of Trustees," *London Gazette*, 15 October 1948.

802. NIOR RGB, f. 343, k. 138, d. 7, l. 63.

803. Ibid., l. 44 ob.

804. Ibid., l. 48 ob.

805. Ibid., ll. 79–80.

806. Ibid., l. 29 ob.

807. Ibid., l. 81.

808. *L'Astronomie: Revue mensuelle d'astronomie de metéorologie et de physique du globe* (Paris, 1924), 500.

809. Poliakova and Poliakoff, *Sem'ia Poliakovykh*, 276 (21 June 1944).

810. Alexander Poliakoff, *The Silver Samovar*, 23.

*The
Diaries*

♦ ♦ ♦ ♦ ♦ ♦ ♦

MY DIARY, 1875-80

13 AUGUST [SOKOL'NIKI][1] [FAMILY DACHA AT SOKOL'NIKI]
For nothing to do, and almost for the hundredth time, I have started to write a diary but have not had the patience to finish this. But this time I am firmly resolved to write, at least on rare occasions, but at least not to abandon it entirely. So I begin.

In the morning the weather was delightful. A soft spring breeze was blowing; the sun of course was not burning so strongly, since at this time of year in our Russia everything is covered by heavy clouds. Despite this, during the entire summer I have never had such a stroll like the one we took this morning. Although it was not long, like those that we usually take when we go with Mama and Papa, it was nevertheless much more pleasant. I do not know whether it was because the weather was so splendid or because I was in a very good mood. By my calculations, this depends on both of these things: when the weather is cheerful, then mankind and all the animals and insects, butterflies, and the like become more animated; if the weather turns foul, leaves with a bright green color take on a boring, unpleasant yellow hue [and] involuntarily make one melancholy. After this wonderful stroll we returned home for breakfast and thought about taking another walk afterwards, but to our great regret it began to rain, and the rain is now continually starting and stopping, so that now it is impossible to go for a stroll. Now I shall go and see if they have collected the eggs of my chickens (at the present time, I have four birds: one is sick, one is not producing eggs, but two are producing eggs almost every day). Now I must finish up and go eat, we have a snack at 3 pm—that is, we have something to eat between breakfast and lunch. I hope that I can soon spend time on my diary.

At last I have again taken up my diary! It has already been a long time since I wrote in it.

"Nauchno-issledovatel'skii otdel rukopisei Rossiiskoi gosudarstvennoi biblioteki" (hereafter NIOR RGB), f. 743, k. 137, d. 27 (13 August 1875–1880).
1. Sokol'niki, located northeast of central Moscow, was originally a pine forest and royal hunting preserve. Formally annexed by the city of Moscow in 1742, a century later it became the site of elaborate summer homes, like that of the Poliakovs.

14 [AUGUST], THURSDAY

As for Thursday I remember almost nothing, so apparently nothing special happened on that day.

15 [AUGUST], FRIDAY

This morning we went with G. Gerts to gather nuts and collected a lot. But since it was time to take breakfast, and Mama had gone for a walk (with Lidiia Stepanovna,[2] Fania, and Masha[3]), Misha[4] and I went with Papa for a stroll and thought that we would not see them. But we had just passed the Panov dacha (which is next to ours), when we saw the governess of the Popovs with Serezha [Sergei Popov], who told us that they had met them at the Sirotinin dacha (which is further) and that Varia[5] is writing me a note to see if she can come to say goodbye at 10 pm (since she is leaving for the city tomorrow and because Serezha has to study at the gymnasium). We left to find the Sirotinin dacha, because we thought that they had dropped in to see some acquaintances. On the road we met the caretaker who held a letter in his hand, and I thought to myself: "Is this not for me?" Then Papa asked him: "To whom are you taking the letter?" He responded, "the Poliakovs." We took the letter and read it. And indeed they did ask whether they could come to say goodbye. I said that we shall reply right away. Then we set out for home and decided that, even if mother and the others are not at home, we shall have breakfast now. But afterwards we arrived home, and they were already there. We told them everything and ate breakfast. Afterwards I sent her a reply, inviting her to come for lunch, but after that she sent a letter saying that the governess is not at home and that she

2. Lidiia Stepanovna Zotova was the Russian governess to the Poliakov children and later described as a "companion" to the family.
3. Fania (the familiar form for Stefaniia) Pavlovna Vydrina and Mariia (Masha) Pavlovna Vydrina were sisters of Zinaida's mother, Rozaliia Pavlovna (neé Vydrina). Zinaida's grandfather Pavel (Pesakh) Vydrin (1825–84) was married a second time (to another woman named Rozaliia) and had children who were close in age to Zinaida and her siblings.
4. Zinaida's brother Misha (Mikhail, Michel, Minandr) was born in 1867 (probably in Riazan, where his parents lived until 1868) and died in Brussels, Belgium. To document his birth, Lazar provided a certificate from the Orsha state rabbi, Borukh Rivlin (who listed the birth date 8 July 1867), and another certificate from Riazan. The Orsha state rabbi provided certificates for all of Lazar's children even though they were not necessarily born in his town. See Irina Ryklis and Andrei Shumkov, "Poliakovy: nekotorye voprosy genealogii roda i soslovnogo statusam," in *Trudy po evreiskoi istorii i kul'tury: Materialy XIX mezhdunarodnoi ezhegodnoi konferentsii po iudaika* 3 (2012): 211–12. For the timing of Lazar and Rozaliia's moves from Orsha, Riazan, and Khar'kov, see Iakov Poliakov, "Istoriia, semeinye nachinaia [s]1748 goda" (hereafter "Istoriia") Central Archives for the History of the Jewish People, ll. 17 and 32.
5. Sergei (Serezha) Popov and Varia Popova were family friends who also had a dacha in Sokol'niki.

cannot respond to my letter and invitation. I waited for her at the appointed time, but there was a downpour, so I thought I would see her the next morning.

16 [AUGUST], SATURDAY

After doing my morning exercises, the Popovs' caretaker came and brought a letter as well as a doll for Khaia.[6] We immediately read it. The governess wrote that, because of the rain, she could not come to say farewell, but that she will accept Mama's invitation for Varia to take a dance lesson together with us, and wants to know when it begins.

17 [AUGUST], SUNDAY

Lidiia Stepanovna was home, visiting her relatives.

18 [AUGUST], MONDAY

The sovereign, Alexander II, came to Moscow for a visit of five days.

19 [AUGUST], TUESDAY

The one thing that I remember, is that it rained cats and dogs the entire day.

20 [AUGUST], WEDNESDAY

They took me into the city today. We wanted to see the sovereign lay the cornerstone for the Historical Museum,[7] but they said that women are not permitted in our carriage, so I stood at the monument for Minin and Pozharskii.[8] We could only hear how people shouted "hurrah!"

21 [AUGUST], THURSDAY

The emperor was present for the dedication of the new *lycée*. Mama did not know whether they would admit women there, and therefore did not want to go. But Lidiia Stepanovna and I advised her to go, so she took Lidiia Stepanovna with her and left. It turned out that there were a lot of women, and Mama liked it all very much. She even regretted not having taken me with her.

6. Khaia (Ksenia, Xenia) was Zinaida's younger sister (1865–1944).
7. The Historical Museum, authorized by an imperial decree of 1872 (in honor of the heir apparent, the future Alexander III) and located on the north side of Red Square, took more than a decade to build and opened its doors to the first visitors in 1883.
8. The famous Minin and Pozharskii monument (dedicated to the commoner Kuz'ma Minin and Prince Dmitrii Pozharskii, heroes of the 1612 national uprising that expelled the Poles from Moscow) was formally opened in 1818 in the middle of Red Square. Because this impeded the military parades through the square, in 1931 the Soviet government moved the monument to the south side of Red Square, in front of St. Basil's Cathedral.

22 [AUGUST], FRIDAY

Today Masha went into the city with Mama and was very pleased. The weather is very bad, and everyone is already moving [to the city]. But Mama wants to stay here for a long time. I am terribly tired. It is no a joke to write four and half pages. It can wait a little.

22 [AUGUST]

Today I again took up my diary, but not for long: I do not have a great desire to write.

23 [AUGUST], SATURDAY

In the morning we took a long stroll. We were on the old route. Then we returned to have breakfast and ate with a large appetite. There was nothing special.

[24 AUGUST], SUNDAY

This morning we went for a stroll on the old path. After breakfast we gathered together to go to the Liamin[9] family, but it began to rain hard. Then Mr. and Mrs. Epshtein came.[10] There is nothing to write about today except perhaps that I had a fight with Khaia. She asked me to dress her doll; I had already begun to do so when she became angry and went to complain about me to Lidiia Stepanovna. Knowing her character, I dressed the doll and combed its hair, and went to show it to Lidiia Stepanovna so that she [would] not think that I had not done so. But she [Khaia] was angry and, as is her wont, turned her back (which she always does when she is mad). Lidiia Stepanovna said that "if you sulk in front of me, then I can imagine how you carry on in front of Zinochka [Zinaida]." And she sat her down on the chair as punishment and told [her] not to get up until permitted to do so. I went upstairs and am writing in my diary. That's enough.

---

9. In the 1860s, Ivan Artem'evich Liamin purchased a large plot (no. 21) in Sokol'niki to build a dacha for his family. The Liamins were a merchant family in Moscow.

10. The family of Efim Moiseevich Epshtein (1857–1939). According to Zinaida, Efim was the chief accountant for the Poliakov enterprises (see the diary entry of 1 July 1881). He became the director of the banking house of the Dzhamgarov brothers in the 1890s, director of the Moscow Branch of the Petersburg International Commercial bank in the 1900s, and board member of the Azov-Don Bank in St. Petersburg in the 1910s. He was also a well-known publicist and writer about the prerevolutionary Russian banking system. For an assessment of Epshtein's scholarship on Russian banking, see S. A. Salomatina, "Trudy Efima Epshteina i razvitie kontseptsii v izuchenii istorii bankov Rossiiskoi imperii," *Vestnik Moskovskogo universiteta*, Seriia: istoriia, no. 8 (2015): 79–94.

24 AUG.[11]

It has been more than a month since I wrote in my diary, and nonetheless much has happened in the interim. First of all, on 2 September[12] we moved back into the city, and were very happy about that.

25 AUG.

This, it seems, was a Monday. To be honest, I do not remember much about these days, but to keep things straight, one ought to write something. We must have been preparing for the move back [to the city].

26 AUG. TUES.

I do not remember anything about this day either.

27 AUG., WED.

I have to stop trying to write every day separately, because I do not remember anything. On 25 Sept. we were at the name day for Serezha [Sergei] Popov. It was a lot of fun because boys and girls were there. We danced the cotillion there, played various games, etc. We wanted to leave at 9 pm, but they did not want to let us go so early. At 9:30 we had to leave because Mama did not permit [us] to stay any longer.

Now there is no time left: they are calling me to breakfast, so next time I'll write about the rest.

Today I again wrote in my diary. We are going today to have a group photograph. I am sitting in a blue, sleeveless silk blouse, Raika[13] in a blue poplin dress, etc. Khaia plans to be photographed together with her doll and therefore is now dressing it; as is her wont, however, the poor thing is sitting in just a blouse—despite the fact that she has a superb dress and hat ordered from Lemercier (together with ours) for Khaia's birthday. This hat is so good that it is worth describing: navy blue, velvety with a splendid white feather, and bronze clasp on the side. It was made by Mme. Foutman (the seamstress who sews dresses for us and made a woolen overcoat for Mama).

That's enough about clothes; it's time to talk about more interesting things.

11. Zinaida stopped writing for a month; the entries for 24–27 August were entered much later. Although she correctly listed the date and day of the week for 1875, she had trouble recalling much detail prior to the entry of 27 August. That also explains why the entry for 27 August suddenly includes information about 25 September.

12. As this and other entries indicate, much here was entered well after the date given.

13. Raisa [Raia, Rachel] (1871–1948), Zinaida's youngest sister, was born in Moscow. Her birth certificate was provided by the Moscow state rabbi, Zelig Minor, for Lazar Poliakov's petition for hereditary nobility.

Tomorrow I have [a lesson with] the music teacher. These have been holidays and so I must confess that I have not been preparing the lesson very well. Today I have a lot of work; I must prepare a lot of lessons. The weather seems to be rather cold today. My dear governess Lidiia Stepanovna is not at home (she went to her relatives). Although I am not very keen on writing, nevertheless I shall absolutely finish this page. The small children are already having breakfast. I have four brothers (of whom Misha is the oldest, while Ronia is two, Il'iushka is three, and the fourth and youngest of all is Satiushka—everyone's favorite). I also have two sisters (Khaia and Raia), but I am the oldest.[14] We shall probably have breakfast now. I am writing without particular desire, as though a cat has been scratching. That's enough!

Yesterday we had a dance lesson. Varia also came. In the evening I read my diary to her; she liked it so much that she even swore to begin writing her own today. She promised to write me a letter, but did not keep her word. However, perhaps I shall receive it tomorrow. Today I had a lesson with the teacher for penmanship and French; I also had a lesson in Hebrew.[15] Then I also prepared lessons for music and arithmetic for tomorrow. The weather is rather good. We strolled for a half hour with Mlle. Eugénie (Mama's maid). But on the way to Uncle Lev [Vydrin][16] (whom we had planned to stop by briefly to say that Mama will not go to the concert this evening) we met Miss Cécilia [Cécelia]. She was coming from church and was then at the dentist's. Today Misha had his first lesson from the French teacher. Masha has been pouting all day (for some unknown reason). Dear Lidiia is not at home. I am hurrying today to read *Grafinia Katia*.[17] Variushka brought me this book to read. I had already given her *Contes de sans pays*[18] and several small books. Recently I have altogether lost the desire to write in my diary, but yesterday I read it and liked it. I think that it is better to write something than to sit on your hands or to quarrel with

14. The ages of Ronia [Aaron] and Il'iushka [Il'ia or Elie] may not be correct here. The metrical book certificates that Lazar Solomonovich included in his petition for hereditary nobility stated that Aaron was born in 6 May 1869 (not 1873). Il'ia was born in 1872 according to Zinaida, but the official metrical records from the state rabbi of Orsha and Khark'kov (where he was born) lists his birth date as 13 May 1870. Since the Poliakovs moved in 1870 from Khar'kov to Moscow, the state record must be accurate. Isaak (Satia, Satiushka) was born on 12 March 1873 in Moscow.

15. It is difficult to say if she was studying Yiddish or Hebrew, since the Russian word *evreiskii* could mean either. Zinaida had some knowledge of both; she wrote letters to her grandparents in Yiddish but read some Hebrew texts (for example, Peretz Smolenskin's novel).

16. Lev Pavlovich Vydrin, brother of Rozaliia Poliakova.

17. A reference to *Countess Kate* (London: J. & C. Mozley, 1862), a novel by Charlotte Yonge (1823–1901), published in Russian as Sharlotta Meri Iondzh, *Grafinia Katia: Roman dlia detei* (Moscow: Tip. Bakhmet'eva, 1866).

18. *Contes de sans pays* was evidently a French novella.

your brothers and sisters. It's true that this is not practice in penmanship because I am just scratching out things; sometimes you have to write so much that your hand even becomes tired. That's enough.

19 OCT., SUNDAY

According to my clock it is 4:20 in the afternoon.

26 OCT.

It is 4:40 pm. On Monday I was at the opera, heard Patti[19] in *Roméo et Juliette*.[20] I liked this opera very much. On Tuesday we wanted to have photographs taken, but have put this off. On Wednesday Varia was not here. It was a holiday. Elizaveta had her name day, but Varka has her friend Liza, so she was her guest. The dance teacher did not come. Yesterday Sasha Miliaev danced with us. We also had Ia[kov] P. Polonskii[21] (Kotia's[22] former tutor) as a guest. Lidiia Stepanovna is at a name day celebration for her friend's husband. I don't want to continue writing because I heard Mama's voice—and I do not like it when they read my diary. No, I was mistaken. Today is a major concert, with the participation of Ms. Adelina Patti. I do not know if Mama is going, because she has an eye ache. I saw a leather notebook at Sokolov's and Belonogov's (a stationer's shop). But I liked it so because it is made of blue leather; I want to ask Papa for the money to purchase it. It costs 1.25 rubles. I received a letter from Varia Sunday evening; she kept her word.

SUNDAY, 1875

Moscow, Tverskoi Boulevard, the Poliakov residence.

P.S. Today Dr. [Grigorii] Zakhar'in[23] came to visit Mama. He ordered me to increase my studies—which I very much disliked.

20 NOV., SUNDAY

Today I prepared all my lessons for tomorrow. Now I am free for a whole day, except for the penmanship lesson at 2 pm and Hebrew at 3. Mama and Papa

19. Adelina Patti was a French-Italian opera singer (1843–1919).
20. *Roméo et Juliette*, an opera by Charles Gounod, was first performed in Paris in 1867. Patti performed the soprano role in the first performance abroad (in New York City) the same year.
21. Iakov Petrovich Polonskii (1819–98) was a romantic poet in the tradition of Alexander Pushkin. He graduated from Moscow University in 1844 and moved to St. Petersburg, where he edited the literary journal *Russkoe slovo*. Later, as his reputation as a writer waned, he worked as a government censor but continued to write and publish.
22. Kotia was the nickname for her cousin Daniil (1862–1914), Samuil Poliakov's son.
23. Grigorii Antonovich Zakhar'in (1829–97), the Poliakov family doctor, was a professor at Moscow University and a privy councilor. He was made an honorary member of the St. Petersburg Academy of Sciences in 1885.

bought us a musical instrument: a Becker piano.[24] I am so pleased with it and now play with great pleasure. We were dancing yesterday, and Varia and Sasha Miliaev were guests. The last time she had a headache and therefore left very early. But since this is my diary, I need to talk about myself.

Yesterday Lidiia Stepanovna gave us two caramels each, but Khaia goes up to her and says (it's so odd: you only need to look at her and you can almost burst out laughing): "*Donnez moi, je vous prie, une longue* [sic]." But Lidiia Stepanovna replies: "*Mais je vous ai donné autant qu'aux autres.*" Khaia says, "*Encore une,*" and Lidiia Stepanovna said that she'll give it later. But Khaia made such a comic face that Masha and I burst out laughing. But Khaia started to cry, and Lidiia Stepanovna scolded me, but not Masha. I asked how I am more guilty than Masha. But Lidiia Stepanovna began to say that she has studied me very well and that I laughed so that Khaia would cry, and that I know that when she cries, everyone will laugh at her. But Masha simply laughed. Of course, I did not want to start a fight over such idiocies, so I responded to everything with silence. But now I will say that I did not have any bad intent, but simply laughed like Masha—simply because Khaia made such a funny face. The accusation ended thus: Masha laughed heartily, while I went for a stroll and made up with everyone in the evening. I don't want to write any more.

P.S. When Varia comes, I'll [tell] her and I'm sure that she will have a good laugh—and, like me, without any evil intent.

Oh, so much time has passed since I last wrote in my diary. I must write that I spent a week in Piter [St. Petersburg]. I was supposed to be here on December 10th. We planned to go again, but did not succeed in going: the reason is that Grandfather and Roman[25] (that is, my uncle) came here. I have long since not seen Varia, but 15 January[26] is my birthday, and I plan to invite her if Mama gives permission. Yesterday her brother Serezha came and kept us occupied the entire time. We danced the cotillion; he and Roman put on bonnets and scarves and carried umbrellas. Both Khaia and I put on gymnasium student hats and danced the quadrille, we like gentlemen and they like ladies. We became mixed up because we were not used to dancing like that. Then they put

24. The Becker piano shop, founded by the German Jacob Becker in St. Petersburg in 1841 (and later expanded into a factory), was famous for the instruments' quality and a patented new design. The Poliakovs apparently purchased an upright, not a grand, piano.

25. Roman Pavlovich Vydrin (brother of Rozaliia Poliakova) later became a first-guild merchant and registered as a resident in the Poliakov home on Tverskoi Boulevard in 1900. He was a board member of the Iaroslav'-Kostroma Land Bank.

26. If Zinaida was citing the Gregorian calendar (New Style) here; this would coincide with 3 January in the Julian calendar (Old Style) used in Russia before 1918. The dates given for her birth sometimes vary depending on which calendar she was using.

the bonnets on [my brothers] Misha and Il'ia and fastened them so that their heads were tied together. And among them was Khaia, who pulled at their scarf. Varia did not come because she was visiting others for the Christmas tree. That's enough [for today]!

28 DECEMBER 1875, SUNDAY, 2 PM, MOSCOW
After My Illness

20 SEPT. 1876–[DEC. 1876], MOSCOW
So long a gap in my diary is due to my protracted illness, then a trip to the Crimea, and finally a stay at the dacha (to which I did not bring my diary). Now I do not know where to begin writing in my diary, since so much has happened with me. First of all, in the Crimea I wrote my "Crimean Impressions" (which I left at the dacha). I was very sick for a long time and did not see my diary at all. Yesterday I was in poor spirits. I had a headache, so I missed my Russian language [lesson] and only dictated, because I do not like it when there are snippets in my diary. And today Lidiia Stepanovna did not permit me to work because I had a slight headache. The weather today seems good, but we did not go for a walk since it was terribly muddy. Tomorrow I have a music lesson, but I still do not know the lesson especially well, so now I need to practice. I also need to prepare Hebrew, although Mama gave me permission not do so (because of my headache). But I am sorry to miss the lesson, which I have only once a week. Bertrand, the French teacher, gave me a medieval history text ("feudalism") to translate. Masha is now in her room, and I do not know what she is doing. She is probably embroidering a monogram on the pillowcase that Mama ordered her to embroider (and about which she has sulked a lot). She does not thank me for this childish expression, which I have applied to her (but how else is one to put it if this is true?). I must study arithmetic tomorrow instead of Monday. In the Crimea we went to see a Tatar house and visited a rich Tatar named Mustafa. That's enough [for today]!

Soon two months will have passed since I wrote in my diary! I am in the mood to write today; that is why I have picked up my boring diary. I have already almost finished my studies; I have only not managed to prepare Russian history. Tomorrow I must work on arithmetic, although this is not my day, but Monday I had a headache. Lidiia Stepanovna said that I shall study on Thursday in lieu of Monday. Yesterday the French teacher Bertrand was here. He is an excellent teacher, but assigns difficult texts. I very much love to study geography, and today I have chosen a very difficult lesson. The weather today is very good, but there is also a frost: I shall hardly go for a stroll! Yesterday morning I also had a headache, but it passed because I went for a walk. Lidiia Stepanovna really dislikes it when we do not want to study. So I sat down to write my diary, without saying a word. I constantly hear how Misha is reciting Russian history today; as usual, things do not come together for him very well. The favorite subject for Khaia and me is geography. She stands out in geography, but Misha does best in Russian history. Enough, I think, for today!

Today, for want of anything to do, I decided to write in my diary, and with a pencil that I still have. . . . Today the weather is foul; yesterday was the same. For the first time in a month, I went for a ride in the sleigh for a quarter hour. On 13 December yet another brother was born; they still have not given him a name; apparently, he'll be called Genrikh.[27] Ronia and I will be his godparents [krestnye]. Lidiia Stepanovna is now attentively listening to Misha's recitation (he and Khaia have a Russian lesson). Ronia is terribly satisfied that he will be the godfather of our brother. Khaia is sulking; I do not know why; she is running out of class and whimpering. Yesterday Misha made me very angry, and I am still mad at him. Yesterday he wanted to take my photograph, but I told him to wait a bit because I was very busy. But he became furious and started to root around in my desk. I had to get up and throw the photo in his face. I was so angry that I did not want to talk to him any more. Enough for today!

20 DEC. 1876

Today (i.e., now) I am in a very sad frame of mind, and here is what caused me, at such a late hour, to write in my diary. Today they gave a name to our young brother: Iakov, in honor of our paternal grandfather.[28] Mama is now feeling well. Lidiia Stepanovna yesterday took to her bed and today has stayed there the entire day—she has come down with a cold. Mama, and I as well, feel depressed. I even cried a little because of the depression and, so that no one takes note, I went into the dining room but everyone was sitting there. Mama remarked that, when I am in low spirits, I get red under my eyes. I said nothing to this and went to my room. Lidiia Stepanovna (who is the main reason that I am now feeling depressed) is dozing at the moment. The doctor saw her this morning, but did not prescribe anything that helped. I do not know what our Iakov is now doing; he is probably "singing" (i.e., crying). I am his godmother; it's hard to imagine how pleased Ronia is.

27. The family ultimately named him Iakov.
28. Her paternal grandfather was Solomon Lazarevich Poliakov. Zinaida may have been referring to a paternal ancestor with the name Iakov, which was also her uncle's name (Iakov Solomonovich Poliakov).

21 DEC., MOSCOW, 2:05 PM, TUESDAY.

Today I am in rather good spirits but not such that I feel perfectly like myself. Lidiia Stepanovna feels quite well, but also not such that she has gotten out of bed. The doctor saw her yesterday and found that she is much better. When he [the doctor] came in, Masha was in a skirt and nightshirt and talking about something when she suddenly hears: "Mar'ia Pavlovna, leave quickly, as I have to come in!" She began to rush around and to hide under our bed, since we could not refrain from loud laughter, which was followed by the same shout from Iulii Osipovich Gol'denbakh.[29] She found my down cloak, flung herself into the room, and locked the door. Yesterday afternoon we had a lot of guests, but we all found it boring. Lidiia Stepanovna did not speak to anyone yesterday; she was visited by her older sister, who lives with the Rantsev family.

WED., [22 DEC.] 1876.

Ron'ka is now being naughty, heedless of the consequences. For some reason, he is very cheerful. The nanny is nagging about something now. Today I did not go for a stroll because of the strong wind. Now Khaia is pouting. Misha is gadding about, and I don't know where he is. Soon it will be my birthday, and it seems that no one except Lidiia Stepanovna has prepared a gift for me. Our little Iakov is getting on very well. Today Mar'ia [Masha] Pavlovna wanted to take a pill that the doctor had prescribed for me, but since she has not finished her schooling, she did not know how to take it and simply spat it out. But Ronchik, like a little squirrel jumping from one tree to the next, is running and crawling across the chairs and tables. I am quite irritated that I have very little news for my diary. Lidiia Stepanovna laughs at me for writing, at times, completely silly things. It is simply for want of anything to do that I sit and write in the diary. Our Satia [Isaak] is terrible rowdy; today, they say, he grabbed Papa by the hair. Raisa is moving to Mama's bedroom. Il'ia has changed for the better; he has not cried for two weeks already. Genrikh[30] now finds that Cervantes's *Don Quixote* is, in his opinion, a silly work. Yesterday Roman inspected my small library and found that I have good books. Of course, I know that myself. Today Fania Pavlovna brought me the works of [Victor] Hugo that I had given her to read.

THURSDAY, 23 DEC. 1876.

Masha read this inscription "23rd," but I did not respond. She asked me to write something about her. She's not dim-witted . . . but it is impossible to

29. Iulii Osipovich Gol'denbakh was the family doctor.
30. Genrikh Pavlovich Vydrin was Zinaida's uncle (Rozaliia's younger stepbrother). He later married Roza Vilenkin.

say that she is bright. Lidiia Stepanovna loves her a little and said that if (God forbid) she falls ill, she personally will look after her. As before, I feel myself [in low spirits]; only today am I in better spirits than I was yesterday. In the evening Papa went to St. Petersburg—a city, not a village. Yesterday Roman mocked my charming diary and found that I have "very short sentences," but that the rest is good. Masha also, at some point, wrote her own charming diary, in which she described all her dreams. Among them one of the main ones was: "I had an extremely strange dream, and this is it: in Roman's room a girl was sitting under his bed and crying, but he packed her mouth full of wheat so that she not cry and told no one that she is under his bed," and so on (which the reader of my diary can judge from its beginning). Yesterday I told him about this, and he laughed, but did not believe that she had written this and said that I had made it all up. I do not write such things and therefore anyone (almost) can read my "daily" journal or, to be more precise, my "monthly"—since I write very rarely, and only recently wrote several days in a row. Today I sent Papa a letter and telegram.

TUESDAY, 4 JANUARY 1877.

Today I want to describe yesterday's celebration of my birthday. I turned 14 years old yesterday.[31] [My uncle] Genrikh says that I shall be 16 in two years. On this occasion, Isaak gave me a box for steel pens; Raisa gave me a little Chinese box for pencils; Il'ia gave me a paperweight with a compass. I liked all the presents. It's just that it was not so merry. In past years it had been very joyful. Genrikh is fooling around a lot. Now he is studying. Yesterday Roman went for a stroll and bought me and Fania [copies of] *Silver Skates* (the Veinberg, not the Stal' version).[32] Roman planned to leave today, but apparently did not manage to do so. Khaia is now going through the rooms to see that they are in order. In recent days we were at the Malkiel' residence[33] for the holiday tree; it was very cheerful there, and the children received gifts. Khaia received a glass box for small items; Misha—an architectural construction; Ronia—little fish, small boats, and tiny ducks with magnets; Il'iusha—a horse with a hussar astride, which is wound up by a key (which they lost, promised to send tomorrow, but forgot to do so). I went for a long ride today and therefore am coughing a lot.

31. This date corresponds to the 3 January (Old Style) cited above.
32. The reference here is to a book by the American writer, Mary Mapes Dodge, *Hans Brinker, or the Silver Skates*, published under the shorter title in Russian as *Silver Skates*, first by P. Zh. Stal' and then by P. I. Veinberg.
33. The Malkiel' family was a wealthy merchant-banking Jewish family in Moscow. The brothers Isaak Mironovich and Samuil Mironovich made their wealth as contractors for the military during the Russo-Turkish War.

Yesterday Uncle came to see me and gave me a box of excellent candies; my aunt gave me a stamp for visiting cards with my name. Fania and Roman [are reading] an excellent book, but I find it too childish for me.

SUNDAY, 9 JANUARY

Lidiia Stepanovna is at home, since she is not quite well. I had been in the office, but Kazakov was there, so I quickly left. Papa is away; he has now gone somewhere. Miss Lemprière is now sitting with us and talking about Mlle. Eugénie,[34] who is now in the hospital. She is very ill; they fear that she will become permanently paralyzed, since she cannot move her right leg and arm. Mama gave Lidiia Stepanovna a small chain (which Papa and I chose) for the holiday. Genrikh is now reading my diary, having of course asked for permission in advance. The weather today is splendid; it is quite pleasant to stroll about. Fania also went with us. Mr. Gerts wrote a wonderful poem for me; it is about a little frog (its picture is glued to my album). Roman signed his name, because he gave it to me. Misha will also write for me but on the topic of "apes." Mr. Gerts also promised to compose something. Khaia is offended that Ronia wrote for my album, but I did not let her write. Genrikh is now examining my album and admiring the splendid pictures that have been pasted there. Yesterday he received an "A" in history and was very pleased.

17 JANUARY

In the evening Lucca[35] will sing in *Mignon*.[36] I would very much like to hear her, but apparently they will not take us, since it is −12 degrees C. in the sun. But they promised to take us, so it is still uncertain.

I just now finished [my lesson] with Klindworth.[37] He waited 25 minutes for me, but no one came to tell me that he [was] here. Masha is writing a letter to Miss Cécilia. Mlle. Eugénie died in the hospital on Saturday night and was buried today. Miss Lemprière and Anna were at the church where the services were held. The weather is good, but not such that one would call it wonderful —it is too cold for that. Tomorrow I have Bertrand [the French teacher]; I have still have not prepared a single lesson for him. If we go to the theater, then I shall have to prepare in the morning.

34. Zinaida used "Miss" and "M-lle" in Latin letters, respectively, for the two women.
35. Pauline Lucca, an Italian opera singer (1841–1908).
36. A three-act opera by Ambroise Thomas, first performed in 1866 and part of Lucca's repertoire.
37. Karl Klindworth (1830–1916) was a German pianist, conductor, musicologist, and music teacher. After studying and working in Weimar and London, he became a professor of piano at the Moscow Conservatory (1868–81), but he later returned to Germany.

Khaia is now having her lesson with Klindworth. Lidiia Stepanovna should be with Mama, so I am now completely alone. Tomorrow morning I have Russian language, but I have still not prepared the grammar (because I did not have enough time). Mr. Gerts brought me an announcement (cut from a German newspaper) that Klindworth is seeking "a young German woman (*devushka*)." He made fun of him and asked: "Is he married?" Mr. Klindworth answered in the affirmative. Then Mr. Gerts said that he read the announcement that he is looking for a "young woman." It was not worth writing about all this, but I have to fill the diary with something.

JANUARY 20TH

It was precisely on this date, in the night, that I fell ill last year. Now it is pleasant for me to recall my illness and to think that, thank God, I am healthy now. Mama promised to take us to the opera when there will be a Lucca benefit, but to tell the truth I don't believe it, since "they are long on promising but short on delivering." This afternoon I have Klindworth at 3:45. I think that he will be very pleased with me because I have tried to prepare the lesson very well for him, so it will be a pity if he is not satisfied. I wrote Miss Cécilia a letter in English and did not even think that I could do it with only two mistakes. We all wrote her that Mlle. Eugénie died so that she knows. Yesterday Anna was at Mlle. Novikova, who recently arrived from abroad.[38] Today the weather is foul so none of us went for a stroll. Bertrand brought a book to show me, *Voyage autours du monde*,[39] which costs 150 rubles. But of course I will not buy it, since that is too expensive for me. Khaia is now writing her own diary as well. Lidiia Stepanovna is now with Mama, because the latter is not quite well and is lying in bed. Tomorrow I have my first recitation in world history, but the lesson is still not ready, so I must hurry. Mama is seeking to hire a French woman as a maid, but today a Russian who knows French and German came and asks whether Mama needs a companion (*compagne*).

21 JANUARY.

Masha and I have quarreled: she took it into her head to call me a tyrant: several years ago, when she broke my watch, I became very furious with her. Miss Lemprière once called Mama the "Grand Inquisitor" because Mama did not

38. Ol'ga Alekseevna Novikova (1840–1925), a writer, came from the famous Kireev family of Slavophiles.

39. There are many books with such a title or subtitle, including a French translation of Jules Verne's *Les enfants du Capitaine Grant: voyage autour du monde*—an 1875 edition published in Paris by the Bibliothèque d'Éducation et de Récréation.

permit her dog to be in our house. I find this not to be terribly smart, since the French have a saying that is quite apt: "*Dis-moi qui tu hantes, et je te dirai qui tu es?*"[40] From this it follows that Miss Lemprière and Mlle. Marie are friends with tyrants and inquisitors, which they themselves are. No that is enough said of stupid things; it's better to focus on what is clever.

Yesterday I did not take a stroll because I did not feel well and it was snowing. Mama is ill and lying in bed. Now Lidiia Stepanovna, Miss Lemprière, Mr. Gerts, Masha, and all the children have gone for a walk. The weather is nasty, but it is nonetheless possible to take a stroll. I am now in an extremely foul mood and, on top of that, I have a headache.

Yesterday Mama, Papa, Khaia, Misha, and I were at the dacha in Komkovskii lycée. I found a small pencil in my pocket and that is why I began to write with it. My pen is good, but I do not have any ink (I gave up my small inkwell for cleaning). I will begin again by telling about yesterday evening. Misha also danced, but could not find a lady. I danced two quadrilles, since my cavalier did not find a partner. I would be very happy to go today to the Galvani[41] concert, which will take place at 2 pm.

Mama very much liked this evening. She said that it is rare to have such a good opportunity for us to have so good a time. Papa very much wanted to visit Spiridonov that evening, but Mama and we did not let him go. I wanted to go tomorrow evening to the Lucca benefit, where they are performing *Les Huguenots*.[42] Naudin[43] [will be performing] as well on January 4, 1877.

5 FEB. 1880, TUESDAY.
A lot of time has passed, a lot of water has flowed since I stopped my memoirs. Now I have to write not in a childish manner, but sensibly, so that I will enjoy reading it in a few years, as that has now happened. First of all, I have entered the final year of my schooling, and with the beginning of 1880–1881 I hope to pass the examination [to qualify] for the rank of a math teacher and perhaps French. This of course is in the future and that is why I shall not expand much

40. "Tell me who you visit and I will tell you who you are." Zinaida is evidently referring to Lidiia Stepanovna's fondness for the dog and, on a rare occasion, taking her mother's side.
41. Giacomo Galvani, born in 1819 in Bologna, was a lyrical tenor who became a teacher of solo singing at the Moscow Conservatory in 1868. He left his position in 1887 to return to Italy, where he passed away a few years later. See N. D. Kashkin, *Ocherk istorii russkoi muzyki* (Moscow: L. Iurgensona v Moskve, 1908), 152.
42. *Les Huguenots* is a French opera by Giacomo Meyerbeer (with a libretto by E. Scribe and E. Deschamps), first performed in Paris in 1836 and one of the most popular grand operas at the time.
43. Emilio Naudin (1823–90), was an Italian tenor of French parentage. He studied with Giacomo Panizza in Milan and performed extensively in France and Russia.

on the subjects that I shall have for a full six months. It is better that I write about the past, about what has long since transpired. Second (since I began to write in this order, then it is necessary to continue doing so), I am very happy that sheer chance has brought me to the idea of again writing a diary as a continuation of the past—namely at a time when I was cleaning out my desk, I came upon this notebook, but the children and my aunt Masha took it to read, and thus I very much regret remembering it so belatedly and that I did not think of this earlier.

We still have the same teaching personnel as before, with the exception of Mr. Gerts, whose place has been taken by Wagner; we have an Englishwoman, a French governess, and L[idiia] S[tepanovna]. Of course it would be strange not to refer to these people, but they apparently have little to do with my diary. But if you look at the essence of things, everyone will of course be convinced that who, if not the parents and then the teachers, are so closely tied with all that can be of interest to a child? That is why I began by listing the three people responsible for our upbringing. As for my personal assessment of their intelligence and knowledge, I think it absolutely superfluous to go into that. Remaining unknown to this point is the ninth member of our family: Aleksandr Lazarevich,[44] whom I shall shortly describe. He is not handsome, but a bright boy. He understands everything even though he is only six months old (in other words, half a year old). I have been practicing piano and am very tired. Today I do not have anything to say so it is quite tiresome to sort through events of past years. But now I remember nothing that could be of interest to others or to myself. So I am ending here.

44. Aleksandr Poliakov (Sasha) was born on 20 August 1879 in Moscow.

JOURNAL OF Z. L. POLIAKOVA (1881)

1 JULY–10 SEPEMBER 1881

1 JULY 1881, SOKOL'NIKI.

I am planning to go into the city to choose a present for Mama on her birthday (the 7th). The weather is overcast; so much the better—it won't be dusty. Yesterday Gorchakov[1] arrived for several hours from Petersburg. He came at 5 and, since Papa and Mama had still not returned from Moscow, I had to entertain him. He and I read old newspapers on the terrace. On Monday (Saints Peter and Paul Day) the Demidovs[2] and Nelli Boldareva[3] came. She is not very attractive but, it seems, quite unpretentious. The one thing about her that I do not like is this: her habit of smoking several cigarettes in a single evening. On Sunday Zak[4] came with Mlle. Mart'ianova, whom Mme. Zak calls her girlfriend.

NIOR RGB, f. 743, k. 137, d. 28, ll. 1–74, ob.

1. This could be either Andrei Aleksandrovich Gorchakov (1798–1883), the minister of foreign affairs in 1856–82, or Andrei Nikolaevich Gorchakov, an engineer. Both were visitors at the Poliakov house.

2. Mikhail Denisovich Demidov (1840–98) and his wife, Praskov'ia Nikolaevna (née Boldyreva, 1851–98). Demidov probably met the Poliakovs when he served as on a special commission under the governor of Riazan province. In 1873, he was appointed advisor to the Moscow Provincial Board. In 1880, he was assigned to the Ministry of Internal Affairs, and in 1882, he was appointed vice governor of Riazan province. The Demidovs were one of the oldest and most prominent noble families in Russia. They were some of the earliest industrialists, who amassed their wealth through mining (gold, silver, and copper) and the production of iron and steel. For a list of the Demidov factories and conditions of work in the Urals, see Basil Haigh, "Ural Factory Hospitals and Surgeons at the Dawn of the Nineteenth Century," *Medieval History* 22 (1978): 119–37.

3. She may be a relative of Praskov'ia Demidova. Demidova's father, Nikolai Arkad'evich Boldarev, was appointed governor of Riazan province in 1866. The Poliakovs and Boldarevs probably met in Riazan.

4. Abram Isaakovich Zak (1826–93) was born in Bobruisk and had a traditional upbringing. He married Ekaterina Iulev'na (née Epstein), a sister of Pauline Wengeroff, and continued to study Talmud with his brother-in-law Ephraim and his father-in-law. Zak eventually moved to St. Petersburg, where he worked as the head accountant for the Gintsburg bank and became the director of the St. Petersburg Discount and Loan Bank. The State Council turned to his expertise on economic and railroad matters. Like the Poliakovs, Zak and his wife were well known for their brilliant salon, to which they invited musicians, diplomats, bureaucrats, and members of high society. At this point, Ekaterina Zak lived in the capital, where people wore the latest fashions—a world apart from their traditional home in Bobruisk, where her mother burned her crinoline in the 1840s. Despite their

For lunch we had the Slezkins,[5] Tsion[6] and Efim Epshtein (who is now the chief accountant).

2 JULY 1881, SOKOL'NIKI.

Yesterday we went to Ovchinnikov and, after a long discussion, we settled on a frame for our general portrait in the office. It is drizzling again today, but we had to go to have the picture taken. Yesterday evening there was music at the circle. I did not expect this and went with Miss Gosh[7] in the simplest dress. Lidiia Stepanovna is not speaking to me after our huge spat on Tuesday during the stroll. Yesterday I received a letter from Il'iusha Vydrin,[8] and I replied to it immediately after lunch. On the walk we saw Shil'dbakh,[9] who works in Papa's office; Papa says that he had a cigar in his mouth, which is unbecoming for his young age. Papa did not think today of going to the village of Maidanovo to N. Vas. Novikova,[10] but did not have time to forewarn her by telegram that we have put this trip off until next week. I am gradually working to put my

---

acculturation, the Zaks kept their feet planted in the Jewish world through engagement in philanthropy and Abram's involvement in organizations such as the Society for the Promotion of Culture among the Jews of Russia. See Boris V. Anan'ich, *Bankirskie doma v Rossii, 1860–1914 gg.* (Moscow: ROSSPEN, 2006), 56; Shulamit Magnus, *A Woman's Life: Pauline Wengeroff and the Memoirs of a Grandmother* (Oxford: Littman Library of Jewish Civilization, 2016).

5. Zinaida refers in later entries to Sof'ia Ivanovna, Mikhail Ivanovich, and Elena Slezkin.

6. Either Moisei Faddeevich Tsion or his brother Il'ia Faddeevich Tsion (1842–1912). Il'ia Tsion (known as Elias von Cyon in France) was a highly controversial figure—a brilliant physiologist, a reactionary who hated revolutionaries, a staunch supporter of autocracy, a conservative publicist, and a financial agent for Russia in France. He eventually received a faculty position at the Surgical Academy of St. Petersburg against the will of the faculty and had to step down after students demanded his removal. Blaming nihilism and nihilists for the problems at the university, he moved to France in 1875. A close associate of Mikhail Katkov, he regularly published articles in conservative periodicals like *Moskovskie vedomosti* and *Russkii vestnik*. He served as an unofficial agent for the tsarist government, using his contacts in Paris to create a political and financial alliance between Russia and France (as opposed to Germany). He came into conflict with Sergei Witte, whom he accused (along with Ivan Vyshnegradskii) of embezzling money from Russia. On his scientific career, see Heinz-Gerd Zimmer, "Ilya Fadeyevich, alias Elias Cyon, alias Élias de Cyon," *Clinical Cardiology* 27 (2004): 584–85. On his dual life as a scientist and political figure, see A. S. Shevelev, "Dve zhizni Il'i Tsiona," *Priroda* 9 (1993): 108–11.

7. Elizabeth Gosh was the children's English governess.

8. Il'ia Vydrin was Rozaliia Poliakova's brother. He was married to Sofi'a (née Sheftel). They had at least twelve children: Abram, Rafail, Fedor, Genrikh, Chaim, Isaak, Roman, Roza, Mariia, Sofi'a (Sonia), Ol'ga, and Anna (Niuta).

9. Konstantin Karlovich Shil'dbakh (1819–92) was a financier with the rank of real state counselor, an honorary citizen of Moscow, and a hereditary noble.

10. Nadezhda Vasil'evna Novikova gained possession of the Maidonovo estate in 1861. She invited Peter Tchaikovsky to spend time there to work on his compositions. In this solitary and quiet place, he began work on the operas *Vakula the Smith* and *The Enchantress* and the Manfred Symphony. See

room in order. They brought me soft furniture and, it seems to me, that this has improved the general view a great deal. Yesterday I played a duet with V[asilii] Bezekirskii. Then he played for me an impromptu à la Chopin, as he put it. Really, he does improvise quite poetically. After breakfast we drove him into the city. Now Raia must be practicing piano, to judge from the uncertain sounds from the keyboard, which is characteristic of all beginners, but especially her.

3 JULY 1881, SOKOL'NIKI.

We are planning to have our photograph taken today, since Papa and Mama are going into the city and therefore we can go without fearing that Mama has guessed. Now Mama has dropped into my room when the nanny was here and asked about children's clothing. Last evening, as we were returning from a stroll, we met Mr. Radzevich, who dropped by and talked about politics and about the fact that the student Starynkevich[11] was sentenced to twenty years at hard labor because they found a [revolutionary] proclamation in his possession. Yesterday we were at the Danilovs.[12] Masha and I played piano, but because I had not memorized the piece (a Chopin waltz), I became confused toward the end. Masha played some kind of waltz by Wollenhaupt.[13] Her teacher, Mlle. Grigorovich, a sister of the boy violinist,[14] said for Jacques to come to show me how he is dressed, but otherwise Mme. Reimonenk [sic] dresses him carelessly. Yesterday *Moscow News*[15] published an article that L[azar] S[olomonovich] Poliakov is allegedly in Athens, when in fact Lazar [Iakovlevich] is there.[16] It is overcast again today—so when will summer finally be here? Two weeks ago bonds and coupons worth 15,000 rubles were stolen in the office. Papa turned this case over to the police, and yesterday morning E[fim] Epshtein came and said that some boy brought a packet to the office with a note "from someone

---

E. M. Koliada and P. I. Chaikovskii, "V istoriko-kul'turnom landshafte podmoskovnykh usadeb," *Vestnik akademii russkogo baleta im. A. Ia. Vaganovoi*, no. 38 (2015): 114–19.

11. Ivan Iul'evich Starynkevich (1861–1920), a member of the terrorist organization Narodnaia Volia (The People's Will) and a student at Moscow University, was arrested in 1881 for disseminating proclamations and sentenced in June by the Moscow military district court.

12. Mikhail Alekseevich Danilov (1831–99) was a railroad engineer who designed the Bender-Galats Railroad and worked with the Poliakovs on their railway projects, serving as the head engineer for the construction of the Poliakov railways. See Iakov Poliakov, "Istoriia," l. 29.

13. Hermann Wollenhaupt (1827–63) was a German composer.

14. Karl Karlovich Grigorovich (see note 73).

15. *Moskovskie vedomosti*, the archconservative paper of Mikhail N. Katkov (1818–87).

16. Lazar Iakovlevich Poliakov (1851–1927) was Iakov Solomonovich's oldest son and Zinaida's cousin. There is a lot of confusion between Zinaida's father and Iakov's son, Lazar, especially when the patronymics are not used.

unknown to you." More than half of the securities have been put on the market and at the exchange rate, kopeck for kopeck, traded for Eastern bank notes. There was also a note: "By mistake I opened the envelope addressed to L. S. Poliakov and, afraid of being held responsible, did not immediately return it but am now returning it in full." In all respects a deft thief, but Papa says even an "honest thief." I have still not taken an interest in checking my numbers against the lottery list, so there is still a chance of winning. I noted that when I write my impressions of the previous day in my journal, Raia is practicing with Lidiia Stepanovna on the piano. Today I have entered a lot into this "book," and I hope that later even all these insignificant facts will give me pleasure as I reread them and imagine every day with complete clarity.

4 JULY 1881, SOKOL'NIKI.

Yesterday we all had our picture taken in Borogrodskoe. They say that the weather today is the same as yesterday. Apparently, the following are coming to lunch: Prince Trubetskoi and his wife,[17] Demidov, and [General] Stefanovskii. The latter, they say, has come into hard times and that is why he has been at Sokol'niki for a long time. Tomorrow, we shall apparently go to the races at Petrovskii Park.[18] I have not seen the races this year. Yesterday I did not like Ksenia's [Khaia's] manner of reading and, when she took my journal to read, I told her this very bluntly, and she became furious. When I told her to give me my journal but say thanks that I let her read it, she said that "she would prefer to spit than to say thanks."

5 JULY 1881, SOKOL'NIKI.

Yesterday we had the Trubetskoi couple, Demidov, and Stefanovskii for lunch, and afterwards Shil'dbakh came and played dominoes. Shil'dbakh related how his ailing son, an officer, journeyed into the city and, in response to his father's comment that this is bad for his health, replied that it is easier to breathe in the city. Apparently, that is because he is always alone, and when he finds himself among the people there, things seem easier for him. Today Lidiia Stepanovna left for Ostankino. I am still not speaking to her. The weather is splendid. I do not know whether we are going to Novikova's today, as had been planned. It is a pity that we shall not be traveling this summer. Yesterday Papa received a letter from Uncle Iakov in Marienbad, where, as he puts it, he reeled off four

17. The Trubetskois were an old gentry family that traced its roots to the Grand Duchy of Lithuania.
18. The picturesque park was developed in the nineteenth century, occupied some twenty-two hectares to the northwest of Moscow, and was the site of sled and horse racing.

weeks of treatment, but without any results. Volkov[19] and his two daughters are in Franzensbad;[20] he has to return from there soon. Yesterday Ksenia received a letter from Rebecca in England, but in the interim we have set her up in the fall with the Demidovs (at 400 rubles per annum). There was some talk of a trip to Yalta, but it's not clear what will come of it. Demidov told Mama that S[of'ia] Iv[anovna] Slezkina asked him to convey that Ivan L'vovich [Slezkin][21] has been summoned to Petersburg. Elena [Slezkina] told me that in confidence, but said that Baranov[22] is summoning him no earlier than 15 August. I am very happy for them; they have been very bored all this time. Yesterday I played a few rounds of croquet, which I do quite rarely, and thus have completely forgotten how to play.

6 JULY 1881, SOKOL'NIKI.

Yesterday during lunch Ia[kov] Polonskii arrived. He brought two boxes of *pastila* [a fruit fudge] and said that he sent remarkable soap as well to the hotel. In the evening we went to the village of Bashilovka and to the park. We met Ekisler, Volodia Akimov, and Mme. Akimova. We had tea at the Slezkins; there we played various games of cards and spillikins. However, I found it to be less animated this time. But present were: Brevern,[23] Dubrovina (very nice young woman), Count Keller,[24] and Vintulov[25] (also a military officer with a very thick, bright nose). Sof'ia Ivanovna became very concerned when Elena went into the garden without a coat, even though it was really quite warm. Everyone thinks that the count's visit will end in a wedding. Today there is a downpour, so it's necessary to send for our group. I told Faitel'son to order for the horses to

19. Lev Nikolaevich Volkov (1825–84) was a collegiate councilor and head of the board of Lazar Poliakov's Moscow Land Bank.

20. Franzensbad was a spa town five kilometers north of Cheb, in western Bohemia (now in the Czech Republic).

21. Ivan L'vovich Slezkin (1818–82) became head of the Moscow Provincial Gendarme Administration in 1867. He assumed control over the investigation of the nihilist Sergei Nechaev, who murdered Ivan Ivanov—a member of his revolutionary cell suspected of being a police spy. This sensational case inspired Fyodor Dostoevsky's 1873 novel *Devils* (also known under the title of *The Possessed*).

22. Likely a reference to Nikolai Mikhailovich Baranov (1837–1901), who briefly served as city governor (*gradonachal'nik*) of St. Petersburg, 21 March–24 August 1881.

23. Either Eduard Karlovich Brevern, who is mentioned below, or Aleksandr Ivanovich Brevern de Lagarde (1814–90), a general in the Russian army.

24. Count Fëder Keller (1850–1904) attended the elite Corps of Pages and the Nicholas General Staff Academy, from which he graduated in 1876 as captain. He served as aide-de-camp for the future Alexander III.

25. Nikolai Aleksandrovich Vintulov (1845–1917) was a general in the Russian army.

be brought from the *manège* [a center for training and riding horses]. Tomorrow is Mama's birthday, and I am rushing to send to Ovchinnikov for the frame that we ordered. Tomorrow we shall have for lunch the following: Demidov (who may stay overnight), General Stefanovskii, the Slezkins (Sof'ia Ivanovna, Elena, Mikhail Ivanovich), and of course the Podgoretskii family. Mama also wanted to invite Shil'dbakh with his daughter. The problem is that our table does not expand and therefore it is impossible to invite many to dine with us. Lidiia Stepanovna did not return yet from Ostankino, from yesterday. I would not wish to invite the Slezkins tomorrow, since I understood from the remark by E[lena] Ivan[ovna] [Slezkina][26] to Eduard Karlovich Brevern de Lagarde ("we face an unpleasant surprise: a change of plans") that it is very boring for her. It turns out that they had arranged a cavalcade for that day, but it had to be cancelled. I very much regret that the rain prevented us from riding horseback today. The boys (i.e., Misha, Ronia, Ilia, and Satia, then Lev, Roman and Mr. Vagner) went on foot to Ostankino, but have returned. Yesterday Elena once more reminded me not to forget to tell her when Papa is going to Petersburg so that she could inform Serezha of this (so that he could see Papa). I of course will keep my word, since she very much desires this; she is hoping that S[ergei] Ivanovich will get a position there.

7 JULY 1881, SOKOL'NIKI.

Today is Mama's birthday. I am hurrying to go down to congratulate her and to give the present from us all. Jacques [Iakov] was in bed yesterday; he had a stomachache. It seems that the weather today is clear. Yesterday we went horseback riding for two and a half hours. When I have my own horse, I shall go riding often. They say that Tret'iakov[27] received a letter, threatening to kill him if he refused to pay 20,000 rubles at 2 am two days ago. But they saw him yesterday, and he asked whether it was we who were riding on horses from the manège. Mama seems to like the brooch that Papa gave her. Today we expect guests for dinner. [Iakov] Polonskii is still here, and Bezekirskii[28] promised Mama that he would come for dinner today.

---

26. Zinaida was very sensitive to any social slights.

27. She is referring to a member of the wealthy Tret'iakov merchant family in Moscow—perhaps Pavel Mikhailovich Tret'iakov (1832–98), an art collector and philanthropist who founded the Tret'iakov Gallery, one of the most renowned repositories of Russian art in Moscow.

28. Vasilii Vasil'evich Bezekirskii (1835–1919), a famous violinst and composer, was the concertmaster of the Bolshoi Theater orchestra until 1891.

8 JULY 1881, SOKOL'NIKI.

Yesterday morning, after breakfast, they sent for Sof'ia L'vovna [Vydrina] and her children. Those dining with us included: Bezekirskii, Grigorovich,[29] Demidov, Slezkin, Amal[iia] Michel, [Iulii Osipovich] Gol'denbakh, the L'vovs, Vydrina, Liliia, Stefanovskii, the Podgoretskiis, Tsion,[30] Roman [Vydrin], and Shil'dbakh. After dinner Ananov and Ms. Akimova came as well. All were in high spirits. Little Karl [the violinist] played before dinner, with Bezekirskii accompanying. After dinner Tsion played the piano. Today we are going to the races. Karl Grigorovich and Stefanovskii stayed overnight. Today the weather is splendid but the temperature is like yesterday's. Last evening it was impossible to sit out on the terrace because of the dampness, and Am[aliia] Ivanovna asked to come inside. They say that Elena is not entirely well, is lying in bed, and therefore did not come yesterday. I very much regret this, although I am still somewhat skeptical about her desire to be at our place yesterday. I drank so much wine yesterday, thanks to my neighbor Bezekirskii, that afterwards I turned completely red and was embarrassed to go where the guests were. I think that this was mainly due to the fact that I am not used to drinking wine; usually, I do not drink anything except seltzer, beer (rarely), and kvass. Next Sunday the Podgoretskii couple will be here to dine with us and then go with us to Bogorodskoe. On the 12th there will be a public gathering in support of a cheap eatery on Tverskoi [Boulevard].

9 JULY 1881, SOKOL'NIKI.

Yesterday morning Stefanovskii and Karl [Grigorovich] went into the city. In the evening we went to the races at Petrovskii Park. There we saw Iakovlev, the Slezkins (including E[lena]), Naryshkin with his brother and wife, and others. The weather was wonderful—demonstrated by the fact that we came home without having to don our warm coats. I am now regularly continuing to write in my journal. I would like to read it in a year and to see whether it is really worthwhile to spend time on it. 27 is Misha's birthday; he will be 14 and is now in the fifth grade at the gymnasium. Today is 9 July; this morning is overcast, but yesterday it was not. Somehow it is boring to think that the summer is starting to come toward an end but we have not seen it in its full radiance. But a weak hope for its artificial continuation runs through my head involuntarily:

---

29. Karl Karlovich Grigorovich (b. 1868), born in Vitebsk, was a student of Bezekirskii and Jozef Ioakhim. He became the leader of the Mecklenburg Quartet—one of the first Russian chamber groups to tour in Europe.

30. Moisei Faddeevich Tsion (Zion) worked for the Poliakov banking house and often performed errands for Zinaida and her family.

to be in the West, where there is no winter, but only two months of autumn. By going abroad, it is possible to extend the summer and [avoid] part of our rainy and muddy autumn. What the proverb says is true after all: it's nice to be a guest, but better to be at home. But unless one has occasionally been a guest, one cannot appreciate being "at home." Sokol'niki is a good place, but after all one occsionally has to go to some place else; otherwise you'll be in the position of returning to those times when Tsar Aleksei Mikhailovich reigned [1646–76]. He came here with his boyars to hunt with falcons. From that comes the name of our place of residence.[31] At dinner, on Mama's birthday, Shil'dbakh said that Iv[an] Kondrat'evich Babst[32] had died at his village estate. They buried him yesterday in the same village. After the races we stopped at Varvara Ivanovna Akimova, but she had gone that evening to Sokol'niki. How pleased I am that Mama likes our present. It is a pity that Lidiia Stepanovna is lying in bed today. I had thought of working on geometry with Nazarov, but I am afraid that Papa and Mama will be opposed. I did not see him at the dacha; otherwise I would have asked him to set aside two and a half hours a week for me. Aleksandr appeared better than all in our group [photograph], but when they took his picture he said "hm"—which caused me to laugh, and that is how the photo turned out.

10 JULY 1881, SOKOL'NIKI.

Yesterday we spent a rather pleasant evening in the company of Julie [Iuliia] Shil'dbakh. Also there was her little brother, Kostia.[33] During a game of cards of "questions and answers," we took alarm: we seemed to hear a man's voice in the garden, but it was totally dark there, so we imagined that a thief had broken in. It all came to naught, but we do not know who had been speaking. Today the weather is splendid—at last! Tomorrow morning I intend to stop for Mlle. Shild'bakh, to bring her back here, and to go for a stroll with her. I am very glad that I have found at least one girlfriend here. Her brother is an uhlan and has still not married; he had proposed to a female relative but, it seems to me, his wedding completely fell through.

---

31. In other words, the name Sokol'niki is derived from *sokol* (falcon).

32. Ivan Kondrat'evich Babst (1823–81), a prominent economist and professor at Moscow University, was also a publisher and editor, historian (who collaborated with Konstantin Pobedonostsev), and head of the Moscow Merchants' Bank.

33. Konstantin Konstantinovich Shil'dbakh (1872–1939), son of Konstantin Karlovich Shil'dbakh and Aleksandra Semenovna Afenas'eva, became a military officer and fought for the Whites during the Civil War.

11 JULY 1881, SOKOL'NIKI.

Yesterday we had pleasant news: Bella is engaged to I[osef] Wilhelmovich [Vil'gel'movich] Landau of Warsaw.[34] I heard that he has yet another brother, younger than himself, and that his parents are alive.[35] What was begun in Biarritz last year has been finished in Marienbad. The weather is very warm today, but since today Stefanovskii, Demidov, a chamberlain, and Iakovlev are dining here, then it seems to me that I should wear a black dress. Yesterday evening we went to the circle where music, under the direction of Kreinbring, had only begun before we left. When we arrived home, we found G. Radzevich in our garden. Yesterday I read telegrams about the amnesty for Gel'fman[36] and the change from capital punishment to life at hard labor. Today I have almost nothing of interest to write in my journal beyond what has already been entered. It turns out that Moisei Faddeev[ich] Tsion was a partner of the banker Landau and knows him well. Mama says that Uncle Iakov Solomonovich has taken all the best cities (Odessa, Khar'kov, Warsaw).[37] In general I am happy with yesterday's news, since many were making fun of Bella because she is very fat. Tomorrow or the day after we plan, it seems, to go to Novikova. Podgoretskii left today for Tver': it is the saint's day for Ol'ga Radkevich.[38] Tomorrow they (he and Sof'ia Frantsevna)[39] will dine with us. No particular walks are foreseen for today (because of the heat). Lidiia Stepanovna has been speaking to me since last Monday, and that makes me very happy.

12 JULY 1881, SOKOL'NIKI.

Yesterday morning I played a lot of croquet, but did not win much against my adversaries; this game is very interesting when the players are divided into two

34. Zinaida's cousin Isabella (Bella) was Iakov Solomonovich's daughter.

35. According to Iakov Poliakov, Iosef Landau's two brothers—Leopold and Daniil—came to the wedding. Zinaida must have been referring to one of them. She also attended the wedding in Taganrog.

36. Gesia Gel'fman (1855–82), a member of the revolutionary People's Will (Narodnaia Volia), was arrested for complicity in the assassination of Alexander II in 1881. Due to her pregnancy and calls for clemency from socialists in the West, the state commuted her death sentence to lifelong penal servitude. See Barbara Alpern Engel, "Gesia Gelfman: A Jewish Woman on the Left in Imperial Russia," in *Jewish and Leftist Politics: Judaism, Israel, Antisemitism, and Gender*, ed. Jack Jacobs (Cambridge: Cambridge University Press, 2017), 183–99.

37. This is a reference to the spouses of Iakov's children: his daughter Liza (Elizabeth) married Lev (Louis) Raffalovich of Odessa; his son Lazar became the second husband of Lev's sister Anna (Annette) Leonino (née Raffalovich); and his daughter Anna (Niuta) married Grigorii (George) Rubenshtein of Khar'kov. Isabella married Iosef Landau of Warsaw.

38. Daughter of Sof'ia and Semen Podgoretskii.

39. Wife of Semen Sergeevich Podgoretskii.

teams. Yesterday the following came to dine here: Stefanovskii, V. Sobolev,[40] and M[oisei] F[addeevich] Tsion. When dinner was over, we found Korobovskii on the terrace with his nephew (a lycée student), who brought us tickets to to-day's holiday in Bogorodskoe. Today the the Podgoretskii couple will dine with us. They repeated to us the intention of the wife of Spiridonov, the head of Mar'inskii [Park]; she came to see Papa about the general plan of Tsurikovo.[41] It is as hot as it was yesterday; today I woke up with a headache—of course because my room in the morning is always facing the sun. If it were possible now to bathe (without going to the bathing pool), it would be very pleasant, especially since, having bathed, one could return home in the same state as before the bathing. Ksenia strolls here a very great deal and yesterday, for instance, she returned from the circle when it was completely dark. I need to write Bella a letter and congratulate her, but I am still mulling this over, since she did not inform me of this even in her own letter. Mishka is hitting the ball with the croquet hammer from morning to night, and for a change I want to introduce to this game what we played so often in Franzensbad. Is it really possible to hear nothing but a game of croquet? After all, everyone will get sick of this, and I think that this is even true of the guests.

[Lev] Volkov returned from Moscow, will take the daughters to the country-side, and on the return come to have dinner with us in Sokol'niki. He told Papa that the people there are terrible (of course he imagines himself to be the best of the public at Franzensbad, where they get water from one and the same source). Ronichka probably has gone for a walk; I infer this from the fact that the croquet grounds are free. However, it seems that I am mistaken; just now the dull sound of a blow has reached my ears. Stefanovskii yesterday said that Mitia is losing all his hair. To that he added that he is very modest (?!) and that they are looking after him. As can be seen, he is not happy about this, since he traveled to Gapsal'[42] for a cure. Sergei L'vovich [Sheftel] (the brother of Sof'ia L'vovna [Vydrina]) fell ill in Kiev and telegraphed Lev to come to him, because he is lying in bed there, sick and completely alone.

13 JULY 1881, SOKOL'NIKI.
Stefanovskii, having spent three nights with us, went yesterday with S[emen] Eibushits[43] into the city. Sof'ia Frantsevna and Demidov had lunch with us

40. Possibly Vasilli Nikolaevich or Vladimir Federovich Sobolev. Both were state officials.
41. The Poliakovs bought an estate in Tsurikovo.
42. A town in northwestern Estonia known for its mud baths.
43. Semen Eibushits (1851–98) was the architect who designed the choral synagogue in Moscow, which was funded generously by the Poliakovs.

yesterday. In the evening we went to the circle in Bogorodskoe. M[ikhail] Mostovskii[44] also had lunch with us yesterday. I learned from him an extremely important fact: our sovereign is to arrive in Moscow or to leave from St. Petersburg tomorrow. This fact is kept, for the time being, as a great secret. Today we will have lunch in [the town of] Klin, but Papa must go to see the deputy ministers Nikolaev and Ermakov, who (they say) arrived with him. Yesterday Demidov stayed to spend the night. The weather is warm, and today my eyes are bothering me from the heat.

14 JULY 1881, SOKOL'NIKI.
Yesterday Papa went to see Nikolaev and Ermakov; they had lunch at Dolgorukov's and in the evening traveled to Petersburg. I think that tomorrow we will not go again to the Novikova estate, because it is the saint's day for Prince Vladimir Andreevich [Dolgorukov],[45] and of course Papa will go to congratulate him. I shall not write about something I have already discussed: the sovereign's arrival. Tomorrow is already Wednesday, and today I want to go horseback riding, but will hardly succeed in doing so, since the housekeeper who was in Moscow yesterday forgot about the errand I had given her. The hot weather is already unbearable, and I regularly have a headache in the mornings. I am now reading Lidiia Stepanovna's [copy of] *The Frigate "Pallada"*[46]—what style! Yesterday Papa, Mama, and I played croquet, and Mama won. Two days ago, in the evening, Il'ia's East Indian canary flew away, but yesterday morning it flew back directly into its cage. It is completely gray with a red beak, as if from sealing wax. Raika gave me an example on how to take a bath: it is so hot that one feels like plunging in. Satin'ka [Isaak] is cross with me: I sometimes criticize his slovenly dress, and he does not in the least like that. Jacques [Iakov] also was not entirely polite yesterday: he placed the wickets for his croquet in the direction of where we were playing, and when I reproved him for this, he began to raise his voice. When I am traveling and thinking about writing a description of a country, I try to borrow from the descriptions in Goncharov's *The Frigate "Pallada."*

15 JULY 1881, SOKOL'NIKI.
Mama was not well yesterday; she lay out on her balcony, and Iulii Osipovich [Gol'denbakh] came by twice. In the evening the horses were brought at 8:45

44. Mikhail Stepanovich Mostovskii (b. 1838) was a Russian pedagogue and geographer.
45. Prince Vladimir Andreevich Dolgorukov (1810–91) was the governor-general of Moscow from 1865 to 1891. His relationship to the Poliakovs is described in part 1.
46. *The Frigate "Pallada"* is a book by Ivan Goncharov that was published in 1858 and recounts his trip around the world in 1852–54 as a secretary to Admiral Evfimii Putiatin.

pm (instead of 6 pm), and [we] went horseback riding for a half hour; when we returned, we saw the coachman leading a horse with a saddle. Through my maid Katia, Mama sent me an order to get up not at 8:30 am, but exactly at 8:00 am. They say that I'm going into the city with Papa—but for what? Perhaps I'll use this to buy Mishka a present. I would very much like to know if the sovereign arrived today in the ancient capital of the Russian state. All these days have been constantly warm, and yesterday everyone referred to this, but did not do anything about it. I practiced piano for 4 hours and 11 minutes. Iulii Osipovich advised me to make shutters that close tightly, and indeed that is good—where is one to find a carpenter now? I intend to wear a gray dress, but with small circles (made from percale), in view of the probable dust from the prolonged hot spell. Tomorrow, if Mama feels well, we may go to Nadezhda Vasil'evna [Novikova]. Sashka has learned to say "Papa" and therefore tries to demonstrate his artfulness to everyone. Our people (the brothers and Vagner) are going to swim in the Iauza River and say that the water is warm. They very much love to swim in the river. Today Papa will be at [Dolgorukov]'s to congratulate him [on his saint's day] and wants to go to the Dashkovs. Count Kutaisov [said] that his son-in-law went to Kiev to investigate the causes of the anti-Jewish movement.[47] Uncle Samuil bought a place for the family crypt in the new Jewish cemetery in Petersburg, and there will also be an almshouse and an artisanal school for Jewish orphans. He will maintain both of these institutions at his own expense and, in addition, has made a one-time contribution of 100,000 rubles to construct a building. This news appeared yesterday in the *Dawn*,[48] but earlier it had been briefly published in all the best Russian organs, including *Moscow News*.

16 JULY 1881, SOKOL'NIKI.
Today is just as hot. Yesterday I went with Papa into Moscow and heard about the sovereign's arrival. [Mikhail] Katkov, whom Papa drove from Dolgorukov's to his apartment, seemingly wants to advise him to be crowned here.[49] The audience at the palace will be either on Friday or on Saturday. They say that

47. Zinaida must have meant Count Ippolit Pavlovich Kutaisov's son rather than son-in-law. Count Nikolai Ignatiev (1832–1908), the minister of the interior, appointed Count Pavel Ippolitovich Kutaisov (1837–1911) to investigate the pogroms. He traveled to many affected areas and met with Jewish delegations.
48. *Rassvet*, a leading Jewish weekly in St. Petersburg published from August 1879 to January 1883.
49. Amid heightened security after the assassination of his father, Alexander III delayed the coronation until 15 May 1883, but he did have the ceremony performed in the Uspenskii Cathedral in the Kremlin in Moscow.

the sovereign and his wife, the heir, and perhaps Vladimir Aleksandrovich[50] are coming. I bought Mishka the works of [Nikolai] Gogol for his birthday; as a present to him from Lidiia Stepanovna I bought him Count Leo Tolstoy's *Military Stories*.[51] In the city I saw Roman. Lev has still not sent Aunt a telegram from Kiev about her brother.

17 JULY 1881, SOKOL'NIKI.

I was at the royal audience in the Kremlin palace and saw the Sovereign, his wife, the heir, and [his brother] Georgii.[52] They very cordially bowed, but the heir and his brother Georgii Aleksandrovich were looking upward. Then we drove to Tverskoi Boulevard to our house and at 5 pm returned to Sokol'niki. Livshits sent a telegram about the birth of a son.[53] Today it rained from the morning and that was good, for the heat was unbearable. The same day Mme. Hortense made me a dress and straw hat. I am very pleased that I saw the Sovereign and his wife and they made a very favorable impression. A. Orlov probably had his name day yesterday, since Afinogen[54] seems [to occur] once a year. The tallest of all was the Sovereign; not a single man was of such enormous height. Everyone was very simply dressed, but the men were in parade uniforms. Genriusha [Genrikh] is still in Orel; he will surely be godfather of Fanechkina's [Fania's] son. I have not had any news even from Misha for a month. If the Sovereign will be here some time, then the name day of Mariia Feodorovna will be celebrated here and in her presence. It would be desirable to dedicate the Church of the Savior[55] now, in the presence of the imperial personages, on the 6th of August.

18 JULY 1881, SOKOL'NIKI.

Two days ago [General Mikhail Nikolaevich] Annenkov[56] was here; he only arrived in the morning and in the evening left for the village. The same day General

50. Grand Duke Vladimir Aleksandrovich (1847–1909) was the third son of Alexander II and the younger brother of Alexander III.

51. Tolstoy's *Voennye rasskazy*, including the Sevastopol pieces, appeared as a separate volume in 1856 (St. Petersburg: Tipografiia Glavnogo shtaba E.I.V. po voenno-uchebnym zavedeniiam). Zinaida probably bought a recent reprinting (Moscow: Tipografiia A.P. Pettsmana, 1878).

52. Alexander III, Empress Mariia Feodorovna, the heir Nicholas (later Nicholas II), and Grand Duke Georgii Aleksandrovich (1872–99).

53. Iakov Isaakovich Livshits and Fania Vydrina's son; Zinaida's relatives on her mother's side.

54. Russian form of the Greek Athenogenes (descendant of Athena).

55. The reference is to the Cathedral of Christ the Savior, planning for which began after the war of 1812. The foundation stone was laid in 1837, and construction took several decades. The church was consecrated on 14 May 1883, the day before Alexander III's coronation.

56. Annenkov (1835–99) was a Russian infantry general, active in the conquest of Central Asia and later involved in the construction of the Zakaspiiskii railroad in Central Asia (1880–91).

Stefanovskii had dinner with us, and in the evening K[onstantin] Shil'dbakh, the engineer M[ikhail] A. Danilov, and M[ikhail] Den[isovich] Demidov came. Today perhaps I will stop by for Mlle. Shil'dbakh and bring her to us; I have long since promised to go. The external appearance of "A" is quite attractive, and it seems that he acts very carefully and sensibly. Bella and all the rest of the Landaus are in Ostend. Yesterday Uncle Samuil Solomonovich sent Papa a dispatch, asking whether it is impossible to organize a deputation to appear before the sovereign emperor. A bouquet from the Moscow ladies was given to the sovereign's wife before her departure to Trinity-Sergius Lavra.[57] Yesterday at the palace, Demidov said he had been told the previous day to remain the entire time in his uniform. His Imperial Majesty, they say, flew past us, evidently to the Cathedral. It is a pity that Ksenia did not see the royal audience. But if they are staying in inexpensive quarters, Mama said that she won't take Ksenia and Misha. Ivan (the heavyset one) told Mr. Vagner that he is seeing our sovereign, but not him. Iosef Landau or Ignatii will live in Warsaw, since Uncle sent a telegram that he be called I[osef] W. Landau. Konst[antin] Karl[ovich] Shil'dbakh did not take his daughter yesterday to the royal reception. It would be interesting to know what they will name the Livshits son. Yesterday Mama wanted to send them a telegram on the occasion of the addition to their family. [Nadezhda] Novikova is probably not especially pleased that Papa forewarned her twice about our arrival and kept delaying it. As for the horseback riding I will let them know in the manège the day before so that they are here at the appointed time. Yesterday Papa was without his ribbon (the green Persian one) and his Persian medals;[58] one has to get really dressed up in all of one's regalia, but either Papa or Mama (I do not clearly recall) [said] that when they award him a red ribbon, then he'll put it on. Raika found that yesterday's hat suits me well. It is a black straw hat; the entire trim consists of a crepe bow and a long crepe veil.

19 JULY 1881, SOKOL'NIKI.

Yesterday Teplov[59] and K[onstantin]. K. Shil'dbakh came to dine, and afterwards (they say) G. Pavlov came, and prior to the meal someone came to see Papa. A member of the *artel'* [an artisan cooperative] brought newspapers and letters from the office, but nothing for me. The weather today is good. A[ndrei]. A. Gorchakov[60] wrote Papa two days ago. I very much fear that I shall spend

57. Trinity-Sergius Lavra is a leading monastery of the Russian Orthodox Church, located about seventy kilometers from Moscow.
58. Lazar Poliakov received the Persian medals as the consul of Persia.
59. Colonel Aleksei Nikolaevich Teplov (1816–91).
60. Andrei Aleksandrovich Gorchakov (1798–1883) was the minister of foreign affairs in 1856–82.

the entire day in the garden; I very much want to go for a stroll. Yesterday evening, I amused myself by giving everyone a surname that matches the individual's traits. For example, I called I[van] L'v[ovich] Slezkin "Kostin," Sof[ia] I[vanovna] "Krestina," our nanny "Staritskaia," and so forth. Mlle. Shil'dbakh will go horseback riding today.

20 JULY 1881, SOKOL'NIKI.

Today is Il'in Day (Il'iusha Paltov's name day).[61] Yesterday we went to [the] roadbed of the Iaroslavl railway and saw how a simple train with two locomotives and many railcars passed by. It turns out that the sovereign returned on this train from Trinity-Sergius Lavra,[62] and a soldier told us that he faced the window and the children on that side, and that no one was permitted to approach until the train had passed. At 3 pm V[asilii] Bezekirskii arrived and said that he had been at the Iaroslavl railway station. Next came S[emen] S. Podgoretskii; along with [Vasilii] Bezekirskii (who had changed clothes), he came to dinner. After lunch Misha and I went riding in a charabanc,[63] but at this time (they say) Mrs. Novikova came for a visit. I dropped by at Julie's, but she had left earlier, with a cousin, to go to the circle. Afterwards privy counselor Shil'dbakh came, as did Demidov and S[of'ia] Podgoretskaia. They managed to play vint[64] and domino-lottery. I won 1.10 rubles. The weather is partly cloudy. Yesterday we were astonished when the train passed that, in the last railcar, a chef stood on the landing in his cook's attire. Yesterday the imperial family left for Nizhnii Novgorod. It is a pity that in Moscow they did not dedicate the Church of the Savior, although they did spend an hour and half inspecting it. Today Novikova is going to Tambov for several days, but Papa had intended finally to visit her today.

21 JULY 1881, SOKOL'NIKI.

Yesterday I went with Papa and Mama for a stroll and, reaching the railroad along Alekseevskii Prospect, we turned to the right into the woods and walked up to the usual road, and from there walked back home. When, two days ago, I went riding in the charabanc, a young man in a cap stopped on our roadway; it seemed to me that this was Novikov, but I did not recognize him and did

61. Il'ia Il'ich Paltov (1838–1915), a member of the Council of the State Bank.
62. The Moscow-Trinity Sergius section was the first part of the line to be completed, in 1862. In 1870 it was extended to Rostov and Iaroslavl.
63. A charabanc was a type of nineteenth-century carriage popular for sightseeing. The name derives from the French char à bancs (carriage with wooden benches).
64. A Russian card game similar to whist.

not bow, while he also only glanced and did not bow, since I was in a thick black veil. Afterward I learned that N[adezhda] Vas[il'evna] [Novikova] was in very much of a hurry since people were waiting for her. Two days ago V[asilii] Bezekirskii stayed overnight with us, and yesterday he traveled to Moscow and to his family in Zhukovka[65] but today perhaps will go with Konshin[66] to the Caucasus. Yesterday morning I told them to bring us riding horses. Mama is going with Papa into Moscow at 9:30 am, and I asked the coachman to go to the manège. I will drop in at Shil'dbakh and ask whether she will come with us. Yesterday Aleksandr played with some kind of stick; during lunch Mme. Reymoneng took it away, since he might accidentally poke someone in the eye. Without saying anything other than "Nanny," he ran offended up to her and left the toy in the hands of Mme. Reymoneng. I am now finishing the first part of *The Frigate "Pallada."* I do not know what else I might cite in my book. Yesterday Papa bowed to one gentleman (Baron Vrangel), who was walking with Mr. Valter and his daughter. His son, a page, earlier had paced back and forth before us. We were sitting on a bench at Stefanovskii's dacha. Today it is already hot, but it is strange that "Elijah" passed yesterday on his heavenly chariot without thunder and lightning.[67] Tomorrow is M[ikhail] Danilov's name day; Zinaida Iv[anovna Danilova] dropped by and asked us to come this evening at 7 pm, and tomorrow she will have a ballroom pianist. She always pays 75 rubles on this day to the orchestra, but this year she will not have music, since "this is no longer in fashion." For the same reason her sister will also not have an orchestra this year.

22 JULY 1881, SOKOL'NIKI.

Today we are waiting for the riding horses. Ksenia wants to let Julie know that, if she wants to go riding with us, we have a horse here for her and we'll go riding. Today the weather is favorable for our proposed horseback ride. Yesterday we went to the circle, where they were playing music. I met Minor[68] and bowed to him, but he probably did not recognize me and did not bow. Upon coming home I found him here on our terrace. On the path, in the darkness, I recognized the Mattern couple (by their different heights) and, if I had not

65. Zhukovka was a village in Moscow province.
66. This could be either Aleksei Vladimirovich Konshin (b. 1859), who was a Russian financier and later minister of finance, or Nikolai Nikolaevich Konshin (1833–1918), a first-guild merchant and industrialist in Moscow province.
67. The reference is to the prophet Elijah. On 20 July Zinaida referred to *Il'in den'* (Elijah's Day), the date it was celebrated by the Orthodox Church (Julian calendar).
68. This may be a reference to one of Zelig Minor's sons (Osip or Lazar), or to Rabbi Minor himself.

loudly said "hello," they would probably have passed by. I heard that, at the manège, the coachman did not talk about having horses for today.

23 JULY 1881, SOKOL'NIKI.

Yesterday we went horseback riding all morning, but Papa, Misha, Raika, and Sashka rode in the charabanc. It turned out that yesterday was Roman's birthday; we went to Aunt Sonechka and congratulated him (he turned 22 yesterday). Aleksandr was very happy to ride in the charabanc; we were all at Ostankino. There was a letter from Mashka to Ksenia; she writes that Friday, the 19th, was her birthday, but to have a more convenient stroll she celebrated it on Thursday. She, grandfather [Vydrin], Sof'ia Iakovlevna,[69] Il'iushen'ka (Il'ia), and Roza[70] are all traveling for a short visit to the Crimea. Volkov and Stefanovskii dined with us yesterday. I did not go to the Danilovs, since I was tired and had a stomachache. She saw us when we drove past the dacha of Julie Shil'dbakh and, they say, bowed to us, but at the time I was galloping and saw only something white on the balcony. The weather is good, but probably will be hot later on, but not right now. It would be very desirable to know why the Vydrins are traveling to the Crimea. Genriusha [Genrikh] will conse-quently go soon to Moscow, although his arrival does not in the least interest me. Today they will name Fanichkina's son Samuil. If this is just an adaptation from "Isaak" (in honor of the father of Iakov Isaakovich),[71] then this will be very original. Yesterday Julie probably would not have gone horseback riding so early. We rode past the dacha of the Baklanovs; the opium [poppies][72] are very beautifully laid out.

24 JULY 1881, SOKOL'NIKI.

Ksenia came now to read my journal, but did not finish because I took it to write. The other day Uncle sent us some candy from Lerfudin in Paris. He him-self is now in Pavlovsk. Yesterday G. Radzevich was here, and in the evening K[onstantin] K. Shil'dbakh came. I was at his daughter's, and Kostia told Mishka that they punished him for making six mistakes in transcription. When we were there, they brought them racing sulkies. In the evening we met the young Shil'dbakh with another gentleman on the sulkies. Today, like yesterday, the

---

69. A relative on Zinaida's maternal side.

70. The daughter of Il'ia Pavlovich Vydrin and Sof'ia L'vovna Vydrina. She later married Isaak Dov Ber Markon.

71. The father of Iakov Isaakovich Livshits was Isaak. Later it becomes clear that Samuil was Iakov Livshit's grandfather.

72. Zinaida wrote "opium."

weather is overcast. I shall give Mishka, in addition to the books, a brown frame of plush with my photograph. Mama is going with Papa into Moscow today and intends to drop in at Princess E[katerina] Andr[eevna] Gagarina's and invite her to have lunch on Monday for Mishka's birthday. Yesterday they gave Papa the usual notes from *conto corrento* [current accounts] with foreign bankers, and these reported that, per Papa's transfer, Mrs. Mina Malkiel'[73] took 10,000 francs in Paris, and N. Kozakova in Nice. Consequently, she reconciled with her mother, for otherwise she would not now be in Nice. When Volkov dined with us, it was the name day of his spouse (M. Mikh[ailovna]), and Mama wanted at lunch to drink to her health, but Ivan (the heavyset one) forgot to fulfill Mama's order to serve Moselle, and Mama forgot her order and did not repeat it. I asked Mama to buy a jardiniere of red wood at Ivanov's and that she not forget to give her the note. Lidiia Stepanovna is already practicing music with Raika again. Mishka and Ksenia, along with Lidiia Stepanovna, will be with me at the Shil'dbakh residence. Yesterday Miss Gosh went to complain about us to Mama: the cause was probably my joke. When Volkov and N. Stefanovskii were having lunch, on the table with the hors d'oeuvres, there was inter alia a bitter English vodka Shtritter [sic]. I said that one should not write "que c'est amerpais que tous les anglais le sont." She replied that "*on voit bien que vous êtes de ce charmant pays ou il n'y a pas de politesse.*" That was the end of it, but yesterday, having collected all the important facts for a complaint, she made use of them.

25 JULY 1881, SOKOL'NIKI.

Yesterday those dining here included Demidov, G. Naumov, K. K. Shil'dbakh, M[ikhail] Mostovskii, and Khotinskii. The weather today was not good. Yesterday Mama was at Princess E[katerina] Andr. Gagarina's.[74] In the evening Ksenia went for a stroll together with Lidiia Stepanovna. Mishka read my journal and came upon the place where I am writing about presents for his birthday. Shil'dbakh is perhaps coming to stay a while with my father. He is not writing me anything more about a fiancé. It is a real pity that I did not know of Mashka's birthday; otherwise, by that time Ksenia and I would have sent her [Sergei Aksakov's] *Family Chronicle* and *Years of Childhood*.[75] But better late than never: we'll correct this oversight and send [the gifts] now.

73. Mina Malkiel' was the wife of Samuil Malkiel' (b. 1836). Samuil and his brother Isaak Malkiel' established the family firm in Moscow with a branch in St. Petersburg.

74. Princess Ekaterina Andreevna Gagarina (1817–1900) was the daughter of Prince Andrei Pavlovich Gagarin and Ekaterina Sergeevna (née Menshikova).

75. Sergei T. Aksakov (1791–1859), the father of the famed Slavophiles Ivan and Konstantin, was a popular naturalist and the author of famous semi-autobiographical narratives, published as separate

26 JULY 1881, SOKOL'NIKI.

Just now I was looking for the geometry textbook by Professor Davydov[76] and did not find it. Yesterday Danilov and General Annenkov dined with us. They say that, before dinner, I. I. Radzevich was here, and afterwards K[arl] Grigorovich and his father arrived from the city and Mr. Shil'dbakh came on foot. Karlush [Karl] will spend the night here and is leaving today for his father's at 3 pm. Yesterday evening, while lying in bed, I thought about how I should work on geometry and French. The weather today is good. Tomorrow is Misha's birthday. Lidiia Stepanovna has left for Ostankino. Yesterday the Murav'evs celebrated their silver anniversary in the city. Yesterday Raika, it seems, was satisfied with Miss Gosh's choice of books for Mishka. A couple of days ago, at breakfast and afterwards D. Fed. Nazarov was here; does he really need money? He says that Mishka has put on weight from the rest, but allegedly I have not. E[katerina] Andr[eevna] Gagarina made Mama a napkin from bows, as if from daisies. Sof'ia Frantsevna and she will be the whole day at Mishka's birthday tomorrow. Karlusha and Mishka have just come to my door to ask permission to go riding on the charabanc. I said that we shall go together later. They laughed, probably because they guessed my response, and left. Indeed, they can damage the charabanc from carelessness, but I would very much regret that. Why was Fanichkina's son called Samuil? They say that it was in memory of Livshits's grandfather. Yesterday I finished volume 5 of [Hugo's] *Les Misérables*.[77] That leaves just as much to read from the total of ten books.

27 JULY 1881, SOKOL'NIKI.

Yesterday afternoon, they say, Iakovlev and Raskin were here (privately). For lunch they expected guests (as always on Sunday), but except for M[ikhail] Den. Demidov no one came. They drank to the health of P. Nikol[aevich] whose name day was yesterday. In the evening G. Shil'dbakh came. Today, on Mishka's birthday, if the weather is good and if it does not rain, for dinner we will have the Podgoretskii couple, Princess Gagarina, M. Stepanovskii,

volumes under the titles of *Family Chronicle* (1856) and *Years of Childhood* (1856). His son Ivan earned some ill repute for antisemitic attitudes, and the Aksakovs generally had close ties to conservative nationalist circles that included Katkov, Pobedonostsev, and of course the new sovereign, Alexander III.

76. Avgust Iul'evich Davydov (1823–86), from a Jewish family in Kurland province and professor at Moscow University, wrote the standard textbooks for geometry and other mathematics in the 1860s and 1870s.

77. Zinaida cites the title in French, suggesting that she read the novel in that language. It appeared in French in 1862; the first Russian translation came out in 1882 (St. Petersburg: Suvorin) with the title *Otverzhennye*.

Mostovskii, G. Demidov (perhaps—since his sister is visiting him), probably K. Shil'dbakh and Karl Grigor'ovich. Today I woke up with a headache; I think it is because at night I plait my hair into a single braid; yesterday and today, it seemed to me, the pillow is hard and painful to the head. Yesterday there was to be riding in the park, but it has been delayed since the 22nd. After lunch the horses were harnessed for two carriages but, with the forecast of rain, we put off our ride. So that the horses were not harnessed in vain, Sasha, the nanny, and I went riding in Sokol'niki, and the brothers and Karl went in the large carriage and overtook us with triumphant shouts. I gave Mishka my presents, and he liked them very much (especially the boxed edition of N. V. Gogol's writings). He, Ronichka, and Satin'ka have now come to me and examined these books. Lidiia Stepanovna has still not returned from Ostankino. My head is still aching. The weather is like yesterday, but more overcast. Annenkov wanted to come yesterday to spend the night with us and to dine with us today, but he sent Papa a telegram yesterday, saying that he is having lunch at Vladimir Andreevich [Dologorukov]'s and asks permission to come this morning, requesting to invite M[ikhail] Alekseev[ich], with whom he would like to make an agreement to travel to the Tekin oasis.[78] Lazar's associate, Mr. Lessar,[79] is still there now: a general received a gold saber for his wound, but he and all the others—because of their love for science and labor—are still suffering in the arid steppe! In general, he is very hardworking and, although only thirty years of age, has already composed a very useful work on railways. Lazar [Iakovlevich] and Annette [Poliakova] are in Athens, conducting reconnaissance for an Athens-Corinth-Patras railway line.

28 JULY 1881, SOKOL'NIKI.

Two days ago, Babin was still with Iakovlev. We had a very good time yesterday evening. In the afternoon Ksenia, Lidiia Stepanovna, and I went to Julie's at Mama's request and asked her to come with her father to dine with us in the evening. In the morning for breakfast M[ikhail] N. Annenkov and M[ikhail] Danilov came. Afterwards Danilov took Annenkov to his house (for some plan), but left us a gold saber. They came back and M. Alekseev said that, if he has time, he will come for dinner, and if not, then after dinner. He did not appear again yesterday. For dinner we had: K. Shil'dbakh, his daughter (for

78. The reference here is evidently to the Akhal-Tekin military expedition of 1880–81, which led to the annexation of the Turkmen territory to the Russian Empire.
79. Pavel Mikhailovich Lessar (1851–1905) was a Russian military engineer and diplomat, a participant in the Central Asian campaigns, and active in the construction of the railway line from Krasnovodsk to Kyzyl-Arvat under General Annenkov.

whom we sent a horse, since he arrived at our house directly from the city), the Podgoretskii couple, and M. S. Mostovskii. In the evening there was dancing, and Sof'ia Frantsevna played the piano.

29 JULY 1881, TSURIKOVO.

At midnight we rode to the village of Tsurikovo in Smolensk district and province. Here we walked around inspecting the estate, which encompasses 800 *desiatines* [2,160 acres]. The peasants say that in 1812 a treasure was buried here (12 casks) and even the place was almost exactly marked. In another direction, in a mount in the field they allegedly find bullets, as a sign that a battle took place here with the French; they have found sabers and other military items. Today the peasants assembled again to excavate and found human bones and even an entire skeleton. After that they refused to dig any more—on the grounds that "our brother is buried here, and one should not disturb him in his grave." The weather is splendid; the moon is now illuminating our house and flower garden in front. The local priest was here, an archpriest (I do not know his surname). The place on which the church stands is very picturesque and the highest point in Tsurikovo. Yesterday on the balcony we gave out gifts to the local women and sashes to the boys as a prize for the three-legged race. S[emen] S[ergeevich] Podgoretskii[80] is now here and evidently much liked. I am sitting in bed (on a hay mattress), but Ksenia deigned to open the door at a time when S[emen] S. said to me, through the keyhole, "pleasant dreams." Ksenia just now said to me: "How awful you are."

30 JULY 1881, TSURIKOVO.

Just now I passed out sweets to peasant women and children. I very much liked the view today: the manor house built on an elevation, with the balcony opening for a view of the mountains that are dotted with peasant houses on the slope (villages that belong to the estate). To the right of our house is an old path leading to the church, and a hill is to the left. With today's overcast weather the landscape is quite poetic. Yesterday evening, the priest, Spiridonov, and of course Semen Sergeevich had tea with us. A conductor from the Kamenka station brought a packet addressed to him and containing *Moscow News*. I do not know which train we shall take to Moscow today (probably the express train). The men in our family and Semen Sergeevich intend to head off for a tour to

80. Semen Sergeevich Podgoretskii (1828–87), who hailed from an old noble family in Tula, was a pedagogue. In the 1880s he was chairman of the commission for the establishment of popular public readings in Moscow.

see the forests. Here in Smolensk province (in Dorogozuskii district Papa has yet another estate, which he acquired from Baryshnikov. Another property in this province (a woods) is called Leonov. Papa is now receiving representatives from the local villages. They are all asking, more or less, that he allot them better land. Prince Vladimir Andreevich Dolgorukov has never been here, but the peasants say that earlier they asked for mercy from the prince, and now from Papa. We also reconsidered, and in view of the cabriolet, harnessed to a pair of horses in traces; we also went yesterday to inspect the land belonging to Papa. The weather here is now poor, as it was yesterday, with a gale in the village. We had to endure a lot of shaking because the carriage had no springs, as we rode through the brush of the forest (where the branches lashed us) and crossed the river, banks, and hillocks. Semen Sergeevich, Ksenia, Mishka, and Ronichka (accompanied by some Leon, a peasant) went looking for mushrooms, while Papa, Spiridonov, the gardener Kliuev, and I (with the peasants) walked through the field. Mama stayed at home, fearing the bad road. In the evening the priest came to say goodbye (we stopped by to see him when we went for the ride). We found the place very picturesque, which S[emen] Serg[eevich] insisted on naming after me ("Zinino"). In general, it is not a bad village, but the main thing is that it has no house and no farmstead. I think that we plan to travel with S[emen] S. to N[adezhda] V. Novikova, whose estate is in Klin district along the Nikolaevsk railway line and two hours from Moscow.

31 JULY 1881, SOKOL'NIKI.
We all returned safely. S[emen] Serg[eevich] left immediately in his own carriage for home. The weather was bad, but is clearing up. I would like to go horseback riding. Lidiia Stepanovna met us at home, with a sleepy countenance. Papa is pleased with the estate. Aleksandr, El'chninov's coachman, explained to us yesterday that his master "absolutely cannot refuse his carriage to a neighbor, but because he had to travel through the townships, he ordered that a stallion be shod and rode in a charabanc." Tomorrow Semen S. promised to be here. Sof'ia Frantsevna did not come to meet him. Most of all I like the view from the hill at the house in Tsurikovo. The river is also quite beautiful, with trees growing along both of its sides.

1 AUGUST 1881, SOKOL'NIKI.
Yesterday I hoped that they would let us go horseback riding, but was wrong. Mama did not want Papa to travel into Moscow and did not tell us to order that the horses be brought yesterday; nor today can we go riding. And tomorrow they are planning to go with S[emon] S[ergeevich] to Novikova: she purportedly in-

vited S[emen] S[ergeevich], and after that it would have been awkward for him to do her the honors. The weather is not good; yesterday it was foul, and today a light rain is falling. I read aloud from *Les Misérables* to Madame Reymoneng. A very good novel has already emerged here. In the morning I had already begun reading it, but there is no time. During a three-hour tea with Ksenia a quarrel erupted as to whether she said an indecent expression about me (about which I had already written here). All her denial consists in softening the word *gada* or *gadina* into *gadkaia*.[81] Yesterday they sent me a frame from Ovchinnikov, which I had given as a present. They say that Shil'dbakh, whom we met yesterday for his trip to Moscow, suddenly realized that his wallet was not in his pocket and immediately sent word to the police; the latter sent agents to search first at his place in Sokol'niki, and it turned out that he had forgotten it at the dacha. Julie went past us and recounted this event to Papa, Mama, and Ksenia. Tomorrow guests are coming to Lidiia Stepanovna. I would like to read aloud the novels of Smolenskin[82] in Hebrew. Misha received a lot of good books, and yesterday I used one of them (*A Collection of Model Works of Russian Poets*).[83]

2 AUGUST 1881, SOKOL'NIKI.

Aleksandr had lunch with me yesterday, but in the middle of the meal he asked permission to get up and moved to the other camp—Ksenia. Bella's wedding, as Uncle Iakov wrote in a letter to Papa, will take place in Taganrog; they will go there in two weeks, along with I[osef] Landau. In general, they obviously are dragging it out on purpose, since the designated date is November or December. Yesterday G. Stefanovskii dined with us and probably stayed overnight; they say that K. K. Shil'dbakh came in the evening. The dacha stay will soon end for us: Mama says that we are moving in the first days of September; if Ksenia's birthday is at home on Tverskoi Boulevard, then we will celebrate this day in a much more festive way. It's a pity that they did not bring Stefanovskii to the countryside! He says that he would go, and indeed with pleasure (gratis). Because Raia is trying to speak English, Lidiia Stepanovna (as soon as Jean placed on the table several pieces of melon brought from the village) took a piece for her and for Jacques [Iakov]. It's a good thing that we had divided it

---

81. The three words differ slightly: the nouns *gada* and *gadina* are variously translated as "reptile" and "vile creature," and the adjective *gadkaia* is "like a reptile or vile creature."

82. Perets Smolenskin (1842–85), a maskilic writer, who founded the Hebrew-language periodical *Hashahar* (Dawn). For his collected works, see Perets Smolenskin, *Kol sifre Perets ben Moseh Smolenskin* (Vil'na: Katsenelenbogen, 1905).

83. The main research libraries do not list the title Zinaida used, *Sbornik obraztsovykh sochinenii russkikh poetov*.

all among ourselves. But they are bringing some more, and Lidiia Stepanovna is again extending her hand to take a second portion for Raika. In a word, she called her a little peasant, but she also began to fire taunts regarding genealogy. Now we are not talking. Il'ia is already speaking English, to his credit, but why privilege Raika over her elders? "Of course, Alexander of Macedonia was a hero, but why smash the chairs?"[84] They say that Iosef Landau is a really excellent person, and this means a lot for a fiancé and still more for a husband. I plan to give Ksenia a brooch for her birthday; she does not have many things that are particularly nice. This morning Lidiia Stepanovna paced back and forth on my balcony to have the waters take effect, and then went for a walk in the garden. Yesterday Mama spent the entire day in an old Worth[85] bonnet, which she acquired when it was in fashion two years ago. We need to go to S[of'ia] Iv[anovna] Slezkin, whom we have not seen for a long time. Papa has still not left for Petersburg, but one must apprise Helene that he [sic] writes Sergei Ivanovich [Slezkin]. Papa asked Uncle Samuil Solomonovich to do all he could about arranging a position for his brother. For the present he is an official serving under the city governor Baranov, but without any compensation.

3 AUGUST 1881, SOKOL'NIKI.

Yesterday was unpleasant for me: slander is a great vice, but Lidiia Stepanovna resorted to it. The Voskoboevs were her guests, but I did not wish to meet them. She summoned Ksenia, and they all went for a walk. They say that in the evening G. Fragovskii was here. After lunch I went with M[iss] Gosh to my aunt and, together with her and Roman, we went for a stroll, then I stopped at her place to drink tea, and again went for a walk in the moonlight with Roman and M[iss] Gosh. At about 10 pm, having returned home, our horses (with the brothers' valet and the heavyweight Tolstoi) went to the railway station for the brothers. They had gone to Pushkino to the Greek teacher, E. Chernyi.[86] I hear that N. Stefanovskii, because of a toothache, did not sleep last night and left early this morning.

84. The quote is from Gogol's *Inspector General*—which (unlike Zinaida) used the present, not the past, tense.
85. Charles Frederick Worth (1825–95), transcribed as Ch. F. Vort in Russian, was the founder of the fashionable House of Worth.
86. Emilii Viacheslavovich Chernyi was a teacher of ancient languages at the Classical Gymnasium No. 3 in Moscow, and she published grammar books for gymnasium students. See E. Chernyi, *Grecheskaia grammatika gimnazicheskogo kursa, chast' 1. Etimologiia po uchebniku* (Moscow: E. Kokha, 1887); E. Chernyi and N. Batalin, *Sbornik materialov dlia ustnogo i pis'mennogo perevoda s russkogo i latinskogo iazykov na grechskii* (Moscow, Universitetskaia tipografiia, 1899).

4 AUGUST 1881, SOKOL'NIKI.

Yesterday Papa, Mama, and I went to N[adezhda] Novikova at Maidanovo. The area is really superb, but the art imprinted on every pathway is even better. We spent the entire day there and made the acquaintance of Prince Golitsyn's family[87] and the family of General Apraksin (consisting of his wife and his son Shura), the family of the Colonel Bandorf (commander of a reserve battalion), and the notary Merts (all of whom reside in St. Petersburg). In Dolgusha we also toured the estate Dem'ianovo, and here one also finds people residing at their dachas: Prince Iu[rii]. Obolenskii[88] and his wife (who is amazingly similar to Marusia Ilovaiskaia), the Vladykins,[89] Feoktistovs,[90] and others. The park there is quite old, but in poor condition. Catherine the Great once came to this village of the Mertvago family. To commemorate the fact that she spent one night here, a granite column with her image on top has been placed here. After returning to Maidanovo, we sat down for lunch, and afterwards the dacha residents converged here, but we soon left (with N. Nik[olaevich] Novikov escorting us to the station). There we were treated to melons. In general, this village is extraordinarily picturesque, and the park is marvelously divided at the point where the sun rises by a pavilion, from which one can admire the sunrise (as at the point in St. Petersburg). At almost the same time, a railway train is visible in the field. Above are the ponds, linked by little bridges like canals in Venice; below is the river, with its mill, and a grotto with a bench at the broadest point. There flows the river Sestra.

5 AUGUST 1881.

Yesterday we dined here with Podgoretskii and G. Demidov. S[ofi'ia] Frants[evna] also wanted to come, since she sent someone to ask whether we would be having lunch at home, but she suddenly received a telegram from Tver to come immediately and left an hour later. S[emen] S. Podgoretskii wants to give in marriage Ol'ga (their second daughter), but does not say to whom. He certainly wants to present to us Mel'gunov,[91] who allegedly plays the piano well.

87. The Golitsyns were an old noble family. Prince Nikolai Dmitrievich Golitsyn (1850–1925) would serve as the last prime minister of Russia before the February Revolution in 1917.
88. Perhaps a reference to Iurii Aleksandrovich Obolenskii (1825–90), a leading member of the Petersburg Musical Society.
89. Perhaps the family of Mikhail Nikolaevich Vladykin, a Russian military engineer, dramatist, and actor in the Moscow Malyi Theater.
90. Perhaps the family of Evgenii Mikhailovich Feoktistov (1828–98), a writer and journalist who served as editor of the official journal of the Ministry of Education (*Zhurnal Ministerstvo narodnago prosveshcheniia*) in 1871–83 and censor in 1883–98.
91. Iulii Nikolaevich Mel'gunov (1846–93) was a music theorist, ethnographer, and pianist. He was

M[ikhail] Den[isovich] is leaving on Saturday for the countryside and then on to the Crimea. Yesterday at dinner we discussed with S[emen] Podgoretskii the kind of excursion that we should make next week; we probably will settle on Arkhangel'skoe, although we were already there once. Yesterday they gave us apples, but because it was not yet Apple Feast Day (*Iablochnyi Spas*),[92] Podgoretskii did not eat any. The rain was a downpour, but the lightning and thunder lowered the temperature (yesterday it was hot all day). At 5 pm we went horseback riding before dinner.[93] Sergei Slezkin (as Novikov, his classmate at the lycée, told us) caroused when he was in Petersburg. Yesterday Aleksandr rode the stick in the garden constantly. N[adezhda] Vas[il'ievna] and her son will perhaps have dinner with us on Sunday. A stomachache forced Satin'ka [Isaak] yesterday for the third day to lie in bed. Vlad[imir] Sem[enovich] Podg[oretskii][94] is still at the dacha. Our gardener Kliuev, who served with Semen Sergeevich, said that he was abroad with Princess Volkonskaia, but is now living with her at the dacha. Genrikh will probably arrive soon, since the gymnasium begins classes on 4 August. Daniil [Samuilovich Poliakov] must take the examination for the second year at the university; he has a fellow student (one year ahead of him) as his tutor. Evgenii Mat[eevich] borrowed 300 rubles with interest from a Jewish loan shark who sometimes sells precious stones to Mama. Zholi, or Solomon Vydrin,[95] has not made an appearance; they say that his wife and son are not well. Baroness Zina Girsh[96] is now undergoing treatment in the environs of Rai [*sic*]. Il'iusha Vydrin recently sent me a picture of himself in a gymnasium uniform. I[osef] Landau is probably with the family of Uncle Iakov Solomonovich, somewhere abroad. Karl Grigor'evich has not been here since Misha's birthday. Lev [Vydrin] met us when, two days ago, we went to Novikova in the village of Maidanovo; he came up to the horse-drawn tram at 8:30 am.

---

the first to transcribe "Russian Songs Directly from the Voices of the People"—the title of his first book (*Russkie pesni neposredstvenno s golosov narodov i s ob'isneniiami izdannye* [Moscow: I. Lissner and Iu. Roman, 1879]).

92. This date (6 August, Old Style) on the calendar of East Slavs is one of the first holidays marking the end of summer and the onset of the harvest and fall. It is a custom not to eat apples (or any dish with fruits of the new harvest) until this feast day, when the new harvest is blessed and eaten for the first time.

93. Zinaida uses *obed* throughout the diary to mean dinner, not lunch. That is evident in this case, when she went riding at 5 pm.

94. The son of Semen Sergeevich Podgoretskii.

95. Solomon Vydrin (b. 1853) was Rozaliia Pavlovna Poliakova's cousin, the son of her uncle Isai Vydrin.

96. Zinaida Samuilovna Poliakova (1855–1909) married Baron James de Hirsch.

6 august 1881, sokol'niki.

Two days ago, in the evening, it seemed to me that a star had fallen from the sky into our courtyard. It was probably a rocket. Yesterday I did not have dinner or drink tea in the evening because of nausea and a headache. For dinner tonight, we shall have Baron Biuler,[97] Makarov,[98] G. Batiushkov, A. Naumov (if he is in Moscow), the chamberlain M. Demidov, and perhaps S[emen] S. Podgoretskii. The weather is clear and warm, like yesterday. Lidiia Stepanovna went to Snegirev, at his request, yesterday. During yesterday's dinner, someone came to Papa from Mr. Paltov, asking that he drop by. Yesterday I read in *Novaia gazeta*[99] that Count [Pavel] Kutaisov ([Vasilii] Dashkov's son-in-law) received a deputation from the Jewish community, purportedly represented by Poliakov and Rubinshtein (at a time when Lazar is in Athens, while one of the Rubinshtein brothers[100] is abroad and the other in the Crimea).

7 august 1881, sokol'niki.

Yesterday Troitskii arrived from Petersburg by breakfast. At 1 pm General Stefanovskii came from Moscow. Dining with us were Semen S. and S[of'ia] Fr[antsevna] Podgoretskii, A. Naumov, N[ikolai] Makarov (who, after dinner, rode with Papa to the Paltovs in Volkov's carriage), L[ev] N. Volkov, [the] chamberlain Demidov, Baron Biuler, P. Batiushkov, Konstantin K. Shil'dbakh, N. Stefanovskii, and the engineer Troitskii. In the afternoon, before 5 pm, Kostia [Nikolai] Shil'dbakh came as a guest of my brothers. Today he will take the examination for the first class at the military gymnasium. It is raining today. S[emen] S. [Podgoretskii] poured Aleksandr chartreuse [a liqueur], and therefore all evening he kicked up a row. Babin's daughter Katia (Mrs. Fedorova, if I am not mistaken), according to the stories [of] Mr. Troitskii, has the same appearance of a girl as earlier. It would be highly desirable for me to see her now. The awful weather continues to torment us dacha residents, but the barometer indicates a change. Even yesterday morning, I wrote, the weather is

---

97. Possibly Baron Fedor Andreevich Biuler (1821–96), a government official, with the rank of "actual privy counselor," and director of the main archive of the Ministry of Foreign Affairs.

98. Nikolai Iakovlevich Makarov (1828–92) was a writer who contributed to progressive journals like *Sovremennik* but later served on the advisory board of the Ministry of Finance.

99. An ephemeral publication, *Novaia gazeta* appeared only 1–8 August 1881, as a temporary replacement for the prominent paper *Golos*, which had been temporarily closed by the censors for its excessive liberalism.

100. The brothers Lev (Leon) and Adolf (Anton) Rubinshtein founded the family firm Roman Rubinshtein & Sons in St. Petersburg with their father, Ruvim (Roman), who had started as a sugar trader in Khar'kov. The family firm included several enterprises such as sugar mills and the First Bank of Khar'kov.

clear, but after 3 pm it began to drizzle and, getting into full swing, it began to rain so hard that it forced us to turn the cart back from the path leading to the circle and head home. Three more weeks at the dacha, and we shall then move back to our winter quarters. It is a pity that the Russian summer is so short; it would not be bad to spoil us with three months of warmth. The Zodiac shows summer, but we see autumn as poetic, rainy, and cold, like the unfeeling verse of a bad poet. Il'ia can now be called a grandfather, since his protégé rabbits have suddenly produced eleven little ones.

The hierarchy of the existing tsarist house is distinguished by its thriftiness. They say that, in their youth, the grand dukes received an allowance of 5 rubles per month; the present sovereign, Alexander [III], always had some money left over, but the others had a deficit.

Yesterday Miss Gosh and I went to Aunt's and invited her and the cousins to go for a walk, and then we went with them. Papa and Mama were in the city; they are seeking something appropriate as a present for the young Epshteins. It seems that they have settled on a samovar from Khlebnikov,[101] if I am not mistaken. For Bella, Papa also ordered a tea service like that which Uncle ordered for cousins Zina and Roza,[102] only somewhat smaller. I advised against this, although Papa says that he will write Uncle directly not to order [the tea set]. Miserable weather; it is raining. Yesterday, after the stroll, we came here with Aunt to have tea, and after dinner Gutenberger was here. Misha must soon begin his studies, although he will not be entering the lycée this year. N[a-dezhda] Vas. Novikova wrote Papa that she is coming for an answer regarding Maidanovo on Sunday or Monday. They say that M[ina] Abramovna Malkiel' has arrived in Moscow and that they (she and he) will soon be here for a visit. His house is being sold for a very great price: 550,000 rubles (with furniture in only five of the main rooms). Papa asked me whether it is better to buy a house or an estate. I said that we have a dacha and that we do not need a house (although, in essence, I very much like Maidanovo). Yesterday I had thought of going for a ride after dinner in my cabriolet, etc. But if September were good and showed to the world that an Indian summer is no worse than the real one, then we would be satisfied. Is it all the same to enjoy warm days in August or in September? They say that Demidov has explained to Mama the reason for the sudden departure of S[of'ia] Frants[evna] to Tver: her son-in-law Radkev-ich was forced to retire and probably asked [her] to intercede on his behalf.

101. The Khlebnikov firm was famous for the high quality of its samovars.
102. Samuil Poliakov's two daughters were Zinaida Samuilovna (who married James de Hirsch) and Roza Samuilovna (who married Leon Varshavskii [Warshawsky]).

They told us that this was a false alarm and that he had a sore throat, that they were cauterizing him, and similar trivia. She made a very strong request of Baron Biuler for some Kireev, who associates with them, but Biuler wants him as a chief steward or future majordomo, and intends to release him from the archive of foreign affairs. M[ariia] Denisovna Demidov[103] is going today for a week to the countryside, but upon her return will go from here to the Crimea.

9 AUGUST 1881, SOKOL'NIKI.

Yesterday, during breakfast, [our doctor] Iu[rii] Osipovich came. It rained all day without ceasing. Lidiia Stepanovna is lying in bed. The daughter of Count Petr Andreevich Shuvalov (the elder)[104] is marrying a Shtakel'berg, Mama told me. They are giving her 400,000 rubles [as her dowry]. Yesterday evening I completed the tenth—and last—volume of *Les Misérables*. The best character there was the hero, Jean Valjean. Today I have to practice piano for at least one hour, since I did not practice either yesterday or Friday. Klindworth will probably return from abroad soon. Yesterday I was pleasantly surprised: in place of the broken and decayed tooth on the side a new tooth is growing. At the age of 18 I had not thought that teeth would still grow in and had even prepared to have Mark. Evans. put in an artificial tooth.

10 AUGUST 1881, SOKOL'NIKI.

Yesterday afternoon the brothers had a visit from Kostia and a German woman, who came and went three times. For dinner we had M[oisei] Tsion, and in the evening M. Vas[il'evich] Sobolev came, and then he went with Mama and Papa to the Nikolaevskii railway station to accompany Princess Trubetskaia (per the telegram that she sent Papa). During this time privy counselor Shil'dbakh came by; upon the return of Mama and Papa, they sent for him, and it seems that he stayed here until rather late. For dinner today there is Sobolev and, it seems, N[adezhda] Novikova and her son. I am working again: I am knitting a blanket, and I am already on the sixth of nine bands. Lidiia Stepanovna has still not gotten up and, rather, is still lying in bed in her room. Miss Gosh and Madame Reymoneng with the small children were upstairs. Tsion is going on 25 August to his family in Paris, and then will go with them to Arcachon.[105] His entire vacation at Papa's is limited to three weeks. On the 20th is Sashka's birthday. I still have not prepared a gift for him. During evening tea Ksenia

103. Mariia Denisovna Demidova (b. 1857) was the half sister of Mikhail Denisovich Demidov.
104. The elder daughter of Shuvalov (1830–1908) was Fekla (1863–1939), who married G. E. Shtakel'berg.
105. In the Gironde area in southwestern France.

told about the planned festivities at the Liamin family. Everything depends on the weather and, if the weather on the 19th [Thursday] is not good, then the music and other celebrations will be put off until the 21st [Saturday]. On Wednesday Shil'dbakh is moving back into the city. K[arl] Karlovich passed the exam to enter the first class of the military gymnasium and matriculates there on Wednesday.

11 AUGUST 1881, SOKOL'NIKI.

Yesterday Sobolev and N. Gorvits from St. Petersburg had dinner at our house. Toward the end of the meal they reported to Papa that Mrs. Smirnova (after purchasing a house) had come, and that she had a half hour to wait. Papa and Misha are going today to Moscow. I will give him the task of buying something for Sashka as a present from me. Miss Gosh rose yesterday, but did not eat at the dinner table (fearing the cold). It's strange that N[adezhda] Novikova did not come either on Sunday or on Monday. Mostovskii, our geographer, is publishing the history of the Church of [Christ] the Savior in every number of the *Moscow News.* But I do not think that many deign to read his articles. I read only the one in the first number, which was shorter and about the church on Sparrow Hills. I am now reading [Goncharov's] *The Frigate "Pallada."* If anyone is especially interested in the description of travels, I do not know of a better work. It is already getting dark now, so I do not know if it will be possible to go for a ride in the cabriolet after dinner. I think that Papa will not decide to purchase the Novikova estate at her asking price (125,000 rubles). Mishka promises me that he will look for and buy a present for Sashka. We shall not stay at the dacha longer than the end of this month. It is damp in the rooms and, although it is possible to heat them, one nonetheless feels that this is a summer place. Madame Levenson is now undergoing a cure abroad with Mania and Sonia, who are also being treated. A[dolf] Rubinshtein is now in Khar'kov or St. Petersburg. Bella's wedding will take place at the end of autumn or the beginning of winter. I intend to give Mr. Tsion the task in Paris [of buying] boots at Ferry's, gloves at Jouvain's, and perfume at Violet's. It seems that Mama wants to have him bring a dress from [Charles Frederick] Worth for herself. Raika is now doing her math lessons on Lidiia Stepanovna's bed. Yesterday I examined my diploma and found that it does not strongly recommend people to the highest administration of the Examination Committee (in order to limit the rights of people who have passed the examination). But why? Because they do not belong to the same confession as they? I would like to pass this year in geometry and French. Will I succeed? This remains an open question for the time being.

12 AUGUST 1881, SOKOL'NIKI.

Two days ago Rabbi Berlin[106] and Zal'man were here in the morning during our breakfast. Yesterday I went with Mama and Ksenia to the guard post to meet Papa and Misha, but they drove past and did not see us. In the afternoon Iu[lii] Shil'dbakh and Kostia (and his German woman) came for tea. He had dinner with us. In the evening K[arl] Karh[ovich] was probably here. Today the Shil'dbakh family is moving. Mishka brought a "carriage" for Sashka's birthday. Today is the birthday for Mr. Vagner (how old is he?!). The weather is good, and we intend to go horseback riding at 6. The Novikovs are coming for dinner on Saturday. Mishka said that she [Novikova] could not open the door to Papa's office and said: "L[azar] S[olomonvich] open the door to paradise!" She is very unique, Mrs. Nad[ezhda] Vas[il'evna].

13 AUGUST 1881, SOKOL'NIKI.

Yesterday we went horseback riding for an hour and half, but Papa had dinner at the English Club[107] and Mama with [Efim] Epstein. In the evening they planned to go with N. Stefanovskii to the garden "Hermitage."[108] The news for today is: rain! I hoped to go for a ride in the cabriolet in the morning, but again the sky is crying. Yesterday, after breakfast, I went for a walk with Nanny, Sashka, and Jacques along the path to the circle, but Mama and Papa soon overtook us, so I went with them. In the evening Ksenia went for a stroll, but took it into her head to leave the keys with Lidiia Stepanovna, without telling anyone. We waited for tea until 9:05, and that resulted in a whole episode. I have a headache again. Probably because of the weather. Tomorrow is Lev's birthday; yesterday the clerk of Mr. Ovchinnikov was here with the estimate and pictures of the service that Papa wants to give Bella for her wedding. It is in the Russian style, and the samovar is on fancy legs. Yesterday during the walk Aleksandr, as he lifted a rock, enunciated the word "rock" perfectly. He is getting used to pronouncing unusual words. Boria [Boris] is now a pupil in the seventh class of the classical gymnasium (at home). In a year Genrikh can be a student at the university. The Vydrins have not yet had a university student [in the family] and he will lay the cornerstone. It seems to me that Il'iusha Vydrin

---

106. Rabbi Chaim Berlin (1832–1912), the spiritual rabbi of Moscow.
107. Founded in 1772 and surviving until the Bolshevik Revolution in 1917, the English Club initially was an elite institution comprised of noble members, but from the mid-nineteenth century on it admitted merchants, financiers, and members of the intelligentsia. It was situated in the center of Moscow in the former Razumovskii Palace, which the Soviet government made into the Museum of the Revolution.
108. A park in central Moscow, in the area of Karetnyi Riad.

will go the same route. It would be a lot better if Roman did not abandon the gymnasium; as for the university, he would clearly not matriculate, but in two years he could complete the gymnasium.

14 AUGUST 1881, SOKOL'NIKI.

We are now going to the wedding of Efim Moiseevich Epshtein and E[lizaveta] Sam[uilovna] Daitsel'man, his cousin. The weather is great. We feared that it would rain, as it did yesterday. I did not plan to go, but the bridegroom's father urgently asked Mama that we come. The wedding will be in the Kogtev hall. The choir and everything else will come from the synagogue. Tomorrow I shall write at length about everything, but now I have to get dressed. I initially thought I would wear my white translucent dress with a train, but Papa convinced me not to do so (because it is too fancy), and the main thing for such a wedding is to make an impression. Mr. Vagner is also invited, but yesterday at tea Mishka asked him why he does not invite me for the first quadrille in the event that there is dancing. Right there he invited me, and I accepted his invitation. In phenomena involving the upper atmosphere another comet has appeared (and even two, it is said). I must observe them; I have not once seen a comet, and only twice have I heard of their appearance.[109] Lidiia Stepanovna is giving Raika her music lesson, and earlier on purpose (so as to have a chance to see us in our attire at departure). It's a pity that my white dress does not have a train. I personally am happy about this, but in view of my age I need to look more like an adult. Today I promised to pay Ovchinnikov the bill for the frame that I gave Mama for her birthday this year (250 rubles). We all joined to pay for this present, but we still have not calculated who gives what. M[iss] Gosh is still not well. I must go to the wedding a bit early: the wedding ceremony takes place at 1 pm, and we are leaving from here at noon. I have only seen three weddings (of people I did not know in a synagogue in Vienna), but here I have never seen any. N. Stefanovskii received the Order of St. Vladimir in the 4th degree.[110] He is invited to the wedding and is probably coming in full parade uniform with the entire regalia—which he especially loves. Yesterday was the day of St. Concordia[111] and therefore the name day of those professing the true

109. Zinaida would be so excited about seeing a comet in Vevey, Switerland, on 3 August 1924 that she would report it to the Astronomy Society of France, which published her observation.

110. Stefanovskii received the order "*v petlitse*," which is smaller and worn in the buttonhole of the uniform.

111. Celebrated on 13 August (Old Style). In the third century Concordia was the foster mother of St. Hippolytus, who was persecuted for his Christian faith. Concordia was flogged and beheaded in his presence, while Hippolytus was dragged to his death by a team of horses.

faith. Tsion will also be at the wedding today. Mrs. Malkiel' is asking him to go with her abroad. He visits them often and dines with them almost every day. They favor him very much, but we are just the opposite; there is no special reason for us to feel any differently.

15 AUGUST 1881, SOKOL'NIKI.

Yesterday was Efim's wedding. After the ceremony they played the music from Natruskin and danced. I danced the quadrille with Mr. Vagner, and opposite was I. Gaberfel'd and his fiancée. The wedding ritual was rather short. Z[elig] Minor[112] made a speech that took up half of the ceremony. Among those invited were: Stefanovskii; Tsion with his *belle mère*; Mozer; I. Gaberfel'd with his wife, and others. E[fim] Mois[evich Epshtein] was not interested; once he looked at someone during the wedding and smiled, which was somewhat comical. Liza [Elizabeta, the bride] looked well and appeared nice. Vagner remained in Moscow with Mr. Chlenov. Today we are dining at home with the Novikovs and General Stefanovskii. Yesterday in Papa's office were V. B. Kozakov, Makarov, and Batiushkov.

16 AUGUST 1881, SOKOL'NIKI.

Dining here were Iakovlev and the Podgoretskii couple (he exited his carriage near Tret'iakov to thank him for the berries). In the evening they went to the "Hermitage" garden. Today K. K. Shil'dbakh with his older son (a guards uhlan) will dine with us. The weather is wonderful. Apparently, Vagner has not returned from Efim's wedding in Moscow, it seems; he will probably tell us everything. Mrs. Mozer told me that Bella's fiancé is not bad looking, but very overweight; I replied that the fiancée is not skinny ("birds of a feather flock together"). Lev (at whose house we had tea yesterday afternoon, and then went with him and S[olomon] Is[aievich] and V. Vlad. for a stroll) says that Ia[kov]. Is. Livshits is coming here soon. Grandfather [Vydrin] is still sick. The other grandfather (Poliakov) is already in Orsha with our grandmother. I asked Mama to sign up for the last season of racing at Petrov Park.[113] Lidiia Stepanovna again began to drink water. Yesterday, in my presence, Lev received a telegram of congratulations on his birthday (which took place two days ago). A. Konst. Shil'dbakh, they say, is the fiancé of the daughter of the baker Bukh in

112. Zelig (Solomon Alekseevich) Minor (1826–1900) was the state rabbi of Moscow and head of the Jewish religious community from 1869 to 1892.
113. This twenty-two-hectare park opened in 1827 in northwestern Moscow (enclosing the area around the Petrov Palace, which had been Napoleon's headquarters in 1812). The park is next to Khodinskoe Pole, the site of the crowd disaster at the coronation of Nicholas II in 1896.

Petersburg. The father apparently opposes the marriage. She is his relative.[114] Uncle Samuil Solomonovich is asking Papa to come to St. Petersburg and to bring along a couple of the children. Uncle Iakov's family is now with him in Vienna. They are probably ordering the dowry for Bella. The long stroll that I took yesterday did not tire me out.

17 AUGUST 1881, SOKOL'NIKI.

Yesterday for dinner came three Shil'dbakhs—the father, the son (the uhlan), and the page. I found that A[leksandr] K. Shil'dbakh has aged somewhat. Kostia [Nikolai] has grown out of the page's uniform such that I thought he will just burst out of it. Yesterday I played the piano for the obligatory hour and more. The weather is excellent. Aleksandr Solomon[ovich], it is said, is similar to V. Vlad[imirovich], like a pig to a 15-kopeck coin. There was trouble with the little boys: we went walking with his mother and father, and Varv[ara] Vl[ladimirovna] was hurrying home to buy [a present for] my godson. V[arvara] Vlad. has put on weight and has become pale. Genrikh must return today and directly begin (in the eighth grade), but he was apparently tempted by some attraction and stayed in Orel today. Lev is giving him a note that attests to his alleged illness. Daniil or Kotia, together with Uncle [Samuil], sent a telegram of congratulations to Efim. Elena Samuilovna (my cousin Roza) and Leon Abramovich Var[shavskii] are probably now in Paris; they had been in Trouville.[115] Zhenia [Evgenii] Tsion, they say, was photographed in a sailor's uniform and sent a card to his grandmother. Zina Girsh [Zinaida de Hirsch] does not correspond with any of her relatives (except for her father and mother). Il'iusha Vydrin, it seems, is already in the fourth class at the classical gymnasium. Iosif Adol'fovich Rubinshtein graduated with a candidate's degree[116] in law from Khar'kov University. Ksenia takes a walk several times a day. Yesterday and the day before (Assumption]) Lev was at the dacha. Masha has completely stopped writing me. Nadia Kazakova, they say, has gotten over typhus and arrived shorn. Ol'ga Leonovna[117] is now in Odessa with her grandfather and grandmother (Raffalovich). Pavel Rafailovich Vydrin[118] in Orel is sick. Roman says that the members of the workers' cooperative brought Efim

114. This is possibly Aleksandr Konstantinovich Shil'dbakh (1853–1915), who married his niece Elizabeta Ivanovna Riting (not Bukh, as Zinaida writes) in 1882.

115. A tourist town in Normandy, in northwestern France.

116. In the period 1804–84 the Russian universities gave three degrees in this ascending order: candidate's, master's, and doctorate.

117. The daughter of Anna (Annette) Poliakova (née Raffalovich) from her first marriage to Edward Emanuel Benjamin Leonino.

118. The father of Rozaliia Pavlovna Poliakova and Zinaida's maternal grandfather.

Moiseevich Epshtein two doves with blue ribbons (I was mistaken; Vagner told this story). Sonia Rubinshtein is still in Khar'kov, not abroad, as I had thought. Aunt Fania is now preoccupied with her son Samuil. Bella's fiancé has one other quality that I have not mentioned: he plays the violin well. Probably, Fania Livshits has completely settled in Orel, and her husband has an office there for the grain trade. Khar'kov is again filling up with the arrival of the Poliakov family from Athens and Odessa: on the 13th they are supposed to have left Greece.

18 AUGUST 1881, SOKOL'NIKI.

I find it strange that yesterday I forgot to write about the fact that two days ago we dined here with Mr. Danilov and K[onstantin] P[etrovich] Troitskii (who in the evening left from our house for St. Petersburg). Now Iakov, the footman, gave me back the six rubles that I had given him to buy the books for Masha's birthday on behalf of me and Ksenia. All the white wool is gone, and I had to order the purchase of more (to continue the knitting). Yesterday, during our dinner, General Apraksin came; I saw him from the window. It is hot today; it would be good if such is the weather until September. Yesterday I sat with Lidiia Stepanovna and Mishka on the bench in front of the dacha, and the Liamins came up to us. Genrikh returned from Orel. . . .[119]

19 AUGUST 1881, SOKOL'NIKI.

Yesterday, for the 3 pm tea, Bertrand came and stayed for dinner. I went with Madame Reymoneng, Raika, and Jacques to the Danilovs, and during this time A[ndrei] Nik. Gorchakov[120] and Princess Trubetskaia arrived for dinner. At 3 pm a city telegram came, but they did not know whether to open it or leave it unopened until Mama returned. It was not opened, and Mama was very displeased with this. I gave Genrikh the task of buying wool and a book for Masha by S. Almazov[121] but also the newest curriculum for university examinations. Tomorrow, if anyone is in Moscow, I shall go riding horseback. Yesterday in the evening N. Paltov came, drank a wineglass of Mouton Rothschild[122] and left, as

119. The end of the line is unclear: "and he managed to be *na akte*."
120. Andrei Nikolaevich Gorchakov (1836–1914), a privy councilor, was an engineer for the Ministry of Ways and Communications and then director of the Department of Railroads. He also worked for the Ministry of Finance and was on the Transport Ministry's Council for Railway Rates in 1896–98). He became the head inspector for the Ministry of Ways and Communications in 1899. See Sergei Witte, *Iz arkhiva S. Iu. Vitte: Vospominaniia*, ed. Boris V. Anan'ich and Rafail Sholomovich Ganelin (St. Petersburg: Sankt-Peterburskii institut istorii RAN, 2003), 1:64 and 88 and 3:583.
121. The main research libraries list no books by "S. Almazov" during this time.
122. A famous claret from the French wine estate, Château Mouton Rothschild.

if he only came for that. Today Arnol'di[123] and some other guests will dine with us. He bought a dacha in Nice and has invited me to visit, saying that he has two spare bedrooms for guests. Yesterday Mama and Papa went into the city and saw him in the office. Yesterday Mishka played two games of chess with me; he made me a stalemate in one game, I [gave] him a checkmate in the second. In the last game Vagner showed me two moves that ended in a black king. I cannot knit the blanket for Jacques now because I still do not have the white wool yarn, which I asked Genrikh to buy in the Hamburg store on Stoleshnikov Alley belonging to Mrs. Leon.

20 AUGUST 1881, SOKOL'NIKI.

Yesterday we had dinner with Arnol'di, Prince Dolgorukii, M[ikhail] D[enisovich] Demidov, and A[ndrei] Gorchakov (who stayed for the night). Prince Dolgorukii is going on behalf of the Land Bank in Moscow to assess the estate of Mrs. Novikova. Today at 10 am Ksenia and I, in the company of a riding master, will go horseback riding. Demidov is leaving for the south coast of the Crimea. At the Danilovs I saw Madame Fisher with her two daughters; she too is planning to travel to the Crimea and is wavering between that and going abroad. Yesterday evening there was a light rain, which reminded me of the summer rainy days that left us bored this summer. I gave Genrikh the task of buying several things, but he forgets everything, since (in his words) he did not travel along those streets where I asked him to make the purchases. I heard how they brought the riding horses; hence the artisan Sidorov accurately carried out my errand. Mishka sent me (through the maid Katia) the money for the frame. Today Sashka turned two years old, and I have a present for him. He has still not come to me. Yesterday, during dinner, Genrikh arrived, and after him M[oisei] Tsion, to whom all was served from the beginning (with some variation—substitutions for what was not available). I need to go get dressed for the horseback ride. M. Tsion said that Maurice Ephrussi of Paris is marrying the daughter of the French baron Rothschild.[124] The young Epshteins have remained in Moscow, replacing the honeymoon trip with a dinner celebration at Natruskin's[125] on the evening after the wedding. Vagner also partici-

123. Perhaps a reference to a cavalry general named Aleksandr Ivanovich Arnol'di (1817–98), but only the dates support this suggestion.
124. Maurice Ephrussi (1849–1916) was a French banker from Odessa who opened a branch of the family bank in Paris. He married Béatrice de Rothschild, the daughter of Alphonse de Rothschild, in Paris in 1883.
125. In the second half of the nineteenth century, Petrov Park came to include famous restaurants. One of them was Ivan. F. Natruskin's Strel'na, which was famed as one of the sightseeing attractions of the city.

pated in their celebrations and caroused there from 1:30 am to 5:30 am, and then arrived at Sokol'niki at 6:30 am. They say that Gerts is getting married to S. Vlad[mirovna], Epshtein's former fiancée. In general, I do not believe a lot of rumors, but to be honest I do not know whether to give credence to such an original, plausible rumor. M[oisei] Fad[daeevich Tsion] is going with Arnol'di tomorrow to St. Petersburg and from there on to Paris. I am giving certain errands to Tsion, but M[ikhail] D. Demidov is asking me why I do not give him things to do in Petersburg. I do not know what I need in Petersburg but if I do need something, I can always obtain this through Kotia or Mr. Khodetskii.

21 AUGUST 1881, SOKOL'NIKI.

Two days ago the teachers were here: Khodobai[126] and D. Nazarov, then Mr. Baryshnikov and some Jew about leasing the Shuvalov apartment in our building. I shall now hurry to get dressed because today Papa is going a bit earlier. Yesterday E. Iv[anovich] Mattern was here, at the same time as the teacher Iu. Khodobai, Iu[lii] Osip[ovich Golden'bakh], and E[milii] Chernyi. In the evening A[vgust]. Iu. Davydov[127] and Ladyzhenskii came. They say that the Jew who came to see Papa about the apartment was here again. Papa said that he will be at home today and that Maliutin (he is leasing) himself should come. They say that it is not cold today and that there is no rain, but neither is it sunny.

24 August is Liza's birthday.

22 AUGUST 1881, SOKOL'NIKI.

Yesterday Papa and I were in the city for a visit to Princess Trubetskaia's. In our absence, Aunt Sonia, the teachers Vinogradov, [Emilii] Chernyi or Iur[ii] Khudobai were here. Today Professor Danilov is dining here, and Papa has also invited the Novikovs. The weather is spectacular, and I am glad that we are living here another two weeks. It seems that Lidiia Stepanovna has left for Ostankino, and I base that conjecture on the fact that I heard talk about a horse. Tsion left yesterday evening and I gave him a letter to his wife, Mrs. Tsion, asking her to do some errands for me. My brother Misha can still matriculate this year in the Lycée of Tsarevich Nikolai.[128] Vladimir Andreevich Dolgorukov

126. Iurii Khodobai was a Latin specialist and the author of many works, including a Russian-Latin dictionary. See Iurii Khodobai and Petr Andreevich Vinogradov, *Russko-Latinskii slovar* (Moscow: Universitetskaia tipografiia, 1882).

127. Avgust Iul'evich Davydov, a Russian mathematician and professor in the physics-mathematics faculty at Moscow University, was the brother of the renowned cellist and composer Karl Iul'evich Davydov, who was the head of the St. Petersburg Conservatory in 1876–87.

128. Tsarevich Nicholas (Nikolai) was the official designation of the successor to Alexander II, who prematurely died in 1865, and in whose honor the lycée was established in 1868.

spoke yesterday with Papa about Ignat'ev[129] and expressed himself in highly unfavorable terms. Genrikh remained yesterday in Moscow, since today he has [his] first lesson not on religion or French, but Latin. Demidov is in St. Petersburg and will probably return in a few days to Moscow. Fania had barely recovered, when Ia[kov] Isaakovich left for Moscow. It is a pity that she and Samuil did not come here for a short time. This means that now she is limited in her travels by the child. Il'ia is constantly playing nurse to his rabbits (which number twelve in all). Iosif Gintsburg,[130] before his death, gave much land in the south or in the western part of Russia to poor Jews and for the development of agriculture among them. Yesterday was the birthday of Aunt S[of'ia] L'vovna. Iakov Isaakovich Livshits came here yesterday, and we saw him at our aunt's. I am again writing the composition for geometry, which I have not written, however; I have only written the one for arithmetic. Yesterday for dinner the following were here: Prof. Shchurovskii,[131] A[vgust] Iu[l'evich] Davydov, K[onstantin] Shil'dbakh, and Podgoretskii. In a word, as an assortment, one is better than the next. Yesterday and today Ksenia has had a toothache. I also forgot to write about Ladyzhenskii, who was also here yesterday for dinner. Today the racing begins at the park, but we still do not have a box. S[of'ia] Frants[evna] plans to go with Mrs. Radkevich, her daughter, to Yalta, but the "fool of a major" will stay in Tver, since during the official inspection he fell from his horse with all his weight and mass, either tearing or pulling a tendon. S[emen] Sergeevich yesterday was sillier than usual, since, for example, [he] ascribed my not wanting to stroll to some kind of "emptiness of heart" and other such nonsense. It is strange that some people, who have nothing substantive to say, are happy to babble if only so that they [do] not "lose the ability to talk." Then I played chess with Miss Gosh and lost to her. But as for Misha: I played him to a stalemate in one match and to checkmate in the other. All went well, just a little boring, that is, little variety. For example, the

<hr />

129. Count Nikolai Pavlovich Ignat'ev (1832–1908) replaced Count Mikhail Tarielovich Loris-Melikov as minister of interior. He served in this office only from 4 May 1881 to 30 May 1882, earning much criticism among Jews for his antisemitic comments and attempts to blame the Jews themselves for pogroms in 1881. He lost favor with conservatives like Konstantin Pobedonostsev, who had initially supported his appointment, when Ignat'ev proposed to convene a *zemskii sobor* (assembly of the land)—that is, revive the Muscovite variant of an estates general with representatives from various groups in society.

130. Baron Evzel' (Joseph) Gintsburg (1812–78) established the I. E. Gintsburg banking house in St. Petersburg in 1859 and a branch in Paris. With a group of merchants, he petitioned the state for the right of first-guild merchants to reside outside the Pale of Settlement.

131. Grigorii Efimovich Shchurovskii (1804–84) was a professor of mineralogy and geology at Moscow University.

conversation and squeaking of Mr. Ladyzhenskii got tiresome. Papa intends to go soon to St. Petersburg. I do not know what I shall do in the winter without my usual studies. They say that the conservatory has invited a new piano professor—Gintsel' to replace K[arl] K[arlovich] Klindworth. I am a little tired of practicing music, so yesterday I did not play piano at all. Prince Dolgorukii who went to V. K. Novikov's estate, says that he very much likes it—and much more than Fon Derviz's estate. It's time to finish. Soon there will be breakfast, but I have not yet begun to get ready. If only we could go to the races today; otherwise you don't see anything. They say that S. I. Slezkin arrived in Moscow and is staying in St. Petersburg at Major General Kozlov's.

24 AUGUST 1881, SOKOL'NIKI.
We got ready to go to the races yesterday, but then stayed home! Mr. Gol'denbakh and D. Fed. Nazarov had breakfast with us. In the morning the young Burges with his tailor Go[t]hlieb (a Jew) and hairdresser came. When it was time to get into the carriage, Shreider came to Papa. At 3 pm N[adezhda] V[asil'evna] Novikova and Prince Shakhovskoi came. But soon Mrs. Malkiel' came, and they stayed for dinner and part of the evening. They are not especially jovial guests. They all praised their son and his riding horse, i.e., the horse Annette. The weather is superb. Yesterday evening they sent for Iu[rii] Osip[ovich] and he stayed a little with us. Ksenia has had a toothache for two days. It seems that today they are fine, in any case compared with yesterday. They had wanted to send for a dentist.

25 AUGUST 1881, SOKOL'NIKI.
Yesterday we were at Liliia [Slezkina's] and congratulated her on her birthday. Iu[rii] Osip[ovich] saw Ksenia three times. In addition, the dentist Depre came; I had the pleasure of not seeing him. Polia, our former housekeeper, came to say goodbye. On Thursday she got married and yesterday left with her husband for St. Petersburg, where she will live. In the evening Messrs. Sobolev and later the young Prince Trubetskoi came. The weather today is fine, but I have a heavy head and see ripples. I must buy Mr. Vagner for his (past) birthday Biblio. . . . [sic]. This year I have not given anyone something for a "red letter day." Yesterday they began to propose that I go to the Crimea. But what pleasure would it would be to go there with Miss Gosh? If Lazar [Iakovlevich] went there with Annette, he is now in Petersburg and the construction of the Greek railway line did not fall to him: the concession has been given to Lekann et Perdu [sic] a French company. Here is what it means not to wish to accumulate a little: the French cut the price and got the concession. Two

days ago at the races, they say, Grand Duke Nikolai Nikolaevich and the empress's uncle (a prince from the Danish royal family) were present. It seems that there will be races in the park on 26 August. Ksenia is still lying in bed. [It is unclear] whether anyone will come today, but in general I take little interest in the guests. I have still not written the letters to Paris, at the request of M[oise] F. Tsion, to various shops: Jouvin (gloves), Violet (perfume), and Ferry (boots).

26 AUGUST 1881, SOKOL'NIKI.

Yesterday in the forest I saw my aunt with Raia and Liliia [Slezkina], and I called to them. Podgoretskii came for dinner and said that afterwards Mr. Spiridonov and his wife will come, but that actually happened during dinner. They took their places at the table, and afterwards we strolled and ran around at Spiridonov's. I sat down to play chess with her father, who gave me a lesson —i.e., he explained how one really plays. Today Col. Orlov is coming; he is here with the grand duke. Yesterday our family's coach broke down and, having met Trubetskoi's manager in a carriage, we transferred to the latter and rode in it. L[azar] Iakov[levich] is now in Odessa and perhaps is thinking of going to Yalta. Mrs. Spiridonova calls her husband "Voldemarchik." Is that not strange? Ksenia has still not gotten out of bed. She has abscesses in various places of her mouth. In general, apparently Iu[rii] Osip[ovich] will still have to lance —which is a pity. Before dinner I went for a ride in the cabriolet with Satin'ka and with Il'ia (in Iakov's place). He clung onto the side the entire time so as not to fall. For today Lidiia Stepanovna ordered water at Redlikh's and in the evening gray horses arrived, harnessed to a carriage, and the master delivered the waters. S[amuil] Malkiel' has asked Papa for a loan of 40,000 rubles. It seems that he has already borrowed from Papa on more than one occasion. In general, I am amazed by his pensiveness and sad countenance. It is bright on the street, and one's spirits are good. As if this sunny light animates one!? In a conversation Mama said that I can go with Papa to Petersburg. It seems that after all things are splendid, but I find that I will be bored, since Papa will be busy, and I shall sit home alone. In acting on my behalf, Mishka ordered from Avanzo a brown sharkskin notebook with a key, and with the letters Z. P. inscribed. Our uncle Livshits yesterday left without saying goodbye to me. Fania may travel to the Crimea in the case she takes it into her head to do so. As to where I would like to travel, it is the Caucasus—and in good company, but also in one's own family, to look at the living spring water of Narzan,[132] at the grave

132. Narzan is a famous spring that produces mineral waters at the town of Kislovodsk.

of M. Iu. Lermontov,[133] and the "mineral waters" public (to use an expression in [Lermontov's] *Hero of Our Time*).[134] But the point is that when you look, you yourself become inscribed into that "mineral waters public." I know that the son of Mr. Osip Gintsburg also went there, but only to be in the Caucasus and to look and laugh at those who travel there to be seen.

27 AUGUST 1881, SOKOL'NIKI.

I am traveling into Moscow today with Papa. In the evening Papa is going to St. Petersburg. I am writing a note about this to Liliia Slezkina. Her brother Serezha needs a position and wants to see Papa there. The weather is good. Everything is fine. Yesterday we were at the races, and Volkov and K. K. Shil'dbakh dined with us. Someone is going down the staircase, so I probably need to get dressed. Today Mrs. Novikova will be at Papa's office. Ksenia will perhaps get out of bed today; her swelling went down significantly. Yesterday Mama forbade me to play croquet with A. Vagner. I find that even silly. Two days ago, at 11 pm, Col. Orlov arrived on four white horses from Petrov Palace.[135] I have already gone upstairs, but Mama is getting out of bed. Yesterday Papa went with me to the Zoological Garden. Grand Duke Nikolai Nikolaevich the elder was there. Professor Davydov wanted to present me to him, but did not find me. Papa initially proposed to present me, but I declined. After the grand duke left, we all had breakfast with music and had a bite to eat. The doctor brought a bouquet of flowers from Fomin to Nikolai Nikolaevich Popandopulo.[136] In the evening we talked about my going to St. Petersburg, but in the end Papa went alone. M[ikhail] D. Demidov had dinner with us; he arrived yesterday from Petersburg and brought a letter for Kotia. Papa hurried to go to Petersburg because my uncle is sick. The weather is good today, and at 5 pm they will bring me a small horse from the manège. Mrs. Malkiel' yesterday morning sent a realtor regarding the sale of her house. A long time ago Papa negotiated for the Gorki estate and they want to sell it to him for the sum that he offered then. In general, it is possible to buy everything, but one should not spread oneself

133. The famous poet and writer Mikhail Iur'evich Lermontov (1814–41) died in a duel in Piatigorsk in the Caucasus, but in 1842—at the order of Emperor Nicholas I—his remains were reburied on the family estate of Takhany (in Penza province).
134. *Hero of Our Time*, the classic novel by Lermontov (first published in 1840), with its "superfluous man" protagonist Pechorin, actually refers twice to the "*vodianoe obshchestvo*" ("mineral waters society"), not the "*vodianaia publika*" (as Zinaida recalls from memory).
135. Constructed in the 1770s and 1780s by Catherine the Great, the palace abuts Petrov Park, which the Poliakovs frequently visited from their dacha in Sokol'niki.
136. This surname exists among some Russian officers of Greek extraction, but an N. N. is not listed in any of the main reference works.

thin on a lot of estates. In my opinion, it would be best to reach an agreement with Malkiel' regarding the house, but not pay more than 500,000 rubles. Il'ia came to my room, and I asked him to bring me some matte writing paper from Papa's desk. Apparently Demidov will have breakfast here today, send off his horse, and then be given a ride. Shchurovskii, A[vgust] Iul['evich] Davydov and N[ikolai] Miliaev drank to my health, and I responded in kind. N[ikolai] K[onstantinovich] Miliaev said that he is inviting me to his funeral, but I replied that I do not accept funeral invitations in advance. The grand duke told Papa that he is taller than his brother and that he has heard a lot of good things about him. Probably from Orlov.

29 AUGUST 1881, SOKOL'NIKI.

Yesterday I forgot to say that, two days ago, when I was in the city, I was shown the original "Magidson from Mogilev." Yesterday Demidov sent a telegram that he cannot visit us because of the sudden arrival of N. A. Boldyreva. Yesterday they did not bring the horse from the manège; I don't know who is at fault —probably the porter Maikov forgot to say something at the manège. Today it is hot in the sun and, if such weather continues for a few more weeks, it will be very pleasant. I bought Vagner for his birthday the first volume of [Friedrich] Schiller's *William Tell* and [Johann Wolfgang von] Goethe's *Faust* (in a cheap two-ruble edition). I can hear the sounds of croquet; I don't know who is playing in this heat, in this sun, and indeed with such strong blows of the mallet. Lidiia Stepanovna is lying out on the balcony; as is her wont, she has not been downstairs and will stay locked in her room for several days. Raika is now with her; she is surprised that Lidiia Stepanovna did not go down today. Yesterday she twice went for a walk with her. Everyone is healthy. Yesterday Ksenia was in the garden with a bandaged cheek. I advised her to say that she had participated in the French expedition to Tunisia.[137] At the races we became acquainted with the Azanchevskii family;[138] the son, despite the injury to his lip by a horse bite, was riding horseback. There are races again tomorrow, and we have a box. If Ksenia removes the kerchief from her cheek and if the swelling subsides, she will go with us. Yesterday I practiced piano for an

137. The 1878 Congress of Berlin assigned Tunisia to French control. Alleged attacks by Tunisian rebels on French Algeria provided the grounds for the French expedition, which lasted through the summer of 1881 and ended in the establishment of a formal French protectorate over the colony. Zinaida's elliptical—and jocular—comments indicate that she was following the international news.

138. Zinaida later names the two sons, from which one can surmise that this was Nikolai Pavlovich Azanchevskii and his wife, Venedikta Kosheleva. Their children were Elizabeta Nikolaevna, Veneditka Nikolaevna, Vsevolod Nikolaevich, and Nikolai Nikolaevich.

hour, and I'm glad that I found the time; it turns out that someone is coming. I have put the *étude* aside, but I have not completely forgotten to play. I paid Ovchinnikov for the frame, but am 50 rubles short, since I did not have a bill smaller than 100 rubles. Today N. Stefanovskii will dine here and he says that his other half (I don't know if it is the better half) has also returned, having put on some weight!? In *Sunrise*[139] I liked a poem, S[emën] Frug's "In the Judgment of History."[140] He makes an excellent presentation of the idea that the Jews in Russia lack civic consciousness (*grazhdanstvennost'*). Papa is in St. Petersburg. Yesterday I sent him a letter and a note to Liliia Slezkina that she write S[ergei] Slezkin, asking him to drop by and see Papa. They say that Roza Varshavskaia is sick. She has been the entire time in Trouville, but has now suddenly moved to Paris. Nothing is forever in this world, they say, but the presence of the Poliakovs in cities changes just as does the most ephemeral happiness.

30 AUGUST 1881, SOKOL'NIKI.
Yesterday we had visits from Stefanovskii (in his new uniform) with his cousin Mr. Palekhin (a professor at the medical academy, which has now been renamed the military academy). Suddenly a woman in mourning came in through the wicker gate, but we could not recognize her. It turned out that it was Mrs. Shirobokova, who was in Yalta when we were there in 1876. She buried her husband a year and half ago. Having left her daughters, she traveled to a hotel for her valise and arrived before dinner in order to spend the night. Today there are races in the park. The Shirobokovs are going today to the Crimea. Natasha, the older one, is very pale. They say that a telegram came from Papa yesterday. Apparently, Demidov, without saying goodbye to us, went to Yalta. In the evening we played various tricks and games.

31 AUGUST 1881, SOKOL'NIKI.
Yesterday morning, we played croquet with the Shirobokov girls. After breakfast they walked to the outpost, and we rode to the park for the races. Podgoretskii arrived before dinner to say farewell; he is going with [his daughter] Mme. Radkevich to the Crimea. The elderly realtor for the Malkiel' house came to see Mama yesterday morning. Mr. Ostroukhov, who came from "Leonovo"

139. *Voskhod*, a prominent Jewish journal published in St. Petersburg in 1881–1906.
140. Semën [Shimen] Grigor'evich Frug (1860–1916) was a Russian and Yiddish poet and essayist from Kherson province. When his Russian poems appeared in *Voskhod* in 1879, he began to attract public attention. He moved to St. Petersburg with the help of Zinaida's relative Mark Varshavskii (the brother of Leon Varshavskii). The pogroms of 1881 pushed Frug to join the Hibbat Zion (Lovers of Zion) movement.

(our forest), was also here. This morning I plan to go and have my photograph taken in my riding habit; Mama told me to do this. I would not go because I think that the riding habit is not becoming for someone thin like me. Papa is still in Petersburg, and I do not know when he will return (but probably in the next few days). On Wednesday the Azanchevskii couple, with their two daughters, promised to dine here. I do not think, however, that from the first visit the daughters will come for dinner. Tomorrow Mama is going to the wedding of [Anna Vadimirovna] Vysotskaia with Mr. [Osip Sergeevich] Tseitlin. Although the invitation was for the whole family, I will not go since I do not know anyone. At the races I saw: Sasha Mil. Azanchevskii, E[lena] Iv[anovna] Slezkin, and many other acquaintances. Everything was very stately to celebrate the name day of the emperor. For one race Princess Khilkova took in 5,400 rubles, since her horse came in first. Everybody was in shock when one of the two racing officers fell; the one who fell came in first in this race, and everybody applauded him madly. As soon as his second began to catch up, he jumped onto his horse and "gave it everything he had," as the common people put it.[141]

1 SEPTEMBER 1881, SOKOL'NIKI.

Yesterday we had news that Baron D. Gintsburg[142] is going to the Caucasus and will stay with us today. Mama must have received a telegram today that David Gintsburg will be here today, and Raika came to tell me this. I hope that Papa returns tomorrow; he wrote me that he ordered a hat for me from Bertrand. The weather is like yesterday's, but Raika said that it is cold and that Mama said for me to put on a wool dress. How strange that Mama wrote me a letter that she is offended by the present from us (me and Ksenia). Today is a half year since the death of the emperor, and because of the requiem, the gymnasium students have been dismissed to go home. I've heard that they (Genrikh is first) will pray very little, but I disparage that; oh yes, G[enrikh] Pav[lovich] is a terrible freethinker. I do not commend him in this, but in minor things, such as the performance of rituals, he is on the level of the high priests of the Jerusalem church. Lidiia Stepanovna lay in bed yesterday and is still there today; she is very weak, and this time I feel sorry for her. As to all my questions for

141. The Russian phrase (*vo vsiu pryt'*) reflects Zinaida's penchant for proverbs and common people's speech.
142. Baron David Goratsievich Gintsburg (1857–1910), son of Baron Horace Gintsburg, was trained as an orientalist who specialized in medieval Arabic and Hebrew poetry. He was the coeditor of the *Evreiskaia entsikopediia* (Jewish encyclopedia) and owned a library of rare books of Jewish and Arab literature. Like his father, David was a prominent communal leader in St. Petersburg. He was involved in the Society for the Promotion of Culture among the Jews of Rusia, Jewish Colonization Association, and Society for Handicraft and Agricultural Work among the Jews of Russia.

Papa, I do not know if he responded to me in the letter. Kotia [Daniil] left for Paris, and Uncle was better yesterday. I had my photograph taken in my riding habit, a long Mockart portrait, and one of [the portraits] will be covered with lacquer. Yesterday, Aleksandr sat down around Vagner, and for that Mama said that he knows where to sit (next to the tutor). Bella, together with her fiancé and all the rest, are now in Odessa, but then will go to Taganrog to their estate. Yesterday we had the pleasure of taking breakfast in the company of V[asilii] Bezekirskii, and he promised to come today to give a violin lesson to Il'ia. It seems that Genrikh wants to get to know David [Gintsburg]; with respect to rites he has just as original [ideas]. It is even strange that a person who serves in the Ministry of Foreign Affairs (in the Asiatic Department) is amusing to such a degree. If one compares him to an old Jewess, that would not be going too far and an exaggeration. It's a pity that Papa is still in St. Petersburg; perhaps he would come with us to the races at the park (although we do not have a box). Throughout all of August there was virtually no rain, but today is 1 September, and one feels a light coolness. And Satin'ka [Isaak] does not want to speak English (the same subject as Jacques) and has started becoming capricious. Yesterday, for that reason, the latter did not receive preserves. Iosef Landau is very interesting to me; if he chose Bella, then I know his tastes, but otherwise. . . [sic].

2 SEPTEMBER 1881, SOKOL'NIKI.

Yesterday we had Barons David and Aleksandr[143] Gintsburg as guests. It is raining today, as I wanted for our move [back to the city]. Yesterday both Gintsburgs and Monsieur Bertrand had breakfast [here]. Together with [Pavel] Vinogradov, A[leksandr] Gintsburg again dined here. We (Mama, David Gorats[ievich] Gintsburg, Aleksandr Gintsburg, and I) went for a ride and drove to the Alekseev water tower. Perhaps Papa will arrive tomorrow. Gintsburg brought us candy. Yesterday Uncle Iakov Solomonovich passed through Moscow to St. Petersburg. We did not see him, since Mama did not send the horses for him. Today, possibly, the Azanchevskii family will not come for diner. D[avid] G[oratsevich] Gintsburg promised to send chocolate from Marquis in Paris. Aleksandr Gintsburg has become more handsome. The former is going as a deputy to the Archeological Congress.[144]

143. Aleksandr Gintsburg, son of Goratsii Gintsburg, married Roza Warburg in 1891, the same year that Zinaida Poliakova married Reuben Gubbay.
144. The Archaeological Congresses, first convened with imperial permission in 1869, met on fifteen occasions before the outbreak of World War I. The fifth, scheduled for 8–21 September 1881, met in Tiflis (Tbilisi).

3 SEPTEMBER 1881, SOKOL'NIKI.

Yesterday morning Sallman on behalf of the Malkiel' house was here and kept asking for an increase of 20,000 rubles. For dinner yesterday there was Mr. and Mrs. Azanchevskii and Lulu (the second daughter). Azanchevskii himself played piano after dinner and gave a splendid performance of a mazurka by Schulhoff.[145] Papa has not sent a telegram to say when he is arriving in Moscow; I hope that he returns tomorrow. Lilii[a] Slezkina sent me a letter yesterday regarding the reception of her brother S[ergei] by Uncle Samuil Solomonovich. It has been raining for two days; perhaps we shall move for our holidays back to the city. Tomorrow is Friday; perhaps I can go horseback riding if they order the horses today. They brought me my portrait in the riding habit, and I will not say that I like one of them. The Azanchevskii girls are coming for Ksenia's birthday in the morning. Yesterday the older one did not come, because she had caught a slight cold, but it has a very strong impact on her, they say, since she is continually sick. Ksenia likes my portrait; she says that I am very beautiful in it (which I do not find). In general, I am satisfied that I appeared to be tall and I ordered a Mockart portrait. Ksenia has still not completely recovered from the sore on her lip, which is going away very slowly. I do not remember Russian orthography and often make mistakes. In St. Petersburg the provincial deputies from the Jewish population are now meeting. They are all spending time at Gintsburg's; ten people once had dinner at Uncle S[amuil Sol[omonovich] Poliakov's. The youngest Azanchevskii son is now studying in the military gymnasium and has already received epaulettes for his excellent behavior.[146] Bertrand, his French teacher, . . .[147]

4 SEPTEMBER 1881, SOKOL'NIKI.

Yesterday morning Mr. Ostroukhov, the steward for the Leonosovo forest (and who has a sharp nose), was here in the morning. We went to the races at Petrov Park and saw the Azanchevskii family, S. Iakovlev, Sergei Popov, and several other of our acquaintances. Papa is arriving today from St. Petersburg, and I am going to the railway station to meet him (I don't know whether Mama is going as well). The weather is changing, and I shall be glad to move to the city, since here things are not very lively. None of us would be against having already moved. For Ksenia's birthday there will be the Azanchevskii daughters, and yesterday we met their brothers Vsevolod and Nikolai. The housekeeper

145. Julius Schulhoff (1825–98), a Franco-German pianist and composer of Czech origins.
146. Vsevolod Nikolaevich Azanchevskii (1864–1914) came from a military family and studied in the juridical faculty of Moscow University. He became the governor of Tomsk in 1904.
147. The entry ends with this incomplete sentence about Bertrand.

Liza came to ask, on behalf of Roman, the Poliakov address in Paris; I no longer know it because they have changed apartments. It's time to get dressed: at 10 I have to go to the railway station to meet Papa, and I still have not brushed my hair. If I go without Mama, then it seems to me that it would be quite sufficient to go with Misha. Katia, my maid, is already losing patience that I am still writing and not dressed, and has gone to her room upstairs. Miss Gosh and Raika yesterday were at Aunt Sonia Vydrin's; my aunt's children had tea with us in the afternoon, and together we went again for a walk. I do not know if they have harnessed the horses; it is already time to go. We are terribly slow in harnessing the horses and getting the coachman dressed. Today S[emen] S. Podgoretskii is probably coming for dinner; his spouse and daughter have left for the Crimea. I heard from Mama that, according to the newspapers, Yalta is burning because of carelessness after the fireworks on the 30th of August. Vitebsk, which is populated with a multitude of Jews, has had the same sad fate: 100 homes on that side of the Dvina have burned. They report that the merchant class has suffered especially, and there probably are a lot of Jewish merchants in their number. Iakovlev told Mama that in his presence they received a note from V. Babin, with a request for a railcar for the two young Barons Gintsburg (from Rostov to the Caucasus). I do not know why it was precisely he who began to tell this (beginning with the fact that the Gintsburgs had traveled from St. Petersburg). Papa can bring me a hat from Bertrand in St. Petersburg; he already bought, if he did not forget, the portrait of Iur'evskaia[148] for E[lena] Ivan[ovna] Slezkina (on my behalf—she asked me to get it for her).

5 SEPTEMBER 1881, SOKOL'NIKI.

Yesterday Papa arrived from St. Petersburg. In the morning Ostroukhov was waiting, but when we went to the railway station. we met him, Ostroukhov, and his tailor P. Burges. It is cool today; we do not know whether we will be here for Ksenia's birthday. Papa brought us hats from Bertrand. I am giving Ksenia a brooch for her birthday. Mama or Papa has still not decided on a bracelet or pendant. Lidiia Stepanovna is sorry not to have seen David [Gintsburg]. It is strange that David is not musical and not an artist, like King David. Our Sasha already knows the entire Russian alphabet, with the exception of "f." Uncle Iakov Solomonovich is very pleased with Bella's fiancé. She is still more pleased since they say she likes him very much—how could it be otherwise?

---

148. Presumably a reference to a portrait of Princess Ekaterina Mikhailovna Dolgorukova (1847–1922), who bore the title "Her Highness Princess Iur'evskaia" after her morganatic marriage to Alexander II in 1880.

6 SEPTEMBER 1881, SOKOL'NIKI.

Yesterday our dinner guests included Stefanovskii and K. K. Shil'dbakh, and after dinner we took seats to play games. Some played checkers, but N. Stefanovskii and I played chess. Today we are invited to the Danilovs for his name day. Z[inaida] Ivan[ovna] dropped by at our house yesterday morning, but because neither Papa nor Mama were home, she gave me the invitation. The weather has decisively changed; the barometer is moving to the left (indicating change). Fanni [Fania] is coming to us today. Two days ago Genrikh was with her in the evening at the Malyi Theater. Someone is making noise in the corridor, probably Roza Kramer.[149] It turned out that the cause of her laughter is the fact that Fania and her son (and wet nurse) arrived here in the rain. Well, that is a good reason for laughter and guffawing, and even for a general ruckus. Everyone has paused in the laughter and demands Roza for stories. F[ania] Livshits came to the nanny to give the baby a bath, but Roza says that it was you who brought Samuil'chik to seek a fiancée for him. As if there were no other reason. Lidiia Stepanovna, wearing fur boots, has appeared looking like a bear. Shil'dbakh is going next week to Yalta. It's a pity that Julie is lying in bed; they say that she has the same (stomach) ailment as before. K. Shil'dbakh and Kostia have been invited on Wednesday for Ksenia's birthday. Ksenia complained that I am inviting little gentlemen, like Kostia. It is interesting to look at a young mother and son; I really am amazed at her. That was something to come for.

7 SEPTEMBER 1881, SOKOL'NIKI.

We stayed at the Danilovs until 2 am yesterday, and I danced more than anyone. My dance is the mazurka. Faina (with Senia [Samuil] and the wet nurse), Mrs. Zel'vina (in the accompaniment of some Jew), and Mrs. Smirnova (with some young man) were here. In the afternoon we went to Lev and had tea; afterward S[olomon] Isaev[evich] Vydrin came. When we encountered rain on the way home, we saw the house of E[fim] Epshtein, who was waiting for the rain to stop before leaving. I gave Roman or Genrikh the task of buying an illustrated album (of one of our[150] Russian writers) for Lev's birthday. The weather is clear, but terribly cold (in the unheated dacha rooms), but finally they are coming to heat my room. Again I hear the loud voice of Roza (the maid's sister and governess). If I were sure that it would not rain, then of course I would order them to send me a horse to go riding, but I do not know if in this case it can be done. Ksenia said that, more than anyone else, she likes some officer

149. Another governess for the children in the Poliakov house, as Zinaida later notes.
150. Note the use of "our."

who was here in the evening and who speaks Russian poorly. Everyone often asks me if I dance often; I answer such questions in the negative. This year I do not hope again to travel so much, and I really do not regret this. Yesterday Mama, with Ronichka and Il'ia, left earlier, whereas Papa, Ksenia, Mishka, and I stayed to dance. Lialiaka Fisher fell down the stairs yesterday and really hurt herself; she was seen by a doctor, who said that it is not dangerous, but that at the very least she must sleep the entire evening. M. A. Danilov (who had the name day) danced in his blue shirt a splendid mazurka, but his [brother-in-law], the brother of Zinaida Ivanovna (his wife), acted more like a fool than [he] in fact. They made some hot punch, which of course I did not try, but I saw that many of them got quite high because of it—including Mr. Sokolov. They commemorated Minin and Pozharskii[151] and impersonated them (if one can call this impersonation): Danilov as Minin, Sokolov as Pozharskii, according to the fantasy concocted by S. Sokolov. Mishka is now coming to pay Ksenia's debt of 1.50 rubles for Masha's present; in general, it's difficult to persuade him to open his *porte-monnaie* although it is sometimes not so fully stuffed.

8 SEPTEMBER 1881, SOKOL'NIKI.

Tomorrow is Ksenia's birthday. In the evening we went horseback riding, but upon returning met S[emen] S. Podgoretskii, who was waiting for us at the gates and who then dined with us. Roza Varshavskaia [Warshavsky] gave birth to a daughter.[152] Uncle S[amuel] Solomonovich informed Papa about this by telegram. The weather is cold and on Thursday, after breakfast, we have decided to move back [to the city]. For today it was proposed that we go to the races, but it seems that we shall not do so (because of rain). Raika is giving Ksenia a silver medallion that has a very beautiful shape. Lidiia Stepanovna is in her room; she is now blowing her nose. Yesterday, when we were riding home on horseback, I strained a tendon in my right leg so that I immediately took the leg from the horn of the saddle and wanted to switch to a horse cab. We were able make do, but the leg still hurts.

9 SEPTEMBER 1881, SOKOL'NIKI.

I gave Ksenia for her birthday a brooch with stones of sapphire and diamonds. Uncle Iakov came yesterday from Petersburg and was here; he showed a photograph of the Landaus. We had breakfast with Uncle and Mr. Khudobai;

---

151. Minin and Pozharskii are the two popular heroes (the former a butcher, the latter a prince) who led the national liberation of Rus' from the Polish occupation in 1612.
152. Roza (neé Poliakova) gave birth to Marie (Maroussia) Leonovna Varshavskaia.

P[etr] Andr[eevich] Vinogradov and E[milii] Chernyi stayed for dinner. The weather is cold; in the morning there was a strong frost, which left icicles on the window in Lidiia Stepanovna's room. Landau's mother is very unattractive, to judge from the photograph; although she is presumably called a *belle femme* [beautiful woman], she does not have a pretty face. We decided to move back to the city tomorrow after breakfast. They gave Uncle our family picture and the portraits of Jacques and Sashka. He probably liked our photographs; he only had time to glance at them, since he was going by express train to Tagan-rog. Bella's wedding will take place in December or even a little later; initially she did not agree to marry earlier than a year. Today for dinner we shall have the Azanchevskii family, and perhaps Mr. Volkov, N. and D. Stefanovskii, S[e-men] S. Podgoretskii, and the Danilovs will come after dinner. It is cold, cold! It's time to move to our winter apartment; otherwise we'll freeze our noses off. Lidiia Stepanovna came into my room; we had agreed, prior to moving to the city, to take a walk in our summer dresses, but today she says that she cannot be held accountable for breaking her word. Today Ksenia is 16 years old; she is two and a half years younger than I. Lidiia Stepanovna came to read the Gospels to me in my room. Mama's former midwife adheres to the apostolic teaching of some Petersburg aristocrat[153] and, because she is a sectarian, she was dismissed from the Foundling Home.[154] Roza was just now here and says that it is time to drag my trunk to the wagon. The snow has entirely covered my balcony and the road. I am glad to move today to our winter quarters. Yesterday, at 3 pm, A[ndrei] N[ikolaevich] Gorchakov was here to have tea and chocolate. Several minutes before dinner, the Danilovs with Madame Diushar (their governess) came to wish Ksenia well on her birthday. For dinner we had: A. Gorchakov, Shil'dbakh and his younger son, D. P. Perevoshchikov, N. P. Stefanovskii and his older son (the student—a fool in the law department). Tomorrow after-noon we have New Year's (a religious [holiday], which we celebrate on a par

153. Presumably a reference to the Protestant evangelical movement initiated by Lord Radstock, a British aristocrat, and propagated by the St. Petersburg circle around Vasilii Aleksandrovich Pash-kov (1831–1902), a retired military officer and founder of a national evangelical movement in the 1870s and 1880s. See Edmund Heier, *Religious Schism in the Russian Aristocracy: Radstockism and Pashkovism, 1860–1900* (The Hague: Nijhoff, 1970); Mark McCarthy, "Religious Conflict and Social Order in Nineteenth-Century Russia: Orthodoxy and Protestant Christianity, 1812–1905" (PhD diss., Notre Dame University, 2004); Samuel J. Nesdoly, "Evangelical Sectarianism in Russia: A Study of the Stundists, Baptists, Pashkovites, and Evangelical Christians, 1855–1917" (PhD diss., Queen's University, 1972).
154. The Foundling Home (Vospitatel'nyi dom) was established in Moscow in 1763 (a similar insti-tution was founded in St. Petersburg in 1771). It took in foundlings and abandoned children. See David L. Ransel, *Mothers of Misery: Child Abandonment in Russia* (Princeton, NJ: Princeton Univer-sity Press, 1988).

with the secular new year). Today I have conclusively donned my winter attire and coat, which were specifically ordered for late autumn. Everything is fine, although we very much feared that one of the children would catch a cold. I forgot about Mr. Grigorovich and his son, who came to the fireworks; the fire-crackers were all damp; only 100 really illuminated the border of the flower-beds with the dropping leaves of the flowers. Everything was beaten down by the first frost; they say that on the 8th of September a splendid rose blossomed in our garden, but undoubtedly it could not withstand the power of the frost. Lidiia Stepanovna is still drinking her water; Shil'dbakh must have left her two bottles, which she wanted to finish drinking. Kotia [Daniil] is at the spa with Zina Girsh [Zinaida de Hirsch], where she is now undergoing a treatment; this year she was sick in Paris, afterwards she was in the vicinity of Cannes, and then went to Spa [in Belgium] for the waters. The [time at the] dacha is finished, and so too is the first volume of the journal. I have been faithful to it the entire time, from beginning to end! I don't know whether I will succeed in writing the next book in such detail. I hope, but after all it's dry here, but there (where it is necessary to write somewhat more . . .[155]), it is more difficult to ex-tricate oneself intelligently and take a different path—such that I understand all that I want to portray, but others do not. D. P. Perevoshchikov and Roman spent the night with us. Roman is leaving for the office in the morning, while the students are going to the gymnasium. I don't know if I have said everything here. I know that Mishka said of this book that my sentences are too short, but he is not my judge, although I do feel that his opinion is fair. Thus, I want for my journal to exist a long time!

155. Missing word.

AUGUST 1883–JANUARY 1887

21 AUGUST 1883 [O.S][1]

I am beginning the new book just before our departure for Baden-Baden and Munich. We had so many plans for this journey that it is simply strange that we have [finally] chosen a route.

Today Papa received from Koti [Daniil Poliakov], in a strange envelope, a notice taken from *Pravitel'stvennyi vestnik*[2] about Papa's new appointment in the Ministry of Interior as a member of the trustee council (*popechitel'stkii sovet*)! Mein is traveling with us. As a result, however, the route is to Munich, and then from there to Schaffhausen.[3]

Edl' [Edel] von Felibinger [Felbinger][4] gave us a group with children, and Karl and Arthur are delightful. They are heading for Russia, but she herself very naively thinks that one has to travel an entire day. They have very strange ideas here. In conversation it happens that one hears "Asia" instead of "Russia."

It is strange that Papa has absolutely no correspondents in Munich, for he has people almost everywhere. Our *Hausmeister* Josef bustles about a lot and, despite his advanced age, himself carries all our baggage to the rail station. For delivering so much baggage and so quickly, Papa gave him an extra tip. He is always very obliging.

I am finishing today's statement with an expression of hope for a pleasant continuation of the journey.

BADEN-BADEN, 24 AUGUST–5 SEPTEMBER 1883

We arrived yesterday at 4 in the afternoon. The town made the most pleasant impression on us.

Source: Zinaida Poliakova and Alexander Poliakoff, *Sem'ia Poliakovykh*, ed. Larisa Nikolaevna Vasil'-evna (Moscow: Atlantida, 1995), 135–212.

1. Zinaida used the Julian calendar in use in prerevolutionary Russia (indicated as "O.S.," or Old Style). When she moved to France, she used both the Old Style as well as the Gregorian calendar date (twelve days ahead in the nineteenth century and conventionally indicated as "N.S.," or New Style).

2. *Pravitel'stvennyi vestnik* was the official newspaper for the dissemination of government decrees and statements.

3. A city in northern Switzerland.

4. E. von Felbinger (not Felibinger, as given in the published text) is the correct spelling.

Today we awoke to the sound of music. Today Papa bought me pictures of the town. We wanted to follow a sightseeing plan, but as always there was a difference of views. Now it is raining, so it is impossible to go out. If we spend our days here as we did today, there will be nothing to boast about.

Along the way, at the station in Stuttgart, Papa and I had lunch, but I felt very nauseated and had a headache the entire way to Baden-Baden. Most likely, I chanced upon something that was not fresh, or after my treatment I should not have eaten Strasbourg pâté.

We spent one day in Munich. The art exhibition is very beautiful. Moreover, the two nights we spent there went very well.

BADEN-BADEN, 27 AUGUST/8 SEPTEMBER 1883

We had time to see the old castle, the Geroldsauer Waterfall and the mountain Merkur. The high towers did not entice me to go up; I am not fond of high, wooden stairs. Traveling with us were two boys of de Hirsh,[5] the nephews of G[oratsii] Os[ipovich] Ginzburg.[6] They are big tourists; they are now living with their grandfather and grandmother, with the exception of Gabriel, who is a soldier.

Here we made the acquaintance of Frau Herzfelder,[7] their aunt. Papa went with Ksiutka and Mishenka to Konversationshaus.[8] Mama wants to go there to see an evening dance. It seems to me that there cannot be anything of interest at such a ball. Life here is very busy if you use it as they all do. From 4–5 at the flower meadow (the best promenades are here) people play lawn tennis and croquet. You have to see how the men are dressed, although they are playing with genteel women and young ladies. Nothing except a white cloth cap, the same kind of pants, and shirts or tunic. The entire society is very animated, and even carriages come to a stop.

A multitude of beautiful villas are tucked away in the mountains of Schwarzwald, where the highest ridge is the mountain Merkur. From the towers one can see the Neckar, the Rhine, and on the left the Strasbourg cathedral.

5. The de Hirsches were a family of entrepreneurs and bankers in Austria, Germany, and England; the founder was Moritz de Hirsch, who received the title of baron for the construction of railroads. Zinaida Samuilovna Poliakova married into this family.
6. Goratsii Osipovich Gintsburg (1833–1909) was a baron and banker who was active in the Jewish community.
7. Spelled "Hel'tsfel'def" in the published text, but probably Herzfelder.
8. The Konversationshaus (house of conversation), since 1914 called the Kurhaus, was the center of Baden-Baden's spa district on the left bank of the Oos River and the center of social life.

Tomorrow we are going to Heidelberg, and from there to Frankfurt-am-Main (in three and a half hours). For one day. Then to West Baden. We'll then get on a steamship and probably travel up the Rhine to Cologne.

Papa received a telegram today from Uncle Samuil,[9] saying that he will depart approximately on 11 September.

Today the weather here was better than usual and even quite warm. So the public took advantage of the weather, and all the coachmen were hired.

I am packing up before breakfast. We are supposed to be accompanied by Rozaliia Gessel'evna Gel'tskhesberg[10] with the nephews of de Hirsch. Today they took tea with us at 6 pm.

Gessel' Rozenberg[11] himself is very weak and has declined mentally. He senses the approach of death; they say that he is very badly off. For dinner today they served us pheasants that had been specially brought from Prague. In general they received us warmly; it is difficult to be any nicer than they.

Yesterday Professor [Heinrich] Graetz[12] paid a visit. He has already left Baden-Baden.

In the evening we wanted to go to a concert featuring the violinist Brodskii, a professor at Leipzig University. Instead, we preferred to stroll around the shops.

Papa received a letter about Doctor Perugia[13] from Trieste (whose daughter was married to Baron Rothschild).

We acquired an almanac for all the barons, with details on the origin of each. It has three pages on the Rothschilds and each individual family. A complement to this book is another that describes their coats of arms, but we do not have a copy.

It turns out that grandfather also knows about the misfortune [the death of Roza Varshavskaia],[14] and Uncle is awaiting our return to describe what happened. We still do not know where and precisely who will meet with him,

9. Samuil Solomonovich Poliakov (1836–88), a banker and owner of railways, was the brother of Zinaida's father, Lazar Poliakov.
10. Rozaliia Gesselevna Gel'tskhesberg was the daughter of Gessel' Markovich Rozenberg and Leonore Gintsburg. Her sister married Goratsii (Horace) Gintsburg.
11. Gessel' [Chaim Yehoshua Heshel] Markovich Rozenberg, a major Kiev entrepreneur, was active in the production of and trade in sugar in the second half of the nineteenth century.
12. Heinrich Graetz (1817–91) was a historian and the author of scholarly works on Jewish history.
13. Achille Perugia was a Trieste merchant whose daughter Marie married Leopold de Rothschild. Her sister Eugenia married Arthur Sassoon.
14. The reference here is to the death of Roza, Zinaida's cousin, the daughter of Samuil Poliakov, and the wife of Leon Varshavskii. She died after childbirth.

since Papa does not want us all to journey to St. Petersburg. But if Uncle does not leave on the 7th, then probably it will have to be done.

MOSCOW, 11 SEPTEMBER 1883

We spent nine days on the trip from Baden-Baden, as we had expected. We traveled 3.5 hours to Heidelberg, and went from there to Frankfurt-am-Main (where we stayed one day). Then we overnighted in West Baden and from Biebrich[15] traveled on the Rhine. We were in Cologne 2.5 hours for the transfer from the ship to the train. We spent three days in Berlin. There we became acquainted with Lakhmann, a young man; he is the brother of the fiancé, M. L. Eltzbacher. He looks a lot like V[ladimir] Podgoretskii.[16] We then went from Berlin to Vil'na for Moscow.

In Orsha[17] we met with Grandfather and Grandmother, and we all then traveled to Smolensk. Yesterday, Papa, Mama, and Grandfather went on to St. Petersburg.

In Frankfurt-am-Main Papa paid a visit to Baron Rothschild,[18] who sent Papa his portrait.

Lazar [Iakovlevich] arrived yesterday from Petersburg!

MOSCOW, 12 SEPTEMBER 1883

Yesterday I received two telegrams from Papa and from Grandmother in Orsha. Uncle and his family will leave for abroad on Wednesday. And our people will also leave on Wednesday. Lazar said that he'll be in Moscow again on the 24th with Annette. And, if she wants, they'll go abroad together from Petersburg. Perhaps, I'll go with them for a short time.

Today Masha hit me in the back when I said that her fiancé's family name begins with the letter "Z." But this pleasure cost me dearly, because Lidiia Stepanovna thought that something in me had snapped.

In telling about the illness and death of the poor Roza, Lazar shed a few tears. They say that Stolz infected her because everything had been going well. They named the young one Ignatii; Bella's daughter was given her name in memory of Roza Varshavskaia [Warshawsky].[19]

---

15. Biebrich is close to Wiesbaden and located directly on the Rhine.
16. Vladimir Podgoretskii was the son of Semen Sergeevich Podgoretskii.
17. Orsha is a town in the Vitebsk area of Belarussia. Solomon and Breine Poliakov were Zinaida's grandparents.
18. Karl Rothschild, a member of the third generation of the Rothschild family, son of Anselm (1773–1855) and grandson of Mayer Anselm Rothschild (1744–1812).
19. Bella's daughter was named Alice [Liulia] Rose (after the deceased cousin Roza) Landau.

The weather today is miserable, and some kind of depression overtook me against my will. I spent the entire day cleaning my room, but something continued to make me anxious. Weighing on my conscience was the thought that tomorrow will be the requiem for dear Roza.

From Baden-Baden I brought a paperweight for Iulii Osipovich [Gol'denbakh].[20] He said thanks and took it, but I do not know if he liked it.

Today I replied to a letter from Luiza [Louise] Gintsburg,[21] and to help with the French summoned M. R. Hugan.

MOSCOW, 24 SEPTEMBER 1883

All the time that I wrote the journal—nothing of interest happened. Our people returned from St. Petersburg. Our guest is now P[avel] P. Demidov,[22] and today Mr. and Mrs. Podgoretskii dined here. They behaved very strangely; he is ill, but S[of'ia] Frantsevna was very boastful.

They say that Katia refused to serve Masha after the 1st of the month—on the pretext that they forgot about her, i.e., did not remember her while abroad.

Mama was very upset over the death of her great-grandfather,[23] which occurred two weeks ago in Mogilev. Grandfather Pavel Rafailovich [Vydrin] and his family only recently returned from there to Orel.

I do not feel all that well, and Iulii Osipovich [Gol'denbakh], an advocate of diversion, advised that I go for a trip.

Today, during a snack, Papa handed me a telegram announcing the engagement of David Goratsievich Gintsburg to his cousin Mathilda. In my opinion, the match is quite good, for each can compensate for the shortcomings of the other.

It is strange that nothing is being said about a wedding for Luiza [Louise Gintsburg]; they say that she is already 23 years old.

Yesterday evening Mama and Papa had D[mitrii] Fe[odos'evich][24] and Alexandra F. Kondrat'ev as guests. As earlier, both of these youngsters passed on Moscow gossip (for example, about the marriages of Mrs. Pustovalova, the departure of Fon Derviz[25] abroad, etc.)

20. Iulii Osipovich Gol'denbakh, the Poliakovs' family doctor.
21. Louise Goratsievna Gintsburg (b. 1862) was the daughter of Goratsii O. Gintsburg. She later married the English entrepreneur Joseph Sassoon (son of David Sassoon and Flora Reuben) and lived in London.
22. Pavel Pavlovich Demidov (1839–85) was from the famous family of industrialists.
23. Rafail Vydrin (son of Ruvim Vydrin) was the father of Pavel Vydrin.
24. Dmitrii Feodos'evich Kondrat'ev (d. 1902) worked in the Ministry of Finance.
25. Pavel Grigor'evich Fon Derviz (1826–81), an entrepreneur of noble origins, was a well-known concessionaire and builder of railroads. The references all say he died in 1881 in Bonn, so the gossip here must refer to an earlier trip to Germany.

The weather is still foul, but Iulii Osipovich insisted today that I go out. But I did not follow his advice. At that very time Demidov, a chamberlain, was in the office, and Arkadii Metskevich was in the blue drawing room. But like the winter sun, these guests brought me neither cold nor warmth. Meanwhile I am constantly alone.

I heard that an Englishwoman has been hired, and Lidiia Stepanovna played an especially active role in this. She knows several aristocratic homes—and I love that.

Miss Gosh[26] plans to go to England as soon as the Lobanovs arrive from the countryside. But she has been planning to do this for a long time, but still lives with them in Moscow. So all this strikes me as somewhat dubious.

ST. PETERSBURG, 1 NOVEMBER 1883

More than a month has already passed since I wrote in my journal. Papa, Mama, and I are all in Petersburg. Mania [Levenson] visited me with the governess. She has become attractive, but Sonia Gorovets appears discontented.

The weather is still poor. Today Krovetskii dined with us. A multitude of people came calling: Trepov,[27] E. N. Zak, Mr. D. Spiridonov, and others. A[bram] Varshavskii[28] also stayed for dinner. He invited Mama and me to go to the grave of my cousin Roza.

We were rather often at the Gintsburgs. Today Mama and I went for a drive, but at that point we met Goratsii Osipovich. Luiza gave me her portrait. Rosette and Uncle Iakov are also here. Only tomorrow do we plan to go calling.

MOSCOW, 18 DECEMBER 1883

To judge from the intervals between each entry, the journal has ceased to be of interest to me. Tomorrow I shall take a break from the multitude of concerts. Today we have two places to go: the Bezekirskii concert and a benefit concert for students. Yesterday Mama reprimanded me over Masha's gossip, so I did not go to the concert with Masha (she told Mama that, because I did not let her have a maid, blood come gushing out of her throat). I was very irate over the slander and, above all, the gossiping. That is why I ate almost nothing yesterday and today. This apparently was not worthy of attention, but that is the way it is.

26. Elizabeth Gosh was a governess in the households of Lazar Poliakov and the Lobanov-Rostoskiis.
27. Fedor Fedorovich Trepov (1812–89), a cavalry general, was the Petersburg military chief in 1873–78. In 1878, in retribution for his harsh treatment of prisoners, he was shot and wounded by Vera Ivanovna Zasulich.
28. Abram Moiseevich Varshavskii (1821–88) was an entrepreneur and railroad magnate. His son Leon married Samuil Poliakov's daughter Roza, who died after giving birth to her son Ignatii.

At 3 we took tea with Dynin, who has fallen very ill and grown old. The beard has greatly changed the contours of his face, and as a result he now looks like a giant.

Several days ago Lev Anisimoivch Raffalovich[29] was here. By now he should be in Warsaw. Yesterday evening there was a performance at our house by Alfred Gr[ü]nfeld[30] and his brother, along with the small female pianist Ebensh[ütz];[31] she was accompanied by her brother, a conductor. A fairly large number of guests gathered. And last Friday both the Gr[ü]nfelds played for almost us alone, but that did not affect their performance in the slightest.

MOSCOW, 19 DECEMBER 1883

At 4 pm today I received Miss Gipson, who conveyed Klindworth's portraits and invitation to a concert. Tomorrow I intend to send her my visiting card, with an invitation to come here Friday evening. Henrietta Klindworth writes that Elsa von Bleichröder was a guest, and expressed her thanks for a pleasant evening. Today Papa sent a congratulatory telegram to the Frankfurt banker Karl Rothschild, "M. Mendelson [Mendelssohn] & Co." in Berlin, and Mr. Gerson Bleichröder[32] (also Berlin).

They say that some financier in St. Petersburg is giving his daughter in marriage to a baron, but that the young people want to mark this occasion properly by ordering colored tails. Ksiiutka [Khaia] thinks that this concerns Luiza Gintsburg, about whom there has already been much talk, and her marriage to a cousin, Jacques Gintsburg.[33]

Singing tomorrow at the Philharmonic will be not Kamenskaia,[34] the prima donna of the St. Petersburg opera, but again Malfrid.[35] We think that she may be from Khar'kov, but are not entirely sure. We have her portrait. We showed this to Polina Ermansderfer and to young Werner. Both think that this is she,

29. Lev Anisimovich Raffalovich was an economist who specialized in the banking industry and a journalist. In the 1880s and 1890s he was on the staff of the newspaper *Birzhevye vedomosti* (Stock market news). His nephew Lev [Louis] Raffalovich was married to Iakov Poliakov's daughter Elizabeth.

30. Alfred Grünfeld 1852–1924) was an Austrian pianist and composer. He was one of the first musicians to make commercial recordings of his music, which are still available today.

31. This may be Ilona Eibenschütz (1872–1967), a child prodigy from Hungary, because she is mentioned below as well. She studied at the Leipzig Conservatory and with Clara Schumann from 1885 to 1890.

32. Gerson von Bleichröder (1822–93) was a Jewish-German banker famous for his close ties to the German chancellor, Otto von Bismarck.

33. She ended up marrying not Jacques Gintsburg but Joseph Sassoon.

34. Mariia Danilovna Kamenskaia (1854–1925), a Russian opera singer whose debut was in Mikhail Glinka's *A Life for the Tsar*.

35. None of the reference works identify "Malfrid"; the only information is what Zinaida provides.

but say that she is more beautiful in the portrait than the woman who sang on the concert stage. But they also describe her with the epithet as being a prima donna of the Florentine and Barcelona operas. It would probably be interesting to find all about this; if true, she probably would receive the invitation to sing here next Friday when young Ilona [Eibenschütz] will play at our house. The latter is apparently inseparable from my female music teacher, who loves to lure everyone into her network.

For now, the weather is not bad. Today Papa offered to take the sled to go for a ride with Miss Owen.[36] But I had a French lesson at 2 and therefore could not go. I hear that tomorrow they are preparing to have the blessing for [the betrothal of] Liza Murav'eva (daughter of Lidiia Stepanovna's friend) with Ini-khov. They say that she is always excited when he appears, and that is already a sign of being well disposed toward him. However, he himself is unattractive, but (according to Lidiia Stepanovna) has means and a relative in the merchant aristocracy (i.e., the Baklanov family).[37]

MOSCOW, 14 JANUARY 1884

Yesterday we spent our time very badly. Mania [Levenson] came to Moscow, and tomorrow Il'ka [Il'ia] has a bicycle tournament. Mania has been here every day since Tuesday, but is leaving this evening. Papa is traveling to Petersburg and has invited me to accompany him.

I am in a really foul mood today: it is amazing how little Mama understands me. They say that opposites attract. Hence in this case I have taken a lot from Mama.

Last Friday M[ax] K. Erdmansderfer[38] and Podgoretskii told our fortune. The former said that I am interested in a married man or in someone who takes no interest in me.

36. A governess in the Poliakov household.

37. Nikolai Baklanov, a big wool trader in Moscow, founded the successful Babkin Brothers Share Partnership with Maria Matveevna Babkina and her son Ivan Matveev. See Galina Ulianova, *Female Entrepreneurs in Nineteenth-Century Russia* (2009; repr., London: Routledge, 2016), 124.

38. The published text has Ermansderhörst, but the reference is clearly to Max Karlovich Erdmans-derfer (Max Erdmannsdörfer in German; 1848–1905). A German conductor, he was active in Moscow and St. Petersburg. From 1882 to 1889, he was the conductor of the Russian Musical Society. He also taught at the Moscow Conservatory, but in 1883 his conflict with the director of the conservatory, Nikolai Gubert, led both to resign. Most notable was his work with Peter I. Tchaikovsky and the premiere of the latter's Manfred Symphony (1885; based on Lord Byron's 1817 poem "Manfred") on 11 March 1886. The composer dedicated his suites for the orchestra (no. 3, op. 55) to Erdmansderfer. The conductor also led the orchestra in the performance of Anton Rubinstein's "Costume Ball." See N. F. Solov'iev, "Ermansdërfer," in *Entsiklopedichskii slovar' Brokgauza i Efrona*, https://rus-brokgauz -efron.slovaronline.com/144971 (accessed 5 April 2019). He was married to the pianist Polina [Pauline Ermansderfer], who is mentioned in the previous entry.

We went to St. Petersburg and, after receiving an invitation to a Gintsburg costume ball, sent for Ksiutka. She came a week later with Miss Owen and on the same train with Grand Duke Peter.[39] For me they ordered the costume of a marchioness.

On Sunday we returned from Petersburg and missed the concert of Max Erdmansderfer. Here, in our absence, were the young Efruski [Ephrussi], for whom the governor-general gave a ball for up to 200 people. Dan[iel] Mein sent Papa a letter expressing regrets that none of us came.

Yesterday we went to the German Theater, which staged the operetta *Der Bettelstudent*.[40] There was almost no one in the theater other than officials: Prince Dolgorukov, A[leksandr A.] Kozlov,[41] and the chief of police, Ogarev.[42] Today Vladimir Andreevich Dolgorukov summoned Papa by phone. Mr. Podgoretskii's daughter died in Tver', and Papa received a telegram from him. How that must shock the poor man—he himself is ill.

There will be a ball at the lycée next week, and the pupils have the right to invite their acquaintances. Papa proposes to invite Baron Gintsburg with his family as well as Mr. and Mrs. Warburg.[43] They are coming here for Shrovetide, and it will be a good time to have fun. Today they will have an evening of music with Professor Davydov.[44] And afterwards there will undoubtedly be dancing. They very kindly invited us to stay, but Papa has to leave on a trip.

MOSCOW, 1 MARCH 1884

All this time I did not pick up my journal for lack of time: we were constantly traveling somewhere. We were at the governor-general's reception[45] and at the lycée for a ball. In addition, we had to take care of the Warburg family, who came from St. Petersburg the day after the ball.

39. Grand Duke Peter Nikolaevich (1864–1931), the youngest son of Grand Duke Nikolai Nikolaevich and grandson of Nicholas I.

40. *Der Bettelstudent* (The beggar student) is an operetta in three acts by Carl Millöcker. It premiered in Vienna in 1882.

41. Aleksandr A. Kozlov (1837–1924) was the assistant chief of police of Moscow in 1878–81 and 1882–87.

42. Nikolai Il'ich Ogarev (1820–90) was the police chief of Moscow.

43. The Warburgs were a prominent dynasty of German-Jewish bankers. The family established M. M. Warburg & Co., which had connections with international banking houses. Goratsii Gintsburg's wife, Anna, was the sister of Theophile Warburg.

44. Karl Iul'evich Davydov (1838–89), called the "tsar of violoncellists," was also a composer and director of the St. Petersburg Conservatory

45. Zinaida says "Forum journée," which is not idiomatic French but seems to mean some kind of reception or gathering.

Moscow now has an opera. We have two subscriptions—the first and third for tomorrow. Today Chebotarev brought me a carved basket for visiting cards that he had made. After the ball we received a visit from Baron Ungern-Shternberg and the officer Stefanov[skii]. On the first day of the [Lenten] fast we went on a troika with the Warburgs (father, mother, and daughter) to Strel'na.[46] Unfortunately, there were not any gypsies,[47] but in their place was a Hungarian chorus of ten people.

On Saturday Papa plans to travel to T-br [sic]. Mama may also go as well. They have proposed that I go (a third time this winter), but of course I declined.

Tomorrow is the [anniversary of Alexander III's] accession to the throne and therefore a celebratory performance is on our subscription tickets. But alas!—it is Friday, so we cannot go.[48] But I am hoping for one thing—to see, at least, Amalia Sual'. She and her sister paid us a visit, and the next day Papa and Mama went to them. In three weeks Mr. Erdmansderfer will go to Berlin, and my music lessons will cease.

Purim[49] was two days ago. Mama gave me a brooch, and Papa gave me (like everyone else) a hundred-ruble note. Everything was like it had always been; the only difference was that two days earlier we received a telegram from George, announcing the birth of a second son.

On Tuesday next the new St. Petersburg commercial bank is opening. Papa is going there on Saturday the 3rd for the opening. None of the uncles will be there.

They say that Lidiia is feeling well. Thank God! I can imagine how everyone feared for her after the stroke. In recent days Mama has been talking about the possibility of a trip abroad, either in the spring or summer. But that will absolutely not do. It would be much better to go in the fall (prior to winter), when [the weather] here [is] so miserable. But talk and plans do not always come to pass; on the contrary, they rarely do.

MOSCOW, 15 MARCH 1884

Yesterday we looked up the meaning of dreams in the *Sonnik*.[50] Today is Mama's and Papa's wedding anniversary. Tomorrow the Stal' sisters will apparently come to visit. Throughout lunch Mama was mad at one person or another.

46. A town in St. Petersburg province located on the Gulf of Finland.
47. Gypsy minstrels are evidently what Zinaida had in mind here.
48. The family observed the Sabbath only on Friday evenings (not Saturday).
49. The Jewish holiday to commemorate the defeat of Haman's plan to destroy the Jews.
50. A *Sonnik* was a book for the interpretation of dreams and fortune-telling. Such books enjoyed considerable popularity. In the years shortly before this entry was written, more than a dozen of

I received a letter from Mama. It says that she spoke with Kotia [Daniil Po-
liakov] about me. He often goes to visit Lidiia Abramovna Malkiel'. Mama and
Elena were at Mrs. Levinson's. I know all this because of a letter from Mania
Levinson.

We plan to go to the Malyi Theater today. Since all the children are coming,
we have reserved two theater boxes. Mama gave me a bracelet; they made two
bracelets out of my old pearl [necklace]: one for Ksiutka, one for me. I did not
gain anything from giving it back to Mama.

MOSCOW, 21 MARCH 1884

Yesterday we were at a Shostakovskii[51] concert and left after the first part. Tomorrow, for the first time in our subscription, Mr. Zonental' will perform.

Today I went with Miss Owen to select gifts for Lidiia Stepanovna. Yesterday the Stal' singers were supposed to take breakfast with us before going
abroad, but they did not come; instead we had breakfast with Iulii Osipovich
Gol'denbakh and the Austro-Hungarian vice-consul [von] Shponer. L. Volkov,
who suffers from an excessive appetite, also came during breakfast. Afterwards,
Fransua Shponer [Franz von Sponer][52] came riding past our house. Spotting
me in the window of my room, he bowed and rode past yet again. Papa plans to
travel again to St. Petersburg in a few days, but will probably not go — Passover
is next week.

Uncle is beckoning us to come to Berlin. Aleksandr Vydrin, my godson,
should be celebrating his birthday any day now. Whether this has already
transpired or is still to come, I simply cannot recall.

A concert will be held in the German club for impoverished Jews. Mr.
Minor told me that he could say that Papa has no time for this, and in that case
they would probably put this off to a later time. They say that even an active
member of the Jewish Artisan School, Aron Efr. Shneider,[53] has no time, but
they paid no attention to this and left everything as it was.

them had been published, such as L. P., comp., *Polneishii sonnik i istolkovatel' razlichnykh primet*
(St. Petersburg, 1872).

51. P. A. Shostakovskii (b. 1853) was a pianist and a professor in and director of a Moscow music
school [note by the editor of the published Russian text].

52. The Austro-Hungarian vice-consul.

53. Aron Efremovich Shneider was a first-guild merchant and warden of the Moscow synagogue.

In the meantime [since the last diary entry], we have had many adventures, but death has taken three acquaintances: (1) Shchurovskii;[54] (2) Nikolai Ustinovich Arapov;[55] and (3) Mr. L[ev] N. Volkov.

We also had visits from Dr. Dynin.[56] And I say "we" because he has dropped by often. Here came the sailor Baron Ungern-Shternberg,[57] who had already come by yesterday to say farewell. I forgot to mention the death of I. Kuranda;[58] I wrote a telegram about his death yesterday.

Yesterday the Stoikovs came for lunch, and Devartovskii (who is going abroad) was here in the evening. Mama spent the entire day riding around —in the morning with Raechka, then with Papa. At the same time there was also Mrs. Zvegintseva.

Tomorrow evening, I think, the entire Devartovskii family, Nora Gipson, and the Messarosh family will be [here].[59]

I have made an album for the signatures of all my acquaintances according to their birth date.

Papa was very distressed by the death of L. N. Volkov, who had been ill for an entire week. The Moscow Land Bank[60] and his fellow workers ordered wreaths for his grave. Now Papa will be the chairman of the bank, but Dolgorukii [sic][61] will be the third director and member of the Appraisal Committee. Ni[kolai Nikolaevich] Pavlov, on the basis of the charter, should be appointed, since he is the first candidate, and Stepanovskii the second. But the former had to decline for reasons of health, and the latter was passed over.

We played four-handed piano with the female pianist E[miliia] I. [Ogus-]

54. Grigorii Efimovich Shchurovskii (1803–84), a Russian geologist at Moscow University, died 20 March (O.S.).

55. Nikolai Ustinovich Arapov (1825–84) had been a police chief of Moscow.

56. Iakov Poliakov mentions the Dynins, with whom the two oldest Poliakov brothers (Iakov and Samuil) took private lessons. David Aleksandrovich Dynin's daughter from his first marriage married Evgenii Gavrliovich Gintsburg, who was already working as a tax farmer in Kamenetsk-Podolsk. His two sons from his second marriage. Aleksandr and Abram, took lessons with the Poliakovs. When Lazar Solomonovich was old enough to start his education, he took lessons with the Dynins' third son, Mark Davidovich. It is unclear if the Dynin mentioned here was related to the Dynins described in Iakov Poliakov's diaries (see "Istoriia," l. 6.)

57. The Ungern-Sternbergs were a Baltic-German noble family.

58. Ignaz Kuranda (1812–84) was a Jewish-Austrian publicist and politician, who died on 3 April 1884 (N.S.) in Vienna. He was elected to the Landtag of Lower Austria as a delegate for the district of Vienna and later to the Reichsrat, where he served for some twenty years.

59. Probably the family of Ivan Vasil'evich Messarosh (d. 23 March 1886).

60. The Moscow Land Bank belonged to Lazar Poliakov. Volkov was head of the bank's board.

61. Presumably Dolgorukov.

Shaikevich.[62] And even Ksiutka was tempted and arranged a lesson. Then they summoned me into the hall to see the coat that they are ordering for Raecha for the summer. It is very boring to sit home alone all day, since there is no one with whom one can talk and share thoughts.

I do not always get along with Mama, and we have little in common. But the governesses avoid me, and I them. As people say, you have to look out for yourself. And each is happy with what is to their advantage.

They say that Iulii Osipovich [Gol'denbakh] was here today, but he did not come in to see me. And in essence he did the right thing. Each time you have to tell about a new ailment. It is boring for him, unpleasant for me, and amusing for others.

Mama noticed that at lunch I was constantly looking at the clock—a sign of boredom. And really it seems as though time stands still, even as the days pass one after another.

SOKOL'NIKI, 18 JUNE 1884

It is strange that I have not written for such a long time. During this time Kokh died; before his death he began to make frequent visits.

Today I had a run-in with Mama. Over newspapers. During this interval Papa was in St. Petersburg for a second time. And as a result things have been extremely boring for us. The Podgoretskiis live in Sokol'niki. I go horseback riding with her pseudoniece Baturina and an officer Binenshtam. It is really a shame that dacha life is so drab. Recently the entire Podgoretskii crew—the nephew, niece, Vladimir Semenov, the brother Binenshtam, and their son-in-law Ratkevich—came for tea.

Aleksandr and Iashka [Iakov] have broken free of the nanny's control, and the nanny is constantly ill.

SOKOL'NIKI, 21 JUNE 1884

Today I am again in a foul mood, because Iashka (probably at the instigation of his worthy teacher) apparently told little Stoikova that Zina [Zinaida], his sister, is mean. Berries were brought to the table, but I asked that they be served on the terrace. Mama has a right to say: oh, children, children, what is with you children! Well, it is not always pleasant for us either.

Mishenka found my red monocle bearing an image of Heidelberg.

62. Emiliia Isaakovna Ogus-Shaikevich, born in Kremenchug in 1872, graduated from the Moscow Conservatory, where she studied with Nikolai G. Rubinshtein (1835–81), and later opened her own music school and gave regular performances.

Yesterday we went to the Podgoretskiis' and drank tea and ate clabber. Something unpleasant is weighing on me, but I do not know exactly what.

Miss Owen told Mama today that, when I am bored, so is she. I made the very same criticism a long time ago about the two inseparables—Ksiutka and Lidiia Stepanovna. To have a more cheerful attitude toward life, I bought some of the poetry by A. de Musset.[63] Two days ago Uncle Iakov passed through on his way from St. Petersburg to go abroad. His family, with the exception of Lazar and his family, are all in Marienbad.

The elder Rozenberg died three years ago in Baden-Baden. Papa came to know him through Baron G[oratsii] Osipovich Gintsburg during his time in St. Petersburg. Like many elderly men he is surrendering his field of endeavor to a new generation. But the youth goes to the grave prematurely—like, for example, our poor cousin Roza.

SOKOL'NIKI, 6 JULY 1884

Last Sunday we went dancing at Fon Derviz's. In the afternoon Mr. Antokol'skii[64] came for a visit.

And this Sunday we were frightened by some man: he ran up to me, waving his arms, as I was talking with acquaintances at the gate. And when I and the others ran into the courtyard, he chased after us and ran into the garden. There L. I. Glazer threw him down and, from zeal, broke the end of our bench. The man started to scream bloody murder.

There was recently a pogrom in Nizhnii Novgorod, where Beselmann perished. He was beaten to death. N[ikolai] Nikolaevich Pavlov died recently in his village, just when Papa and Mr. Dolgorukov had been thinking of inviting him to replace temporarily the latter during a trip abroad. Dolgorukov (among others) came for lunch on Tuesday for Mother's birthday.

On Sunday afternoon we received Demidov (vice-governor of Moscow) and M. Malkiel' with their young. On Monday we went in a carriage drawn by four horses to the Devartovskii's in Kuz'minki for their silver anniversary. We had lunch there and then went for a stroll. After that there was dancing, and we did not arrive back home until 2 am.

63. Alfred de Musset (1810–57) was a prominent French romantic poet, novelist, and dramatist.
64. Mark Matveevich Antokol'skii (1843–1902), a sculptor, was the founder of the realist school in Russian sculpture. He exhibited at the World's Fair in 1867 and received his first major commissions when *Ivan Grozny* was purchased by Alexander II. See Olga Litvak, "Rome and Jerusalem: The Figure of Jesus in the Creation of M. M. Antokol'skii," in *The Art of Being Jewish in Modern Times*, ed. Barbara Kirshenblatt-Gimblett and Jon Karp (Philadelphia: University of Pennsylvania Press, 2006), 441–96; Musya Glants, *Where Is My Home? The Art and Life of the Russian-Jewish Sculptor, Mark Antokolskii, 1843–1902* (Lanham, MD: Lexington Books, 2010).

Iulii Osipovich Gol'denbakh unexpectedly came today after returning from abroad. He is very dissatisfied with his trip and came back without feeling any better.

Uncle Samuil plans to come to Moscow with Katkov who is now there. It struck me as very strange that in his telegram Uncle referred to him as "Mikhailov." He had lunch with Uncle in Tsarskoe Selo[65] and probably agreed to travel together with him.

Just now a charabanc with two horses and driven by some man flew past.

The 8th [of July] is Masha's birthday, a few days later is Roman's, and then Mishen'ka's on the 23rd. I have already prepared a present for them: Wagner's book in a shagreen binding. Lidiia Stepanovna, after the incident with the stranger, has begun to talk to me again.

Miss Owen gave Mishen'ka the task of bringing her some cream caramels from town—which he did.

SOKOL'NIKI, 2 AUGUST 1884

Since I last wrote in this journal, a lot of water has flowed under the bridge: and there have been many events, both good and bad.

First, Luiza [Gintsburg] became the fiancée of Esner [sic] Sassoon[66] from London, which we learned from a telegram sent to us. Second, Miss Owen has left. This latter circumstance, precipitated by a whole series of incidents on Mama's part, upset me greatly.

Third, Papa went to St. Petersburg on the anniversary of Roza's death and wanted to take me with him. Everything was packed when the trip was put off until the following day (the eve of the anniversary), but the requiem—according to newspaper reports—was scheduled for 10 am. I did not have a mourning dress and therefore had to stay behind. Moreover, Mama did not want me to go the cemetery, where the train made a stop for Papa.

Today we escorted Miss Owen to the train stop, but hired two carriages when a rainstorm overtook us.

There are moments in life that, while in themselves of no great significance, become deeply embedded in one's memory. Thus, for example, the pity that I felt on the occasion of Miss Owen's departure (and especially because I was convinced of her innocence)[67] will not soon disappear from my memory.

---

65. Tsarskoe Selo (now Pushkin) is a town twenty-four kilometers from St. Petersburg. It was an imperial residence, the site of a famous palace constructed in the mid-eighteenth century.
66. She married Joseph Sassoon.
67. Zinaida explains below in this entry that her mother suspected Miss Owen of having a romantic interest in her son Mikhail.

Al'fred Gintsburg[68] paid us a visit during Papa's absence. A few days ago Baron Gintsburg came by as well. Yesterday we received Derenburg, who publishes the Berlin newspaper *National-Zeitung*, with a letter of commendation to Papa from Mr. Bleichröder. Derenburg is already elderly; he has a very unattractive appearance and very twisted nose.

Today Papa went to the train station to accompany Prince Dolgorukov. Papa was given the prince's portrait with the inscription "it is a matter of railway cars," i.e., it is a question of whose car he will travel in, that of Fon Derviz or ours. In the end he traveled as usual in a Fon Derviz car and, thinking that Papa will be offended by this, made his apologies and invited Papa to lunch.

I forgot to mention the specious reason for our parting with Miss Owen: a pseudo-love story in our house. Mama imagined that she [Miss Owen] was chasing after Mishen'ka, but more likely the envious L. S. [Lidiia Stepanovna] perpetrated this because of her animus toward me and her desire to get rid of anyone who was my friend.

SOKOL'NIKI, 7 AUGUST 1884

Yesterday we traveled to Trinity-Sergius Lavra and spent the whole day there, returning home (with the Podgoretskiis) at 11 pm. As a historical site, the Lavra deserves attention, and also because of the incalculable riches in its sacristy. Semen Sergeevich Pogoretskii cannot sit still in the presence of a pretty woman. In the railway car, for example, he kept trying to strike up a conversation with one woman. Having arrived at the Lavra and famished from the trip, we ate some small cakes and then went directly to the monastery. After seeing both cathedrals and other churches, we asked whether it was possible to see the sacristy, and were told that it is not possible until vespers are over. The director then ordered that his visiting card be taken to the prior, with a threat to complain to the metropolitan. After lengthy monologues by the director and a monk, open sesame!—the people (but not all) were admitted to the sacristy under the pretext that "they are from the [imperial] Court." His visiting card bore the inscription, "Chamberlain. DEV."[69] After viewing the sacristy (where I especially liked the portraits of Alexander I, Alexander II, and Nicholas I that had been given to the metropolitan), there was the icon of the Mother of God [made] from rose coral with precious stones donated by the late empress on the first confession of Mariia Aleksandrovna.[70] There was an unusually natural

68. Al'fred Goratsievich Gintsburg (b. 1865) later became head of the Lena gold-mining enterprise.
69. "DEV" is probably an abbreviation for "Dvor Ego Velichestva" (Court of His Majesty).
70. The "late empress" is a reference to Mariia Aleksandrova (1824–80, the wife of Alexander II). The "M.A." refers to their daughter and the empress's namesake, Princess Mariia (1853–1920).

depiction of Christ's head on one stone, and also an agate bearing a natural portrayal of a praying monk at the feet of the cross of crucifixion. From there we went to the skete [monastic community] of Bethany, bypassing on the left the Chernigov [skete with its icon], Mother of God. There we saw the original church and small house of Patriarch Nikon.[71] Then, after dining in the Lavra hotel and buying some toys for the children, we set out on our return journey. And this too did not pass without some adventures. The conductor opened the door in the passageway between cars and dropped the cane of Semen Serge- evich Podgoretskii. We heard about the impending marriage of Mikhail Katkov with the older Princess Lobanova-Rostovskaia. I have seen the groom; as for the bride, Miss Gosh had lived in her household and praised her highly.

That is everything that transpired during the time when I did not write in my journal.

However, there is some news: Papa bought a riding horse called Drob'. Al- though he is old (18), they say he is a good horse. He has turned white because of age and resembles the legendary horse of the "White General" Skobelev.[72]

SOKOL'NIKI, 8 AUGUST 1884

I was home the entire day. I had just decided to take a walk with the little chil- dren and Miss Veler [Veiler] when a funeral cortege went past us. They say that it was the Germans from Bogorodsk[73] since pastors were in front. Mama has now invited me to go for a walk. Papa rented our old apartment to M. M. Bernard, the French consul. Ksiutka went horseback riding with an equestrian instructor.

I still have not written to Miss Owen, but did receive a letter from her. They say that Raechka [Raia] has already replied to a letter. Podgoretskii has come and called for me. I intend to give him the cane that I bought in Baden-Baden; he will find it useful while he waits for a new one—otherwise he will probably continue to mourn the old one. I will have to hurry to finish in order to re- spond—very reluctantly—to the summons to appear.

SOKOL'NIKI, 13 AUGUST 1884

Yesterday we had guests, including Malkiel' and her daughter. Today the air was fresh, and the sky was overcast all day. Nonetheless, Il'ka and I went horse-

71. Patriarch Nikon was head of the Russian Orthodox Church from 1652 to 1666 and famed for his role in precipitating the movement of Old Believer dissenters.
72. Mikhail Dmitrievich Skobelev (1843–82) was renowned as the daring "white general" (he led cavalry charges in a white uniform on a white steed) in the Russo-Turkish War, but he later became infamous for the slaughter of Turkmen at Geoktepe in the conquest of Central Asia in 1881.
73. Now called Noginsk, a district to the east of Sokol'niki and Moscow.

back riding. E[miliia] Is[aakovna] Ogus[-Shaikevich] will come tomorrow instead of today. Today is the birthday of Tonia Shaikevich. The day before yesterday Lidiia Stepanovna made up with me and began to apologize if she had wronged me in any way.

Today I sent Miss Owen a letter with the card showing little Il'ia on a bicycle. Miss Veler is complaining of a headache. Miss Owen wrote her and asked to come and see her on Saturday, but I advised against this. And indeed why should she go anywhere since we will be leaving soon. Again there is some vague talk about a trip abroad, but I do not know what will come of all these conversations. Most likely, the mountain will give birth to a mouse, as often happens.

They say that in the countryside Genrikh fell from his carriage and injured his leg. They all had taken it into their heads to go visit someone, but this happened—as if on purpose. Mama says that this occurred on almost the same date as the time when we were thrown from a carriage in Khar'kov. At that time Fania broke her leg and was nearly killed, but recovered.

On Thursday classes begin at the Lycée of Tsarevich Nikolai.[74] S. Mir. [Malkiel'][75] and Mina Abramovna Malkiel' have invited us for Wednesday evening, but this is a holiday,[76] and Papa never goes into town on this day. It is as if, once Papa and Mama drive off, the house will fall in.

SOKOL'NIKI, 3 SEPTEMBER 1884

All this time I have not been in a very good mood. The reason is the incessant spying of Lidiia Stepanovna.

74. The Moscow Imperial Lyceum in Memory of Tsarevich Nikolai, was an institution of higher learning that operated in Moscow from 1868 to 1917. The reference is to the eldest son of Alexander II, who died prematurely. The lycée, located on Ostozhenka Street (a prominent street in central Moscow) and reserved for the children of the nobility, was informally known as the Katkov Lycée (after the principal donor, Mikhail Katkov, whose contribution was supplemented by donations from such figures as P. M. Leont'ev, Samuil S. Poliakov, Pavel G. Fon Derviz, and other entrepreneurs).

75. "S. Mir" may be an abbreviated reference to Samuil Mironovich [Meerovich] Malkiel' (b. 1836), who made his money as a contractor for the military during the Russo-Turkish War; settled in Moscow; and opened several enterprises, including a foundry. He was married to Mina Abramovna Malkiel'; his son Matvei Samuilovich, a technical engineer, founded a leather factor in Moscow, while his daughter Sof'ia Samuilovna, a children's book writer, supported the artist Isaak Levitan and was a close friend of Anton Chekhov—who carried on a correspondence with her sister Mariia Samuilovna.

76. In 1884 the next Wednesday after 13 August was two days later—15 August, which is one of the twelve great feast days in the Russian Orthodox Church—Dormition (Uspenie Presviatoi Bogoroditsy). That would preclude a business meeting and explains why her father would not go into the city on this holiday.

The guest now is Antokol'skii, who is simultaneously making the busts of Mama and Papa. I also made my first attempt at sculpting (a bas-relief of the late emperor)—which people say was not so bad.

Today is a momentous day in the history of the future: the meeting of the three emperors.[77] Papa, Mama, and M[ark] Antokol'skii were in the city and looked at antiquities.

The day after tomorrow is Ksiutka's birthday; she will be 19 years old. I intend to go tomorrow to buy her a present.

On 20 August we went to the wedding of our coachman in a church, and for that we received an earful.[78] Miss [Maria] Mein[79] was exceedingly insolent today. Ksiutka thought that I had sat down on her picture; Miss Mein—who was at the other end of the room—stood up and with the utmost impudence confirmed that.

Tomorrow the Senate will hear a report about one of Papa's matters. It will be interesting to know whether it goes through.

At Emr. Khugon's I bought a small *khinouzeri*, a small Chinese statue from ivory, for 8 rubles. I shall try to justify Mr. Antokol'skii's opinion that I have a talent for making models. Tomorrow I shall begin working on a small head if I do not go into the city with Papa.

S. Shaikevich[80] invited me to his home to view the collection of engravings that he recently acquired. He bought them secondhand for 4,000 rubles. They had previously belonged to the well-known Likhachev.

They say that Luiza's[81] fiancé is neither nice nor handsome. Those are the words of the sculpture Antokol'skii and, consequently, someone well versed in physiognomy. Absolutely nothing is known about the wedding other than the fact that it will be in Petersburg.

Papa was in Petersburg and invited me to go, but this time I declined. I learned that the young Lakhpan married [M. L.] El't[s]bakher, the sister of his

77. The emperors of Russia, Germany, and Austria-Hungary met at Skierniewicz on 15–17 September 1884 (N.S.) as members of the Three Emperors League, which was intended to bolster stability and affirm the neutrality of the three great Central and Eastern European powers. The league's renewal in March 1884 and the emperors' meeting in September of that year seemed to ensure peace and order. The league lapsed three years later, a direct casualty of the irreconcilable differences between Russia and Austria-Hungary over the Balkans—the issue that ultimately led to the outbreak of World War I.

78. Zinaida does not say who did the scolding—wedding guests or Jewish acquaintances.

79. Mania is the diminutive form for the given name of Mariia Aleksandrovna Mein (1868–1906), the daughter of Aleksandr Danilovich Mein (1836–99). Mania became the second wife of Ivan Tsvetaev and mother of the renowned poet Mariia Tsvetaeva.

80. Possibly Samuil Solomonovich Shaikevich (1842–1908), a Moscow lawyer.

81. Luiza [Louise] Goratsievna Gintsburg, who married Joseph Sassoon.

elder brother's wife. P. [sic] is in Galicia, where his brother is ill with typhus, and that is why he is there now.

There is nothing else new; all is just as it was. It would not hurt to have less squabbling in the house.

In the short span of time since I last wrote, nothing good has happened. It seems that our plans to go abroad have come to naught.

Mark Matveevich [Antokol'skii] is sculpting busts of the sovereign and Count Tolstoi.[82] There were student disorders here yesterday: a crowd of 150 students gathered in front of Katkov's residence, but were surrounded and taken off to prison. They say that all those detained will be expelled.

There is nothing to note except incessant troubles. The weather changes frequently and for the most part has become colder. Miss Veler [Veiler] [the governess] was supposed to go away, but Mama changed her mind and asked [her] to stay. The latter, without noticing, is completely under the thumbs of the hangers-on: Lidiia Stepanovna and the old nanny.

I went with Papa and Mama to St. Petersburg and stayed there ten days. Today Professor Gevartovskii died of stomach cancer; he had been ill for a long time, and Zakhar'in had said that the illness was incurable.

Antokol'skii's wife arrived in Petersburg from Paris. Kuznetsov, the grandson and heir of Gubkin (the former tea merchant),[83] wants to order a bust of his grandfather. M. Antokol'skii says that he can make a bas-relief, but not a bust, from a picture.

Yesterday Fomin sent me photographs and a description of the paintings that are for sale.

Luiza [Louise] Gintsburg's fiancé is very ugly, to judge from his picture. Moreover, today Papa told Mr. Raffalovich that he had also heard the same thing. Uncle was very attentive to me and very much wished that I would stay. But we agreed that it would be better to come back.

Luiza's [Louise's] wedding will be soon, and perhaps Ksiutka and I will go then (although we do not have any more information from them).

The daughter of Lidiia Stepanovna's friend Niuta [Anna] Murav'eva will

82. Given that Antokol'skii did sculptures of writers and high officials, the reference here may be either to the writer Leo Tolstoy or to the high-ranking official Dmitrii Tolstoi (then the minister of the interior).

83. Aleksei Semenovich Gubkin (1816–83) was a Russian tea merchant and philanthropist.

marry Liders. Everything else is proceeding as usual. Were it not for the incessant gossip, life would be better. "If you live with the wolves, then learn to howl like them"—as the saying in old Rus'[84] has it. I hope, however, that this does not mean that I should gossip like them.

On the last day of the year I am taking up my journal to enter several incidents. P. was here, spent three and half days in Moscow, and left yesterday. Everybody liked him, but his politeness toward Khellei caught everyone's attention. I am very glad that he was not here for long. Everything is for the best, and I hope that is the case here.

Tomorrow is a new year. Will it bring me anything good? I am not complaining, but I hope that I have a better year.

Saturday, 5 January, is my birthday, but we have been invited to Savinkova's, Prince Dolgoruskov's, and Zinaida Ivanovna Danilova's for the first three days of January.

Today I went to Ksiutka and Mishen'ka to write addresses on the envelopes for the holiday visiting cards.

I hope that January 1st will be a joyous occasion. Right now I do not know; we will see what tomorrow brings. [Mariia] Mein is again a fiancée, and we learned of this in a very strange way. Papa and I went to visit them, and she introduced us to her fiancé: a young man named Dubovitskii, who completed the university with a candidate's degree in law (along with a gold medal). He is not very good-looking, but apparently smart and clever.

Many weddings have been announced, although not in the upper circle. The daughter of Shopel'skin, a second Daitsel'man, Boris Poliakov, and John Lane—almost all of these are unbeknownst to us and therefore do not interest me in the least.

Mr. Gerts has married, and they are already inviting him to serve as our tutor. The future for me is entirely unclear: nothing planned earlier has come to pass.

Luiza [Louise] and her husband were in Moscow after our second visit to them in St. Petersburg. Goratsii Osipovich [Gintsburg] invited us by telegram to a ball on Friday, and we stayed overnight at their place.

---

84. Rus' is the form used before the modern Rossiia (Russia) came to prevail in the eighteenth century.

Although I have not written for almost an entire quarter of a year, I am nevertheless not abandoning my journal. As yet there is nothing new. We were in St. Petersburg and only returned from there yesterday. It turned out that Mama not only has been opening my letters but has not even been giving them to me. I said that was swinish, and she hit me with blows to the head. I don't care in the least about all this, but yesterday she came into my room twice and left notes: "I don't give a damn about you, Zina." They were dated 11 March 1885. I tore them up and threw them into the wastepaper can.

Luiza [Louise] and her husband are still in Petersburg. She is in an interesting position.

Sasha [Aleksandr] Gintsburg is an officer and very pleased with his uniform.

MOSCOW, 13 MARCH 1885

I forgot to write yesterday that during this interval Gol'dberger was again in Moscow. Yesterday Mark Antokol'skii was here; today he came for breakfast and said good-bye before departing for Petersburg.

All the children have forgotten how to speak English; Russian now reigns in our household.

The weather is warm again. I went out with Papa this morning.

Mama complains constantly about her life. Well, what am I to do? After all, I am totally dependent on her—to the point where I cannot even go for a stroll. But as the proverb says: "Rely on the Lord, but do what is right!"[85] And following this adage, I try to do everything possible to avoid being constrained in my actions. I have an album that has twenty-five questions on each page; you have to write the answers yourself. I wrote in such journals in Berlin (at George Gol'dberger's) and in St. Petersburg (at Il'ia Rubinshtein's). But my album is in German; those were in French and English.

Everything in this world is so perverse. And I hope that the present state of my spirit will change; otherwise it will be unbearable.

MOSCOW, 15 MARCH 1885[86]

Everything passes (as is to be expected). And therefore my mood has somewhat improved, as far as I am concerned.

Today *Moskovskie vedomosti* and *Russkie vedomosti* carried an official an-

---

85. "*Na boga nadeisia, a sam ne ploshai.*" The proverb was indeed widespread.
86. The published text gives 25 March, but given that the entry is between 13 March and 21 March, this evidently should read 15 March.

nouncement about the bankruptcy of Malkiel'. One feels sorry for them: it is difficult for anyone to go from riches to rags—all the more in their case.

This week all the newspapers, both Russian and foreign, wrote about the impending marriage of Topper. But yesterday's issue of *Neue Freie Presse*[87] announced that her father had forbidden the marriage. And that is very surprising. In my opinion, this will only make things worse for him and her. In any case, the matter had already gone too far.

Lidiia Stepanovna again seized upon an opportunity to quarrel with me. Somehow they are talking about a trip. At lunch today Papa asked Mr. Fridman whether things are going well in Vienna. I do not know what they decided about Professor Zakhar'in's advice for Mama. It seems that he advised her to go to West Baden and then from there to the waters for the spas.

I sent a birthday telegram to Ida Rubinshtein[88] and also signed for Ksiutka. We did not receive any response, but it seems that none is required in such cases.

A[dolf] L. Elmenik's daughter is marrying the lawyer Dr. Dekhshberg. I sent them a telegram. The first one did not have a [street] address; I received a reply about nondelivery, since Vienna has several Adolf Elmeniks.

Yesterday was the burial for the elderly Gil', who had died the previous night. They say that a lot of people came to the funeral. [G]rigorii Zakhar'in went in our place; the deceased was in the final stage of heart disease. But we all have the same end and face making this journey.

The new dresses—ordered from a Lyon shop for the holiday but arriving too late—were only now delivered. This is a strange transition from philosophy to real life, but my thoughts are all jumbled.

MOSCOW, 21 MARCH 1885

I had a chance to see Zakhar'in again today. He was visiting Papa and asked that I be called.

We received a telegram from Jerusalem. All the words on the address, other than "Poliakov," were incomprehensible. What does the signature "Poliakov" mean? Did grandfather and grandmother travel there? To this point it remains a mystery. We hope to receive an answer soon.

---

87. Mistitled by Zinaida as *Neue Freue Press*, this leading Viennese paper (1864–1938) had a strong Jewish orientation and included, among its correspondents, Karl Max, Stefan Zweig, and Theodor Herzl (in Paris, starting in 1891).

88. This is not the dancer and actress Ida L'vovna Rubinstein (who was born in 1883 and would have only been three years old at this time) but a relative of Grigorii (George) Rubinshtein, who was married to Zinaida's cousin Anna (Niuta) Iakovlevna Poliakova.

S[amuil] Mir[onovich] Malkiel' came to see Papa today. They say that he was weeping and had changed greatly.

There are few people on the streets—contrary to what is usually the case. Papa explains this by the fact that business is bad. Masha was late for breakfast and got an earful from Mama.

MOSCOW, 25 MARCH 1885

The holidays—ours as well as the Russian—were rather boring. The question of our trip abroad will probably be settled in the next few days. Upon the advice of Zakhar'in, yesterday I took two strolls and today went for a ride twice. Lidiia Stepanovna was a guest at her relatives for two days, and returned in the evening of the day before yesterday. She says that Niuta L[ieders] has become very attractive since her marriage.

The father has once again denied permission for the elder Topper to marry, as I wrote earlier. Confirmation of this has now appeared in the German newspapers.

A ticket to the English amateur concert came. A theater box costs 25 rubles; this means that Mama apparently does not want to agree to this. This event is to support a church that they have recently opened (to have benches made).

I was in our synagogue with Papa, Mr. Shaikevich, and I. Solo. Gal'bershtadt.[89] Today I went to the Manezh[90] and from there to Petrov Park. At the Manezh we saw the young Kil'khen and V. Akimova with her daughter; the latter had become somewhat unattractive and was wearing a straw hat.

Baby [Beniamin] is using extremely strange expressions in Russian (for example, *nevozmozhno* instead of *nel'zia* for "it is forbidden").

Just now a stormy scene with Ksiutka occurred. She showed me the display from her supplier Lur'e. And when I chose a Mora Stande, without asking about its price, she told me that his price is high. I asked whether she was paying with her own money or using Mama's account, she declared that she was paying herself (but that in fact was not true).

89. Isai Solomonovich Gal'bershtadt (1842–92) a lawyer and graduate of the juridical faculty of Moscow University (1864). He collaborated with Osip Rabinovich on the first Russian-language Jewish periodical, *Rassvet*. He served in the archives of the Ministry of Justice and the Moscow Department of the Senate. As a lawyer, he helped Jews who were expelled from Moscow in 1891.
90. This exhibition hall, located next to the Kremlin and Alexandrov Garden, was constructed in 1817 to mark the fifth anniversary of the War of 1812. At the time of Zinaida's visit it was the site of a polytechnical exhibition.

During the [intervening] time I did not see, hear, or learn of anything particularly interesting. In a few days the Rozenbergs are coming from Petersburg. For a long time they were guests at Baron Gintsburg's. They say that Aleksandr [Gintsburg] is still wearing his officer's uniform and is not thinking about a trip abroad. Poor Anna Warburg: she is apparently very interested in him, but he keeps putting everything off.

In our family everything is fine, but not quite with Uncle Samuil: Kotia has come down with typhoid.

We went to the Danitskii girls, but were told that they were out (a horse, however, was standing at the entrance). N. Danilov was a guest today. On Saturday we went to their house for a ball and danced a lot (almost three and half hours). If it were not for our schedule the next day and evening, we would have stayed for the mazurka.

There was no reason to feel sorry that we left early: others also began to leave then as well. There was a buffet dinner, but with an extraordinarily large sturgeon.

Il'ia came to the defense of the horses today: they had wanted to harness them to the barouche after lunch, but listened to him.

Iosef Landau has an heir, who was born in the last few days.[91] I learned about this indirectly. Ksiutka told Papa, but I heard this from Raechka [Raia] so I cannot vouch for its veracity. It would in any case be better to give birth to a boy than a girl (all the more since, thank God, they already have a girl).

Fania invited Masha to accompany her to visit the Dubel't family.[92] Masha was so happy that she nearly went through the ceiling. It is important to give her a diversion: if we do travel abroad [without her], she will probably be sour.

There is nothing to write about myself. Uncle reports that the weather in Paris is very changeable. Therefore we shall not go there in any case; most likely, we shall again put off the trip until the summer. It is really just Mama who wants to heed Grigorii A. Zakhar'in's advice that we go to West-Baden [Baden-Baden]. Initially I thought that we will not go, but now the wind has begun to blow in another direction. Papa has said directly that he will go during Holy Week, immediately after Passover.

91. George Iosefovich Landau (b. 1885) later married Lina Levi, of Florence, Italy.
92. This family presumably derived from the Baltic noble clan of the same name, whose members had been in Russian state (especially military) service since the eighteenth century.

Antokol'skii submitted a proposal for a monument in honor of the [late] sovereign, Alexander II. Apparently, the proposal was in principle accepted.

I made some visits today. We were at Mrs. Zakhar'ina's, and in the evening we will go to the Spechinskii's. Liza Danilova was here. The weather is constantly fresh, and the Moscow River is flowing. Tomorrow we shall have a lot of guests, and we shall apparently have dancing. Uncle, Aunt, together with Zina [de Hirsch] and her husband, have gone to Petersburg; this will be the second time since their wedding.

On Tuesday there was a performance at the Conservatory. They performed some passages from the opera of R. Rubini.[93] Nothing else special now is being planned.

MOSCOW, 8 APRIL 1885

I do not know why I was terribly on edge today and in a bad mood. Perhaps because of yesterday evening spent at a performance of the Meininger company.[94] I just now gave Raechka the task of finding the journal *Grazhdanin*.[95] It has the interesting diary of Ol'ga Alekseevna.[96] But she did not find it in my room, so I'll have to look for it myself. O[l'ga] Novikova, the writer,[97] was a guest at Mrs. Chertova's yesterday at the same time that we were there. [Prime] Minister Gladstone[98] wrote her that we shall not have a war.

Our travel abroad has become very bogged down, and all our (more precisely, Mama's and Papa's) intentions are coming to an end. If it were really necessary, that would be a different matter. But, thank God, that is not the case.

Today the youngest children went to view the plan by M[ark] M. Antokol'skii for a monument. There are still some others that have been exhibited at the competition.

---

93. No information could be found about R. Rubini.

94. The reference is to the Meininger Theater, a German theater in the Saxon city of Meininger. In 1885 and 1890, the company toured Russia, where it had great success.

95. An archconservative weekly, a vigorous advocate of government policies, and a recipient of state subsidies, *Grazhdanin* at this point was edited by Prince Vladimir P. Meshcherskii (1839–1914), a close confidant of Alexander III.

96. Presumably Ol'ga Alekseevna Novikova (see the next note).

97. Ol'ga Alekseevna Novikova (1840–1925) came from the Kireev family, which included Aleksandr Alekseevich Kireev (1833–1910), who had close ties to conservative Petersburg circles (including Konstantin P. Pobedonostsev).

98. William E. Gladstone (1809–98) was then completing the second of his four terms as British prime minister.

Yesterday evening M[ikhail] N. Katkov came to see us while we were at the theater. I did not like Franz Mauer in Schiller's *The Robbers*. They want to think that the Antokol'skii proposal has been accepted, but it probably will be decided only after approval at the highest levels. An entire council has been assembled for this purpose; among others, it includes the respected director and Ananov.

In a month Mishen'ka has exams. If he is successful, he will become a [university] student in the fall. One cannot say that he has great abilities, but he does meet the requirements.

MOSCOW, 9 APRIL 1885

They have all gone to the Malyi Theater, which is presenting the play, *The Ruble*.[99] Ksiutka arranged everything, but did not ask my opinion. Therefore I declined the pleasure of going with them. At breakfast she asked whether the horses had been sent for.

Rozenberg and his wife came today and purportedly were here but did not find Mama and Papa at home. Apparently, someone else came with them: I heard the phrase "with an additional person."

Aunt Sonia came by for me today so that we could take a walk together. She was on the avenue and sent Ustin'ia; the latter then took a stroll with Lizonka, not together with us, but separately.

Family discord is unpleasant, but what can I do when Mama forgets that I am already an adult? Although I often try to overcome pride, I do not always succeed in doing so—as was the case today. This year seems like a whole century to me. Never have I been so morally tormented.

In a month it will be summer, but nothing has been done to calm me down. May the prescription of G[rigorii] A. Zakhar'in (take some fresh air to calm my soul) not come to pass. The antics of my younger sister often cause me leg cramps and similar ailments. The adage that "a pike lives in the lake to keep all the fish awake" is quite apropos for our situation and for my hypochondriac temperament. Shall I travel to Samara for koumiss or to Franzensbad —that is the question that interests me now. If we go: paradise is wherever it is nice for us. Thus it is impossible to say that it will be more enjoyable to be abroad.

Iulii Gol'denbakh was here yesterday with a cane and complained of an ailment that kept him from going out. I completely believe him; he has lost a lot of weight and appeared to be utterly enervated—so much has he changed. I

99. A drama written by Aleksandr F. Fedotov (1841–95), a prominent actor and director.

do not like the Fekla in Schiller's *Kolomine* [Wallenstein];[100] she has only one striking trait—performing a duty. But Max is a truly chivalrous character. It is no accident that Mania Mein likes him.

I do not have anything else to write today. I do not feel well, and I am not in good spirits. It is always necessary to accept things as they are.

MOSCOW, 16 APRIL 1885

I heard that Malkiel' will come to our house. Aleksandr Gintsburg was here with his uncle. He is a big man—and a big fool. On Sunday he left for Hamburg.

G[rigorii] A. Zakhar'in was here yesterday. He stayed for a long time and asked a lot of questions. Naturally, if a medicine helps, there is no need for another. He canceled the iron for me, but ordered that the arsenic be continued.

The trip abroad has already been canceled. Apparently they will not be going to the Crimea either.

I. Fridman was at the consulate today. F[ranz von] Sponer has apparently gone to Paris. Love is not a potato, [you cannot just throw it out the window], and it is true that Mel'd Kheiuzei made a major contribution to having him leave with her.

MOSCOW, 22 APRIL 1885

Iu[lii] Gol'denbakh came to breakfast yesterday and said that measles has appeared in Moscow, but much weaker than usual. That is why he said: if someone is fated to catch it, then better to do it now.

The children (the boys) say that a lot of people are sick with measles at the Lycée clinic. Only yesterday, at dinner, Il'ia had red eyes and a severe head cold. It is a pity that this turned out to be measles and, most surprising of all, for a second time. His exams begin in a month, but he will not be released earlier than six weeks. At the Lycée he is called "Don Quixote," to which is added: "the knight."

Georgii Khes [Hess] is complaining to all the doctors about a heart problem, but Professor Zakhar'in, they say, found that he has the gout. What a pity for N. Miliaev,[101] and K–ni [sic] amputated a leg in two sessions. This caused him extra suffering, since his life is in danger.

---

100. *Wallenstein* is a play set during the Thirty Years War. Wallenstein, the ambitious general of the imperial Habsburg forces, treacherously plans to bring his army over to the opposing side in exchange for recognition as the king of Bohemia, which destroys the love affair between his daughter Fekla (Thecla) and Max, the son of a lieutenant who seeks to overthrow Wallenstein.

101. Nikolai Konstantinovich Miliaev (d. 1885), served in the office that administered Empress Mariia's various charitable institutions.

In the spring we will probably not go traveling and will limit this to moving earlier to the dacha. There was no point to consulting so extensively and making plans. I also did not think about myself, but now must occupy myself with something. Papa asked me today where I prefer to go afterward: for the koumiss or to Franzensbad.

Raechka went with us last week to the opera. They presented Serov's *Uriel' Acosta*. The wife of the well-known composer staged this opera, and it was a great success.

Today I went with Papa to see Miliaev, who is near death. His gangrene has now gone higher; they say that he has no more than a day to live. Papa stayed with him for quite a long time. He is fully conscious and ordered us to bow. I waited for Papa in the carriage.

Fedotova[102] has typhoid. It is apparently now an epidemic in Petersburg. It would be good if she survives this illness, since she does not have a strong constitution. It has been almost a year since we saw her; she went abroad and was ill there.

Chebotarev, Mishenka's comrade, dedicated a short poem to me yesterday. In a jocular mood, he imitates Pushkin's poem *Upas Tree* and titled his own poem *Two Upas Trees*.[103]

Shchi and kvass are the favorite food and drink of most of the acquaintances who wrote in our album. Some inscriptions were acerbic but apt, while others were supremely stupid and spoiled the album.

Emiliia Isaakovna [Ogus-]Shaik[evich] said that I probably wrote a letter yesterday because I did not have anything else to do. Iulii Gol'denbakh wrote, promising that tomorrow, or the day after, Il'ka will get out of bed. I would be happy for him to come up here so long as he does not give me measles.

Fedotova was at the theater for the final performance of the Meininger company. Aleksei Nikolaevich Teplov came today to see Mama when Papa and I were gone. It is a misfortune when one has no traveling companions. That is why I did not go anywhere for two days, despite the orders of Professor Zakhar'in. In particular it is necessary to go out when the weather is good. But Mama takes the horses for the entire day. It would be much better if I rode in the droshky and did so every day. The countryside plan—Samara—is very

102. Glikeriia Nikolaevna Fedotova (1846–1925) was a famous Russian actress.
103. Alexander Pushkin's poem (*Anchara* [1828]) is a political allegory: it recounts how an evil, tyrannical ruler forced his subjects to risk their lives by collecting the tree's poisonous emissions (which would be smeared on the tips of arrows to make them more deadly).

much in doubt, since the Levinson family at most will spend three weeks there. If I go there, then I would stay in a koumiss-processing facility, which is not particularly pleasant.

Plans for the summer are not at all settled. It is unpleasant not to know in advance. But perhaps they will think of some way to combine *utile dulci*[104] —i.e., the pleasant with the useful—and come to see that the spas are equally useful for me.

MOSCOW, 30 APRIL 1885

They buried Miliaev yesterday. Mama and Papa were at the funeral. Dr. Golubov was here today. He described his life in Samara in detail. I hope that this trip will be useful for my health, for otherwise, I shall not go. Today Ksiutka took the horses, and I sat at home. Now the three of them have gone again to the park and then to the concert. And that is almost always the way it is.

M[ikhail] A. Boldyrev, M[ikhail] Demidov, and Kolia had lunch with us today. Mikhail Denisovich is taking Kolia to Petersburg to enroll in a cavalry school.

The squabbling at home is terribly depressing. One wants to get away from here. Lidiia Stepanovna constantly takes Ksiutka's side.

MOSCOW, 8 MAY 1885

I still have not decided whether to go to Samara for the koumiss treatment. We were on the verge of canceling this treatment when suddenly, one fine morning, Guboni[105] came to Papa. His wife is going there and will gladly take me. It all depends on how much the young Guboni likes the village that Mr. Ushakov is letting him have. It will all be decided in eight to ten days: I shall go either to that village or to Franzensbad.

Kotia [Daniil] is apparently better, although uncle has telegraphed that the fever is very tenacious.

I forgot that I am writing my journal today. I have to hurry up and finish, or otherwise I shall catch it. Nevertheless, I do not feel like giving it up, so I shall hurry and finish.

The weather is splendid—it is hot, as in the summer. I walked over to Manshen'ka Perevozchikova[106] but did not find her at home. Any day now Papa will

---

104. "The useful with the agreeable" (Latin).

105. Possibly Petr Ionovich Guboni (1825–94), a first-guild merchant and entrepreneur who came from a family of masons. He received a commission to build the stone bridges of the Moscow-Kursk railway. He also participated in the building of other railways, including the Orel-Vitebsk line.

106. Mariia Petrovna Perevozchikova (later Alekseeva; 1866–1943) was an actress with the stage name of Lilina. In 1889 she married Konstantin Stanislavskii (1863–1938), the famous director of the Moscow Art Theater.

probably go to Petersburg on some kind of business. I read Uncle's telegram inviting him to come.

Zina and James Girsh [de Hirsch] are apparently still in Petersburg and do not want to come to Moscow. Aunt Amaliia[107] sprained her foot in Warsaw. Bella was very sick, but today Uncle Iakov went to [his son] Boris in Khar'kov to meet with Auntie.[108]

MOSCOW, 13 MAY 1885

The next day, as I wrote in my journal, I fell ill—in all likelihood, with measles. I say "in all likelihood" because Vul'fius says this is simply German measles. Ksiutkia fell ill Wednesday evening, but took her dancing lesson. I think that I caught it from her. Iashka and Benjamin were ill at the same time and only today got out of bed.

They brought a riding horse to show Il'ka. He won and wants to buy himself a horse. It is called Kristall from the stables of Prince Trubetskoi, who recently married Princess Obolenskaia.

All these days we have been confined in quarantine. Today Iulii Osipovich [Gol'denbakh] allowed us to go into the other rooms. But I made little use of this permission—I only went into the drawing room.

Zina [de Hirsch] and her husband are leaving for Petersburg tomorrow. This means that they will not see Moscow. But the main thing is that Moscow will not see their cross-eyed dog, which is a permanent fixture at the old baron's side.

Papa, Mama, and Raechka went to the park, and I saw them drive past. They say that yesterday many of our acquaintances were in the park on the occasion of Whit Sunday [Pentacost]. Vladimir Obolenskii and V. Oganchevskii will ride for the prize this season. The former has evidently never raced here before, and the latter is a backup rider.

They plan to go to the dacha on Friday, but it is doubtful whether they will actually be able to do this. The opening of the handicrafts exhibition is this Thursday (instead of last Thursday), because a lot was still not ready.

The weather is superb, but they say that the people in Vienna are freezing to

107. Amaliia Poliakova (1840–1906), Iakov Solomonovich Poliakov's wife.
108. According to Iakov Poliakov's diary, Boris failed his university examinations in Khar'kov because the "nihilist Professor Ditiatin" had a penchant for persecuting "sons of well-to-do parents, in particular Jews." The professor "was dismissed for his political unreliability," but Iakov's son lost a year as a result of the failed exam and had to enroll at a university in Warsaw. Iakov's wife had joined him in Khar'kov after her injury in Warsaw. Iakov's daughter Niuta (Anna) and her husband, George, also lived in Khar'kov. See Iakov Poliakov, "Istoriia," l. 97.

death like flies. Of course, it is difficult to determine whether this is a canard or the absolute truth. In any case this news is taken from *Noie froe press* [*Neue Freie Presse*].

Papa has an invitation to attend tomorrow's opening of the Hospital of St. Ol'ga, built through contributions by a brother of Count Orlov-Davydov.[109]

I was in such a terribly nervous state today that I did not even go for a ride in the park. The weather is good, but blustery. Moreover, several times there was a drizzling rain.

Yesterday Mama did not want to hear my explanation. It all comes to this: since I do not receive good wine, I buy it with my own money, but Ksiutka also drinks it. They all were up in arms against me. There is nothing left for me to do but to starve.

SOKOL'NIKI, 5 JUNE 1885

We have been at the dacha since last week and very much regret it. It has been terribly cold every day and rarely has it been tolerable. Papa and Mama were of course in the city today, and we are here alone. Tomorrow Mishen'ka has his last exam and then a lunch the day after that. His friends are gathering in the Hermitage to celebrate the end of school.

Uncle Samuil plans to come here on Friday. He wants to consult with G[rigorii] A. Zakhar'in. Ogus-[Shaikevich] visited me today and was really obstinate. When I schedule a lesson with her, she can never do it. Masha spent all this time in town because of her fiancé. She likes I. P., but Mama does not want to agree [to the match]. Everything else is just as it was. They have decided to go to Franzensbad. Apparently, the departure is set for Sunday, 16 June. I still do not know what and how they make the decisions. Ksiutka is going with them. There is only one disagreeable thing: she is terribly spoiled.

Lidiia Stepanovna is going mad over her thinness, not obesity. She keeps telling me that I am lying. I have no idea just what the lies are. It causes other people to laugh, but makes me sad. Well, we shall soon part with her. She is pious and will travel to monasteries (even as she curses me and others).

If only it would stop raining! The foul weather at the dacha can only induce depression.

MOSCOW, 23 DECEMBER 1885

More than six months have passed since I last wrote in my journal. During this time, however, there has not been the slightest change in our way of life. We

109. The reference is to a children's hospital established by Count Sergei Orlov-Davydov (1849–1905).

spent five months abroad. Thus I was two and a half months with Mama in Paris after the treatment in Franzensbad and in Nachhut (in the Swiss mountains)[110] and made a pleasant new acquaintance. I initially did not like the Gabbe [Gubbay][111] family, but later became close to them.

In our absence Papa fell ill here; he is better now, but still not entirely himself. Upon arriving in Moscow, I came down with a cold and as a result have not left the house for about two weeks.

After yesterday's evening at the Italian opera for Van-Zandt[112] and then the dances I did not feel well. Only today did I feel like going to Zhenia Boldyreva[113] to invite her to dine with us. But because they kept Papa at home, I restricted myself to a simple ride in the sleigh—under the light of the barely flickering twinkle of the tedious streetlights of Moscow.

Everything here is somehow unique. Even the people think and talk in their own way. That is not how it is in Paris, the world's capital.

Tomorrow is Christmas Eve, and it is the name day for all the Evgenii's. Since we returned from Paris, Masha has not deigned to talk to me. But why? Uncle wrote me a letter, saying that soon she will become more respectable and cease to quarrel with me. And what do I have to do with all this?

Today at breakfast Mama said that she should go to Amsterdam to the masseur Mettgert, but meanwhile Uncle Samuil is constantly urging Papa and me to come to Nice for the health of us both. And just yesterday I received another letter from him in the same vein. Papa originally planned to go in February, but Mama's plans have left us in a cul-de-sac. But I do not regret this in the least.

MOSCOW, 24 DECEMBER 1885

Good news is always nice. Such was the case today, when they told me about the appointment of M[ikhail] Demidov to the rank of a full state councilor. Moreover, Papa received a telegram from Leon Abramovich[114] informing him that Kotia [Daniil] passed his exams brilliantly and has already left for Nice.

Papa and I went to the name-day party of E[vgeniia] Nik[olaevna] Boldyreva, the finacée of Shelkovskii. There we came upon Countess Gendrikova;[115] she

110. Zinaida may have meant to write Nax.
111. The Gubbays were an Iraqi-Jewish family from India, who married into the Sassoon family. The oldest son, Reuben Gubbay, whom Zinaida called Ruby Gabbe, would eventually marry her.
112. Marie van Zandt (1858–1919), an American opera singer, toured Russia in 1885.
113. Evgeniia Nikolaevna Shilkovskaia [née Boldyreva] (d. 1906).
114. Leon Abramovich Varshavskii, son of Abram Varshavskii and husband of Roza Samuilovna Poliakova, who died after she gave birth to Ignatii.
115. The Hendrikovs (the family of Countess Gendrikova, or Hendrikov or Hendrikoff) were closely linked to the imperial family as their ladies-in-waiting. The most famous female member of

is a very prominent woman and apparently looks down on everyone, but that does not prevent her from being very attractive. The head of the family presented her to me as their guardian angel.

Everything else is unchanged. I just cannot get around to writing a letter to Flora Gabbe [Gubbay].

MOSCOW, 25 DECEMBER [*SIC*] 1885[116]

All Orthodox Christian people celebrate Christmas today. But we belong to the Semitic family, also to the Poliakov clan, and celebrate Kotina's birthday today and my birthday tomorrow.

The year 1885 will be over in a few days, but it brought us nothing good. Thank God, however, it did not bring anything bad. One hears so many various complaints from all sides that it becomes quite dreadful. The only thing one can do is to take a philosophical view of life.

I'll write now about what happened today, since these days I accurately write down everything.

Having changed my mind about taking a stroll with Mishenka (as I had earlier planned to do), I went for a ride with Papa. Samuilchik[117] is coming tomorrow to Moscow. Since that is a holiday for me, I hope that he will stay with us and not depart directly for St. Petersburg.

At lunch, with Beniamin present, there was talk about a present for me. He says that it is not in good taste to wish happy birthday with empty hands, and I fully agree. But this is the second day of the holiday and the stores are closed, so he decided not to go to my room and to wait until I come into the dining room.

At this very same time Fridman proposed to cut Beniamin's hair in order to give him a more masculine appearance. It is good that everyone takes such a lively interest in him.

MOSCOW, 5 JANUARY 1886

Everything is just as it was—so there is nothing new under the moon, to quote a great man.[118] We greeted the year 1886 in a close family circle. On [New

---

the family was Anastasiia Gendrikova, daughter of the Grand Master of Ceremonies of the Imperial Court and a lady-in-waiting at the court of Empress Alexandra.

116. The published text evidently has an apparent typographical error, giving the date as "24 December," but the textual reference to "today" indicates that it should be 25 December.

117. Samuil Iakovlevich Poliakov, Zinaida's cousin.

118. This is taken from Nikolai Karamzin's poem, "Opytnaia Solomonova mudrost'" (1797), the first line of which is "*Nichto ne novo pod lunoiu*," drawing upon a classic Latin expression, *nil novo sub luna*.

Year's] Eve God gave us guests: Rozenberg[119] and his wife arrived from Kiev. But they did not stay long: on January 1 they only took lunch. By the way, she came in a black dress and was not in good spirits: that same day she fell on the street on the way to Ovchinnikov's shop and crashed into a pillar.

We found amusement in two albums: *Confession* and *Erkenn Dich Selbst* [Know thyself].[120]

Today N. S. Stoikov came for lunch, and he is traveling with his wife to Nice, which, they say, is an earthly paradise. Uncle Samuil very much wants us (especially Papa and me) to go there.

The weather has changed drastically: it has become warm, so there was a thaw on New Year's day. The reception at Prince V[ladimir Andreevich] Dolgorukov's was especially interesting, because all strata of society were there, representatives and deputations, who expressed congratulations on the twentieth anniversary of his governor-generalship.

Today I finally sent a letter to Flora [Gubbay], thanking her for the New Year's present. Day after day I put this off and, although I probably wasted a hundred sheets of paper, I nonetheless could not write all that I wanted to express. But my efforts ended in success. It is as though a great weight were lifted from my shoulders.

Russians have the custom of fortune-telling on the eve of Epiphany, but in my opinion it is all nonsense.

Aron Bek graduated from the university, purportedly with an excellent record and bachelor's degree in law. However, one cannot conclude much from all that: some of those who hold the bachelor's degree are stupid. At Aron's advice, Fridman went to Prince Urusov and obtained an invitation to the ball —which he very much wanted. Moreover, the invitation was hand delivered by a courier from the governor-general. They first looked for him at the building on Nikitskii Avenue, then in all of Papa's other buildings, until they finally found him at our house. He was very happy. The English officers there were very striking. One of them very clumsily fell with his partner during the waltz and dragged down others with them.

MOSCOW, 9 JANUARY 1886

Yesterday Anna Aleks[sandrovna] and N[ikolai] Ark. Boldyrev[121] celebrated the wedding of their daughter Zhenia. For the most part those present were rela-

---

119. Markovich Gessel' Rozenberg.
120. Zinaida badly transcribed *Erkenn Dich Selbst* as "Erkendikhzel'ts."
121. Nikolai Arkad'evich Boldyrev (1826–1904), governor of Riazan from 1866 to 1873.

tives, but we also were invited to St. Sergius Church on Kozitskii Street[122] and afterwards to a reception at the hotel France.[123]

Yesterday, before our departure, I received a letter from Nora Gipson in Moscow telling me that she had arrived from Berlin but had not called on me because she had caught a cold during the trip and then developed such a strong case of bronchitis that the doctor ordered her to stay at home. Deva-torskaia was also sick (typhoid). Uncle [Samuil] recently wrote Papa that he came down with a cold in Nice. If they have already had snow there, it is not surprising that it is −16 degrees here (although this is only the second day of the frigid cold—previously there was a thaw).

MOSCOW, 12 JANUARY 1886

Yesterday, at the housewarming for the young Spiridonovs, we danced until morning. There were far more gentlemen than ladies, and all were brilliant dancers. We again saw English officers there; one was a colonel, the other a captain.

Today Mama went for a ride with Papa, and then I went with Mishenka. I found that, despite the cold, the weather is wonderful. The trees are so covered with frost that they looked like snow-covered mountains. And the thick fog made it difficult even to distinguish close-up objects. Nevertheless it is wonderful to go for rides. The entertainment tomorrow is an amateur performance. Thus do we spend the evening somewhere, away from home, during the holidays.

Today Papa again talked with Mr. Sergeevich about how he should travel —with or without a leave of absence. Of course, this is just talk; it is still a long way from actually happening.

The English, and especially their striking uniforms, have captured everyone's attention. One of them is the same person who last year was in the theater box with Mania Levinson, when she came here with her father for two days and went to the German theater. We sat alongside them and assumed him to be her fiancé (I myself do not know why we did so).

I wrote a remarkable letter. I am hardly likely to receive a reply, since I completely forgot to mention this. A distinctive feature of the epistle was the red color of the paper—identical to the uniforms noted above.

122. This street in central Moscow was notable for its prominent business offices as well as St. Sergius Church (built in 1621 and demolished in 1934–35 during the Stalinist antireligious campaign).
123. The luxury hotel France, which had just opened, was located at 10 Tverskaia Boulevard. After the revolution, it was renamed Liuks (Deluxe) and used extensively by the Comintern. In the 1930s it became the main residence for German Communist refugees who had fled Nazi Germany.

Yesterday we received from Nice two small boxes of violets from Uncle. Papa offered me the right to choose first. I took the closest box and opened it—inside were rosebuds. Tomorrow we have an invitation to go riding with a troika. The number of participants is said to be about 30 people. We will gather at Spiridonovs, from there go to the Zoological Garden (where they plan to sled down the hills), and then go to Strel'na to dine and dance until 11. It will evidently be a very merry group.

Today Raechka began serious music lessons with Mrs. [Emiliia Ogus-] Shaikevich. Now she will have to prepare well for her lessons. It seems that I have a new desire to play piano with Emiliia Isaakovna [Ogus-Shaikevich]. Until now I have played only once in public and by myself, but now I especially want to distinguish myself by my artfulness.

Themis, the goddess of justice, very often shifts one cup of the scales in a particular direction. Thus today, for example, I had a great problem with the chambermaid, who has become so spoiled that it did not occur her to tidy up in advance, and she will be away tomorrow. Of course, others are involved in this maneuvering. Lidiia Stepanovna told me that I should ask Katia to stay. But I absolutely do not want to humiliate myself—despite the fact that, after she has spent six years with me, it will be difficult to adjust to someone else. I hope that this misfortune will not be so great and that I will soon find someone better than she.

It is always necessary to know how to endure the smallest difficulties, in order—insofar as possible—to be master of one's own will. Where there is an intellect, there is a will. And since I am reasonable (according to my own opinion), I want to know how to control my thoughts. And for this I shall look upon the surrounding world with a dispassion worthy of any sons of Albion (whom, by the way, I admire). Then all of life will be easy.

It is surprising that I cannot be completely cold-blooded. Whatever the case, I want to show my will and therefore I wish to appear calm and completely contented.

MOSCOW, 15 JANUARY 1886

Yesterday we went to a concert of Anton Rubinstein.[124] This pianist-giant distinguished himself in his performance of nine sonatas of L[udwig] Beethoven, and of these I very much liked the *Appasionata*. Why is there no one like him

---

124. Anton Grigorievich Rubinstein [Rubinshtein] (1829–94), world-famous pianist, composer, and conductor who founded the St. Petersburg Conservatory.

up to now? Not one of the young pianists gives great hopes for such a brilliant talent in our nineteenth century. Perhaps the lone exception is D. Albert Elzhen [Eugen d'Albert],[125] who has strongly distinguished himself and perhaps will achieve the Rubinstein heights. For now only Liszt[126] could compete with him, but after all he has renounced the world and plays only in a close circle of beautiful women.

MOSCOW, 16 JANUARY 1886

Angels, as we know, do not exist in this world. But there are imitation demons. Unfortunately, my chambermaid Katia—under the incitement of the evil spirits located in our home—has left, and that was absolutely unexpected.

Yesterday we did not go out for a picnic, since this *partie de plaisir* was somehow canceled. But in the morning of this same day we received a letter from M. M. Simashko, who expressed a thousand apologies and regrets because of the cancellation. And so we did not take the sleigh route after all. We will apparently not succeed in going to all the places where we have been invited.

Daniil [Poliakov] has already left for Petersburg from Nice and, probably, will soon inform us about his trip. If Papa decides to go there soon, then of course I will join him for a short period. However, I do not wish this. I am awaiting a response to my red letter to Flora [Gubbay]—I hope to receive it today. To judge from the lack of a response, I think that she is angry at my long silence and, for her part, wanted to demonstrate to me her own indifference.

Today Il'ka liked the food at breakfast. He usually complains (and justly so) about our gastronomy. After all, this concerns the health of each person. If someone is hungry, then of course even someone who is in ill humor is ready to eat everything. That often occurs with us. Iosef Landau, because he eats a lot, received the order of Stanislav.[127] When we were in Warsaw on the way to Moscow, I had breakfast with them. Their breakfast normally consisted of four dishes, not including sweets.

MOSCOW, 25 JANUARY 1886

Our own people (i.e., Papa and Mishenka) went to St. Petersburg for several days. However, we had a reception both yesterday evening (Friday) and today.

125. The convoluted reference here is probably to a young artist who gained international prominence in the 1880s—Eugen François Charles d'Albert (1864–1932), a Scottish-born pianist and composer in Germany.

126. Franz Liszt (1811–86), a virtuosic pianist, composer, conductor, and music teacher.

127. This is probably an ironic reference to the Order of Stanislav, awarded 1831–1917. It was the lowest-ranking medal, given virtually to all civil servants who served a lengthy term. From 1844 onward a modified medal, in black, was given to non-Christian recipients.

Incidentally, [Franz von] Sponer, Neildt, Novikova, and M[aria or Masha] Perevozchikova were here yesterday. After dinner [von] Sponer went to a ball of the nobility, while Mashenka Perevozchikova (who apparently is very much drawn to it) talked with us at length about the worldly vanities and about materialistic inclinations that dominate in it. She substantiated this story with facts from the life of a relative who had married for money and for looks. Is that really so rare? All you hear are stories like that.

I myself made a gesture of reconciliation with Lidiia Stepanovna today by going into her room. The only thing left to do now is to make up with Mama, who continues to sulk about something.

We unexpectedly received mandarins from Nice, and as usual these were locked up. The famous French novelist, Heyel [sic], has left me in raptures with his novel, which I just finished reading in French. The novel has many thoughts, which are expressed eloquently. And it ends with the triumph of religion over an individualistic nonbeliever.

I have not gone to the Symphony three consecutive Saturdays. In an hour and a half Mama and Ksiutka are going there, but I shall deny myself that pleasure: I do not wish to make my cold even worse. It is often harmful to one's health to fool around, and I once did something similar: the next day after Anton Rubinstein's concert I went out in the evening and caught a cold.

The click of the lock and the crackling from a fireplace very often frighten me. And at night I wake up from a strong pounding of the heart. Food does not provide much support, all the more since it is not nutritious, and I am becoming weaker and weaker. I myself do not know how I feel.

Edmond Rudnitskii danced the first quadrille with me again at the Spiridonovs. Mashen'ka Perevozchikova finds him similar to a pig, because he says "gm . . ."—like that very animal.

I have bad dreams. One of them last week made a strong impression on me: it was as though I were sick, and over my window, in the next house, Roza— our deceased cousin—was smiling at me.

MOSCOW, 26 JANUARY 1886

All the same, I am reading zealously and continue to write my journal.

They say that Fedotova[128] and the actress Ermolova[129] will perform together

128. Glikeriia Nikolaevna Fedotova [née Pozdniakova] (1846–1925), a famous Russian actress, was married to Aleksandr Filippovich Fedotov (see note 130). She was considered one of the best actors of the Ostrovskii Theater.
129. Mariia Nikolaevna Ermolova (1853–1928), a well-known dramatical actress of the Malyi Theater.

in the play *The Wolf*, written by Mrs. Fedotova's husband,[130] with a tendency toward the matter of the Menitskii children.[131]

Today they buried Count Gudovich,[132] who lived in our building on Nikitskaia St. He was buried in the Trinity-Sergius Lavra, and his children traveled there. Standing at the window, I saw how the funeral procession passed along the other side of Tverskoi Boulevard. Only the deceased's children were there. Thus, in a flash, does the physical life end.

I received a note from A. Andr[eevich] Devartovskii in response to my own. It is said that one can catch typhoid even this way, but I am not afraid.

MOSCOW, 30 JANUARY 1886.
We arrive punctually at the Rubinshtein concerts, which give me a strong sense of the Schumann[133] mood.

Every day we have guests: G[essel] Rozenberg and his wife, and L[azar] Izr[ailevich] Brodskii[134] with his male cousin. The latter is not attractive: he wrote yesterday in my album, and I found him more stupid than I previously thought. First, although he is Russian, he does not know how to speak Russian. Second, despite the fact that he has a law degree, he cannot answer the simple questions posed in my booklet. I invite all young people to write in it.

Dr. Gol'denbakh was in a particularly good mood today and sent me out to go riding. But for a long time I did not know how best to organize this. I did not have anyone to go with, since Raechka went with Miss Gosh to Moura. In the end, however, I went in the pleasant company of Lidiia Stepanovna.

For some reason it seemed to me that I will receive a letter today from Paris. And I was slightly surprised when Papa received a response from [Rachel] Gabbe [Gubbay]. She did not write anything special: she thanks him for the kind invitation to come to Russia, but regrets that they cannot accept, on the grounds that they are now leaving and will be receiving [guests at her salon] in Paris.[135]

---

130. Aleksandr Filippovich Fedotov (1841–95) was a prominent Russian actor, director of the Moscow branch of imperial theaters, and playright. The play is reprinted in A. F. Fedotov, *Polnoe sobranie dramaticheskikh sochinenii* (Moscow: Tipografiia D. A. Bonch-Bruevicha, 1890), 1:263–362.
131. Possibly a reference to the opera by Aleksandr Onisimovich Ablesimov (1742–83), *Mel'nik, koldun, obmanshchik i svat* (Moscow, 1782) that figured in Fedotov's work.
132. Vasilii Vasil'ievich Gudovich (d. 1886).
133. Robert Schumann (1810–56).
134. Lazar Izrailevich Brodskii (1848–1904), a prominent entrepreneur in the family's sugar businesss in Kiev. See the memoirs of Alexandra Fanny Brodsky, *Smoke Signals: From Eminence to Exiile* (London: I. B. Tauris, 1997).
135. Rachel Gubbay, Reuben's mother, had a salon at their home on Boulevard Malesherbes in Paris.

Papa again had a headache and has still not fully recovered. [Dr.] Zakhar'in prescribed cinchona[136] for him.

We are finally free of tiresome guests, who did send us a bouquet today as a reward. Truth be told, the bouquet was of such monstrous proportions that a person could easily fit into the box in which it was delivered.

I went with Mama for the first time since the season for visits resumed. By the way, we were at Countess Brevern de Lagarde[137] and learned that yesterday evening her older daughter fell and injured her leg (kneecap) and chin. It was so serious that the doctor ordered her to stay in bed for three days.

The weather has changed very quickly from a thaw into frost and also become rather windy.

After riding in the sleigh, I came inside with a red nose and ears—which is not especially attractive. And I think that one should make visits in a carriage.

Brevern de Lagarde (along with the Zakhar'in family and the young ladies of the Donetskii family) will apparently come to our soirée next Friday. And what will we do about young men? Mama does not want us to be in the world of Mariia Pavlovna Spiridonova, so we will not have an opportunity to invite them. Nevertheless, a large group will assemble this time.

I can now read L[eo] Tolstoy's novel, *War and Peace* with a clear conscience. I have an original edition with the French phrases. I intend to acquire all his works.

In the coming days I expect a letter from Flora Gabbe [Gubbay] in Paris. She has forgotten me, but I remember her very well and am unable to understand why she has not written in such a long time.

Today I spent the entire day pleasantly, listening to students in the conservatory. Where else is it possible to see so well and to hear an opinion about the performance of these future maestros if not in the institution of Rubinstein's late brother?[138] It must be said that they are all rather weak, with a few minor

---

136. Cinchona (*khina*), or China bark, is the dried bark of the cinchona tree; it is the source of quinine and other medicinal alkaloids.

137. Maria Aleksandrovna Boeikova Brevern de Largarde [Lagardi] was the wife of Count Aleksandr Ivanovich Brevern de Lagarde [Lagardi] (1814–90), a member of the State Council, a lieutenant general, and commander of the Moscow district in 1879–88.

138. Anton Grigor'evich Rubinstein's (1829–94) brother Nikolai Grigor'evich (1835–81)—"the late brother"—was cofounder of the Moscow Conservatory (along with Nikolai P. Trubetskoi).

exceptions—for example, Koreshchenko, who very successfully performed variations on the Händel piece for violin that was suddenly placed before him and sung to him by Anton Grigor'evich [Rubinstein]. The latter was quite satisfied and said that this youth has talent.

A telegram from Kotia [Daniil] came today, expressing his regret that Papa and Misha did not wait for him in Petersburg.

MOSCOW, 5 FEBRUARY 1886

I did not write in this book yesterday because I went to the Rubinstein concert in the evening. The enchanting sounds of his powerful genius were resounding somewhere far away. And when he played, I thought that this was not his fingers striking the keys, but that he has wings, fluttering in the air.

Today I went on visits with Mama, and we were at the [homes of] Vanssherpentsel'pkhin [Wanscherpenzel'pchin], Princess Sofiia, Petr Dolg[orukov],[139] and Fon Derviz, but did not find them at home. Therefore I shall speak with them by telephone and invite them to come Friday to dance. But there are not enough young men: last Friday there were too few of them. S. Fon Derviz[140] is married to a poor girl, who always goes with him to concerts.

Mishenko surprised me yesterday: despite an unoccupied seat [in our box], he sat in the seventeenth row. One has to find a middle ground between luxury and modesty, but this is too exaggerated, even ludicrous. After all, self-abasement is more than pride.

Papa thought of going with me to Nice, but the dull ones are interfering. Namely: since Mama announced to me from abroad that she will never travel with me, I cannot lower myself to the point of causing her this displeasure. I am therefore declining to go, but then Papa will not go either.

MOSCOW, 6 FEBRUARY 1886

The Gonetskiis have a reception on Thursday. Earlier we thought of visiting them today, but since they will be here tomorrow, we have put this off until next Thursday (to avoid being together a bit too often).

Papa went out today for the first time since returning from St. Petersburg (where he spent just two days with Mishenka), as he had promised us. Tomorrow it will be exhausting for him to sit until late, and moreover they will play cards and smoke in his office, which makes the air in that room unbearable.

139. Prince Petr Dmitrievich Dolgorukov (1866–1927), a political figure and later one of the leaders of the Constitutional Democratic Party.
140. This is probably a reference to Sergei Pavlovich Fon Derviz (1863–1943), who graduated from the Moscow Conservatory and was later an honorary member of the Imperial Russian Musical Society.

Infrequent gatherings are still more onerous. I bought ribbons and other things (for example, nuts with surprises) for the cotillion. The local toy stores have absolutely nothing luxurious and new for the cotillion.

Mama went to ride in the park but did not find it cold. But it seemed like a severe frost to me so I donned a hood, something that I only do in exceptional circumstances—when it is very cold.

They told G. Azanchevskii, the horseman, to come to us tomorrow morning to dance. For some reason he wore a student's uniform, not a suit (as is normally done in the afternoon). And he was with Papa on some kind of business. Papa set a time for an audience tomorrow. They must have invited his brother as well.

We had barely returned from our wandering when we saw A. Al. He came to skate with Masha Danilova on our pond. That was the designated rendezvous. Then, having seen the funeral coachman and footman, we asked who is here; we were told that it is the widow, Countess Uvarov. It turned out that she did not need anything but simply came to visit Mama. They say that she was very nice. And should she not be?

Zhukovskii,[141] an employee in the credit chancellery in St. Petersburg, is marrying the daughter of A. Zelenbakhov, whose oldest daughter also lives in Petersburg and is married to the young Spiridonov. Today they sent us an invitation to the wedding, which will take place on the 9th of this month. Uncle is asking, by telegraph, when we will arrive. It is still unknown, actually, whether we shall go at all. I have to stop now; as it is, I have written utter rubbish and I am tired.

MOSCOW, 9 FEBRUARY 1886

Today passed quickly, for I spent a whole two hours at a quartet concert. Especially successful was the vocal section of Schumann with the lyrics of Chamisso (my favorite poem).[142] But in my opinion Mrs. Miller-Svetlovskaia did not sing them poetically enough.

Yesterday I took up *I des deb*[143] and the first thing that caught my eye was

141. Iulii Galaktionovich Zhukovskii (1833–1907) was a privy councilor, economist, publicist, manager of the State Bank (1889), member of the Council of the Ministry of Finance (1894), and senator (1901). See Witte, *Iz arkhiva S. Iu. Vitte*, 1:281, 298, 323, and 325 and 2:590.

142. *Frauenliebe und -leben* (A woman's love and life) is an 1830 cycle of poems by Adelbert von Chamisso (1781–1838), a German poet and writer. The work describes a woman's love for a man from their first meeting through marriage to his death. Schumann's version (opus 42) became the most widely known.

143. This garbled title evidently refers to a German periodical on debutantes.

the announcement of the engagement of Evelyn Kann[144] with Reinach.[145] Her fiancé is a lawyer and, as Mama and Papa later told me, very wealthy.

Yesterday I had the pleasure of hosting N[ora] Gipson.[146] In the evening F[ranz] Sponer and Baron Vrangel' stayed for dinner. And during the lesson, we danced!

MOSCOW, 10 FEBRUARY 1886

Artists and admirers of A[nton] G. Rubinstein today honored him at the Bolshoi Theater. It was very festive and interesting. The theater was illuminated by E. Koorno; despite the fact that it was daytime, the hall was completely full. Having returned home, I began to cut the [bound] pages of [Leo Tolstoy's] *Complete Collection of Works* given to me by Countess Tolstoy. In fact Naumenko had sent me *War and Peace*, but I wanted to have all of Count Tolstoy's works in their original form, but in the last edition. Mr. Uvarov wrote her on my behalf.

It is even strange to think that G[rigorii] Zakhar'in is giving a ball. If it were not for the printed invitation, one might think that it is just an evening dance. It is a pity, however, that there is a European concert the very same evening. Tomorrow is the penultimate concert by Rubinstein and Surel' de Chopin—which should be entrancing (as evidenced by the fact that all the tickets have been sold). One sometimes wants to rest from the worldly bustle but, as if on purpose, this is precisely the time when one must go out the most.

Joseph Sassoon[147] and his small family are in Petersburg. When we are there, I will tell him that I read his *Profession de foi*.[148] People can be stupid, clumsy, and ridiculous, but he combines all three shortcomings in an unusually successful way.

MOSCOW, 12 FEBRUARY 1886

The balls end in a week, and then a magnificent season begins. Yesterday there was again the penultimate Rubinstein concert, but today we will rest from the daily round of evening trips.

Mr. [George Daniel] von Weisweiller is here now. Kotia highly recommended

---

144. [Charlotte Marie] Evelina Kann (1863–89) was the daughter of Isaac Eduard Hirsch Kann and Henrietta Kann.

145. Theodore Reinach (1860–1928) was an archeologist, laywer, and later an advocate for Captain Alfred Dreyfus. For their engagement, see *L'Universe Israélite*, 1 February 1886.

146. Nora Gipson, Klindworth's assistant.

147. The husband of Luiza Gintsburg.

148. As an example of Zinaida's awkward transliteration, *profession de foi* appears as "profes'en defo."

him to us, and Papa therefore wants to receive him with the customary Russian cordiality and hospitality. It turns out that he is a widower and has a thirteen-year-old daughter, the niece of Sulzbach[149] of Frankfurt-am-Main—whom Papa has included in the list of [potential] fiancées for Mishenka. It is even known that this man—already a widower—was a [potential] fiancé for Zina. Egor or Iurii (that is the same as Georgii)—but they explained to me long ago that the last form was not used under Ivan the Terrible. The life of that epoch does not have the current character, and therefore the historical novel of Nina Germet is regarded as too weak to be published. Her work lacks eloquence, and one even finds mistakes in the choice of appropriate adjectives.

For my birthday, Il'iusha is offering to give me a beautiful old edition with prints from the galleries of Florence and Orléans.

Mama is inviting François de [Franz von] Sponer to come. It is superfluous to add that this, in my opinion, is not quite appropriate. Mama did not even know that he has already come once to skate; I did not come out to him. But today they called me twice, since he came to apologize that he cannot go riding. He is going to E[katerina] Zakhar'ina[150] for a visit before the ball (having received an invitation at the Pushkins).

Papa is also planning to go there (that is, to G[rigorii] A. Zakhar'in). There will be a daytime ball at the Nobility's Assembly, which will be to his detriment, since those of his acquaintances there will be too tired to go to him.

MOSCOW, 23 FEBRUARY 1886
This was the day of the Zakhar'in ball. I did not feel well and could not dance the mazurka. Grigorii Antonovich [Zakhar'in] was very attentive to me and even left all his guests to occupy himself with my "treatment," as he put it. The daytime ball at the Dolgorukovs was not today, but instead there was an evening ball on Thursday; I practically did not dance at all for fear that my dizziness—to which I am apparently subject—might recur. Moreover, there were not enough young men. Only this evening remains, and then the theater and the amusements will end.

It is a pity that Baron Leopold Koch has died. I learned this from the newspapers. We all have to die. Mr. Messarosh is in poor health.

149. Sophie von Weisweiller [née Sulzbach]. She had two daughters: Marie Jean Kohn (b. 1872), who was the mother of Armand Kohn (a close friend of Zinaida's during World War II), and Mathilde Sophie Henrietta de Rothschild (1874–1926).
150. Ekaterina Petrovna Zakhar'ina (née Apukhina), daughter of a landowner in Orlov province and wife of Grigorii Antonovich Zakhar'in.

MOSCOW, 24 FEBRUARY 1886

They say that the synagogue will open next Friday.[151] Grandfather [Solomon] and Grandmother [Breine] are coming from Orsha the day after tomorrow specifically for this occasion and will stay at an apartment that has been prepared for them. If Kotia [Daniil] and Leon Abramovich [Varshavskii] also come, then at least that will improve our usual life somewhat—which has been a little interrupted by the appearance of von Weisweiller in our drawing rooms. He assumed that the opening of the synagogue occurred last Friday and sent a telegram. They were waiting for some kind of festive occasion, but in the end did not wait.

It is noteworthy that Uncle Iakov is now in Warsaw and thus did not travel to Paris, where I have developed a new friendship with the Gabbe [Gubbay] family.

Joseph Sassoon is still in Petersburg (in the words of G. G. Shul'ts of Odessa); the plenipotentiary and partner of the banker Maas,[152] having returned from there, were today at our house. Apparently, G. [von] Weisweiller is very much enamored with one of his daughters and left there earlier than expected, only to avoid being obligated to keep his word to travel to Odessa. They are apparently good people, but very plain in my opinion, since they are remarkably similar to the Riga German men and women selling wool kerchiefs and small cartons made of small, glued pieces. The mother is particularly similar to this.

MOSCOW, 25 FEBRUARY 1886

The theme assigned to me two years ago—to write verse about the onset of spring—has now been prepared. And it was very easy to do, since this is entirely a matter of imagination and poetic inspiration at the given moment. Life is so full of various impressions that it is sometimes pleasant to make a small reflection of them or simply to imagine them.

The Onset of Spring
The beauty of spring is gleaming around me,
Young life is playing, voices are more resounding.
The last snow is already melting, in the sun glistening.
The land is fragrant, and brighter than daybreak.
The lark is flying, the forest is already filled with noise.
All of nature is prophesying that spring is already here.
The sky is transparent, clear, drawing to itself.
Everything in the world is wonderful and brings us happiness.

151. A reference to the private Poliakov synagogue on Bronnaia Street that opened in 1886.
152. Baron Ernst Maas [Mahs] (1807–79) established the family firm Mahs and Co. in Odessa.

Earlier I wrote "The Dnepr," a poetic rendering of Gogol's *Dnepr*.[153] G. Babin is here from St. Petersburg and dined with us today. Sonia Meis married his cousin, the young Grinevich, a month ago.

James Girsch [de Hirsch]—Papa told Misha—sent a telegram about the tenders scheduled for 4 April for Moscow's water supply. This apparently interests him, and he would like to participate in this undertaking and even asked Papa to provide detailed information.

Lidiia Stepanovna evidently had a fight with Katia about the new order for a dress. I heard the voice of the tailors from Minangua[154] and do not know what it was about, but I presume that it concerned some secret for the reception at Countess Brevern de Lagarde. We have an invitation for 4 March. In the next days our grandfathers [Poliakov and Vydrin] from Orsha and Orel are expected in Moscow. They will, of course, come with the greatest joy to celebrate the dedication of the synagogue.

Papa again is quite weak, and the old order of life has resumed. Rarely does a brilliant meteor flash by, forcing one for a time to sink into reverie and fall asleep, as one poet expressed it.[155]

MOSCOW, 26 FEBRUARY 1886

Grandfather and Grandmother had hardly entered the apartment before we set off for the choir rehearsal at the synagogue. Waiting for the reception are about 100 invited guests—consisting exclusively of representatives from the Moscow Jewish community and its entire intellectual component. The only thing to note is that the newly created choir does not sing well and therefore individual voices sometimes ring through—as for example, that of a boy with a very strong soprano, who reaches high notes no worse than Kochetova.[156] The cantor Maten'ko[157] is similar to a priest in his broad black cassock. And the boys are all dressed in black as well.

Georgii Essel', the former manager of the bank, will probably be invited too. Except for the architect Chichagov[158] and servants, there will not be any non-Jews.

153. Gogol's passage on "Dnepr" appeared in his short story "A Terrible Vengeance," which is part of his well-known collection *Evenings on a Farm Near Dikanka* (first published in 1831–32).
154. A clothing firm located at Kuznetskii Most in downtown Moscow.
155. Probably a reference to Mikhail Lermontov's 1843 poem "I Am Going on the Road Alone."
156. The reference here could be to either Aleksandra D. Aleksandrova-Kochetova (1833–1902) or her daughter Zoia R. Kochetova (1857–92), both of whom were soprano opera singers who lived in Moscow.
157. Nahum Maten'ko was the cantor of the Poliakov synagogue. He attended the Moscow Conservatory.
158. Dmitrii Nikolaevich Chichagov (1835–94), a prominent Moscow architect.

It is a pity that no foreigners are at the opening of the synagogue. This means that everything will be simple and modest, as is required. The authorities will be invited at some other time on an appropriate occasion.

Il'iusha expresses sharp criticism of the architectural shortcomings of the new house of worship and is even excessive in his abuse of its builder, Chichagov. However, the latter is really not qualified to design a Jewish synagogue: he himself is [Russian] Orthodox and has hardly seen such buildings.

Giun goes horseback riding twice a week. Hence he is afraid, and in general he is a big coward.

Leopold Popper[159] was buried at the castle Naziu on his estate in Hungary. They have a family crypt there.

Mama let [me] write to M-m. Ermansderherst to have the Italian woman she recommended come to us tomorrow evening to play the harp. I hope that it will be pleasurable to listen to her; otherwise, to tell the truth, this instrument is monotonic and boring. I heard from them about the illness of Mme. Polina [Pauline] Ermansderherst, since Misha did not convey anything of what she had ordered him to say on the phone. Namely, that she cannot give lessons today because of her illness, but should come for my lesson tomorrow at 2 pm. But that probably will not come to pass.

Papa asked that he be given an account—written out in all its splendor—of all his relatives and wives, and husbands, but with the children listed separately. It is amusing to read that a daughter (or, more likely, a daughter-in-law) is a born marchioness.[160]

MOSCOW, 1 MARCH 1886

The opening of the synagogue had a remarkable impact. Especially that moment when both grandfathers, Papa, Misha, [Efim] Epshtein, the rabbi, and some other elderly man carried the Torah. And Misha was in his uniform with the sword, giving a unique quality to the entire ceremony—which, even without that, was very original.

Iosef and Bella did not delay [the arrival of] Uncle [Iakov], Aunt [Amaliia], and Niuta, whom we expected any day in Moscow. They are already in Petersburg and, most likely, will leave tomorrow evening to see Grandfather, Grandmother, and us. But they do not get along with Mama.

159. Perhaps Leopold Popper [von Podhragy] (1826–86).
160. This list was probably for his petition for hereditary nobility, which required certificates of births of all the family members.

When we returned in the evening from the house of worship, it was already seven o'clock. We had barely stood up from the table when people arrived for tea—Nechaev, Baron Vrangel, Balliutin, N. S. Gol'denberg, and the Chiarkone family. We were delighted with their performance on the harp and hope to hear them again next Friday.

We have an invitation for Tuesday evening. It reads as follows: "Count and Countess Brevern de Lagarde most humbly ask that you come on Tuesday evening, 8 March, at 9 pm." I think that after the music part there will be dancing —despite the Lenten fast. Therefore one should be dressed décolleté. But I am happy to say that it does not have to be a tulle dress. I simply do not have such, but there is a blue silk dress, very beautiful, from the famous Worth. Of course I shall use this occasion to wear the dress.

Today we had several people visit, some for the first time: Mme. Daragan, Bogoliubov (a member of the appellate court),[161] and Mr. Bezobrazov. Also present was S[of'ia] Fr[ansevna] Podg[oretskaia] wearing a leather coat and jersey. Her son is skating. It is amazing how she has become so thin and changed this season; her figure has really become like that of a sylph. As Papa says, the only thing left to do is to change the head—i.e., the face with the sagging wrinkles. How good it would be if everyone knew how to touch up their appearance as well as she does. After all, many take her for a young woman; only those who know how she looked earlier are surprised by this sudden metamorphosis.

MOSCOW, 3 MARCH 1886

Thus Uncle [Iakov], Aunt [Amaliia], and Niuta stayed here for a day at the hotel Dresden.[162] According to them, James received an inheritance of 750,000 francs from the late baron Joseph de Hirsch, his father, who had lived in Planegg.

Khaia and Niuta went to Grandmother, but I stayed the entire day at home. I did not go out either yesterday or today. Only in the evening did I go to the theater of Korsh[163] and watch the Shakespeare tragedy *Hamlet* (with the famous Barnai[164] in the lead role). No one plays this part better than the artist Possart.[165] Mama arrived in the middle of the performance and soon went

---

161. Possibly Victor Alekseevich Bogoliubov, who eventually served in the Ministry of Justice.
162. A fashionable hotel on Tverskoi Boulevard in central Moscow.
163. The Russian Dramatic Theatre was the creation of Fyodor A. Korsh and operated from 1882 to 1933.
164. Liudvig Barnai [Ludwig Barnay] (1842–1924) was a German actor and, in the 1880s, a member of the Meininger theatrical company.
165. Ernst von Possart (1841–1921), a German actor.

home. But Miss Gosh and I stayed until the end of the performance and were very satisfied.

Niuta very much likes [Bella's husband] Iosef Vil'gel'movich Landau.

Khaia somehow caught a chill and yesterday thought that she would not be able to go to the reception at Count Brevern de Lagarde's. Only in the evening did this pass, as the doctor kept her home for several days for fear that the cold might lead to complications. Today I went with Mama to visit the Zakhar'ins and N[adezhda] Trubetskaia (who is going tomorrow to St. Petersburg for the anniversary of General Gedeonov[166] and very much regrets that our family is not going). Mama, apparently, also regrets this. One must conclude that she is more interested in this kind of festivity than in her own family.

There is nothing special to report about yesterday evening. Except for one thing: they were very attentive toward us.

Next week Papa is planning to go to St. Petersburg and of course will go with Mama. It is rare that I accompany him. Such belongs to a remote happy past, when (as the popular tale has it) "the mushrooms fought under Tsar Pea."

It is very cold today. I was afraid that I might get frostbite on my ears, since I went for the ride without a scarf. But I smeared on glycerin and apparently it will be all right; however, Sasha did get frostbite on his ear, and they are putting some kind of compresses on him (three cloths with some ointment). He also had a temperature of 40° C [104° F].

They will play the harp for us on Friday. I feel terribly sorry for the Italians (more precisely, the Italian women).

Khaia went to Mama to find out who else should be invited for tomorrow evening. It would be wrong to invite a large public if one wants to hear the playing of the artists and the little Levin.[167]

Mama and I went today to von Sherentsel' Khin, Countess Brevern de Lagarde, S. Shaikevich,[168] and Madame Mafern. I invited a few people for

---

166. General Ivan Mikhalovich Gedeonov (1816–1907) was a Russian military and state public figure.

167. Iosif Arkad'eivch Levin [Joseph Lhévinne] (1874–1944), a pianist, was a student at the Moscow Conservatory and later had a brilliant career, first in Russia and later in Berlin (1907) and New York (1919), where he joined the faculty of the Juilliard School of Music. He made his debut with his performance of Beethoven's "Emperor Concerto" with an orchestra conducted by none other than Anton Rubenstein. Zinaida met him before he became famous.

168. Samuil Solomonovich Shaikevich (1842–1908), a Moscow lawyer.

tomorrow, and Shaikevich for Saturday and Sunday. It is necessary to divide society according to classes and various strata. However, I think that a fair number of people will come tomorrow.

Papa plans to go to St. Petersburg on Tuesday, but it is still not known who will accompany him. Today Raia strongly praised my visiting attire. She especially likes the matching dress and hat. It would be a wonderful dress if it were better draped ([that is,] the skirt, but it is too fluffy),

The theater and concerts no longer appeal to me, for I fear that the Zakhar'in story might recur with me.

Grandfather Solomon Lazarevich [Poliakov] is sitting here with us now, but Papa will have a meeting of the Jewish Committee.[169] Filipp Rozental' and his wife attended the performance of *Hamlet*. Although he converted for her sake, she is apparently not worth it.

It has been ages since I last saw Lelia Messarosh.[170] She is very upset by her father's illness. According to the oracle Iulii Osipovich [Golden'bakh], he should be joining his forebears shortly. Such predictions, made in jest, are at the very least inappropriate, if not malicious.

Shchukin[171] is now the complete master at the former home of Princess N[adezhda] Bor. Trubetskaia,[172] and to this day she is still living there.

Today we are going to the anniversary in the company of the Spiridonov family and K[arl] Iul['evich] Davydov. The celebration must be unpleasant to the person being honored—given his extremely advanced age.

MOSCOW, 8 MARCH 1886

We did not observe Purim pleasantly. I need to think of something to bolster and strengthen my weak nerves so that some nasty story not ensue. I shall not

169. The Jewish Committee was the Supreme Commission for the Review of Existing Imperial Laws on Jews, established on 4 February 1883, eventually chaired by K. I. Pahlen (1833–1912), and closed on 24 May 1888. Comprised of high-ranking officials, the commission also included "experts" from the Jewish community as advisors, including Samuil S. Poliakov.

170. Daughter of Ivan Messarosh.

171. Sergei Ivanovich Shchukin (1854–1935) was a Moscow merchant and collector of art. He owned the house in which Nadezhda B. Trubetskaia (see the next note) was given a rented apartment for her services to the Humane Society.

172. Nadezhda Borisovna Trubetskaia (née Chetvertinskaia; 1812–1909) came from a well-known noble family whose members had fought in the Napoleonic wars. She received an excellent education at home and later audited university courses. She became a lady-in-waiting for Empress Alexandra Fedorovna (the wife of Nicholas I). In 1834, she married Prince Aleksei Ivanovich Trubetskoi (1806–55), the vice-governor of Vil'na province. Her son Aleksei had misused state funds, and she was forced to sell her immovable property, including her home. Due to her philanthropic service, the Humane Society rented an apartment for her in Shchukin's home.

expatiate about myself and my kin today; I shall only say that the nanny fell ill and apparently has pneumonia, according to the diagnosis of Dr. Gershovskii, who dined with us today. He is extremely amusing, but does not have what (according to his stories) was felt to be lacking during the war: strength.

For now there is no word on gatherings in the capital. It is rare for them to meet on time, and all those coming have been forewarned.

We had Jewish musicians three times today. They made an effort in the performance of dissonant selections.

Miss [Nora] Gipson must be an amazing housekeeper: she keeps the house so clean that there is not a speck of dust anywhere. And even the chambermaids are wearing caps with rose ribbons. In this respect, Flora [Gubbay] is similar: her room in Paris also exhibits a remarkable order and neatness—which, unfortunately, is not to be seen among any of us (and me in particular).[173] To my shame, I must confess this, and I would very much like to be similar to the English woman in this respect. At least I ought to tidy up everything—that would be enough.

Whole days pass by unnoticed for me. I am constantly occupied with reading. I am reading Tolstoy's *War and Peace*.

MOSCOW, 13 MARCH 1886

A collection of sundry works in the field of literature is rarely useful. Hence I do not want to read all the new novels that make up the inundation coming from Parisian book dealers and publishers.

Papa sent Il'iusha to [Nikolai] Boldyrev, who is ill with rheumatism and is in the former Shevaldyshev hotel.[174] He has a daughter, Mrs. [Evgeniia] Shilovskaia, who is purportedly ill as well and is not in a village but in the city of Riazan. We were at her wedding this winter, and I felt sorry for her: I did not find her husband attractive. She must have been driven by need to marry him. He could very well be a good young man, but appears to be very stupid. Thus she chose the lesser of the two evils that she faced. Nonetheless it is an evil, since this union is forever.

---

173. The Poliakovs were not known for their neatness. In fact, Alexander Poliakoff recalled in his memoirs the terrible condition in which the family left their rented apartment: "Sir Stuart Samuel, head of the Bank, used to lend them his house on Hill Street, off Berkeley Square, and I believe that he was less than pleased with the state it was left in when they left" (Alexander Poliakoff with Deborah Sacks, *The Silver Samovar: Reminiscences of the Russian Revolution* [Moscow: Atlantida Press, 1996], 23).

174. In the mid-nineteenth century this was a fashionable, elegant hotel on Tverskoi Boulevard in central Moscow, and it attracted prominent guests, including Leo Tolstoy. But later it lagged behind the luxurious, aristocratic Dresden, came under new ownership (hence Zinaida's "former Shevaldyshev"), and disappeared completely by the turn of the century.

Tomorrow the young pianist Levin-Fel'dman [Iosif Arkad'eivch Levin] will play for us again. If his auditions were not too expensive, this would really be a perfect way to diversify the program of our *jour fixe*.

Although Daragan proposed that Papa and Mama invite him, nothing will apparently come of this, because we are very indecisive in both petty and serious things—and especially with things like travel and similar undertakings. It is much easier for me to make up my mind, since I am a fatalist. A whole three weeks have passed since I last received a letter from Flora Gabbe [Gubbay]. I am now reading quite a lot, especially novels, primarily French novels.

Sherbiul'ev[175] writes very well. I have now begun to read *Le Monat* by R. G. Bonir [sic], a writer completely unknown to me. This novel is taken from the life of Parisian Jews. The stuffy upper society of this world capital finds it difficult to befriend our brethren. Herein lies the so-called high point of the story, which centers on details and a description of all the petty trivia of this life.

Food strengthens the body, reading the human mind. This axiom serves as clear proof for the following axiom: a strong mind means a weak body, a strong body a weak mind. The south develops the physical side of life, but suffocates the moral, in exchange for stimulating the sensual side. I personally feel a need for such a life so as to strengthen the body and to give a rest to thinking and the mind, which are consuming all my strength.

MOSCOW, 15 MARCH 1886

Yesterday, Zakhar'in questioned me closely about my condition. At least he told me that unpleasant sensations are a consequence of nervous perturbation and anemia, not a weak chest. Of course this is better than another cause, since, if one energetically follows a treatment, then it is possible to regain one's strength. Otherwise there is little hope and one must accept one's lot without the slightest complaint, and simply submit to one's fate.

Today we had a daytime reception. Kim and the adjutant Shamshekh were the most elegant guests. I find it amazing that a personality like Mina Abr[amovna] Malkiel' can resign herself to her lot. She has not studied philosophy and consequently does not know much.

MOSCOW 16 MARCH 1886

On Thursday Papa plans to go to St. Petersburg for several days.

The story of Le Man is not as good and engaging as *Genrikh Laube* by

---

175. Presumably this is a reference to Charles Victor Cherbuliez (1829–99), a popular contemporary French novelist.

D. Shomeruben that I read last spring. I myself do not like novels that are based on Jewish life and involve an intrigue between a Christian man and Jewish woman (or vice versa). Society is so segregated today that such stories have little verisimilitude, and the denouement of such a novel in life is too enigmatic.

Today I wrote a letter to Fania in Orel. Her husband was recently here, but I saw him only briefly. Khaia, Mama, and Raia are going to a concert this evening. A whole legion of boy and girl pupils of Kochetova[176] will be participating. There were even plans for Mel' Nazarov to perform. Because of ill health she will have to disappoint her public by her absence and be conspicuous by her absence, as a great Frenchman put it.[177] Aleksandra Dormidontova invited Khaia to participate in the choir. She is presenting a picture of her face to the teacher. Although Mama was initially opposed to this, she agreed (after Khaia insisted) to allow her to be photographed.

They have given me no orders at all to practice music. Jokes aside, it is unpleasant to be sick, if quietly as in my case.

MOSCOW, 17 MARCH 1886

Zakhar'in permitted me to go for a drive, but said that he cannot cure the problem of my nerves.

Today I received from M[ark] Antokol'skii in Paris the marble busts of Papa and Mama (but smaller than before). Only I do not know whether it is because of the size or because of the more precise finish, but these seem to resemble [my parents] more than those that were originally done. Moreover, I like this size: approximately one-third of the real size. Miniatures turn out to be more delicate.

Khaia regrets that she did not go to Nice this winter. She came to feel that way upon seeing the pictures of Aivazovskii.[178] A whole series of his sea paintings are exhibited in the Petrovskii arcade.[179] Five of them definitely merit special attention, but the main picture, "The Eruption of Vesuvius," bears absolutely no resemblance to reality. The boats in the sea, overloaded with people saving themselves from the flying sparks of the eruption, absolutely do not (in my opinion) correspond to the character of the entire picture, which already —because of its artificial illumination—does not look real and makes an impression through its sheer size more than anything else. A new method is used to portray the shields and coats of arms of knights.

176. Aleksandra Dormidontova Aleksandrova-Kochetova (1833–1902), an opera singer.
177. The French phrase is *briller par son absence*.
178. Ivan Konstantinovich Aivazovskii (1817–1900), a Russian-Armenian painter.
179. Petrovskii Passazh was a shopping arcade located on Petrovskii Street in central Moscow.

On the trip home we stopped at the window in the same arcade where these images were displayed. Edzhubov, the stockbroker, also has his bureau there, on the upper floor; the building that is hosting the exhibition is intended for a large banking house.

Iulii Osipovich [Gol'denbakh] did not apparently come to our house today. I, at least, did not see him.

I was summoned twice during the Zakhar'in visit and the second time it was recommended that I drink foul red wine.

Fedotova, an actress at the Malyi Theater, will read from the text of [Goethe's] *Faust* with the music of F. Liszt. This interesting concert of the Twelfth Symphony will be on Friday, 21 March—precisely when it is impossible for us to attend. I personally could not be there in any event, but the others will forfeit [the opportunity].

They say that Yokahama, Japan is a very beautiful place. Il'iusha has developed the desire to visit China at some point.

MOSCOW, 19 MARCH 1886

I myself did not think that I would receive a letter today from Flora in Paris, where there is one wedding after the other. Last week she collected donations for the wedding of the clerk G. Reinach,[180] of whom she holds a very high opinion. It is surprising that a mixed marriage could take place in Paris for Leoni Goldschmidt and Viscount Deforfie [sic]: she is Jewish, the groom a Catholic serving as a secretary at the French embassy in Berlin. In recent days I read about this pair in the *Nord et art*,[181] which we receive.

Fani's husband will pass through here again. Although it would be nice to take a trip, I nonetheless declined to accompany Papa and Mama to Petersburg.

For a whole week, one day after the other, Khaia has gone to concerts, but I have sat at home.

MOSCOW, 22 MARCH 1886

It is amazing that the nanny's suffering has lasted so long and that she is still alive. Flora has not answered the letter that I sent here a week ago. She has become very lazy about writing and probably will no longer continue our correspondence.

Khaia is somehow very upset by the nanny's illness. They say that last night

---

180. Possibly a reference to a relative of the brother.
181. This is the title as given in Zinaida's transcription; it is not clear what periodical she had in mind.

she could not fall asleep because she had gone in to see the nanny and saw her suffering face—which greatly frightened her. I visited her yesterday morning and was very sorry for her, since every impression of such sadness makes a powerful impression on me.

A cycle of Rubinstein concerts begins soon in Paris. Some of them have probably already been performed. Abbé Liszt is now conducting in the churches there.

The elegantly dressed P[raskov'ia] Nik[olaevna] Demid[ova][182] was here, went on a drive with me, and dropped in at Mlle. Messarosh. At dinner they called the idiot Shchapov a baron, but then explained that one only needs to change a [single] letter to make it *baran* [ram].

Papa and Mama arrived safely, and today I received a telegram from Papa asking about the nanny's condition. I sent a reply. This is an enigma to us all: how long can a person—even someone as weak and old as our nanny—fight off death? Today she nearly stopped breathing, but then began again. However, this is the third day that she has neither eaten nor drunken anything; when they tried to pour a drop into her mouth, she swallowed it with the greatest difficulty.

Iulii Osipovich [Gol'denbakh] is no longer coming. I do not know why it is already unnecessary to see Dr. M. Iak. Girsh.

They say that yesterday Fedotova read not from Goethe's *Faust* but from his *Egmont*.

Today Aleksandr Vasil'evich Khlebnikov, along with Gonetskii,[183] dined at our house. The chronicle of balls is coming to an end and giving way to simple, more intimate gatherings—for example, the hypnosis experiments of Mr. Fel'dman. This tomorrow evening S. F. P[odgoretskaia] has a Feld'man reception; we are invited but will not go—notwithstanding the kind service of A[leksandr] D. Mein, who wanted to drop by and escort us (otherwise we could go with Miss Gosh).

Where will our people be in St. Petersburg? Have they left long ago? Misha received a letter from Mama. If I had not written Mama yesterday, then I could wait until tomorrow, but that would not be good on my part.

MOSCOW, 26 MARCH 1886

Yesterday I sent a letter to Flora, describing in detail all that is going on here. Although it was impossible to bury nanny yesterday (because of the holiday

---

182. Praskov'ia Nikolaevna Demidova (née Boldyreva) was the daughter of Nikolai Arkad'evich Boldyrev, governor of Riazan.

183. Nikolai Stepanovich Gonetskii (1815–1904), a Russian general who fought in the Crimean war.

of Annunciation), they did so on the morning of the third day after her death. We spent a whole four hours undergoing this depressing experience. [Ivan Vasil'evich] Messarosh also died on Sunday at 2.30 pm; he was buried today, and Mishen'ka went to the cemetery on foot. At the nanny's funeral he and also Sasha walked to Vagan'kov Cemetery,[184] and we were afraid that their feet would get soaked.

To show respect to the memory of Messarosh, on Monday Khaia, Misha, and I went to the funeral service. Death is no joke. The horror of it all is overwhelming: it is amazing how people live while knowing that death awaits each of us mortals.

MOSCOW, 27 MARCH 1886

Today Khaia and Miss Gosh went for chocolate at the home of A. Fed[erovna] Kondrat'eva.

A fine, splendid death is the goal of life. In my opinion, the path to this goal —life—must be strewn with good deeds that lead us to immortality.

In a short time we shall again start making plans for the summer. Having recognized the insignificance of all human existence and its consequences, one does not want to ponder how better to arrange one's life. The end and lot of human life mercilessly pursues us. Someone with an expansive spirit is more likely to succumb to sadness. A generous spirit is inclined to take all that life gives; such a broad character precisely accepts one's fate and inevitably ponders the meaning of life.

I went for a drive but shivered greatly because of the dampness and overcast weather (which is probably due to the drifting ice).

Egoism in *War and Peace* was embodied by Julie Karagina, the friend of Princess Maria Bolkonskaia. I very much dislike Julie, to judge from her letter to a close friend. I am absolutely convinced that real friendship cannot be manifested in such pathetic expressions.

MOSCOW, 29 MARCH 1886

Today I spent the entire day away from home. I went to Saltykova, and then Lidiia Stepanovna and I read the well-written and skillfully selected sketches of Juliette Lambert. In a jocular way, she shreds into little pieces all of London and English society, especially those who oppose her opinions and views of people. However, she says that the Jews go into the financial sphere and im-

184. Vagan'kov Cemetery, established in Moscow in 1771 amid an epidemic of the bubonic plague, is a large site where many prominent figures in Russian intellectual and cultural life are buried.

mediately fall into extraordinary materialism, but [this] does not deny their intelligence and abilities.

Our people usually go for one week, but stay for two. This has happened in this case as well—they should have already returned.

Iulii Osipovich Gol'denbakh promised to make the most convenient arrangements with Ermansderfer for me. I sent her a few words to make clear what they need to do.

Anna Pavlovna Messarosh is concerned about poor Lelia after the death of her husband and Lelia's father. She is such a nervous person and impressionable to the highest degree. I had been on the verge of visiting them, but on Miss Gosh's advice put this off for several days—until she has calmed down at least a bit, but even that is still too early, and it is difficult to think of any way to console them. Later they will not find this consoling, but will be more resigned.

Yesterday I went for a ride with Miss Gosh. They say that Papa has some meeting scheduled for Tuesday in Petersburg. Hence they will not return home soon, and we shall be left here alone. Jews are a multifaceted people, like well-cut crystal: they can polish and perfect any aspect of their capabilities.

At times you wait for something (or perhaps someone) to free you from a situation that has become intolerable. Yesterday evening Mashen'ka [Mariia Petrovna] Perevozchikova and the young, talented pianist [Iosef] Levin (recommended by Countess Brevern de Lagarde) came for tea. Once again he delighted us with the charming, but as yet imperfect sound of his playing on the piano. He will be a great pianist if his small height does not become an impediment. Of course, I am talking about his character—i.e., I mean his sloth, which is characteristic of all mankind. Finis! I hear the sound of the pianist. I love to watch the dance lessons of the children.

MOSCOW, 31 MARCH 1886

In twenty-four hours Papa and Mama will leave. The farceur Orlov[185] should leave Moscow today and see them tomorrow.

Yesterday we went to the Malyi Theater for a performance of boy and girl students from the Moscow Drama School. This evening had been arranged with great diversity, and General Orlov came specifically for this occasion.

Iulii Osipovich was at our house today and ordered me to put iodine on the

185. Count Anatolii Orlov-Davydov (1837–1905) was a lieutenant general and held an appointment at the imperial court as *ober-shtal'meister* (in the second highest tier of servitors in the Table of Ranks).

side where I feel the pain. I heard of the miraculous cure of Serafima by the hypnotist Fel'dman, who allegedly healed her completely by inspiring her to think that she was not at all ill and that she should be healthy.

MOSCOW, 1 APRIL 1886

The children performed Ostrovskii's[186] *Shaluny* very well.

Food constitutes a vital necessity for every living creature. Why is it made into a joy and necessity when, for example, you come as a guest and they force you to eat. I do not like this custom. Today I was at the name day for M[a-riia] Perevozchikova, and a large number of people gathered. But the chocolate they served was so thick that it was impossible to drink. Levin was also there and played some sweet pieces on the piano. At Perevozchikova's I saw a picture of Iulii Osipovich; he was not bad looking in his youth. I immediately recognized him.

Yesterday Grandmother and Grandfather had lunch with us, and then Aleksandr Danilovich Mein[187] came. Yesterday I went for a ride in the park, and then went to a confectionary (Al'bert) to buy candy for Mashen'ka.

Genrikh, a former pupil at Mr. Shlesinger's gymnasium, is not bad, and I like him. He is already graduating this spring from the juridical faculty of the university. He brought Mama a wonderful bouquet (in their natural state, not bundled up in paper). Even M[aria] P[avlovich] Spiridonova brought her a basket of flowers (albeit a very paltry one).

MOSCOW, 13 APRIL 1886

The Shchapovs, they say, are already living at their dacha in Sokol'niki. But "laws are not written for fools."[188] It would be good if others followed their example.[189]

Our family members are now in St. Petersburg, and then (on the first day of our Passover) Kotia [Daniil] arrived here for three days and very much cheered us up. It is even amazing how the presence of a single person can have such an impact on others and on my mood.

The jeweler Lor'e made, per an order from Khaia, a gold brooch for Lidiia Stepanovna, with her initials "L. S." It is well done.

---

186. Presumably, Aleksandr N. Ostrovskii.

187. Aleksandr Danilovich Mein (1836–99) was a Baltic-German writer who published in *Russkii vestnik* and headed the provincial and Moscow branches of *Golos*. His wife, often called Mania, and daughter were both named Mariia.

188. A popular proverb, expressing disapproval of someone's conduct.

189. This contradicts the negativity in the previous sentence. Perhaps Zinaida meant to say instead that "it would *not* be good."

I was inclined to ask Fel'dman to perform several experiments with me. It is good, he says, that I am easily hypnotized.

Mark Varshavskii [Warshawsky][190] from St. Petersburg was a guest yesterday and spent almost the entire day with us. However, he did not wish to write in my album.

They say that Uncle will soon come here and perhaps will live at a country house in Tsarskoe Selo. Even Leon Abramovich and Lazar [Iakovlevich] have rented summer lodgings there. It is only our plans that remain unclear. If we travel abroad, then as the first, necessary condition I shall insist on traveling with Papa.

I am waiting for news from Flora, who has still not responded to my letter.

Here the general flow of life has again come to somewhat of a halt, but there is still some hope. Sometimes it is as though you have been aroused from a deep sleep and look on your surroundings with completely different eyes.

MOSCOW, 16 APRIL 1886

I went out for a ride with Mishen'ka and was at Devich'e Pole,[191] where I met Slezkin. This is even strange: in a short period of time he has changed and aged.

Iu[rii] Gintsburg[192] (so-called I. Ru.), apparently is choosing Russia as his place of residence—that is, at least, what they are saying about his family, and therefore about the relatives of Baron David, who married his [Iurii's] second daughter, his cousin [Mathilda]. They already have a daughter, but what is her name? I heard about the birth of Lelia's daughter, and then wrote them a letter of congratulations. They named her Roza. The former contender, Felix Kuranda (son of the late member of parliament [Ignaz Kuranda]), is marrying some Elena Karpeles.[193]

MOSCOW, 18 APRIL 1886

Indil'gart is invited to participate in the *tableaux vivants* in the presence of the emperor and empress in Moscow at Prince [Vladimir] Dolgorukov's.

Iulii Osipovich [Gol'denbakh] has been ill throughout the holidays and, they

---

190. Mark Abramovich Varshavskii [Warshawsky] (b. 1845), Leon Varshavskii's brother, was head of the joint-stock companies Gergard i Gei and Stroitel'. He served on a committee at the Society for the Promotion of Enlightenment among the Jews and was a member of the board of the chorale synagogue in St. Petersburg.

191. Devich'e Pole (Young Maiden's Field) is a district in Moscow to the north of the Novodevichii convent.

192. Iurii Iosifovich Gintsburg, son of Joseph Gintsburg and brother of Goratsii [Horace] Gintsburg.

193. Helene (Elena) Karpeles (1865–1938) was the daughter of Moriz and Emma Karpeles. She married Felix Kuranda (1852–1917), son of Dr. Ignaz Kuranda, a member of the Austrian parliament.

say, is still lying in bed. A[leksandr] Mein visited him on the second day and said that he is quite ill.

Today Papa and I were at the art gallery of the Itinerant Exhibition[194] on Miasnitskaia Street (opposite the post office).

Princess Golitsyna[195] fell ill with typhoid and died from that terrible disease yesterday morning. Today I saw from my window the funeral of Prince Urusov,[196] a chamberlain! Where did they all become infected with this disease? Petrova-Solodova and Baroness Sheppening, young ladies, also have typhoid. Dmitrii Mikhailovich Golitsyn, they say, had moved to the hotel Dresden, for fear of contracting the disease. But the burial service will be at the cemetery church of Donskoi Monastery, and the coffin will be tin and soldered. I feel terribly sorry for the poor parents and relatives of Princess Golitsyna, but perhaps she is better off now. Jews are quickly done with funerals. For them life consists of the human soul being in darkness. Thus the more quickly that the remains are buried, the greater is the respect shown to the memory of the deceased. Is that perhaps true? Either way is bad. The only thing is not to wake up in a grave; otherwise, in my opinion, it does not matter.

MOSCOW, 20 APRIL 1886

They have sent for Iulii Osipovich [Gol'denbakh] to see Sasha, who is somewhat listless today. Today I went to see Del'vis and to the young Arsharumovs but did not find them at home. Then I met them on the street.

To judge from the newspapers, Fedotova and other artists of imperial theaters were at the university for a festive meeting for the Society of Lovers of Literature. We were not there because the meeting was on Saturday, not Sunday (as is usually the case). An artist who is dedicated exclusively to waltzes —J. Strauss[197]—will soon be in Moscow.

Lidiia [Nikolaevna] and Tat'iana [Nikolaevna] Gonetskaia[198] were at our house today. G. Zaichenko, Kondrat'ev, and Rozentsveig (a suitor for Masha) were also here. He has a very pleasant appearance, reportedly completed the sixth class of the gymnasium, and works at his own exchange office in Khar'kov.

194. The Association of Itinerant Art Exhibitions was a private organization formed in 1870 to display the works of nonofficial artists.
195. Princess Anna Dmitrievna Golitsyna (1860–86) was a lady-in-waiting in the Court of Her Imperial Majesty. She was buried in the Donskoi Monastery, as Zinaida notes below.
196. Prince Aleksandr Mikhailov Urusov (1839–86), state councilor and chamberlain in the Court of His Imperial Majesty.
197. Johann Strauss II (1825–99), a composer.
198. Lidiia and Tat'iana were daughters of Nikolai Stepanovich Gonetskii, a general who had fought in the Crimean War.

They say that, in our absence, M[aria] P[avlovna] Spiridonova and Bavin came. I am sorry that I did not see the former.

Johann Strauss will give two concerts at the Noble Assembly. How I would like to hear him—if I am well. I absolutely must put on some weight, since I am often ill.

Ludwig, the king of Bavaria, conferred the regency on Prince Luitpold[199] —because of the king's grave nervous breakdown, the prince was designated regent. The king has long been nearly insane; only art has flourished under him. During our recent trip we did not go to the Pinakothek, but did see an international art exhibition open at the time.

MOSCOW, 21 APRIL 1886

I was very sorry to hear about the death of Iugan. Because he was a French teacher at the Lycée from the day it opened, the two upper classes went on foot all the way to the church. His poor wife, they say, wept a lot in the church and wove him a wreath of his favorite flowers (which had been ordered from a florist's shop). She is a very pathetic, pitiful creature.

Everyone is still talking about the cruelty of Prince Golitsyn, who did not see his daughter before his death. What they say (and embellish) is such that it is hardly credible. It must be the case that a lot of slander is being directed at her poor father.

MOSCOW, 22 APRIL 1886

We are planning to go to the Novikovs for tea. They are home on Tuesday afternoons and evenings. They regularly come to us, and it has been such a long time since we paid them a visit that it is outright shameful. As recently as Saturday Ivan Alekseevich came here; Mama dropped by there yesterday, but did not find them at home. They lead a completely secluded way of life.

I did not ask for a telegram regarding our plans to go to Franzensbad. I hope that we do not go there at all this summer. Are the Gabbes [Gubbays] planning to go there? Why not? After all, Flora asked me if we are going. Uncle probably wants to know this in order to settle his own future plans.

In this respect, my aunt [Avdot'ia] does not agree with me, and she is apparently angry because I am so well disposed toward the Gabbe [Gubbay] family. Her animus toward them and her inclinations are none of my business. I am far more sympathetic to Uncle [Samuil]'s attachments. The Epshtein[200] breed

199. Luitpold (1821–1912) was prince regent of Bavaria from 1886 to 1912 due to the incapacitation of his two nephews, King Ludwig II and King Otto.
200. Dana Avdot'ia Taikhilovna came from the Ephstein family in Rudni.

is not to my liking either, but I do not know why she suddenly began talking about them.

I must now rush to finish writing and get ready to leave—which is now often tiresome for me.

MOSCOW, 23 APRIL 1886

We went to the Novikovs, where there were a lot of people—contrary to our expectation. As a result, we arrived home somewhat later than we had thought. At Novikovs we played questions-and-answers as well as *mantevizm* [muscle reading]. At 11 am [our tutor] G. R. was given a farewell audience in Mama's blue office, where Mama, Roman, Masha, G. R., and I assembled. He left for home in Khar'kov until he is called back to Moscow—after the requisite information about his person is received (in response to a written request from an acquaintance Fainberg). Then he whispered something with Roman. Originally they received him in Aunt's red room, which Mama believes to be more successful than the blue room.

Uncle [Samuil] is still at [his daughter Rachel] St. Paul's at the Château de Saint-Germain-en-Laye where she[201] gave birth to her daughter. Thank God, both she and the daughter are healthy. Everything is going well with them.

Tomorrow, it is probably necessary to go for visits, including to the Belgian consul's wife, who was at our house during the holidays. Her husband was also here on Saturday and met with Countess Brevern de Lagarde, who arrived to show us her new hat (which had been brought from Paris by M. I. Fon Derviz).[202] It is really very beautiful—a gray hat from tulle, which suits her about as much as a saddle does a cow. But it is a splendid saddle.

It is now getting too dark to write. Grandfather has come to me, so I have to finish—though I am sorry to do so. They say that Grandfather has a plan to resettle here permanently.[203] But the question is whether this will pan out or not.

MOSCOW, 27 APRIL 1886

During all this time we have gone almost nowhere. However, two days in a row we did go to Strauss concerts, which were absolutely enchanting for me.

They are starting to talk about a trip abroad—which I regard as something

---

201. In 1886, Rachel St. Paul (Samuil Poliakov's daughter) had a daughter named Georgette (who later married Bentley Mott).

202. Maria Ivanovna Fon Derviz (née Kozlovskaia), wife of Pavel Grigor'evich Fon Derviz (1826–81), a railroad entrepreneur.

203. Solomon Poliakov, his wife Breine, and two of her nieces did move to Tverskoi Boulevard in Moscow.

stupid, which I cannot explain to myself or set right. Mama managed to cause me so much unpleasantness in Paris and other cities that I simply shrink before the mountain of woeful memories. In addition, they are asking me to travel with them again. But it has to be done as if Mama is traveling not with me, but for my sake. It is difficult to deny her this pleasure, which has to be satisfying for her: egoists love to be considered philanthropists, and it is impossible not to see that Mama is the former.

MOSCOW, 28 APRIL 1886

Today I read the entire day, mainly Tolstoy's *War and Peace*. I especially liked Pierre's induction into the "free masons" [Freemasons],[204] which is written with such power that every kind of thought occurs to one, like the following: "But perhaps the world has tests so that the soul after death has access to paradise if it passed them well on earth."[205] I have now begun to read more quickly, but especially after yesterday evening when I did not sleep but read in bed. True, not much—one chapter. Nonetheless I have finished a definite and legitimate number of chapters. Until now I had had the task of reading only one chapter a day, but then I rethought this (to avoid an interminable period of reading). Papa gave me several letters to read today, namely: from [Mikhail] Katkov, Vil'basov, and Leon Abramovich [Varshavskii]. There was also one open letter from Turin from the correspondent of the *Jewish Chronicle*,[206] who proposes to purchase some rare collection. That means: publish in various organs about one's activities—that is, not we of course are writing, but correspondents from Moscow, who through reading become acquainted with the powerful in this world. And that is how this man learned of our existence.

MOSCOW, 2 MAY 1886

On the evening of 1 May, in accordance with the Muscovite custom, there was a mass outdoor fête in Sokol'niki park. Our people went, but I remained at home for several reasons (viz., I had a headache). But as they were leaving, I noticed Khaia wearing a hat similar to the one that I had bought for myself. The affair with this hat began already in Paris. I was the first to claim the hat, but Khaia wanted to buy it. And when I proposed to them (i.e., Mama and Khaia) to transfer my right, Papa gave me his word that he would not buy

204. Zinaida uses the literal *svobodnye kamenshchiki* in quotation marks, not *masony*.
205. In quotation marks, without attribution.
206. The *Jewish Chronicle* (transcribed by Zinaida as *Dzhevish kronikl*) was founded in 1841 in London and remains the oldest continuous periodical in the Jewish community.

Khaia exactly the same hat. Despite this, Mama deliberately—to do something unpleasant to me—bought it for her. But her forehead is so resonant from the internal vacuity that she does not in the least profit from this. I alone win from this, since I am now convinced that I do not have to travel with Mama—not only now, but ever again in the future. Having given rein to my wounded self-esteem, I could no longer sit until the end of breakfast, rose from my chair, and walked out. What can one say about the fact that it is difficult to fix something—Mama's inclination to rip from my grasp everything precious to me and to give it to Khaia. In these heartfelt matters I am offended by her and therefore do not wish to entrust myself to her in whatever is of greatest interest to her (for example, the choice of a prospective suitor, if such appears, that I do not wish). All this grief is gnawing at my soul. How bad it is to be proud and not to submit to one's fate. I realize that I neither know how nor wish to resign myself so long as it is given to me to live. To live means to fight. And so long as struggle is possible and I am alive, then I shall not bow down to higher injustice. My mother does not want to know me, and in fact I cannot be her scapegoat. Her love for Khaia means nothing to me; so be it. But only do not pity me, for otherwise I will completely wither and fade away.

MOSCOW, 7 MAY 1886

I am still not going outside and am sitting in my room. This is already the second week since I have been languishing from a deep depression, caused by the epitome of injustice in my parents' treatment of me (as I see it). Tomorrow I shall not go out again and thus am never fated to rid myself of the burdensome order of life that is caused by Mama's egoism and other consequences that ensue from this source. However, I feel that something bad will happen with me and, if this drags on, I may well acquire the affliction that the English call spleen. May God will that I be able to endure this trial without pernicious consequences.

MOSCOW, 18 MAY 1886

During this interval I was at the court for a festive occasion. The next day I watched the parade on Theater Square (in Sereda's apartment). Near this house the sovereign, his wife, and the suite made a stop. The heir, the tsarevich,[207] was on a small Cossack horse and dressed in the blue uniform of that same regiment (which was very becoming to him). Georgii[208] and the Grand

207. The emperor's oldest son, Nicholas Aleksandrovich (1868–1918), the future Nicholas II.
208. Possibly the emperor's younger son, Georgii Aleksandrovich (1871–99).

Dukes Sergei[209] and Pavel[210] were alongside and on white horses. The grand duke's wife, Elizaveta Fedorovna,[211] initially sat in the carriage of the empress, but then moved to another coach.

Today Mama carried out an "exile of peoples"—i.e., she expelled Laletr [*sic*], Miss Gosh, Fritsman, and Polin. But soon, having grown bored, she went to seek happiness at Gordkha.

As far as I am concerned, I can say that no one can [endure] what has long been on my mind: whatever is hidden and secret is bad. But Mama thinks it necessary to mete out a good lesson to all who are dependent on her. Today she sank her teeth into poor Fritsman, who really got it—for precisely what, I do not know. He should have defended himself, and I was an involuntary witness to Mama's scene with him. He first explained something in the drawing room; then she went into the hall, probably having seen me at the tea table, and made a completely innocent, even oppressed look. As he continued his explanation, I walked away—I did not wish to witness this dispute.

MOSCOW, 30 MAY 1886

All this time I have not written in my journal, because I went riding in the park after lunch. But since today is Friday, I found it convenient to remember my journal. And I have thus begun to write in the journal, even though M[ark] Varshavskii is here. He came for lunch, when we had a snack and Mama had already finished her soup. Today I was anxious because I had to go and be measured for a dress, so I ordered that the horses be harnessed. But "the early bird gets the worm." Ksiutka had already left with the charming Lidiia Stepanovna, who is always in the mood to pull some dirty trick.

Miss Gosh remains for now—until Mama finds a new governess. The cause of all this is an egoism of such a stupendous magnitude that it can prevent her own reason from adopting the proper perspective. That egoism is the supreme misfortune that a person can be fated to possess. It not only makes the egoist unhappy, but by taking over that someone's will, denies happiness for those around this person. Such scoundrels as L. S. and Kh.[212] are rarely encountered without egoism, and still more rarely with a mind. Most often this is some

209. The emperor's younger brother Grand Prince Sergei Aleksandrovich (1857–1905), who was assassinated during the revolution of 1905.
210. The emperor's younger brother Grand Prince Pavel Aleksandrovich (1860–1919), who was executed during the civil war.
211. Elizaveta Fedorovna (1864–1918), wife of Grand Prince Sergei Aleksandrovich, who was excuted after the Bolsheviks killed members of the royal family in July 1918.
212. Lidiia Stepanovna and Khaia.

kind of swinishness incarnate. . . . [sic] And never can it be guided by personal spiritual qualities and feelings.

Papa thought of traveling with me to Petersburg for a couple of days, but has now changed his mind. As soon as I perked up (because of a glimmer of hope), Mama—because of the egoism in her nature—gets out of sorts. It is awful! As they say: drive nature out the door, and it will come in through the window. And that is the truth—at least, in my opinion. And what was there to be angry about when the cause is envy? Of the latter Mama has too large a dose. That is a misfortune.

Yesterday I finished Tolstoy's *War and Peace*. Shortly after that I began to read Goethe's *Edmont* [*Egmont*] (as Flora Gabbe [Gubbay] had recommended). She has not answered my letter. I do not understand what her indifference means.

MOSCOW, 3 JUNE 1886

The month of June has now arrived. What good will it bring us? May is the month that poets have celebrated as the month of love, but it gave me absolutely nothing new. There was only constant solitude and nothing else. Books are my true friends. I am now reading [Alexandre] Dumas, a short collection of stories, playfully composed and put together well. Today I feel a yearning, as if for my homeland. But since I am home, I do not know the causes.

SOKOL'NIKI, 6 JULY 1886

I have not written the journal during the entire time that we have been at the dacha, so I do not know where to begin. During these days I went with Papa to Petersburg, and we stayed with Lazar [Iakovlevich] at Tsarskoe Selo. We were there just three days, but I do not regret going. Papa was very weary from his business affairs. I did not do anything there except go for rides; on one occasion I went out for music. I was also at Kraevskii's[213] dacha at Pavlovsk, where he has settled very comfortably—with flowers and a charming view. But his old housekeeper is very unlikable. The bagels I saw there were of extraordinary size, and for some reason are called "Moscow bagels." That is probably because they are so large, and they take Muscovites (because of their generous hospitality) for gluttons.

Uncle [Samuil] and Kotia [Daniil] were here until our trip to St. Petersburg. Unfortunately, I had gum boils and therefore virtually did not see them. At the time Uncle expected us in Tsarskoe Selo, but Papa—as if deliberately putting it off—arrived there on the day after their departure.

213. Andrei Aleksandrovich Kraevskii (1810–89), prominent Moscow publisher (most famously of the journal *Otechestvennye zapiski*).

Leon Rubinshtein dined here without us. His wife, the charming Ernestine, was also with him, and she amazed everyone with her inordinate stupidity.[214]

Today I went to town and spent the entire time going around to the stores. First, with Papa and Mama I looked at the newly acquired building for a Jewish school (the former Saarbekov home).[216] Tomorrow I am planning to rest from the daily excursion and just do nothing. I visited Grandfather and Grandmother and talked to them briefly about everything. However, I also spoke of Uncle Samuil and Kotia. He (i.e., Kotia) is going from Amsterdam to Petersburg and back. Papa still has not decided anything. They say that Mme. Gabbe [Gubbay] asked Uncle Samuil about our whereabouts. Her son has already been in London for some time and probably will come to them.

The weather is changeable. Several times a day it starts to rain. Today it drenched us a few times while on the road and in town; there were even several claps of thunder.

All this time we had M[ania] Mein as a guest, but yesterday Aleksandr Danilovich took her: she had caught cold, was coughing, and was even wheezing a lot. Quite unexpectedly, we got along very well and even became friends. They say that Khaia was very upset by the fact that, in a letter to Raia, Mania sent me a kiss. All winter she was friends with Khaia, but in the end totally changed her way of thinking. Because of this, the camp of Lidiia Stepanovna and Khaia became completely isolated. Now they are my enemies. For my part, I did nothing to provoke our cold relations. Amazingly, I am indifferent to this. Except perhaps when they make me feel this too strongly. Then it is necessary to put up a self-defense and resort to every possible means (but of course honest ones) to prove the slander. However, this also is not always successful. All my life I have fought this squabbling, and it is ruining my health. I am now reading [Charles] Dickens's *Dombey and Son*, and which has already managed to bore me to death. The author's jokes, however, are sometimes rather amusing.

SOKOL'NIKI, 7 JULY 1886

Today I am in an absolutely hypochondriacal mood. Why? Mama is just the opposite, as often—for some reason—happens with us. But the main thing is

---

214. Leon Rubinshtein (d. 1892) and Ernestine were the parents of the dancer and actress Ida Rubinshtein.

215. The published text gives the same date for this and the following entry.

216. The reference here is to the wealthy Armenian merchant Moisei Semenovich Saarbekov (b. 1855, d. after 1917), a hereditary honorary citizen in Moscow.

that I sense the impossibility of a pleasant trip. Mama has nonetheless insisted on having her way, despite the entire winter, when I felt like someone who had been sentenced to death.

As the proverb has it, "what a woman wants is how it will be decided." Unfortunately, I feel my spleen growing strong because of something that does not depend on me. One has to forgive and forget everything. However, that is sometimes more difficult than it seems. It is much easier to write verse. Because of that I cannot follow this wise Christian verity.

SOKOL'NIKI, 11 JULY 1886

Today I received a letter from Lelia Messarosh in Troitskoe.[217] She writes that she is now very satisfied with the fact that N. Zanchevskii was a guest for a whole ten days and will come again. I am now guilty before her: today I did not congratulate her on the day of her angel St. Ol'ga (11 July). But I did not want her to think that I am pestering her. So I put off dealing with this.

I have come down with "verse-mania," if one can say that. It is amazing how I produce these like pancakes. Fon Derviz is going to Vichy and then to Biarritz.[218] Today Semen Sergeevich Podgoretskii talked about their plans to travel on the 20th of the month. Papa also decided to leave on that day.

It is a great pity that Papa and I did not go to Nice last winter, because now it will again be necessary to satisfy all the whims of Mama and Khaia. Flora Gabbe [Gubbay] does not write me and for good reason: she knows that we are now in turmoil over the trip abroad and probably does not want to interfere at this time. At the present moment everything is totally up in the air. Khaia is simply thriving. All week they are all talking about getting ready for abroad. I am finishing the Dickens novel, which has a good ending.

SOKOL'NIKI, 15 JULY 1886

There was chaos after breakfast today. Papa and Mama went to congratulate the prince,[219] and for lunch we had the company of Mr. Demidov, who came from Riazan specifically to congratulate His Excellency on this occasion.

James Girsch [de Hirsch] recommended an excellent table wine, which had been recently bottled. It is cheaper and better than last year's Bordeaux, which was very sour, and does not have any impurities.

217. There are numerous villages called Troitskoe (Trinity), taken from the name of the local parish church.
218. An oceanic resort town, on the extreme southwest corner of France.
219. Possibly Vladimir Dolgorukov.

I would very much like to go with Misha or Papa along the Volga—they say that it is very picturesque there. But Mama wants to go abroad and with Papa, me, and Khaia thrown in. Why not? After all, it is better to live as a double than not at all—as I do, for example, when I renounce everything and live on hope. Right now, I have absolutely no future prospects. It is the same general egoism that burdens me—and nothing else.

Miss Gosh is very happy that together we will read Saint Mar[220] after Dickens, who, I must confess, has become boring for me (even if, basically, his work is well written). Of course, the French writers are easier to read.

I did not do anything substantial today except play piano. Tat'iana even said to me that I ask nothing for myself with respect to dresses—a dresser [cabinet], etc. Khaia has much more of all this than I do.

It is good if I am satisfied with everything that I wish. But God does not know what I desire. First, tranquility, and then a happy family hearth—that is, family happiness, as I imagine it. That I can achieve through my own efforts alone. A whole week has passed since I saw Iulii Osipovich. Part of my ailments has passed, but the rest have increased. I am often naughty when I am too busy intellectually, and I alternately read and write.

I. Shchapov is leaving the Lycée of Tsarevich Nikolai.[221]

SOKOL'NIKI, 16 JULY 1886
Yesterday Aleksandr Danilovich brought me a letter from Mania. It is a misfortune if she writes me more often than Khaia. Now there are rumors that I said or whispered something bad.

All the preparations for the departure are being actively carried out. I alone have not yet prepared, since it is better not to think about the future—so gloomy is my present. All that one hears about concerns the various squabbles and troubles with Mama. Meanwhile, she and Khaia get along famously.

They say that they are going to Bad-Ischl[222] for Mama. But Bad-Ischl does not have mineral waters, so it is possible to remain in Sokol'niki. If earlier it had been decided to go to the sea, to Biarritz, that would have been something quite different.

---

220. I could not identify this author.
221. See note 128.
222. A spa and resort town in upper Austria.

Yesterday we were very much animated because of dinner—eleven people came. Moreover, the chief of police dined along with [Gennadii V.] Grudev[223]— the youngest person of the ancient capital. Also present were the Podgoretskiis, the engineer [Andrei Nikolaevich] Gorchakov, P. Naumenko, Kondrat'ev, Semen S., Sof'ia Ivanovna Slezkina and her sister, and Iu[lii] Gol'denbakh. And that was all our guests. I will say one thing: I was very flattered by the fact that it fell to my lot to entertain A[leksandr A.] Kozlov, and they say that I performed the role well. Because Mama was busy with Grudev, I had to hold a conversation with my neighbor so that he not become bored. For this occasion Lidiia Stepanovna was really dressed up. Miss Gosh put on a dress that she wears only on festive occasions. But I wore something very simple and modest: a dress of pink crepe de chine[224] which apparently suits me well (and in any case I really love crepe de chine).

Today Papa suggested that I go with him for a ride in the charabanc. But I declined, given that Mama would be left alone.

Now they are talking about when and where to go. They say that Lazar and Annette [Poliakov] are not traveling abroad, but want to stay in Tsarskoe Selo all summer. That is very, very reasonable if one takes into account the fact that their children are still very young for a big journey.

All this time, one week altogether, nothing interesting was to be heard here. They say that we will go to Warsaw on Sunday etc. But I do not want to travel together with them all, as previously. And for the same reason.

[Samuel] Montagu[225] and his doctor Asher[226] from London paid us a visit. They came to Russia to improve the conditions of Jews here. But I do not think that they can do anything for them: they wanted to expel the Jews from Moscow, and if it were not for Papa, the Jews would have had to clear out while the going is good.[227] These are very typical Englishmen. One of them is a banker, a member of Parliament, and a very intelligent person. As for Asher, who performs the role of a surgeon, I cannot say anything other than "ludicrous." But

---

223. Gennadii Vasil'evich Grudev (1796–1895) was an honorary justice of the peace in Moscow. Zinaida uses her wit here to describe him as the "youngest person of the ancient capital."

224. A fine, lightweight silk, cotton, or worsted fabric with a plain weave and crepe-twist filling.

225. Samuel Montagu (1832–1911)—the first Baron Swarthling of England, whose father had immigrated from Kempen (near Posen) in 1775—founded the bank Samuel Montagu & Co.

226. Asher Asher (1837–89), a physician from Glasgow, Scotland.

227. Fears of expulsion from Moscow ensued after the removal of Jews from Kiev in that year.

he does have a gift from Baron Adolf de Rothschild, who gave him a gold watch with a long inscription engraved on the inside cover. Both are going to Nizhnii Novgorod today, and will return to Moscow on Wednesday and dine with us in their traveling clothes: they will leave for Petersburg that evening, from there travel to the Baltic provinces, and then on to Finland, Hamburg, and England. For this entire trip they have set aside just five weeks.

The poor Jews! Today is the beginning of the holiday. Our family stayed in the city on purpose—in order to go to the synagogue. Now only the boys go there, returning late in the evening.

The majority of our family is fasting today. The weather is extremely foul. It has been pouring rain all day, incessantly, in buckets, and makes one depressed: you really do not know what to do on such days at the dacha, as you sit alone in your room. Only verse is saving me. I wrote the following poem:

Angel
The angel, still young, is flying to heaven,
An evil fate loved him not,
There he has seen clear, eternal peace
Sending his memory back to earth.

I wrote this a long time ago, with the initials A. Z. P. in memory of my deceased brother.[228] I have one small musical work, and now I am beginning to compose a waltz, etc. Otherwise writing poetry is beginning to bore me.

In our home there is still such monotony and tedium.

SOKOL'NIKI, 29 JULY 1886
Our Englishmen arrived this morning from Nizhnii Novgorod. They are fasting and therefore did not come today to dine. But they promised to come tomorrow instead.

It is now drizzling rain, and one senses the dampness in the air, but in the morning the skies were clear. It was not even noticeable that all yesterday there had been a heavy downpour. But the paths were somewhat wet, so I did not go for a walk and only strolled in the garden.

In recent days the newspapers have written about the arrival of a Jewish philanthropist, a relative of the Englishman, Lord Salisbury.[229] They are full of lies, with no basis in fact, and make insinuations about Montagu.

---

228. Zinaida's brother Avgust (Azi) died in Geneva, Switzerland, in 1872 at the age of eight.
229. Presumably a reference to Robert Arthur Talbot Gascoyne-Cecil, third Marquess of Salisbury (1830–1903).

SOKOL'NIKI, 19 AUGUST 1886[230]

We were supposed to leave today, but because of me did not—despite the fact that Mama had announced that she is going with Khaia. Yesterday I had a very stormy day. From early morning Papa and Mama began trying to persuade me to go abroad, but I categorically refused. Danilov [the engineer], who arrived in the midst of our lunch, is here now; the day after tomorrow he is going with General Annenkov to Akhal-teke.[231] His uniform, as usual, is very original: a red shirt instead of dicky and a frock coat. Given that he is overweight, this is not very elegant.

All this time I was very anxious—two poor English Jewish women came and brought photographs (*kartochki*) from Montagu. For some reason this seemed suspicious to Khaia and Lidiia Stepanovna, who hastened to warn Mama about this. That happened precisely as they were first meeting the women on a bench.

Sometimes one has to grieve about what cannot be fixed. I am terribly sorry about the time lost (in vain) as well as the drab winter, when in fact one should have been earnestly seeking the means to achieve my future goals, not cry about what is a past youth that is of no use to anyone. That, at the very least, is out of character and induces spleen. Thank God for all that is so good, but may God make things better in the future. If this hope did not give me strength, then I could not accept my fate with equanimity and be prepared for all [that may come].

SOKOL'NIKI, 13 AUGUST 1886

Whatever happens, I will staunchly stick to my opinion: not travel abroad as a party of four. I am not tempted to travel and suffer; since I cannot foresee anything else, I do not wish to travel at all. This is not the first time: at the departure they seek to persuade me and make every possible promise not to make things unpleasant for me, but in fact things turn out differently. The result is that all—except me—flourish and enjoy themselves. That is why I clarified this clearly in advance and have no intention of retreating. Iulii Osipovich [Gol'denbakh] has not visited us for a long time.

I rode in a boat on the Iauza River today. There were twelve people in all. It was very pleasant to go boating, for the weather was very good today. We went in three boats up to Ekho, where we drank milk and ate *prostokvasha*,[232]

230. The date given in the published version precedes the date of the next entry by six days.
231. An oasis in the Aral-Caspian basis of modern Turkmenistan, a key site in the Russian conquest of the region in the early 1880s.
232. Thick soured milk.

and—then reinvigorated—returned home. The children went with Khaia and Katia for a walk on the old strolling area, which has a toy shop, where they bought a harmonica to entertain me. I am waiting with impatience while they cut the "Gordion knot"—i.e., when we think up something with regard to our trip. Everything here is proceeding at a quiet pace. That is, except for Lidiia Stepanovna, no one is undertaking anything. And she has seemingly become more reserved and pouts less than usual. Iosif Arkadievich Levin left our house a couple of mornings ago. I did not say goodbye to him, but think that I shall see him here before we leave. He has exams during these days. The conservatory professor Safonov,[233] who is married to the daughter of Vyshnegradskii,[234] will admit him directly into his class.

Khaia has already packed everything, and she is now sitting at the sea and waiting for the weather.

SOKOL'NIKI, 17 AUGUST 1886
I finally received a letter from Mania in Gurzuf,[235] but—other than wonderful descriptions—it contains nothing of substance. And now I am very unhappy that I stupidly decided to travel abroad together again. I am certain that nothing good will come of it.

They have decided to leave next Tuesday morning, first taking a courier train to Warsaw and then going from there to Vienna. We will stop for one day in Warsaw (to rest) and then two days or more in Vienna. As for the rest of the journey nothing will be decided before we arrive in Vienna.

Rosenshtein will probably oversee the trip. He so often interferes with my plans and does not let me arrange things. Tomorrow I shall pack; so far I have not packed at all.

VIENNA, 22 AUGUST/3 SEPTEMBER 1886[236]
We arrived today after one day to rest in Warsaw. So far we have not encountered here anyone we know. The only acquaintance is Rozenshtein, the usual visitor of the hotel.

Yesterday we did not spend the day in Warsaw badly: we went to Saxon

233. Vasilii Il'ich Safonov (1852–1918) was a Russian conductor, pianist, public activist, and leading figure in Russian musical culture in late imperial Russia. His wife was Varvara Vyshnegradskaia, daughter of the future minister of finance (see the next note).
234. Ivan Alekseevich Vyshnegradskii (1832–95), a Russian engineer, entrepreneur and minister of finance (1887–92).
235. A town on the southern Crimean coast, eighteen kilometers from Yalta.
236. Zinaida gives dates using both the Old Style (Julian) and New Style (Gregorian) calendars.

garden, and in the afternoon we had visits from Boria,[237] Mr. Odynes, the gendarme officer Gorskii, and his nephew P[avel] Mikh[ailovich] Khotinskii,[238] who had received a telegram to meet us.

The weather is marvelous. Arriving in Warsaw, it had already become noticeably darker, and on the trip from Warsaw to Vienna it was very hot—despite the fact that we had a separate railway car (which aroused everyone's attention in Warsaw because it was painted a bright yellow color and had been specifically sent for us from Vienna). Therefore all possible respect was given to us along the way, and we traveled in the most comfortable manner possible. If it had not been so hot, it would be really excellent. Instead we were all sweating and suffered terribly from heat and the lack of air.

Vienna seems to have become dirtier—or so it seems after Paris. Nonetheless, this is a nice city and quite beautiful.

BIARRITZ, 15/27 SEPTEMBER 1886

During this long period, we were in Vienna and Paris, and we will also pass time pleasantly somewhere [else]. Until now, however, we were not particularly bored. Yesterday I was in Bayonne and watched the bullfights.

On the road from Paris to Biarritz Khaia got coal into her eyes but only felt the pain on the second day after we arrived here. She went yesterday and today to V. Esker, who removed a small piece of coal and now, thank God, it no longer hurts. But it gave us a fright. Today is her birthday—she is now 21 years old. It is a pity that Ida Rubinshtein and her friend [Mania] Levinson leave tomorrow.

We saw here Leon A., the same person we knew eight years ago and who is now courting Ida Mel'. True, Mania Levinson said that he is rather stupid. Flora Gabbe [Gubbay] very much likes Ida Rubinshtein; Flora wrote us here in one day (i.e., she wrote her the day after me, but since my letter was forwarded from Vienna, it arrived here on the same day as Ida's).

Today, for her birthday, Mama and Papa gave her a brooch with the image of a partridge and with diamonds in a gold hoop. This dear little thing is very original in both its idea and execution. (I had thought that it showed a chicken, not a partridge.)

Leon is not bad, but I like R[euben] Gabbe [Gubbay] more. Mama finds him even good-looking, which means too much. Of course, one must be closer to acquaintances in order to compare one with the other.

237. Boris Iakovlevich Poliakov (b. 1865), Zinaida's cousin.
238. Pavel Mikhailovich Khotinskii was Dolgorukov's right-hand man and head of the governor-general's secret chancellery.

G[ubbay] sent us candy in Paris. All have a good opinion of him. Only his pockets are empty. Papa talks only about that; the main thing, he says, is that he has neither shelter nor a fortune—and this is also a lot. One definitely does not know what should be given more attention.

In Vienna we received the Schossberger [Schôszberger] de Tornya family from Budapest. Both sons are very wealthy, very much wanted to please us, but did not succeed in achieving that—and returned home to Hungary dissatisfied.

BIARRITZ, 16/28 SEPTEMBER 1886
Yesterday evening Uncle received Antokol'skii and the elderly Leon, the father of August. They say that Ida Rubinshtein and A. Abr. Levinson left today for Paris, but I did not see them because I am not quite well. For that reason too we even delayed moving to an apartment until tomorrow; otherwise, we would already have resettled there this evening, since we were only waiting until the apartment had been vacated. This house is well situated, with a direct view of the beach. If it had a couple more rooms, it would absolutely perfect.

I am waiting for letters from Misha in Moscow. He has not written me to give his opinion of the portrait. Abroad people quickly get together, especially fellow countrymen, and there are lots of Russians here, so we have rapidly made a lot of acquaintances.

BIARRITZ, 22 SEPTEMBER/4 OCTOBER 1886
All this time I have not yet begun to swim, but I think that I shall try to do so tomorrow. They say that, with each passing day, the water is becoming colder, and then it will be impossible to begin—especially for me, as someone who has not been in the sea for a long time. Even people who constantly swim are now gradually beginning to stop, for fear of catching a cold.

The weather is warm, but change is frequent and adverse, even with rain and thunderstorms. If it is like this all the time, that will not be much comfort. It is a pity that we stayed so long in Sokol'niki. The season began here long ago. But we thought that Uncle will be alone here in the summer.

Ida Rubinshtein for some reason broke with Leon and found a young man. Stupid. James [de Hirsch] and Zina will arrive in Paris by the day that Uncle and Aunt get there. That is probably in a week. Khaia is somewhat out of sorts because yesterday, as Papa and I were discussing whether one should send a telegram to Kh. Schossberger, we expressed the view that it is none of her business to interfere in my private affairs (which are absolutely none of her concern).

Leon, our vice-consul, dined at Uncle [Samuil's] residence yesterday. We are also invited there, and therefore I declined to eat today. It is important that their son [Kotia] be there—he is so splendid!

BIARRITZ, 25 SEPTEMBER/7 OCTOBER 1886
Papa and I swam in the sea today and yesterday, and we plan to continue. Mr. Mende came here this morning. We met him on the beach and afterwards talked with him for a long time on the seashore. Even Mama found that he is more interesting than Gubbay—despite the fact that he is quite unreligious, observes none of the Jewish rites, did not even know that one does not pray on Saturday, and said that he does not intend to spend the whole day in a house of prayer. Torsz is leaving him an inheritance.

The hot weather has passed, and today was one of the most pleasant days. Now only Russians are arriving; earlier the Spanish and French elements predominated.

The game of baccarat[239] is flourishing here, and all the grand dukes play it.

Joseph Sassoon Eloiz[240] is now with Baron [Goratsii] Gintsburg . . . [sic] or perhaps already in Paris. He has written to M[ark] Antokol'skii.

Khaia has stopped bathing—that is, swimming in the sea—for several days. She is not quite well. Strangely, this happened just at the time when I began to go swimming. So we are not going at the same time. Papa also began to swim with me.

I would very much like to go to Zaragoza, where there will be bull fighting. But it seems that I will not manage to go there, since this festival takes place precisely on the day of Uncle's departure. For now there is no talk of this, and it will be necessary to stop thinking about it. As it is, Papa is already in a hurry to return home, so one should not complicate matters and in any case it would be better to travel to Brighton.[241] Of course, if we like it there, we could stay longer. But I swore that I would not remain alone with Mama or together with Khaia so as to avoid the misunderstandings and other troubles like those in Paris.

I have to hurry and finish this page: Mama is going now to Uncle's to get Papa, who dined with us today.

BIARRITZ, 30 SEPTEMBER/12 OCTOBER 1886
Yesterday we were at the Bernardine nuns[242] and Ile de Ré. In the convent of the former they take a vow of silence; they are very coarsely dressed and in

239. A parlor card game popular in the late nineteenth century.
240. Joseph Sassoon (1856–1918) married Louise de Gintsburg and had seven children.
241. Brighton, England, the home of the Sassoons.
242. A female religious order established in the late fifteenth century.

general inspire melancholy thoughts. They even ask visitors not to talk loudly among themselves and, as soon as they see outsiders, hide and reluctantly come out of their cells. This is a refuge of penitence for Magdalene sinners of the present time, and only women under age 25 are admitted. They have a garden and very nice flower bed. It is a pity that they did not repent for their transgressions in this world.

BIARRITZ, 5/17 OCTOBER 1886

Last night everyone here was thrown into a panic by a fire in the casino. They say that even those living in the hotel Angleterre left their apartments and at night began to help put out the horrible conflagration.

Uncle left for Paris today. We accompanied him to Bayonne and then went to the confectionary shop Dominique and drank coffee. After that we looked at the cathedral (where a service was under way) and the entire town. Then we rode along the banks of the Adour River and returned in a carriage to Biarritz and went for a stroll along the beach. We had hardly finished the walk when it began to rain. It is a pity that Mama has decided to go to Paris on Tuesday. I would rather stay here. We do not have any particular acquaintances here, but the days pass pleasantly. I spent all of yesterday with Uncle. And Mende is also bored to stay here for a long time and will probably leave earlier.

Khaia is being very coquettish with M. Mende, who also seems to take an interest in her. Today, under the moonlight, we walked to the sea, but did not see or hear anything other than the sound of the waves and spray. And the poetry did not inspire us—as we expected.

The politeness of the young Spiridonov is boundless. He constantly led Mama by the hand and is generally very attentive toward her.

I need to pack for the journey if we are leaving on Tuesday.

BIARRITZ, 6–8 OCTOBER 1886

Today Mr. Mende went with us to Roye, which has a splendid view. Uncle and Aunt telegraphed us that they arrived safely in Paris, and we immediately replied that we are remaining here until Sunday. The Evreinovs[243] are leaving tomorrow for Moscow; this is well-matched couple. And, in terms of external appearance, I never saw two people who were better fit for each other than this couple. But, as to their character, that I cannot judge.

It was not hot today, and the weather was excellent. There is no one here

---

243. A noble family, several of whose members held high government posts in the second half of the nineteenth century.

who is especially interesting for us. I do not like even Richard Mende, and Khaia seems to like him less than before.

Robin Gabbe [Reuben Gubbay] is much more to my taste. [Joseph] Sassoon, Luiza's husband, is much less attractive. Khaia finds attractive anyone who courts her even slightly, and since Mende seems to be very attentive to her (and even gave her a little doll), she is ready to see him as positively splendid.

The horses that I had for the charabanc today were very docile, so I drove the entire way to Biarritz. We spent the day pleasantly and did not even notice how it began to get dark—the south has no dusk and turns immediately into night. This is sometimes pleasant, but not always, especially since this circumstance impeded my driving. We are spending our last days in Biarritz. I am amazed by how sorry I am to leave this wonderful country with its poetic sea.

BIARRITZ, 11/23 OCTOBER 1886

All this time we did not once take a long stroll through the environs. As to where we did go, it was the lighthouse near Biarritz. We went there on foot with Mende. Once we also played roulette: I lost 15 francs, Mama 8, Papa about 2, whereas Mende won 80 francs. The former minister, Nabokov,[244] lost 35 francs, but N. Spiridonov about 100 francs. The entire [local] community went with us.

It is hardly likely that we will go to Zaragoza. A pity: the town will have bullfights.

The English have come in quite large numbers. Russians have gradually begun to leave for home while the getting is good.

BIARRITZ, 13/25 OCTOBER 1886

Genrikh [Vydrin] has again written a letter to me here and, inter alia, says that the Machines [sic] are in a bad way, and indeed we are also not in a brilliant situation. I think that nothing better will come of it now, but do not regret it.

Foreign Jews are very stand-offish, especially toward us Russian Jews, who regard themselves as not the least better or worse than they (the "cibilized"[245] ones, as Mme. Malkiel' says). She always tries to use pompous, stilted words. But it is excusable for her not to know how to speak Russian.

I am sorry to part with Biarritz—it is so good here. But today it was even hot, and the strong sun gave Mama a headache. Uncle and Aunt are leaving from Paris on Sunday to return to Petersburg. Ida Rubinshtein wrote Aunt

---

244. Dmitrii Nikolaevich Nabokov (1827–1904), a state official who was a member of the State Senate and minister of justice from 1878 to 1885.

245. Malkiel' evidently mispronounces "civilized," and Zinaida sardonically reproduces her mistake.

Avdot'ia a letter, but will hardly receive an answer. How pleasant it is to have nice acquaintances everywhere. Today Mr. Nabokov came twice, and then General Seliverstov and the old Baron Sherping.

It is better to be healthy than to have the sympathy of friends.

Mende also came by. Now Khaia and I have candy for the road. Nice wicker baskets, which one can only obtain here by special order. He probably ordered them earlier at a confectionary.

Last week the Lyon Stock Market brought Mama a large box of candies. The kindness and attentiveness toward us is amazing. To be honest, I do not understand why they are so solicitous toward us.

PARIS, 19/31 OCTOBER 1886

Uncle and Aunt are now here, and we arrived last Wednesday morning. We only had time to look around when, on the second day, Papa got a headache. Since then we have seen no one; we have only left visiting cards with a few people. I am awaiting the arrival of Flora with the greatest impatience and hope that she comes today or tomorrow. For now I am constantly sitting at home, since we cannot do anything (because of Papa's illness). Mama and Khaia are buying things and take considerable advantage of the stay in Paris, where they (and especially Khaia) pass the time splendidly.

The Gabbes [Gubbays] are also here. Yesterday they dined at Uncle's with the young Meyer Sassoon,[246] who makes himself at home. I talked with him very little yesterday, since I was hoarse and still had a cold. Jacques, the son of R[osa] Gintsburg,[247] will probably not be here tonight. Papa asked his mother to tell him that we will be very glad to see him.

Khaia has already ordered herself a jacket and two hats. She managed to do this! But I have been absolutely nowhere and ordered nothing.

It would be better to go directly home rather than, for no good reason, to sit and pay for a hotel. And to meet no one, see nothing, do nothing—as in our case. Mama is now completely overjoyed that I am quite stranded and cannot even go out. That does not mean going to the dentist and the like. She is in a state of bliss when we (i.e., Papa and I) cannot go out to do things; she knows perfectly well that there is nothing that she and I can do together, but it is also impossible to do nothing. Yet I must accept my lot a second time. God alone knows how much I suffered last year because of her.

---

246. Meyer Sassoon married Reuben Gubby's sister Mozelle.
247. Gabriel Jacob (Jacques) Gintsburg (1853–1929) known as "Jacques" was the son of Joseph and Rosa (née Ettinger).

Papa is now dining at Uncle [Samuil]'s with Zina Girsh [de Hirsch], her husband, D[mitrii] Nabokov, and General Seliverstov.

I have absolutely no idea when, whither, and for what purpose we will now travel. It is ludicrous to think that we have also been away from home for a long time and that they nonetheless did nothing necessary for my health—indeed, not only for my health but also for my amusement. Papa has begun to ail more and more, and I am left without any moral support. When Papa was healthy, Mama did not let him go out with me and ascribed to him the vilest acts, and we even had a fierce quarrel about this recently. That happened a month ago —during our stay in Paris. She has virtually no conscience and no sense of fairness toward others.

PARIS, 4/16 NOVEMBER 1886

We still have not decided when to leave and return to Russia. Or what else we shall do. It would be desirable to determine how useful it would be to remain here and whether it would not be better to be in Paris than Moscow. I do not think so. Here we became acquainted with Kann[248] and Jacques Gintsburg, who is very handsome, but does not intend to marry, so we have not seen him at our house for a rather long period of time; earlier he visited Papa three days running and once had breakfast with us. Mr. Kann also visits us, but he is a complete contrast to Jacques. Even his physical appearance is the diametrical opposite. Jacques—Baron de Gintsburg—is a handsome brunet, but Kann a blond. Kann is short; his eyes are large, blue, bulging.

PARIS, 6/18 NOVEMBER 1886

Unfortunately, we still do not know conclusively where we shall go from here. To England or to Russia? Zina Girsh [de Hirsch] today is going to the *variété* with Cherukova, who is dining with us today. I saw her this morning at Rue de la Paix.[249]

In a letter to Mama and Papa, Ida writes that Miss Gosh very much opposes our trip to London. She says that if we go to her country this time of year, we shall see the English fog, and that this will suffice to quash any desire to go there again.

James told Papa that even the son-in-law of the President Jules Grévy of France, Wilson, is in police custody. Kann was also in custody, and that has

248. This may be a reference to one of the sons of Isaac Eduard Kann (1830–87), a French public figure and influential leader of the Alliance Israelite Universelle. After she moved to Paris, Zinaida became close to his second wife, Julie Kann née Koenigswater (1845–1917).
249. An elite, high-fashion shopping venue in Paris.

apparently not been lifted. People who caroused in their youth sometimes get into serious trouble later on. I would very much like to know Robin Gabbe's [Reuben Gubbay's] opinion of me. I think that he is very cool toward everyone, with the exception of I[da] A. Rubinshtein. It is essential to ascertain the veracity of all this and what is specifically true here. I presume that Aunt [Avdot'ia] deliberately gave me and Khaia [his] photograph, taken with them together, to eliminate any desire on my part to pay attention to him.

As for Papa, I wrote long ago that he is not well. At present there is nothing of interest here, and I do not think that there will be.

BRIGHTON [ENGLAND], 24 NOVEMBER/6 DECEMBER 1886

We all arrived here from London last Thursday, 21 November (3 December [N.S.]) We had breakfast this morning at Sarah Sassoon's.[250] No matter where we go, we run into Robin Gabbe [Reuben Gubbay] almost everywhere. Today he was summoned by telegraph to his grandfather in Crauworth [sic]. Later we went to his uncle, R. D. Sassoon,[251] to have tea, and he came there as well. Apparently, everyone is disposed to ensure that we are together as much as possible. And I am happy about that: Gabbe [Gubbay] is a very nice, handsome young man, in my opinion. One regret: he is without means. He is very strongly praised by his relatives and by those who know him.

I rather like English life. But the climate is bad. Here in Brighton there are severe storms and morning fog; it is impossible to go outside because of the foul weather.

Joseph and his wife Louise [Sassoon] kindly received us at Ashley Park, which we reached by train and we spent the day. When we returned, Sasha [Aleksandr] Ginzburg accompanied us to London, where we spent the night. On Tuesday he and Warburg dined with us at the hotel Metropole,[252] and then we went to the Royal Albert Hall, where we heard Albani and a very poor performance of orchestral works.

London did not make a distinct impression on me. Mama liked it very much and would want to live there.

In a few days we are supposed to leave from here in order to attend a large dinner at [Samuel] Montagu's on Wednesday. He invited us two weeks prior to the dinner, and we recently replied that we will be there.

Papa has come down with a severe cold here, as did we all, but worse than

250. Sarah Sassoon, the daughter of Elias David Sassoon, married Nassim Sassoon.
251. Reuben David Sassoon (1835–1905), Reuben Gubbay's uncle, served as the director of David Sassoon & Co. in India and China.
252. A prominent London hotel, which had only opened in 1885.

I—and I have been coughing in Paris and here. Naturally, I did not stop coughing in Brighton, which is so favorable for colds, where the wind blows through the windows as if one were outdoors.

I am not fond of inconveniences. After arriving here, Khaia became capricious and complained that she was given a bad room and rushed to have it changed.

The Sassoons are very nice toward us and give us endless invitations.

LONDON, 2/14 DECEMBER 1886

It is bad for me everywhere. Even here, which I very much like, I suffer spiritually; for example, I am now sitting alone at home. There is little happiness on earth, and even that small amount is quite vulnerable. And all people strive, in every possible way, to ruin the lives of those closest to them. For example, Mama oppresses me to the utmost and totally ignores her promise to restrain herself.

It would be desirable to know when my family is coming back. There is a kosher restaurant Silver here, and they have gone there with Baron Gintsburg and Aby Warburg.[253]

LONDON, 3/15 DECEMBER 1886

If we were here for a long time, it would make absolutely no difference to me how the days are spent. But since we are leaving on Sunday, I cannot be indifferent to this. It would be desirable for Mama to have some conscience about how she fulfills her promise to treat me pleasantly in all things and at all times. But such is her way. Today she even ordered Papa not to promise to go on strolls with me, since she had promised that to me above all.

Beyond that, I also suffer from something else—something that is not complicated, but holds great significance for me.

Mama very much likes people who court Khaia, but despises anyone who pays any attention to me. So she is always an obstacle for me. So who knows a daughter better than her mother? And since she herself upbraids me and puts me in a bad light, then of course no one wants to get to know me.

VIENNA, 10 DECEMBER 1886

We arrived in Vienna already on Monday evening and will remain here until Sunday. It would be desirable for Richard Stern to look on me as I do on him—

253. Aby (Abraham Moritz) Warburg (1866–1929) became a German art and cultural historian. Perhaps the Poliakovs were hoping he would marry one of their daughters (Zinaida suspected they had Khaia, not her, in mind as she suggests in the next entry).

that is, not from a positive point of view. I find him unsatisfactory. He also has a physical shortcoming: loss of hair, which is combed back in an Eastern fashion. As for the rest of his appearance, he is an entirely normal person and even not bad looking, but not to my taste. The fact is that he is a milksop, as they say, and not an entirely independent person. Joseph is, of course, much worse than he, but comparison is not the point. How should one look at all this? If one is not too demanding, then of course it is a good thing: it is better to have less glitter and more substance, in my opinion. But I regret to say that it is all a waste of time, because I have already sorted out things and have come to the belief that it is all or nothing: either everything is irreproachable, or I will not at all have any pretense of marrying.

Papa's birthday was yesterday. We learned of this in the evening. Of course, I am at fault here. Still, I blame Misha for failing to tell us earlier. This morning I went for a walk with Papa and stopped at a shop. Things are not very lively here, despite the approach of the holidays and the best season. In Russia things are much better; even on the eve of Christmas and Easter it is impossible to move through the best, most populous streets of Moscow. It is different here. Well, this is explained by the size of Vienna.

I think that Flora is not writing me, because I did not include our address when I wrote her from London. Our correspondence did not achieve its goal, so there is no point in striving to do that and bore her with my letters for no good reason.

VIENNA, 11/23 DECEMBER 1886

Georg[e] von Weisweiller's sister came for a visit today and went with us to the exhibition. We stopped at a fur shop and bought three pairs of muffs for Mama, Khaia, and me (two lambskin and one sealskin in the current fashion). I find everything cheaper in Vienna than in Paris. To be sure, nothing here is especially new, but still these are beautiful things and the leather goods are better than anywhere in the best capitals of the world. Everything is very well made, even remarkably so. The leather is Russian. The workmanship here is better than anywhere else.

Christmas [Eve] is tomorrow evening. How strange that foreign Jews observe this event.

Liulia's husband George is bald like Mende, but better than Richard Stern.

VIENNA, 14 DECEMBER 1886

This morning, after lunch, there was a rendezvous with Rippe von Bouhau [sic]. I cannot form an opinion of him, since I had to sit with my back to him.

Iosif Isaakovich Ziberding and his son came for a visit one evening and even gave Papa his old fur coat to sell in Moscow, since it is not needed in Vienna. Papa will use it on the journey, since he did not bring along a fur coat with him.

Today Papa gave me a letter from Flora Gabbe [Gubbay]—which he had assumed was from L[ouise] G[intsburg] Sassoon. My joy was more than if it had been a letter from Sassoon. How nice of Flora to write me. "Love is not a potato," as the proverb says, and a new sign of love is always pleasant. I had to show my gratitude, and I immediately responded to her brief note. We have managed to become acquainted with several new families here. It is wonderful to make an acquaintance without a definite goal and even without a prior opinion. But when the contrary holds, that is unpleasant.

Today we went to Hofmannstahl[254] but had difficulty finding his apartments. After searching for a long time we arrived at the appointed place and, on the sidewalk, came upon Malkiel'.

MOSCOW, 21 DECEMBER 1886

So, we finally arrived home on Friday, 19 December. Iosef [Landau] and Boria [Boris Iakovlevich] met us in Warsaw at the railway station, and from there we went to their apartment while we waited for our train. Khaia was very rude to me during the entire trip from Vienna to Warsaw. I could not even sit quietly in the lounge of our railcar. She and Mama stirred up Papa against me, and thus I remained entirely alone, without any defender. But this was hardly anything new for me.

Love is a conditional thing. It seems to me that Khaia's feeling for Mama does not deserve this term. But Mama nonetheless helps Khaia in all her quarrels and confrontations.

I was very happy to see all our relatives. For now it is not yet apparent that my future has become somewhat clearer. On the contrary, once again Mama does not exchange greetings with me. It is a joy to see how the young children missed their parents, but the latter (and especially Mama) does not seem in the least concerned: she even wanted to remain for the season in Vienna, where the balls and soirées are most probably at their peak.

Today I saw a lot of people here—for example, Dolgorukov,[255] Ladyzhenskii, and Petrovskii[256] were guests. I am astonished that none of them congratulated me, given that rumors have allegedly been circulating about my wedding.

254. Possibly Hugo August Peter Hofmann Edler von Hofmannsthal (1841–1915), director of Bank of Vienna (Wiener Bank).
255. Presumably Prince Vladimir Andreevich Dolgorukov, governor-general of Moscow.
256. Poliakova described Petrovskii as an editor below.

Flora Gabbe [Gubbay] is in Brighton, but there has been no news from her. Khaia left her brooch with Flora to have it exchanged for one with emeralds instead of a sapphire.

The cycle of our wandering has come to an end. And I must say it has been highly unsatisfactory for me, all for the same reason: Mama's disfavor and dislike for me. This is, again, offensive, for the years are passing one after the other. And it is all the same tedious, imperturbable life. The fatal hour is approaching and it will say: time to retire.

Shaikevich came up to us at the concert yesterday. I. Shchukin[257] visited Papa today and asked how our trip to England went. We are now eating better, because Il'ia orders much greater variety.

MOSCOW, 27 DECEMBER 1886

Jerusalem and Russia are celebrating Christmas.[258] Nevertheless, things here are extremely quiet. Earlier it had seemed to me that Vienna does not have as much liveliness on the streets as Petersburg and Moscow, but now I am no longer convinced of that. Mama is constantly pouting, and the atmosphere has not improved. But I absolutely do not care: I am used to it.

MOSCOW 28 DECEMBER 1886

How I would like to see Uncle Samuil and tell him so much!

Lidiia Stepanovna does not say spiteful things as she used to do at the summer house in Sokol'niki. So I gave her a brooch that I brought back from abroad. But she is very unpleasant toward me and in general displays last year's extremely disagreeable attitude—sulking, sulking, sulking. She forgets that everything she told me before our departure for abroad proved a lie. But after all everything is transient, nothing is forever.

As for Tret'iakova,[259] they say that she is the fiancée of Zelobki. This is a good match, in my opinion; one could not think of anything better for both of them. It is extremely rare for people with the same views to come together. I am happy for them: it is so unusual to see happiness on earth, so one involuntarily has a warm feeling about it. Today we had several acquaintances come, but one more boring than the next—the editor Petrovskii, I. I. Zaichenko,[260]

257. Ivan Vasil'evich Shchukin (d. 1890), a prominent Old Believer industrialist.
258. This is not a slight directed at European churches: Zinaida is merely referring to areas that still used the Old Style calendar—hence the omission of Catholic and Protestant countries.
259. Possibly a relative of Pavel Mikhailovich Tret'iakov (1832–98), Russian entrepreneur and founder of the Tret'iakov Gallery.
260. Ivan Ivanovich Zaichenko (1844–1920) was a first-guild merchant, cofounder of the South

Ladyzhenskii, and others. So I had to sit for several hours in the office and listen to all kinds of business and dry conversation—for example, about the Persian railroads, about the future appointment of a new minister of finance, etc. That is why I do not like to be present at a reception.

MOSCOW, 29 DECEMBER 1886

An additional kindness never hurts, and I am very glad that I sent Flora a New Year's greeting. Misha found her letter to be very dry, and I think that he is absolutely right, but she also sent me and Khaia greeting cards. On my note she added a large seal with a cupid, along with a greeting in Old English. She sent Khaia a small note, the kind that is attached to a suitcase. Khaia does not like it, and rightly so. Flora does not write anything interesting about herself.

Papa is ill today, again with a headache. He is not up to working now. As if on purpose, he has people sitting in his office from morning to night. He apparently went for a stroll in the morning; perhaps the cold had an effect on him—driving the blood into his head.

Flora writes that she ordered my things. She has Khaia's brooch in Brighton and asks what she is to do with it. Sukki's example of fasting has infected Misha, who has stopped eating meat. They keep telling him that this is very enervating, but he pays no attention whatsoever. Charcot,[261] a Parisian professor, has been mentioned in this case, and there was talk of sending Misha to him. But of course they were joking. Food constitutes something in life; on an empty stomach, nothing reaches the brain. Of course, people like Dr. Ganner and others fast virtually their entire lives, but there are very few such people.

MOSCOW, [30] DECEMBER 1886

Miss Gosh frequently complains of weakness and ill health. She says that she will not go to England until the days are long and fears traveling in the winter. It is a pity that I was able to read so little of Flora's letters: she wrote me only several lines. I am thus a little angry at her, although I also wrote her only a few words from Vienna, with a New Year's greeting. Yesterday Papa was not completely well; I am happy that he is better today—thank God. Aleksandr Danilovich Mein, it turns out, came here twice yesterday.

Russian Winemaking Society, director of the Moscow Guardianship of Prisons, and honorary member of the Moscow Council of Children's Shelters.

261. Jean-Martin Charcot (1825–93), a pioneering French neurologist at the famous Salpêtrière Hospital, had a major impact on the fields of neurology and psychology. After her marriage, Zinaida became friendly with Charcot's daughter Jeanne Edwards.

At last the year is over, and I am very happy that it is. It did not bring anything particularly pleasant. It is a great pity that, with the coming New Year, my relations with Mama are extremely strained. But what else might I wish? Thank God, all is alright, and we cannot complain about unduly great troubles. To be sure, Papa was sick several times during the year, but thanks to God he now feels better (although for the third day he does not feel well and is again lying in bed). I hope that he will be healthier in the coming year and that Mama will not pester him with all kinds of nonsense. His work really exhausts him. Today we will welcome the New Year as in years past: the same situation as on this day last year, and the same phony faces. Everyone has something in [his or her] heart and each has something to wish for. Khaia is very much given to sulking; she and Lidiia Stepanovna, with Mama at the head, comprise an original fourth triumvirate, which is known in the chronicle of our home. They very much like to belittle all those around them and, simultaneously, act in a vile manner.

MOSCOW, 1 JANUARY 1887

We are older by one year, and 1886 brought nothing new. True, it is unknown what this year will bring and whether it will be better than last year. But I hope that some of my wishes come true.

Girls tell their fortunes on Epiphany eve, and we will enjoy ourselves at the Novikovs on that day, for they have invited Misha and me, without Mama. Only the youth, without their elders, will be present. The Novikov mother is not well and will not participate in receiving guests, and all that will be the responsibility of Novikov and his daughters.

Today we had a New Year's reception—but much smaller than last year. Surprisingly, neither A[leksandr] D. Mein nor General Kondrat'ev, nor S[emen] Podgoretskii came. The physiognomy of some showed dissatisfaction and others even exhibited boredom. Khaia poured tea as usual, while I occupied people with conversation so far as I could. At the same time, my thoughts were far away. The Tsurikovo registry office sent Mama a new year's greeting. Gabriel Gintsburg sent me two visiting cards from Bombay (India), where he is now located. Amazingly, these cards came just today. At 1 pm we were still serving breakfast. D. Sheleshevskii was in tails and very interesting, but he speaks Russian very poorly—and suffers on that account. Also here was [Ivan] Shchukin, the elder son of the merchant Shchukin, who was with us abroad. The Perlov brothers[262] ate and drank: today they are celebrating the hundredth

---

262. The tea house of Vasilii Perlov and sons in Moscow, the history of which is recounted in *K stoletiiu chainoi firmy. V. Perlov s synov'iami 1778–1887* (Moscow: Izdanie I. C. i N. C. Perlovykh, 1898).

anniversary of their tea trade. This was a huge celebration at their home. Breakfast from Oliv'e [Olivier] (Hermitage [Restaurant])[263] was served for 600 people. I[van] Zaicheno brought the menu to show us: it listed twenty dishes, at the very least, and had been lithographed by the Levinson typography. Fedor Knaev, it turns out, is the cousin of V[asilii] Bezekirskii. They met at our house today and found this out.

MOSCOW, 3 JANUARY 1887

For the time being, there is nothing new. And thank God. Everything is all right. Of course, everyone was asking why none of us was at the ball yesterday (because of Friday [Sabbath]), and we were conspicuous by our absence. This afternoon we had a reception in the red drawing room and many people were there, including: Naumenko, General Biskupskii,[264] G[rigorii] A. Zakhar'in, and others. Both young countesses Brevern de Lagarde also came to thank us for the *côte de bal[eau]*. Since she [Countess Brevern de Lagarde] sent Mama a figurine, it was necessary to send them something. S[of'ia] Slezkina's son-in-law was made a chamberlain, and she is in ecstasy. Fedos'ev is moving up in the world through Liliia.

MOSCOW, 4 JANUARY 1887

The order of the governor-general to eject a man who kissed someone at the Sorokoumovskii[265] concert yesterday is highly rational. It is shameful to think that such a scandal could occur at the Noble Assembly, indeed with a very nice young lady and after the first part (just after Mrs. Arnol'tseva sang an aria from *The Marriage of Figaro*). Then cries were heard: "Throw him out!" There was, simultaneously, a commotion at the exit. It turned out that some scoundrel had taken it into his head to kiss Sorokoumovskii's wife on the lips, with the words: "We have not kissed for a long time." Is it surprising that, after this, he was immediately ejected by the police?

The brother-in-law of the baker Fillipov has married [the daughter of] Ga-briel' Gerikker. Although he is also a swindler (*shuler*) and forbidden to enter Moscow, his wife nonetheless loves him and has a happy mien. At the cost of her parents' disfavor, she entered into this union. People often encounter her

---

263. Lucien Oliv'e (Olivier) was the French master chef at the Hermitage, a prominent Moscow restaurant.

264. Probaby General Konstantin Ksever'evich Biskupskii (1834–92), who was decorated for his role in the Russo-Turkish War.

265. Presumably the concert had been funded by the family that owned Pavel Sorokoumovskii and Sons, so famous for its fur fashions that the clientele even included the imperial family.

in a cab, and when she sees acquaintances, she turns away to avoid acknowledging them with a bow.

P. Shostakovskii[266] should be satisfied that the history of the kiss did not occur at his concert: people would say that every kind of rubbish occurs at his performances. But at a symphonic concert it is impossible to blame anyone; Strizhevskii[267] behaved insolently, forgot himself, and committed such an impudent act.

MOSCOW, 5 JANUARY 1887

This morning I went skating and then took a stroll—thus I exercised twice, which is extremely useful for me but which I especially dislike. The number of notaries in Moscow decreased with the passing of Perevozchikov, who died of heart failure on 2 January. They say that earlier he was sick with an adipose heart, and the doctor ordered him to eat and drink only milk. But he did not observe this regimen.

Shakhovskoi[268] recently became the father of a daughter named Sof'ia, who, according to Miss Gosh, is the spitting image of her mother. The Fedotovs, who bear the princely title, attended the opening meeting of [the] psychiatrists' [congress],[269] and Mama was there as well. I did not want to go: to attend and listen to everything about the insane would be very unpleasant for me. It is already enough that Mama and Papa apply this epithet to me.

I did not see Iulii Osipovich [Go'ldenbakh] yesterday at the congress, but almost all the doctors we know were there. However, I was seated in the back and cannot guarantee that he was not present. The actress [Glikeriia] Fedotova, it seems, was also there, and in general a lot of ladies were present (mainly the wives and relatives of doctors). I came at the invitation of a future doctor, Uncle Genrikh, who obtained the admissions ticket to the Noble Assembly with difficulty. He himself was with the medical students in the gallery, but came down to us. The large auditorium was filled to capacity. It was all very festive, but boring for a layman.

266. Petr Adamovich Shostakovskii (1853–1917), a pianist and conductor.
267. Possibly Aleksandr Ivanovich Strizhevskii (1866–1911), a baritone opera singer in Moscow.
268. Prince Dmitrii Ivanovich Shakhovskoi (1861–1939) was a public figure, historian, publicist, prominent member in the liberal Constitutional Democratic ("Kadet") Party, and deputy in the first State Duma in 1906.
269. Held in Moscow in 1887, this congress was the first national meeting of psychiatrists and neurologists.

MOSCOW, 6 JANUARY 1887

On Saturday the theater Paradizo is presenting the Tyrol performance of *Krasavitsa*. People say that they all have excellent voices, and a third also have comedic talent and make everyone laugh.

Today I finally sent Flora Gabbe [Gubbay] a letter, addressed to Brighton —to her grandfather, Albert Sassoon.[270] She is probably not very pleased with me: for a long time I did not reply to her few words and did not thank her for sending the original greeting card. Khaia asked me to request that she keep the brooch until an occasion presents itself. It takes 45 days for a letter to go there, so I shall not receive a letter soon. Crossing the sea just now must be a difficult trip, so the postal service is irregular.

MOSCOW, 7 JANUARY 1887

The danger that an illness posed for Elena (Liza) Raffalovich[271] has passed.

Today Khaia and Mama went to visit the Perevozchikovs, who are in deep mourning and very sorrowful, it is said.

Yesterday evening we danced the entire evening at the Novikov residence, where thirty couples were dancing. Despite the large number of people, I was not happy, because now I am not glad to dance to no purpose. No one, nothing is attractive for me, even if only for conversation. The officer Chaplin, who appears at Z[inaida] Danilova's, was not there. A noisy ball is fun only when there are a lot of friends present. Shchepkina, they say, skates extremely well with A. Postnikov at Lazar [Poliakov]'s in the garden. I only went sledding twice this winter. This extremely pleasant activity is much more attractive than other outings, and I am very willing to exchange a sleigh ride for a ball. For some reason Iuferov[272] is not to be seen—as if he dropped out of the conservatory and no longer attends any concerts. Earlier, however, he did not miss a single concert. I empathize him for this surfeit. For Fedotova, the actress, there will be a benefit concert, which will present *Antony and Cleopatra*. But I think it will be impossible for us not to see Iuferov there.

---

270. Sir Albert Abdullah David Sassoon (1818–96) was the son of the entrepreneur David Sassoon (who was active first in Baghdad and later in Bombay). He was Reuben Gubbay's grandfather on his mother's side.

271. Daughter of Iakov Poliakov.

272. Sergei Vladimirovich Iuferov (b. 1865) was a Russian composer. Among his works is the opera *Antony and Cleopatra*.

French newspapers and journals are of little interest to me. Although I receive *Journal des débats*,[273] I hardly look at it and instead prefer reading in German. For a whole two weeks I have been reading Krishevskii and soon will finish this novel, which involuntarily reminds me of certain incidents in my own life. The description of everything is remarkably accurate; it often happens that you see yourself as in a mirror.

[Princess] Shakhovskaia is getting married to the architect Rodionov.[274] Mama and Papa are traveling to Petersburg; perhaps Grandfather and I will also go there. This will, in any case, be more pleasant than going with Mama. I think that Mr. L. I. Brodskii,[275] who dined with us today, came to talk again about his cousin Aron. The former is apparently trying to arrange a marriage, but absolutely refuses to grasp the fact that one cannot like the cousin.

I have begun to take music lessons. This morning Mme. Erdmansderfer came and we set a time. Where are the [de La]gardes[276] now, and where did they go after England—perhaps to Cannes or Nice, as they planned? In any case I shall not see them, since I shall not be making a journey under the usual circumstances. Mama, as always, will prevent this, so that we shall wait for a ray to appear on the horizon in the future. Were it not for this, I could go with Papa. It is a pity that things are so unpleasant for me, that I must fight against fate. Il'iusha is now here and says that he could not write so much as I do. And because of laziness he does not even read anything.

MOSCOW, 9 JANUARY 1887

Because the wind is too strong, today I decided not to go out and do not have the slightest regrets. That is because I intend henceforth to look after my health above all else on earth. It is possible to buy everything else, but good health cannot be bought at any price if you did not have it or do not know how to take care of it.

Today we drank black coffee with sugar instead of cream. This did not taste very good, but meets all the prescripts of the Law of Moses.

---

273. A French newspaper published from 1789 to 1944.
274. Sergei Konstantinovich Rodionov (1859–1925) was a Russian architect and master of the Moscow modern style.
275. This could be Lev Izrailevich Brodskii.
276. Probably a reference to the Brevern de Lagarde family.

The entire day was spent in conversation with Jacques and in critical remarks. Across the table Lidiia Stepanovna asked me whether I like his comment that children should pay attention to their food if the parents fail to do so.

Six people came to our reception today, with the exception of Daragan and Slezkina's sister. The latter came at my invitation; I sent her a note yesterday that I would be very happy to see her, and if she is inclined to come in the evening, then we are at home on Friday. Instead of that, however, she came today. The Star of David decorates all the windows at the synagogue. They are going to the theater, but Khaia and I are going to a concert of the Philharmonic Society. That concert is all the more interesting, because a singer of the Dutch court, Mme. Bemmer, will be performing there.

Fedor Fedorovich Knauf is a frequent visitor to Papa upstairs. He does not look well and even has a sickly appearance. Since we arrived, he has already managed to lose weight, but I remember how he was overweight, when we teased Lidiia Stepanovna, but now only a shadow remains of him. No more balls are envisioned, and I am very content with that.

In a few days my 24th year will come to an end. I must confess that I am very sorry about this. Joking aside, I do not want to get married, all the more since I have two adult sisters who can be a hindrance for me. As the Russian proverb says, "a pike lives in the lake to keep all the fish awake," and hence I should [not] rush and give up my place to others, who only thirst after this with the greatest impatience. Indeed, I have given everyone carte blanche without the slightest pretensions.

They went out today for visits, but I sat at home. This is not the first time that the rats ate the boots.[277] It is amazing: youth passes so quickly that one grows old without noticing, and without taking advantage of all the worldly blessings. However, I am not complaining of my lot, but only regret the unjust state of affairs. Thucydides is for good reason called the father of history, but history itself is a monument of the past. After all, with these things, all that once was would disappear without a trace. At the same time, forgetting is the greatest blessing. There are moments (few such in life) . . . [sic] etc., about which it is pleasant to remember, but these are so few; it is better to forget the remaining years and never think about them. Such is the disillusionment

---

277. This is the literal translation of the text ("kogda sapogi s"eli krysy"), which corresponds to no well-known proverb and which may be an error in the published text.

to which one sometimes comes; it is said that life is a puzzle, and death is the solution. And that is not so terrible. While we still try to do divine things, it is necessary to endeavor—so far as possible—to find a solution. If I had to seek this myself my entire life, then I would rather reject this wise solution.

I wait impatiently for winter to pass in order to have the opportunity to follow Mama's intentions and best wishes for me. For lack of her own sense of dignity, she takes it away from others in the most merciless fashion. Understandably, she does this only among those who permit her to take it. Consequently, she can do this with Papa, but not me.

MOSCOW, 12 JANUARY 1887

[The lawyer] Shaikevich was here today, sat for a long time, and talked. D. Shchukin, they say, wants to marry Mashen'ka Perevozchikova, but she allegedly does not want this and therefore things are not going well. Today we are going to the opera and will hear G. Sil'va and the singer Diuran—two stars of the first magnitude. They are giving several performances here, and there are subscriptions for these. We are not going with subscription tickets, although this is the first in the subscription series. Elvis—the wife of the general —ordered quite miniature photographs in the English shop. The jewelry section there is not distinguished by new things, and I did not find anything there.

MOSCOW, 13 JANUARY 1887

Shchukin and the lawyer Shaikevich are currently the luminaries of the local court.

Misha and I went to go sleigh riding today, and then we had a conflict with Khaia because she did not permit me to watch how they took my things from the trunk.

Emiliia Isaakovna [Ogus-]Shaikevich is now giving lessons to almost all the boys, including Misha, who has become very interested in music. Although not especially talented, he nonetheless practices very willingly. It is a pity that he gave up this art as a child.

The South has strengthened my Mama only in terms of her caprice.

I wanted to acquaint Masha [Levinson] with [Osip Grigor'ievich] Khabas, an army doctor, who came to the congress [of psychiatrists].

The benefit concert for Glikeriia Fedotova has still not been given and will take place only in the course of this month (i.e., January). Since she will probably choose Friday for some reason, I do not think that we shall go. The Brevern [de Lagardes] will be in our synagogue this Friday and then dine with us the same day. Everyone says that our synagogue choir is very good, all the more since they sing so badly at the temporary house of prayer on Solianskaia Street [in central Moscow] that [the singing at] ours is of course relatively good. So it is not surprising that people like our choir.

MOSCOW, 15 JANUARY 1887

I do not know whether Nora went to the rehearsal yesterday evening, or if this is only a pretext. With this she excused herself so as not to be bored at our house in the evening. As if on purpose, Colonel Tolmachev came for tea. But this was a misunderstanding.

Nature in the South does not attract me as much as tranquility, and hence I would be very happy to be in Nice this winter if Uncle [Samuil] travels there now. But it seems that this will not transpire, because he will stay on in Petersburg.

I celebrated my twenty-fifth birthday yesterday. The historian Thucydides could not write a better history than what transpired yesterday. I had thought that everything was over now and that we could make peace. It turned out differently, entirely differently. It is necessary to be very attractive [*sic*] so as to exorcise from my memory all the troubles that I am now experiencing.

Countess Brevern, the wife of the military commander, will be at our house tomorrow, and I am very displeased with this, especially because it happens that I am not on speaking terms with Mama and Khaia. Yesterday they did not even wish me a happy birthday, and Mama wore a black dress. Well, after all, everything in the world is absolutely perverse. Perhaps, if our roles were to change, then we would have to sing a different tune. It is a pity that one has to have so many failures in life and that there is now so much sorrow. Tomorrow a lot of guests will gather, including Anichkov. Ivan Ivanovich Zaichenko very much praises his Baron Norman, who arrived from Persia. Iosif Khabas today had a meeting with Masha in Papa's office. He was not in a full parade uniform, but in military stripes, and I commented to him that now they have narrow, no longer wide, stripes (as earlier), and that consequently he was not correctly attired. It seems that he made a favorable impression on Masha—better in any case than Mr. Tsetlin.

MOSCOW, 17 JANUARY 1887

The Efros wedding was held at our synagogue. But they say that everyone conversed in very loud voices.

Yesterday I had to entertain all the guests because Khaia refused to come to dinner (claiming to have a headache). I was nevertheless dissatisfied with her rude behavior toward the honored guests who were here at our house.

Themistocles[278] in ancient history for some reason is embedded in my memory.

I think that Papa is nevertheless going to Petersburg with Mama. Today the cavaliers[279] came to our house to apologize that they could not come yesterday (which was quite impolite). We all danced with our brothers.

MOSCOW, 18 JANUARY 1887

Iuliia [Julie] Konstantinovna Shild'bakh no longer shows herself in public. I myself would willingly pay her a visit, but her father is ill, and I think that right now it would not be appropriate to go to her.

Thrace is apparently a province of Greece (if I am not mistaken), but I know ancient Greek history and geography so poorly that I simply cannot remember all the Greek provinces. There was a time when we could learn all this by heart, and I knew chronology especially well . . . [*sic*]

278. Themistocles (524–459 B.C.), an Athenian politician and general, was a nonaristocratic politician who played a major role in the early development of Athenian democracy.
279. "Cavalier" has multiple meanings, but here Zinaida uses it in the sense of dance partner.

NOTEBOOK 2

They say that, at the start of every endeavor, one should ask for divine blessing. Even in so unimportant a matter as the new notebook of a journal (which I continue to write)! But actually that is not really a beginning; rather, it is the continuation of a diary. Just today I managed to finish the last page of the old notebook, immediately began a new one, and turned a page in the history of my life. At least that is how it seems to me, when I begin a new section of my journal (which has little interest even for me, not to mention other people!). I would want my journal to be a good one! I suppose that only one thing might be an obstacle here: my carelessness. So, if by the end of this notebook there is a break from a monotonous, drag[ging] life, then thank God! Job prayed to God and did not complain about his poverty—despite the fact that he was among the poorest. The beginning and end of each matter are the important points.

ST. PETERSBURG, 26 JANUARY 1887. MONDAY.
I am writing here [in Petersburg] today and, apart from the monotony and Muscovite boredom, here too there is nothing. Today Kondrat'ev gave me the notes and letters that Misha sent with him from Moscow; he only just arrived and hastened to deliver what had been sent. Today I was visited by the Messarosh family (mother and daughter) and by Mme. Epshtein (born Dynina and from the city of Tula). The latter has become quite ugly and changed. As for Lelia Messarosh and her mother, the former looks very good, but her mother has grown terribly thin and become simply unrecognizable. To be sure, she has had much grief from her husband's death, and that is probably her spiritual infirmity.

The weather is bad, and only yesterday was it tolerable. Mr. Constant Dreyfus,[1] who is married to the second Gutman[n],[2] came to Uncle Iakov from Vienna. Dreyfus was with him at the hotel yesterday, and Papa found him there when he dropped by to pick up Uncle for a meeting. Time passes imperceptibly, and even here I have not seen any of my acquaintances. But, I hope, today Papa will dine with I. A. Zvegintsev, whom we visited yesterday and sat along

1. Daniel dit Constant Dreyfus (1852–1907), a banker and stepbrother of the entrepreneur Leopold Dreyfus.
2. Hermine de Gutmann (b. 1864).

with Mariia Aleksandrovna [Mein]. She was wearing a red bonnet, a circumstance that was especially strange, because just a few days ago she arrived from the burial services in Moscow for her uncle, who left her a substantial inheritance (300,000 to 500,000 [rubles]). So, out of propriety, she could have worn something black, if not a mourning dress, then at least some thing made of silk or velvet. But apparently the victors are not judged. Kotia [Daniil] is now intensively occupied with preparing for the exam that he must take on Friday. So he is almost not to be seen or heard for the simple reason that he is constantly in his room below. And each day Grandfather goes to drink tea down at Leon Varshavskii [Warshawsky] and his uncles.

Tomorrow I promised to be at Mme. Messarosh's at two o'clock, and if Papa has to go anywhere, he will drop me off and leave me there. I have a lot of lunches to do. Yesterday I declined to stay at Lazar and Annette [Poliakov]'s, but Mr. and Mrs. Zvegintsev urged us stay and dine with them; but we preferred instead to come today rather than yesterday. Moreover, on Thursday there is musical soiree at A[bram] Zak's with the participation of Evgenii Al'ber [Eugen d'Albert], who recently performed in a concert in Moscow. Babitta is still the same old muddle. No one was at her house yesterday, and she received us alone in her drawing room. Then we stopped at the residence of David Goratsievich Gintsburg and his wife, where her mother is now visiting—in expectation of a great occasion. She looks fine, but she has turned completely pale over the past year since I last saw her. Matil'da Iur'evna Gintsburg [David's wife] also, despite the fact that she is now in an interesting condition [pregnant], looks splendid.

ST. PETERSBURG, 28 JANUARY 1887, THURSDAY.

We are contantly idle here, all the time, and not doing anything worthwhile. From Spiridonov I just learned about the engagement of Ekaterina Aleksandrovna Spiridonova to Baron Russov, an officer in the Sumskii dragoon regiment. He has been courting her for a long time, and only in Moscow were rumors to be heard that he will marry either her or her younger, unattractive sister Elena (who is very homely, but that is simply a matter of luck). They say that everything depends on fate, and I think that is absolutely true. But the question is when is fate decided? It seems to me that everything comes at its own time. Uncle Samuil is again ill; he is coughing blood, and Professor Botkin[3] sees him twice a day. My aunt does not get out at all and is here all the

---

3. Sergei Petrovich Botkin (1832–89), a premier doctor and a professor at the St. Petersburg Medical Surgical Academy.

time; she went out just five or six times and caught a cold. Most probably, they will soon leave for Nice or Paris.

Today the Georgievskiis, mother and daughter, were my guests, and it was very nice. They stopped by for only a minute in Uncle's office, where he is resting, talked with him a bit, and then set off on their visits. Tomorrow evening, apparently, we will leave here for our home in Moscow, and it is indeed time to go: instead of being here five days, as planned, we have already been here more than a week, and if we leave tomorrow (i.e., Sunday), we will have been in St. Petersburg ten days—exactly twice as long as planned. But today I have to go to Masha [Mania] Levinson's. Masha became engaged during our absence from Moscow. Her fiancé, Dr. Osip Grigor'evich Khabas, serves as a junior physician at a military hospital in Helsingfors [Helsinki]. He is only 27 years old, she is already 26 and a half, but he said that this does not matter to him. Grandfather [Solomon] Poliakov was partly her matchmaker, and this happened in a very strange way: he came to the congress of doctors in Moscow and presented him the next day to Papa, and [Khabas] began to visit. It occurred to Papa that this would be a highly appropriate match for Masha and asked me what I think about this. I replied that it is very easy to make them acquainted, since Masha often comes to visit me. And that is how this serious thing came about! He is a court councilor and wears a colonel's epaulette, since this is assigned to doctors. And of course it is better to marry an educated person than some clerk. May God grant them happiness! And yesterday M[asha] Levinson teased me that I am allegedly the fiancée of Mr. Gabbe [Gubbay]—how about that!

I just returned from the opera, where I was with Aunt [Amaliia Poliakova], Mlle. Fanny, Niuta, Samuil'chik, and Ol'ga.[4] They performed [Mikhail] Glinka's *Ruslan and Liudmila*. Yesterday evening we three went to the symphonic assembly of the St. Petersburg Musical Section, and I came back very pleased with the evening. This evening we will apparently be at the Spiridonovs, our Moscow acquaintances, and the fiancé and fiancée—Baron Russov and Ekaterina Spiridonova—will also be present. The latter is very lovely, but the fiancé is a short redhead with a stupid expression on his face; he is a baron, because his grandfather received that rank and title for fifty years of trading, as Semen

---

4. Her cousins Niuta (Anna) and Samuil were children of Iakov Poliakov. Ol'ga was Lazar Iakovlevich Poliakov's stepdaughter (Annette's daughter from her first marriage).

Sergeevich Podgoretskii told me. He is a rich young man and has a mother. The weather here has changed drastically; it has suddenly become dark because of a snowstorm. And just two days ago it was quite warm, with a smell of rot in the air, as always in Petersburg. Aunt Amaliia [Poliakova] is very attentive toward me and in every possible way tries to entertain me. Thus, yesterday and today we painted the town and even talked about going tomorrow evening to the theater, but I think that one should not abuse one's health and so I should not do this. It seems that we will not leave here earlier than Tuesday evening because they are summoning Papa about the case of Mr. Savin from Moscow and because he has other urgent business that he must put in order now (and while he is here). However, I think that no sense whatsoever will come from the rest of it and thus it would be possible to return home. Yesterday Mania [Masha] told me that F. Morgulis will marry some unnamed man, but people write that he is very smart, as indeed is she. Thank God, all the old maids are getting married! She is already 40 years old and, in my opinion, that is a bit late, but "better late than never." Thus she is entering into the bonds of Hymen[5] before death! Well, something will come of it.

Yesterday evening I received a letter from Miss Elizabeth Gosh,[6] who describes Masha's betrothal and, inter alia, says that everyone likes the fiancé. True, he is quite ordinary and not very bright, but the bright ones can be penniless, and the dullards are just dullards. If you please, the same thing now ensues here, and I am counting on this, since I very much would like for this to work out for her. Masha [Mania] Levinson is such a kind girl that she should finally have God-given happiness. All this is in the hands of the Almighty! A professor from Berlin, Dr. Bermann, is now here (having been summoned by Abram Isaevich Gorvits). The latter has gangrene; they thought that his leg would have to be amputated, but the professor found this to be impossible. The point is that he is already very weak and, according to all indications, will not survive. May God allow him to live a little longer, and people are looking after him very closely.

ST. PETERSBURG, 2 FEBRUARY 1887, MONDAY.

I have just returned from the shops with Aunt Amaliia—I had gone to buy some presents for the children in Moscow. I even managed to buy Baby [Beniamin] a paperweight lamb for one ruble (at the Knopp shop on Nevskii Prospekt); he will probably be very pleased with this, although it is very tiny and

---

5. The Greek god of marriage.
6. Spelled out in Latin letters; usually given in Cyrillic transcription.

rather modest. I bought Misha a red leather porte-monnaie with a silver lock, something quite nice, and for Raia a silver and gold-plated brooch with dried forget-me-nots inside: it is very nice and especially original! So it is only Khaia to whom I shall give nothing, because she did not congratulate me on my birthday and gave me nothing; indeed, Mama encouraged this, so in the end "everything comes out in the wash." For now, they are still making things difficult for me and creating obstacles for me. But for my part I have a clear conscience and mind. I do not know what Mama and her dearest daughter (and my most gracious sister, Ksenia Lazarevna Poliakova) would say, but their dirty tricks cannot be an obstacle for me.

ST. PETERSBURG, 3 FEBRUARY 1887, TUESDAY

At last, I managed to go with Papa to an exhibition of Aivazovskii's paintings on Vasil'evskii Island. There was a total of twenty-two paintings. I did not particularly like any of them, but the best, in my opinion, is "The Surf at Gurzov Cliff," a small but precise painting. In addition, we went to Mme. Messarosh, and it turned out that today is her name day. In honor of this solemn day we had chocolate at their house, but quite inadvertently: tomorrow at 1:00 or 1:30 Lelia promised to come to me for an hour, and we shall talk to our heart's content. But as if on purpose all is not fate: either she or I for some reason cannot receive each other.

Uncle Samuil is not receiving anyone today, with the exception of relatives. Apparently, he feels better; it turns out that he was bleeding because of some laceration in his nasal passage. Khabas, Masha's fiancé, was here today on his way to Helsingfors, and he is very satisfied. For some reason they have delayed the wedding for four or five weeks—in a word, until March; he is taking along his sister, who lives in Vil'na, and wants her to live with him. Masha, apparently, plans to be a doctor's spouse again in Moscow, since Osip Grigor'evich told us this morning that she wants him to be transferred to any military hospital in Moscow. But Papa is apparently opposed, and quite justly so. After all, life in the capital is much more expensive than in a small city, and Helsingfors is a very good city in Finland. They say that she was very nice on the day of their engagement. What is surprising is the fact that Mama and Khaia paid them a visit. After all they both always make a scene for some reason. Oddly, at the very same time, the doctor became Mama's beau-frère [brother-in-law]. Everything in the world is so perverted, but there was a time when Mama did not even want to hear of this. Thank God, all this has been finally settled.

I finally received a long, detailed letter from Masha about the engagement. She is very grateful to me, Papa, and Grandfather—the three main culprits responsible for her happiness (I am using her own expression). And I hope this will be happiness. Today Zinaida Perel'man wrote me two letters from the railway station Durovo,[7] with a detailed account of her desperate, unhappy marital life. The marital breakdown with her husband is complete, apparently because of jealousy toward her predecessor (some other woman), but she purportedly was always passionately in love with him. Evidently, nothing lasts very long now. Tomorrow we finally hope to leave for Moscow, which had been holding its balls in my absence. Hence I absolutely would like to leave here, mainly because my aunt [Avdot'ia] is apparently irritated. One encounters obstacles everywhere in life, and even here as guests. She is jealous that Uncle Samuil is well disposed toward Papa and Uncle Iakov and always perceives an alleged hostility toward her and believes that various secrets are being withheld from her. For now there has not been anything particularly unpleasant for me, but it suffices that, in my presence, she complained to Grandfather about my father for allegedly urging Samuil not to travel to Nice but to remain in St. Petersburg (where he has a lot of business). And she reiterates that he should leave sooner. All this really upsets me. Spiridonov paid us a visit today and sat with me and his aunt. He asked whether Papa is corresponding with Mr. Mende of Vienna, whom he befriended through us. Lelia Messarosh wrote me a brief note asking me not to be angry. The point is that she cannot come to visit because of the cold she caught while ice-skating, but I think that this is all an invention of her imagination. Papa is still traveling, first in one direction, then in another. Now I would like to go out with Miss Blues [sic] for a stroll, but unfortunately she also has no time today, and she is very apologetic that she cannot visit me this afternoon, but can come and talk only in the evening. However, I myself already have an invitation from Mrs. Messarosh. I do not know whether I should go there, since Lelia has not written me. All the same, I think that it is better to stay home. My aunt went to Grandfather, and there we together read Masha's letter about her fiancé. She is now in seventh heaven, has completely gone crazy over him, and even says that he is very smart (contrary to what I thought). I need to hurry and finish writing, since I am going for a ride with Papa. He has finally returned home, and I am very happy that I can breathe fresh air, if only in a carriage.

---

7. Probably the Durovo station in Smolensk province, on the Moscow-Minsk railway line.

At last we are packing up to go home to Moscow, which makes me very happy. Tomorrow, after synagogue, we shall serve dinner to Panaeva[-Kartseva][8] and her husband as well as Baron Biuler;[9] they should come in the evening, since Friday is our jour fixe. It is surprising that the Frenchman and his wife are also traveling today to Moscow; they are not dropping by to visit Uncle and Aunt but only sent their visiting card with regrets that they cannot make their acquaintance, and a letter from Zina Girsh [de Hirsch]. If we meet them today at the railway station, it will be fun to travel together. Mr. Antokol'skii is also going with us. This evening we have a ball at Fon Derviz's, and on Saturday at Professor Zakharov's. Last year I fell ill at their house and was not even able to dance the marzurka. Here I spend all my time at home, since there is no one to go out with (Papa is constantly busy).

MOSCOW, 6 FEBRUARY 1887, FRIDAY

Only now have I found time to drink tea and talk with Masha about her goings-on and fiancé. They arrived here safely, and our guests for dinner will be Panaeva-Kartseva and her husband, along with S[ofia] F[ranstevna] Podgoretskaia and Baron Biuler. The weather is perfect! The frost is crisp, and in the morning the trees will be covered with snow—and in my opinion that is especially beautiful! Our Russian winter is so wonderful! All the charms of the South pale in comparison with the beauty of winter and its marvelous view. Masha has also become animated and happy after her betrothal with O[sip] Khabas. He has departed, and she misses him. Apparently, it was fate that she marry soon. However, two weeks have already passed since we became acquainted with them in Papa's office, and I helped bring this about. In the evening it will be necessary to sit up late again, and thus impossible to rest from the journey. It would be wonderful to lie down in my own bed after the trip and to sleep deeply, without a care—as one does from exhaustion. Papa felt very well during the entire time that we were in St. Petersburg; only on the eve of our arrival did he begin to complain of a headache caused by the excessively intensive conversations about business matters. But, thank God, this all passed without further consequences. If only he would not become so exhausted here!

They say that Ida Rubinshtein is going to [St.] Petersburg on Sunday. It is a great pity that things turned out that we missed each other, but I would be

---

8. A. L. Panaeva-Kartseva (1853–1941), a famous opera soprano.

9. The reference here is probably to Baron Fedor Andreevich Biuler [Bühler] (1821–96), a Russian-German diplomat and state councilor, who was known for his publications about the history and literature of peoples in the Russian Empire.

happy to see them there. Uncle Iakov and his family are leaving St. Petersburg in two weeks. Although they do not have a good time here, they nonetheless find it better than Petersburg.

MOSCOW, 7 FEBRUARY 1887, SATURDAY

Yesterday after dinner, as should be the case, we also had guests in the evening. After the concert at Count Olsuf'ev,[10] a general in the reserves, Ofrosimov, came as a guest and played on a zither that he obtained from Vienna through Bauer. This evening there is a ball at the G[rigorii] Zakhar'in residence, but I do not think I shall go, since last year I fell ill during the ball, frightened everyone, and caused trouble for all—myself more than anyone. They could not have been nicer to me, which forces me to avoid an awkward scene that might reoccur. He told Papa that he asks that I come. Here the atmosphere is far from clear, and I do not think that it will become brighter afterward. Only Masha is exulting because of her impending marriage to Dr. Khabas and hopes to become a general's wife soon.

Whatever good there might be remains an unknown, but now the season is coming to an end and Lent will begin in a week. Fasting faces and physiognomies replace the happy, shiny faces from the morning hotcakes, and the mournful church bell ringing will call the sinners to repentance. But the weather is splendid! Bright and clear in the courtyard as one would like so that all are in high spirits! But not every wish is fulfilled, especially those that do not depend on us. Hence we shall be content with our present mood and not wish for something better.

I just now returned from my stroll with Papa. M[ikhail] Katkov came on foot from the [Katkov] Lycée on Ostozhenka Street, and we walked together with him. He walks a lot for his health. He also told me that he lives in both Petersburg and Moscow, since he has a lot of business in both places. Miss Gosh is now visiting his daughter-in-law, born Princess Lobanova-Rostovskaia. She is an extremely attractive person; although not pretty, she is very bright and pleasant in society, which has given her the reputation as a favorite among Muscovites. They say that the wedding of Masha Vydrina will take place in April, and [the wedding of] Mlle. Spiridonova, the fiancée of Baron Russov (the Sumskii officer), will also be about that time, so we shall feast. The former is now busy ordering her trousseau. I told her to order it for 800 rubles (from the interest on her funds, and I think that Mama and Papa will probably cover the difference).

Today there is a concert at the Philharmonic Society and a ball at the

10. Possibly Count Aleksei Vasil'evich Olsuf'ev (1831–1915), a general and philologist.

Zakhar'ins, and tomorrow there is a quartet. In the evening there will also be something at our place, it seems, but I still do not know anything about it and have no idea what it involves (nor am I interested). All of Shrovetide is merry-making, mainly as evening dances. I am not even talking about them, since I get very little enjoyment from spending my time at dances with young people whom I find [un]interesting.[11] I have to conclude my chronicle for today, since it is time for dinner.

MOSCOW, 8 FEBRUARY 1887, SUNDAY

I have already had time today to go to the quartet performance, which was held in the hall of the conservatory. Safonov[12] played the piano accompaniment; the quartet performed a piece by Eugen d'Albert, and I liked the third part the most. I can now say something about the evening ball in the home of G[rigorii] A. Zakhar'in; it was very pleasant (contrary to every expectation), since I danced every dance and waltzed a lot especially with all the most outstanding chevaliers, who for this purpose asked their acquaintances to be introduced to me—something that had happened earlier. However, this was not fun for me. Prince Vladimir Andreevich Dolgorukov told me that we had not seen each other for a long time. He gave me his hand during the first quadrille when I curtseyed to him without at first understanding what he had said to me. Z[inaida] Esipova, when I passed by, exchanged scornful winks with the procurator Murav'ev.

MOSCOW, 9 FEBRUARY 1887, MONDAY

Yesterday evening, I lay down to sleep after the ball and therefore had an excellent night of rest. But today is a very long day, and I simply do not know what to do: first I play the piano, then write in my journal, next take a stroll, and so forth. Papa is again preoccupied with business, and it was virtually impossible to see him the entire day (except at breakfast and lunch, when he is free). Otherwise it is just a great misfortune. It is only [possible to see him] when he does not have a headache; his brains are constantly working and have no rest! Does he really have the strength for all that? But there are people who can do the work for him.

Tomorrow evening, we shall apparently go to the Russian opera, where they are performing *A Life for the Tsar*.[13] Mrs. Panaeva-Kartseva, who will

11. Zinaida wrote "interesting" but clearly intended a negative.

12. Vasilii Il'ich Safonov (1852–1918), a Russian pianist, conductor, and public figure.

13. A famous opera (renamed *Ivan Susanin*, for ideological reasons, in the Stalin era) about the events of 1612, composed by Mikhail I. Glinka and first performed in 1836.

debut in the role of Antonina, sent us tickets through her husband. I do not think that they had much fun during Shrovetide, but they say that there will be balls. Tomorrow is the opera, and the next day (Wednesday) Mrs. Anna Aleksandrovna Sazikova[14] is holding a ball for the first time since Liudmila's coming out as a debutante (at age seventeen). Nothing further is planned for Thursday; we shall host a gathering on Friday and, if there are really a lot of people, then we shall perhaps dance; on Saturday, apparently, there will be a ball at the residence of the governor-general, Prince Dolgorukov (however, we still do not have an invitation—although I shall not regret it if one does not come). Despite this, he was very polite. In St. Petersburg, at Bolin's,[15] I saw his daughter and her husband, General Voeikov.[16] She seems to have recognized me; for my part, I did not recognize her, and only later did Papa tell me who she was. Things at home have now been settled, to some extent; I am on speaking terms with Mama. She constantly complains of her ill health and has already begun saying that she is going to England in the spring for treatment.

MOSCOW, 11 FEBRUARY 1887, WEDNESDAY

At last I can write in my journal after missing a day! I forgot about it. During this time, however, nothing of interest happened, and I intend only to convey my impression of yesterday's debut of A. Panaeva-Kartsova. Today she is again performing in a matinee show to benefit inexpensive housing, but I found that her voice was not in top form after yesterday's performance. To be sure, it is no easy matter to sing in the Bolshoi Theater, and therefore I am not in the least surprised that she was tired. Although no one shouted "Encore!," she did receive a bouquet as a sign of gratitude for her performance, and they did call her back [for more applause]. Tomorrow evening we are invited to the Beskupskii residence where people are gathering to dance with students, and I do not think that it will be very much fun. But this evening it is necessary to "get the legs ready" (as Papa puts it) to dance at Anna Aleksandrovna Sazikova's. What fun! We could never expect such fun—honest!

Mr. Antokol'skii is now here, the doorman told me, and is sitting with Papa

14. Presumably a member of the Sazikov family, which operated a world-famous jewelry firm that served the imperial court and produced some famous works of art.
15. Probably a reference to a member of the Swedish Bolin family in St. Petersburg, which included Wilhelm Bolin (1835–1924)—a philosopher and historian who later taught at Helsingfors University.
16. The reference is to Nikolai Vasil'evich Voeikov (1832–98), a cavalry general and courtier, and his wife Varvara Vladimirovna (née Dolgorukova), daughter of the governor-general of Moscow, Prince Vladimir Andreevich Dolgorukov.

in his office. Mama has already left, probably to inspect a new building at the hospital. Masha sent me the announcement of her betrothal, and two days ago, in the evening, she brought the portraits of her fiancé and them together to show us. The pictures turned out well; it is just that she seems to hold him so firmly in her grasp as though she feared that he would leave her. He, by contrast, is quite passionless and displays a look of insouciance on his face. But perhaps it only seems that way to me; I even hope that such is the case. In any event, from that point of view the portrait is not successful. Today Khaia did not go in the afternoon to the theater of Prince Shakhovskoi-Streshnev[17] because she was busy making preparations for a ball this evening. She always loves to plan her attire in advance and always takes a long time to get ready. The last time she was still not ready at midnight, but when Papa made a slightly critical comment, she went into her room and people had to coax her to come out. And we have to suffer all that! First Mama, then I, did not want to go to the ball hosted by G[rigorii] Zakhar'in; next Khaia began to carry on. In a word, only Papa was in a position to reason with everyone, and consequently he alone has to bear it all—evidently, that was his lot at birth! Still, reconciling everyone is a noble task in life.

The weather is still very frigid. At times it is really cold. Even in my absence Raia got frostbite on her ears. Il'ka has the mumps, which he caught in the Lyceum of Tsarevich Nikolai, and unfortunately he has missed out on Shrovetide. The doctor, Wulfius [sic], came to see him today; in the morning Belousov, the doctor from the Katkov Lyceum came (because Iulii Osipovich [Gol'denbakh] has severed relations with us because of some spat with Mama during our absence).

MOSCOW, 12 FEBRUARY 1887, THURSDAY

Yesterday, along with Khaia and Misha, I was at the Sazikovs, but in my opinion it was not very much fun. Those dancing consisted only of gymnasium pupils and students, with very few exceptions; one gymnasium pupil who danced with me mistook me for Satia's [Isaak's] mother. Such is the compliment he paid me! He asked if I know V. N. Nikiforov, and I said yes, and he then observed that I probably know him because he gives lessons to my son!? In all seriousness I replied that he gives lessons not to my son, but to my brother, and he became very embarrassed and turned redder than a boiled crayfish. This

---

17. Probably a reference to the estate theater of Prince Mikhail Valentinovich Shakhovskoi-Glebov-Streshnev (1836–92), a lieutenant general, governor of Estland and Tambov, resident of Moscow, and honorary member of the charity incorporated as Empress Mariia's Council of Guardians.

evening we have both the theater and dancing. This *bénéfice*[18] for Possart[19] is staging *Die Tochter des Herrn Fabrizicusi* [Fabricius] and *Mein Freund Fritz*.[20] I think I shall go first to the theater and then to the Biskupskiis (whom we shall visit for the first time). Tomorrow people will come here, and then on Saturday there is a ball at the governor-general's.

MOSCOW, 13 FEBRUARY 1887, FRIDAY

I just now received a letter from Flora, and I cannot say how happy it made me. Masha is sitting here and in a very humorous vein has begun to ponder my love life. First she began to analyze Robin Gabbe [Reuben Gubbay] and then even tried to convince me that it will come to pass. Tomorrow evening we shall be at the governor-general's ball and, I think, this will be very interesting (at least, I hope so). Yesterday at the Biskupskiis', by contrast, it was extremely boring, and I terribly regret not staying to the end of the Possart bénéfice, where there was much of interest. I especially liked the first act of *Freund Fritz*, which I had still managed to see before the dances. I regret missing the last two acts, so I was very sorry that I had to leave. "A promise given is a promise kept." This afternoon I went with Miss Gosh, Raia, and Jacques to the manège, the site of a festive gathering organized on behalf of Christian aid. Jacques was beside himself from joy, and after the manège we went to the booths and carousels at Devich'e Pole. Unfortunately, Il'ia, with his swollen glands or mumps, cannot leave his room for fear that he will catch cold and make the illness still worse. All this time Papa does not feel well, and Mama also complains about every kind of ailment and weakness (as is her wont). She did not even take breakfast with us this morning. First Papa, then Mama comes to the table —as if they had agreed to take turns being absent and not constantly spoil us. A concert is being given tomorrow at the English church. Some organist is coming from St. Petersburg specifically for this purpose. It is a pity that this is our receiving day and that I cannot hear the spiritual music and singing of the English—it would be interesting. Flora Gabbe [Gubbay] writes that she had a good time in Brighton and has only now returned. She is so apologetic about not responding to my letter for so long that I agree to forgive her and will write her soon.

---

18. A bénéfice is a performance to honor an artist, with all profits going to the honoree.
19. Ernst Heinrich Possart (1841–1921), a German actor and stage director.
20. Adolf von Wilbrandt (1837–1911), a German writer and the director of a theater in Vienna, wrote *Die Tochter des Herrn Fabricius* (1883).

Yesterday, Saturday evening, we went dancing at Prince Dolgorukov's, and it was not very boring. I did not dance the first quadrille there, since we had just arrived; many ladies and chevaliers arrived after us, so we were not the last to come. Great Lent begins tomorrow, so we shall say goodbye to Shrovetide! That is not bad, since it is unhealthy to eat a lot of hotcakes, and I think that Moses established the fast so that people not gorge themselves excessively on tasty foods. And he was right. But what was good and appropriate for our predecessors is not good for us, and therefore I do not observe [these rules].

In Nice there was an earthquake and panic: A. R. D. traveled there to enjoy Carnival, so he has probably already returned. During yesterday's mazurka they passed out bouquets of violets that the prince [Dolgorukov] had received from Nice, and I was given one of them. I was very annoyed that the chevaliers did all this with so little tact. For example, my neighbor, Rakhmaninov (who danced with Mlle. Novikova) received not three but four bouquets; indeed, he wanted to take as many more, claiming that he had not taken any. But he did not succeed in pulling off this trick and was a little embarrassed, since he knew that I saw this, as did his lady (who, however, would probably encourage him in this); she favors him a lot and says that they are all very nice people. That may be, but "let's suppose that Alexander the Great was a hero, but why smash the chairs?"[21] Why act so self-important?

Today I went skating. I saw many of the young men who were at the ball yesterday and who gathered today. A. I. Postnikov concocted a lot of difficulties and, amid an enormous gathering of the public, danced a waltz on the ice.

Lidiia Stepanovna found that both of our ball gowns are fine. It is hardly surprising that they turned out so well: [Charles Frederick] Worth is eager to make ballroom gowns and often does so personally. Although my gown did not fit me perfectly, in my opinion it was really excellent, and even Mr. Podgoretskii said that mine and Mama's gowns were the most beautiful of the entire ball. Khaia's was less impressive, despite the fact that her white gown with green ribbons and roses was very good and more original than a blue dress with roses. But that is simply a matter of a person's taste.

Then one and the same dress always repeats, first with one, then with another. Why did civilization invent attire? After all, savages got along perfectly well without it and did not waste money on this! James de Hirs[c]h inserted an apt comment in my notebook of thoughts. After all, what he said is true: gowns were invented for plunderers like Mr. Worth and company; everything

21. This quote is from Gogol's *Inspector General*.

is for their benefit. So too *all other deeds of the human mind* are for someone's benefit.

Only now have I begun to assign roles for the show at the silver wedding anniversary [of my parents]. At last we found *Les lundi[s] de Madame*,[22] a very old play, but one that Baron Vrangel thinks will be very appropriate. Tomorrow I shall finish the letter for Flora; I think that I shall send it soon to Paris, but I very much want to avoid giving her reason to laugh at my haste in responding! For a long time she did not answer my letter sent to Brighton (to her at the address of her grandfather, Sir Albert Sassoon: 1 Eastern Terrace). According to her own account, she had a good time there. Here we are beginning to prepare celebrations for the silver anniversary. I first want to order a porcelain tea table with our images from Mr. Goldschmidt in Vienna. Then I am preparing to play, as a duet, the wedding march by Mendelssohn-Bartholdy.[23]

I can finally take a break from the seasonal chores, the entertaining, and the balls! Yesterday, they say, Khaia received a letter from Flora Gubbay in Paris, but for some reason she did not show it. I'm jealous! Tomorrow is Wednesday, but nothing interesting is currently planned, because I must now be more occupied with music and the like so as not to become overly bored after the balls and concerts. The latter, however, will then resume, and I think that I shall go to few of them—I've already had enough. At some point I shall listen more attentively. But for now I am devoting little attention to music. Mme. Erdmansderfer was here at our home for the lesson and says that there will have to be a No. 1 *baignoire* [a groundfloor box at the theater] for Possart. Since there was a misunderstanding about our theater box in the morning, we do not want to be there in the evening for the second performance of *Manfred*[24] with the orchestra under the direction of M. K. Erdmansderfer. How annoying that I took so few lessons from his wife [Polina] this winter, but Papa and I had to go to St. Petersburg for two weeks and I did not practice during the entire time! It must be said that I am not properly preparing the lesson with her and even now I shall still perform with E[miliia] Ogus-Shaikevich. It is somewhat

22. A reference to Feu Alart's *Les lundis de madame: Comédie en un acte, en prose*, which is available in various editions (for example, Paris: Lévy, [ca. 1854]).
23. Felix Mendelssohn-Bartholdy (often known simply as Felix Mendelssohn; 1809–47), a German composer, pianist, and conductor of the early Romantic period.
24. Presumably a reference to Tchaikovsky's *Manfred Symphony*.

better with her than with Raia, all the more since the latter often misses my lessons. The weather is uninspiring: dampness and slush, as is approprirate for this time of year in Moscow. Nice debased itself: its battle of the flowers (*bataille des fleurs*) was held in the snow. As a rule, the flowers [in Nice] are already opening up in February, but now there is a cold spell and, on top of that, an earthquake.

MOSCOW, 18 FEBRUARY 1887, WEDNESDAY

I have finally decided to resume the reading of Dickens in English! Otherwise I was about to discard him entirely and read absolutely nothing; I had only been looking through a few journals in all languages. Fania is asking me why Mama is angry with her. Of course, I am not in a position to answer this question, but she claims that Masha allegedly wrote her husband that Mama gave her diamond earrings, but allegedly gave her nothing for the betrothal. What trivia can cause discord! Today Papa is again feeling sick; he has a headache and sent for G[rigorii] A. [Zakhar'in]. It is apparent that all winter he has not managed to free himself from the unpleasant visits of a guest. That is why he needs complete rest and tranquility.

Tomorrow morning at 11 am we will have E[miliia] Ogus-Shaikevich, and at 3 pm Mme. [Polina] Erdmansderfer, so I shall have two music lessons in a single day. Yesterday, during the German carnival, E. Mattern hosted a concert, and many Russians were present among the public there. The pianist Shesta-kovskii [Shostakovskii] played *Consolation[s]* by Liszt[25] (which I have played) as well as some boisterous piece unknown to me. We passed several hours pleasantly, but this did not do Papa any good. Of course, he should not be going out. Even the entire Konshin family[26] was at this concert as well as the one with the glass eye. He recently played Chatskii in *Woe of Wit*[27] and, probably for that reason, shaved—which does not become him. A comedy sometimes requires sacrifice by the actors—at the price of their beauty. For some men the beard grows rapidly (as in the case of Vladimir Podgoretskii), but that is probably not true for all, and I do not think that this was pleasant. That is especially so when the beard enhances the personality and is not a luxury. I do not justify this archaic law, which would ruin many if they all followed and observed it. In England, for example, no one has a beard. Only in Russia are there people with

25. Liszt composed two versions of a work titled *Consolations*, the second of which was published in 1850.
26. A reference to the Konshin clan of Moscow, known for their commercial as well as their philanthropic activities.
27. The reference is to *Gore ot uma*, a classic play by Aleksandr S. Griboedov.

originality, such as the barons Gintsburgs and people like them. The weather is absolutely terrible. You choke from the stench both outside and in the house. And a terrible infection is also here. They say that dear little Il'ia, thank God, is getting better and the swelling has gone down. Probably, he did not have the mumps but simply swollen glands, and we feared for him for no reason at all, since that latter condition is not contagious. It is odd that the Lyceum pupils did not give a ball this year.

MOSCOW, 19 FEBRUARY 1887, THURSDAY

I now have to make a lot of preparations for my parents' silver anniversary in March. I think that tomorrow I shall write Flora or Misha von Weisweiller[28] and ask them to order dance figures for that day and cards for the menu at lunch and dinner. I am also thinking of sending their photographs to the same place to have them made as medallions in the corner of the cards; if we choose some kind of appropriate play to perform, then perhaps we shall perform on the stage of our home theater. But I have my doubts about that, and it seems that this proposal will not prevail among us, because there are few plays appropriate for us. It will be possible to write something in verse. Baby and Sasha must memorize the words of congratulation: the former in Russian, the latter in English. But we have little practice speaking German, unfortunately, since none of the Germans are now with us. Lidiia Stepanovna, contrary to every expectation, has remained with us and did not depart.

MOSCOW, 22 FEBRUARY 1887, SUNDAY

Today Aleksei Nikolaevich Teplov came to my room for a visit. He said that he is planning to come with Possart to our box for the performance of *Manfred* and that they purportedly promised to give him a seat with us. The performance will be given this afternoon and tomorrow evening, and Prince V[ladimir] A. [Dologrukov] gave us his theater box. I hope that Mama has not invited so many people that you cannot see anything (as she often does when there are unoccupied seats that one does not have to pay for). Yesterday evening [Panaeva-]Kartseva was at the concert; she could not have been more beautiful in a red velvet dress with a train. They say that her husband was in a bad mood, and I think that he is angry with us because we have not yet paid for the box. In the morning of the same day I went to the train station and then to the hall of the Noble Assembly, which was the site for a benefit concert (by

<hr/>

28. It is unclear who Misha [Michael] von Weisweiller is. Zinaida may have been referring to her brother Misha as a joke; he is the only one she calls Misha in her diaries.

male and female conservatory pupils) for their poor fellow students; a lot of people came, including Mr. Hill. He is everywhere that offers something to listen to; in the evening he was again in the hall of the Sabashnikov[29] heirs; only there did he see me as we left the concert at the end of the evening. So I can say that yesterday I spent the entire day and the evening with him. Misha says that he is a music lover. Meanwhile I still have not received a letter from Flora Gabbe [Gubbay]; she is probably not planning to respond quickly to my last letter. Yesterday morning Uncle Iakov, Aunt Amaliia, and Niuta passed by Moscow, stopping at Grandfather's but not at our house. After breakfast Raia, Miss Gosh, and I went to a student concert at the hall of the Noble Assembly.

MOSCOW, 24 MARCH 1887, TUESDAY

Iulii Osipovich Gol'denbakh came to see me today after a long period of time and a row with Mama. He now has a third child, a son, who was christened Sunday (22 March); I know of this from Mania Mein, whose father had been invited to him in the evening of that day. I received a letter from Masha Levinson with a photograph enclosed; I found that she is not at all interesting in the picture and turned out to be such a large girl that it is somewhat exaggerated, since in reality she does not appear to be so heavyset (whereas the photograph makes her appear heavy, in my opinion, and in a hat three stories high). Their business affairs are now very poor, and they have changed apartments. Yesterday evening we were at the concert of Aleksandrova-Kochetova,[30] and found that her pupils sing very well. One can say that, despite some shortcomings, she is a very talented teacher.

Papa's and Mama's silver wedding anniversary turned out very well, and in the evening there was dancing. Even Count Brevern de Lagarde with his wife and daughters, came; true, he did not stay long, but one must admit that it was very kind of him to come. Lidiia Stepanovna celebrated her name day with her relatives yesterday and only today did she bring some refreshments for us to commemorate that day, which we usually celebrate here (as the only day each year when we receive her relatives, including her female friend and family). She did very well, since she soon plans to leave completely. For our evening Misha was quite ill and did not look well. He has been recovering very slowly, because—prior to contracting mumps—he fasted for a long time because of

29. Sabashnikovs were a Moscow business clan. Nikita Filippovich Sabashnikov (b. 1785) had gold-mining operations; he was succeeded by his sons Vasilii (1819–79) and Mikhail (b. 1824), with two grandsons of the former (Mikhail and Sergei) becoming prominent publishers.

30. Kochetova's married name was Aleksandra Dormidontova Aleksandrova-Kochetova (1833–1902). She was a Russian soprano opera singer.

some silly theories. Our family will probably return from St. Petersburg to Moscow tomorrow evening, possibly Thursday. There too the weather is apparently bad, and I think that ours is still better because at least there is no early spring. The climatic conditions in Petersburg are similar to London, where the fog contributes significantly to increasing the number of people with depression (i.e., with the English national spleen). But Petersburg, although one cannot say it is completely similar, is nonetheless somewhat analogous in the winter, when there is slush and fog with its own white shroud. By contrast, however, the people of Petersburg have a cheerful disposition. Incidentally, I would note that the Katkovs (through Miss Elizabeth Gosh) inquired whether they could be with us in the synagogue on Friday. We, of course, replied that we are happy to send tickets for Friday.

MOSCOW, 25 MARCH 1887, WEDNESDAY

I was just now with Misha at a concert of religious music at the manège. I saw many acquaintances there, but only from a distance; no one apparently saw us, since we were not in our own seats. Friday evening marks the beginning of Passover, and I have not properly prepared for it—that is, I did not buy anything tasty for myself, but then everything will be forbidden except for unleavened bread and what is homemade. I have now entered into a religious crisis; yesterday I read the Gospels, today I went to a concert of church music, and so forth. Mania Mein finds that the rites of all religions are superfluous. It is simply that I seek something higher on earth and, of course, never find it. I even have moments of asceticism, but never fanaticism.

MOSCOW, 16 APRIL 1887, THURSDAY

Today I intend to make up for the lost time and to tell about everything. First of all, on Sunday April 12th, there was Masha [Vydrina]'s wedding, and the young are still in Moscow at the old apartment of Masha, Roman, and Genrikh. Then yesterday they sent the porcelain table on bronze legs with the portraits of us all and our parents (which had been ordered in Vienna for the silver wedding anniversary) in the middle of the table that Rosenstein had given a factory owner. It turned out amazingly well; it is just that I appeared on the last level, behind the backs of my parents. It is not a matter of honor, but I am offended. Masha and her husband are very happy and completely satisfied with their new position. All these days she had a very animated look, but today appears tired, even if content. In any case, I hope that God brings happiness and joy to the young couple. It seems that they entirely deserve this and they need only not deviate from the right path to be good spouses. Papa came from Petersburg in time for the wedding day, on Sunday morning. The wedding ceremony itself was set for 4 pm, but was somewhat later than the appointed hour. All those invited thus waited with the greatest impatience for it to begin, since a Jewish wedding was something new for them. It went very well, and only our relatives remained for dinner. Yesterday I picked up Mania Mein to take her along to Mr. Makart's[31] art gallery, where his *Spring* and *The Five Senses* are on exhibition, along with several paintings by various contemporary artists, primarily German.

MOSCOW, 3 MAY 1887, SUNDAY

Poor Ogus[32] died a week after the weddings of Masha and Roza Shaikevich. He suddenly fell ill and developed gangrene, so they made incisions to stop the disease from spreading.

Yesterday evening our family members (i.e., Papa and Mama) went to St. Petersburg for several days. This morning Miss Gosh went by courier train to old London and somehow will get there. After the train she will board a steamship and travel six hours by sea only in order not to stop. She intended to leave a long time ago, but they kept restraining her. In the time after the wedding of Masha and Dr. Osip Grigor'evich Khabas, I have not gone out. The reason: there is no one to go with. Mama does not allow me to go with Papa, since she herself wants to ride with him. As a result, yesterday I did not even go to accompany them to the railway station. True, today I also did not accompany Miss Gosh to the Smolensk rail station. But that was because of my systematic decision not to go anywhere for the time being. Papa has proven to be a wet rag in Mama's hands; she twists him as she wants, uninhibited even by her duty to love her own friends. This has become positively intolerable for me, and that is why I do not wish to expose myself to various unpleasant things. But this is still more difficult for me to do, so I have to regard myself as unfortunate. I do not even have any basis for hope. Tomorrow is Monday, and I intend to play a duet with Miss Ogus-Shaikevich. She has somewhat regained her composure, even came for a visit today, and gave Khaia a piano lesson so as not to begin on Monday. Miss Gosh asked me to give her a card for Mrs. A[sher] Asher in London (whom she would like to meet). She has a very smart, attractive husband —Dr. Asher, who is engaged in journalism, but also medicine and especially the performance of religious duties.

Completely sympathizing with the sadness of Sof'ia Frantsevna Podgore-

---

31. Hans Makart (1840–84), an Austrian painter.
32. Iakov Moiseevich Ogus (1851–87), professor of mathematics at Göettingen University.

tskaia (whose husband is very ill), I recognize that she does not sufficiently suffer for him, but mainly talks about her own grief and how she threw herself on Sklifosovskii's[33] neck and implored him to save Semen Sergeevich. But her husband grabbed Sklifosovskii and said: "I won't let you, I won't let you," until the doctors seized and chloroformed him. He is still very ill, but the operation was a success. Thank God! He is a wonderful person, and it is quite surprising how quickly he fell gravely ill. God is the source of all—both grief and joy! So one has to hope that God will always protect us from everything bad. Misha, Raia, and Jacques accompanied Miss Gosh to the railway station this morning.

MOSCOW, 4 MAY 1887, MONDAY

Yesterday I did not go out again, but in the evening Mariia Aleksandrovna Mein paid me a visit and had tea. She is very bored, apparently because Aleksandr Danilovich has retired (due to the ill will displayed toward him by all, with no exceptions). Khaia and Lidiia Stepanovna Zotova get along perfectly and do not in the least even miss Papa and Mama when they are away; by contrast, I positively do not come out of my monastic cell. I have now taken up reading and want to finish Dickens' *David Copperfield*, which I began shortly after arriving from abroad. It is very well written, but quite long. As if to spite me, the weather is splendid; I think that one should regard this as a mockery of fate. But the time will come when I will at least break free of my voluntary imprisonment!

MOSCOW, 7 MAY 1887, THURSDAY

Yesterday, for the first time since my imprisonment, I went out with Misha to the park. There we met many of our acquaintances, including Baron Vrangel', who escorted us as usual. Then, after arriving home, I drank tea and, before falling asleep, managed to read another chapter from my novel (by Dickens), but today I have managed to read just one chapter and am already eager for the ending (which interests me very much!), all the more because this writer has very interesting denouements. All the knots are cut at once. Papa and Mama are not thinking of returning home from Petersburg. They are apparently having a good time as guests and do not agree with the saying that "it is nice to be a guest, but better to be at home." But we think that they will finally return tomorrow! It has already been a week since they left. Papa, to be sure, always has a ton of business, and that is why they stay there such a long time before they can break free. That is why Mama loves to travel so much. Uncle Samuil never

33. Nikolai Vasil'evich Sklifosovskii (1836–1904), a surgeon.

stays for long in St. Petersburg by himself: he always has relatives as guests — among whom Papa is particularly conspicuous, while Uncle Iakov and his family stay at the hotel Angleterre[34] (on the corner of [Great] Morskaia Street, not far from English Embankment). When I was there, I did not like it. Kotia [Daniil] must now pass his final examinations at the juridical faculty. Because he has not had time to make up for his earlier transgression, they have added some supplementary examinations for him and scheduled them for autumn.

MOSCOW, 9 MAY 1887, FRIDAY

I did not write my parents the entire time they were in Petersburg, because I am not on speaking terms with them. They were very nice to me, especially Papa; if Mama did not prevent our rapprochement — that is, if she permitted me to be with him. But that is the point: because of her power she seeks — through every possible means — to block our spiritual union. By sheer force she wants to become nice (which of course no one has never achieved through orders and commands). In general, the more she separates me from Papa, the more detestable her system becomes for me.

Incidentally, now they are again making plans. Summer lies within her [Mama's] rights: she will seek excuses to travel abroad. I have already informed Papa that I shall not go anywhere if Mama and Raia[35] go too — given their constantly ruinous influence on me. Nonetheless, I am convinced that they will offer me various conciliatory terms. But I have learned too well from previous trips [not] to believe their words, and the fact that, unfortunately, Mama fears neither God nor man. But all [her] religion rests only on "fat" — i.e., kosher — foundations that one could successfully replace with more salutary conditions and with love for one's fellow man and for me specifically. It is not difficult to love one's kin, and the law of nature prescribes maternal love for her children. Unfortunately, such is not always the case! Khaia still complains about her unfortunate situation?! But she herself lives like a queen. Well, the devil with her and with all her friends — my enemies! I do not wish them anything bad or evil. But if only they would leave me, sinner that I am, alone for a short time, while they themselves do whatever they wish. Papa very quickly gives in to outside influence, and therein lies the entire misfortune. Were that not the

---

34. Built in the mid-nineteenth century in the very center of St. Petersburg (facing St. Isaac's Cathedral), Angleterre was a premier hotel, with many famous guests on its record books — from Anton Chekhov to Isadora Duncan.

35. The entry was probably about Khaia, not Raia, since Zinaida's main sibling rivalry was with Khaia. There may have been an error in the transcription of the published diaries, since in the extant manuscript diaries "Khaia" looks like "Raia."

case, I would be the happiest of daughters, having his love and the support of an honest, honorable person. Everything comes from God! And I do not know when my long ordeal will end; although I must thank Him for the worldly blessings bestowed on me, I do not know how to use them. Mama is jealous of my well-being, compares her own childhood and youth with mine, and therefore tries to compensate for the fact that she had so little happiness, wealth, and abundance in her youth.

MOSCOW, 11 MAY 1887, MONDAY

Uncle Iakov came through Moscow yesterday, and we accompanied him to the train station in the evening. Raia met him with Grandfather and Il'ia; Misha, Raia, and I accompanied him to the station, where he was met by Liliia *et toute lec sainte famille* [sic], with the exception of M. I. Slezkin. The latter lives with his family in Tula, which explains his absence yesterday; otherwise, he would have been at the station with those accompanying her [Liliia] and her husband (Grigorii Ardal'onovich). Papa has still not seen him. Notwithstanding the fact that they are expecting visits when we are in Petersburg (Papa and I always drop by their home), I was not given the honor of a return visit on her part. But I do not feel in the least offended, since my acquaintance with her is no honor, and I only visit her because I am on close terms with Sof'ia Ivanovna Slezkina.

MOSCOW, 19 MAY 1887, THURSDAY

Our family members did not manage to leave for Moscow yesterday evening, but their things have already arrived. We expect them here only tomorrow. Like tsars, they sent Franziska[36] with their things ahead, but were late (not through some fault of hers). They should probably arrive tomorrow, because the next day is Saturday, followed by two days of holidays. So they do not want to remain there for the holidays, and in that case they would inevitably be guests for eight to ten days! Papa needs it, and Mama wants this; everyone has his own system for raising a family. Tat'iana is now cleaning my room. My things are in terrible disarray, and even yesterday dresses were lying around the whole day. Dynin is here. He arrived from Tula and today will dine with us, according to Misha, who invited him.

Yesterday Grandfather, in a very secretive way, summoned me in order to say a few words. It turned out that the mountain gave birth to a mouse—it was utter trivia, something that does not merit anyone's attention: arranging

36. Franziska was a domestic servant in the home of Lazar Poliakov.

my marriage. He came to an agreement with Nemzer,[37] who teaches religion (*Zakon Bozhii*) and began to conduct negotiations with him regarding my favorite subject—i.e., my marriage. Nemzer is writing to everyone, and that pleases the old man [Grandfather], who thinks that something sensible will come of all this. Papa is very eager to listen to everything. And that gives rise to the fact that even the lowliest teacher at the Glebov compound[38] has access [here]. But I have great antipathy toward this, since—under no circumstances—do I believe in happiness that has been prearranged, calculated, and decided in advance.

SOKOL'NIKI, 1 JUNE 1887, MONDAY

Yesterday our family members left again for St. Petersburg and will be there three days. But of course it will be not three but six days (at the very least), as is always the case; they have probably already arrived there. Today, during breakfast, Misha received a telegram from Mama, in which she asks how things are with Sasha and Baby. But she spends so little time with them at home that this question evokes laughter and astonishment because of the sudden tenderness—to which we are not accustomed. She is always busy with other things! Yesterday, Papa suddenly proposed that I travel with him to St. Petersburg. Uncle Samuil invited me to come (in a letter to me as well as in a telegram to Papa). Unfortunately, however, for various reasons I could not. The first reason is that Mama herself wanted to go (and she and I are not good company); there was yet another reason that did not depend on anyone and that prevented my going.

Misha is in Moscow every day—not only during workdays, but also on Saturday, when he goes on foot during lunch. This has turned out not to be terribly convenient—since at lunch we had guests—Teplov and Mr. von Krause from Berlin (a banker). He (Misha) promised to accompany me there tomorrow. I love to spend the summer at the dacha, and still more would like to live in the countryside. But the kind of weather that we now have makes it impossible to be in good spirits: from early morning a downpour and dark (like evening). Masha [Khabas] has not written me for a rather long time about her life and goings-on. She must have begun to live there and does not want to know me any more! The ingrate! As people say, however, I am the one who arranged her happiness.

37. Mark Osipovich Nemzer (1833–1912), a historian who was a teacher at the Vil'na Rabbinical School. After the school closed down, he taught at a woman's gymnasium in Vil'na.
38. The Glebov compound (Glebovskoe podvor'e) was an inn located in the impoverished Jewish area of Moscow called Zariad'e. Zinaida expressed her indignation that any Jew—certainly not of her class—now had access to their home on the pretext of matchmaking.

Grandfather S[olomon] L[azarevich] Poliakov is now here with us in So-kol'niki—that is, he only came for a visit and plans to stay for lunch, but then wants to spend the night in Moscow. But he is absolutely correct: it is very miserable here in this dismal, humid weather. But it is pitch dark in our house: the rooms are very dark because of the terrace. Almost the only bright room was mine. Papa and Mama, in accordance with their plans, were to leave tomorrow. They will probably remain here until Uncle goes abroad, i.e., until Saturday or Sunday evening. Vladimir Vasil'evich, the boys' teacher, is very happy that little Il'ia passed the examination: he received a 4 on the oral exam and 3 on the written (Greek) exam; it turns out that these were his best grades. The weather is making me positively depressed and putting me in a melancholic mood.

SOKOL'NIKI, 2 JUNE 1887, TUESDAY

Today I have already managed to read chapter 3 of the German book by Felix Dahn, *Ein Kampf um Rom*.[39] It is too long and in four volumes, admittedly with a rather large typeface, but all the same it is quite a long historical novel about ruling personages. Two days ago Papa read the letter that I received from Uncle Samuil, with an invitation to come for a visit in St. Petersburg before he leaves for far-off destinations. To my regret, I could not fulfill this request: first, I did not feel quite well; and, second, I knew very well that Mama would be happy to travel herself. So now I have afforded her that pleasure. Uncle Iakov and Aunt Amaliia are asking me to come to the countryside, to Novomar'inskoe;[40] people say that it is very nice there, on the seashore, and perhaps I'll go.

FRANZENSBAD, 16/28 JULY 1887, THURSDAY

I am here now, and today we accompanied our Aunt [Avdot'ia] to the Girshs' [de Hirsches'] in Russigen. She will stay there for a little and then go either to Marly-le-Roy [Marly-le-Roi][41] or even to Paris itself if Uncle Samuil is there. Yesterday Aunt and I went to Bad Elster and spent the entire day there, but to our dismay, it rained, so we did not manage to see anything. We had dinner at Wittiner [Wettiner] Hof, went to buy some mother-of-pearl, and bought something as a keepsake. By the way, the shell makes a very loud sound when placed

39. Felix Dahn (1834–1912) was a German nationalist. His 1876 *Ein Kampf um Rom* ("The struggle for Rome," subtitled "a historical novel") recounts the succession struggle in sixth-century Rome. The multivolume work has been reprinted several times; the 1885–87 edition, in four volumes, describes itself as the twelfth edition.
40. Iakov Poliakov had an estate in Novomar'inskoe near the Azov Sea. See Ia[kov] S[olomonovich] Poliakov, *Statisticheskaia svedeniia za 20 let ot 1774–1894 po imeniiu Novomar'inskoe* (St. Petersburg: Tipografiia i litografiia Berman i Ko., 1897).
41. A commune on the periphery of Paris, some eighteen kilometers from the city center.

next to your ear, and this proves that it is genuine. On the road from Elster to Franzensbad there was nothing of interest other than perhaps the fact that we met a baroness at the railway station. This is the sister of von Schönberger, and she looked after me the entire time that I was here. She is now going to her mother in Marienbad, and I am very happy, because I have no interest in her brother. But she apparently wrote from Karlsbad so that we make his acquaintance. But, as if on purpose, on these days I shall not take the water and therefore did not have a chance to see them in the morning, as is usually the case in Franzensbad, where everyone meets and is seen at the waters.

FRANZENSBAD, 17/29 JULY 1887, FRIDAY

Since I did not do anything today except play piano, I intend to write at least three pages in my journal. Madame Goldberger came to visit us; she was here with her children, but without her husband. But he promised to come here from Berlin on Sundays. Tomorrow we intend to return the visit, which is not tiring, since she occupies an apartment of Bleichröder[42] and Aunt's salon. I asked her to give me a neighboring room for my maid Franziska, and I think that she does not care if her Englishwoman will be further away. The weather is constantly very hot. We received several letters, including one for me from Flora Gabbe [Gubbay] in Paris. She writes that her brother will soon leave for India, and therefore she is remaining in Paris. Uncle now has a secretary, Il'ia Dynin, from St. Petersburg. Flora Gabbe [Gubbay] has cousins, Miss Sassoon and Mlle. Ezekiel of London, who probably arrived here today from Paris, to judge from Flora's letter (which says that they left on Wednesday).

Papa was ill the entire time after his return from Franzensbad; he caught a cold on the journey to Berlin and could hardly make his way to Moscow. In Petersburg he was bedridden an entire Saturday, according to Adolf Romanovich Rubinshtein, who saw Mama and Khaia before their departure here. He assures us that the fever has passed. But I do not like the fact they kept us uninformed all this time. Papa has not written me once since he left us together with Misha. Now I received Misha's present[43]—a young man of bronze. It is called a "Dandy" or the first ball. Oh, it is done in the nicest way possible; a paperweight or simply a bibelot, which is very amusing. But the fact is that as soon as I saw this at the colonnade, I said that I shall buy it, but it happened that, after a certain time, when I did have the opportunity to acquire it,

42. Presumably Gerson Bleichröder (1822–93), a German-Jewish banker, with powerful connections to Otto von Bismarck and the German government.
43. The text has pari (in Latin letters), evidently intended to mean "present."

I learned that it had already been sold. And so they sent me another one from Vienna. Misha bought some kind of brooch. Here he is reading poetry and Russian books that are banned. I must finish my long German novel, and I can hardly wait for it to end. Madame Bornemisza, the sister of von Schossberger, has still not visited us. She has probably left, without saying goodbye, and was angry at me for my coolness.

FRANZENSBAD, 20 JULY/1 AUGUST 1887 MONDAY

I was very surprised yesterday when I met Mme. Sassoon and her niece [Mlle.] Ezekiel. I did not know of the latter, but her mother had breakfast with us at Sir Albert Sassoon's in Brighton when we were in England. She is a real Indian type. Tomorrow the Rubinshteins have invited us to travel with them to Marienbad, but I really do not know if I will go with Misha: I do not feel well today and do not think that tomorrow I could undertake such an excursion, which will take up some time. Misha went to bathe today. Mama and Papa have not written us a line since we have been here. That is, on their part, very unkind to say the least, and in all likelihood they intend to go abroad themselves soon.

FRANZENSBAD, 4 AUGUST 1887, THURSDAY

Yesterday, it turns out, was Misha's birthday, and he turned 20, but we thought it was today. The point is that the fast of Tish b'av [to commemorate the destruction of the First and Second Temples in Jerusalem] was deferred from Saturday to Sunday, and Misha figured that three days after that is today, but in fact it was yesterday. To judge from a telegram, Papa is now much better, thank God, but he still is in bed—so his illness is serious, probably real typhus, as Adolf Romanovich Rubinshtein told us upon his arrival from Russia. He was at Sokol'niki, but saw only Mama. I received a bouquet from him today. Since I agreed in the morning to go to a concert with Mrs. Sassoon, I do not know if I shall go to the theater. Ida Rubinshtein sent me a note with an invitation to go with them to an operetta, where they are presenting *Gasparone*.[44] Tomorrow I hope to take my thirteenth bath; that leaves two more baths, and after that we shall leave. I think that it is necessary to leave together with Ronia and with Uncle Genrikh for Ostend, where Liza [Poliakova] now finds herself, among other guests. That is how unfortunate my trip abroad this year has been: Papa had not managed to come and be here with me one week when he returned sick to Moscow. And now when will he be able to go abroad? And Misha is sour

44. An operetta in three acts by the composer Carl Millöcker.

and yearns for home. Well, no point in complaining about one's fate! Yesterday or the day before, Misha received a letter from Baron Gedalii. He is seeking the position of secretary at the Danish embassy and hopes to receive it in a month. Everything is just as it was when we arrived in Franzensbad. The crown princess is still here, but we arrived with her at the same time.

SOKOL'NIKI, 6 AUGUST 1887, THURSDAY

Only yesterday did we arrive safely in Russia, and Papa does not yet know of this. But they say that he often asks about us and today even ordered that a passport be sent to me abroad. Mama even told him that she will write us today or will have Katia do this, but she brought Papa our cards to show together with Misha. Papa looked at them for a long time and did not know that we are also so close to him. Professor Nothnagel[45] from Vienna is now here, and we arrived later in the afternoon. He was in Vienna when they sent him a telegram. That is how things are in the world! You do not have time to look around, and he had already fallen ill. Dr. Vul'fis [Vulfius or Wulfius] today left a card for Nothnagel; today he and Mikorel made a visit. Aunt Amaliia and Uncle Iakov were called to Taganrog by telegram. Iulii Osipovich Gol'denbakh was very attentive during the entire time of Papa's illness; Zakhar'in, on the contrary, showed himself to be a real swine. Thus, they say, he ordered Papa to have a massage after the illness, as a result of which he developed a peritoneal inflammation. But at the most difficult time he told Mama that he can do nothing and that the only thing one can do is pray to God, and hence there is no point for him to come—and no kind of entreaties could make him to reconsider. Now that is gratitude for all that he has received! Then they wrote Kotia to bring Botkin[46] to Moscow, but he was not there. They sent a telegram to Professor Leideck in Berlin and simultaneously to Nothnagel in Vienna. He answered that he can come immediately to Moscow. Such was done, and thank God, in his words, there is not yet an apparent danger, although the situation is very serious. Papa, fully conscious, says that it is necessary to write us to come, and therefore immediately to send me a passport to where he thinks I am (that I am now with Misha, Ronia and Genrikh, since they told him that we have already left Franzensbad). He also said that I love to write in Yiddish (po-evreiski). Aunt Amaliia told him that I wrote Uncle. She added that she read my letter to him and that I write well. Kotia has also been here since Sun-

45. Carl Wilhelm Hermann Nothnagel (1841–1905), a famous German internist and a professor at a university clinic in Vienna.
46. Sergei Petrovich Botkin (1832–89), a famous Russian doctor, social activist, and professor at the Medical Surgical Academy.

day, but Papa saw him only yesterday morning, since he also has not shown himself. Hence we have to wait at least several days more. But the main thing that God gives is this: may Papa get well more quickly, and there is no time to think now about the rest, not to mention talk about it. Nothing matters except health and peace of mind.

SOKOL'NIKI, 15 AUGUST 1887, SATURDAY

Today we again met with Papa, and the meeting yesterday evening went well. Uncle Samuil sent a telegram that he wants to come here, but they do not order him to do so on the grounds that Papa could not see him for a certain time. Yesterday I went with Misha, Ronia, and Genrikh to Papa when they told him that we have arrived, but because he had not heard the sound of the wheels, he was surprised that we have so quickly arrived and did not expect us. Now he has completely calmed down and spoke with us (me and Misha) for a rather long time. They say that there is someone new—Robi [sic] de Castro from Amsterdam, a Spaniard by birth. Everything is now in God's hands, but so far as the baron is concerned, I definitely do not like him. He is an old fogey, although a young man, without any means whatsoever.

SOKOL'NIKI, 17 AUGUST 1887, MONDAY

Mama has now called me to come down to show Dr. Gurvich that I have something on my head—that is, the hair and skin of my head are not right and that I have some kind of ringworm. Now that's something! Yesterday a telegram came from Uncle Samuil, informing us of his arrival here on Thursday, not Friday, as he had told Uncle Iakov. Flora sent me a letter, writing that, rather than await my reply, she has written me again to learn about the current state of Papa's health; she sent Mama a telegram last week to find out the same thing, but Mama directed me to reply by telegram, which I did, but again they are not satisfied. So that is why she wrote me. Tomorrow I shall write Mrs. Sassoon in Franzensbad to thank her for thinking about us. She replied to my telegram with such kindness, likewise without waiting for my reply.

Professor Nothnagel, who came here for a consultation, had a truly terrible experience. During the journey he wanted to open the door of the railcar, but instead, in the night, flew out the external door and landed on the roadbed of the railway tracks. Because Mama was concerned after reading about this in the newspapers, we wrote him to write about his miraculous rescue; today Mama received an extremely kind and detailed letter from him, with a full description of what happened to him and how, by some miracle, he remained alive and completely unharmed. That is how fragile our life is! Grigorii

Antonovich Zakhar'in told Mama today that he is not taking Genrikh. He even broke his promise and said that he now has too many assistants. However, because of his respect for us, I think that he will be ashamed not to do this. Papa said that he would do better to arrange this.

SOKOL'NIKI, 18 AUGUST 1887, TUESDAY

Today I talked about Gabbe [Gubbay] with Papa, who finds that Jacques Rozenberg is better. To be sure, the former is much more attractive, but the latter is much wealthier and better-looking (if one ignores the attractiveness of the personality). So when Uncle Samuil comes here shortly, we will find out what Robin Gabbe [Reuben Gubbay] intends to do and whether, after the wedding of his uncle (a Sassoon), he is really going to China, to which he "is drawn by some unknown power." I think he will go, since he has no work or business here in Europe, and he is just twiddling his thumbs. At the same time, I am surprised by his sister Flora. It is probably necessary to write a letter to A[by] Warburg in Hamburg. It has already been a rather long time since she [Flora] last wrote me, and therefore I do not know where she is right now. I presume that she is somewhere on the seacoast, most likely in Ostend.[47] However, since I do not have exact information about her whereabouts, I think that she is more likely to receive my letter if it is addressed to Hamburg. Yesterday evening I went to bed early—without even waiting until Papa had awoken and we could drink tea or milk. He did not even see me again that evening since I dropped by after dinner, and he was resting, so I quickly left him, and he did not ask about me at all. Uncle Iakov has scheduled duty watches. My share consisted only of daytime watch, which is tantamount to zero. All this is trivia; the main thing is that Papa get well quickly, but I shall tell him about these insults later. Kotia has already told me that he knows how hard my life is. Uncle [Samuil] has probably completely changed his opinion of me because of the caviling and gossip from Uncle Iakov, who is against me. However, sooner or later, all this prevarication and desire to serve Mama will become apparent, and then we will speak with him about the past and together will recall his wonderful deeds allegedly on behalf of Papa's health (I absolutely do not believe any such thing, for I know Uncle perfectly well). Now that is everything I have on my mind! Only Gurvich is now with Papa, because Iulii Osipovich [Gol'denbakh] is leaving. He is departing next Tuesday for the Crimea, but promised to delay the trip for three days because of Papa. Aleksandr Danilovich Mein, together with his family, is also traveling to the Crimea (that is, to Gurzuf). The Pod-

47. A city on the Belgian coast.

goretskii family (husband and wife) also went there last Friday, but none of us even accompanied them to the railway station. Nevertheless, no one has any reason to complain about this.

SOKOL'NIKI, 1 SEPTEMBER 1887, TUESDAY

I received a letter today from Flora in Paris, and it included news about Ruby Gabbe [Reuben Gubbay]. He is still in Royat[48] with his grandfather and will accompany him to England; he will then go to his uncle Edward's wedding in Paris.[49] The weather is splendid—warm, as though it had been ordered. And the sun glows radiantly from morning to night. This is such good fortune! All day yesterday it was rather cool and one might even say cold; hence I did not leave the house to walk in the garden. But today Papa sent for me to go on a stroll with him in the sunshine. Mama has already gone off to the city today. Misha and Ronia wore their student uniforms and went to the university. Misha seeks to be admitted simultaneously to the reserve squadron; for the time being, it is as yet unclear whether that is possible.[50]

SOKOL'NIKI, 2 SEPTEMBER 1887, WEDNESDAY

Papa is gradually growing stronger and recuperating, and he is already walking unassisted. Tomorrow (Thursday), Mama will probably go into Moscow, since she has nothing here to do; when she is home, only sighs and curses are to be heard. Grandfather is here but plans to leave shortly for the city. He has his own pair of horses and does well to have them and not to wait until Mama gives him ours (since, to be honest, our horses are being heavily worked at the present time—transporting first university students, then the Lycée pupils). Mrs. Katkova, they say, was in our office and withdrew some money; altogether, they have 800,000 rubles left, all of which was left to S[ofia] P[etrovna] Katkova (i.e., the widow of the late Mikhail Nikiforovich [Katkov]).[51]

Everything now depends on how she invests this capital. It was quite tactless, on her part, to take the money so quickly from our office, for Katkov had complete confidence in Papa. All this wealth was in a current account in Papa's bank, although it is rumored (by Tsarevich Nikolai) that he has money in an English bank. However, that is untrue, according to Papa—who has excellent knowledge of the Katkov finances and monetary assets.

48. A spa town in the central French department of Auvergne.
49. Edward Sassoon (1856–1912) married Aline Caroline de Rothschild (1867–1909). They had two children: Philip (1888–1939) and Sybil (1894–1989).
50. Evidently, he wanted to be simultaneously in the university and in the reserve squadron.
51. Katkov had died in February 1887.

Yesterday, at last, we received a wire from Uncle. It turns out that he will not leave Paris earlier than Friday. In that case, it will be awkward for me to travel with him because the impending holiday of Rosh Hashanah begins on Sunday evening. Professor Zakhar'in showed himself in the worst light during Papa's illness; he also withdrew money from his current account.

SOKOL'NIKI, 3 SEPTEMBER 1887, THURSDAY

Mama and I now fight almost every day, and I am suffering terribly. It is amazing how she still does not understand that for Papa it is most important that everything be tranquil (in moral terms), but Mama is constantly angry with someone. Fania came here this morning and, what is most stupid of all, began to lecture us that it is impossible to disturb Papa, that we are allegedly killing him. If she were not crazy,[52] it would of course be easy to understand completely the repulsive role that she is now playing. It is she and Mama, not we, who make Papa distressed. Although I tolerate much from her, I am getting tired of it; I pass entire days anxious that no great scandals occur. Today Misha caused a terrible uproar: Zakhar'in, as he was leaving, responded to a question by Misha ("Can Papa eat meat fried in oil?"[53]) by ordering that Mama be summoned. A commotion and yelling were to be heard on the balcony when Mama did not want to go see him. "A pike lives in the lake to keep all the fish awake." Yesterday Mama swore at me because I had spoken up against this, but it turns out that I told G[riogrii] A. to fry the chicken in pig fat. This made her so furious that she brazenly even went in to Papa and began to curse us every possible way, so that Papa asked her to leave his room in order to avoid any further problems that might occur.

But she is still revolving, as the astronomer Galileo put it—like meat patties in lard! . . . [sic] Iulii Osipovich Gol'denbakh did not allow this. I am totally convinced that Mama's fanaticism will enter into the history of Yid-ism (zhidovstvo).

F. F. Knauf[54] is now one of the directors at a new rubber factory, in which he is also an investor. We are now hoping to leave shortly from the dacha. There

52. Zianida meant this literally: in 1903, she wrote that her aunt Fania had to be placed in the care of a Mrs. Smolensk in Vienna for care due to her mental illness for fifteen years.

53. The published text reads "meat in the village (selo)" but Zinaida clearly wrote "meat in fat (salo)," as the following text shows. The issue was obviously about kosher food, and Zinaida ridicules her mother's kosher demand as "Yid-ism."

54. Feodor Feodorovich Knauf served as the director of the Poliakov rubber factory. In 1888, with two others, he established the Moscow Company for Hemp Production. See *Vestnik finansov, promyshlennosti i torgovli: Ukazatel' pravitel'stvennykh rasporiazhenii po ministerstvu financov* (St. Petersburg: Tipografiia Ministerstva Finansov, 1893), 126.

is no reason to stay here any longer; only a few people are still at their dachas, and they too will probably leave soon for the city (in the first days of September). Everything here is just as it was in olden times: the dogs howl at night, the guards are now gone, the police are sleeping, and in general dubious types are wandering around Sokol'niki. Even Il'ia is afraid to take an evening stroll in the woods or on the paths around the house, where there were always a lot more people than anywhere else.

They say that Uncle Samuil leaves tomorrow. May God help see that he gets to Biarritz in time, since that is very useful for me. If it were not for Papa's illness, I would certainly accept his invitation to go with him. A pity that everything turned out so badly, yet I must say, thank God! It is now very boring, not to mention the fact that in the evening and at night it can even be awful to be alone in one's room. Yesterday I read the entire evening (to midnight).

SOKOL'NIKI, 4 SEPTEMBER 1887, FRIDAY
Aleksandr Danilovich Mein is probably already in Gurfuz, at the place where they want to live in the Crimea, and Mania is sick there. Although that is never pleasant, it is nonetheless better [there] if one is fated to be sick during one's lifetime. Papa is very happy that he did not stay in St. Petersburg. Yesterday we had a pure "Sodom and Gomorrah" because of Mama's impossible and quite fanatical, stubborn tendency to deny Papa nutritious and easily digestible food that is contrary to the Law of Moses. For her, that is more important than the question of love for one's neighbor and anonymous benevolence (charity that does not trumpet oneself). It is said that fanaticism is stupidity. Indeed, I agree totally, all the more because it makes people stupid. If one calculates the number [of] Jewish fanatics, it is easy to compile a percentage for the level of intellectual development. Life teaches one to be hardy and not to condemn the blind for their foolishness.

SOKOL'NIKI, 5 SEPTEMBER 1887, SATURDAY
"There are moments, rare in life, about which you tell neither other people nor God," etc. It's true that I often experience such a moment, because I become so depressed that I no longer even wish for anything. Genrikh is already unemployed and, while waiting for something better, still has the status of a medical student. In other words, he does not yet want to think about practicing his profession. Apparently, he does not have a very high opinion of his knowledge. But, my God, look how he fusses when anyone lays a finger on him. The fool always thinks that he is a sage. Were it not for Papa's illness, I would probably be in Biarritz now. It is such a pity that thus far I have not settled my affairs so

that, if need be, I could go alone! But it is still good here and, one might say, quite fresh. Yesterday for Raia's [Khaia's] birthday[55] we did not go into the garden at all. I recently wrote to Iosif Grigor'evich Khabas and Masha in response to their letter; they live quietly and, although they are not amassing wealth, at least they live well—thank God for that! But some, like Fania, begin to complain of their ill-starred fate just two weeks after the wedding.

The Katkovs are still in the countryside. People forget all joy and sadness, and thank goodness for that: forgetting is a treasure. It seems to me that the longer you remember the last minutes of a beloved person, the longer the consolation lasts. But not everyone shares that view; some think precisely the opposite. And I am very sorry about M[ikhail] N. [Katkov]—a patriot and famous statesman of our time.

SOKOL'NIKI, 9 SEPTEMBER 1887, WEDNESDAY

Yesterday was the second day of Rosh Hashanah, and we were not in the city at our synagogue on Bronnaia Street. They say that huge throngs of people were there, and that there was not even room for all of them to stand, let alone sit, and that they did not even admit everyone, but only those who had tickets and previously assigned places.

Dynin arrived here from Odessa with his younger brother Vladimir, who graduated from the Odessa classical gymnasium and will now enroll in the Lycée of Tsarevich Nicholas as a student in the university division. He has still not visited us for some reason, and today only Iakov Abramovich Dynin is dining with us. There are several other such types. It is just a pity that they are mentally underdeveloped but physically overdeveloped. Yet some people suffer in this respect and pay more attention to mental development, as in my case. To be sure, one without the other is bad, and everything should be in moderation.

Iosif and Masha Khabas sent us a holiday card instead of a telegram (which had long been their custom). Raia[56] is very much anxious about today's dinner; she apparently likes L. Dynin. As for me, I think that number one is Robin Gabbe [Reuben Gubbay], then the widower Rozenberg, followed by today's hero of our tragedy (who is not bad, but does not satisfy all the criteria of my ideal). It is better to let your heart choose than otherwise. Mama is at her wits' end trying to cause the maximum trouble for us. To her dismay, she is not

---

55. This was probably Khaia, not Raia as in the published version of the diaries. Khaia's birthday was celebrated at various times in early September, as seen in the diary entries.
56. This may have been Khaia, since she and Zinaida were both looking for spouses.

particularly successful, because we all know how to cope with this (it is like "water off a duck's back"). I am very glad that Yom Kippur will soon be over, for then we shall be free. For the present there is still nothing new in our way of life, and I wonder when we shall finally be ready to move back to the city. Of course, if the weather were still good, it would not be right to grumble about this, but now, amid a downpour, we sit in our rooms, so of course that is not a source of great joy. I am afraid that Papa may even catch another cold, which would be extremely unpleasant for him, all the more given that he is still weak. Today it was necessary to reply to telegrams. Since we are very liberal in this regard, we accumulate a plethora of dispatches. It is surprising how all our foreign acquaintances now send letters, not telegrams, and that is much better. Fania Livshits, our aunt, is here today and asking for a loan of 100 rubles. Although I could fulfill her request, Mama is not giving this to her (so that she not stay longer), and I therefore declined. We spend entire days sitting with Papa, but then go to bed early.

SOKOL'NIKI, 10 SEPTEMBER 1887, THURSDAY

Mr. Dynin dined with us yesterday, without his young brother Vladimir Abramovich. With good reason they say that he is very corpulent and rather dumb, so it was probably pointless to bother getting him admitted as a student at the Lycée of Tsarevich Nicholas. If we are here for Yom Kippur, it will be impossible to spend the entire time alone: on September 1st all the police guard posts will be removed, and the chief of police will not permit the policeman to guard our house, as was done with [Aleksandr] Kozlov earlier, if there is no particular necessity for this. I am waiting for a letter from Flora Gabbe [Gubbay]. It has become very boring here, and I would be very happy to move back to the city as soon as possible. To be sure, one cannot guarantee that there will not be a sudden onset of cold weather and even frost. Joseph Sassoon lives constantly in the countryside (Ashley Park)[57] with his family.

SOKOL'NIKI, 12 SEPTEMBER 1887, SATURDAY

Today all the children favor moving from the dacha as soon as possible (because of the rain). If such miserable weather persists for long, then one can see why that, the sooner we leave, the better and more pleasant it will be for us and even for Papa, who is also becoming bored here.

57. Joseph's father, David Sassoon (1832–1867), purchased the estate Ashley Park, a private residential neighborhood at Walton-on-Thames.

We are waiting for Kotia [Daniil] to come from St. Petersburg for the fast of Yom Kippur—if only he really fulfills his promise to come here for the holiday (as he said before his departure to Tsarskoe Selo, when Papa was still very sick). But then, as grounds for his departure, he cited the fact that Uncle Samuil was supposed to arrive in Petersburg from abroad, and he wanted to forewarn him [about Papa's illness].

My dear Samuil'chik [Samuil Iakovlevich Poliakov] from Taganrog is here. This evening he is going to Petersburg to study at the university there.

Iosif Zaiberling did not reply to the holiday card that Papa had us send.

Raia and her cousin sang sentimental songs in the dining room (in an undertone).

Lidiia Stepanovna has not been here since my return from Franzensbad. They say that she fears infecting her sister's children, and therefore has not come during the entire time of the illness. I am quite amazed that the Danilovs recently arrived from the countryside and still are going somewhere as guests; they are all half-wits, beginning with Mikhail Alekseevich and ending with the governess, who allegedly acquiesces to the home situation as it is (where there are also a lot of impossible, inappropriate things). But they now have a young German woman. A very simple woman, but from Courland,[58] but like a real person. Papa has asked Professor Zakhar'in whether it is possible to move to the city earlier than prescribed. It is amazing that some people are still living here! Fania left (or in a few days plans to leave) from Moscow to go to her family in Orel.

MOSCOW, 23 SEPTEMBER 1887, WEDNESDAY

Had Papa not insisted on moving back from the dacha, we would still be there. We are waiting for a decision about going abroad, and in the very near future it will probably be settled—when and where we shall go. Grigorii Antonovich Zakhar'in is here for Mama and Baby, whom—no matter what—they want to take abroad (because of Mama's fantasy). Since he too is very weak (like me), Mama wants to build up his strength in Paris, where she will no doubt be. And so now they are hearing what Zakhar'in has to say. Iosif Grigor'evich [Khabas] sent us a telegram on Sukkot. As I thought, he and Masha are prospering and, although they are not wealthy, they live modestly but well. People are a lot happier when they live in shacks than in palaces. It seems to me that it would not take a lot of effort to get used to a modest (but of course comfortable) life, surrounded by people whom one loves. But perhaps I am wrong, since, as they

58. Courland (Kurliandiia), one of the Baltic provinces, was in western Latvia.

say, the "*sated person does not understand someone who is hungry*" [emphasis by Zinaida]. And it is quite possible that I will now not be able to deny myself luxury and the like. It is of course a matter of habit. It is no accident that one hears the proverb "habit is second nature," and that is true.

What a great pity that the weather has turned bad. Papa has not gone out once since we returned to the city. Of course, in the foul weather that we have had during all this time, one cannot think about going out for a ride or a stroll. I was very sad today; I myself do not know why. Since I have not received a reply to my two letters to Flora Gabbe [Gubbay], I do not know what I should think about her past periods of silence. I am surprised, all the more since of late she has written me very often, and I did not even have time to answer all her letters. Thus they crossed each other, and we corresponded almost every week, and suddenly *tout passe, tout casse, tout lasse* [nothing lasts forever], as the French say. Fania Livshits wrote me. Although she is not particularly bright, she writes well. She spent a whole month in Moscow, where they admitted her daughter to St. Vladimir's [Children's] Hospital. One year after her first operation she had to undergo a second one. It is no joke for a poor child to suffer so. I think that she may not survive all this suffering and torture and that she may give up her soul to God. The Shcherbatovs are also renovating their house (on Sadovaia Street) into a children's hospital.[59]

MOSCOW, 24 SEPTEMBER 1887, THURSDAY

I am expecting a letter from Flora Gabbe [Gubbay] in Paris, but do not know whether it will come. Sitting here now are Lidiia Stepanovna, Mrs. Reymond, and Emiliia I. Ogus-Shaikovich; the latter came because of the letter I sent earlier from Sokol'niki.

We have still not been anywhere since moving back to the city! True, we are very happy, but for now we do not go out because there is no one to accompany us, and our brothers are at the university (and cannot be distracted from their studies). And we should not go out alone, as this is contrary to etiquette and the rules. Iosif Zeiberling sent a letter. How strange that earlier I did not know the house number where Messarosh lives. Lelia [Messarosh] wrote me today from St. Petersburg, saying that she visited us here. Mama did not tell me anything about this when we were at the dacha.

---

59. The reference is to Prince Aleksandr Alekseevich Shcherbatov, who built a children's hospital on Sadovaia-Kudrinskaia Street.

A lot of people came here today, and Dr. Gurvich and Lidiia Stepanovna are sitting here now. For the first time Il'ia and I went out in the carriage for a half hour and breathed the fresh, but not clean air of our dear capital, mother Moscow.

Iosef Landau is probably now at Uncle's place in the countryside, since he should go there after his treatment in Marienbad. He wanted to be there after his dear parents come back from abroad. Bella spent the entire summer in the countryside, which was the site of the betrothal of Niuta [Iakovlevna Polaikova] to Grigorii Isaakovich Rubinshtein from Khar'kov.

Raia [Khaia][60] was again in the company of her friend. Lidiia Stepanovna, her former governess, is with her for the third day in a row. Mama has still not recovered completely from her sore throat and speaks not in a loud voice but in a whisper. Not because she cannot, but because she has been ordered to speak softly.

I am quite amazed that thus far I have not had any news from Paris; apparently, everybody there has forgotten me and stopped caring about me.

Papa is talking about going abroad in October, but somehow I do not believe this. It seems to me that there will be a lot of talk before anything is decided once and for all. And I am even beginning to be a little afraid of traveling because of the endless rebukes from Mama. It is really only for Papa's sake that I will do this. Therefore Mama should be more reserved, for I am not doing anything to her and do not wish her ill. I do not know what she and I have to argue about. It is amazing how she simply hates me and idolizes Raia.[61] Here is a fact: I have still not managed to answer all the letters asking about Papa's condition.

MOSCOW, 26 SEPTEMBER 1887, SATURDAY

I went for a stroll with little Il'ia today along the boulevard and stopped at Shilling's on Tverskoi Boulevard. Joe [sic] has now sharply raised his prices—that is, his stock has risen because Aline de Rothschild married his cousin, Edward Albert Sassoon.

Khaia had a fit at breakfast today and was in a very foul mood the entire time. She even quarreled with Il'iusha because he somehow irritated Lidiia Stepanovna, saying that yesterday, in her presence, he spoke of Mr. Gringmut[62] and that he had not noticed his presence at the dinner table, and Khaia be-

---

60. This was probably Khaia, not Raia, given the former's close relationship to the governess.
61. This was probably a reference to Khaia, not Raia. Zinaida consistently believed her mother loved Khaia more than her (as is evident in the Paris diaries as well). The following entries were also most likely about Khaia.
62. Vladimir Andreevich Gringmut (1851–1907) was a right-wing publicist, chief editor of *Moskov-*

came angry. Lidiia Stepanovna Zotova stayed overnight at our house. Mama was already at the synagogue today and did not seem to be at all ill. Khaia has a sore throat now, but Raia is completely healthy, thank the Lord. It is very unpleasant that I must now constantly remain silent in Mama's presence! Papa is still so weak that of course he is in no condition to intercede on my behalf; indeed, even earlier he did not have the strength for that and avoided doing so. I do not intend to make my parents quarrel, and therefore I hope that God will help me bear my cross, so that I should bear it as long as necessary—up to my emancipation perhaps from Mama's yoke by means of marriage (about which I have my doubts).

Today I met Baron Vrangel'. Since the Fon Derviz family moved nearby, we shall see them. It is terribly difficult to imagine how they must be saddened by the death of the father and husband. Fania should answer my kind letter soon. Although she does not write me often, I have to think that she sometimes remembers me and wishes everyone all the best. I did nothing all day and dropped in to see Papa just a few times—where there were guests, who, other than exhausting him, bring nothing useful through their presence. He becomes so tired during the day that it is even impossible to imagine this. In an hour I'll go have dinner.

N. Shirobokova writes me nothing at all, and I even think about her.

Shchukin's youngest son is studying at the Lycée of Tsarevich Nikolai together with our brothers.

It is still undecided whether we shall go abroad and where precisely we might go. This of course will depend on the advice of Professor Nothnagel in Vienna, who to be sure will be there with us. Iulii Osipovich, our doctor, is still in Yalta.

MOSCOW, 27 SEPTEMBER 1887, SUNDAY

Iosef Vil'gel'movich [Landau] and Bella are of course now together at Uncle Iakov's. I allegedly do not want to write them! They have not written me since I was abroad (in Franzensbad) this year. Lidiia Stepanovna was with Khaia yesterday (or the day before, I do not really remember); I only know that she visits us very often and is not shy about spending the night here, in her former room, where she stays as if in an apartment, and no one dares to occupy her room.

Today Mama told Papa the news. But I do not very much believe these rumors—namely, that the Demidovs are getting divorced.

---

skie vedomosti in 1896–1907, and a prominent figure in the "black-hundredist" movement in the 1905 revolution.

They say that Mlle. Nikiforova is marrying an officer Leslie, a nephew of Prince Shakhovskoi. For now, no news regarding my own personal affairs.

MOSCOW, 29 SEPTEMBER 1887, TUESDAY

How pleasant it is to read a few pages of one's journal after several years have passed! Lidiia Stepanovna has not been here for several days, and I think that little Il'ia's speech had an effect on Raia [Khaia], who no longer sends a horse to bring her, as was done earlier.

I would very much like to know when the young Gabbe [Gubbay] leaves for India or China; he stayed for the marriage of his Uncle Edward, which should be next Wednesday, 7/19 October in Paris, where of course there will be a great celebration, since he has married a Mademoiselle [Aline] de Rothschild, the daughter of Gustav. But they say that she is not very pretty. Papa does not like him, but I always said that he is very worldly and *distinqué* [*distingué*]. And there are few such. To be sure, he is not good-looking and does not even have an intelligent face, but it is pleasant all the same.

I spent the entire morning with Papa, together with Khaia, who—probably as a result—did not go to synagogue (so as to avoid leaving me alone with Papa). Since Mama constantly makes things difficult for me, she imagines that I will complain about her to Papa. I always just sit there and do not even talk with him in order to avoid an unpleasant subject of conversation (for example, the trip abroad) that might upset him.

But now I have to get a hold on myself. Flora Gabbe [Gubbay] has still not written me, and I think that someone is the reason for this. Khaia did not even respond to her letter last spring, but I always replied promptly to her letters. The purpose of this correspondence between us cannot now be achieved. As a result, I look upon the correspondence simply as a pleasant way to pass time, not as serious proof of love.

MOSCOW, 7 OCTOBER 1887, WEDNESDAY

Having lived here for three weeks, I have been unable to go out and escape from the bickering and troubles. While glad that, at last, I could breathe fresh air, I did not foresee my helpless fate, but I hope soon to stroll here everyday once our people go abroad. I wish this with all my heart—in my monotonous life, amid complete tranquility—to forget the troubles that I have experienced in the best part of my twenty-four years. One thing would already be entirely sufficient in this loathsome situation: to change my way of life (of course, for the better). But there is absolutely no reason to think about the rest of it; life does not agree with me.

The streets impressed me as very animated; many new buildings are going up in Moscow!

Today the French Jews of Paris are celebrating the marriage of A[line] de Rothschild and Edward Albert Sassoon (whom we know). Although we do not know Baron Gustave de Rothschild,[63] he nonetheless sent us an invitation. The entire day we involuntarily thought about Gabbe [Gubbay] and his relatives, who have probably come to Paris for the celebration, which is both religious and secular. However desirable our presence at this wedding (as was planned), I will be much more pleased if the object of my thinking does not go off to China, where he lives "like a god in France." But I do not think (and of this I am convinced) that this will not come to pass, since *qui vout pont, a il le vent* [sic] and he has a strong character (unfortunately, more than I thought; I thought him a wet rag, from which one could make whatever one wishes). He does not have much style, but *c'est une bonne pâte.* I will shout to him, "Bon voyage," when he departs for the Heavenly Kingdom of Bogdkhan.[64] It takes a whole five weeks to travel there by sea—which is no joke; after all, it is possible to drown doing so. Summoned by his mother to Paris two years ago, he traveled nonstop.

Iulii Osipovich Gol'denbakh was still in Yalta when we went abroad, and I am continuing to write this journal in Vienna, where we now find ourselves.[65] I would very much wish to be at home right now and not to know that I am completely superfluous in my own family—in an alien environment, far from my beloved brothers and Raia, who likes me much more than do Khaia and Mama (the only female representatives among us here).

E. O. accompanied us to the railway station, but Glazer came as well, despite the fact that this was a business day. The poor children, with tears in their eyes, accompanied us as we set out on the long journey; as for me, I wept the entire time. By evening I had somewhat calmed down, lay down to sleep, but the next day was again crying. The voice in my heart sang something sad; the silence of the night terrified me; I could not even completely regain my composure when we arrived in Vienna. In other words, this time I experienced an unpleasant feeling that I had never before known.

63. Gustave Samuel de Rothschild (1829–1911), a prominent French banker.
64. Bogdkhan was the Russian term for the Chinese emperor in the sixteenth through eighteenth centuries.
65. Zinaida evidently started this entry in Moscow but then continued it (at some later point) in Vienna (as confirmed by the next entry).

Today a whole crowd of people were at our place, and a mass of people called on us. For example, Mr. and Mrs. Fon Derviz came now; they live here, in this very hotel, and she is our guest for the first time. She is not bad looking and one could even say that she is beautiful; the only thing is that she speaks very unclearly and lisps. Since she was born a von Gutmann in Vienna, she has her entire family here. Despite this, here they live with greater freedom and so as to avoid imposing on her parents, as her kind husband put it.

Today Mama consulted with Professor Nothnagel. He found so many guests here that he was even dissatisfied. Armin Popper[66] fell ill in Budapest with peritonitis, and he also went to him there. He is now recovering; a daughter or son (I do not know which) was born in his family.

PARIS, 4/16 NOVEMBER 1887, WEDNESDAY

It is now very cold here, and we plan to go to Nice on Saturday (7/19 November). Il'iusha competed in a bicycle race in our town manège; he stood out, since (as the newspapers report) only he and Blok—of the eight competing—did not fall. Yesterday evening James Girsh [de Hirsch] babbled a lot about fiancés and so loudly that I did not know where I should go to save myself from the embarrassing situation into which he thrust me (in front of all those present in the room). Since I have a certain habit of *ne faire semblant de rien*, at the time I was conversing with A[leksandr] D. Mein, who was here. What a nice Sassoon! I became acquainted with him here. Lidiia Stepanovna does not write anyone; nor does her favorite write her—what does that mean? I finally saw my Franzensbad friends, Mme. Rachel Sassoon and her cousin Ezekiel who is very nice. They say very little about their cousin's marriage to Mlle. de Rothschild, and I find this supremely tactful and modest on their part, and indeed appropriate. Two weeks have passed since we arrived in Paris, but I have not ordered anything for myself and have acquired just one wool dress at the Rauff store (13 Boulevard Haussmann) for 500 francs; that is my only purchase during our stay here, but I hope to finish shopping on the way back. They say that the difference between the climate here and Nice is enormous. The cold itself is unbearable because of its aridness and fog, which sometimes is no worse than that in London. I find myself completely out of my depth here, and I do not know what will become of me in Nice, to which we are going on Saturday evening. The streets are packed with foreigners; we are rarely at home; and therefore I cannot get used to Paris.

66. Possibly the baron who built a hotel in Trenčín (in modern Slovakia).

We arrived yesterday morning by train after an eighteen-hour overnight trip—how convenient. Papa does not want to remain here in the Hotel des Anglais, where we are temporarily staying until we can rent a villa (which, it seems, they have already seen). Miss Gosh does not praise these villas, saying that it is impossible to take a stroll from there; indeed, for me in particular, it will be terribly boring to be in the company of three people who do not need me, who have no intention of doing anything nice for me, and who always annoy me in every possible way.

The weather was poor yesterday, but excellent today. In general, Nice has made a very strange, special impression on me. I myself do not know why, but the more beautiful and luxurious the nature, the more alone I feel. True, I would like to be completely satisfied and happy here. But we sinners are so rarely given such happiness; moreover it is always so relative that I am honestly afraid of angering God because of my dissatisfaction.

Aleksandr Danilovich Mein is arriving here today. He is expecting a response in Petersburg from the prince regarding the disposition of his inheritance (which he, or more precisely his wife, received from her brother Prince Aleksandr Wittgenstein,[67] who visited us last year in Paris). Uncle Samuil summoned Mein for this. Baron James de Hirsch is partly managing this business, through his brother. But Georges[68] is still going to the Conseil d'État, notwithstanding the fact that they have such a scandal in their ministry—which is resigning as a consequence of Mr. Wilson.[69] The latter, together with General [Louis Charles] Caffarel, the former minister of war, sold military decorations and have been badly compromised. Hence people are hawking printed fliers on the street: *quel malheur d'avoir un tel gendre* [sic] (what a misfortune to have such a son-in-law), an allusion to the president's son-in-law and to this whole sordid story; they say that this has already been compiled into a pamphlet that has some very successful parts. It will be necessary to read this, since Mama bought two copies. Our family members went for a ride around town, apparently. I have already gone with Elizabeth Gosh for a stroll but saw nothing special. I have managed to write Raia a letter today, but in the morning, while still in bed, wrote a poem. Khaia is in a good mood today, but it could hardly be otherwise: everyone is at her beck and call. Tomorrow we will probably move

---

67. Mariia Lukinichna (née Bernadskaia) was the wife of Aleksandr Mein.

68. Georges Boulanger, the minister of war and a central figure in a conservative, nationalist movement in 1887–88.

69. The reference is to Daniel Wilson, who had trafficked in medals of the Legion of Honor. The scandal forced Wilson's father-in-law, President Grévy, to resign on 2 December 1887.

from the hotel to a villa, where we all cannot have a good time, and that is especially true for me. In Paris I met with E. I. Fedos'eva.

NICE, 10/22 NOVEMBER 1887, TUESDAY

It has been raining the entire day, ever since morning, and it is also such a nasty rain, like ours in the fall. Tomorrow I hope to take the carriage for a drive to see the city; otherwise I still have not been anywhere or seen anything. Meanwhile, nothing has turned out successfully. It seems that Papa is in a bad mood here! Yesterday evening Mein came here and stayed in our hotel, where he will remain until Saturday or Sunday; then he will probably travel again to Strasbourg, where he is negotiating with the prince about the management of his inheritance in Russia, the castle Vert. The weather is far from good, and I am bored. What a blessed corner they dragged me into now! To be honest, the place itself is splendid, but this is just not the right season. Virtually no one is here now; people come here only in the month of January.

NICE, 11/23 NOVEMBER 1887, WEDNESDAY

No matter what I looked at—the sea, where sails are visible, or the beach, where palms are growing—it is all splendid. Both places are amazingly picturesque, like Biarritz, with its southern Spanish sun or its Spanish traders. So Italian Nice[70] is also wondrous and delicate. It is impossible to go out in the evenings here, and one must always be careful when the sun goes down: each locale has its own peculiarities, good and bad. For one thing, they say that there are strong winds from the sea; these are apparently unhealthy because of the thick dust that is stirred up in town and along the seashore.

The conversation about Mama's unfairness is annoying for me. It is now impossible to discuss this with Papa, who takes everything that Mama and Khaia tell him to be the absolute truth. I wanted to go for a stroll with Miss Gosh right after coffee, but it was 11 o'clock and I was afraid of being late for breakfast.

Yesterday Papa, Mein, and I had dinner together, but I did not talk to them the entire time. The French cuisine here is not as delicate and delicious as in Paris—especially at the Ritz Hotel, where dinner is 12 francs, which is expensive but tasty.

It is so, so good here in Nice! As though one has moved to another part of the world! And how soft and light one breathes here, just as in Montreux, but perhaps even better, because here it is much more southern and the vegetation

---

70. Nice had been part of Piedmont-Sardinia but was ceded to France in 1860. Zinaida is describing the city in cultural, not political, terms.

richer: palms, orange and lemon trees, oleander, cypress, cactus, in a word, all the southern trees. The goal of our stay here is to bolster our health. In an hour Miss Gosh will go for lunch, and I shall remain alone in my room. The stormy waves quickly carry the boats between the waters gleaming in the sun, and their sails shine white in the distance, like the wings of flies. *Das Leben ist Ernst*, said the poet.[71] Unfortunately, I completely recognize that. I am now waiting for lunch; I write and yearn for home, but there I am sometimes bored and want to go somewhere.

NICE, 12/24 NOVEMBER 1887, THURSDAY

Personally, I have only good things to say about Nice, but other circumstances [are at work]. In the evenings I do not spend much time in the salon but am always more in my room, where I read each evening.

The fish and crustaceans here are very good, and oysters—which are [from] Marenne, not Ostend—are much smaller than the latter, but delicious all the same. Papa, Mein, and I went to the restaurant of our hotel and had a rather good breakfast. But we put off the trip to Monte Carlo until tomorrow: we were running late today because of the need to lease the apartment (on Place Grimaldi). I really like this city; it is a pure paradise. Since we have come to stay for two months, it is necessary to set up a kitchen for Mama and Khaia. I have already managed to see the Sassoon villa ([called] Theresa), but I am unhappy that they still have not arrived. The French fade completely into the background here; only the English are to be seen. The owner of our new apartment is apparently an Italian, and his wife is English.

One problem is the difficulty in renting the apartment: it does not have enough rooms. The goal of renting is that everything be nearby and especially be close to the Promenade des Anglais. The entire local community assembles for music in the public garden, where an excellent orchestra performs. A lot of people gather there at that time of the day, and things become very lively as a result.

Now, in anticipation of moving, it is necessary to pack up everything, and one cannot say that this is much fun. I still have not recovered from the flu (a cough, head cold, and above all a sore throat). *Vraiment si le climat de Nice ne me guérit pas, je crois qu'il n'y a plus de salut pour moi, que mon temps est arrivé, quand je dois quitter cette vie, quoique cela ne me paraisse pas probable* [sic].[72]

---

71. Presumably Zinaida's version of a Schiller aphorism in *Wallenstein*: "Ernst ist das Leben, heiter ist die Kunst" (Life is earnest, art is gay).

72. Indeed, if the climate of Nice does not cure me, then I think there is no saving me, that my time has come, when I must depart this life, however improbable this might seem.

Mr. Arnoldi is offering us his villa and has found an apartment for us that fits our taste. But it lacks a room for Miss Gosh and an office for Papa (as well as a good bathroom for him). Although there is a toilet, it is near the kitchen and of course not very good. There is also an apartment on Victor Hugo Boulevard, but it is as bad as the one on Place Grimaldi. It is a pity, however, that one cannot remain at the seashore, given that this is the epicenter of life for foreigners. Tomorrow morning we are planning to travel to Monte Carlo to play roulette. It is a place famous throughout the world, where people have amassed—but more often have lost—enormous sums of money.

NICE, 13/25[73] NOVEMBER 1887, FRIDAY

I am of course very tired after the ride to find an apartment. It goes without saying that the three of us—Aleksandr Danilovich Mein, Miss Gosh, and I—rode all over the city. At the very time when we were out, Miss Arnoldi was here. Immediately upon returning I ordered Russian tea and with genuine pleasure drank a cup after such a prolonged ride in this rainy weather (although in an enclosed landau). Still, I was the entire day in fresh air until sundown (until it became necessary to light candles). It is time to finish; Saturday is now approaching. The French, in this regard, are not so strict and are less observant. It is so, so good that we are here! It would be still better if the entire family were here—it would be less boring than it is now.

NICE, 14/26 NOVEMBER 1887, SATURDAY

This morning we went with Miss Gosh to the seashore for a stroll—it was so charming. Mein left for Monte Carlo without us, and we asked him to play roulette on our behalf, and I probably lost a whole 10 francs. He returned and said that I lost the 10 francs (Mama did as well), but that Khaia won (that is, she neither won nor lost, but broke even and got her 10 francs back (saying that this was the same as Papa). The latter gave them to me, remarking that he allocated them to lose in gambling, but that I can have them.

Iurasov, the Russian vice-consul,[74] was here. This is a pathetic, sick old man, who was recommended to us by A. P. Bogoliubov.[75] Tomorrow we shall go again to look at apartments, as well as the Bashkirtseva or Romanova villas. They say that the rent for the villa that we saw today is 50,000 francs. The artist

---

73. The published text has "19/26," but given the dates of the preceding and succeeding entries, it should read "13/25." And 13 October 1887 was indeed a Friday, as Zinaida wrote at the head of the entry.

74. Nikolai Ivanovich Iurasov (1836–1906).

75. Perhaps the painter Aleksei Petrovich Bogoliubov (1824–96), who lived in France in the later years of his life until his death.

Makovskii[76] lived there last year, thanks to his friendship with the Marquise di Ormesson,[77] who was connected with the embassy in St. Petersburg.

The weather today is glorious! At least, we have been compensated for yesterday's rain and dreariness; this is horrible—it is so boring when it rains all night and all day! It is impossible to become reconciled with the idea that we traveled so far to come here for such weather. But, thank God, today was wonderful. Papa is gradually getting better and becoming much stronger. That is already apparent from the fact that he walks a lot here and for a long time does not get at all tired. It is necessary to continue this lifestyle to become stronger. I myself have not completely ceased to cough and must admit that I am a little concerned about this.

NICE, 15/27[78] NOVEMBER 1887, SUNDAY

Villa 63 has a very beautiful garden. It is amazing, however, the Corinaldi house has a nice park with orange and lemon trees in the courtyard and right in front of the house.

Flora Gabbe [Gubbay] has not written me here a single time, nor have I written her. However, I did not have time to write a letter from here to Paris; I will put that off until I am settled and then will send the details of my address (which I cannot yet do, since we have not chosen a place to stay). It is good that the choice is now between two places. The goal of today's excursion was to examine the apartments. They are better, warmer, and healthier than where we are now in Nice. It is all the more regrettable (for Mama) that neither Baby nor Sasha is here.

Switzerland, Montreaux, and Vevey are also pleasant winter sites, but not like Nice. [Nikolai] Shcherbatov of Russia, according to the newspapers, is also here with his son and daughter, and they are staying in the Splendide Hotel, which I apparently have not seen. We went again to examine the Corinaldi house on Place Grimaldi, where Count Loris-Melikov is living; he occupies the entresol and is residing in this house for the second winter. Hence it must be good and healthy there; otherwise, one would have to assume that he would not have taken it for all this time and would have found something better. Like me, Iuliia Shil'dbakh is losing her hair.[79] Today I made the acquaintance

76. The reference may be to either one of the two Makovskii brothers—Vladimir Egorovich (1846–1920) or Konstantin Egorovich (1839–1915).

77. Olivier d'Ormesson (1849–1923), who served as French ambassador to St. Petersburg in 1886–88.

78. The published version of the diaries has "15/24," which—to judge from the sequence of entries—is wrong. And Sunday was indeed 15 November 1887 on the Julian calendar.

79. Zinaida continued to have problems with her hair, as she noted in her later diaries.

of Mrs. Demidova, the widow of A. B. Kozakova.[80] Fedor Fedorovich Knauf wrote Papa recently and described all the business affairs in detail. Yorick, the Shakespearan buffoon,[81] was probably no more stupid than us bright people. I am continuing my literary activities here, but other than two small poems, I have written nothing else; indeed, there was no time for it. More than a week has passed since we arrived in Nice, but we are still camping out and cannot set up housekeeping and spread out our trunks, even briefly; the point is that so far we have taken almost nothing from the trunks other than what is most essential and necessary. After all, we shall be here three months. Mr. Arnoldi wanted us to move into his villa, but we declined. The long garden leads from the promenade to the dacha of Mrs. Bashkirtseva (a Russian) and her sister (Romanova). If it is not good to be close to the sea (I think not), then this is a godsend. The desire to be as close as possible to the sea would be realized, yet all hygienic demands would be met. Here are churches of all confessions, even a synagogue (which, they say, is very luxurious). . . . [*sic*].

80. Aleksandr Borisovich Kozakov (1808–70), a privy counselor.
81. A character in *Hamlet*.

APPENDIX

Family Trees of the Poliakovs and Gubbays

THE POLIAKOV (POLIAKOFF) FAMILY

LAZAR SAMUILOVICH POLIAKOV (1748–1833)
- *Married* first wife (name unknown)
    - SAMUIL (1783–1868, d. in Shklov)
    - VENIAMIN (d. in Dubrovna)
    - MORDUKH (d. in Rudni)
    - Daughter (name unknown, *married* Magidson)
- *Married* second wife Yegudka
    - AARON (d. in Dubrovno at the age of 71)
        - SAMUIL
        - NATHAN
        - MIKHLIA
    - VUL'F (d. in Shklov at the age of 73)
        - SAMUIL
        - Daughters (names unknown)
    - MOISEI (d. in Mstislav)
        - Many sons and daughters (names unknown)
    - SOLOMON (SHLOMO) (1812–1897, d. in Moscow; see below)[1]
        - IAKOV (1832–1909)
        - SAMUIL (1837–1888)
        - LAZAR (ELIEZER) (1842–1914)
    - KHAIA *married* ZAK (first name unknown)

SOLOMON LAZAREVICH POLIAKOV (1812–1897)
- *Married* first wife ZLATA RABINOVICH (1812–1851), daughter of Iakov and Malka Rabinovich
    - IAKOV (1833–1909; see below)
    - SAMUIL (1836–88; see below)
    - MALKA (d. in infancy in Beshenkovich)
    - LAZAR (ELIEZER) (1843–1914; see below)[2]
- *Married* second wife BREINE (BRAYNE) (d. 1900)

---

1. These are the dates provided in Iakov Poliakov, "Istoriia, semeinye nachinaia [s]1748 goda," Central Archives for the History of the Jewish People, ll. 2 and 248–49.

2. These are the birth dates of Iakov, Samuil, and Lazar provided in ibid., l. 2. Iakov wrote, "I was

IAKOV SOLOMONOVICH POLIAKOV (1833–1909)

   Married first wife KHASIA MERI MOISEEVNA BERLIN (d. 1857), daughter of Moisei Nakhimovich Berlin of Rudni

      MOISEI IAKOVLEVICH (b. 1850, d. in infancy)

      LAZAR IAKOVLEVICH (1851–1927) *married* ANNA (ANNETTE) ANISIMOVNA (1852–1929), daughter of Anisim Raffalovich and Nadine née Lowensohn and widow of Edward Emanuel Benjamin Leonino, with whom she had two daughters, Ol'ga Lucie Warburg and Rosa Eleonora

         VLADIMIR (VOLODIA) LAZEREVICH (1880–1956) *married* KSENIA LEOPOL'DOVNA LEON (b. 1883)

            VERA VLADIMIROVNA POLIAKOFF (stage name Vera Lindsay, 1911–1992), *married* first husband PERCY BASIL HARMSWORTH BURTON RICHARD (1933–2017)

            Married second husband GERALD BARRY STEPHEN LEON REID (1945–2000)

            Married third husband JOHN RUSSELL (1919–2008)

         VICTOR LAZAREVICH (1881–1906, suicide)

         DMITRII (IONA) LAZAREVICH (1883–1944) *married* MATILDA (MANIA) ISAAKOVNA SOLOVEICHIK (1890–1944), daughter of Isaak Solomonovich Soloveichik and Anna Abramovna née Bronshtein

         MARIIA (MARY) LAZAREVNA (b. 1889)

         NADEZHDA LAZAREVNA (b. 1895)

         OL'GA LAZAREVNA (b. 1906)

      ELIZABETH IAKOVLEVNA (Liza, Elena; 1855–1937) *married* LEV (LOUIS, LEON) ANISIMOVICH RAFFALOVICH, son of Anisim Raffalovich and Nadine née Lowensohn

         SERGEI (SEREZHA) LVOVICH (1873/5–1943), *married* or cohabited with first partner, his cousin ALEXANDRA (ADA) RAFFALOVICH[3]

            OL'GA RAFFALOVICH (buried with Maria [Marie] Varshavskaia [Warshawsky])

         Married second wife, PRINCESS CHOLOKAEV (TCHOLOKAIEFF)[4]

         NIKOLAI (NICOLAS, KOLI) LVOVICH *married* first wife MARIA (MARIE) RAFFALOVICH

            HELENE RAFFALOVICH *married* JACQUES DE SOGONZAC

---

born on 30 July 1833." Based on archival documents, Irina Ryklis and Andrei Shumkov list Iakov's birth year 1832, Samuil's as 1837, and Lazar's as 1842 ("Poliakovy: nekotorye voprosy genealogii roda i soslovnogo statusam," in *Trudy po evreiskoi istorii i kul'tury: Materialy XIX mezhdunarodnoi ezhegodnoi konferentsii po iudaika* 3 [2012]: 190, 201, and 206). The Poliakov brothers reported earlier birth dates in the official documentation, which Ryklis and Shumkov relied upon for their article.

3. Zinaida wrote that Sergei Raffalovich was marrying Ada Raffalovich in a Russian Orthodox Church in Geneva ("Nauchno-issledovatel'skii otdel rukopisei Rossiiskoi gosudarstvennoi biblioteki," f. 743, k. 139, d. 1, 18 ob.). This is confirmed in "Mariages," *Le Figaro*, 18 October 1901. However, Ol'ga Raffalovich's death certificate notes that her parents cohabited and were not married.

4. The obituary of Elizabeth Raffalovich mentions her two sons and their wives, Princess Tcholokaieff and Katharine Tinsley Lightner ("Deuils," *Le Figaro*, 18 March 1937).

Married second wife KATHARINE TINSLEY LIGHTNER

ALEXIS (ALESHA) LVOVNA

Married second wife AMALIIA (MALKA) MOISEEVNA LIVSHITS (15/27 January 1840–12/25 August 1906)

LIUBA MUSHA IAKOVLEVNA (1861–1869)

ISABELLA (BELLA) IAKOVLEVNA (1863–1922) *married* IOSEF (JOSEPH) VIL'GEL'MOVICH LANDAU (1846–1900)

ALICE (LIULIA) ROSE IOSEFOVNA (1883–1968) *married* OSMOND ELIM D'AVIGDOR GOLDSMID (1877–1940)

SIR HENRY JOSEPH (1909-1976)

CYNTHIA ODETTE (1910–1915)

SIR JAMES ARTHUR (1912–1987)

SIDNEY (b. 1913)

GEORGE IOSEFOVICH (b. 1885) *married* LINA LEVI

BORIS (BORIA) IAKOVLEVICH (b. 1865; baptized in 1900) *married* ELENA KONSTANTINOVNA NÉE FOTI, the divorced wife of Pen'kovskii

SERGEI BORISOVICH

ELENA BORISOVNA

ANNA (NIUTA) IAKOVLEVNA (1867–1942) *married* GRIGORII (GEORGE) ISAAKOVICH RUBINSHTEIN (1863–1929), son of Isaak Osipovich and Revekka Rubinshtein

SAMUIL IAKOVLEVICH (1869–1943)

SAMUIL (SHMUEL) SOLOMONOVICH POLIAKOV (1836–1888)

Married AVDOT'IA (DANIIA, EVDOKIA) TROFIMOVNA (TAIKHILOVNA) EPSHTEIN (d. 1899)

ZINAIDA SAMUILOVNA (1855–1909) married JAMES DE HIRSCH

ROZA (ROZALIIA) REVEKKA ESFIR SAMUILOVNA (1859–1883) *married* LEV (LEON) VARSHAVSKII (WARSHAWSKY)

MARIIA (MARIE, MAROUSSIA) LEONOVNA (b. 1881 in Paris, d. 1964)

IGNATII LEONOVICH (IGNACE) (1883–1916)

RACHEL SAMUILOVNA (1861–1929 [her gravestone reads 1859–1929]) *married* GEORGES ELIE ST. PAUL

ROBERT (1884-1924)

GEORGETTE MOTT (1886–1943)

GEORGES REN (1898-1900)

EDOUARD

THIERRY

DANIIL SAMUILOV (Daniel, Kotia; 1862–1914) *married* ALMA ANTOINE REISS (1879–1940), daughter of Eduard and Fanny Reiss

LAZAR (ELIEZER) SOLOMONOVICH POLIAKOV (1843–1914)

Married ROZALIIA PAVLOVNA VYDRIN (1842–1919), daughter of Pavel (Peisakh) Raphailovich Vydrin

ZINAIDA (ZINA, ZLATA) LAZEREVNA (27 January 1863 [Old Style]–28 April 1952) *married* REUBEN GUBBAY (*see below*)

ANNETTE (1896–1986)

AVGUST (AUGUST, AZI) LAZAREVICH (28 April 1864–72, d. in Geneva)

KHAIA (KSENIA, XENIA) LAZAREVNA (1865–1944) *married* GEORGES LEVI (both d. in Auschwitz)

MIKHAIL (MINANDR, MINAIDOR, MISHA, MICHEL) LAZAREVICH (8 July 1867, d. in Brussels) *married* VERA NIKOLAEVNA BOITCHEVSKY

AARON (RONIA) LAZAREVICH (6 May 1869–5 May 1895)

IL'IA (IL'IUSHA, ELIE) LAZAREVICH (13 May 1870–1943)

RAISA (RAIA, RAIKHL, RACHEL) LAZAREVNA (22 May 1871–1948) *married* ADOLPHE DE HIRSCH (d. in Geneva)

ISAAK (SATIA) LAZAREVICH (12 March 1873–1823 March 1937)

IAKOV (IASHA, JACQUES) LAZAREVICH (b. 13 December 1876) *married* CLAIRE (CLAIRETTE) NÉE BRODSKAIA, daughter of Leon Israelevich Brodskii (d. in Auschwitz)

> OLGA *married* LEO LINDENBAUM
>
> ELIZABETH (Lily; d. in Auschwitz)
>
> HÉLÈNE (d. 1940)

ALEKSANDR (Sasha; 20 August 1879–1942) *married* KLARA (CLARA, CLAIRE, VISHA) SOLOMONOVICH, divorced from Khishin

BENIAMIN (BENJAMIN, BABY) LAZAREVICH (4 December 1881–1942, d. in Auschwitz

AARON MOSES GUBBAY (1832–1894)

    Married RACHEL SASSOON (d. 1913), daughter of Sir Albert Abdullah David and Hannah Sassoon

        REUBEN (1860–1931) *married* ZINAIDA LAZAREVNA POLIAKOVA, daughter of Lazar (Eliezer) Solomonovich Poliakov (see above)

            ANNETTE (1896–1986)

        FLORA (b. 1863) *married* JULES ISAAC RUEFF (1853–1907)

            LEON CHARLES EDGAR (b. 1892)

            IRÈNE RACHEL (1894–1971) *married* JEAN DENNIS MONFERRATO

            ALICE ERNESTINE (b. 1896)

            GASTON ALBERT (1901–1977) *married* DÉNIE JOSÉPHINE ROHOZINSKI

        DAVID (1865–1928) *married* HANNAH EZRA

        MOZELLE (1872–1964) *married* MEYER ELIAS SASSOON

            REGINALD ELLICE (1894–1933)

            VIOLET (1894–1970) *married* DESMOND RICHARD FITZGERALD

        MAURICE (1873–1929)

        LOUISE (1875–1928) *married* ANTOINE "TONY" DREYFUS (1867–1926), son of Emile Auguste and Laura Dreyfus

            BÉATRICE ADÈLE FLORA HALPHEN (1898–1983) *married* HENRY JULES HALPHEN

                FRANCINE RACHEL (b. 1919) *married* CHARLES CLORE

                PHILIPPE (1920-2010)

                FABIENNE

INDEX

Page numbers in *italics* indicate illustrations; page numbers with "n" indicate notes.

interwar losses, 105–6; Jewish mourning rituals, 40–42, 43–44, 45; of Reuben Gubbay, 106; of Reuben's grandmother Sassoon, 78; of Reuben's mother, 79; suicide, 13; telegrams as forms of condolence, 124; WWII losses, 111–12, 121–22; of Zinaida Lazarevna Poliakova, 128; of Zinaida's brothers, 18, 45, 106, 111, 307, 307n228; of Zinaida's grandmothers, 9, 98; of Zinaida's parents, 76, 105–6; of Zinaida's paternal grandfather, 43–44; of Zinaida's sisters, 122; of Zinaida's uncles, 13–14, 15; Zinaida's views on death and burial, 258, 280, 292, 296

de Hirsch, Adolphe de (brother-in-law), 60, 126, 144–45n255

de Hirsch, Baron James, 55, 144–45n255, 373

de Hirsch, Baroness Zinaida Samuilovna (née Poliakova) (cousin), 55

de Hirsch family, 237, 237n5

Della Rocca, Princess Maria, 86

Dem'ianovo estate, 209

Demidov, Mikhail Denisovich, 185, 185n2, 198

Demidov, Praskov'ia Nikolaevna (née Boldyrevna), 185, 185n2

diaries, xi–xiv, 4, 5, 39, 173n11, 174–75, 177, 188, 202, 235

Diskin, Yehoshua Yehudah Leib, 44

Diskin orphanage in Jerusalem, 44–45

divorce, 90, 146n276, 155n515, 337, 369

Dolgorukov, Vladimir Andreevich: close friendship with Lazar Solomonovich, 22–23, 25, 35, 51; conservative critiques of, 51, 62; dismissal as governor-general of Moscow, 62, 65; support for Jews, xii, 4, 16–18, 62; Zinaida's mentions of, 195, 196, 220, 221–22, 244, 249, 251, 270, 280, 295, 320, 340, 341, 344, 347

Dolgorukova, Ekaterina Mikhailovna, 231n148

dolls, 81, 171, 172, 173, 314

domestic servants: hiring and firing of, 39–40, 272, 301; maids, 174, 181, 182,

353; nannies, 27, 91, 179, 204, 232, 248, 255, 287, 290–92; as potential romantic rival in household, 91; Zinaida's cook, 114. *See also* Gosh, Elizabeth; Zotova, Lidiia Stepanovna

Dostoevesky, Fyodor, 67, 141n178

Dreyfus, Alfred, 101

Dreyfus, Antoine (Tony), 85, 90, 101

Dreyfus, Louise (née Gubbay) (sister-in-law), 85, 100

Dreyfus, Ruben, 85

Dreyfus affair, 84, 101

Dreyfus family, 85, 113

Dubrovno, Russia, 8, 45–46

Dynin family, 247, 247n56

Eban, Zeev, 34

education: music and dance, 30–31, 34, 92, 171, 174, 175, 177, 181–82, 187, 196, 272, 293, 309, 327, 345–46; philanthropic support for, 35, 47–48, 66; Poliakov males' exposure to Jewish and secular, 9; private tutors and lessons, 26–27, 30–32, 91–92, 174, 177, 177, 178, 181, 182, 184, 192, 203, 243; state examinations, 214; as ticket to escape Pale of Settlement, 136n86

Edwards, Jeanne (née Charcot), 83

Eibenschütz, Ilona, 33

Eibushits, Semen, 51, 194, 194n43

Elzhen, D. Albert, 32

emancipation, Jewish, 47

Emden, Marthe (née Vanderheym), 112, 162n693

England, WWII repatriation and residence in, 118–24

entrepreneurship, Russian Jewish, 9–10, 30. *See also* banks and banking; women

Ephrussi, Charles, 83

Ephrussi, Maurice, 92, 220

Epshtein, Efim Moseevich, 172, 172n10, 186, 187, 216, 217–18

Erdmansderfer, Maks (Max), 31, 243, 243n38, 244, 245

Erdmansderfer, Polina (Pauline), 242, 327, 345, 346

Livshits, Stefaniia Pavlovna (Fania) (née Vydrina), 170, 170n3, 197, 197n53, 232, 253, 362, 362n52

London, England, 120, 318

Louis-Dreyfus, Léopold, 85

L'vov, E., 62–63

Maidanovo estate, 186, 186n10, 209, 212

Makovskii, Konstantin E., 36–37

Malkiel', Mina, 146n277

Malkiel', Samuil, 224, 259, 263

Malkiel' family, 180, 180n33, 230, 258

manège, defined, 190

Marienbad. *See under* spas

Markovich, Andrei N., 68

marriage: cultural differences in, 8, 77, 86–87, 89; dearth of upper-class Jewish marriage partners, 54–57, 192, 242, 277, 282, 295, 312, 368; of Iakov Poliakov's children, 55–57; ideals, 243; intermarriage, 56–57, 80, 286, 290; of Lazar Poliakov's children, 57–60; loss of servants to, 223; matchmaking and arranged, 9–10, 32, 55–57, 58, 93–94, 209, 217–18, 258, 259, 327, 335, 338, 353–54; of Samuil Poliakov's children, 54–55; Zinaida's views on marriage, 57–59, 94, 256, 274, 328, 343, 353–54, 356, 359, 360, 363–64, 369, 370. *See also* weddings

Marrot, Jacques (Ricardo), 80

Maten'ko, Nahum, 49–50

Maze, Iakov Maze, xiii–xiv, 52–53, 105, 144n244

Mein, Aleksandr Danilovich, 373, 374

Mein, Mariia (Mania) Aleksandrovna, 254n79, 256, 303, 333, 349

Mel'gunov, Iulii Nikolaevich, 209, 209–10n91

merchants, 6, 20, 35, 71, 172n9, 190n27; female, 29–30, 90; Jewish, 8, 9, 16, 17, 18, 23, 26, 45, 46, 63, 64, 66, 130n4, 132n27, 132n39, 136n86, 176n25, 180n33, 222n130, 231

Meshcherskii, Vladimir P., 63–64, 66

Messarosh, Ivan Vasil'evich, 247n59, 280, 292

Miliaev, Aleksandr (Sasha), 175

Miliaev, Nikolai Konstantinovich, 226, 263, 263n101, 264, 265

Minor, Lazar, 47

Minor, Zelig (Shlomo Zalkind), 46–47, 52, 143n212, 200, 217

Montagu, Gerald, 72

Montagu, Samuel, 306, 306n225, 317

Montefiore, Sonia (née Antokol'skaia), 84

Moscow: expulsion of Jews from (1891), 7, 64–65; industrial banks of, 20–21; residency restrictions for Jews in, 17, 132n27, 136n86; urban development of, 17; Zinaida's love of, 29, 271, 368

Moscow Jewish School for Poor and Orphaned Children, 47

Moscow Land Bank, 18, 21–22, 25, 137–38n111, 189n19, 220, 247

Moscow State Bank, 71

Museum of Fine Arts, Moscow, 35

music: choir, 289; concerts, 183, 241, 246, 259, 272–73, 277, 278, 290, 328, 329, 334, 339, 340, 343, 346, 348, 349, 375; musicians, 32–35, 85–86, 230, 242, 277, 283, 284, 287, 296, 296n197, 297, 309; music lessons, 30–31, 92, 174, 177, 181–82, 187, 196, 272, 309, 327, 345–46; music teachers, 30–31, 34; opera, 33–34, 97, 175, 181, 183, 242–43, 244, 245, 261, 268, 341; patronage, 33, 34–35; purchasing a piano, 176; sacred, 49–50, 329; at social events, 186, 193, 200, 217, 244, 284, 302, 333, 339; Zinaida's performance of, 32–34, 85–86, 92, 176, 187, 213, 218, 247–48, 272, 307, 343, 345

Nadezhda, 69

Nancy, France, 114, 115–16

Nazi occupation of France, 107–22

newspapers: Jewish, 64; Russian press, 62–64, 211, 211n99; society pages on Poliakovs, 32, 35, 55, 59, 81–82, 83, 84–85, 91, 92, 96, 104–5, 158n580

Nice, France, 270, 289, 344, 373–78

Nicholas II, Emperor of Russia, 36, 72, 101, 221, 221n128, 253n74, 300

Nickel of New Caledonia, 89–90

Nikiforov, Dmitrii, 18, 21–22

Nikolaevan soldiers, 46, 64

Nikolai Nikolaevich, Grand Duke, 224, 225

nobility. *See* hereditary nobility

Novikova, Nadezhda Vasil'evna, 186, 186n10, 206, 209, 214, 220, 223

Novikova, Ol'ga, 37

Ogus-Shikevich, Emiliia Isaakovna, 31, 33

Old Believers, 21

Old Yishuv, Palestine, 44–45

Oulman, Esther, 113, 117, 162n702

Pale of Settlement, 7, 8, 17, 45–46, 102, 131n14

Panaeva-Kartseva, Aleksandra, 33

Panjdeh incident, 141n179, 261

Paris, France: visits described in diary (1886), 315–17, 372; Zinaida's married life in, 76–106; Zinaida's post-WWII return to, 124, 127

patriarchy, submission and obedience rule for unmarried daughters, 40. *See also* gender; women

patriotism, 29, 171, 195, 196–97, 227, 251, 300–301

Persia: Persian Railway and Tram Company, 106; Poliakov investments and losses in, 68–70, 76, 149n344; Poliakovs as consuls of, 69, 149n345, 198, 198n58; railroads in, 322

philanthropy: Jewish, 45–46, 142n209, 191, 196; for music and theater, 33, 34–35, 246, 259, 341; for Palestine, 45; Poliakov family's reputation for, 3, 81, 140n171; Russian, 16, 23, 66

Pobedonostsev, Konstantin Petrovich, 66–67, 144n238, 148n336

Podgoretskii, Semen Sergeevich, 39, 190, 194, 205–7, 209, 210, 244, 251, 252

poetry and poets, 36, 264, 281–82, 304, 307

pogroms, 6, 64–65, 102, 131n14, 196, 249

Poliakoff, Alexander, xi, xii–xiii, 72, 129

Poliakoff, Elizabeth (Lili) (niece), 111, 161n678

Poliakoff, Martyn, xi, 129

Poliakoff, Vera (Vera Lindsay) (grand-niece), xi, 118

Poliakoff, Vladimir (Volodia), 118

Poliakov, Aaron (Ronia) (brother), 18, 45, 53–54, 141n190, 178

Poliakov, Aleksandr (Sasha) (brother), 18, 22, 60, 105, 107, 111, 184, 192, 200, 215, 220, 229

Poliakov, Avgust (Azi or August) (brother), 18, 141n190, 307n228

Poliakov, Beniamin (Baby or Benjamin) (brother), 18, 110–11, 121, 335–36

Poliakov, Boris (cousin), 56–57

Poliakov, Daniil (Daniel, Kotia) (cousin), 12, 112, 145n268, 146n270, 175, 175n22, 210, 260, 268

Poliakov, Iakov (Iasha or Jacques) (brother), 18, 60, 96, 102, 111, 178, 190, 248

Poliakov, Iakov Solomonovich (uncle): bank failure of, 73; on Biarritz synagogue, 96; on Borki train accident, 13; business activities of, 15–16, 133n44, 133n46; on "consuls of Persia" designation, 69; on continued associations with conservative antisemites, 66–67; diaries of, xii; on family losses, 9, 41–44; hereditary nobility status campaign, 68, 149n346; on increased discrimination against Jews, 65; and Lazar and Rozaliia, 9–10, 30; on marriage matches of children, 55–57; sculpture commissions, 36

Poliakov, Il'ia (Il'iusha or Elie) (brother), 18, 29, 48, 60, 74, 82, 111, 139n138, 179, 263, 283

Poliakov, Isaak (Satia) (brother), 18, 22, 60, 74, 106, 179

Poliakov, Lazar Iakovlevich (cousin), 55, 141–42n191, 145n259, 204, 223–24

Poliakov, Lazar Samuilovich (great-grandfather), 8, 131n23

Poliakov, Lazar Solomonovich (father): death of, 76, 105; financial empire, 16, 18–26, 70–71, 75–76; illnesses, 16, 42, 244, 268, 276, 315, 317–18, 322, 356, 357, 358–59, 361, 363, 365, 369; and Ivan Tsvetaev, 35; Jewish criticism of, 15; and Rabbi Maze, 52–53; move to Moscow, 18; portrait, *19*; relationship to Russian conservatives, 63–64, 66; relationship to state, 236; risky investments and financial crisis (1890s), 68–71; as target of antisemitic attacks in Russian press, 63; and Vladimir Dolgorukov, 22–23, 65; Zinaida's relationship to, 3, 41, 74, 105, 302, 315, 323, 352, 356

Poliakov, Mikhail (Misha or Michel) (brother): birth of, 170n4; and death of Solomon (grandfather), 44; education of, 178; interwar banking career, 159n620; marriage of, 60, 62; relationship to Zinaida, 220, 262, 329, 336, 348–49, 357–58, 361; role in family businesses, 22, 76; sibling order, 18

Poliakov, Samuil Iakovlevich (cousin), 57, 73, 112

Poliakov, Samuil Solomonovich (uncle), xiii, 9, 10–15, *11–12*, 36, 55, 133n46, 135n63, 143n213, 196, 218, 333

Poliakov, Solomon (Shlomo) (grandfather), 8, 9–10, 43–44, 65, 281, 282, 355

Poliakova, Alma (wife of Daniil Poliakov), 112

Poliakova, Amaliia (Iakov Poliakov's second wife), 43, 142n193

Poliakova, Anna (Niuta) (cousin), 56

Poliakova, Avdot'ia (née Epshtein) (aunt), 9, 297, 337

Poliakova, Breine (step-grandmother), 281, 282

Poliakova, Claire (Keta) (née Brodskaia) (sister-in-law), 60, 96, 111, 113, 161n678

Poliakova, Elizabeth (Liza, Elena) (cousin), 55, 56, 99

Poliakova, Isabella (Bella) (cousin), 56, 193, 193n35, 214, 215, 217

Poliakova, Khaia (Ksenia, Ksiutka, Xenia) (sister): on forced evacuations in Italy, 101; loss of in Holocaust, 121–22; marriage of, 59–60; rivalry with Zinaida, 37–38, 40–41, 97, 172, 176, 178, 188, 207, 215, 259, 262, 299–300, 303, 320, 336, 352; in Russia during WWI, 81; sibling order, 18; Zinaida's worries about safety of, 111

Poliakova, Khasia (Iakov's first wife), 9, 43

Poliakova, Raisa Lazarevna (Raechka, Raia, or Rachel) (sister), 18, *31*, 60, 83, 107, 111, 121, 122, 126, 173, 336

Poliakova, Rozaliia Pavlovna (née Vydrin) (mother): business skills of, 22, 29–30; death of, 105–6; dedication to charity, 44–45, 47–48; education of children, 30–31, 137n93; family background, 9–10; government seizure of assets, 72; illnesses, 182, 183, 195, 341; patronage of the arts, 35; portrait, *24*; religiosity of, 42–43; Zinaida's relationship with, 40, 42–43, 74, 96, 243, 245, 248, 250, 257, 262, 277, 299–302, 303–4, 315, 318, 320, 321, 329, 330, 336, 352, 362, 368

Poliakova, Vera Nikolaevna (née Boitchevsky) (sister-in-law), 60, 62

Poliakova, Zinaida Samuilovna (cousin), 55, 98, 134n58, 145n255, 210n96, 212n102, 218, 261, 266, 311, 316, 338, 355

Poliakova, Zinaida (Zina) Lazarevna: birth of, 16, 129n1; death of, 128, *128*; elite habitus of, 4, 7, 18, 32, 97–98; financial circumstances, 108–9, 111; illnesses, 110, 119, 124, 177, 182, 237, 266, 268, 288, 289, 297, 338, 339, 375; losses during Holocaust, xii, 110–12, 121–22, 163n723; love of Moscow and Russia, 27–28, 29, 171, 195–97, 205–6, 209, 227, 251, 271, 300–301, 338, 361, 368; marriage, 4, 8, 74, 77, 79, 86–87, 89, 91–92, 130n8; motherhood, 90–94, 232; philanthropic activities, 36, 77, 101–2, 106; photos, *61*, *88*, *119*; poetry, 281–82, 304, 307; in post-war France, 125; Russian identity, 27, 38–39, 43, 53–54, 185, 197,

349–50, 370, 371; invitations to, 278;
plethora of announcements at start
of 1885, 256; prospects and plans for
Zinaida's, 320
Weill, Julien, 91, 107
Weisweiller, George Daniel von, 110, 281
Witte, Sergei, 13, 71, 73
Wittenberg, R. Moshe, 45
women: in business, 9, 10, 30; diaries as
outlets for emotional expression, 5;
exclusion from family business, 22, 29,
30; property rights of Russian, 30

World War I, 81, 95, 101–2
World War II, xiii, 29, 107–22
Wright, Reginald, 104

Yalta, 80, 189, 222, 224, 231, 232, 369

Zak, Abram Isaakovich, 185, 185–86n4
Zakhar'in, Grigorii Antonovich (family
doctor), 175, 175n23, 263, 280, 358
Zotova, Lidiia Stepanovna (governess), 37,
39, 170n2, 179, 186, 188, 193, 208, 228,
241, 249, 251, 253–54, 267, 274, 292, 321